THE EVOLUTION OF
SOCIAL INSURANCE
1881–1981

THE EVOLUTION OF SOCIAL INSURANCE 1881-1981

Studies of Germany, France, Great Britain, Austria and Switzerland

Edited by Peter A. Köhler
and Hans F. Zacher
in collaboration with Martin Partington

Published by
Frances Pinter (Publishers), London
St. Martin's Press, New York
on behalf of the Max-Planck-Institut für ausländisches und
internationales Sozialrecht

©Max Planck Institut für ausländisches
und internationales Sozialrecht, Munich, 1982

First Published in Great Britain in 1982 by
Frances Pinter (Publishers) 5 Dryden St., London WC2E 9NW
ISBN 0 86187 242 8

Published in the United States of America by
St. Martin's Press, New York

Printed in Great Britain
First published in the United States of America in 1982
ISBN 0-312-12780-4

Library of Congress Cataloguing in Publication Data
Main entry under title:

The Evolution of social insurance, 1881-1981

   Includes index.
   1. Social security--Collected works. I. Köhler,
Peter A. II. Zacher, Hans Friedrich, 1928-
HD7091.E86 1982   368.4   81-23258
ISBN 0-312-27285-5   AACR2

Typeset by Westview Press, Boulder, Colorado
Printed by SRP, Exeter

Contents

GENERAL INTRODUCTION

Precursors of social insurance have existed since the Middle Ages. During the 19th century, social conditions underwent a change. Henceforth many countries attempted increasingly to solve sociopolitical problems by social insurance. In 1881 the German Reich enacted legislation introducing social insurance to an extent unknown up to that time. Many countries followed sooner or later, introducing similar or more selective schemes. In the 1930's and 1940's the idea of "social security" gave a new impulse to social policy. However, it has proved that social insurance has remained an important part of social security policy.

It is therefore justifiable to take into consideration the year 1881, which symbolizes the beginning of the first social insurance legislation on a large scale, in order to discuss developments during the next hundred years and from this to draw conclusions for the future as far as possible. However, such reflections should not be limited to one country; rather they should be extended to an international level.

In the Federal Republic of Germany the Max-Planck-Gesellschaft zur Förderung der Wissenschaften e.V. (Max Planck Society for the Advancement of Science) founded a Projektgruppe für internationales und vergleichendes Sozialrecht (Project Group for International and Comparative Social Law) in 1976, which has been transformed into a permanent Max-Planck-Institut für ausländisches und internationales Sozialrecht (Max Planck Institute for Foreign and International Social Law) in 1980. It seems quite "natural" for the Project Group — and later the Institute — to draw attention to the development of social insurance. Accordingly a research programme has been worked out containing three parts.

The first part consisted of a colloquium on the "Conditions relating to the Origins and Evolution of Social Insurance" which was organized in 1978. The proceedings have been published in the Schriftenreihe für Internationales und Vergleichendes Sozialrecht, Vol. 3, "Bedingungen für die Entstehung und Entwicklung von Sozialversicherung" (Duncker & Humblot, Berlin 1979).

The second part consists of an analysis of the evolution of social insurance in five countries: Germany, France, Great Britain, Austria and Switzerland. This analysis is intended to juxtapose theoretical reflections with the actual course of history in countries being considered as models in this field.

   The third part of the project consists of an international and interdisciplinary colloquium being held in Berlin in autumn 1981 trying to give an account in various ways for the development and trends in social insurance as regards national, European and international legislation.

   The present volume contains the work done for the second part of the project. It contains parallel studies on the evolution of social insurance in Germany, France, Great Britain, Austria and Switzerland during the last hundred years. Germany is listed among these countries because of the importance of its social insurance legislation introduced in 1881. France and Great Britain for a contrast to this as two important industrialized countries going their own way. Austria and Switzerland are included in the studies because they are Central European and mainly German-speaking neighbours of Germany and they both represent in some way good comparative models.

Professor Hans F. Zacher
Munich, 1981.

GERMANY
by Detlev Zöllner

CHARACTERISTICS AND SPECIAL FEATURES
OF SOCIAL LEGISLATION IN GERMANY

Most of this work is devoted to describing the origins and development of a social security system which is considered throughout the world to be both comprehensive and efficient. Nevertheless, it is curiously difficult to explain the German system to those with little previous knowledge of it. The diversity of its institutions, special features of certain sectors and its many legal sources frequently cause confusion.

Social Expenditure and Extent of Protection

The German social security system involves vast monetary turnover. Total expenditure on all the benefits prescribed by law to substitute income or avoid additional social hardship amounts to almost one-third of the gross national product. With such a range of social benefits, the Federal Republic of Germany ranks high among countries in this field.

Social benefits embrace the following spheres (expressed as a percentage of total social expenditure in 1975): old age and surviving dependents 36.2, health 31.7, family 16.1, employment 6.2.[1] This functional division of social benefits takes no account of which institutions are responsible for the respective benefits, the laws on which they are based or the ways in which they are financed. Thus, the first feature to note about social legislation in Germany is that it provides for a comparatively large distribution of money. Compared with other countries, it is to be noted that expenditure on old age pension schemes dominates.[2]

In view of the vast expenditure on old age and health schemes, it may be assumed that everyone is protected against these basic risks. Broadly, this is true. A determining factor for social security is compulsory insurance prescribed by law or the possibility of voluntary insurance as provided for by law. Fundamentally, all employed persons are compulsorily insured in social insurance pension and accident insurance schemes; health insurance is only compulsory up to a certain income level. Over two-thirds of independently employed persons participate in the social insurance scheme for employers or in independent insurance schemes. In 1973, 93 percent of gainfully employed persons were covered against illness, and 86.8 percent participated in pension schemes.[3]

However, one of the peculiarities of the German system is that even after 100 years of development, the whole population is still not protected against basic risks. Compared with other countries where the principle of residence was used as a basis for defining the groups of persons eligible for social security, the principle of need for protection is still in force in Germany today. A technical way of applying this principle is to mark the limits of compulsory insurance horizontally according to definable groups of persons and vertically according to the level of income. A profusion of literature and legal decisions serves to define who is eligible. As a result of countless legislative measures, with a gradual shift of emphasis away from the principle of need for protection to that of eligibility for social security, the position is not unlike that of countries following the principle of residence. Nevertheless, there are still gaps which are the legacy of the principle of a need for protection. The problem of how to fill these gaps is still being discussed; how, for example, can housewives without an income, artists or handicapped people be covered by the social security system?

Institutions

The great variety of institutions is both a characteristic and special feature of the German system. The institutions responsible for the classic branches of social security — pension, health and accident insurance — provide almost two-thirds of all the direct benefits. In view of the numbers of people covered, the level of expenditure and the numbers employed, they form the heart of the system. Other institutions deal with unemployment, old age assistance for farmers and professional pension schemes. Compensation payments for disabled ex-servicemen, refugees and persecuted persons are made by special government bodies. Public assistance benefits are paid by local authorities.

The social security institutions in the Federal Republic of Germany are not government bodies but are, from an organizational and financial point of view, independent corporations under public law. This is the result of historical circumstances, as are the following subdivisions. There are approximately 1400 sickness insurance schemes; 54 industrial and 19 agricultural cooperative associations cater for accident insurance and 21 for pension insurance. This reflects the division of social security institutions according to the type of insurance. Other divisions reflect the economic structure: trade associations exist for the various trade branches; there are special schemes for agriculture, the mining industry and shipping and guild sickness insurance schemes. There are further divisions according to the social status of the insured person in his or her working life: pension schemes for both manual and white-collar workers, private (substitute) sickness insurance schemes for employees (Ersatzkassen), and old age pension and sickness schemes for the self-employed in agriculture. Apart from the local sickness insurance schemes (Ortskrankenkassen), there are also a large number of works' sickness insurance schemes (Betriebskrankenkassen). Finally, the social security institutions are organized at a regional level; the local sickness insurance schemes, the insurance schemes of the individual federal states (Landesversicherungsanstalten) and some of the industrial and trade associations and institutions concerned with social insurance for the agricultural sector. This unsystematic network of institutions has provoked criticism ever since it began and yet it has shown a high degree of continuity. The reasons for this development will be dealt with later.

Ever since they were founded, the social insurance institutions have been self-administered; both the insured and their employers take part in forming the policies of the institution. The honorary representatives chosen by these groups form bodies — an assembly of representatives and an executive board — which decide on the constitution and budget of each institution, appoint the director and, within a statutory framework, establish administrative procedures. There is usually equal representation of insured persons and employers, although there are exceptions — usually of historical origin. In the federal miners' provident fund (Bundesknappschaft) there is a two-thirds majority of representatives of insured persons and in the private sickness insurance schemes (Ersatzkassen) there are only representatives of insured persons; in the case of the agricultural associations, one-third of the seats are held by the employed, one-third by employers and the remaining third by the self-employed.

Benefits and their Finance

About 40 percent of the social benefits in the Federal Republic of Germany are financed by state funds and about 60 percent by contributions. Social insurance itself is financed predominantly by contributions; the Federal Government only subsidizes expenditure on pension insurance for workers and employees by about 15 percent. A large proportion of the total expenditure is financed by contributions; correspondingly, the insured persons' and their employers' contributions (half each) are high. Up to the limit of assessment of contributions (the so-called 'Beitragsbemessungsgrenze'), 18 percent of wages and salaries go on old age pension insurance, 11.3 percent (on average) on sickness insurance and 3 percent on unemployment insurance, amounting to almost a third of wages and salaries.

The level of finance is high because of the comprehensive system of benefits. In case of sickness, the insured person and members of his family who are entitled to receive benefits, receive all the medical attention deemed appropriate by medical standards of the time. This also includes the use of specialists and hospitals and the prescription of medicines. The insured person has a free choice of registered panel doctors. These doctors have formed associations (kassenärztliche Vereinigungen) which provide the medical services under the sickness insurance schemes. They are party to an agreement with the sickness insurance scheme through which they receive their medical fees. Thus, there is no financial or legal relationship between the individual doctor and his patient. Economic security is ensured in the case of sickness as the employer is bound to continue to pay the wage or salary for a period of 6 weeks. Thereafter the insured person receives sickness benefits from the sickness insurance scheme amounting to 80 percent of his usual wage or salary. In the case of an accident at work or an occupational disease, the injured person receives medical attention and vocational assistance. If the injured person's fitness for work has been reduced by at least 20 percent after the thirteenth week following the accident, he then receives a pension. In the case of total disablement this corresponds to two-thirds of the last wage or salary; otherwise it is a percentage of the full pension in accordance with the degree by which the person's ability to earn a living has been reduced.

Upon reaching retirement age or in the case of disablement, the insured person (or in the case of his death, his surviving dependants) receives a pension which is calculated according to the duration of insurance contributions and to the individual earned income during that person's working life. Upgrading the level of this previously earned income ensures that the insured person's position in the income structure during his working life is reflected in the level of his pension.

Thus, old age pension insurance is designed to ensure a relative standard of living. An insured person, who has always earned an average income, receives a pension after 40 years of insurance amounting to 60 percent of the current average income.[4] Pension levels are adjusted each year in relation to changes in the average wage in order to avoid a drop in the pensioners' standard of living owing to increases in wages and prices.

One of the prominent features of old age pension insurance is the principle of equivalence between duration and level of contributions on the one hand and the level of the pension on the other hand. There are several exceptions to this principle of equivalence — such as pensions based on a minimum income, family allowances, allowance for periods when contributions have not been paid. However, these are pragmatic adjustments to ensure a fair distribution between young and old; they are not intended to lead to redistribution between rich and poor. Surprise is sometimes expressed at how little the German social insurance system is characterized by the motive of 'redistribution' in its proper sense. This applies particularly to old age pension insurance. In sickness insurance, however, there is a considerable amount of vertical redistribution as, on the one hand, contributions are paid strictly in proportion to the level of income, but, on the other hand, 90 percent of the expenditure goes on benefits in kind and services which, quite independent of income, are based on medical needs alone.

The foregoing is only an incomplete summary of the basic features of German social legislation.[5] However, one point that must have become clear is that these features — however one chooses and evaluates them — depend largely on their historical development. Thus, one has to return to the historical roots to gain a deeper understanding of German social insurance. The following historical survey is limited both in its scope and intention. It incorporates only a selection of the vast range of literature available.*

The developments described in the following pages are reflected in a large body of legislation. Since 1883 about 400 laws have been passed and over 1000 decrees issued on social insurance in the narrow sense of the term. Many of these laws must be mentioned in the course of this survey; but to make the text more readable, only a brief annotation and the year of publication of the various laws are given.[6]

HISTORICAL DEVELOPMENT

THE INITIAL POSITION

Legislation on social insurance in Germany arose from a given social, economic, legal and political situation and was intended to influence it. Any attempt to analyse this situation retrospectively involves selecting those circumstances which are of relevance to the initial development of social legislation. However, this selection cannot merely be made by considering those circumstances which are relevant today, but must take into account circumstances which influenced people at that time. Furthermore, such an analysis must include an account of changes of circumstances, as it was these changes which gave rise to social legisla-

---

*Interested readers are referred to the contributions, and the sources quoted in Zacher (ed.), 1979, see Bibliography.

tion. Finally, this account is to be completed by answering the questions whether, to what extent and in what way people were aware of the changes at the time.

Economic and Social Change

Population Growth and Urbanization

In the nineteenth century the population of Germany increased from 23 million to 56 million people. In the second half of the century the growth rate was far greater than in the first half. Between 1850 and 1900 the population increased at an average rate of 1.2 percent per annum. Although the birth rate was clearly on the decline, the population expanded as life expectancy increased due to medical progress — particularly the control of epidemics — and the standard of living was raised. Famines which had regularly reduced the population in previous centuries no longer occurred because of increased agricultural activity and improved means of transportation.

The growth in population was closely connected with an increase in the urban population. Between 1850 and 1900 village populations hardly grew; small towns between 2000 and 30 000 inhabitants grew at a rate of about 60 percent; and towns with over 30 000 inhabitants multiplied about five-fold.

Increased Wage Dependency

The growing population meant an increased need for jobs. Two major reforms during the first half of the nineteenth century further increased this need: the emancipation of the peasantry and the introduction of freedom of trade.

The emancipation of the peasantry consisted essentially in the abolition of personal ties to the lord of the manor, the transformation of duties and levies in kind into monetary payments and the distribution of property rights instead of usufructuary rights. However, relief from farming duties had to be compensated. Either part only of the area previously used by the farm became the farmer's property (half, or in the case of an already existing right of inheritance, two-thirds) or the former duties were transformed into a redemption price which the farmer had to pay off with interest. In other words, the farms were weakened or further encumbered with debts. These events took place at a time of low grain prices. The owners of larger farms, who were usually the former lords of the manor, were not affected because of their wealth and solvency. The principle of profit became increasingly popular among them and they began to employ paid workers (day labourers). By applying rational, capital-intensive methods of cultivation, they were able to compensate for losses of income through increased yields. As a result of these various conditions, many small properties were bought up by larger farms. This led to rural unemployment. Unemployed farm labourers who no longer had any ties as vassals fell on bad times.[7] At the beginning of the nineteenth century about 85 percent of all families had at least a limited right to farm land; by the middle of the century the number of families had dropped to about 60 percent.[8] As time went on, the numbers of families without or with very little land continued to grow. The proportion of people employed in agriculture dropped from about two-thirds around 1800 to about half by 1875.

Freedom of trade was introduced in the areas west of the Rhine under French occupation in 1790, in Prussia in 1807 and in all German states by 1868. This also led to the release of workers. At first the number of master craftsmen increased, and thus the number of their workshops; but overall the market for craftsmen had become overcrowded by guild regulation. The release of such workers created an important precondition for the initial development of industry, in particular regarding the quality of their skills.

Against this background of widespread unemployment, a job in industry was extremely coveted.

> Compared with the lower strata of farm workers and craftsmen . . . industrial workers were considered a favoured class in the 1830's and 1840's. To many, factory work meant the security of a minimum living wage, personal independence, the chance of establishing a family, indeed even relative security and social standing.[9]

However, for a long time industry was unable to provide sufficient jobs. The increase in wage-dependent people, due both to population growth and the release of workers, forced many to emigrate. Between 1815 and 1835 over 400 000 people emigrated from Germany.

> During times of food shortages (years of price increases, periods of famine) the number of emigrants increased (1816/17, 1828, 1831). Surplus food supplies and low agricultural prices curbed emigration. Evidence of this can be seen in the fact that it was not the more well-to-do classes (farmers, affluent craftsmen and tradesmen) who emigrated, but wage-dependent groups of the population, including artisans with poor wages, who had no or very little use of land.[10]

Emigration further increased over the next few decades from an average of 15 000 people per annum in the period from 1831–40 to 82 000 from 1861–70.

Industrialization

Industrialization was one of the crucial factors for the beginning of social insurance legislation. It started in Germany in the 1830s, and was characterized, and to some extent conditioned by, the following factors:

growth in the number of impecunious and wage-dependent people (employed persons);

progress in production techniques, particularly the replacement of manual labor by machine work;

increased use of capital (net investment);

foundation of the German Zollverein (1834) and within this the patent agreement (1842);

development of the banking system;

development of transportation, in particular the construction of railways (from 1835 onwards).

The type and extent of industrialization is characterized by the following development:[11]

the number of steam engines used in Prussian industry rose to about 2000 from 1835 to 1850 and to about 30 000 from 1850 to 1875;

the number of engineering works rose in Prussia from 180 to 1196 between 1852 and 1875; the number of people employed in these factories increased over the

same period from just under 10 000 to over 160 000. Thus, the factories were
not only more numerous but also larger; the average number of people
employed in each concern rose from 54 to 133 in these 23 years;
pig-iron production increased six-fold in Germany between 1850 and 1870;
railway construction developed as follows; 1845 about 2000 km, 1860 about
12 000 km, 1880 about 34 000 km.

Technical progress and increased use of capital and larger factory units
resulted in a rapid increase in productivity; for example, between 1835 and 1875
the peak capacity of a blast furnace rose five-fold (from 2000 to 10 000 tons of
pig-iron); and the railways reduced transportation costs to a tenth of the costs by
road.

Industrialization brought about radical changes in the employment market.
The number of people employed in industry (including manufacture and mining)
increased by an average of about 17 000 per annum from 1835 to 1850, by
almost 50 000 from 1850 to 1865 and by over 200 000 from 1865 to 1880. The
absolute number of industrial workers was, 1835 500 000, 1850 800 000, 1867
2 000 000, 1882 6 000 000.

In the period, 1835–1900, it has been calculated that 38 percent of industrial
workers came from actual growth within the existing industrial population and
62 percent came from the primary sector, i.e. predominantly from agriculture.[12]
Almost two-thirds of those newly employed in industry changed their job. For
many of these people this also meant a change of house and environment, as jobs
in industry were created mostly in the west of Germany, while rural unemployment was predominant in the eastern parts of the country. In 1899, of the
205 000 miners in the Ruhr area, 44 percent came from East Silesia, West and
East Prussia and from other countries in Eastern Europe. These decades have
been referred to as the years of 'industrial migration of nations'.[13]

Economic Conditions and Income of the Employed

Improvements in Employment. Although new jobs were created by industrial growth,
for some time demand exceeded the number of jobs available. Various factors — complaints about the slim chances of gaining employment, low wages, increased expenditure by the cities on relief for the poor, high numbers of
emigrants — indicate there were decades of substantial unemployment. The
employment situation only began to improve after about 1855 as the number of
jobs increased, particularly in the metal industry and in railway construction,
and grew in prestige.

Constant Real Income. The same circumstances may well explain why growing productivity in these sectors was reflected in a greatly increased national
income. From 1850 to 1900, national income rose (in real prices) 3.5-fold, and
because of the increased population per capita 2.2-fold. However, this increase in
income largely benefitted people who drew ground rents and unearned income.
The increase in income from ground rents was based on rising agricultural prices
from 1825 until the 1870s, as well as the rapid rise in income from building sites
associated with city growth. Unearned income increased — with a long term, constant interest rate of 4 percent — particularly as a result of increasing capital funds
and industrialists' earnings. Consequently, the share of personal earnings within

the national income fell in the nineteenth century. The real per capita personal income remained constant from 1840 to 1880.[14]

Thus, the social questions which were being raised from the middle of the last century onwards were not solely the result of increased poverty among workers as compared with the pre-industrial era. Although rents for housing were a great burden on the wages of workers who moved into the towns from the country, they did not lead to a drop in their previous standard of living. Conditions in the towns were to be seen against a background of earlier rural conditions. Industry was thought to be not only a place of poverty but also the cause of it. However, when Friedrich Engels published his book *The Situation of the Working Classes in England* in 1845, in which he portrayed industrialization as the cause of the plight of the workers, his ideas were immediately contradicted by the view that in Germany, poverty was most widespread in areas without industry. This view has been confirmed by recent historical research:

> The 'intact world' of yore, the 'pre-industrial harmony between town and country life', compared with the world of factories and machines, was exaggerated. This image took no account of the crises which also rocked the pre-industrial world: it ignored the hunger which befell the poor at frequent intervals, gradually leading to increasing destitution of the populace.[15]

Poverty was not restricted to industrial workers. In 1850 in an essay about the 'fourth estate' the following was written:

> The proletarians of intellectual work are the real 'ecclesia militans' of the fourth estate in Germany. They form the mighty army column of that stratum of society that has openly and self-confidently broken with the social order which has been handed down so far. . . . I include in this group of the fourth estate the civil servant proletariat, the school master proletariat, perennial Saxon candidates for the ministry, starving academic university lecturers, men of letters, journalists, artists of all kinds.[16]

Thus, as always, poverty was a characteristic of the unpropertied classes and not just of factory workers.

From the middle of the century onwards there were signs of a gradual improvement in the standard of living in the towns. The consumption of animal (and thus more expensive) products increased while the number of calories derived from vegetables decreased. The average working hours of wage earners had risen in the first few decades of the century (from about 65 to 90 hours per week) but from the middle of the century they fell continuously.[17] When social questions were raised both in literature and politics, the situation of the employed began to improve, at least as regards employment opportunities, real income and working hours.

The Problem of Income Maintenance. Despite this, and perhaps because this improvement had led to greater social awareness, workers were faced with new problems. These included unaccustomed working speeds, the routine and monotony of industrial work compared with farm and handicraft work; furthermore, working conditions were frequently detrimental to health. Although employment of women and children was hardly less widespread than in the pre-industrial era, however, work in factories had far more devastating effects on them both physically and psychologically. The sense of strain was aggravated by a lack of social ties in the cities. Many workers had been separated from their primary groups (village community, extended family) and now lived, in many cases, only with their immediate family in strange surroundings. Without exception they were poor, and they suffered loss of income continuity in cases of disablement and unemployment.

Geographical Concentration of and Increased Political Awareness of Industrial Workers. The coincidence of three factors makes it easier to understand how social questions became political ones: the quantitative importance of industrial workers from the middle of the century onwards, their concentration in certain areas and the speed of this development. One must understand 'that the German industrial labour force is a product of merely 50 years' and that it 'suddenly appeared as a unified colossus in the midst of society'. The size, concentration and rapid growth of the industrial labour force changed the response of society to their problems. To begin with, however, it was the awareness of the workers themselves which changed.

> For 30 years they were drawn into the whirlpool of prodigious economic expansion, the aims and meaning of which remained unknown to them for a long time, until the political and trade union movement gradually banded them together into groups and made them aware of their social, economic and cultural position.[18]

This banding together of the workers into a new social group leads on to a discussion of the interplay of political forces.

The Political Forces

The Foundation of the German Reich: the Aristocracy and the Middle Classes

The introduction of social legislation in Germany in 1881 is connected with the foundation of the German Reich 10 years earlier. Compared with neighbouring European countries, this political unification occurred late; thus, there was neither a tradition of behavior *vis-à-vis* the Reich nor a tradition of Reich legislation. The German Reich was not founded spontaneously but was the result of a systematic policy lasting several decades and shaped to a large extent by Bismarck. This policy was extremely risky and was faced with considerable opposition. For contemporaries, and particularly for those who were politically active, the Reich was not a given fact but something 'created'. They still remembered the main events which led to the foundation of the Reich:

1833	The foundation of the German Zollverein under Prussian leadership.
1848	The meeting of the National Assembly in the Paulskirche in Frankfurt, which elected the Prussian King as German Emperor. The King, however, repudiated his election because of lack of support from other princes.
1862	Bismarck became Minister-President of Prussia and from then on worked towards the foundation of the Reich under Prussian leadership. He opted for the 'kleindeutsch' idea of a German Reich excluding Austria, contrary to the strong movement for a 'grossdeutsch' or pan-German solution including Austria.

1866   As a result of the war against Prussia, Austria acceded to the
            reorganization of Germany without its own participation. The North
            German Confederation was founded with Bismarck as Chancellor.
1870   The war against France strengthened national feeling and created the
            necessary conditions for the south German states, particularly
            Bavaria, to join the North German Confederation to form the Reich.
1871   Creation of the German Reich. Bismarck became Chancellor of the
            Reich.

The German Reich was a federal state with 41-million inhabitants at that time.
The Bundesrat (Federal Council), representing the princes and the towns, had
sovereign power. The Reichstag, however, was the supreme legislature. The
Chancellor of the Reich was appointed by the Kaiser.

The middle classes, with their liberal attitudes and ideals, contributed considerably to the movement which culminated in the unification of Germany. The
(liberal) German Progressive Party, founded in 1861, had a majority in the Prussian Lower House elected according to the three-class electoral system. In 1871
when the Reichstag was elected for the first time by general, equal, direct, and
secret ballot, the Liberal Party was the strongest group with 119 out of 397 seats;
it represented the nationally oriented, west German middle classes and advocated
a liberal, constitutional state. Other parties in the Reichstag were the liberal-
conservative German Reichspartei, the Progressive Party, the Old Conservatives
(representing the Prussian aristocracy) as well as the Centre Party representing
middle class catholics.

The balance of power in the Reich was determined to a large extent by the
Prussian aristocracy which held leading positions in the army and administration, and by the upper middle class which had a firm grip on industry, trade and
the monetary system. While members of the aristocracy were predominantly
conservative, strong liberal-democratic traditions and tendencies were very much
alive among the middle classes. However, these tendencies were disguised and
delayed in their political impact. The reasons for this were the failure of liberal
reform attempts in 1848 and Bismarck's brilliant nation-state successes until the
Reich was founded, which — along with the economic expansion — resulted in the
middle classes adopting to a large extent aristocratic patterns of behavior and
monarchic, authoritarian concepts of order. The feudalistic character of the
young Reich was one reason why it was more difficult for workers to become integrated in society in Germany than in neighboring countries.

The Labour Movement

There was no political labour movement in Germany until 1848. Workers'
education associations had been formed in the 1830s and 1840s; however, their
importance lay not in their political influence at the time but in the fact that early
organizational experiences were gained which were of use later.

Following the revolution in France in 1848, which influenced political events
in Germany, the General German Workers' Fraternity (Allgemeine deutsche
Arbeiter-Verbrüderung) was founded from the local worker associations in
Berlin. This can be seen as the first German political workers' organization. The
Workers' Fraternity was banned by federal law in 1854; only non-political and
denominational workers' associations were allowed to continue. However, from it

there emanated clearly recognizable organizational and personnel connections until, in 1863, the General German Workers' Association (Allgemeiner deutscher Arbeiterverein) was founded.[19] This association, under the leadership of Ferdinand Lasalle, which was an amalgamation of workers' associations (though by no means all of them), had a political programme and regarded itself as a party.

In 1869 a second party, also based on already existing workers' associations, was founded under the decisive influence of August Bebel and Wilhelm Liebknecht. This was the Social Democratic Labour Party. In 1875 leading members of the workers' association joined the Social Democrats; the Socialist German Labour Party was founded which was called the German Social Democratic Party from 1891 onwards. The political weight of the workers was expressed in the voting during the Reichstag elections as follows, 1871, 3.2 percent; 1874, 6.8 percent; 1877, 9.1 percent; twelve Social Democrat deputies became members of the Reichstag for the first time in 1877.

The Printers' Mutual Improvement Society (Fortbildungsverein für Buchdrucker) founded in 1862 (whose forerunner was the German National Printers' Association, 1848) can be classed as the first trade union organization to regard representing workers' interests *vis-à-vis* the employers as of primary importance. Further trade unions were founded after the prohibitions on association were removed in Prussia in 1867 and in the remaining German states in 1869 (by the Trade Act, 'Gewerbeordnung'). They were founded by Hirsch (Hirsch-Duncker trade unions) who had been influenced by the trade union movement in England. 'Free' trade unions were also founded, some of which, however, were disbanded again in 1879.

The passage of the anti-Socialist bill in 1878 was a decisive turning point for the labour movement. After two assassination attempts had been made on the Kaiser, Bismarck introduced and forced through the Reichstag the 'law against the aims of social democracy which are a menace to the public'. Because of this law the organizations of the German Socialist Labour Party were dissolved, and nearly all their publications prohibited. It is estimated that about 1500 people were sentenced to detention, 900 were deported and many others were forced to emigrate.

The anti-Socialist law was also applied to the trade unions, with the exception of the Hirsch-Duncker trade unions, whose members had to state in writing that they were neither members nor followers of the Social Democrat Labour Party. Moreover, reasons were found 'to deprive thousands of workers, the majority of whom were harmless, of their associations and funds, at which point they really became Social Democrats'.[20] Organizational activities continued in secret. When the anti-Socialist law was repealed, the socialist (free) trade unions joined together in 1890 to form the General Commission of German Trade Unions (Generalkommission der Gewerkschaften Deutschlands). The number of its members rose from about 200 000 to 1.8 million in 1908, and soon permanently left other trade union organizations way behind.

In retrospect it is difficult to understand the anti-liberal aggression of the steps taken against the political labour movement. According to the Gotha programme, the Socialist Labour Party aimed at 'a free state and a socialist society, the breaking of the iron law of wages by abolishing the system of paid labour, an end to all forms of exploitation, the elimination of all social and political inequality'. However, these goals were to be achieved 'by using lawful means'.[21]

The uneasiness of the ruling powers in the Reich about the growing labour movement has been explained as follows: 'objectively, in view of the practical policy of the Socialists, there was no reason to fear revolution in the Reich. Subjectively, however, neither Bismarck, the aristocracy nor the middle classes had any doubts about the impending danger to the state and to society. . . .'[22] Fear of revolution could have come from the Socialists' revolutionary terminology and the aggressive language of their publications, but not from their programme or political action — if only because the Socialists were too weak in face of the anti-Socialist law for such action. (In 1877, they had 493 000 voters out of a total population of 44 million.)

Bismarck's reaction to the labour movement, in the form of the anti-Socialist law and also of the social legislation which followed shortly afterwards, has its origins in reasons which will be explained in more detail. At this point, it is important to add that the labour movement at that time neither demanded legislation on social security as a matter of priority nor contributed towards its content. In the period until the Kaiser's special message, the workers 'seldom voiced their opinions on national insurance legislation'.[23] In the Gotha Programme of 1875 only two demands were made concerning social security neither of which were innovatory: 'An effective Employers' Liability Act' and 'complete self-administration for all worker relief and benevolent funds'.[24]

The trade union associations at that time also advocated only an extension of the Employers' Liability Act. In 1864 the second meeting of the German labour associations decided to develop a 'general old age pension insurance scheme for German workers'. This scheme was to pay out funds to a worker when he reached a certain age; the worker was free to choose whether or not he wished to contribute to the scheme and the employer was to feel morally obliged to assume part of the costs of the contributions. When this scheme was not put into effect, the view was expressed that state assistance was necessary. However, this view made no headway against the distrust felt among the leaders of the Social Democrats about state administration of the workers' insurance funds. They called upon members of the workers' associations to club together, like the trade unions in England and the German Printers' Association, to form cooperative associations and to let these attend to the establishment of insurance funds. The Social Democrats firmly supported in principle the protection of workers, but were critical of insurance schemes for workers, even after they were introduced, until about the turn of the century. They thought that such schemes did not constitute true social reform but were merely an improvement of the poor relief system which, furthermore, was used only as a device to distract the workers from the right course.[25]

Bismarck and the Labour Question

Motives, Readiness to Act and Openmindedness of Approach. It is generally agreed that Bismarck did not consider social legislation an end in itself but rather as a means to an end. In his detailed *Reflections and Reminiscences* (*Gedanken und Erinnerungen*) he did not discuss the labour question as a real problem. Nevertheless, there is other evidence that he repeatedly concerned himself from an early date with the labour problem and with methods of solving it and that he decisively influenced social policy.[26]

Bismarck's fear that the workers could become a danger to the state constituted his initial motive for concerning himself with social policy. As early as 1849, when he was still a young deputy in the Prussian Chamber of Deputies, he said that the factories 'reared a mass of proletarians, of poorly fed.workers who were a danger to the state because of the insecurity of their very existence'.[27] Fear of the Socialists had been intensified by the events of the Paris Commune insurrection in March 1871, which members of Prussian and German Government circles had experienced firsthand and 'of which Bebel's glorification had made a very great impression on Bismarck'.[28] The dominant motive for passing the anti-Socialist law in 1878 was to ward off this danger to the state. This same motive comes through clearly in the Kaiser's message of 17 November 1881: it expresses the conviction 'that the cure of social ills will not only have to be sought along the road of repression of social democratic excesses . . .' and the wish 'to bequeath the fatherland new and lasting assurances of internal peace . . .'[29] but also by satisfying workers' demands. Later, one of Bismarck's staff expressed this idea somewhat less majestically; he stressed that social policy was not born of love but of fear among the ruling classes, especially among government circles'.[30]

Bismarck had long recognized that the labour question could not be countered with repression alone. In a controversy with his Minister of Commerce, he wrote in November 1871: 'The only means of stopping the Socialist movement in its present state of confusion is to put into effect those Socialist demands which seem justified and which can be realized within the framework of the present order of state and society'.[31] This was also the trend-setting motive behind the Kaiser's message which stated that the cure of social ills 'will not only have to be sought along the road of repression . . . but by meeting the positive demands for the well-being of the workers' and that it was desirable 'to ensure the needy greater security and assistance to which they have a right'. It is known that Bismarck not only sketched the outlines of the Kaiser's message but also edited it thoroughly himself. Bismarck expounded his two-fold aim of suppressing the Social Democratic Party by force but at the same time putting an end to workers' complaints and ill-feelings by bringing in social legislation, in so far as this seemed justified to him, in a public speech in the Reichstag in 1884.[32]

Bismarck's basic idea of tying workers to the state by providing welfare benefits seems to have been particularly original at that time in Germny. There is reason to believe that he embraced this basic idea in France. During visits in 1855 and 1857 and as ambassador in Paris in 1861 he had been extremely interested in the regime of Napoleon III, particularly regarding the way Napoleon won support from among the workers and sections of the rural population by the introduction of state pensions, measures to counter unemployment, producers' cooperatives, workers' funds, etc.[33] In 1889 when the disablement bill was tabled, he said in the Reichstag: 'I have lived in France long enough to know that the faithfulness of most of the French to their government . . . is largely connected with the fact that most of the French receive a state pension. . . .'[34]

Since Bismarck considered social policy primarily as a means to an end, he was quite open-minded in principle as to how it should be implemented. However, there was one important reservation: he rejected a policy of protecting workers during their working life. His motives for this were his concern about the competitiveness of industry compared with other countries and about maintaining the workers' will to work and their chance of earning a living. Thus, he rejected the prohibition of work on Sundays and during the night as well as the limitation of work done by women and children. 'All his staff, apparently without exception, regretted that Bismarck could not be moved from arguments which were so characteristic of the Manchester school of thought'.[35]

Shortly after accession to office as Prussian Minister-President in 1862, Bismarck began to consider how he could win over the workers as allies against the liberals. The introduction of universal, equal and direct suffrage and state assistance to producers' cooperatives seemed one way of doing this. He discussed this matter both personally and in letters with Ferdinand Lassalle. Later Bismarck said of Lassalle: 'a distinguished man with whom one could talk'. They agreed on the demand for universal, equal suffrage, although Lassalle expected an increase in urban, proletarian votes to result from this while 'Bismarck hoped for an increase in votes of farmers and farm labourers who were still under the spiritual and political influence of the landowners. Thus, there were points of contact.' Lassalle assured Bismarck that from the very beginning he had wished to carry out the social programme of the labour movement as far as possible, except 'its political aspects'.[36]

In the 1860s Bismarck also turned his thoughts towards assisting producers' cooperatives, restricting child labour, promoting old age pension institutions on a communal basis and savings banks. However, these ideas were not new even then and displayed none of the characteristic features of later legislation.

There are many examples of Bismarck's open-minded approach. In the Reichstag in 1878, referring to state assistance for producers' cooperatives, he said:

> I do not know whether it is because of Lassalle's reasoning or my own conviction which is partially due to the impressions I gained during my stay in England in 1862, but it seemed to me that by creating producers' associations, such as are flourishing in England, there was a chance of improving the workers' lot, of channelling a considerable proportion of business profits in their direction.

Even with reference to his own social insurance bill he said in the Reichstag in 1882 that he was sure of the aims but not of the choice of means to achieve them. 'I am partly not clear about this myself yet and partly not as clear as I was in the past, as I still need more information.'

Bismarck's openmindedness of approach must not be interpreted as a lack of interest or indifference. He was anxious to arrive at better solutions. Such openmindedness did not mean indifference towards certain principles of organization which were of national relevance in Bismarck's eyes. Here, as will be seen, he repeatedly showed great determination and exercised a decisive influence. However, it is difficult to arrange Bismarck's key principles systematically. 'Bismarck's social policy consists of a strange medley of personal experiences and disappointments, patriarchal, state socialist and economic points of view influenced by the Manchester School.'[37]

The Influence of Social Reformers. Bismarck's quest for suitable solutions is also manifest in his continual interest over several decades in the opinions and proposals of men of learning for solutions to the labour question. One has the impression that he was continually in search of politically feasible proposals without committing himself to particular schools of thought or concepts. Here too one is confronted with Bismarck, the 'realpolitician'.

Until after the middle of the century the doctrine of free competition predominated. This aimed at limiting state power to the execution of legal procedures and to the maintenance of legal order. A change only occurred with the founding of the historic School of National Economics which published *Jahrbücher für Nationalökonomie und Statistik* (annuals of national economics and statistics) and with the appearance of the academic socialists in the Association for Social Policy which received considerable publicity in the 1870s and which opposed liberalism. Gustav Schmoller was one of the spokesmen of this group. He did not see the state as an evil whose powers had to be limited as much as possible but as 'the most splendid moral institution for educating mankind' which had a 'socio-political calling'[38] in keeping with Prussian tradition. This view was also typical of other social reformers of that time (Ketteler, Schäffle, Rodbertus, Wagner, and Wichern). It was also characteristic of a group of socio-conservative authors (Roesler and Meyer) who expressed their opinions in the *Berlin Revue,* published until 1873, of which it was said that the articles were written 'more for Bismarck's consumption than for that of a wide reading public'.[39] This explains why a movement for social reform did not arise from the practical efforts of the social reformers — as was the case in England. These reformers turned to the state, considered it responsible and expected it to take the appropriate measures.

Scholars discussed a multitude of proposals — many of which were controversial — to solve the labour question, often including the question of worker insurance. One cannot tell whether or not the government's bills which were finally introduced were definitely influenced by the scholars' new proposals. Nonetheless, by the beginning of the 1870s the commitment and activities of these men of learning, going far beyond their official duties, contributed decisively to creating a political climate which paved the way for later legislation. In this respect they too are to be considered as an important factor in the political scene in the 1870s. Otherwise, Bismarck had hardly any reliable allies.

Legislation on workers' insurance schemes took shape

> even though major interests of both a practical and ideal nature were opposed to this change. Private insurance, the individualistic national economy and political liberalism competed to portray the advantageous consequences of free business and association activities and the damaging effect of bureaucratic patterns and compulsory measures.[40]

The arguments of the liberals against social legislation were (even at that time) essentially that it interfered with personal freedom, slackened family ties, weakened personal responsibility, and destroyed initiative to save.[41]

Connections with other Reich Policies

Bismarck's basic motives regarding social policy — to fight social democracy and to tie the workers to the state — did not change with time. However, to realize his social policy he had to wait for a favourable moment, or else to create the right situation, so that the Reichstag was likely to support his policy. The right opportunity did not arise in the first Reichstag (1871) with its national liberal majority and a strong conservative element. Agricultural insterests with their conservative attitudes were set against any kind of social legislation.

Apart from certain individuals, industry also rejected insurance legislation or at least opposed it for the time being. Workers' demands on the state were considered of dubious validity, state socialism was feared, and the costs were thought to be prohibitive. The attitude of industry shortly before the Kaiser's message was expressed thus:

> If it were not for gratitude towards the princely Chancellor of the Reich, and perhaps even more for fear of forfeiting that mighty pillar of our trade policy and of losing once more the customs duties for which we fought so hard, industry would now show a united front against the project.[42]

Private insurance companies also argued against the idea of a socialist state and in favour of self-help.

From 1872 onwards Bismarck was concerned with the so-called 'Kulturkampf', a struggle for power between the imperial government and the Catholic Church. The legislative result of the 'Kulturkampf' was governmental control of schools (1872) and compulsory civil marriage (1874). Catholicism was represented politically by the Centre Party which formed the second largest group in the Reichstag in 1871. In order to reduce the influence of this party Bismarck was advised in 1874 to put the social question forward as 'perhaps the only effective means of combatting ultramontanism'.[43] However, he saw no chance of realizing his plan at that time as he could not count on the support of the National Liberal Party which had been his parliamentary mainstay since 1866. The 'Kulturkampf' was ended in 1878, partly because it had not proved politically successful. The number of Centre Party deputies in the Reichstag rose from fifty-eight in 1871 to ninety-one in 1874 and ninety-three in 1877. Furthermore, there were changes in the political situation.

1873 had brought economic crisis to Germany. Until then industrial production had expanded by leaps and bounds, creating a surplus, which led to a drop in prices, a narrowed profit margin and the collapse of many companies. Industries affected by the cuts in prices reacted in several ways: by fixing prices, sales volumes and sales areas so as to reduce competition, by founding the Central Federation of Industry (Zentralverband der Industrie) (1875) and by demanding the reintroduction of customs duties on iron which had been abolished between 1869 and 1873. In 1879 customs duties on pig-iron were reintroduced; this measure was directed against English competition in particular.

Agricultural prices also fell in the 1870s largely because of a drop in grain prices due to drastically falling transportation costs from overseas. Thus, in agricultural policy the trend began to move away from the free trade policy (the import of grain had been free of duty since 1865) and from 1880 onwards the duty on grain was reintroduced and import duties were imposed on animal products. Although the agricultural protectionist policy was contrary to the interests of industry, it was supported by the latter within the framework of its general protectionist policy. Moreover, a further motivation of the imperial government for a tariff policy was that customs returns were its only direct source of revenue;

otherwise it had to rely on previously negotiated levies payable by the federal states to the imperial government.

Bismarck exploited the change in the situation by trying to divorce industry from the liberal parties and to gain it as an ally.

> In the field of home affairs Bismarck broke with the National Liberals as they did not want to take part in his protectionist policy; he turned to the Centre Party with which he had just feuded during the 'Kulturkampf', and to the Conservatives.[44]

In 1877/8 an alliance was forged under his leadership between the big industries and large property owners for the purpose of 'mutual protection by tariffs'.[45]

This change of course had far-reaching political consequences. The tariff policy enabled Bismarck to create a different political situation. He turned away from general political and politico-economic liberalism and thereby gained freedom of action for the anti-Socialist law (October 1878) and for legislation on social insurance.

Forms of Social Security

German social insurance, as it developed after 1881, contains four elements, each of differing importance, which together represent the beginnings of social security; (1) saving, (2) welfare (by the community or state), (3) employers' liability, and (4) insurance. In order to understand how and why social insurance in Germany took its specific shape, existing forms of social security must also be borne in mind particularly with regard to methods and institutions.

Saving was of no political importance. Saving was extolled and recommended in contemporary literature but workers neither got into the habit of individual, voluntary saving, as they did not earn enough money to save, nor was there compulsory saving along the lines of the English provident fund system. However, the idea of saving did become incorporated in the later disablement insurance in as far as its benefits — in the case of a claim — were graduated according to the duration and amount of contributions paid. Saving will not, however, be further considered here.

Welfare

Welfare has its origins in the Christian charitable ethos. For a long time the Church alone was responsible for measures which are now called 'social policy.' Church parishes, monasteries and convents set up hospitals and homes; they gave relief to the poor, to the sick and to old people. Thus, persons who were not gainfully employed were given a chance of survival. Alms were the only means of assistance. Usually no-one questioned the causes of poverty. The type and amount of assistance was left to the almsgiver. Thus, on the one hand aid might be given generously and without any obligation, while on the other hand it was haphazard and uncertain so that bad harvests and famine regularly demanded sacrifices of the needy.

The spirit of Christian charity lived on in the towns when they flourished and liberated themselves from the church and from landlordism. Originally, the founding of hospitals (usually by religious orders) was subsidized by the towns. Later the towns took over and ran these charitable institutions themselves. Town poor laws were passed from 1520 onwards. The 'Reichspolizeiordnung' (Police

Order of the Reich) of 1530 stipulated that towns and communities were to sustain their poor. This meant that the public authorities recognized their obligation to provide maintenance; it also meant that the sovereign was relieved of his responsibility.

Official recognition of the former aspect was taken up in the era of absolutism, put into concrete terms and transferred to the state. The 'Allgemeine Landrecht für die Preussischen Staaten' (Common Law for the Prussian States) of 1794 postulated: 'The state is responsible for the provision of food and lodgings for those citizens who are unable to support and fend for themselves, and who cannot obtain such assistance from those private persons who are obliged to provide it by law.' Though poor relief was delegated to existing corporations (guilds and trade associations), to the towns and communities, and though the type and amount of assistance as well as methods of financing it remained unsettled, this law demonstrated that the state recognized its responsibility towards the poor and the needy, with all its far-reaching consequences.

In the wake of growing liberalization in the nineteenth century, laws were passed governing freedom of movement. This meant that the question of local responsibility for poor relief had to be settled at the same time. The Prussian law on poor relief of 1842, for example, was passed for this very purpose, and was later used as a basis for the federal and imperial law of 1870. It stipulated that the local associations for the poor, consisting of one or several communities, were officially responsible for poor relief. The communities' obligation to provide welfare included maintenance of the subsistence minimum. However, support entailed the temporary loss of the right to vote and to hold a public appointment.

Present-day social assistance has developed institutionally from these early welfare measures. Furthermore, certain welfare characteristics combined together with aspects of insurance to form German social insurance. This applies in particular to financing from public funds (state subsidies) and the application of the 'principle of need' (social equalization). The preamble to the first accident insurance bill shows that this connection is not merely technical and methodical but that the legislator was aware of welfare (known as 'poor relief' in those days) being a sphere of responsibility and a tradition. The preamble also reminds us that the modern state recognizes the statutory regulation of assistance to the poor as a duty and that measures to improve the situation of the unpropertied classes 'are only a further development of the form on which state assistance for the poor is based'.[46]

Employers Liability

The provision of social benefits by the employer for his employee goes back to the old patriarchal traditions of landlordism, of guilds and seafaring. Such patriarchal behaviour, which was often criticized because of the restrictions it imposed on personal freedom, continued into the era of early industrialization and led to a large number of works' welfare institutions, the importance of which is often underestimated nowadays.

According to a survey by the Prussian Ministry of Trade, Industry and Public Works there were welfare institutions in 4850 firms in Prussia in 1876. The largest number of these institutions was concerned with accident insurance (2828 firms), followed by sickness and relief funds. In 1860 there were 779 relief funds for factory workers in Prussia with 171 000 members to which the employers also paid contributions. By 1874 this figure had figure had risen to 1931 with 456 000 members. Such funds existed in 3.6 percent of all industrial and commercial enterprises with more than five workers; their members comprised 35.8 percent of all the employed.[47]

Later legislation carried on earlier traditions. The Prussian 'Gesindeordnung' (Servants' Ordinance) of 1810 placed a duty on masters to ensure that care and medical attention was given to their servants in case of illness. The General German Code of Commerce of 1861 obliged shipowners to assume the costs of care and treatment of a sick sailor for up to 3 months in his home port and up to 6 months in a foreign port. The law provided for the continued payment of a salary for up to 6 weeks in the case of illness of clerks. Both clauses were linked to existing conditions and customs.

Employer responsibility applied particularly clearly in the case of employers' liability for damage caused in connection with activities at work. This idea first entered Prussian legislation when the railway companies in 1838 became liable to pay damages to persons conveyed, unless the damage was due to their own negligence or an unavoidable event. A supplementary law in 1869 provided that the liability of the railway companies could not be limited or excluded by contract. This was the first law prohibiting private agreements *vis-à-vis* companies under public law.

For other works accidents the 'Reichshaftpflichtgesetz' (Liability Act) of 1871 brought about an extension of employers' liability compared with the provisions of civil law. Until then the owner of an enterprise had been liable for damages only if he or one of his employees, whom the employer had failed to choose with due care, was at fault. Now such a defence was removed in those enterprises cited by law as having particular accident risks. The employer was liable for damages even if he had chosen his supervisors with care. However, the onus of proof continued to lie with the injured party.

Employers reacted to the extended liability by taking out insurance against accidents with assurance companies or newly founded mutual companies; while the former assumed obligations against previously agreed payment of fixed premiums, the latter apportioned costs after the event. Contributions were usually graded according to danger groups and calculated according to the aggregate wages. It has been estimated that in 1879 about a third of all factory workers were insured against accidents in this way.[48]

This leads to a discussion of the institutions — based on the insurance idea — which existed before social insurance was introduced. It must be borne in mind that the method of employer liability, which was taken over in the development of social insurance in the form of the employer's contribution and the employer's financing of accident insurance, goes back to earlier traditions:

> Moreover, it was an ancient social principle that the master, the lord of the manor, the shipowner and mine owner had to look after his sick, old and needy people. This responsibility was transformed . . . into the employers' compulsory payment at public law of subsidies to the workers' insurance funds or even into liability for certain damages (accidents) which represented part of the production costs.[49]

Insurance

The beginnings and further development of social insurance in Germany are characterized by the principle of insurance. Insurance usually features

the formation of societies of persons exposed to similar risks (insured);
the payment of contributions (premiums) by the insured person depending on the
    level of likely risk;
compensation of risks among the insured when a claim is made upon occurrence
    of an event for which an insurance has been taken out.

The method of insurance was used long before social insurance came into being. From an institutional point of view, three lines of development can be traced which influenced later social insurance legislation and in part determined it; private assurance companies, benevolent or relief funds and miners' provident funds.

Without going into the development of private assurance companies in detail, insurance — starting in particular with maritime and fire insurance — expanded considerably in Germany in the first half of the nineteenth century as did life insurance, mostly in the form of assurance of a lump sum in the event of death. Between 1833 and 1857 alone, fifty assurance companies were founded in Germany. However, private assurances were overall of little practical significance for social security and of none whatsoever for workers. Nevertheless, while legislation on social insurance was being prepared, the idea of insurance was very much in evidence; previous decades had also brought progress to technical aspects of insurance, even if these were not restricted to the private assurance sector.

Relief Funds. The insurance idea was applied at an early stage by the guilds for socio-political aims. The feeling of solidarity which existed and was encouraged in the guilds led to the formation of 'guild collection boxes', i.e. funds to which each member of the guild had to contribute at regular intervals. In case of illness, these funds met the costs of hospitals with which they had an agreement; in the case of death, they paid for funeral expenses; and in the case of disability and old age they covered the costs of food and lodgings. The socio-political activities of the guilds were sporadic at first. However, they were gradually institutionalized and from about the middle of the fourteenth century they were governed by 'statutes' and 'regulations'.

The journeymen also belonged to the guilds at first and were thus bound to contribute to the guild funds. Later, however, there was an organizational split. Apart from the guilds, journeymen's fraternities were formed to which all journeymen belonged and had to contribute. Like the guilds, these fraternities paid for hospitalization in the case of illness. Apart from hospitals under contract, the fraternities also had a few hospitals of their own and later even their own doctors. The fraternities improved on the benefits of the guilds by providing sick pay.

All guild privileges were abolished with the Prussian 'Allgemeine Gewerbeordnung' (General Factory Act) of 1845. However, the journeymen were allowed to maintain existing fraternities and funds for mutual assistance. Moreover, this law contained two innovations of great significance for the future: first, the communities were empowered to declare that it was compulsory for journeymen to contribute to the funds; secondly, it became possible to start new funds for factory workers as well.

A further important development was in the form of a decree made in 1849. The communities were authorized by local byelaws

to declare that it was also compulsory for factory workers to contribute to relief funds,

to oblige the factory owner to pay up to half of the workers' contributions to the relief funds for the workers he employed,

to oblige the factory owner to pay the workers' contributions in advance, subject to deduction from the next wage payment.

A series of such statutes was passed which established the individual rights and duties of fund members and employers. Benefits took the form of assistance in the case of illness, namely medical attention, medicines and meal allowances, as well as funeral expenses. The communities supervised the local relief funds.[50]

While the establishment of relief funds had so far depended upon the initiative of those concerned, the law on industrial relief funds of 1854 authorized the introduction by local byelaw of the compulsory establishment of funds. Furthermore, as 'the local authorities hesitated, handicapped by the industrialists' reluctance',[51] the regional governments were also authorized to pronounce membership of sickness schemes compulsory.

The legal status which had been created in 1854 was essentially taken over by the 'Gewerbeordnung' of the North German Confederation in 1869. There were no innovations until the law on registered relief funds of 1876. This set certain standards and on satisfaction of these conditions, free funds (i.e. those which were not formed in accordance with local byelaws) were provided with a legal framework. They remained corporations under civil law at the same time as acquiring under licence the rights of a 'registered relief fund', i.e. the status of a corporate body with limitation of liability on the fund's means. The statutory standards applied to the charter, executive organs, management and the upper and lower limits of contributions and benefits.

On the eve of social insurance legislation the situation was as follows: there were about 10 000 relief funds of all kinds in Germany in 1874 with about 2 million members.[51] Thus, only a minority of the 8 million workers were members of a relief fund. About half of the total number were registered relief funds. The greater proportion of funds was for workers in certain jobs and trades for which there was local compulsory membership (local sickness funds — 'Ortskrankenkassen') and for workers in certain industries (works sickness funds — 'Betriebskrankenkassen'). Apart from the fact that too few workers participated in these schemes, the confusing coexistence of various funds as well as the discrepancies in types of benefits and their prerequisites were considered deficiencies in the system.

Miners' Provident Funds (Knappschaftskassen). As early as the Middle Ages miners had been 'free', i.e. they were not beholden to a lord of the manor. Their living conditions were similar to those of industrial workers later, in so far as they were often not tied to one place, they were concentrated in a particular area and they depended on wages. The miners joined together to form associations, following the example of the town guilds. These associations, the miners' provident funds, took over, *inter alia,* the care of miners who had fallen ill or had had an accident and also the care of their dependants. Initially, assistance was financed by a voluntary 'pfennig in the moneybox'. Later compulsory contributions by miners and employers (mining companies), as well as the type, amount and duration of benefits in the case of illness, accident, disablement or death, were arranged according to mining rules issued by the sovereign. Although membership of miners' associations was voluntary in principle, when they were replaced in the age of absolutism by the state management system, 83 percent of the miners still belonged to these associations in Prussia in 1852.[52]

The Prussian law of 1854 on the organization of miners, foundry workers and workers in salt mines into miners' associations (Knappschaften), brought decisive innovations. It contained the following provisions:

compulsory insurance for all miners with obligatory miners' provident funds
    which were to be largely self-administered;
free 'treatment and medicine' and sick pay during illness;
lifelong assistance in the case of disablement of death of the breadwinner;
compulsory contribution for the insured person and the employer;
payment of contribution through employer.

Because of these elements, in particular the compulsory insurance, the employer contribution and the self-administration, it has been said that later social insurance legislation was patterned on the miners' insurance. After presenting some of the shortcomings of the miners' insurance, a contemporary summarized his opinion thus:

> Overall, however, it has proved so successful that in the eyes of the best German industrialists and the government, it set a pattern for insurance for all workers. . . . Reference was repeatedly made to it in the course of public debates from 1850–1890.[53]

In 1876 there were 88 miners' provident funds with 255 000 insured miners.

THE FIRST LEGISLATION

Even before the Kaiser's message, the need for an initiative was recognized and demanded. In principle the Chancellor had been willing to act for some time. From 1876 onwards the political situation augured well for such initiative. Those whose efforts for reform were directed towards social security were aware of three models which might be the basis of reform: poor relief, employer liability and insurance. The last of these had developed in a characteristic way from the principles of solidarity and cooperative self-help and had already become compulsory in some sectors. During the preparatory phases prior to legislation, discussions were centered around these starting points, their further development and supplementation.

Crucial Developments

Civil servants responsible for drafting bills took a major part in discussions on how the proposed social insurance should be organized. At first these civil servants were by no means favourably inclined towards the new plan. The majority of them were 'convinced of the correctness of the doctrine of free interplay of forces and of social harmony and disinclined towards direct government assistance'.[54] However, one of the special features of German social policy was that apart from any political aims there existed 'the feeling of responsibility of high civil servants, who worked as representatives of social progress and as advocates of the introduction of social institutions to safeguard workers' existence'.[55]

Indeed, Bismarck appointed new staff (Hofmann) to enforce his protective tariff and social policy. As this did not pose any problems and as he later severed relations with staff committed to social policy with whom he had basic differences of opinion (Lohmann), one may conclude that civil servants did not play an important political role. But in view of the Chancellor's open-mindedness about methods as well as the widespread feeling among socially committed politicians that the state must be active, civil servants did influence the shaping of the bills to a large extent.

The crucial political developments were centered particularly on the questions of compulsory insurance, organization, and finance.[56]

Compulsory Insurance

The liberal zeitgeist in bureaucracy, science and journalism, as well as the opinion of the majority of industrial employers, opposed the extension of compulsory insurance via miners' provident funds and the communal decision on relief funds (1854). Either they were against social reform on principle, or they wanted to retain a free hand in industrial social policy.

In November 1872 a Prussian and Austrian Government delegation, convened by agreement between the two chancellors, conferred on measures to counter the dangers of the international labour movement. They agreed 'on the Prussian principle of compulsory funds with obligatory contributions by both workers and employers'.[57] Extension of this principle to general compulsory insurance was not anticipated at this stage.

Outside the government, compulsory insurance was demanded for the first time by scholars and effectively proposed, for example, in a book by Albert Schäffle in 1870,[58] by Adolph Wagner in a 'Speech on the Social Question' in the Garnisonkirche in Berlin in 1871[59] and by Gustav Schmoller in the opening speech of the Association for Social Policy in 1872.[60] However, even in 1874, after a survey among its members, the Association for Social Policy did not advocate general, compulsory insurance but only an indirect, compulsory fund system based on existing models.[61]

Apart from academics, two industrialists — both in the coal and steel industry — pleaded for general compulsory insurance. In 1878 von Stumm-Halberg proposed a motion in the Reichstag for the establishment of government old age and disablement funds with compulsory membership. In 1880 Baare, the general manager of the Bochum association, drew up a memorandum at the request of the Chancellor's Office, in which a proposal was made to replace employer's liability for on-the-job accidents by an accident insurance scheme.

In 1880 Bismarck seems to have decided on compulsory insurance, but initially only with regard to accident insurance. When the majority of the authorities opposed the idea of general, statutory, compulsory insurance in Stumm's motion, on the grounds that it was too difficult to enforce, Bismarck's comment on the appropriate report of the Imperial Office of the Interior in July 1880 was: 'quite right'. Nevertheless, at the same time he had statutes of the miners' provident funds presented to him which Stumm had recommended as a model.[62]

Thus the starting point of governmental work on social insurance legislation was accident insurance. The much criticized and acknowledged shortcomings of the 'Reichshaftpflichtgesetz' (Liability Act) of 1871 demanded a solution. The fact that the burden of proof lay with the worker meant that employers and insurance companies usually let the matter go to court. Even if the worker won his case, he received only a single cash indemnity. The high costs, vast amount of paper work and many trials were a source of dissatisfaction to employers. Two motions to revise liability legislation had been under review since 1878.

At the beginning of 1880 the Imperial Office of the Interior presented bills on the revision of liability and on the notification of accidents. Bismarck had misgivings about these bills, stopped them and sent them to the Central Association of German Industrialists (Zentralverband deutscher Industrieller) for an opinion — which was negative (March 1880). In April, Baare's memorandum was submitted with its proposal for accident insurance. When the Imperial Office of the Interior pressed Bismarck for a decision, particularly with regard to the proposed reversal of the burden of proof, Bismarck noted on the bill in July: 'State where "culpa" not verifiable'. When the fundamental change in the liability bill was discussed in August 1880, Bismarck set forth his directives:[63]

no revision of liability, but insurance;
limitation to amount of damages but increase in number of cases in which assistance is granted;
establishment of an imperial or state insurance.

Bismarck gave instructions for a bill to be drafted which — using the Baare memorandum — provided for the replacement of civil liability by general accident insurance. These instructions were not made in agreement with but against the advice of the responsible Undersecretary of State (Lohmann). Thus, the decision for compulsory insurance had been made. Afterwards, even with reference to sickness and disablement insurance, it was no longer questioned in government circles.

From a legal point of view, compulsory insurance was to be incorporated in the work contract. In view of the circumstances at that time, this incorporation has been described as a breach of the work contract. Yet the thought of including arrangements in the work contract for insuring the worker was 'both a simple and also brilliant idea which ought to meet with tremendous response'.[64]

Organization and Finance

The First Accident Insurance Bill. In 1880 Bismarck intended to implement accident insurance by means of a government insurance institution (Reichsversicherungsanstalt). This was in keeping with his view of the role of the Reich as patron of the workers. For the same reason he gave instructions for provision to be made for a government contribution, as well as employer contributions, to the costs of accident insurance.

An accident insurance bill was submitted to the Reichstag in this form on 8 March 1881. At the opening of the session on 15 February 1881 a speech by the Kaiser was read in support of the bill. It emphasized the necessity for the law and appealed to the Reichstag to cooperate. However, the Reichstag did not agree to the bill without reservations. While it approved of compulsory insurance, the Reichstag rejected the proposal for a state subsidy, wanted to replace the 'Reichsversicherungsanstalt' with institutions in each German state (Landesanstalten) and wanted to introduce a contribution by the employed person. The government of the Reich did not agree to these modifications and thus the bill became obsolete when the legislative period came to an end.

The Kaiser's Message. Bismarck was determined to try a new approach in the newly elected Reichstag. The Kaiser's speech at the opening of the first session of the 5th Reichstag on 17 November 1881, later known as the Kaiser's message,[65] supported Bismarck's policy. Its general aims and ideas followed on from those given in the speech from the throne in February of the same year: namely, that the curing of social ills is not to be found in the repression of social democratic excesses exclusively but also in the furtherance of workers' well-being.

The content of the message, however, went much further. Whereas an insurance against the consequences of accidents only had been mentioned in February, now the idea of an insurance against sickness as well as 'a higher degree of state welfare' in the case of old age and disability was being considered. The accident insurance bill that had failed in the summer was to be revised 'in light of the debates which had taken place in the Reichstag'.

However, on one decisive point, a new organizational aim was also clearly stated: "A closer connection with the real forces of the people's life and the concentration of the latter in the form of cooperative associations under state protection and with state assistance. . . .' This was Bismarck's reaction at being unable to gain a majority for the 'Reichsversicherungsanstalt' he had originally planned. From then onwards he set great store by cooperative organizations, motivated once more by several overlapping political considerations. His staff reported (1883):

> Accident insurance in itself is of secondary importance to him. His main aim at this point is to create cooperative associations which should gradually be introduced for all classes of productive society so as to acquire a basis for future representation of the people which — instead of or as well as the Reichstag — will play an important role in shaping the law, even if in the most extreme circumstances it could involve a coup. . . .[66]

Bismarck wanted compulsory trade associations for related businesses and industries in the form of corporations at public law — and he forced his plan through.

When debating the first accident insurance bill, the problem of paying for the large number of industrial accidents which caused only temporary incapacity to work had proved difficult. Such accidents resulted in extremely high administrative costs. Thus, the idea evolved of transferring them to already existing relief (i.e. sickness) funds. Furthermore, as welfare in the case of illness was usually inadequate and it was thought that welfare institutions needed to be put in order, the government decided to table a bill for sickness insurance at the same time as the second accident insurance bill on 8 May 1882.

Sickness Insurance Law. The heart of the sickness insurance law was the introduction of compulsory insurance by law. From an organizational point of view, the already existing relief funds had so left their mark that only legal provision and no reorganization seemed necessary.

Two thirds of the contributions were to be paid by the worker and one third by the employer. Bismarck's original idea that the employed person should not have to pay any contributions, as in the case of accident insurance, otherwise 'he would gain nothing from the scheme',[67] did not meet with government approval. His staff saw this as a violation of the insurance principle. It was probably more important that the payment of contributions by workers to the relief funds was already in practice.

The sickness insurance law was debated by the competent board of the Reichstag first of all, perhaps because there were few basic differences of opinion about it. It was separated from the accident insurance bill, as it was thought that the two together were too much to contend with, and thus it was presented to the Plenum alone. The bill was passed with 216 votes in favour and 66 against (mostly Social Democrats and the Progress Party) on 31 May 1883. The law was promulgated on 15 June 1883 and came into force on 1 December 1884. The government had to table the accident insurance bill in the Reichstag for the third time on 6 March 1884. This time Bismarck abandoned the Reich subsidy as it did not seem practicable. The law was promulgated on 6 July 1884 and came into force on 1 October 1885.

'Basic Features' of a Disability Insurance Pension. The government now embarked upon disability insurance. The 'Basic Features', published by the Imperial Office of the Interior in 1887, proposed that the trade associations should be responsible for the organization of this insurance. This plan met with the massive disapproval of industry which feared the supremacy of the trade associations. The plan to establish a Reich insurance institution (Reichsversicherungsanstalt) once again — as was originally planned for accident insurance — failed because of opposition by the Bundesrat (Federal Council) which rejected an increase in federal government power. Thus, insurance institutions were established which were run by the different German states (Landesversicherungsanstalten). The bill presented to the Reichstag at the end of 1888 was debated quickly. 'Bismarck brought pressure to bear for its acceptance once again; he stood up for this bill with the full strength of his personality.'[68] The law was promulgated on 22 June 1889 and came into force on 1 January 1891.

Bismarck proposed that half of the contributions should be paid by the employed and the employer each plus a government subsidy. The government bill had provided for Reich participation amounting to a third of pension expenditure. The government is said to have been motivated by its interest in the purpose of insurance being fulfilled, by the danger that the burden on individual branches of work was too high and by its expectation that insurance would bring considerable alleviation to public poor relief. To reduce the burden on the Reich, the Reichstag stipulated that a fixed amount of 50 M per annum was to be paid to each pension.[69] Thus, for the first time Bismarck's old plan for Reich participation in social insurance was realized.

Self-administration — a Feature of German Social Insurance. One of the characteristics of German social insurance is its self-administration by the insured and their employers. As a matter of principle, this idea was not as controversial as compulsory insurance itself and the organization of the insurance bodies. The tradition of cooperative self-help, as well as communal self-administration, was very much alive and recognized on all sides. The numerous relief funds which existed were run by their members. The Kaiser's message had talked of a 'closer connection with the real forces of the people's life' and of 'corporative associations'. As sickness insurance legislation was dealt with first and was linked with the relief funds for reasons of expediency, there was neither the occasion to introduce self-administration nor the possibility of putting an end to it. The self-administrative bodies now had to include employers who were bound to pay contributions in accordance with their share (one third).

Thus, when the trade associations were established shortly afterwards, it seemed natural for the employers to take over administration as they alone paid compulsory contributions. The government had proposed integrating workers' committees in the boards of management; 'the employers' influence knew how to counter this in the Reichstag'.[70] Provisions were made only for consultation of chosen workers for accident investigation and for accident prevention and safety regulations.

Under the disability insurance law, a committee was established, in addition to the full-time board of management, as a control body that could pass resolutions and was composed of equal numbers of employers and employed, reflecting the provisions relating to finance. Furthermore, the law permitted employers and employees to join the appointed board of management in an honorary capacity.

The Bases of Further Development

By 1889 the foundations of German social insurance legislation had been laid. This had taken place in several stages both from a timing and organizational point of view.

The timing arose from the urgency of settling accident compensation on the one hand and from Bismarck's tactical considerations on the other. In 1881 he wrote:

> If the government were to come forward now with the whole plan for reorganization, numerous circles of society would be horrified by the size of the tasks ahead and would be driven into the arms of the opposition. Thus, the field of social reform must be trodden gradually, step by step. . . .'

The organizational structure was based on already existing relief funds and on Bismarck's tactics. It was the result of compromise and not of a planned policy. In 1905 the Secretary of State, Posadowsky-Wehner, said in the Reichstag:

> If we had 'res integra' now, no reasonable being would think of creating a special organization for sickness insurance and a special organization for old age and disability insurance. I believe it must be left to the future to give these three major insurances one homogeneous form. . . .[71]

In view of this early and weighty opinion which has found supporters up to this very day, the basic organizational structure of German social insurance has shown incredible continuity.

The basic structure of financing social insurance has also shown continuity. The division into three sources of finance, namely employed person's contributions, employers' contributions and state subsidies, has often been modified in its details or subject to shifts in emphasis; however, it has never been questioned in principle.

In summary, Bismarck's original ideas on organization and financing were only realized in part and with modifications. The only plan which he realized fully was the introduction of general, compulsory insurance. Such an achievement at a comparatively early date, with considerable opposition both in theory and practice, makes it possible even today, notwithstanding certain reservations regarding his motives, to agree with 'eyewitnesses' who claimed it was 'highly unlikely that workers' insurance would have been carried through without the Prince's titanic powers'.[72] And: 'The giant strength which pushed legislation through against the trends and currents of the day was purely political and was not based on a particular understanding of the matter at issue.'[73] Regardless of this judgment, when 'pushing through' politically motivated legislation, enough understanding of the matter was incorporated so that German social insurance became workable and, above all, capable of further development.

The fundamental decision-processes had led to previously existing ideas and methods being consistently and considerably extended:

compulsory insurance originated from insurance;
employers' contributions originated from employer liability;
state subsidies and institutions under public law originated from state responsibility;
self-administration originated from cooperative self-help.

Substantive Law

The first three laws on social insurance contained a wealth of detailed provisions which are set out systematically below with special reference to their socio-political significance. The following subdivisions into persons insured, eligibility for benefits, financing and organization will be repeated in the following chronologically ordered sections as far as seems expedient, so as to show the development in each sector.

Persons Insured

Sickness insurance: compulsory insurance by operation of law for workers who were employed in certain legally defined types of industry. Employees were subject to compulsory insurance if their yearly income was less than 2000 M. Right to insurance for persons employed in the designated industries who were not subject to compulsory insurance and whose income did not exceed a certain level.

The sickness insurances were entitled by statutory resolution to include dependants of the insured, either at the expense of all members of the scheme or against payment of a supplementary contribution by the individual insured person (without employer participation).

Accident insurance: persons who worked in certain types of industry were insured (employees up to an annual income of 2000 M).

Pension insurance: compulsory insurance for all wage earners and employees whose annual income did not exceed 2000 M. Possibility of voluntary continuation of insurance; self-insurance for tradespeople and industrialists.

Benefits

Eligibility:
Sickness insurance: for sickness (without legal definition).
Accident insurance: for accidents caused by dangers which arose from the branch

of industry in which the insured person was employed, excluding intentional accidents.

Pension insurance: Incapacity for employment: when the insured person was not in a position to earn a wage corresponding to one sixth of the average annual income of his wage bracket plus one sixth of the usual, local daily wage. Thus, the insured person's capacity to work had to be reduced by two thirds. Qualifying period: 200 weekly contributions (5 years). Old age: 70 years of age and 1200 weekly contributions (30 years).

Monetary Benefits:

Sick pay: 50 percent of the wage from the third day of incapacity to work until the thirteenth week.

Injury pension: two-thirds of the annual income in the case of total incapacity for employment; partial pension corresponding to the reduction of earning capacity; in the case of needing care, increase to 100 percent.

Widow's pension: 20 percent of the annual income.

Disablement pension: basic amount of 50 M (government subsidy), fixed amount of 60 M and a further amount depending on the length of time contributions had been paid and on the wage bracket in which these were paid.

Benefits in Kind and Services:

Sickness insurance covered free medical treatment, medicines and auxiliary treatment. Instead of sick pay and medical expenses, it could cover hospital treatment and partial sick pay. Maternity benefits were granted for 4 weeks after delivery. The insurance institutions met their obligations of paying for medical treatment by making contracts with individual doctors who practiced at district level. Thus, the principle of benefits in kind held true. Instead of the usual two-sided relationship between doctor and patient, there was a three-sided relationship between the sickness insurance institution, doctor and patient. This type of insurance system was completely new and 'had never existed anywhere in the world before'.[74]

The trade associations provided for treatment from the fourteenth week onwards. They were authorized to issue regulations on accident prevention. If these were not observed, the industries concerned could be forced to pay contribution supplements; the insured could be fined.

The insurance institutions of the individual German states (Landesversicherungsanstalten) were empowered to cater for the welfare of insured persons who were not insured against sickness if such illness led to incapacity for work which was the basis of pension eligibility.

Finance:

Sickness insurance: contributions, two-thirds of which were to be paid by the insured and one-third by the employer. In the case of relief funds the insured person bore the costs of the contribution himself. The contribution varied between 1.5 percent and 6 percent. The sickness insurance institutions were to accumulate money amounting to 3-years takings.

Accident insurance: employer contributions; financing through allocation procedure.[75]

Pension insurance: contributions, half paid by the insured and half by the employers. The payments were fixed nominally as weekly contributions for four wage classes to which the insured belong. These classes provided for gradual decreases: the average contribution amounted to 1.7 percent; in the lowest wage bracket it was over 2 percent and in the highest only about 1 percent.

The Reich paid a subsidy to each pension amounting to 50 M per annum and ensured a government guarantee. Financing by means of level premium system.[76]

Organization

The sickness insurance law provided for the following types of funds:

local sickness insurance funds (Ortskrankenkassen) by resolution of the community for insured persons in a branch or type of trade or industry;

works sickness insurance funds (Betriebskrankenkassen) by resolution of the works;

guild sickness insurance funds (Innungskrankenkassen) by resolution of the guilds;

miners' provident funds (Knappschaftskassen) according to provisions existing so far;

builders' sickness insurance funds (Baukrankenkassen) which are to be established by the employers under certain conditions;

community sickness insurance schemes (Gemeinde-Krankenversicherung); a community institution (not a sickness insurance fund) which is to be established by all the communities (or else together with other communities); people who are not covered by one of the other funds are to belong to this scheme.

The 'free' relief funds which continued to function could be recognized by means of an official certificate as sickness insurance institutions, provided their benefits corresponded to those of the local community sickness insurance schemes. This meant that membership of a relief fund freed persons from membership of the statutory insurance funds. (These were known as 'Ersatzkassen' which literally means 'substitute insurance funds').

Local sickness insurance funds were administered by the honorary elected board of management and the general assembly (if there were more than 500 members, the assembly of representatives), in which employed and employers were represented in a ratio of 2 : 1. The minimum benefits of the sickness insurance funds could be extended by statutory resolution.

In the case of disputes over rights and duties, the supervisory board decided first, according to the law; ordinary legal proceedings could be taken against their decision. The local, regional insurance offices (Landesversicherungsanstalten) with their own legal status and administrative autonomy were responsible for pension insurance.

The trade associations created by the accident insurance law were managed by a board of elected representatives of industrialists.

The duties concerning accident prevention, assigned to the trade associations, ran parallel to the duties of the factory inspectors who had already existed previously. The government's attempts to introduce uniformity by empowering the trade associations to commission factory inspectors to work for them failed.[77] Since then dualism has existed between the state factory inspectorate and the accident prevention measures of the accident insurance institutions.

The 'Reichsversicherungsamt' (Imperial Insurance Office) was established by the Accident Insurance Law. This was the highest forum for legal decisions and for the supervision of accident and pension insurance. Later, this office also became the supreme forum for verdicts and resolutions concerning sickness insurance (1913), employees' and miners' insurance schemes (1923) and unemployment insurance.[78]

The Socio-political Result

The first legislation on social insurance improved decisively the condition of many employed persons. Before the sickness insurance law came into force about 2 million workers had been members of relief funds. In 1885 sickness insurance schemes had 4.3 million members. About the same number of workers were insured against accidents and also shortly afterwards for pensions. Thus, at first go, the number of employed with insurance protection doubled. The maximum wage of 2000 M for compulsory insurance for employees was comparatively high judging by present-day standards; it corresponded to about three times the average worker's income in 1882.

The situation also improved decisively for people who had previously been insured in some other way. In the case of an accident at work, the injured person had a claim under public law against the trade association without carrying the burden of proof and without consideration of the question of guilt. Absolute liability had replaced civil liability for intentional and negligent acts. A claim to a pension had replaced the single compensation payment and permitted the injured person to maintain his standard of living even in the case of total inability to work. In the case of illness, the insured person was guaranteed medical attention free of charge instead of the reimbursement of costs which had been customary hitherto. Sick pay prevented the person concerned from suddenly plunging to the depths of financial need.

In the case of disability and old age, the insured person had a claim to a pension for life. The first old age insurance legislation had a modern approach to eligibility for benefits. Interim provisions guaranteed payment of a pension to persons over the age of 70 right from the beginning, notwithstanding the level premium system. This was achieved by waiving the qualifying period for a limited time. As every pension received a fixed state subsidy and a basic amount, useful amounts were paid out as pensions even after a short period of insurance. Already in the first year of disablement insurance (1891) 133 000 old age pensions were granted and after 10 years there were some 600 000.[79]

Progress was undeniably great compared with the previous state of affairs, from both a quantitative and qualitative point of view. Compared, however, with present-day standards of social security for all, the achievements appear more modest and gaps and defects emerge. Several important factors were not covered by insurance, such as protection against unemployment, protection against illness of dependants of the insured or protection against loss of income in the case of the breadwinner's death. Although the absolute number of people insured had risen by leaps and bounds, the relative proportion of people actually covered by insurance was small. The number of people insured (4.3 million in sickness insurance in 1885) corresponded to about 40 percent of all people employed and a mere 10 percent of the population. Pensions were also modest. In 1891[80] the average pension corresponded to 18 percent of the average annual earnings of an employed person. The old age pension for the worker was considered as 'an additional payment for his reduced earnings or other income'.[81]

Further Developments (1883–1900)

Further development of the social security system began at an early date and took place in a series of quick, successive measures. This was because the deficiencies and imperfections already mentioned demanded rectification. The modest beginnings made the gaps and limitations of protection stand out more clearly. Furthermore, the legislative and executive powers gained more confidence in the 'manageability' of the problems as time went on. The new system which had first found its description in 1893[82] proved workable and financially feasible surprisingly quickly. Many fears of difficulties and negative consequences proved exaggerated or of little substance.

The legislative measures taken to complete, extend and clarify initial legislation will not be discussed chronologically but selectively with reference to their problems and effectiveness.[83]

Persons Insured

Development relating to persons insured was tremendous. Apart from introducing compulsory insurance by operation of law, the sickness insurance law had empowered the communities, the German states, the Bundesrat and the Chancellor to extend compulsory insurance to further groups of persons. This measure took administrative practicability into account, as it is often and systematically applied in a stage by stage extension of social security in less industrialized countries today.[84]

Due to the extension of these categories, and to the extension of compulsory insurance according to law, and to a considerable degree to the increasing number of people employed in sectors which were subject to compulsory insurance, the number of members of compulsory sickness insurance schemes rose from 4.3 million to 9.5 million between 1885 and 1900. The insurance schemes made increasing use of their right to include members of the insured person's family for eligibility for benefits. By 1900 family insurance had already been introduced for about half of all employed insured persons and this was done predominantly at the expense of the general contribution. Only 11 out of 201 sickness insurance schemes charged supplementary contributions for family insurance.[85]

Several laws were passed quickly to extend accident insurance to other types of industry, for example to a series of imperial and state enterprises (1885), to agricultural and forestry undertakings (1886), to the building trade and to shipping (1887). The number of persons insured against accidents rose from 4.1 million in 1887 to almost 19 million in 1900. This was also the result of a rise in the wage level for compulsory insurance from 2000 to 3000 M.

Pension insurance did not expand so briskly. Nevertheless, the number of insured persons rose by about one-third as the work force grew and because the Bundesrat passed several resolutions and an amending law in 1900.

Benefits

As far as eligibility for benefits was concerned, the concept of disability was newly formulated in the Disablement Insurance Act of 1899. The two-thirds ceiling remained but for the first time the reasonableness of referring disabled persons to other forms of employment was limited. The yardstick for such employment was that 'which can be expected of the disabled person, with reasonable consideration of his training and previous employment'. Originally only the 'strength and capabilities' of the insured person were rated as the decisive factor.

In the sphere of benefits in kind and services, the pension insurance institutions made prompt use of the possibility of taking over sickness benefits in certain circumstances. The fight against tuberculosis, often a cause of disablement, was of primary concern. In 1894 the first consumptives were treated in santoria; one year later the first sanatorium belonging to a pension insurance institution was opened and others soon followed.

Based on initial experience, the fundamental legal provisions of the Disablement Insurance Act were extended in 1899; the insurance institutions were authorized to arrange for medical treatment such as was deemed necessary. However, it was still the case that the condition which constituted a claim for a pension that 'following illness, incapacity to work is to be feared'. In 1900 nearly 30 000 cures were carried out. The cost amounted to about 7 percent of the pension expenditure (cf. 4 percent in 1977).

Accident prevention activities on the part of the accident insurance institutions also developed rapidly once begun. The first accident prevention regulations were drawn up in 1886. When the trade associations were legally obliged to employ safety advisers in 1900, most of them had already done so.

By amalgamating the arbitration tribunals for individual trade associations and the arbitration tribunals for disablement insurance, similar tribunals began to operate in the field of workers' insurance in 1899, thus setting a pattern for later social jurisdiction.

Financing

It soon emerged that original estimates on the frequency of disablement had been too high. Thus, pension insurance schemes had considerable surpluses. At the turn of the century they held about ten times as much as they gave out each year. However, there were considerable differences between the different pension insurance schemes; there were soon relatively 'rich' and relatively 'poor' institutions as the age structure of the insured and their distribution in the different wage brackets varied a great deal. The original assumption that the risks would balance within the institutions was not borne out by the facts. Thus, a limited common charge fund was introduced in the Disablement Insurance Act in 1899 to create a financial balance among the insurance institutions; four tenths of the contributions were paid into the common charge fund. This was the beginning of financial centralization while maintaining, organizational decentralization. The permanent importance of this decision was that in pension insurance, unlike sickness and accident insurance, contributions and benefits were uniform throughout the Reich.

DEVELOPMENTS SINCE THE TURN OF THE CENTURY

Improvement and Codification (1900–1914)

Continuation of Socio-economic Changes

The socio-economic factors which had characterized the beginnings of social insurance legislation continued to play a significant role up to the eve of the First World War. In the last two decades prior to the Great War, Germany finally completed the transition from an agricultural to an industrial society. The population of the German Reich had grown by about 40 percent from the time it had been founded to the beginning of the First World War. Moreover, the increase in big business and the further development and extension of the railway network also resulted in rapid urbanization. From 1880–1914 the number of people living in towns with over 30 000 inhabitants trebled.

With the growing population, the number of people employed in the secondary (industrial) sphere of production also continued to increase. In 1914, 38 percent of the working population was employed in industry. There was a trend towards increasingly large industrial units: from 1882–1907 the proportion of people working in concerns with less than 6 employed halved, while that of people working in concerns with over 1000 employed increased two-and-a-half-fold.[86]

Industrial production rose two-and-a-half-fold between 1890 and 1914. Expansion in steel and pig-iron production, the chemical industry, the electroindustry and the shipbuilding industry was particularly noticeable. Because of this fast growth, Germany caught up with developments which had been accomplished in other western European countries—particularly in England—decades earlier. Germany increasingly became an exporter of industrial products.

Development towards a society of employees and workers continued. From 1882–1907 the proportion of the self-employed as a percentage of all gainfully employed persons fell from 32 percent to 22 percent; correspondingly the number of employed rose from 68 percent to 78 percent. During the same period, the number of office workers greatly increased in larger concerns to meet growing needs. Their number multiplied seven-fold owing to diversification; their proportion of the gainfully employed rose from 1.9 percent to 5.2 percent. The number of women employed also increased, particularly among office workers. The proportion of women in trade, industry and transportation (without agriculture) of the whole labour force rose from 13 percent to 20 percent from 1882–1907, and among white-collar workers from 2 percent to 12 percent. The degree of worker organization into trade unions also rose considerably. About 6 percent of all employed persons (excluding agriculture) were trade union members in 1890, about 11 percent in 1900 and about 32 percent in 1913.

Industrial expansion led to a clear rise in national income. From 1891–1900 this rose by 20 percent per capita and in the following decade by almost 30 percent. The average yearly earnings of people working in trade, industry and transportation rose from 1895 = 100 to 163 nominally and 125 in real terms in 1913. Average daily working hours dropped from 12 hours around 1870 to 9.5 hours in 1914.[87]

The Political Forces

The turbulent restructuring of the economy and of society was reflected in political representation and social patterns of behaviour, though in clear-cut phases. Of the main political groups represented in the Reichstag from the time the Reich was founded until the First World War, only the Centre Party maintained a constant proportion of votes (around 20 percent) in Reichstag elections. The conservative parties received 25 percent of the votes until 1887 from which time, however, the percentage dropped steadily to 12 percent. The proportion of Liberal votes also fell by half. At the first Reichstag election these parties had gained almost half the total number of votes; in 1890 they only had one-third and in 1912 a mere quarter. The Conservative and Liberal losses were SPD gains. At the first Reichstag election the SPD had only gained 3 percent of the votes; this figure rose to 10 percent in 1884 and with a sudden leap to 20 percent in 1890 — after the anti-Socialist law was abolished — and then steadily to 35 percent in 1912.

However, this change in the proportion of votes was not reflected proportionally in the distribution of seats in the Reichstag. As a result of the direct voting system and the constituency distribution, which had remained unchanged since 1871, the internal migration of the population led to industrial centres and cities being at a disadvantage compared with country areas. Because of this, in the 1903 elections the Conservatives gained 13.5 percent of the votes but 18.9 percent of the seats, the Social Democrats, in contrast, had 31.7 percent of the votes and only 20.4 percent of the seats.[88]

The legal, and conscious integration of workers in society and state lagged even further behind than the election results and the distribution of seats. Committed, well-informed social politicians characterized the situation at the turn of the century thus:

> With the 'monumental feat' of worker insurance the German Reich takes the lead by international standards, in worker protection it is wrestling with other countries to carry off the palm and with regard to equality of the workers, that jewel of social reform, we have long been overtaken.[89]

Freedom of association was considered to be the principal item of equality of rights by social reformers, trade unionists and Social Democrats alike. The demand for freedom of association and a legal basis for collective bargaining were clearly matters of priority for the leaders of the labour movement. Demands for the development of social insurance were not made with such urgency. This arose from the fact that the merits of existing social insurance legislation were stressed both by the government and by middle class political writing and used as an argument against further socio-political activities. While opposition to further development of social insurance consisted merely of delaying tactics and was predominantly undogmatic, the opposition to freedom of association and to the right of collective bargaining was firm and a matter of principle.[90]

At the turn of the century the way was open for further development of social insurance. Although there was no political driving force, there were also no important opposing forces. The conservatives had come to terms with social insurance; the government pointed to its successes and thought a period of consolidation appropriate; the labour movement affirmed the achievements so far and pointed out that the system had to be developed further.

From 1899 (following an amendment to the Disability Insurance Act) the SPD faction of the Reichstag gave its assent to social insurance laws, in particular because its supporters would not have understood a rejection, and because the increasing influence of the pragmatic thinking and active trade unions made the party less dogmatic. However, additional impulses were required to achieve further development of social insurance.

A book entitled *Undesirable Consequences of German Social Policy,* which was published in several editions and was the subject of lively discussion, reflects some of the attitudes and thoughts of the time without referring to politics. The book deplores pension hysteria, party-political misuse of socio-political institutions as well as state regularization.[91] The arguments collected in this book against social insurance have been used repeatedly by conservative elements in more or less modified form ever since. Despite these discussions, the social insurance system was consolidated in this period.

Consolidation of Social Insurance

Continued industrialization, growth of the labour force and the increase in wages during the first decade of the twentieth century provided fertile conditions for further development of social insurance. First, the existing system was to be further developed and experience gained was to be utilized. In general this was good both from the point of view of the administration and that of the insured.

The number of insured persons rose from 9.5 to 15.6 million in sickness insurance and from about 19 to about 28 million in accident insurance in the period from 1900–1914. About 35 percent of the population was protected against the consequences of illness (insured persons and their dependants also covered by insurance schemes). In 1903 an amendment to the law extended the period of eligibility for sick pay from 13 to 26 weeks. The pension insurances paid out about 1.2 million pensions in 1913, predominantly for cases of disablement; less than 10 percent of all pensions were old age pensions. The number of sickness insurance schemes, originally totalling about 18 000, had risen to about 23 000 in 1910. This was due to the increase of local and works sickness insurance schemes.

The insurance institutions formed associations to safeguard their common interests. The 'Verband der Deutschen Berufsgenossenschaften' (Federation of German Trade Associations) had already been founded in 1885; the 'Centralverband der Ortskrankenkassen' (Central Federation of Local Sickness Insurance Schemes) was founded in 1894, the 'Hauptverband deutscher Innungskrankenkassen' (Central Federation of German Guilds' Sickness Insurance Schemes) in 1910 and the 'Verband kaufmännischer eingeschriebener Hilfskassen' (Federation of Commercial, Registered Relief Funds), which were 'Ersatzkassen', in 1912. Such federations had not been envisaged by the legislature. But they served practical needs and were the result of initiatives by the insurances' self-administering bodies.

The consolidation of social insurance was particularly marked in the financial position of the insurances. From their very beginning until 1914 all three insurance branches had had considerable annual surpluses. This led to an accumulation of wealth which in pension insurance was about 8 times the respective annual expenditure in the whole period from 1894–1914. From the present-day perspective of a modified allocation procedure, these were enormously high reserves. From the point of view of the compulsory level premium system at that time, the accumulation of wealth remained far behind the amounts actually required. In sickness insurance the surpluses accumulated to a level which was just short of the expenditure of one year from the turn of the century onwards. The average rate of contribution to sickness insurance schemes rose from 2 to 3 percent by 1913.

The consolidation of relations between sickness insurance schemes and doctors was less difficult. The legislature had considered these relations so unproblematic that originally no provision was made for them at all. From 1892 onwards the insurance institutions were entitled by statute to determine the medical system and to stipulate the number and types of panel doctors working for the schemes. Individual contracts of employment were the norm. In practice, sickness insurances had predominantly used the services of district doctors by contract to realize the principle of benefits in kind. Thus, to a limited extent, a free choice of doctor was assured. Only some of the doctors, however, were permitted to treat members of insurance schemes. The conflict arising from this situation was described thus by a contemporary:

> The medical profession maintains that insurance legislation has ruined the doctors' social standing. However, these much lamented grievances are due less to compulsory insurance than to the overcrowding of the medical profession. . . . Thus, doctors have started to undercut one another, which the sickness insurance schemes have used to advantage.[92]

The background to this statement was very true: from 1876–1900 the numbers of doctors had increased by 50 percent.[93]

In the 1890s discussion centred around two main questions, namely whether the insurance schemes were to allow all doctors or only a selection of them to practice for them and whether individual or collective contracts were to be concluded. Faced with this situation the 'Verband der Ärzte Deutschlands' (a doctors' association in Germany, known as the 'Hartmannbund') was founded in 1900. One of its aims was to ensure that all established doctors would be allowed to practice for the insurance schemes without limitations. This association created a lot of publicity but even the 'Reichsversicherungsordnung' (Imperial Insurance Decree) of 1911 provided no further legal regulation other than to make written contracts compulsory between doctors and sickness insurance schemes. The 'Berlin Agreement' between doctors and sickness insurance associations was only made after it was announced that the doctors were planning a general strike in 1913. The 'Berlin Agreement' recognized the 'Hartmannbund' as the insurance schemes' contractual partner; the trade unions had not achieved this kind of recognition at that time. The 'Berlin Agreement' also stipulated:

certification to practice (Zulassung) of at least one doctor per 1350 insured persons (in the case of family treatment per 1000 insured persons);

that doctors permitted to practice for the sickness insurance schemes had to be chosen by a registration board;

that the individual doctor's contract required the approval of a contract board made up of an equal number of doctors and representatives of the insurances.

Thus, after long and heated arguments, self-administration established basic principles which so far had not been governed by law. These principles became more sophisticated and modified by subsequent legislation but basically could not be altered. At the same time fundamental alternatives, such as doctors employed by sickness insurance schemes, which continued to be possible from a legal point of view, were in fact excluded.

The 'Reichsversicherungsordnung' (Imperial Insurance Decree)

Socio-political debate centred around three themes at the beginning of this century: the desirability and feasibility of including more groups of people in compulsory insurance, the lack of insurance of surviving dependants and also the complexity and lack of uniformity of the law and organization of social insurance. However, discussions on these matters were not as extensive and far-reaching as those at the initial stages in the 1880s. It remains to be seen whether this was in spite of or because of the consolidation successes of social insurance. One important reason was undoubtedly the fact that questions of labour legislation were uppermost in the minds of people in the labour movement and of social reformers. Nevertheless, the development of social insurance did not come to a standstill.

Course of Codification. The wish to simplify the law and the organization of social insurance intensified in 1903 and resulted in a Reichstag resolution 'to consider whether the three types of insurance . . . could be joined organically for the purpose of simplification and reduction of costs and whether the existing laws on worker insurance could be united in a single law'.[94]

The government took its time over these considerations. Four years later, when it finally expressed its views on the subject, it rejected unification of the three forms of insurance but considered codification. In March 1908 it presented the 'Reichsversicherungsordnung' to the governments of the German states. The draft of the decree reached the Reichstag in March 1910; the bill for an introductory law for the transitional period followed. Both laws were accepted and promulgated in 1911. They came into force on 1 January 1912 for pension insurance, on 1 January 1913 for accident insurance and on 1 January 1914 for sickness insurance. The 'Reichsversicherungsordnung' comprehended all existing workers' insurance laws in a systematic arrangement. However, it also contained a series of pertinent innovations.

Innovations. Compulsory sickness insurance was now extended to include all agricultural workers who had previously been covered only occasionally under local statutes. Furthermore, servants, casual labourers and people employed in household and itinerant trades — accounting for almost 7 million people — were included. The maximum salary for compulsory insurance for employees was raised to 2500 M. In real terms, however, this was a decrease; since the average earnings had almost doubled between 1883 and 1913, the relation of the compulsory insurance ceiling to the average income (= 1) had dropped from 3.0 to 1.8; it was now raised to 2.3.

The wage ceiling for compulsory accident insurance was raised to 5000 M. Further innovations were the introduction of appeal proceedings when fixing the level of pensions, and the Bundesrat's authorization to extend the protection of accident insurance to certain occupational diseases.

The 'Reichsversicherungsordnung' put an end to about 8500 community sickness insurance schemes; people insured with them (about 1.7 million) became members of the local sickness insurance institutions for the most part. Thus, the proportion of people insured with local sickness insurance schemes, which had been about one-third in all in 1885 (two-thirds belonged to works sickness insurance schemes), rose to about 60 percent. A new form of insurance scheme was created at this point, namely the 'Landkrankenkasse' (insurance scheme of the agricultural workers). As their number was less than the number of community institutions which had been abolished, the 'Reichsversicherungsordnung' marked the beginning of a process of concentration of sickness insurance institutions which has continued up to this day.

The registered relief funds were not included in the 'Reichsversicherungsordnung'; since then they have been differentiated from the insurance schemes covered by the decree as private (or substitute) sickness insurance schemes (Ersatzkassen). In 1911 a special law repealed the early Relief Fund Law and placed registered relief funds as mutual insurance associations under the law on private assurance companies. However, the 'Reichsversicherungsordnung' settled the relationship to the statutory insurance schemes and the conditions for permitting relief funds to function as private sickness insurance schemes (Ersatzkassen).

There had been many complaints that social democracy dominated in sickness insurance because two-thirds of the administration and self-administration were taken up by representatives of the insured. To counter this, a provision of the 'Reichsversicherungsordnung' stated that the chairman and senior employees of the insurance institution had to be elected by the majority of both the insured and the employers. The same applied to modifications to the insurance statutes. Failing agreement, the supervisory board was to make the decision. 'These innovations were made to provide an effective stop to abuses of a party-political nature which had formerly occurred in some local sickness insurances as long as the unrestricted majority principle was in existence.'[95] It was because of these innovations, *inter alia,* that the SPD faction of the Reichstag voted against the 'Reichsversicherungsordnung'.

Finally, the 'Reichsversicherungsordnung' brought uniformity to the procedural law of the insurance institutions: It also ensured that the insurance authorities were uniformly structured. It was stipulated that there should be insurance offices at the lower administrative authorities and higher insurance offices at the higher administrative authorities. These replaced the former arbitration tribunals and other authorities which had been competent to deal with disputes.

However, the insurance for surviving dependants in the case of the insured person's death, introduced simultaneously with the 'Reichsversicherungsordnung', was even more important for the progress of social policy.

Insurance for Surviving Dependants

Initially, legislation provided only for the payment of a pension to surviving dependants of a deceased insured person in the framework of accident insurance; the widow received 20 percent of her husband's annual earnings. There was no provision for pensions for surviving dependants within the pension insurance schemes; such a benefit was considered desirable but impracticable for financial reasons. The law only provided that the widow should be paid the contributions of the insured, if the deceased had not already drawn a pension.

The introduction of insurance for surviving dependants was demanded both by the public and in the Reichstag. During debates on social and political issues the evidence brought forward to indicate such a need was that the mortality rate, suicide rate and involvement of widows in property offences was markedly higher than among married women.[96]

A specific parliamentary event stimulated progress in this matter. In 1901 the government presented a tariff bill to increase the tariffs on agricultural products in particular but also on industrial goods. The proposed bill was highly controversial both among the public and in the Reichstag. The Conservatives (agriculture) wanted higher tariffs; the Social Democrats were against tariff increases because of the effect on the cost of living. The Centre Party's stand held the key to the fate of the bill. The agriculture-oriented supporters of the bill in this party could only gain the approval of their 'leftish' party colleagues by making a concession in favour of the consumers (i.e. the employers). It was agreed that the pension for surviving dependants was to play a compensatory role. Centre Party members of the house proposed the motion both in committee and plenary sessions, which led to the incorporation of section 15 in the tariff law of 25 December 1902.[97] This stipulated that revenues from certain agricultural tariffs exceeding the average for the years 1898–1903 should be set aside to facilitate the introduction of insurance for surviving dependants. Furthermore, the Reich was bound to create such an insurance by 1 January 1910.[98] This is why insurance for surviving dependants was already included in the first draft of the 'Reichsversicherungsordnung' of 1908.

Eligibility for a widow's pension depended on her 'disablement'. It was implied that a worker's widow could usually be expected to work herself, even if she had children to bring up and had not been gainfully employed previously. It was estimated that about 75 percent of able workers' widows had to go out to work after their husband's death.[99] A pension was not granted if the widow was herself insured against disablement; in this case she received an annual amount of the widow's pension as compensation. Finally, the new provisions were only valid for cases of death after 1 January 1912. In 1912, based on a minimum provision, widows' pensions amounted to 87 M per annum. That corresponded to 47 percent of the average disablement pension and to 9 percent of the average yearly earnings. Thus, pensions for surviving dependants were inadequate in every respect. Nevertheless, these deficiencies aside, a foundation stone had been laid for continuous development up to the present.

Insurance for Employees

After social insurance legislation had become effective and was considered an improvement by practically everyone concerned, employees who were not insured because they earned over 2000 M per annum began to show an interest in being included in the insurance system. In 1901 a syndicate was founded for employees whose main aim was to acquire compulsory insurance. Its efforts were spurred on by the fact that a law on the insurance of employees was passed in Austria in 1906 (where, incidentally, there had existed no insurance for workers). After debating two memoranda, the government submitted the bill for an employees' insurance law to the Reichstag in May 1911 — only a few days before the plenary meeting on the 'Reichsversicherungsordnung'. The bill was discussed briefly and became law in the same year; coming into force on 1 January 1913.

One of the main questions in pre-parliamentary debates was whether disablement insurance ought to be extended to include employees or whether a special institution ought to be established for them. At first employee opinion was divided; however, as time went on the majority inclined towards the creation of a special institution. Both the government and parliament favoured the special institution for financial reasons — inclusion in the workers' insurance would have entailed extending the government subsidy to the new group of persons — and also for political reasons. 'Apart from meeting the employees' wishes, political factors were decisive for the establishment of a special insurance. It was hoped that the middle classes could be swelled by separating employees from the broad masses of workers.'[100] The 'Reichsversicherungsanstalt für Angestellte' (Imperial Insurance Institution for Employees) was founded and administered by the employees themselves.

The Employees' Insurance Act covered both employees with an annual income of between 2000 and 5000 M and all employees who had so far been subject to compulsory insurance (altogether some 1.4 million people). The latter group, however, remained in the workers' insurance and was doubly insured. The employees' insurance institution did not receive a state subsidy. Contributions, half of which were paid by the employers and half by the employees, were disproportionately higher than in the workers' insurance scheme: in lower income brackets 8 percent of the salary (including the contribution for disablement insurance), in higher income brackets 7 percent. The contribution rates, which were about four times higher than for the workers' insurance, provided a financial margin which made decisive improvement both in the pension level and in pension eligibility possible:

retirement age: 65 years (70 for workers);
unconditional widow's pension (disablement in the case of workers);
less stringent criteria to establish disablement (incapacity to work);
orphans' pensions until the age of 18 (15 for workers).

These qualitative differences strengthened the employees' opinion of their own special status for a long time, just as the supporters of the special ruling had hoped. At the same time, workers were given cause to strive hard for equality, a struggle which continued step by step until its attainment in 1957. Thus, the decision in 1911 to establish a special insurance scheme for employees became a pacemaker — quite unintentionally — which had far greater repercussions than was the case in the more developed provisions for civil servants.

The Great War

Surprisingly for observers of the socio-political scene, the workers were integrated into the war in 1914 without friction. Socio-political debate faded out for the moment, but returned again as the war dragged on and caused greater hardship, physical, economic and psychological. In order to ensure cooperation, the military administration, which was endowed with far-reaching powers, worked with the trade unions without prejudice and thereby recognized their existence *de facto*. During this period, social insurance legislation was not a priority for trade union leaders but rather questions of individual and, even more so, collective labour law which had been postponed since Bismarck came to power. In this respect,

> the First World War proved a mighty pacesetter for social policy along the lines of social reform before the war. . . . Recognition of the trade unions, complete freedom of association, workers' committees, collective bargaining, arbitration tribunals . . . all began during the war, and either took shape during this period or were at least outlined for the future.[101]

The 'Reichswirtschaftsamt' (Economic Office of the Reich) was set up in 1917 to deal with the state's duties which had expanded during the war to include socio-political commitments, formerly the concern of the Reich's Office of the Interior. In October 1918 a 'Reichsarbeitsamt' (Labour Office) was established, headed by a trade union leader, Gustav Bauer.

The consolidated social insurance systm proved how well it could function, even under the difficult conditions of the First World War. There were no serious problems in meeting commitments. Legislation at the time provided mainly for adjustments to the special circumstances of the war and was not of a fundamental nature.

In December 1914 the introduction of maternity benefits for the wives of insured servicemen and in April 1915 for the wives of all servicemen, as well as the lowering of the retirement age from 70 to 65 for workers' pension insurance in 1916, was of greater significance.

The Weimar Republic (1919–1932)

Background

The events at the end of the First World War led to the collapse of the monarchy in November 1918 and to the signing of the Weimar constitution on 11 August 1919. The constitution created a parliamentary democratic republic; Social Democratic personalities and the trade union movement left their mark on it in spite of violent opposition by left- and right-wing extremists. The importance that social insurance had gained in domestic politics was reflected in the fact that it was firmly anchored in the Weimar constitution as the duty of the state (art. 161).

Policy-making in the Weimar Republic was influenced to a far greater degree than before the war by economic developments. Basically, the trends characterizing the pre-war period continued:

decrease of the number of employed in the primary sector and increase of the number employed in the tertiary sector;
growth in real incomes;
increasing urbanization, in particular growth of the cities;
increase of average size of businesses and factories.

Furthermore, there occurred a shift in the age structure of the population; this was an entirely new development. Between 1911 and 1934 the proportion of 45–65-year-old people rose from 15 percent to 21 percent; that of the over 65's from 5 percent to 7 percent.

Changing economic conditions during the Weimar Republic, and not continuous trends, are relevant for an understanding of the influence of economic development on political and socio-political processes

the post-war years (1919–1923), adjusting to peace-time production and inflation; the latter had been caused by enormous state debts amounting to three times the national income of the year 1914;
the stabilizing phase (1924–1929) with currency reform, extensive investments and high growth rates;
the world economic crisis (1929–1933) with declining economic activity, sinking real wages and catastrophic levels of unemployment.

The dependency of the majority of the population on wages, along with a new awareness among workers due to the war and the many political changes, made the labour market a particularly important internal political force. After the war the steep rise in unemployment (nearly 3 million) caused great concern and led to the implementation of a series of remedial measures. However, during 1919 this figure sank dramatically. A further rise in the number of unemployed (to about 4 million) during the inflation period was only temporary. However, the continuous rise in unemployment from 1929 onwards had catastrophic repercussions on both the economy and on politics. In the winter of 1931/2 it overstepped the 6 million mark; about one-third of the work force was without a job. This situation was reflected in the results of the NSDAP in Reichstag elections: 20 May 1928 2.6 percent; 14 September 1930 18.3 percent; 31 July 1932 37.3 percent; 06 November 1932 33.1 percent; 5 March 1933 43.9 percent.

During the period of falling revenues and growing deficits in the national budget, the government under Brüning pursued a deflationary policy. It was based on the principle of reactivating the economy by lowering costs and prices; deficits were to be avoided. Taxes were lowered, salaries and pensions in the civil service were reduced, people were dismissed from their jobs and a building stoppage was imposed. This policy was carried through mainly by means of emergency decrees bypassing the Reichstag, based on art. 48 of the constitution.

During the first years after the war general socio-political development was marked initially by the fulfilment of old demands in the labour law sector.

Immediately after the war the 'Gesindeordnung' (Servants' Ordinance) and emergency laws on farm labourers in the different German states were abolished and the industrial safety regulations which had been suspended at the beginning of the war were brought back into force.

Art. 165 of the Weimar constitution provided for collective bargaining autonomy for the settlement of wage and working conditions on equal terms; an earlier decree of 23 December 1918 on collective bargaining agreements, workers' and employees' committees and the arbitration of labour disputes had already defined the term 'collective bargaining agreement' and the possibility of such agreements having binding legal force for all concerned in the particular branch of industry (Allgemeinverbindlichkeitserklärung).

Introduction of the 8-hour working day in November 1918.

The Works' Council Act of 1920 improved the chances of employed persons having their interests represented at their place of work.

In 1920 a law on the employment of severely handicapped persons stipulated that concerns employing a certain number of people were bound to engage such persons.

During the stabilizing phase the following regulations were made:

former poor relief was reformed and developed into state welfare (now social assistance) (1924);

the miners' provident funds were standardized in line with Reich legislation (1923);

the introduction of labour jurisdiction (1926);

the introduction of unemployment insurance (1927).

During the world economic crisis the deflationary policy of the national budgets was also applied to the social security sector. Eligibility for benefits became more difficult and monetary benefits were reduced.

Social insurance passed through unusually stormy times during the first years after the war and again during the world economic crisis with an ever-changing financial situation and frequent amendments to the laws. The years 1930–1932 saw a reduction of social insurance. Nevertheless, its fundamental structure remained intact. Social Democrats and trade unionists had long seen social insurance as 'their' business and one which was worthy of their defence; no decisions could be taken without their consent at that time. Employers and industry were still intent on keeping financial burdens to the minimum; they had not only come to terms with the existence of social insurance, but even approved of it. Members of the insurances' self-administrative boards and officers of the social insurance institutions had a stabilizing effect; at the same time they made themselves heard by the public more than in the years before the war.

It is only of academic interest to mention that in 1928/9 — during the stabilizing phase — there were several publications which expressed basic dissatisfaction with social insurance.[102] Moral corruption, the molly-coddled society and pension neurosis were used as arguments which had already been articulated in the decade prior to the First World War (another stabilizing phase[103]) and were to be voiced again later — during a stabilizing period — when discussions on reform were revived in the 1950s.

The Development of the Classic Branches of Social Security

During the early years of the Weimar Republic, much social insurance legislation was passed despite the priority given to reorganizing labour legislation. From 1883 to 1918 an average of one law was passed per year; from 1919–1932 six laws were passed on average per year. The majority were passed in 1921 (twelve laws), 1922 (twenty-two laws) and 1923 (sixteen laws).[104] This great number of laws gave rise to the reissue of the 'Reichsversicherungsordnung' of 15 December 1924.

However, these figures by no means reveal significant developments in social policy. The majority of the statutory regulations were adaptations of existing laws; questions of definition, procedure and organization and a few laws on the nominal levels of contributions and benefits were adapted to the special, multi-facetted and rapidly changing economic, social and legal conditions of the postwar years and the years of inflation. The following rules reflected socio-political developments.

Persons Insured. As far as the insured persons were concerned, double insurance of employees with a low income, who were also covered by workers' pension insurance, was abolished from 1923 onwards. At the same time the possibility of an employed person insuring himself (up to the age of 40) was introduced. The income level for compulsory insurance was raised in several stages (to 8400 RM by 1928) to four times the average earnings; this level had never been reached before and has never been achieved since then.

The income level for compulsory sickness insurance was adjusted in 1925 and 1927 and corresponds approximately to current levels. A limit to accident insurance depending on the level of income was abolished in 1923; other types of industries were included in accident insurance.

The inclusion of persons who had had an accident while saving another person's life was completely new (1928). This separation from industry-oriented activities to actions in the public interest was the first step towards drawing up a long list of persons who are now insured according to section 539 of the 'Reichsversicherungsordnung'. Nowadays, this list is occasionally discussed under the heading of 'unreal' accident insurance.

Eligibility for Benefits. Further developments regarding conditions of eligibility for benefits were:

The introduction of a right to maternity benefits for all females covered by sickness insurance (1919).

The payment of orphans' pensions from pension insurance up to the age of 18 (1923).

The extension of accident insurance protection to occupational diseases, official recognition first of eleven occupational illnesses (1925) and later of twenty-two (1929).

Right to a widow's pension in the workers' pension insurance scheme at the age of 65, without being disabled.

Right to a pension because of incapacity to work from the employees' insurance scheme, also at the age of 60 after one year's unemployment (1929).

In miners' pension insurance schemes a pension was granted for cases of incapacity to work if the following conditions were fulfilled; (a) 300 monthly contributions, (b) 180 monthly contributions when actually working as a miner, (c) 50 years of age, and (d) no insurance for a wage-earning job of equal value.

Monetary benefits were raised repeatedly in all branches of insurance. However, these rises did not bring any permanent improvement in relation to earned incomes but were merely later adjustments — particularly during inflation — to higher wages and prices. Even when the currency was stabilized, pensions were still low. Thus, in 1929 30 percent of the pensioners in the towns (22 percent in rural districts) received welfare relief in addition. A further 20 percent were simply not eligible for welfare relief as they had an additional source of income from working.[105]

In 1928 the possibility of receiving a lump-sum settlement to buy or keep up property instead of being paid a pension was introduced within the framework of accident insurance.

Benefits in Kind and Services. In the sphere of benefits in kind and services, vocational training assistance was introduced as a new benefit of accident insurance in 1925. Training and further training schemes were intended not only to prepare people to find a job of the type which they had had previously, or to help them advance professionally, but also to prepare them for an entirely new job. The insurance institutions could use funds to provide opportunities for work and make appropriate arrangements for vocational training assistance. This was indicative of both individual and institutional promotion in its early stages and was a significant step towards a number of measures which developed rapidly. After the Second World War this sector was handed over to the pension insurance schemes and the 'Bundesanstalt für Arbeit' (the Federal Labour Office); it is sometimes popularly known as 'rehabilitation'. (For the relationship between doctors and sickness insurance schemes see below.)

Finance. As far as finance was concerned, the sickness and accident insurances could adapt to changing conditions by means of the allocation system. Thus, fundamental legislative amendments were not necessary until the world economic crisis.

In 1917 the workers' pension insurance had funds amounting to 2500 million M; this corresponded to just under ten times the annual expenditure. However, these funds were subscribed almost exclusively to war loan. After inflation practically none of this money was left (250 million RM). Over 30 years after the establishment of insurance, the institutions were back to square one as far as the demands of the level premium system were concerned. As circumstances demanded continued payment and an increase in benefits while considerable rises in contributions were impossible, a contributory (or allocation) system was practiced *de facto*, even though the level premium system continued *de jure*—until 1957! Without prejudice to numerous amendments regarding the state subsidy, until 1931 the proportion of state expenditure on pension insurance remained as high—at about 30 percent—as it had been at the end of the war.

Effects of the Deflationary Policy. It has already been mentioned that the government's procyclical deflationary policy during the world economic crisis was also applied to social insurance. In order to bring expenditure into line with revenues which had declined because of the reduction in employment and wages, several measures were introduced by means of emergency decrees from 1930–1932, including:

Abolition of the injury pension from accident insurance in cases where ability to work is reduced by less than 20 percent (formerly 10 percent); some 130 000 pensions were abolished; expenditure was thus reduced by 10 percent.
The injury pension was reduced by 7.5 percent to 15 percent.
Current pensions already being paid out were reduced by 6 RM, new pensions by 7 RM per month (a saving of 410 million RM per annum).
Child allowances and orphans' pensions from pension insurance were to end when the beneficiary was 15 years old.
Interruption of pension when sick pay, accident pension or other pensions payments were received.
Introduction of a sickness certificate fee and a prescription charge of 50 Rpf. each. (In 1923 a 10 percent contribution towards the cost of medicines had been introduced.)
Introduction of a maximum basic wage (10 RM per day).
Beginning of sick pay with the fourth day of incapacity to work (previously: with onset of the illness).
Limitation of sickness insurance benefits to the regular benefits.

The deterioration in benefits had tremendous repercussions. The total expenditure on social insurance, which had continually risen in absolute figures until then, dropped by a quarter, from 4400 million RM in 1930 to 3300 million RM in 1932. Thus, social insurance experienced its greatest reduction.

From the perspective of today, these measures are comprehensible only insofar as they were necessary to avoid increasing contributions at a time of declining wages and growing unemployment. They are no longer comprehensible so far as pension insurance is concerned. By 1930 the workers' pension insurance had again amassed funds amounting to 1600 million RM (= 13 months of expenditure) which could easily have covered the deficit of 1931 and 1932 of some 180 million RM per annum. The employees' insurance never had a deficit because its members tended to be younger and less affected by unemployment. Thus, from 1929 to 1932 it built up its funds to 766 million RM; this figure corresponded to almost three times the expenditure of 1932. It was directed to invest some of its capital gain in Reich railway shares only so as to relieve the state. Decision makers must have experienced both horror of deficit spending and fascination at the unearned premium reserve calculated as technically necessary for insurance (18 000 million RM for the workers' pension insurance in 1931).

Organization, Administrative Autonomy and the 'Reichsknappschaftsgesetz' (Law on Miners' Provident Funds). As far as organization was concerned, the consolidatory process in sickness insurance continued. By 1932 the number of sickness insurance schemes had dropped to about 6600. Sixty-two percent of the insured were members of local sickness insurance schemes (Ortskrankenkassen), 14 percent of works' sickness insurance schemes (Betriebskrankenkassen) and 9 percent of private sickness insurance schemes (Ersatzkassen).

Miners' insurance schemes were completely reorganized. Initial legislation in the 1880s had left the miners' provident funds largely untouched. They continued to be subject to the laws of the individual German states. Reich law only stipulated that miners' provident funds were to provide at least the level of benefits of the works' sickness insurance schemes. They could also provide pension insurance on application, instead of the insurance institutions of the respective German state (Landesversicherungsanstalt); most miners' provident funds made use of this ruling. A miners' provident fund association covering the entire Reich had been established only for accident insurance. At the end of the First World War there were 110 miners' provident fund associations. This lack of unity and — above all — the fact that the transfer from one association to another was only partially regulated, had for a long time exacerbated the demand for legislation to unite miners' provident funds.

A draft bill to meet this demand was promulgated as law under the name of the 'Reichsknappschaftsgesetz' in 1923. A national miners' provident fund association (from 1926 onwards the miners' provident fund — 'Reichsknappschaft') carries out sickness and pension insurance for all persons (workers and employees) employed in the mining industry. Accident insurance remains the concern of the miners' provident fund association (Knappschaftsberufsgenossenschaft).

With reference to the principle of self-administration, it is of interest to mention that the separate election of insured and employer representatives for the administrative bodies of the sickness insurance institutions, introduced by the 'Reichsversicherungsordnung', was abolished in 1919. Thus, a two-thirds majority of representatives of the insured was once more the determining factor. This became significant later for the political persecution measures of the Nazi regime.

Standardization of the Law on Panel Doctors

The main outlines of the present-day panel doctor law were formulated during the world economic crisis. These were, however, the result of a long development fraught with many conflicts. The 'Berlin Agreement' between doctors and sickness insurance schemes (see above) settled their relationship and also proved satisfactory during the first few post war years, apart from a doctors' strike in 1920. Tension mounted once again when the limited 'Berlin Agreement' expired at the end of 1923. In October, the most important regulations of this agreement were incorporated in the 'Reichsversicherungsordnung'. The doctors protested against this.

In November 1923 the doctors went on strike. This lasted until January in most places and until June 1924 in Berlin. During this time the Association of Sickness Insurances in Berlin set up outpatients' units with employed doctors so that medical treatment was guaranteed. This step, born of necessity during the dispute, later gave rise to many discussions on principles. The associations of independently practicing doctors immediately considered it a threat and fought it vehemently. The thirty-eight outpatients' units and the doctors working there had in the meantime so grown in importance that they were to continue to function even when the strike was over.

New tension developed when the government, reacting to the reduction in sickness insurances' receipts, passed an emergency decree in July 1930. According to the decree, the insurances had either to form medical examination units or to employ health officers to give second medical opinions. The decree did indeed improve the ratio of doctors (who were to be certified to practice for the insurances) to insured to 1 : 1000 ('Berlin Agreement' 1 : 1350); moreover, at that time there were already over 1000 health officers working for the sickness insurances. However, this increase and the fact that they were protected by law met with the doctors' opposition. Many doctors were worried that the idea of introducing a system of employed doctors into sickness insurance schemes was being considered.[106]

However, it was remarkable that the doctors' reaction — when faced with the insurances' financial predicament — proved both aggressive and constructive at the same time. At a doctors' congress in 1931, overall remuneration was demanded, i.e. the medical profession wanted to be assured of a certain share of the insurances' receipts even if these were to show an absolute drop.

The basic idea was adopted by the government in a decree in 1932[107] and developed along the lines of equal ranking self-administration. The domestic political situation encouraged the government to improve the ratio again in favour of the doctors (1 : 600); in addition, it established a closed system settling the relationship between doctors and sickness insurance institutions:

The establishment of Panel Doctors' Associations (Kassenärztliche Vereinigungen) as corporations under public law; these were responsible for ensuring medical treatment.

Obligation to conclude contracts between the Panel Doctors' Associations and the sickness insurance schemes.

The sickness insurance pays a fee which has been agreed (flat rate per capita) to the Panel Doctors' Association with no obligation towards the individual doctor (total remuneration). The flat rate per capita is coupled with a basic salary.

The Panel Doctors' Association establishes a scale of distribution of fees and assumes responsibility for prescriptions of drugs and medicines.

Certification (Zulassung) to work as a panel doctor to be granted by certification boards composed of equal numbers of representatives of the insurance and of the medical profession.

Many of the details of this system, regulating the relationship between sickness insurance institutions and doctors, have been modified, further developed, or partially abolished since then. However, its fundamental features — self-administration, overall remuneration, assurance of medical treatment and control of panel doctors' activities by the Panel Doctors' Association — continue to exist to this very day and have continually proven their workability in ever-changing situations compared with possible alternative solutions.

Introduction of Unemployment Insurance

The introduction of unemployment insurance or even of state-run employment exchanges seemed impossible to the pioneers of social insurance. This question was not seriously discussed as a problem for legislation in the 1880s and 1890s. It was the trade unions and communities which first became active in this sphere; commercial employment agencies and labour offices were opened by employer and industrial associations. Before the First World War over 2000 public or association labour offices and some 7000 employment agencies were set up. In 1910 the Reichstag passed a law stipulating the conditions required of commercial employment agencies. Relief funds for unemployment had also been started by trade unions and some towns; other towns paid subsidies to existing institutions (Ghent system).

After the First World War broke out, the number of unemployed soared.[108] In August 1914 this led the government to establish a 'Reichszentrale für Arbeitsnachweise' (Central Labour Exchange). This played a co-ordinating role and improved the transparency of the labour market but did not alleviate the burden on existing relief funds which was growing enormously. Trade unions and towns thus demanded state participation in their expenditure. However, during the war legislative measures were not taken, presumably as the number of unemployed dropped after only a few months; from then on recruitment of labour became the focus of interest.

This situation changed fundamentally at the end of the war when some 6 million soldiers were discharged. At the beginning of 1919 there were over 1 million unemployed. On 13 November 1918 a decree was passed providing relief for the unemployed; this provided that the communities were to be responsible for unemployment relief (without fixing an amount) and established that the Reich would contribute 50 percent and the respective German state 33 percent of the outlay. From 1923 onwards employers and employed had to pay contributions to unemployment relief. However, benefits remained subject to a means test.

In December 1918, parallel with the decree on unemployment relief, the government declared that labour exchanges were to be further developed with the Reich's financial assistance. Competence for job placement was first transferred from the Demobilization Office to the Minister of Labour and then to the 'Reichsamt für Arbeitsvermittlung' (National Employment Exchange Office) established in 15 January 1920. On 1 October 1922, a law came into force which prescribed matters of organization of labour exchanges, and the principles of impartiality and free services. It forbade commercially run employment agencies.

Unemployment insurance had been discussed since the end of the war. The principle of insurance, as opposed to the welfare principle which applied hitherto, soon made progress. However, it proved more difficult to decide whether and to what extent risk compensation should differ between the various branches of industry. From an organizational point of view the original idea of combining the new insurance with sickness insurance soon lost ground compared with the idea of combining insurance and placement as a matter of priority.[109] It was generally agreed that such an insurance was to be financed by contributions. However, the matter of Reich or community participation in the scheme remained controversial.

Legislation was delayed because of inflation; bills had been withdrawn and amended several times since 1919. In 1926, as an interim measure, a law introduced 'crisis relief' to provide assistance upon expiry of unemployment relief. This assistance was to be borne by the communities; three quarters of the costs were reimbursed by the Reich.

Finally, on 1 October 1927, the law on labour offices and unemployment insurance came into force. Its fundamental features were:

The establishment of the 'Reichsanstalt für Arbeitsvermittlung und Arbeitslosenversicherung' (National Institution for Labour Offices and Unemployment Insurance) in the form of a corporation under public law, self administered, (representatives of employers, employed and of the state), with a substructure of public authorities dealing with unemployment (labour exchanges of the individual German states and towns).

A legal right to unemployment benefit; the previous system of unemployment relief was repealed; crisis relief upon expiry of the maximum period of receiving assistance (26 weeks) continued as part of the work of the 'Reichsanstalt'.

Labour offices and vocational guidance were the duties of the 'Reichsanstalt'; establishment of the monopoly of the 'Reichsanstalt' on job placement (with exceptions).

Those persons included in sickness and employees' insurance schemes were insured.

Financing solely by employers' and employed persons' contributions (together 3 percent) to be collected by the sickness insurances.

Shortly after the new law came into force, the number of unemployed rose far above the figure which was considered normal. The 'Reichsanstalt' was already in financial difficulties during 1929. The state—itself in the midst of a financial crisis—had to help with loans and subsidies. The alternative was either to reduce benefits (supported by the employers and in particular by the Deutsche Volkspartei—the German People's Party) or to increase contributions (supported by the trade unions and the Social Democrats in the government). As an inadequate compromise, benefits were cut at the end of 1929 and contributions were increased for the period until June 1930 to 3.5 percent. When a decision had to be made once again at the beginning of 1930, the grand coalition collapsed as the Social Democrats would not accept any further deterioration of benefits and the other parties in the government would not agree to further increases of contributions or state debts.[110]

In the meantime the number of unemployed continued to rise at the expected annual average. When the new government under Brüning failed to win its case in the Reichstag with proposals for the improvement of the state's finances and unemployment insurance, the Reichstag was dissolved. An emergency decree of 26 July 1930 provided for a reduction in benefits, an increased state subsidy and a contribution of 4.5 percent. Nevertheless, the deficit rapidly continued to rise still further. To stop it from being a burden on the state budget, contributions were raised to 6.5 percent in October 1930. At the same time the state deliberately limited its expenditure on crisis relief, which meant that the communities' welfare costs grew. An ever-increasing number of unemployed went from unemployment insurance via crisis relief to general welfare. At the end of 1931 about one-third of the total 4.5 million unemployed were supported by each of these branches.

Even the drastic rise in contributions did not bring financial equilibrium. An emergency decree of 5 June 1931 directed that there would be drastic reductions in the benefit rates of unemployment insurance and crisis relief as well as other cutbacks. The suspension of unemployment insurance and the return to unemployment assistance depending on need were publicly discussed at this time. In June 1932 benefit rates were reduced yet again and the payment of benefits was limited to 6 weeks; after that benefits depended on needs. To counteract the catastrophic burden on the communities, the curtailment of crisis relief was repealed in November 1932 until March 1933. However, this solution which had been planned for the winter only was to become permanent.[111]

The fate of unemployment insurance during the first few years of its existence is but one aspect of the general situation which led to the change of political system in 1933. This change had catastrophic consequences, which also influenced the development of social insurance, if not in so far-reaching a way.

Beginnings of Social Assistance and Social Compensation

Apart from unemployment insurance, two further items of social relevance were regulated fundamentally and in a new way if not for the first time in the Weimar Republic. Both poor law and subsistence law were decisively developed compared with the time of the monarchy and were given a basic structure which has lasted to this day irrespective of further developments.

Based on the origins of poor law (cf. above p. 17) welfare had to provide what was considered necessary for subsistence; the type and scope of assistance was left to the legislation of the individual German states (the 'Länder'). Until 1918 people receiving such assistance were frequently denied the right to vote. The need for social assistance was not considered by reference to the needy person, but as an aspect of public order. As recently as 1901 one could read in a decision of the 'Bundesamt für Heimatwesen':

> The poor man has no obligatory claim to assistance. It is not the poor man who is holder of the claim; it is the general public, the state. The poor man is only the object of eligibility for relief, which latter is imposed on the relief organizations in the public interest.[112]

This attitude no longer prevailed in the new republic. In 1924 a decree on obligatory welfare and the bases for eligibility, type and extent of public welfare, was issued. With this, a uniform, modernized welfare law and efficient welfare institutions — sponsored by towns and rural districts — were created. Because of individualization and the subsidy principle of assistance, disenfranchisement was abolished; assistance with self-help was brought to the fore and day-to-day subsistence aid was calculated according to standard rates. These rates were to ensure 'essential needs' and not only the 'strictly essential necessities for life' as previously.

Apart from general welfare, there was also an 'enhanced' type of welfare which had already been introduced earlier for special groups of persons: disabled ex-servicemen, surviving dependants of servicemen killed in action, social insurance pensioners and small pensioners (certain people who had been badly affected by inflation). For the latter type of welfare there were less stringent conditions of eligibility, less stringent regulations on other qualifying criteria and standard rates for subsistence were 25 percent higher. The greater part of the costs was covered by the state.

Welfare for disabled ex-servicemen and surviving dependants of servicemen had been regulated in 1906 by the Soldiers' Welfare Law and the Officers' Pension Law.[113] Different rates of benefit applied for both groups and this met with a lack of understanding among many disabled servicemen during the war who came from the same types of professions and had suffered similar disablement.

First of all, in 1919 the new government transferred responsibility for military pension and welfare schemes from the military authorities to the National Ministry of Labour. In the Welfare Act of 1920, the differentiation of pensions according to military rank was abolished, as were other differences according to whether there were internal or external consequences of injury and according to whether they were war and peace injuries. The basis for assessing the pension level was impairment of the ability to work. Moreover, the meaning of disablement for work and for loss of income of the injured person was to be considered; this was done by means of a compensation allowance, predominantly a lump sum. In certain circumstances there also existed an allowance for the severely disabled, an allowance for nursing and the possibility of a lump-sum settlement. The right to receive treatment was introduced and its implementation was entrusted to the sickness insurances.

The Era of National Socialism (1933–1945)

Background

When the National Socialist Party came to power in Germany in January 1933, it had no particular policy for social insurance. Its influential leaders were far more absorbed in other matters. Development of social insurance during this period followed along the lines of logical necessity and of previous development. The group of insured persons was extended, the restrictions on benefits imposed during the depression were lifted gradually and the organizational structure remained essentially the same. The new regime's intervention in social insurance was motivated not by a desire to introduce its own social policy but derived from its general policies which particularly had an anti-democratic and racist content. This intervention can be described simply as power politics and was part of the regime's staff policy.

The lack of interest of the new regime in social policy was due to the fact that the National Socialist Party had neither tradition nor experience of the labour world. Apart from its anti-democratic and racist interventions, its interest was not aroused later either, as social insurance did not contain any politically relevant problems. The growing national income and the drastically declining number of unemployed soon overcame the deficit problem and, indeed, soon provided a source of finance for other state expenditure. In the people's eyes, the fall in unemployment pointed to a successful social policy which overshadowed other needs, thus making them seem less important—quite apart from the fact that such necessities could not be articulated either politically or in the press. This also explains why the quota of social benefits dropped drastically, compared not only with that of the depression but also with that of the Weimar Republic. The quota of social benefits (public social benefits as a percentage of the national income) was as follows:[114] 1927, 10.4; 1932, 20.7; 1939, 8.7.

In view of the political circumstances, ideas for reform elaborated by the German Labour Front (Deutsche Arbeitsfront), which aimed — as part of the party programme — at introducing a general old age pension scheme and at abolishing the employer contribution while raising wages accordingly, remained a subject of discussion without political relevance. Because of the lack of 'political tailwind', social policy was predominantly discussed only among civil servants in the National Ministry of Labour. The staff of this ministry remained largely unchanged; it was either Prusso-Conservative oriented or Christian Social and averse to fundamental reform. The debate on reform was of a defensive nature between 1935 and 1940; it was tough and fought with the weapons of superior knowledge and flexible tactics but was nevertheless without any dramatic climax.[115]

Abolition of Self-administration, Political and Racial Persecution

State intervention during the first years of the NS regime, motivated by power politics, and anti-democratic and racist policies, was indeed dramatic. As early as May 1933 — only a few days after the trade union movement was destroyed — a law was passed to 'reestablish the professional civil service' and another law was passed on 'honorary posts in social insurance'. The first of these laws provided the legal basis for dismissing 2500–4000, or at least 10 percent of all sickness insurance employees.[116] This primarily affected local sickness insurances. In their association publication, 'Die Ortskrankenkasse', a Nazi official justified these measures by saying

> that following the Führer's seizure of power, changes also had to be made in the local sickness insurances. It was important to regain the local sickness insurances, which at that time had been largely in the hands of Marxists and Jews, for their real purpose, namely for the insurance of the working population of Germany.[117]

Grounds for dismissal were, *inter alia:*

Marxist activities (communist or social democratic);
non-Aryan descent;
no guarantee of wholehearted backing for the national state because of previous political activities.

According to the second law, holders of honorary posts could be dismissed if they had been elected on the proposal of an industrial association — trade union — and if the association or its successor — in the case of trade unions these were NS organizations — declared that the holder of the post in question did not have their trust. The majority of representatives of the insured on the boards of local and works sickness insurances was affected by this law. The posts in administration and self-administration which thus became vacant were filled by NS followers according to plan.

Self-administration had ceased to exist *de facto* in May 1933; it was formally abolished by the Reconstruction Act (Aufbaugesetz) of July 1934, an omnibus act which was built up and completed by a total of seventeen decrees from 1934–1942. The insurance institutions were run by state appointed 'managers' who were answerable to the supervisory authority. The self-administration bodies were abolished; there was only an 'advisory board' to assist and advise the 'manager'.

Persecution also spread to the doctors working for the sickness insurances. In 1933 decrees by the Minister of Labour excluded 'non-Aryans' and persons who had been involved in communist activities, from working as doctors for the sickness insurances. It has been estimated that this affected about 2800 doctors or 8 percent of all practising panel doctors by the end of 1933. The decision to 'exclude' individual doctors lay in the hands of the Associations of Panel Doctors; the excluded doctor had a right of appeal to the Minister of Labour. The Ministry did indeed repeal many 'exclusion' decisions of the doctors' associations Not being allowed to practise as a panel doctor was tantamount to ruin, as the panel doctors' associations also informed the private sickness insurances. The association of private sickness insurances circulated a list of doctors excluded from practising under the heading 'List of doctors who are hostile to the state'.[118]

Legal Development

In other respects, social policy[119] ran largely along the usual lines and in some ways can be said to have brought about further developments.

The circle of persons included was clearly enlarged. Further groups of self-employed persons (artists, people in home industries, midwives) were included in sickness insurance as well as people receiving pensions (1941) for whom the pension insurance institution deducted a lump-sum contribution per pensioner for sickness insurance. Compulsory accident insurance was extended (1939) to all farmers and their wives since this had been regulated only by bye-laws until then.

There was a further significant qualitative change in accident insurance. Since its beginnings, insurance protection had been extended by incorporating further industries into the insurance. The injured person had to prove that he had suffered an injury in an insured concern. This obligation was abolished in 1942. From then on the work itself was insured (for all persons employed on the basis of a contract of employment, service or apprenticeship). The works insurance was replaced by a work insurance. Thus, the term 'industrial accident' was replaced by 'accident at work'.

In 1937 all citizens up to the age of 40 were entitled to voluntary pension insurance (self-insurance).

In 1938 the Law on Old Age Pensions for German Craftsmen was passed. For the first time it extended compulsory insurance for cases of old age and disablement to a large number of self-employed persons, without claiming that they were in a similar need of protection to other employed persons.

The self-employed craftsmen had to contribute to employees' insurance; they did not have to pay into the insurance if they paid as much in premiums to a private life insurance as they would have had to contribute to the employees' insurance.

As far as benefits were concerned — as already mentioned — a large number of the reductions and limitations imposed during the depression was gradually lifted. Further improvements in sickness insurance were the abolition of a time limit for medical care and the introduction of maternity benefits as a wage substitute for 6 weeks before and after the birth of a child with costs reimbursed by the Reich (1942). In pensions insurance, increases in benefits were essentially adaptations. The ruling introduced in 1942, that pensions were to be based on certified wages and salaries and no longer on the amount of contributions paid in, was to be of lasting effect.

There were no serious problems financing social insurance because of the economic boom and a restrictive benefits policy. The contribution rates remained stable. Although a law was passed in 1933 'to maintain the performance ability' of pension insurances and the Extension Law (Ausbaugesetz) of 1937 also contained financing regulations, these were basically intended to improve conditions for having a full funding system (Anwartschaftsdeckungsverfahren). The reasons for this were mathematically calculated insurance deficits, not actual deficits; on the contrary, the funds of the pensions insurance grew steadily and considerably; however, they had, in fact, to be paid to the Reich against letter or debt register claims.

The state subsidy for workers' pension insurance was settled and increased in 1933, a state subsidy for employees' insurance and a state guarantee for the funds of pensions insurance was introduced in 1937. Moreover, the unemployment insurance was to transfer funds to the pensions insurance. With the drop in unemployment, contributions could have been drastically reduced. Instead, the high contribution rates of the depression (6.5 percent) were maintained and the surpluses were disposed of. Thus, from 1938 funds amounting to 18 percent (workers' insurance) and 25 percent (employees' insurance) of the revenue from contributions were transferred to pensions insurance. The surpluses were otherwise used for building motorways, for child allowances

> as well as funds for other nationally important tasks of the Reich. Whatever was left of these surpluses after that was paid to the Reich to cover general state expenses. . . . In reality, contributions were collected and used like taxes for the Reich's budget.[120]

An important and permanent new feature was the method of collecting contributions. Instead of the previous system of stamps, contributions were deducted directly from wages from 1942 onwards. The sickness insurances deducted the total amount, including the contributions for pension and unemployment insurance; the basis for calculating the level of contributions and wage tax was standardized. This simplified administration considerably.

As far as organization was concerned, the abolition of self-administration has already been mentioned above (p. 53). The Reconstruction Law of 1934 and the decrees deriving from it brought about further changes. However, these were not of a fundamental nature:

The community tasks of sickness insurance were transferred to the insurance institutions of the respective German state (Landesversicherungsanstalten); the same applied to the work of the health officers of the sickness insurances.

The private sickness insurances (Ersatzkassen) became corporations under public law.

The sickness insurance associations became corporations under public law.

In retrospect, it is surprising that these modifications were not more far-reaching when one considers that previous debates, even in expert circles, had often started with the catchword 'fragmentation' and that the political spirit of the time tended towards uniformity. Nevertheless, the Reconstruction Law was unequivocally in favour of keeping the structure of the social insurance system as it was. The reasons for this were presumably the flagging interest of the party leaders after the abolition of self-administration and the removal of the politically undesirable staff; and the attitude of the ministerial bureaucracy towards maintaining the existing system. In addition to these, the NS functionaries who had moved into administrative posts in social insurance in 1933, often with extensive influence, were soon absorbed into the existing system and advocated its upkeep so that they could maintain their newly gained positions.

The Federal Republic of Germany

Background

The consequences of National Socialist rule and the war were catastrophic: the German Reich ceased to exist; legislative and executive power was transferred to the military authorities of the allies; the economic capacity of what was left of Germany had sunk in all sectors to an average of 70–80 percent and in the industrial sector to 30–35 percent of the 1937 level.[121] In spite of high losses during the war, the poorly fed population, suffering an acute housing shortage, greatly increased with the influx of refugees and displaced persons. In 1939 there were 39 million inhabitants in the area of the present-day Federal Republic; in 1949 there were 47 million.

The state was rebuilt stage by stage, starting at the lowest level. First, in 1945/6, community and district administration was re-established; this was followed in 1946/7 by the establishment of the 'Länder' (states) and zonal administration was created in the occupied zones. At the beginning of 1948 a bizonal administration was set up for the British and American zones. At the same time legislative and executive power was gradually transferred from the military to the German authorities. In July 1948 the Minister-Presidents of the 'Länder' were given the authority to convene a constituent assembly to establish a federal state. This 'parliamentary council' established the Basic Law (Grundgesetz) for the Federal Republic of Germany which came into force on 24 May 1949. In the autumn of 1949 the first German Bundestag was elected and the first federal government was formed. The German Democratic Republic was created at almost the same time in the Soviet occupied zone.

Associations were also re-established at the lowest level at first, and followed to a large extent the traditions of the Weimar Republic. The trade unions were an important exception as they did not take up the idea of sectoral trade unions again. The industrial trade unions amalgamated in 1949 to form the 'Deutsche Gewerkschaftsbund' (the German Trade Union Federation) which has played a decisive role in the formation of social policy ever since.

While the state was being reorganized and reconstructed, the economy was also rehabilitated. It would have been impossible to survive the first years of acute shortage without the help of the occupying powers, particularly without food imports from the USA. After the currency reform of June 1948 industrial production also began to increase by leaps and bounds. One of the reasons for this was that the currency reform and the simultaneous easing of a state-controlled economy, was an expression of a policy favouring a free-enterprise system based on competition (a social market economy). The economic growth rates for 1948/9 were over 20 percent; they remained above 10 percent until the mid-50s and have fluctuated around 5 percent ever since. In 1953 the population's provision with goods and services for private consumption had again reached the same level as shortly before the war.[122] The initially high level of unemployment could soon be reduced because of this rapid growth. The unemployment quota fell from 12.2 in 1950 to 9.5 in 1952 and 5.6 in 1955; from the beginning of the 1960s onwards there was full employment in the Federal Republic of Germany. The trend towards a society of employed persons continued; the proportion of dependently employed out of all gainfully employed persons rose from 69 percent (1950) to 86 percent (1979).

The 20 years of economic expansion were interrupted by a recession in 1966/7 and by another starting in 1973. The unemployment quota rose from below 1 to 2.3 in 1967, then sank again below 1, but reached 4.7 in 1975, a level not registered for 20 years. These recessions were not grave compared with those of other countries. Given the earlier background of economic expansion, these recessions resulted in a change of awareness within Germany which cannot yet be described conclusively. In this context, however, it is significant that they had a notable impact on social insurance.

Developments Prior to the Basic Law (Grundgesetz) (1945–1949)

The word 'catastrophic' has been applied repeatedly to the situation of social insurance at the end of the war. True, its wealth had been lost — as after the First World War — and its central jurisdiction at state and association level had been abolished. However, the local institutions lived on and still received contributions, even if greatly reduced. The military authorities left the social insurance law in force and abolished only purely National Socialist rulings. Furthermore, NS-incriminated staff were removed from administrative posts. However, apart from some local exceptions, these circumstances did not prevent insured persons from being looked after. The lack of revenue from the Reich and the reduced revenue from contributions resulted in restrictions and reductions of benefits. Social insurance experienced another phase of contraction. Yet as early as 1946/7 some of these reductions, and in 1948/9 nearly all of them, were revoked. Social insurance passed by far its most severe test of continuity. Its institutions proved durable; its functions were fulfilled.

This overall assessment of the past excludes a large number of legal regulations in the occupied zones and 'Länder' which are not to be discussed in detail here[123] as they were incorporated into federal law or were amended by this later.

However, it is of interest to mention a Social Insurance Adjustment Law (Sozialversicherungs-Anpassungsgesetz) passed by the Economic Council of the combined British and American zones on 17 June 1949. This brought about considerable changes and improvements one year after the currency reform which later became federal law. Apart from the abolition of a series of special regulations dating from the war and the early post-war period, the adjustment of the amount of benefits and an increase in pensions through lump-sum bonuses, and the introduction of a minimum pension of 50 DM (widows: 40 DM), these improvements also included the introduction of an unconditional widow's pension within the workers' pension insurance (however, only for cases of insurance since June 1949), and the reduction of the disablement limit for workers from 66.6 percent to 50 percent of their earning capacity. Thus, on two important points the workers' position was brought into line with that of the employees.

The contribution rate for pension insurance was raised from 5.6 percent to 10 percent but reduced for unemployment insurance from 6.5 percent to 4 percent, while the previous subsidies were abolished. The contribution for sickness insurance was shared equally between the employer and the insured person (until then the employer had paid one-third). The Social Insurance Adjustment Law marked the end of zonal legislation and also the beginning of the expansive legislation of the federal government.

Questions have since been raised as to whether the situation in Germany in 1945, known as 'zero hour', provided an opportunity for the radical reform of the social insurance system and if so why this was not exploited. Plans were made to establish a standard insurance. However, as little is known about the authors of these plans as about the politics behind them.

The primary reason why no fundamental reform of social insurance occurred may well have been that the Western Occupying Powers had already decided on the continuation of the existing system in principle before the end of the war. In guidelines for the future policy of the American occupying power of December 1944, it had been stated that: 'social insurance will be continued according to existing laws and regulations, in so far as German funds are available.' One of the parties concerned commented as follows:

> German emigrants to the USA during the Nazi era, who had taken part, heart and soul, in the development of an exemplary system of social security in Germany during the Weimar Republic, had advised that first of all every effort should be concentrated on quickly re-establishing social benefits for the old, for those who are incapable of working and for surviving dependants.[124]

> As far as the British military government was concerned, the policy had been decided before the occupation: all existing systems of German social security were to be maintained as far as possible. This decision was not surprising as the German system was greatly admired in Great Britain.[125]

In spite of the opinions outlined above, the Allied Control Council approved principles for a standardized organization of social insurance in March 1946. The reasons for this cannot be reconstructed. Apparently the Western Allies were not politically motivated as far as social insurance was concerned.

> We had, indeed, approved the principles for a standardized insurance in the Allied Control Council, but we were of the opinion that the organizational redevelopment of German social insurance, which is of such decisive importance for the future of German social insurance, ought to be decided by the Germans themselves.[126]

The Germans, however, were not very keen on reform. The thoughts of people who might otherwise have had influential expert opinions on the subject, were absorbed in the daily reconstruction work.

As reaction to the NS-period there was a strong trend against centralization. Moreover, no one felt that there was any urgent cause for far-reaching change. Social insurance fulfilled its functions, incompletely at first, but improving all the time; there was confidence in further improvement. These circumstances explain why conservative elements rejected the reform plan. Another reason was that the plan also included a policy of cut-back by reducing pensions for workers and employees to the lower level of workers' pensions. The trade unions did not support this, and some even opposed it (British zone).[127] Thus, the draft plan stood no chance of being realized.

Foundations of Federal Legislation (until 1955)

Social Insurance in the Basic Law (Grundgesetz). If one asks why no organizational guidelines were incorporated in the 'Grundgesetz' — as in Art. 161 of the Weimar Constitution — considering the general consensus on the necessity for the existence and basic structure of social insurance, an answer will only be found by examining a far broader context. The legislators of the 'Grundgesetz' set great store by the standardization of personal basic rights, the regulation of relations between individuals and the state, and the establishment of state procedural rules. By comparison, the legislators were extremely reserved as far as fixing economic, social and labour structures was concerned. In these respects the 'Grundgesetz' remained 'open' for future developments. This reflects not only wisdom but also the fact that at the time of debating and passing the 'Grundgesetz', *de facto* decisions had already been taken in favour of a social market economy, on working conditions in accordance with collective bargaining and on the continuation of the previous social insurance system. There was hardly any need for further decisions; neither proponents nor critics of the existing state of affairs saw any urgent need to discuss the principles again.

Later, the Constitutional Court (Bundesverfassungsgericht) defined social insurance as a generic term of constitutional law which incorporates all aspects of social insurance. This also expresses the 'frankness' that has proved helpful for further development. Public discussion, the legislator and legal decisions were less preoccupied with discussions about terms and legal structures; the 'Grundgesetz' left plenty of scope for discussions and decisions 'in relation to the subject matter'.

The Newly Founded Bundestag. The German Bundestag (Federal Parliament) which assembled in the autumn of 1949 turned its attention directly to such matters. It was faced with a mammoth task which it set about with great application. In the first legislative session fifty-two laws were passed on social insurance, a figure which was in no way matched even approximately in later legislative periods. First of all the existing fragmentation of laws which had occurred after 1945 had to be remedied; this was almost completed during the first legislative session. Moreover, income scales for rating contributions and benefits had to be adapted to changed circumstances.

The benefits also had to be raised to adapt to the new situation; average wages had gone up by over 80 percent during the period from 1948 to 1953. The 'Rentenzulagegesetz' (Pensions Increase Law) and the 'Teuerungszulagengesetz' (Cost of Living Supplement Law) of 1951 as well as the 'Grundbetragserhöhungsgesetz' (Law on the Increase of the Basic Allowance) of 1953 were passed for this reason; laws on improved benefits for accident insurance were also passed in 1952 and 1953.

A number of laws regulated the legal status of special groups of persons, as can be seen from their titles: the 'Heimkehrergesetz' (Law on Home-coming Prisoners of War) 1950, the 'Schwerbeschädigtengesetz' (Law on the Severely

Disabled) 1953, the 'Häftlingshilfegesetz' (Law on Assistance to Prisoners i.e. for political prisoners) 1955. The 'Bundesversorgungsgesetz' (Federal Pensions Act) of 1950 served social security in the broad sense of the term. It regulated pensions for the war-disabled, largely according to the principles of the Welfare and Pension Act of the Weimar Republic (see p. 52). The 'Lastenausgleichsgesetz' (War Burden Equalization Act) of 1952 not only provided for compensation for damage to property or financial losses but also for pension benefits according to social criteria, particularly in cases of old age and incapacity to work, for about 11 million refugees and displaced persons.

Integration of Refugees. The 'Fremdrenten- und Auslandsrentengesetz' (Foreign Pension Law) of 1953 served to integrate refugees into the social insurance system. The law was based on a principle of compensation, i.e., insurance institutions in the Federal Republic of Germany took over the obligations of institutions outside the Federal Republic in certain circumstances. The benefits, particularly pensions, conformed to the law of the country of origin. As the refugees had come from many different countries, particularly from Eastern Europe, with very different legal systems as far as compulsory insurance, the rating of contributions and benefits were concerned, a high degree of inequality of benefits resulted among the refugees themselves and in relation to non-refugees.

'Errichtungsgesetze' (Establishment Laws). Apart from laws designed to standardize the law, to adapt to the changed economic situation and to regulate the consequences of the war, laws were soon issued which paved the way for further structural development. These were the 'Errichtungsgesetze', the laws on panel doctors and on self-administration. First of all (as of 1 May 1952) the 'Bundesanstalt für Arbeitsvermittlung und Arbeitslosenversicherung' (Federal Office of Employment and of Unemployment Insurance) was founded. By transferring labour administration, which had previously been under the jurisdiction of the 'Länder', to this federal institution, the situation reverted to that of the Weimar Republic with its similar institution, the 'Reichsanstalt'. The 'Bundesversicherungsanstalt für Angestellte' (Federal Insurance Institution for Employees) was also re-established in 1953 in accordance with the earlier model; from 1945 until then, employees' insurance had been administered by the workers' pension insurance.

Social Jursidiction. The 'Sozialgerichtsgesetz' (Social Court Law) of 1953 corresponded to the demand in the 'Grundgesetz' by creating a special social jurisdiction (Art. 96) and separating legal decisions and administration (Art. 20), It created a three-stage legal system with a new type of cost-free court procedure with lay judges. Later amendments to this law served only to simplify and accelerate the procedure without affecting the basic structure of social jurisdiction, which has proved very successful according to everyone concerned. When social jurisdiction came into being, the state authorities were no longer responsible for legal decisions. Until 1945 such authorities had been the 'Reichsversicherungsamt' and afterwards the 'Ober-' or 'Landesversicherungsämter' (upper or state insurance offices) in the 'Länder'. These now had only an administrative and supervisory role according to the division of responsibility between the federal government and the 'Länder'. The federal government transferred its rights of control (with exceptions) to the 'Bundesversicherungsamt' (Federal Insurance Office) which was established in 1956 as an independent, federal, supreme authority.[128]

Panel Doctor Law. The federal law on panel doctors of 1955 regulated the relationship between sickness insurance and doctors. Similar principles were used to those which had been developed during the Weimar Republic (see above p. 47). Panel doctors' associations and a Panel Doctors' Federal Association were formed as corporations under public law. These ensured the availability of medical treatment by doctors and are the contractual partners of the sickness insurance schemes. The schemes formed associations in each 'Land', also based on a law passed in 1955, and a federal association of the respective type of insurance in the form of a corporation under public law. The basic structure, developed in the early 1930s and continued in 1955 — namely the guaranteed availability of doctors through self-administered medical organizations, the contractual agreement of total payment by the insurance and distribution of fees among the doctors by the Panel Doctors' Association — has proved its capability, irrespective of modifications and difficulties, right up to the present phase of curbing costs.

Law on Administrative Autonomy of 1951. One of the first laws of the German Bundestag of social and political relevance was the Law on Administrative Autonomy of 1951. This also followed old traditions. However, an important development was the transition to the self-administration of associations. The original cooperative principle of representation of individual members in the various governing bodies was no longer followed, but rather the principle of representation of the insured and the employers through their respective associations.[129] In the case of the social insurance institutions, assemblies of representatives are elected, drawn from the associations' list of nominations, and these in turn elect an executive board. The self-administrative bodies elect the director of the institution. The members of these bodies are composed in principle of equal numbers of insured persons and of employers. There are exceptions for miners', agricultural and private sickness insurance schemes. This led to innovations for the administrative bodies of both sickness and accident insurance, where the insured so far had played no part. Up to two-thirds of the administrative bodies were composed of representatives of the insured in accordance with the division of contributions into three parts up to 1949. Trade union demands for sole or at least majority representation of the insured in these bodies, were not supported sufficiently in the Bundestag;[130] the majority adopted the 'Sozialpartner-Modell' (social partner model) which still forms the basis of the law on self-administration.[131]

Summary. The above, brief portrayal of legislative activity in the first years of the Federal Republic may give the impression that the content of legislation was predominantly restorative in nature. Indeed, many things were re-established and continued. It is easy to understand this phenomenon if one considers the following factors. There was a need to give institutions and mechanisms which functioned satisfactorily *de facto*, legal status and uniformity again. Germany had been cut off from international discussion for over a decade; this is apparent from the fact that the term 'social security' only entered the German language at the beginning of the 1950s. Moreover, it is presumably even more significant that many of the decision- and policy-makers in the new republic were either people who had been condemned to having no influence whatsoever since 1933 or who had survived the NS-era and wished to preserve the remaining good features of the past while hoping to prevent worse developments. For these people — many of whom were no longer young — it was only too natural to adopt the thoughts and ideals of the Weimar Republic. Indeed, the legislature was extremely active in the new Federal Republic. The number and content of the laws which were passed and administered show that legislation, administration and self-administration were all part of unusual activity during the first years of the new 'Grundgesetz'. This must also be taken into consideration when judging the hesitant start to discussions on reform and further developments

Pension Reform 1957

Discussions on Reform and Political Action. Discussions on reform began in the early 1950s when scholars criticized the complexity of social law and social institutions. This led to demands for a new concept, for rational social planning.[132] In the political arena, the demand for a social plan related to ideas on the quantitative and qualitative development of social security was advanced by the Social Democratic Party.[133] Later, and without practical influence on the reform legislation of 1957, the Social Democratic Party (SPD) elaborated a 'social plan'.[134]

In January 1952 the SPD had proposed a motion in the Bundestag with the same aim, namely to appoint a 'social study commission' of independent experts to

> examine current social institutions and benefits in Germany and to investigate the possibilities of disentangling these social benefits and of consolidating them systematically and to elaborate a plan for social security in Germany.

This motion was dismissed by a majority vote of the government in February 1952. However, at the same time, an advisory board was appointed.

> In order to prepare legislative measures on financial security, reform and progressive development of social benefits, clearly delimiting insurance from poor relief and welfare, the Federal Minister of Labour is commissioned to apppoint an advisory board at the Ministry of Labour.[135]

Until 1958 this advisory board dealt with a multitude of questions, particularly in its study groups — above all on sickness insurance and on the poor relief system — and a large number of these questions were settled by mutual agreement.[136] This matter-of-fact investigation fertilized and facilitated later legislation up to the 1960s. However, the advisory board did not develop fundamental ideas on reform nor did its work lead to a homogeneous concept or social plan.

At the beginning of the second legislative session in October 1953 the declaration by the government spoke of 'comprehensive social reform'. The new government pointed to the preliminary work of the first federal government for implementing social reform and declared: 'The new federal government will promote this preparatory work vigorously and submit a comprehensive programme for social reform'.[137] Such a programme never came into being. A 'reduction of social reform took place after the reform of individual branches of social insurance, beginning with statutory pensions insurance'.[138] The term 'social reform' had already been reduced in scope. For the labour movement, it originally meant a far-reaching cut in the power and dominance of capital interests. In the last two decades of the Kaiserreich, it had been connected with the demand for freedom of association and wage bargaining power. In the early days of the Federal Republic, a conservative-led government could also use the term 'social reform' partly because it covered the emotional content of both Socialist and Christian Social ideals, and partly because only reform of social benefits was a concept that was widely understood as a basis for political action.

As far as the content of reform was concerned, the government did not rely on the advisory board it had appointed but mobilized further experts. In 1954, upon the instigation of the Federal Ministry of Labour, the Bogs Report[139] was compiled and in 1955 the Rothenfels memorandum[140] was presented, initiated by the Federal Chancellor. However, irrespective of all demands, suggestions and assistance, no official government social programme was created. Discussion at that time tended either to get bogged down on matters of principle — concerning terms such as the subsidiary principle, the insurance principle, industrial or prudential insurance — or, when it was more concrete, it provided nothing tangible from a political point of view.

The need for political action grew, not just because of the complexity of the law, criticized in particular by scholars and journalists, and of pension accumulation, the practical repercussions of which were often overestimated, but because of the low level of pensions compared with earned incomes, in spite of several rises. Pensions amounted to 28 percent to 32 percent of comparable wages and salaries.[141] It was generally thought that pensioners were not participating enough in the economic boom. The 'basic ideas on the overall reform of social benefits',[142] submitted to the cabinet by the Minister of Labour in April 1954, referred predominantly to reform of pensions insurance, with emphasis on a change of function of the old age pension from that of a pension in the form of a subsidy, to one which maintains a certain standard of living. Once these basic ideas had been expressed, discussion was soon concentrated on pension reform.

Chancellor Adenauer recognized the need for political action. In the first few months of 1955 a cabinet committee, the 'Social Cabinet', was formed under his chairmanship and a secretariat general for social reform was established in the Federal Ministry of Labour, which was given new staff. The activities of the secretariat general in connection with discussion on social reform at that time and the groups involved, were later described thus:

The Federal Ministry of Labour (the secretariat general for social reform) finally formed a fourth authoritative group which had begun to work intensively on pragmatic (i.e. potentially legislative) proposals for reform after hesitating for some time. Three groups worked towards a fundamental rearrangement of social security (even if with varying content, motives and tendencies); the fourth group paid more attention to current, urgent needs, or at least to those thought to be most urgent, while not considering questions of principle to any large degree. However, this conception cannot be designated as 'pragmatic', i.e. lacking theory and principles. It seemed to me to be based on insight into the procedural nature of social policy, into its dependence on society's development and on so-called 'Sachnotwendigkeiten', i.e. decisions which have to be made because of practical considerations.[143]

Work on concrete proposals for legislation was an essential but not sufficient pre-condition for political decision; opposition, particularly from the Minister of Finance, remained strong. In a session of the Social Cabinet in 1955, Adenauer gave the author of the Schreiber Plan an opportunity to speak.[144] This plan broke boldly through usual ways of thinking and proposed an annual, automatic adjustment of pensions to wage levels by using an indexing procedure. Summoning an author who had been little known until then to present the case was understood as a political event.

The Chancellor returned the proposal of the secretariat general of 27 December 1955 on major alternatives of decisions with marginal notes during the first week of January. The proposal prejudged important points of future reform. In the margin next to the passage on adjusting pensions in accordance with the development of wages and salaries Adenauer had written 'Yes'. On 13 January 1956 the Chancellor assured himself of the support of the executive committee of the CDU and on 18 January and 17 February 1956 'he correspondingly converted his policy into resolutions of the Social Cabinet'.[145] This and later adherence to the basic principle of the indexed pension in the face of immense opposition is one of Konrad Adenauer's personal achievements. It provoked a

> positively panicky reaction among powerful pressure groups which immediately began to organize opposition after hearing Schreiber's speech to the cabinet. Apart from renowned figures from the Neoliberal School and the redoubtable Bank deutscher Länder (Bank of the German 'Länder'), practically the whole of industry—from the insurance companies and banks, through whose insurance schemes a considerable part of the capital for pension insurance had flown so far, to the employers' associations—formed a long phalanx of opponents against 'the frivolity of a wage-indexed pension'.[146]

Like Bismarck's, Adenauer's motives were of a general political nature.

It is certain that Adenauer planned and used pension reform for his election campaign, to show that his party was concerned with social policy. The indexed pension—a type of positive addition to the rallying cry of 'No experiments'—was not only to affect old age and disabled pensioners materially and psychologically, but also coincided with the expectations of people who were still working by promising to extend the economic boom through into individual retirement.

Referring to the Chancellor's speech to the CDU Executive Committee in January 1956, it was said that

> it was also certain that Adenauer did not just have short-term election aims in mind. Among his long-term aims, apart from the conservative wish to

maintain the existing social system by reducing social tension, there was one which must be seen in the context of a long-term policy of German reunification: the Federal Republic of Germany was 'to remain attractive' for 'people in the eastern zone'.[147]

Adenauer's political aims were achieved. In the elections for the third Bundestag in 1957 the Union Parties won landslide victories and gained an absolute majority. Opinion pollsters reported: 'So far no example is known of a law, institution or even a constitution and symbol of the state, which has had so positive a response as pension reform.'[148]

Content of the New Rulings. The indexing of pensions was central to the pension reform laws passed by the Bundestag in February 1957. Specifically, pensions were no longer to be calculated on the basis of the nominal value of contributions or wages but were to be based on relative values. Thus, an insured person's pension is calculated by assessing the relationship of his earnings to the respective average earnings. The percentage which results on average during a person's working life is compared with the current level of average wages (general basis of assessment) and updated. Pensions already being paid out are adapted to changes in the general basis of assessment each year.

This is not the place to discuss whether or not the indexed pensions system had precursors in other countries. If it had, the initiators of this reform were not aware of them so that they could later say 'that stimuli for introducing indexed pensions came only from within the country. . . .'[149] The fact that there had been a systematic breakthrough with the 'Renten-Mehrbetragsgesetz' (Pensions Appreciation Act) of November 1954 suggests this. Until then, rises in pensions had entailed overall increases; their relative benefit for insured persons was greater, the less and the more recently payment in advance had been made. Insured persons who paid higher contributions and had been so doing for far longer were at a disadvantage. This problem was recognized at an early date — at least by 1953. 'The reason for such systematic increases was largely due to administrative considerations.'[150]

According to one of those instrumental in reform from 1955 onwards, the 'Renten-Mehrbetragsgesetz' was

> the first socio-political, post-war law to derive from the long-term wage trend, following increased productivity and taking into account the fact that statically assessed pensions were bound to fall behind rising earnings. It provided that as insured person's earnings and contributions rose, increases in pensions were to be adjusted to suit current values, regardless of when contributions had been paid. Thus, the earlier contributions had been paid, the more the pension had to be increased to approach corresponding current values.[151]

Apart from indexing pensions and reorganizing the law extensively, the reform laws of 1957 introduced a series of new rulings. The new calculation formula and the abolition of fixed component parts of the pension led to a greater differentiation of pensions depending on the length of insurance and individual average earnings during the insured person's working life. The aim of ensuring 'that the employed person's individual situation during his working life continues correspondingly when he receives a pension'[152] was achieved.

Disability insurance was divided between disablement and incapacity for employment. It was hoped that this would put an end to the 'all or nothing' decision of granting pensions. Security in cases of premature disability was improved by the introduction of a 'Zurechnungszeit' up to the age of 55. Possibilities for implementing measures to promote health and better opportunities for employment were increased while a reduction in disability frequency was aimed at. Such benefits were raised to the status of a regular benefit instead of merely being a possible benefit.

The introduction of a retirement age of 60 after one year's unemployment and an unconditional widow's pension for widows whose husbands had died before 1949, aimed at assimilating the law for workers with that of employees. The introduction of a retirement age of 60 for women who had paid insurance contributions during the course of employment for the greater part of the last 20 years was also new.

Finally, methods of financing pensions were also changed. Instead of the full funding system (Anwartschaftsdeckungsverfahren) which had been tried in vain since 1891, another system (the so-called 'Abschnittsdeckungsverfahren') was introduced. In practice this means that funds amounting to a year's expenditure must always be available. The considerable rise in pensions entailed an increase in contributions from 11 percent to 14 percent; at the same time the contribution rate for unemployment insurance was decreased from 3 percent to 2 percent. The government increased its subsidies without, however, any rise in the proportion of government funds for its whole expenditure on pension insurance.

Further Developments and Analysis of Social Reform (until 1965)

Discussions on reform during the second legislative session of the Bundestag had concentrated so hard on pension reform that less attention was paid to other parallel developments than they deserved. Within the social insurance system these included the introduction of a family allowance; the modernization of the poor law; within its own sector, the extension of social security for the self-employed; and the reform of the pension law for displaced persons. Moreover, at the end of the second legislative session a further significant improvement to workers' economic security in cases of illness was brought in (cf. p. 69 below).

Family Allowance Act (Kindergeldgesetz). The social disadvantages for families with numerous children had been the subject of debates on family policy since the beginning of the 1950s. These discussions had to be started anew as the population policy of the NS-regime (dependency allowance from the fifth child onwards from 1935, later from the third child onwards) had been ended in 1945. After long debate, particularly on the financial aspects and on the underwriting of the measure, the Family Allowance Act was enacted in 1954. This entitled gainfully employed persons to a family allowance from the third child onwards. Family equalization funds were established at the trade associations and allowances were financed by contributions from employers. The system proved inadequate and was completely reorganized in 1964. The federal government took over the financing; a family allowance department to handle allowances was established at the Federal Labour Office (Bundesanstalt für Arbeit). Since then family allowances have been increased several times. From 1961 family allowances also applied to the second child; since 1975, to all children. The amount of the allowance per child increases with the number of children.

Federal Law on Social Assistance (Bundessozialhilfegesetz). Public welfare institutions had to bear an enormous burden in the first years after the war. When this burden began to decrease as social insurance was built up, discussion on reform began. These were triggered off by a judgment of the Federal Administration Court (Bundesverwaltungsgericht) in 1954, which held that a basic legal claim to welfare exists. This represented a change from a law which only concerned administration to substantive public law. The discussions were included in the reform efforts as the advisory board for the reform of social benefits appointed a committee on welfare questions. In this committee the basis for the 'Bundessozialhilfegesetz' of 1961 was elaborated — quietly but effectively and in concrete terms. Social welfare or assistance is to enable those in need to lead a life worthy of a human being. Based on the subsidiary principle and on the principle of individualization, the law was summarized, modernized and extended. Apart from the evolutionary elements, the extension of possibilities of 'assistance in particular situations' merits special mention as this introduced a strong emphasis on benefits in kind as opposed to just monetary benefits.

Housing Allowance Law (Wohngeldgesetz). In 1960 a housing allowance financed by the federal government and the 'Länder' was introduced to relieve social hardship as housing controls were relaxed.

Old Age Assistance for Farmers. The lively discussions on the problems of old age security had also included the self-employed. Gradually everyone recognized that earned income is crucial for the majority of the self-employed and that unearned income is not a sufficient basis for old age security. In the agricultural sector there was a growing need to create a balance between the older and the younger generation which went beyond the right to an annuity on transfer of the farm to a descendant. The predominantly small size of the farms in the Federal Republic made cash provision for the older generation difficult, and led to delays in farm transfers. This in turn stood in the way of the extremely popular aim at that time of improving the structure of agriculture. Thus, the discussions on old age security for farmers, which began in 1955, were based on the idea that a solution had to be found which combined socio-political aims with those of agricultural policy.[153]

The Law on Old Age Assistance for Farmers of 1957 provided more than one innovatory solution. An old age allowance was only granted if the farm was transferred (by handing it over to heirs, alienating or letting it). This soon accelerated the process of transferring farms and resulted in a clear reduction in the average age of farm owners. With this in mind, but also to achieve the required socio-political effect, the whole of the 'old burden' was included for entitlement to benefits when the law came into force. Older farmers only had to prove that they had worked as farmers instead of making contributions; they were treated as if they had paid contributions in the past.

Farmers' old age schemes were set up for this purpose at the farmers' associations. Old age assistance was financed with contributions from farmers and later, for structural reasons and because of agricultural and political aims, it was subsidized in increasing amounts by federal funds.

Old age assistance for farmers with its new structural features has proved successful and has been considerably extended since then by a series of amendments:[154]

The old age allowance has been raised several times and since 1975 it has been automatically adjusted in accordance with increases in employed persons' pensions.

Introduction of a premature old age allowance in cases of incapacity to work (1963).

Introduction of measures to preserve and restore earning power (1965); a relief worker can be provided instead of relief money.

Introduction of an additional pension for owners who relinquish very small farms, as in such cases the proceeds of such a transfer and the old age allowance do not seem to be adequate (1969).

Sliding scale of the amount of old age assistance — which was originally a standard amount — in accordance with the duration of payment of contributions (since 1974).

Craftsmen's Insurance law (Handwerkerversicherungsgesetz). The craftsmen's insurance, introduced in 1938, was not satisfactory. On the one hand registration and the payment of craftsmen's contributions was incomplete, and on the other hand employees' organizations demanded organizational separation from the employees' insurance as this was burdened unreasonably by the craftsmen's insurance. An amendment to the law in 1956 provided for the clarification of the financial situation by stipulating separate accounts for receipts and expenditure as well as a different type of contribution stamp for craftsmen's insurance.

The Craftsmen's Insurance Law of 1960 entailed fundamental changes. It abolished the possible choice between social and private insurance while limiting compulsory insurance for all craftsmen to 18 years. Similar to the case of the farmers, the legislature guaranteed the craftsmen basic security only. The workers' pension insurance scheme became responsible for implementing craftsmen's insurance.

Foreign Pension Law (Fremdrenten- und Auslandsrenten-Neuregelungsgesetz). The improvements of the pension reform of 1957 exposed the deficiencies of the pension law for displaced persons, based on the compensation principle, even more clearly. The reference of the compensation principle to the law and economic conditions of the country of origin, led to differences which were difficult to understand, compared with the indigenously insured and even among displaced persons from different countries. The Foreign Pensions Law of 1960 replaced the compensation principle with that of integration. This was based on the bold, yet simple idea of treating displaced pensioners as if they had spent the whole of their working life in the territory which had become the Federal Republic. Contributions paid into a non-German insurance scheme are treated as if they have been paid according to Federal German law; employment abroad is the same as employment in the Federal Republic of Germany, entailing compulsory pension insurance if such employment would have been subject to compulsory insurance in Germany. The wages and salaries paid for the respective forms of employment in the Federal Republic are used as a basis for calculating the pensions. Thus, integration and equal treatment of displaced persons were achieved instantaneously as far as old age pensions are concerned. To facilitate the administration of implementing such a law, insurance documents from inaccessible countries of origin were no longer of paramount importance; facts (of the working life of the applicant), that could be elicited, were sufficient if credible.

After the election victory in the autumn of 1957, to which pension reform contributed, the re-elected Chancellor Adenauer said in his government declaration of 29 October 1957; 'Social reform will be continued. Apart from amending some of the deficiencies which have come to light in the legislation so far, the reform of sickness and accident insurance primarily will come under consideration.' Clearly the government declaration showed a change of stance after the political and financial drive of pension reform.

> However, social reform cannot be exhausted by developing social security institutions based on solidarity. . . . The federal government is determined to promote self-help and private initiative in every way and . . . to prevent the country from sinking to the level of an all-embracing welfare state.[155]

This new aim was predominantly directed towards sickness insurance. As has been shown, it did not prevent the reform of social welfare, craftsmen's insurance and foreign pensions law and the development of farmers' old age assistance from following pension reform and along similar lines. The same also applies to accident insurance which provided few possibilities for self-help and private initiative.

Accident Insurance Reform Act (Unfallversicherungsneuregelungsgesetz). The federal government had proposed a bill to the second Bundestag on the reform of accident insurance. However, there was no time for it to be passed. An amended, revised bill submitted to the third Bundestag was not passed either; apparently it was felt that there was no urgent need for reform. The Preliminary Laws (Vorschaltgesetze) of 1957 and 1960 brought about improvements to benefits which seemed necessary. The Accident Insurance Reform Act was not passed until 1963. It modernized and systematized the law, stressing the importance of accident prevention — an innovation — extending possibilities of curative treatment and careers advice as well as of compensation for occupational diseases and, lastly, providing for benefits to be continually adjusted in line with wage developments, as in pension insurance. Since then the federal government has had to submit a report on accident prevention at regular intervals.

Reform of Sickness Insurance. The aims formulated by the government declaration of 1957 regarding sickness insurance are reflected in the reform which followed. In 1959 a proposal submitted by the government on the reorganization of sickness insurance included the payment of doctors according to each individual treatment and the patient's own financial participation in all medical treatment. Thereby it was hoped to dissuade insured persons from making thoughtless use of medical treatment; medical attention was to be directed from minor to more severe, long-lasting cases of illness and sickness insurance was to be relieved of the expenditure incurred from so-called 'bagatelle cases'.

This plan was rejected by the SPD parliamentary group in the Bundestag and — of greater importance — outside the Bundestag, by the trade unions and doctors' associations. The former protested at the limiting of medical treatment and the doctors opposed what they publicly called the role of 'debt collectors' which they were to assume. The government majority in the Bundestag was not strong enough to enforce the plan in the face of this unusual coalition. The proposed bill was left until the end of the session (1961).

However, the government was unflagging. In its communiqué of 29 November 1961 the government stressed that social policy was not to be an aim in itself and that it would take care to strengthen the individual's own sense of responsibility. 'Social reform will be continued; that is a matter of course. The federal government will table bills for the reform of sickness and accident insurance, following the afore-stated principles.'[156] In 1962 another sickness insurance bill was proposed. While providing for another form of self-participation, the main issues of the bill remained unchanged. To facilitate its acceptance politically, this bill was tied into a 'social package' which in addition provided for the continuation of full wage payment by employers to workers who fall ill, and for the shift of costs of family allowances from the employers to the federal government.

Opposition by the SPD, the trade unions and doctors to self-participation and by the employers to the continuation of wage payment was so strong that once again nothing could be resolved. In October 1963 Ludwig Erhard, the new Federal Chancellor, withdrew the government's plans. In his government declaration he said that social legislation had to be thoroughly examined and announced the setting up of an official social enquiry. The term 'social reform' did not arise again. A 'pause for thought' was obviously intended and requested by the government. The Bundestag reacted by improving family allowances in April 1964 and by deciding that they would be financed by the federal government. The controversial items in the 'social package' remained unresolved.

During the fourth legislative session, a pensions insurance amendment was passed in 1965 without any real public involvement. It complicated the law considerably but a series of hardship and inadequacies, which had arisen after the pension reform and which had been summarized in a report by the federal government, known as the '"Härte"-Novelle' ('Hardship' Amendment), were ameliorated.

"Economic Orientation" and Adaptation (1966–1969)

In 1966 a recession began which reduced economic growth almost to nil and rapidly increased the number of unemployed. This setback was a new experience for the Federal Republic; it had far-reaching psychological and political repercussions. At the end of the year a 'Grand Coalition' between the CDU/CSU and the SPD was formed. Social policy had to be tailored to the needs and consequences of the recession. A general spirit of disillusionment and a need for rationality also manifested themselves politically.

Socio-political discussion had already resulted in a shift in emphasis which can be described as 'economic orientation'. It was triggered off generally by the increasing amount of finance that was redistributed by the institutions responsible for social security, and in particular by discussions on the economics of indexing pensions. In 1955–1957 a series of pioneering publications on social security were written by economists.[157] Soon afterwards an *Economic Theory of Social Policy* appeared with the following introduction: 'Social policy has become the policy of redistributing incomes'.[158] An attempt was made at explaining the immense rise of the social benefits quota — in international terms as well — through the interaction of socio-economic determinants.[159]

The report presented in 1966 by the social enquiry commission was also highly economic. For the first time, sickness insurance was analysed using economic methodology and concrete proposals were made for drawing up a comprehensive medium-term social budget which was to be calculated in advance.[160] Preliminary work soon started; at the beginning of 1969 the first social budget was published and presented to the Bundestag.[161]

A composite work entitled *Social Budget-Social Planning* introduced in 1968 clearly went beyond the official social budget. Here a calculation for 10 years in advance was drawn up which was not based on the law in force but on a specially elaborated, rationally structured socio-political concept which nevertheless kept political options open. Aside from its new methodological approach, this work showed that the social benefits quota would rise, particularly in view of demographic factors, but would not become prohibitive.[162]

The pause from action and for thought which the government had introduced in 1964 was immediately followed by the economic recession. The reduction in revenues from taxes and contributions which the recession caused, made consolidatory measures necessary, particularly for the federal budget. In 1967 (Finance Amendment Act — 'Finanzänderungsgesetz') government subsidies for pension insurance were reduced and the contribution rate was increased in stages (1968, 15 percent; 1969, 16 percent; 1970, 17 percent). A substantial increase in contribution would have been necessary in any case because of the increasing number of old people by the mid-70s. A sickness insurance contribution of 2 percent for pensioners was abolished again in 1970.

Two further measures, proposed for some time, were triggered off by financial pressure. The first was the discontinuance of reimbursing contributions to women in the case of marriage. The second was an amendment law at the end of the legislative session (1969) which served to ensure that pensions could be financed in the longer term. Such a measure seemed necessary in view of the experience of the recession and was facilitated by the beginning of the economic boom in 1968 which was in full swing by 1969. Methods of financing were brought increasingly in line with the allocation system. The government has to submit a comprehensive 15-year calculation of pension financing every year; the minimum reserve amounts to 3-months expenditure. Since 1972 the contribution rate has been 18 percent.

At the same time the problem of unequal financial development between the various pension insurance schemes, which had existed for a long time, was settled. Among the workers' pension insurance institutions a so-called 'common charge' system had already existed earlier (first of all in 1899) to balance regional differences in the ratio between those who pay contributions and those who are entitled to benefits. As not all expenditure flowed through the common charge system, the reserve funds of the individual institutions continued to develop differently. Thus, in 1969 a deficit distribution system was also introduced.

Since 1969 there has been far-reaching financial adjustment between the pension insurances for workers and employees, which are separate organizations. This became necessary as the number of employees was greatly increasing compared with the number of workers so that the ratio between contributors and pensioners is far more favourable in employees' insurance than in workers' insurance. To avoid having to introduce different contribution rates to maintain the same benefits and financial independence, the discrepancy was balanced by means of an appropriate government subsidy (1964). Since 1969, direct equalization payments are made whenever the funds of a particular branch of insurance exceed a certain ratio to expenditure and those of the other branch of insurance exceed a certain proportional value. Furthermore, provision was made for mutual liquidity assistance.

˜The financial integration described above does not affect institutional differentiation but offers the advantages of a central organization. Changes of an economic and structural nature and demographic differences can be cushioned better by such an organization. In this respect, financial integration is essential to uphold the organizational structure. The arrangements which were made for pension insurance in 1969 are currently being discussed with a view to solving the problems of the sickness insurance sector.

The recession over, the Grand Coalition passed two more laws of sociopolitical importance in 1969: the Job Promotion Act (Arbeitsförderungsgesetz) and the Law on the Continuation of Wage Payment (Lohnfortzahlungsgesetz).

Workers demanded that they should be treated in the same way as employees who had a claim to their full salary for 6 weeks in case of illness. An important step in this direction had been taken during the second legislative session. The 'Lohnfortzahlungsgesetz' of 1957 had increased sick pay for the first 6 weeks from (usually) 50 percent to 65 percent (with allowances for dependants up to 75 percent) of earnings and stipulated that the employer should pay the difference between the sick pay and 90 percent of the net earnings. This was raised to 100 percent in 1961. The 'Lohnfortzahlungsgesetz' of 1969 provided that the worker was entitled to be paid his full wage by his employer for a period of up to 6 weeks; thus, this law provided for the equal treatment of workers and employees in this respect. An equalizing fund, financed by contributions, was set up for businesses employing less than 20 persons in order to spread the financial risks of this new law for small businesses.

As a drop in unemployment was followed by full employment, at that time unemployment insurance was not a public issue. In spite of many improvements to monetary benefits, the contribution rate, originally 6.5 percent, was lowered to 4 percent in 1949, 3 percent in 1955 and finally to 2 percent in 1957. An amendment and supplementary law of 1956 standardized the legal aspects of unemployment insurance objectively and formally, while maintaining the content of the old law which had existed for nearly 30 years. In 1959, in view of seasonal unemployment in the building trade 'bad weather pay' and measures to promote building in winter were introduced.

The recession of 1966/7 resulted in a new awareness of the problem of labour administration, which it was realized, must not only relieve unemployment but must also prepare to meet emergencies far more than before. With this in mind, a bill was tabled at the end of 1967 which led to the 'Arbeitsförderungsgesetz' of 1969. The Federal Labour Office (Bundesanstalt für Arbeit) was to aim at maintaining a high level of employment, improving the employment structure, and promoting industrial growth. The tools required for this—careers advice, employment offices, promotion of professional training, promotion of job acceptance, research and information—were considerably expanded. Since then the Federal Office has become a modern administrative service which, apart from playing its traditional role in relation to social security, fulfils its tasks of actively influencing the labour market. This new approach has proved successful in the period since 1974 with its difficult labour market.[163] This economic situation also led to the introduction of a new type of benefit in 1974, a bankruptcy allowance, which employed persons receive as a wage substitute when their employer becomes insolvent.

Further Developments (1970–1975)

After the Bundestag elections in the autumn of 1969, the foundation of a 'Social Liberal Coalition' government led by the SPD sparked off political responses, long-felt wishes and activities which were later designated as 'reform euphoria'. After the previous phase of strong dependence on the economic situation and of measures to adjust to the consequences of recession, expectations rose that traditional Social Democratic goals might be realized, especially as economic conditions seemed so propitious because of the boom. These goals were coupled with phrases such as: social planning, active and preventive social policy, comprehensive social security for everyone.

The new government not only specified its intentions in its declaration of October 1969 but also shortly afterwards (April 1970) in its *Social Report 1970*. The latter contained a comprehensive description of the problems and tasks of social policy plus a further developed and extended social budget, broken down into functional categories. The report starts with 'the necessity for internal reforms and tries to show where a new start could be made and where there is potential for the further development of social policy'.[164]

The term 'further development' used in this context and often repeated later referred to the general attitude of expectation but it also showed that the government intended developing its social policy on the basis of existing institutions; no new approaches were attempted. However, little time was spent clarifying terminology and 'further development' soon took shape.

It embraced a social code as well as quantitative and qualitative extensions in all branches of social insurance. However, these matters which will be described in more detail were only part of a whole range of activities. The federal government appointed four commissions in 1970: the Commission for Economic and Social Change, which submitted a concluding report in 1976,[165] as well as commissions of experts to prepare a labour code, a social code and to further develop social sickness insurance.

In April 1970 a rehabilitation action programme in particular initiated development of institutional capacities in this sector. In the same year bills were tabled to increase family allowances (passed in 1970), to automatically index pensions for war victims (passed in 1970), to extend and standardize the promotion of vocational training (passed in 1971), to extend and increase housing allowances (passed in 1970) and to reform 'shop rules' which came into force in 1972.

Further development on a European level was also considered desirable. Until 1969 the German attitude on European socio-political matters had been minimal because of the very limited powers of the EEC institutions. For many years discussion was ensnared in the problem of 'harmonization'. On this it was said:

The federal government is of the opinion that harmonization of social policy at all costs would be just as disadvantageous for European integration as absolute insistence on the multiple forms of social systems which have developed in the course of history.

Upon German initiative, the Council of the European Community decided in November 1970 to clarify 'which common goals are to be striven for in future while the systems of the member states maintain their individual differences'.[166]

At home, the commissions appointed to work on various aspects of social insurance set about their task speedily. The social code commission, established in May 1970, was to assist the federal government in elaborating a draft for a social code. This was the start of a plan, first mentioned in the SPD's Godesberg Programme in 1959 and again in the government's declaration of 1969. The codification of social law was intended to clarify and simplify the law. The government and the commission of experts agreed that such a goal could only be achieved in stages. First, a 'General Section' of the Social Code was started; it was presented as a draft by the government in February 1972.[167] However, it was only passed by the following Bundestag in 1975. One year later the second stage of the Social Code — General Regulations for Social Insurance — was passed. Further stages — Administrative Proceedings and Assistance for Young People — are currently before the legislature.

The work of the commission of experts appointed in April 1970 for the 'Further Development of Social Sickness Insurance' soon brought concrete results which were also reflected in amendments to the law. The further development of sickness insurance was assisted by the introduction of the law on the continuation of wage payments at the beginning of 1970; this relieved the financial burden of sickness insurance considerably.

A further Development Law (Weiterentwicklungsgesetz) of December 1970 made it possible for all employees voluntarily to become members of the statutory sickness insurance. The level of income for compulsory sickness insurance was indexed to 75 percent of the respective assessment level for pension insurance. Voluntarily insured employees were granted a claim to an allowance towards their sickness insurance from their employer. Furthermore, this law introduced a new type of sickness insurance benefit, namely facilities for the early diagnosis of disease. Apart from the discretionary service of disease prevention which had existed since 1923, the insured now had a right in certain circumstances to medical examinations aimed at the early diagnosis of disease. This was clearly a change in the concept of sickness insurance: it now aimed at securing good health.

In 1972 a Law on Sickness Insurance for Farmers also included the self-employed, their dependants and people who receive old age assistance in sickness insurance. This group of persons does not receive sick pay, but in certain circumstances substitute labour is provided to continue the 'business'. The agricultural sickness insurances wre set up — like the old age funds previously — at the agricultural associations.

In December 1973 a Law on Improved Benefits (Leistungsverbesserungsgesetz) accorded the insured in certain circumstances the right to home help during hospitalization as well as to time off work and sick pay on the illness of a child of the insured. The time limit for hospital treatment was abolished.

Finally, in June 1975 a law was passed to include all students in statutory sickness insurance and a supplementary Act on criminal law reform of August 1975 introduced 'other forms of assistance' such as medical advice on contraception, and assistance pertaining to sterilization and abortion.

Further significant development of accident insurance led to the inclusion of schoolchildren, students and children at kindergarten and thus to more widespread measures for accident prevention (1971). Furthermore, farm and household assistance was introduced as a new service in agricultural accident insurance.

The consolidatory financial measures of pension insurance of 1969 have already been discussed. In retrospect they proved over-cautious. Measures taken following the recession meant that calculations for the future boom years, 1970–1972, showed continually growing surpluses. Thus, the government could also set about further developments in this sector. In a draft bill on the further reform of statutory pension insurance in 1971 it proposed:

the introduction of a flexible (lowered) retirement age;[168]
the calculation of pensions according to a minimum income to balance out lower wages in the past;
the allowance of an additional year of insurance for women per child ('baby year');
the accessibility of pension insurance to all citizens.

The law was debated in parliament at a time when the coalition government's majority was on the decline and shortly before the Bundestag elections (which had been brought forward). This factor and the improved financial calculations for the immediate future led to decisions which doubled the originally planned excess expenditure. Once more there was an over-reaction to economic circumstances which were favourable this time. Of the proposed measures, two — the flexible retirement age and the pension according to a minimum income — were resolved. The accessibility of pension insurance was extended by providing generous possibilities for backpayments of contributions. In addition, adjustment of currently paid out pensions was brought forward by 6 months. This latter measure in particular considerably burdened later calculations of the future financial situation.

The following laws also belong to the further development phase, even though they were passed at the beginning of economic recession in 1973:

the Rehabilitation and Assimilation Law (Rehabilitations-Angleichungsgesetz) (1974) which improved and standardized benefits for the disabled;
the Law on the Social Insurance of Disabled Persons (1975) which included in sickness and pension insurance disabled persons employed in workshops and institutions under certain conditions;
the Law on the Establishment of an Additional Relief Fund for Persons Employed in Agriculture and Forestry (1974);
the Law on the Improvement of Works' Old Age Schemes (1974) which brought conditional non-forfeiture of qualifying periods for works pensions as well as the prohibition of cuts in works pensions due to increases in social insurance pensions.

Consolidation and Cost Reductions Since 1975

With the first oil crisis in the autumn of 1973 it became apparent that economic decline had begun. The number of unemployed rose monthly from the summer onwards and was clearly higher than the corresponding figures for the previous year. In January 1974 there were over 600 000 unemployed, almost double that of a year earlier. At the same time the number of foreign workers continued to grow. In view of these circumstances, the Federal Minister of Labour and of Social Order decreed a ban on the recruitment of foreign workers in November 1973 which is still valid to this day. This measure helped to relieve the situation on the labour market but did not prevent the number of unemployed from increasing further. In January 1975 it exceeded the million mark.

Following the sudden increase in the price of oil, a law was passed in December 1973 granting recipients of housing allowances and social assistance a single heating-oil allowance. This procedure was repeated in the winter of 1979.

Sickness Insurance. Once the development phase of sickness insurance had been completed (by 1973) the government turned to regulating financial, organizational and structural matters. There was, for example, a need for more uniform medical treatment in rural areas and on the periphery of cities because of a lack of panel doctors in these areas. Thus, a draft bill was tabled in November 1974 and passed in December 1976 which improved the possibilities of panel doctors' associations by ensuring that panel doctors were available to provide treatment. It also provided for planning according to need and the participation of the sickness insurances.

At the end of 1974 a trend became apparent in the health service which was designated a 'cost explosion'. This was triggered off by the decline of contribution receipts. At the same time expenditure grew increasingly; heated debate ensued as to whether the main reason for this was the increased number of health benefits or structural factors, such as the rise in the price of services, the increased use of expensive technical equipment in medicine, the higher average age and the growing health consciousness of the population. In view of the rising contribution rates for sickness insurance, the government endeavoured to bring in a policy of cost reduction by talking to all groups concerned during 1975. It aimed at

> exploring the scope of activity of all concerned and at developing the structures more efficiently and economically and in keeping with needs. . . . All participants agreed to explore every possibility of cost reduction in their respective sectors.[169]

However, the success of these efforts was neither rapid nor far-reaching enough. The contribution rates continued to rise on a large scale. The average contribution rate of 10.4 percent in 1975 reached the 1969 level before the law on the continued payment of wages was introduced. After that, in 1971, it had dropped to 8.2 percent. In 1976 it rose to 11.3 percent. The government considered legislative measures at the end of 1975 and at the beginning of 1976, but could not come to any decision.[170] However, the very threat of legislative intervention led to a restrained fee policy by the medical organizations.

It was not until after the Bundestag elections of 1976 that the newly formed government tabled a bill on sickness insurance cost reduction; this was passed in June 1977. Apart from a series of service limitations which appeared reasonable, its major points were as follows:

The development of basic aggregate wages is to be considered in negotiations on the total remuneration for medical services.

A maximum amount is to be agreed for medicines prescribed; when this is exceeded, certain control mechanisms are to be put into operation.

Contracts can be concluded on pre-inpatient diagnosis and post-inpatient treatment in hospitals.

The establishment of a 'Concerted Action' in the health service.

The sharing of the financial burden of pensioners' sickness insurance was also introduced. A draft bill on the revision of the hospital financing law, aimed at better cost control, has not yet been passed.

Contribution rates of sickness insurance remained stable from 1977 to 1979. There are indications that this is not primarily the direct result of changes in the law but rather an indirect consequence. The vehement public debate and the fact that the legislature was so active made everyone concerned behave in a way which affected cost reduction.

Pensions Insurance. During the period under discussion, pension insurance reached the height of the demographic 'pensions peak'. As the population stagnated, the number of pensioners rose from 9.5 million to 12 million between 1969 and 1978. The pension reform of 1972 had caused considerable additional expense. The high wage increases during the years of economic boom were now reflected in high adjustment rates for pensions with the expected time lag. At the beginning of the recession from the end of 1973 onwards expenditure was rising more quickly than income. However, the situation was not disturbing at first as the pension insurance reserve (a reserve for fluctuations) had been created for this very purpose. At the end of 1974 there was still a surplus revenue of 6600 million DM. In 1975 there was a deficit of 600 million DM but this was more than balanced by a reserve of 45 000 million DM. In these circumstances political decisions depended on what assumptions could be made in relation to future economic development.

The public debate which now began on the financing of pensions insurance concerned possible, probable, or feared future developments. This discussion grew more intense and was part of the electoral campaign for the Bundestag election of 1976. On the one hand it was pointed out that the pensions insurance reserve was in danger of being completely used up within a few years if assumptions were made on a 'realistic' basis. On the other hand, the federal government had to stress the possibility and desirability of more favourable assumptions if only to avoid giving negative signals in relation to the actual development of the economy. The government's statement, 'Pensions are safe', was based on the current and future solvency of the insurance institutions which assure the nominal amounts paid out and the purchasing power of the pensions. If doubts were expressed about pensions being safe – political polemics of the day aside – these referred solely to the time and scope of future pension increases.

When economic factors did not improve during the course of 1976 and pensions insurance ended the year with a deficit of some 6000 million DM, it was time for a decision to be made. The new federal government tabled a bill for a 20th Pensions Adjustment Law (Rentenanpassungsgesetz) in February 1977, which was passed in June of the same year. Apart from adjusting pension levels as of 1 July 1977, it provided for the following consolidatory measures:

the change of time for adjusting pensions to the 1st January of every year;
the reduction of expenditure for pensioners' sickness insurance at the expense of the sickness insurance (for which the Cost Reduction Law was passed at the same time);
the payment of contributions for the unemployed through the Federal Labour Office (Bundesanstalt für Arbeit);
the premature repayment of deferred government subsidies;
the reduction of minimum reserves to the expenditure of one month.

Furthermore, a series of improvements were made with regard to the minimum contribution to voluntary insurance, family allowances, limits to additional income and rehabilitation measures.

The hope that this law would permanently consolidate the financial situation of pensions insurance was not fulfilled. Based on new overall economic assumptions on the medium range development of the economy, the calculations for the future, made in January 1978, once again pointed to a financing gap. The government had to propose further measures for consolidation in a draft bill of the 21st Pensions Adjustment Law. The law passed in July 1978 provided for an increase in contributions from 18.0 percent to 18.5 percent in 1981 and, deviating from past procedures, it established a discretionary adjustment rate for pensions. In keeping with the policy of updating pensions in accordance with wage increases, pensions would have had to be raised by 7.2 percent, 6.9 percent, and 6.1 percent from 1979 to 1981. The new law reduced these rates to 4.5 percent, 4.0 percent and 4.0 percent.

This participation of pensioners in consolidating the financing of pensions was considered economically feasible as the pension level had increased considerably since 1975 compared with net wages. Thus, this measure was criticized not so much because of its economic result but

because of its political significance. The level of pension adjustments had always been controversial in the past. However, the (quasi-automatic) adjustment process had become such a matter of course that it even prevailed under highly conservative influences. Thus, one aspect of social security evaded *de facto* the arbitrariness of politics; the continuity of pensions development followed its own socio-political aims within the limits of economic development. The breaking of this dogma by the introduction of the 21st Pensions Adjustment Law restored the situation which had prevailed in 1957; pensions policy is once again exposed to political machinations and is again included in party-political deliberations and electoral campaign tactics. It is reasonable to assume that this will not help to advance any measures that are considered.[171]

Other Significant Measures: Pension Equality and Security for Women. Since 1975 sociopolitical discussion has been characterized by endeavours towards deflating costs and consolidation. This has largely excluded making financial improvements to benefits. Nevertheless, in 1978, predominantly due to the employment situation, the flexible retirement age for the severely disabled was gradually lowered from 62 to 60 years of age. Two plans were passed during the seventh legislative session which were hardly effective financially but which will leave a permanent mark on the structure of the social services. The Co-determination Law (Mitbestimmungsgesetz) of 1976 affected some 500 firms; according to this law the number of representatives of the employed on company boards was extended to just below parity.

In December 1975 pension equalization was introduced in the context of reform of matrimonial and family law. In future, based on the idea of an equal share of both partners in the pension-qualifying periods acquired together, there will be equalization of claims and the prospect of disability and old age pensions in the case of divorce. Equalization is provided for the weaker partner from a social security point of view — thus, usually for the wife — by the transfer or establishment of pension-qualifying periods within the statutory insurance scheme. Thus, in the case of inability to continue a certain job or to work altogether, and in the case of old-age, qualifying periods to that person's credit result in a pension from the statutory pensions insurance scheme.

Social security for women and surviving dependants will be an important topic in the near future. The reorganization of this sector will probably be one of the first socio-political reforms in the second century of the history of social insurance. In 1975 the Constitutional Court (Bundesverfassungsgericht) decided in a fundamentally important decision that the current legal sitaution, according to which different conditions apply to widows' and widowers' pensions, cannot be upheld because of the increase in the number of working married women. The legislature was committed to reform welfare for surviving dependants by 1984. A commission of experts appointed by the federal government in October 1977 made its report in May 1979.[172]

The debate on the last-mentioned problem will probably raise a number of sociological arguments, as did the confirmation of the Constitutional Court's verdict in 1975, and thus strengthen a trend which has been recognizable for some time. This can be designated the 'sociological aspect' of scientific social policy which has followed the economy-dependant phase mentioned earlier (see above p. 70). For a long time sociologists had barely taken social security into account and had rarely made it the object of their studies. However, after the pension reform of 1957 they began to criticize the 'legal' and 'monetary orientation' of social policy.[173] Apart from many interesting points of view expressed, their study gave the impression that only sociologists had suitable means of dealing with socio-political problems.[174] Empirical studies were carried out[175] which have rapidly multiplied recently. It is striking, however, that most of the recent studies and reflections by sociologists are concerned only with marginal aspects of the field of social security, relating to institutions, staff and financial arrangements. A sociological look at the central questions is more likely to help improve understanding of the situation, the sooner it is realized that the important measures of monetary redistribution which have been developed over the last 100 years are based on legal security and are fundamentally indispensable.[176]

EXPLANATORY ASPECTS

This brief account of the history of German social insurance over almost 100 years raises questions of whether and how its origin and development can be explained. An attempt to understand what has happened so far, and what was aimed at, could help in comparative studies on future development as well as with advice on setting up and developing new social security systems. Such an explanatory attempt would require a far broader scope than this study allows. Thus, only a few aspects can be mentioned as an introduction for a more comprehensive discussion. An important distinction must be made between those aspects which refer to the emergence of social insurance and those which refer to its further development.

Origins

The conditions for the emergence of social insurance have already been discussed in detail.[177] Opinions are broadly unanimous about the type and effect of the various factors although the importance of each individual factor is less clear and also less easily explained because of national characteristics. About the middle of the last century, a series of conditions prevailed in Germany which were similar to those in other western European countries: industrialization, liberalization, population growth, urbanization, increasing wage dependence, geographical concentration of the new industrial workers. Such factors undermined older forms of social security and created new needs which these older forms could not satisfy. At the same time, the work force which was most affected by the new situation, began to mobilize politically. With the nineteenth-century trend towards rationalization, individualization, and democratization, such political awareness led to the spread of the idea — which deviated from liberalism — that the state should be responsible for the solution of social problems. 'Thus, social distress became a factor in politics.'[178]

The 'intrusion' of the above-mentioned conditions into political awareness of the issue was new and decisive for further events in Germany in particular. As far as economic development and the level of industrialization were concerned, Germany was by no means in the lead when the Second Reich was founded, but took fifth place after Great Britain, Belgium, Switzerland and France. Thus, the early start of social legislation in Germany cannot be sufficiently explained by the economic level of development. 'Social conditions and political "constellations" tipped the scales.'[179]

It is impossible to decide here whether social traditions were so different and above all older and more effective than in neighbouring countries. It must be pointed out that the early introduction of social insurance was not due to the 'modernity' of Bismarck's Reich

> but to the specific, lasting instability of the foundation of the Reich; in addition there were older traditional concepts of political understanding and also of administration. In any case, it was easier in Germany than anywhere else to revert to the modernity of pre-liberal thought with the swing to conservatism in 1878. The fascinating part about this turn to conservatism, as a reaction to the internal crisis, is that it had 'progressive' results.[180]

Looking at the political constellations it is easier to arrive at a judgment. It is important to remember that 'not the parliamentary parties but the political leaders and civil service at that time were the decisive motive powers behind the development of a national social insurance system in Germany'.[181]

Studies have been conducted on why the political leaders in Germany pressed for the development of a national social insurance system with special reference to political systems and the effect on them of changes in socio-economic data and to the effects of political mobilization. Germany is described as having an authoritarian system as opposed to a parliamentary system in those days. 'Germany's headway in this field is explained by the fact that early political organization of workers in this authoritarian state was combined with relatively progressive socio-economic development.'[182]

This point of view seems feasible if one realizes that the political leaders and the bureaucracy belonged to a newly founded Reich. This Reich lacked democratic legitimation; it had neither grown gradually nor arisen spontaneously but was a creation of public law, 'forged' politically in the face of opposition of particular interests and to the disappointment of people with hopes of a 'grossdeutsche' (Pan-German) solution. This situation was described as the 'immaturity and uncertainty, the continuing problematic state of the new Reich, its endangerment both from within and without'.[183] There was thus great need for integration and stabilization and a high degree of sensitivity to any destabilizing forces. This applied particularly to the creator of the Reich who assumed a stabilizing role and who was given the time and authority to play this role to the full. Bismarck gave priority to this stabilizing task at foreign policy level; however, he also recognized the need for stabilizing policies at a national level. Such needs made him act. One stabilizing measure was the creation of social insurance. This 'brainchild' of his has survived 100 years.

Expansion

The history of social insurance in Germany is the history of its expansion. It originally covered 40 percent of the employed or about 10 percent of the population; today all employed persons and about 90 percent of the population are covered. The original workers' insurance expanded to include white-collar workers, thus becoming an insurance for all employed persons; later with the inclusion of large groups of the self-employed and the accessibility to pensions insurance, it became a people's insurance.

As the group of insured persons expanded, there was an increase in and differentiation of factors influencing benefits, as well as a rise in the rate of income substitution in all branches. Whereas social insurance originally provided minimum protection against destitution, it now ensures the basic standard of living in most cases. Classic social insurance of the early years has been complemented by further types of benefits such as unemployment insurance, social compensation, family allowances, training promotion and special systems for the self-employed. Today social insurance is part — indeed the most important part — of a comprehensive system of social security. The growth in the number of people affected, the sectors and types of benefits and the level of benefits, together with an increase in the quota of old people from (originally) 5 percent to (now) 15 percent of the population have resulted in an immense increase in expenditure. The quota of social benefits of about 2 percent originally rose to 10 percent in the 1920s and is now over 30 percent.

The expansionary trend was partly due to the inherent automatic mechanism of the system itself in so far as the quota of employed and thus the number of insured persons rose continually at the expense of the self-employed and working members of their families. At the same time new legislation repeatedly brought about further sporadic expansion, such as the extension of accident insurance to farms (1886), the extension of sickness insurance to people employed in

agriculture (1914), the introduction of employees' insurance (1913), the extension of old age insurance to craftsmen (1938) and farmers (1957), the opening up
of pension insurance to all citizens (1972). Generalizing, one can say that
legislative extension of the circle of people affected took place in times of
economic prosperity.

Staff expansion of the system which was also sporadic was followed by
monetary expansion with stabilization effects and delays. This again was partly
the automatic result of the enlargement of the circle of people included or eligible
for benefits. From a long term point of view one can understand the vast
numbers of 'adaptive' legislative measures which only cause adjustments to
changed economic conditions and thus uphold or restore the content of earlier
decisions. These include standards which adapt levels for assessing benefits to
changed wage levels or maintain the relative purchasing power of benefits.

Compared with legislation of this type, the number of 'inductive' regulations,
i.e. those which really change the level of benefits, are far fewer.[184] These include: the introduction of employees' insurance with an increased level of benefits
(1913), the introduction of an insurance for surviving dependants in the workers'
pension insurance (1914), the raising and indexing of pensions (1957), the raising
of sick pay in proportion to the wage (1957, 1961), the indexing of accident pensions (1963), the lowering of the retirement age (1916, 1957, 1972). Such
measures also coincide with times of economic prosperity.

Financial expansion has often been interrupted by phases of reduction which
all coincided with times of economic depression. During the inflation of
1921-1923 and during the post-war years 1945-1948 there were real reductions
in benefits as adaptive legislation took unusually long to be enacted. During the
world economic crisis of 1929-1932 and the recessions of both 1966/7 and from
1974 onwards, reductions were brought about by legislation. Benefits were only
lowered in the first instance; in the two latter cases there were only reductions in
the increases of benefits which were expected according to legislation.

The reasons for the expansionary trend which has continued until very recently are surely not only to be found in the increasing quota of employed and people
of retirement age but are also due to many other factors. These can, however, be
summarized in the statement that social insurance had considerable functional
deficiencies at the time of its introduction, as now seen from today's point of
view.

If one takes as a basis the concept for old age insurance which was considered
right by the social enquiry commission, whereby security in old age was to be the
norm for all citizens,[185] then it is clear from what has already been said that this
aim has not yet been achieved.

A look at the beginnings in 1891 reveals a series of successes, to progress, to expansion. From a present-day perspective, however, history appears as only a
gradual reduction of deficiencies.[186] One no longer asks why something happened at a given time but why it happened so late and incompletely. The answer to
the latter question is certainly difficult and complex but perhaps more accessible
than in the case of the former question.

A line of approach with regard to the functional deficiencies of social insurance
which were immense at first and were only gradually reduced and to increasing
claims to social security is also suggested by the following observation: as
statutory old age security expanded, individual insurance[187] and works' pension
schemes also developed.[188]

Functional Change

As staff and monetary requirements of social insurance expanded, several changes of function also occurred. The structure of expenditure shifted from monetary benefits to benefits in kind. Of the total expenditure on sickness insurance in 1885, 60 percent comprised monetary benefits, whereas these only account for about 10 percent nowadays. The proportion of benefits in kind of total social expenditure rose between 1950 and 1978 from 14.1 percent to 21.0 percent.[189] These figures point to the trend towards a rise in expenditure on health meaures in cases both of illness and disability, on job promotion measures of the Federal Labour Office and on benefits in kind provided through social assistance. At the same time they reflect the development of preventive measures. Examples of how social insurance institutions have extended their range of services and benefits in kind are: the further development of accident prevention measures, the extension of measures to retain and restore a worker's capacity to work through the pensions insurance scheme, measures of early diagnosis financed by the sickness insurances as well as the provision of substitute labour and household help.

The development of preventive measures indicates a trend which has been described as the transition from social security's task of maintaining existing structures to that of modelling the structures themselves. 'One can speak of a change from the subsidiary function of social insurance to that of an institution of major significance to daily life.'[190] This point of view is not only supported by the development of preventive measures but also by the development of control mechanisms in the health service, the special regulations on financing and eligibility for benefits in the mining industry and in agriculture, the financial equalization mechanism in old-age security and the special retirement ages for the unemployed, women and the severely handicapped. In many ways social insurance is also an instrumental feature of structural policy nowadays.

A further trend which may be observed is a shift towards the 'Finalprinzip' (principle of finality, i.e. earmarked for a definite purpose). Originally, German social law was characterized by the causal principle; the type and amount of social benefit depended on what had been paid in previously and on the cause of the claim to benefits. This shift towards the 'principle of finality' can be seen from the following examples:[191]

According to the original law, sick pay was denied to persons whose illness was caused by brawls or heavy drinking; a disability pension was not granted if the disability had been caused on purpose or had arisen while committing a felony. These causal restrictions were only abolished after many decades, indeed only recently for sickness insurance.

The 'Lastenausgleichsgesetzgebung' (legislation on the equalization of burdens) of 1952 which mainly aimed at the compensation of losses of property was also designed to ensure that damaged persons received subsistence.

The 'Fremdrentengesetz' (Foreign Pensions Law) originally conceived as a compensatory measure was remodelled in accordance with the integration principle. Contributions paid earlier in the country of origin are not used as a basis for calculating benefits; rather the situation of comparably employed persons in the Federal Republic of Germany is taken into account.

Pensions according to minimum incomes (1972) place the insured after quite a long period of insurance in the same position as if they had always earned 75 percent of average earnings of all insured persons. With this, a modification of pension calculation has been carried through in accordance with the 'Finalprinzip'.

After the dissolution of a second marriage, the widow's pension used to be granted again only if that marriage had been dissolved without the widow being the guilty party. This condition was abolished in 1972.

The 'Rehabilitationsangleichungsgesetz' (Rehabilitation Equalization Law) of 1974 was expressly designed to adjust benefits for disabled persons according to the principle of finality. The disabled are to receive promotional benefits according to uniform criteria, regardless of the cause of the disablement, and of which institution bears the cost.

The 'Schwerbeschädigtengesetz' (Law on the Severely Handicapped) of 1974 included not only the war and labour disabled but all severely handicapped persons regardless of the cause of their disability.

The above developments point to a change of function which is particularly clear in the sickness insurance sector. This 'can be described as the development of the former Reich's insurance law against sickness, lasting for nearly 100 years, towards a nationwide system to safeguard health in the Federal Republic of Germany'.[192] An account of those insured and the benefits available through sickness insurance, clearly shows the scope of development. Furthermore, this change is made clear by noting the continually increasing degree of differentiation as well as the increasing problems, associated with safeguarding health.

When creating social sickness insurance the definition of sickness and the range of medical treatment which could be offered appeared unproblematic for the legislature. In those days illness was considered part of one's fate; it seemed definable in principle, even if the legislature did not lay down a definition. Sickness insurance was designed to safeguard the insured against the economic consequences of illness—lost pay and the costs of medical treatment. There was a real need for the medical benefits available. Neither the number nor type of available doctors and hospitals was considered a problem.

A great many changes have taken place since this initial situation. The term 'sickness' was legally defined at the turn of the century as an 'irregular state of body or mind requiring medical treatment'. A need for treatment was legally recognized, primarily to cure and prevent the disease from becoming worse and later to relieve discomfort or pain, if such an irregularity could be cured and if treatment was deemed sensible. Thus, medical treatment served to ward off sickness; nowadays, it works towards maintaining good health.

The catalogue of statutory sickness insurance benefits extended considerably beyond the original sickness assistance. In 1920 family assistance (maternity allowances) were added, followed by preventive measures (treatment in spas) in 1923, early diagnosis (as a right) in 1971, household help in 1974, other forms of assistance in 1975 (in cases of sterilization and abortion).

It has become far more difficult to define sickness and health. The more sickness insurance becomes involved with preventive medicine, the more it is directly confronted with the insured persons' behaviour and habits appertaining to health.

The range of medical benefits and services has also become a problem. The choice of treatment has grown enormously. The density of doctors (per 10 000 inhabitants) rose from 3.2 to 19.8 between 1876 and 1976; the density of hospitals (hospital beds per 10 000 inhabitants) rose from 26 to 150 between 1886 and 1976.

Parallel to the above-mentioned developments, all doctors have been permitted to practice as panel doctors. Briefly, this came about as follows:

1883	sickness insurances employ individual doctors in the various districts;
1913	the Berlin Agreement: at least doctor registered per 1350 insured persons;
1931	the proportion was lowered to 1 : 600;
1955	the proportion was lowered again to 1 : 500;
1960	verdict of the Constitutional Court: every practicing doctor is to be allowed to practice as a panel doctor.

According to recent forecasts the number of doctors will double in the next two decades. Thus, changes in licensing procedures for doctors to practice medicine and in the income policy of the medical profession seem inevitable.

This applies all the more as the belief in a finite level of need for medical services has been shaken. The number of doctors and hospital beds has multiplied six-fold while the productivity per doctor, and intensity of treatment per patient, has increased constantly. Nevertheless, doctors have neither become unemployed nor even underemployed. This is predominantly because the type and scope of medical service is largely determined by those who offer such services. The confidence of the legislature of 1883 — and of many subsequent generations of lawyers — that need for treatment could be assessed objectively, has been shaken.

The discussion on the so-called 'cost explosion' of the health service since 1974 has shown clearly the variability of those who offer treatment. This plus the rapidly increasing number of doctors will probably affect the nature of discussion on concerted action within the health service. It will affect the scale and method of assessing incomes for professions within the health service.

If one compares the situation at the beginning of health insurance with the present one can say that the term 'sickness' is no longer considered a 'pretext' but has become a problem and an object of discussion. The constant extension of its meaning has led to the recognition that good health must be maintained whatever the permanent difficulties of definition. The new concept and the insurance institutions' shift towards measures for ensuring good health pose a fundamental question — apart from many other questions of a technical and organizational nature — namely, what demands can and should an insurance institution providing multiple benefits make on those who are eligible for benefits with regard to health-oriented behaviour?

The range of medical services and benefits also no longer seems a pretext but a problem. Analyses and decisions are required on a series of questions, such as the training capacities for medical professions, the number, type and distribution of hospitals, the production and distribution of pharmaceutical products, criteria on income for all those who are involved in medical treatment, and control of type and quantity of medical benefits and services.

Although sickness insurance has turned into health insurance and although it has changed from an institution which gives concessions into one that provides services, this does not mean that the process of development is complete. Indeed, it is more than likely that it will continue to develop even more in the second century of its existence.

Final Remarks

The expansion and change of function of social insurance over the last 100 years can be understood primarily, if not exclusively, as the gradual reduction of originally inadequate functions. Their increasing quantity necessitated an understanding of the interdependence of socio-political measures with other political spheres. The policy of social security increasingly affected economic, financial and legal policies and was, in turn, increasingly affected by repercussions from these sectors. Moreover, the increase of activity focussed attention on remaining deficiencies. This may explain a stronger shift to the purpose-oriented approach and also to the wish for reform — still very much alive — quite apart from the reduction of faults which has already taken place. These are reinforced by the goal of equal opportunity which gained political recognition during the whole period. From this arose the differentiation and qualitative improvement of benefits in kind and services in particular which in turn led to increased insight into the conditions influencing the actions and reactions of all concerned.

Thus, all the main present and future problems have been mentioned. However, it does not look as if a satisfactory solution to such problems will require fundamental restructuring of the German social insurance system. This system, linked with Bismarck's name, has shown incredible continuity in its institutions and legal structure when one considers the many, partly catastrophic, circumstances it has endured.

'In spite of the frequent changes in social insurance law, there are few public legal subjects whose basic forms have been subjected to so few, far-reaching changes — irrespective of their functional changes — as social insurance law.'[193] The legal form of this basic structure has shown a flexibility which has meant that the system could react to changed circumstances and has made and will continue to make possible adjustments and further developments.

NOTES

1 *Sozialbericht 1976*, Bundesminister für Arbeit und Sozialordnung (ed.), Bonn 1976, p. 105. Quotations from other social reports (from 1970 to 1978) refer to the publication of the BMA.
2 Detlev Zöllner (1978). *Alterssicherungssysteme im internationalen Vergleich, Schriftenreihe des Deutschen Sozialgerichtsverbandes*, vol. xvii, p. 146.
3 *Sozialbericht 1972*, p. 2, Krankheit: gesetzliche Krankenversicherung, Anspruch auf Beihilfe oder Heilfürsorge, ohne private Krankenversicherung, Alter: gesetzliche Rentenversicherungen (ohne latent Versicherte), Altershilfe für Landwirte, Beamtenversorgung, ohne betriebliche Altersversorgung.
4 This 'pensions level' fluctuates in the course of time depending on wage developments; the figure for 1977 was 66.4.
5 For more detail see the Survey on Social Security by Dieter Schewe and co-authors which is an impartial, complete, and correct account: Bundesminister für Arbeit und Sozialordnung (ed.), 10th edn, Bonn 1977.
6 For more detail see chronological table of socio-political laws and decrees from 1839–1939 in Syrup-Neuloi: *70 Jahre Sozialversicherungsrecht*, Bundesarbeitsblatt 1953, p. 751; from 1954 onwards cf. annual lists in the *Bundesarbeitsblatt;* catalogue of amendments to the *Reichsversicherungsordnung* since 1925 in '*Sozialgesetzbuch. Reichsversicherungsordnung*' of Beck-Verlag; cf. also Michael Stolleis: *Quellen zur Geschichte des Sozialrechts*, Göttingen 1976 and Horst Peters: *Die*

Geschichte der sozialen Versicherung, 3rd edn, Sankt Augustin 1978. Florian Tennstedt also provides an extremely detailed compilation of material of the insurance institutions and their associatoins: 'Quellen zur Geschichte der Sozialversicherung', in: *Zeitschrift für Sozialreform*, 1975, pp. 225, 358, and 422.

7 A. von Lengerke: *Die ländliche Arbeiterfrage*, 1849.
8 Henning, vol. 2, p. 45.
9 Grebing, p. 22.
10 Henning, p. 107.
11 Henning pp. 116, 118, 130, 150, 154, 163, 238.
12 Henning, p. 126.
13 Syrup-Neuloh, p. 50.
14 Henning, p. 28.
15 Wilhelm Abel: *Massenarmut und Hungerkrisen im vorindustriellen Deutschland*, Göttingen, 2nd edn, 1977, p. 6; reference is made to the Engels critic of the day, Bruno Hildebrand.
16 Wilhelm Heinrich Riehl 1850, cit. after Abel (n15) p. 12.
17 Henning, pp. 195, 231.
18 Otto Neuloh: *Arbeiterbildung im neuen Deutschland*, Leipzig 1930, p. 18.
19 Grebing, p. 46.
20 Schmoller, p. 464.
21 Art. II of the Gotha Programme of the German Socialist Labour Party of 1875; quoted from: *Programme der deutschen Sozialdemokratie*, Hannover 1963, p. 74.
22 Grebing, p. 74.
23 Vogel, p. 51.
24 Programme (n21), p. 75.
25 Vogel, pp. 52, 54.
26 From the broad range of literature on Bismarck: Hans Rothfels, *Zur Geschichte der Bismarckschen Innenpolitik*, Archiv für Politik und Geschichte VII, Heft 9, Berlin 1926.
27 Herkner, p. 98.
28 Herkner, p. 347.
29 Relevant extract from the Kaiser's message, cf. last note.
30 Reference to Theodor Lohmann, cf. Vogel, p. 135.
31 Syrup-Neuloh, p. 55.
32 Vogel, p. 149.
33 Karl Thieme: *Bismarcks Sozialpolitik, Archiv für Politik und Geschichte*, 1927, Heft 11, p. 385.
34 Herkner, p. 102. Bismarck seems to have exaggerated or was inadequately informed. The benevolent funds (sociétés de secours mutuelles) paid out about 30 000 pensions in 1872 and about 200 000 pensions in 1896. Cf. Schmoller (n20) p. 388.
35 Vogel, p. 164. This fundamental disagreement on the necessity of a policy of industrial safety and labour law later led to the break with Lohmann. Cf. Hans Rothfels: *Theodor Lohmann und die Kampfjahre der staatlichen Sozialpolitik*, Berlin 1927.
36 Vogel, pp. 148, 149.
37 Above quotations cf. Vogel, pp. 132, 144, 169.
38 Gustav Schmoller: *Die soziale Frage und der preussische Staat*, Preussische Jahrbücher, 1874, vol. 3, Heft 4. Schmoller had stressed that the reform he wanted did not aim to change science, overthrow existing conditions and promote socialism; 'we protest against all Socialist experiments'. Cf. *Jahrbücher für Nationalökonomie und Statistik*, 1873, p. 11.
39 Vogel, p. 87.
40 Schmoller, p. 392.
41 Syrup-Neuloh (n13) p. 120, with reference to contemporary sources.
42 Opinion expressed in a letter by the editor of the *Deutsche Volkswirtschaftliche Korrespondenz*, by Roell, 1st May 1881, quoted from Vogel, p. 41.
43 Hermann Wagener to Bismarck 1874, quoted from Vogel, p. 156.
44 Vogel, p. 158.
45 Herkner, p. 104.
46 Motive zum Unfallversicherungsgesetz, Reichstagsdrucksache 1881, No. 41.
47 Wolfram Fischer: *Die Pionierrolle der betrieblichen Sozialpolitik im 19. und beginnenden 20. Jahrhundert*, Zeitschr. f. Unternehmensgeschichte, November 1978, p. 32.
48 Schmoller, p. 400.
49 Schmoller, p. 368.

50 As far as we know, statutory, compulsory contributions were demanded for the first time by Wilhelm Wagner: *Denkschrift über Allgemeine Hülfskassen für Arbeiter mit gesetzlicher Beitragspflict der Arbeitgeber und Arbeiter*, Berlin 1851.

51 Schmoller, p. 391.

52 Joseph Höffner: *Sozialpolitik im deutschen Bergbau*, Münster 1956, p. 48.

53 Schmoller, p. 390.

54 Vogel, p. 30.

55 Syrup-Neuloh, p. 56.

56 Cf. also Rothfels (n35).

57 Vogel, p. 28.

58 Albert Schäffle: *Kapitalismus und Sozialismus*, 1870.

59 *Jahrbuch f. Nationalökonomie und Statistik*, 1872, p. 219.

60 *Jahrb. f. Nat. u. Statistik*, 1873, p. 9.

61 *Schriften des Vereins für Sozialpolitik*, vol. v, 1874.

62 Vogel, p. 39. It is difficult to assess how much influence a report on relief funds set up by the friendly societies had on policies of the day (Vogel, p. 13). It was drawn up by the German consul general in London upon the request of the Chancellor's Office.

63 Vogel, pp. 33, 152 with reference to papers of the chancellery.

64 J.-J. Dupeyroux: *Entwicklung und Tendenzen der Systeme der sozialen Sicherheit in den Mitgliedsstaaten der Europäischen Gemeinschaften und in Grossbritannien*, Hohe Behörde der Eur. Gem. für Kohle und Stahl (ed.), Luxemburg 1966, pp. 35 and 64.

65 The Kaiser's message of November 1881 (see extract at the end of these notes) was neither the first nor the last speech from the throne which dealt with social insurance (cf. the speech of 15 February 1881): a speech from the throne of 14 April 1883 urged the politicians to attend to the bills on accident and sickness insurance, a further speech of 22 November 1888 announced the bill on disability insurance.

66 Vogel, p. 158 with reference to Lohnmann.

67 Vogel, p. 151.

68 Syrup-Neuloh, p. 124.

69 This plan did not come to fruition; in the 1890s the share of Reich funds on the expenditure of pensions insurance amounted to 40 percent.

70 Schmoller, p. 402.

71 Syrup-Neuloh, p. 125.

72 Herkner, p. 105.

73 Schmoller, p. 414.

74 Maximilian Sauerborn: *Kassenärzterecht in der Entwicklung*, Bundesarbeitsblatt 1953, p. 205.

75 Bismarck had rejected the level premium system which the civil servants originally planned and staunchly defended so that there would be only a gradual increase in burden on industry; cf. Vogel, p. 98.

76 The level of contribution was to be calculated for a 10-year period in such a way that it covered administrative costs, funds to form a reserve fund, contribution reimbursements 'as well as the capital value of those proportions of the pensions which are to be provided by the insurance institution and which will probably be granted in the period concerned' (Section 20 of the Disability Law).

77 More details in Syrup-Neuloh (n13) p. 75.

78 More details in Walter Bogs: 'Das Bundesversicherungsamt im Rückblick', in: *Die Praxis des Bundesversicherungsamtes*, Dieter Schewe (ed.), Bonn-Bad Godesberg, 1977, p. 195.

79 *Reichsarbeitsblatt*, 1905, p. 339.

80 *Reichsarbeitsblatt*, 1905, p. 340.

81 Schmoller, p. 411.

82 Heinrich Rosin: *Das Recht der Arbeiterversicherung*, Berlin 1893.

83 From 1885–1900 ten new laws were passed to amend the three first laws.

84 Detlev Zöllner: 'Planung und Durchführung von Gesundheitsmassnahmen in Entwicklungsländern, in: *Soziale Sicherung durch soziales Recht, Festschr. f. Horst Peters*, Hans F. Zacher (ed.), Stuttgart 1975, p. 239.

85 Horst Peters, p. 57.

86 G. Hohorst, J. Kocka, and G.A. Ritter: *Materialien zur Statistik des Kaiserreiches 1870–1914*, 2nd edn, Munich 1978, p. 58.

87 Details partly calculated and partly taken from *Materialien*, pp. 67, 69, 107, 135, 156.

88 All details on Reichstag elections from *Materialien*, p. 173.

89 Ernst Francke, in: *Soziale Praxis*, ix, 1899, Sp. 865.

90 Numerous sources in Rolf Neuhaus: *Die Gesellschaft für Soziale Reform 1901–1914, Magisterarbeit*, Bonn 1978.

91 Ludwig Bernhard: *Unerwünschte Folgen der deutschen Sozialpolitik*, Berlin 1912. Contrary arguments in Herkner, p. 365; discussion at that time involved England: Lewis S. Gannet (1914), 'Bernhard, Unerwünschte Folgen der deutschen Sozialpolitik and its critics', *Quarterly Journal of Economics,* vol. xxviii, p. 561.

92 Herkner, p. 361.

93 During the same period (1876–1900) the number of hospital beds per inhabitant doubled.

94 *Verhandlungen des Reichstags*, vol. 188, p. 9201.

95 Herkner, p. 353.

96 Material on this subject in Wolfgang Dreher's *Die Entstehung der Arbeiterwitwenversicherung in Deutschland*, Berlin 1978, p. 39.

97 So-called 'lex Trimborn': the motion was accepted with the votes of the Centre Party and the SPD against those of the Conservatives and the Liberals; for further details cf. Dreher (n96), p. 41.

98 This deadline was extended twice with regard to the imminent 'Reichsversicherungsordnung'.

99 Dreher (n96), p. 73.

100 Syrup-Neuloh, p. 134.

101 Ludwig Preller, p. 85.

102 Gustav Harz: *Irrwege der deutschen Sozialpolitik*, Berlin 1928; Erwin Liek: *Die Schäden der sozialen Versicherung*, München 1928; Ernst Horneffer: *Frevel am Volke*, Leipzig 1929.

103 Cf. note 91.

104 The author will present a more detailed analysis of the relative incidence of legislation on social insurance elsewhere.

105 Wolfram Fischer: 'Wirtschaftliche Bedingungen und Faktoren bei der Entstehung und Entwicklung von Sozialversicherung', in: *Bedingungen für die Entstehung und Entwicklung von Sozialversicherung*, Zacher, p. 95.

106 Sauerborn (n74), p. 211.

107 Decree of 14 January 1932 (RGB1. I, p. 19).

108 More details and reasons in Preller (n101), p. 6.

109 Walter Kaskel: *Die gesetzliche Regelung der Arbeitsnachweise als Voraussetzung der Arbeitslosenversicherung*. Schr. d. Dt. Gesellschaft zur Bekämpfung der Arbeitslosigkeit, 1921, Heft 6; the combination of both tasks in one law is also demanded here.

110 One often reads that the grand coalition collapsed 'because of a contribution increase of 1/2 %'; this is an oversimplification. For details of the extremely complex connections between economics and politics see Preller (n101), p. 428.

111 For the history of unemployment insurance until 1939 cf. Syrup-Neuloh (n13) pp. 303, 326, 455.

112 Quoted from Wilhelm Bangert: *Die Sozialhilfe*, Stuttgart 1961, p. 4.

113 A first military pension law had been passed in 1871.

114 Detlev Zöllner: *Öffentliche Sozialleistungen und wirtschaftliche Entwicklung*, Berlin 1963, p. 21.

115 This assessment was given during the author's talks with former civil servants of the Ministry of Labour.

116 Florian Tennstedt: 'Sozialpolitik und Berufsverbote im Jahre 1933', in: *Zeitschrift für Sozialreform,* 1979, p. 140.

117 Quoted from Tennstedt (n116), p. 137.

118 Tennstedt (n116), pp. 217, 223.

119 Also cf. Karl Teppe: *Zur Sozialpolitik des Dritten Reiches am Beispiel der Sozialversicherung, Archiv für Sozialgeschichte,* 1977, p. 195.

120 Syrup-Neuloh, p. 456.

121 Henning, vol. 3, p. 184.

122 *Wirtschaft und Statistik*, 1954, p. 167. One wonders how social security would have developed after 14 years of peace.

123 Cf. details in Peters (n85) p. 128; for details on the special development in Berlin where a single institution was set up, cf. essays by Baker, Foggon, Noetzel, *inter alia*, in: *Bartholomäi*.

124 Herbert W. Baker: 'Beginn der deutschen Sozial- und Arbeits-politik unter der Militärregierung', in: *Bartholomäi*, p. 24.

125 George Foggon: 'Alliierte Sozialpolitik in Berlin', in: *Bartholomäi*, p. 35.

126 Baker, p. 30.

127 A detailed description by Hans Günter Hockerts: *Sozialpolitische Entscheidungen im Nachkriegsdeutschland: Alliierte und deutsche Sozialpolitik 1945–1957,* Stuttgart 1980.

128 *Die Praxis des Bundesversicherungsamtes,* Dieter Schewe (ed.), Bonn-Bad Godesberg, 1977; cf. especially W. Bogs: 'Vom alten Reichversicherungsamt', and H. Schirmer: 'Selbstverwaltung und Aufsicht'.

129 Walter Bogs: *Sozialversicherungsrecht (unter dem Obertitel: Versicherungswissenschaft und Versicherungspraxis in den zurückliegenden 75 Jahren),* Zeitschrift für die gesamte Versicherungswissenschaft, 1974, p. 31.

130 More details by Alfred Schmidt: Zum Entstehen der Selbstverwaltung in der Nachkriegszeit, in: *Sozialpolitik* nach 1945, p. 391.

131 On current discussions cf. *Sozialpolitik und Selbstverwaltung,* WSI-Studie Nr. 35, Köln 1977.

132 Walter Auerbach: *Modell eines Sozialplans, Die Krankenversicherung,* Heft 5, 1952; Gerhard Mackenroth: *Die Reform der Sozialpolitik durch einen deutschen Sozialplan, Schriften des Vereins für Socialpolitik, N.F.,* vol. 4, Berlin 1952; Hans Achinger: *Zur Neuordnung der sozialen Hilfe. Konzept für einen deutschen Sozialplan,* Stuttgart 1957, cf. bibliographic details in Richter: *Anhang V.*

133 *Die Grundlagen des sozialen Gesamtplans der SPD,* Bonn 1953; resolved on 14 September 1952 by the socio-political board of the SPD in agreement with the executive committee of the party. Similar decisions were made at party meetings in 1952 and 1954.

134 Social plan for Germany. Instigated by the SPD executive, presented by Walter Auerbach, *inter alia,* Berlin/Hanover 1957.

135 *Die Sozialreform,* F I, p. 3, F II, p. 4.

136 Compilation of results in: *Die Sozialreform,* C.

137 *Bundesanzeiger* 1953, Nr. 204, p. 3.

138 Erich Standfest: *Sozialpolitik als Reformpolitik, WSI-Studie* Nr. 39, Köln 1979, p. 30.

139 Walter Bogs: *Grundfragen;* the manuscript was available to the ministeries and the advisory committee from 1954 onwards.

140 Hans Achinger, Joseph Höffner, Hans Muthesius, and Ludwig Neundörfer: *Neuordnung der sozialen Leistungen,* Köln 1955.

141 Harmut Hensen: 'Zur Geschichte der Rentenfinanzen', in: *Sozialpolitik* nach 1945, p. 138.

142 Reprinted in: *Die Sozialreform,* B III, 1.

143 *Standfest* (n138), p. 29.

144 Wilfried Schreiber: *Existenzsicherheit in der industriellen Gesellschaft,* Köln 1955.

145 Hans Günter Hockerts: p. 366. This is a fundamental work on this period because of its comprehensive coverage and use of original sources and its balanced description.

146 Hockerts, p. 367.

147 Hockerts, pp. 370, 371.

148 Report on trend observations of the 'Institut für Demoskopie', Allensbach, in: *Bundesarbeitsblatt* 1960, p. 66.

149 Hensen (n141), p. 138.

150 Karl-Heinz Orda: 'Im Vorfeld der Rentenreform', in: *Sozialpolitik nach 1945,* p. 101.

151 Hensen (n141), p. 139.

152 Kurt Jantz in the introduction to Jantz/Zweng: *Das neue Recht der Rentenversicherung der Arbeiter und der Angestellten,* Stuttgart 1957, p. 7. For more details on the emergence and further development of the indexing principle see also Kurt Jantz's: 'Die Rentendynamik 1957 als Vorbild im Sozialleistungsrecht', in: *Sozialpolitik nach 1945,* p. 109.

153 Resolution of the committee of the 'Agrarsoziale Gesellschaft' (Agro-social Society) in: *Soziale Sicherheit für das Landvolk,* Heft 15, *der Schriftenreihe für ländliche Sozialfragen,* Hanover 1956, p. 138.

154 Heinz Frehsee and Detlev Zöllner: 'Die Entwicklung der Agrarsozialpolitik', in: *Sozialpolitik nach 1945,* p. 263.

155 *Die Sozialreform,* B II, 4, p. 13.

156 *Die Sozialreform,* B II, 5b, p. 19.

157 Thus especially: Harmut Hensen: *Die Finanzen der sozialen Sicherung im Kreislauf der Wirtschaft,* Kiel 1955; Wilfried Schreiber: *Existenzsicherheit in der industriellen Gesellschaft,* Köln 1955; Horst Jecht: *Ökonomische Probleme der Produktivitätsrente,* Stuttgart 1956; Wilhelm Hankel and Gerhard Zweig: *Die Alterssicherung in der sozialen Marktwirtschaft,* Ordo 1957, p. 157.

158 Elisabeth Liefmann-Keil: *Ökonomische Theorie der Sozialpolitik,* Berlin 1961, p. 1.

159 Detlev Zöllner: *Öffentliche Sozialleistungen und wirtschaftliche Entwicklung,* Berlin 1963.

160 Walter Bogs, Hans Achinger, Helmut Meinhold, Ludwig Neundörfer, and Wilfried Schreiber: *Soziale Sicherung in der Bundesrepublik Deutschland.* Bericht der Sozialenquête-Kommission, Stuttgart inter alia, 1966; the term 'social budget' originates from Mackenroth, cf. n132.

161 Social budget 1968, *Bundestagsdrucksache* V/4160. For more details on the emergence and methodology cf. Hermann Berié: *Das Sozialbudget,* Bonn-Bad Godesberg 1970.

162 *Sozialbudget-Sozialplanung. Apprails of a working group of the 'Gesellschaft für sozialen Fortschritt' (Society for Social Progress),* Berlin 1971. The working group was headed by Willi Albers.

163 From 1961 onwards the contribution rate was less than 2 percent; in 1975 it had to be raised to 2 percent in 1976 to 3 percent and in 1982 to 4 percent.

164 *Sozialbericht,* 1970, p. 3.

165 *Wirstchaftlicher und sozialer Wandel in der Bundesrepublik Deutschland,* published by Bundesminister für Arbeit und Sozialordnung, Bonn 1976.

166 *Sozialbericht* 1971, p. 42; cf. Detlev Zöllner: *Formen internationaler Zusammenarbeit in der sozialen Sicherung,* Bundesarbeitsblatt 1971, p. 229; cf. also resolution of the Council of the EC of 21 January 1974 on a socio-political programme.

167 Hans F. Zacher (for the first few years Chairman of the Commission of Experts for a Social Code): *Das Vorhaben des Sozialgesetzbuchs,* Percha 1973.

168 The inclusion of this programme point, which proved so successful both from a socio-political and—from 1973 onwards—labour policy point of view, in the government speech of 1969, and its popularity was, to an unusual extent, the result of the personal involvement of the Federal Minister of Labour at the time, Walter Arendt; cf. Walter Arendt: *Kennzeichen Sozial,* Stuttgart 1972, p. 198.

169 *Sozialbericht,* 1976, p. 28.

170 The law on regulations on the medicine market of August 1976 was an exception; a moderate price reduction of medicines resulted through a decrease in the trade profit margin.

171 *Standfest* (n138) p. 92. In view of the 'danger that adjustment in accordance with gross wage increases will not be made again after these exceptional years', half of the members of the social committee present at the vote had recommended another possible concrete solution. Cf. appraisal of the social committee of 10 March 1978. Deutscher Bundestag, Drs. 8/1665, quote p. 7.

172 *Vorschläge zur sozialen Sicherung der Frau und der Hinterbliebenen,* Bundesminister für Arbeit und Sozialordnung (ed.), Bonn 1979.

173 Hans Achinger: *Sozialpolitik als Gesellschaftspolitik,* Hamburg 1958.

174 Christian von Ferber: *Sozialpolitik in der Wohlstandsgesellschaft,* Hamburg 1967, p. 26. This opinion is based on Ferber's special understanding of the term 'social policy', 'Social policy is not a systematic but a historical concept. . . . Social policy designates concensus, it forms a basis for political action.'

175 Franz-Xaver Kaufmann: *Sicherheit als soziologisches und sozialpolitisches Problem,* Stuttgart 1970.

176 Hans Braun emphasizes the importance of legal security for the confidence of those concerned, from a sociological point of view: *Soziale Sicherung, System und Funktion,* 2nd edn, Stuttgart 1972. p. 40. For a critique on the economic and legalization syndrome cf. also Volker Hentschel: *Das System der sozialen Sicherung in historischer Sicht 1880 bis 1975,* Archiv für Sozialgeschichte, 1978, p. 307, especially p. 351.

177 Zacher (ed.) 1979.

178 Jens Alber: *Modernisierung und die Entwicklung der Sozialversicherung in Westeuropa,* Dissertation Mannheim, 1979, p. 22.

179 Fischer, in: Zacher, p. 91.

180 Michael Stolleis: 'Die Sozialversicherung Bismarcks. Politischinstitutionelle Bedingungen ihrer Entstehung', in: Zacher, p. 394.

181 Michael Stolleis: *Diskussionsbeitrag in Bedingungen,* p. 222.

182 Alber (n178), p. 181.

183 Hans Rothfels: 'Prinzipienfragen der Bismarckschen Sozialpolitik', in: Hans Rothfels, *Bismarck, der Osten und das Reich,* Darmstadt 1962, p. 166.

184 To differentiate between inductive and adaptive legislation cf. Detlev Zöllner: *Öffentliche Sozialleistungen und wirtschaftliche Entwicklung,* Berlin 1963, p. 22.

185 *Sozialenquête* (n160), TZ 340, 347, 388, 390.

186 Detlev Zöllner: 'Die Funktionserfüllung der gesetzlichen Alterssicherung im Rückblick', in: *Alterssicherung als Aufgabe für Politik und Wissenschaft,* Festschrift für Helmut Meinhold, Klaus Schenke, and Winfried Schmähl (eds.), Stuttgart 1980, p. 195.

187 Karl Hax: *Die Entwicklungsmöglichkeiten der Individualsicherung in einem pluralistischen System der sozialen Sicherung*, Stuttgart 1968.
188 Detlev Zöllner (n2), p. 149.
189 *Sozialbericht 1971*, Teil B, Anhang 2, Tab. II-1 and *Sozialbericht*, 1978, p. 72.
190 Hans F. Zacher in the introduction to Zacher, p. 11.
191 Here reference is made only to changes which have been carried out: cf. also Willi Albers: *Möglichkeiten einer stärker final orientierten Sozialpolitik*, Göttingen 1976.
192 Walter Bogs: 'Entwicklungstendenzen im neueren Recht der gesetzlichen Krankenversicherung', in: *Sozialpolitik. Ziele und Wege*, Alfred Christman *inter alia* (eds.), Köln 1974, p. 319.
193 Bogs (n129), p. 37.

BIBLIOGRAPHY

Bartholomäi, Reinhart (ed. *inter alia*) (1977). *Sozialpolitik nach 1945*. Festschrift für Ernst Schellenberg, Bonn-Bad Godesberg.

Bogs, Walter (1955). *Grundfragen des Rechts der sozialen Sicherheit und seiner Reform*, Berlin.

Bogs, Walter,. Achinger, H., Meinhold, H., Neundörfer, L., and Schreiber, W. (1966). *Sociale Sicherung in der Bundesrepublik Deutschland*. Bericht der Sozialenquête-Kommission, Stuttgart *inter alia*.

Braun, Heinrich (1955). *Motive sozialer Hilfeleistungen*, Frankfurt/Main.

Grebing, Helga (1966). *Geschichte der deutschen Arbeiterbewegung*, München.

Henning, Friedrich-Wilhelm (1978). *Die Industrialisierung in Deutschland 1800–1914* (vol. 2) and: *Das industrialisierte Deutschland 1914–1976* (vol. 3), 4th edn Paderborn.

Herkner, Heinrich (1921). *Die Arbeiterfrage*, vol. 2, 7th edn, Berlin.

Hockerts, Hans Günter (1977). 'Sozialpolitische Reformbestrebungen in der frühen Bundesrepublik', *Vierteljahreshefte für Zeitgeschichte*, p. 366.

Peters, Horst (1978). *Die Geschichte der sozialen Versicherung*, 3rd edn, Sankt Augustin.

Preller, Ludwig (1978). *Sozialpolitik in der Weimarer Republik*, Düsseldorf (re-ed.).

Richter, Max (ed.) (1955–70). *Die Sozialreform. Dokumente und Stellungnahmen* (11 volumes), Bad Godesberg.

Rosin, Heinrich (1893). *Das Recht der Arbeiterversicherung*, Berlin.

Rothfels, Hans (1927). *Theodor Lohmann und die Kampfjahre der staatlichen Sozialpolitik*, Berlin.

Schmoller, Gustav (1918). *Die soziale Frage*, München/Leipzig.

Syrup-Neuloh (1957). *100 Jahre staatliche Sozialpolitik 1839–1939*, Stuttgart.

Tennstedt, Florian (1975). 'Quellen zur Geschichte der Sozialversicherung', *Zeitschrift für Sozialreform* pp. 225, 358, and 422.

Vogel, Walter (1951). *Bismarcks Arbeiterversicherung*, Braunschweig.

Zacher, Hans F. (ed.) (1979). *Bedingungen für die Entstehung und Entwicklung von Sozialversicherung*, Berlin.

FRANCE
by Yves Saint-Jours

GENERAL OUTLINE

The development of social legislation in France has been characterised by four fundamental features which define its principal phases:

a) the original abstention of the State from the field of social welfare;
b) the encouragement of private initiative through financial aid;
c) the progressive creation of legal obligations; and
d) the extension of a general system of social security.

The pattern of this historical development is not linear; it gave rise to bloody confrontations in the nineteenth century before becoming the subject of major political debate with both breakthroughs and setbacks prior to new advances taking place.

ABSENCE OF STATE PARTICIPATION
IN THE FIELD OF SOCIAL WELFARE

Until the end of the nineteenth century, the State refrained from creating obligation lost any stake in the means of production and were thrown into fearful misery. will of the individual, that is to say, the freedom of each person to guarantee his own security on the basis of the right of property and through saving. This was a logical consequence of the ideology of natural law which had inspired the French Revolution in 1789 and the codification of civil law by Napoleon I. Indeed, out of nearly 2300 articles which make up the Code Civil, more than 1700 are devoted to the law of property in its various manifestations, a little over 500 concern the law of persons, and the principle of the autonomy of the will underlies the entire theory of the law of obligations.

However, as the industrial revolution developed, large sections of the population lost any stake in the means of production and threw them into fearful misery. In 1791 the Law Le Chapelier[1] abolished the old *corporations,* which had become an obstacle to the development of the nation's productive forces, and prohibited workers and journeymen from grouping together to regulate their common interests, thereby placing workers in a relationship of inequality towards employers who owned the means of production. Article 1781 of the Code Civil, which was not repealed until 1868,[2] provided, contrary to the principle of civil equality proclaimed in the rest of the code, that in the event of disputes concerning the payment of salaries 'the master is to be believed upon his affirmation'.

In this context the working class had no other way to affirm its identity than to rebel against its living conditions, a rebellion which was savagely repressed by the bourgeoisie as is demonstrated by the revolt of the silk-weavers of Lyons in 1831, the events of June 1848 and the Commune of Paris in 1871, to cite only the best known examples. Rare exceptions apart, the French bourgeoisie refused to deal with the issue of social welfare otherwise than by bloody repression.

It was only after the Commune of Paris that a section of the bourgeoisie, generally of Christian inspiration, recognised the necessity of social reform in order to contain and control the working class, which had become a political force in spite of everything. The politics of compromise thus prevailed over the politics of the sabre.

The Financial Encouragement of Private Initiative

Isolated from the rest of the nation, the working class developed in secret, during the nineteeth century, solidarity and its own forms of resistance to the brutal exploitation to which it was subject. It achieved this by creating benefit and resistance societies. These more or less clandestine organisations were opposed by the authorities, who, unable to reduce their activities, endeavoured, especially from the Second Empire onwards, to gain political control over them as distinct from providing financial aid.

The financial institutions which were created in order to facilitate the development of social welfare provision — a national pension fund guaranteed by the State in 1850 and a national employment accident insurance fund in 1868 — did not enjoy the success hoped for. Gradually the State had to start providing financial aid for private initiative. Conversely, the principle of the autonomy of the individual will will progressively gave way to a subsidised freedom in matters of social welfare.

Following the same pattern as the State, employers turned to the creation, and sometimes even to the financing of works' pension schemes, in order to counteract the influence of the trade unions. Those had been tolerated since the abolition in 1864, of the delict of *coalition* (unlawful combination), and given legal recognition in 1884 by which they were charged with the responsibility of protecting the professional interests of their members.

With the exception of the law of 1893 on free medical aid, and the legislation of 1898 on compensation for accidents at work, which simply substituted the notion of professional risk for that of fault as the basis for liability (in order to impose a system of fixed compensation for damage suffered by victims which excluded other remedies and was paid for by the employers) the nineteenth century ended without the State having created any true legal obligations in the field of social security. The law of 1898 regulating friendly societies was still based entirely on the principle of the autonomy of the individual will, to the extent that membership of a benefit society remained purely optional.

The experience of the social insurance system set up in Germany by Bismarck in the years 1880–1890 had been observed in France, but from a distance, for two reasons: first, the fall of the Commune of Paris allowed the working class to be physically removed from the political scene for several years, thus leaving the field open for the French bourgeoisie until the end of the nineteenth century; after its defeat in 1871; the French socialist movement was divided and was not unified until 1905; secondly, the bitterness of the French defeat in the war of 1870-71 generally meant that any experience coming from the other side of the Rhine was of little interest to the French.

The Gradual Creation of Legal Obligations

The legislation on accidents at work led employers to insure with insurance companies which began to grow considerably from this time. As a result, the practice of insurance spread among a population which was opposed to it in principle.

Moreover, the abuses committed by employers in connection with works' pension funds, with the worker losing all accumulated rights in the event of leaving that employment or if the enterprise became insolvent, compelled the authorities to intervene on several occasions, and by 1910 they set up a compulsory system of pensions for industrial and agricultural workers. This was the first time a legal obligation to establish a social welfare institution as a financial charge on employers and wage earners was imposed, apart from the poor laws which only imposed obligations on local bodies, principally the communes.

However, the system of industrial and agricultural pensions ran up against opposition both from employers and from wage earners, though for different reasons. Established on a capitalisation basis, these pensions were markedly undermined by the effects of inflation and were utterly rejected by the workers themselves.

After the 1914-1918 war and the return to France of Alsace and Lorraine, endowed with the German system of social insurance, the question of extending social insurance throughout the country was raised. This was not finally achieved until July 1, 1930, however. The French system was strongly influenced by that of Bismarck and was directed solely towards the working class. For those with resources above a specified level, insurance remained optional, so that the system was still seen by the public as one of public assistance. The legislation on compensation for accidents at work remained on the fringe of social insurance, since it dealt with the question of liability, not compulsory insurance.

In 1932 a statute was passed which extended to all wage earners the family allowances which had been developed from the end of the nineteenth century. These had been introduced at the instigation of employers and under the influence, originally, of the theory of the just wage, put forward by the Church to counter Marxist theories.

However, at the very moment when the French system of social insurance was set up, the economic crisis broke and plunged whole new sections of the population in addition to the working class into need.

The Extension of a General System of Social Security

The end of the 1939-1945 war saw the beginning of the extension of social security to the entire population, necessitated by the effects of the economic crisis of 1929-1930, aggravated as they were by the war. A French plan to this effect had been drafted by the National Council of the Resistance; its general ideas were influenced by the Beveridge Report and sought to ensure that all citizens would have the means of existence whenever they were incapable of providing them for themselves. Nevertheless, the application of the plan had to take account of the realities of French society, notably current social forces, which, after the rise of national resistance to fascism, divided along class lines and sometimes on narrowly corporatist lines.

In face of the refusal of the non-wage-earning population (whose resistance to the idea of public assistance was as great as to the idea of worker solidarity) to be involved in a general system of social security, the French plan collapsed, leaving a patchwork of special, independent and complementary schemes surrounding the core of a general scheme for wage earning workers.

It was not until the sixties that two major independent schemes were established, alongside the general scheme for wage earners in commerce and industry: one for those engaged in agriculture, whether self-employed or as wage earners, and the other for non-agricultural independent workers, that is to say craftsmen, industrialists, tradesmen and those engaged in the professions.

In spite of the existence of these three major schemes, about 2 percent of the population were still not covered by any form of social insurance. A statute of 1974[3] put the extension of social security to all on the agenda once again in cases of sickness, maternity, old age and family allowances, but the application of these provisions in practice remained optional, contrary to the intention of the legislature. The extension certainly made it possible for workers employed abroad, Catholic clergy and other categories of persons formerly excluded, (concubines, prostitutes, prisoners, etc.) to join some scheme of social security, but it did not achieve its threefold objective: that all French men and women should be covered by social security provisions; that benefits should be harmonised; and that there should be financial adjustment between the different schemes on the basis of changes in their relative demographic positions and the capacity of participants to contribute.

Instead of the French plan of 1945–1946 for the unification of social security and its extension on the basis of social equality to the entire population we have in practice at the present day a spread of social security provision based on diversity and social inequality.

INTRODUCTION: THE SOCIAL SITUATION IN THE
MID-NINETEENTH CENTURY

In France, the nineteenth century, which began ideologically with the Revolution of 1789, was dominated by the principles of individualism: the right to property, the autonomy of the will, and thrift, all precisely designed to ensure the material security of the individual. The problem of social welfare came more and more to the fore as industrialization proceeded, provoking a bloody repression of workers' revolts by a victorious bourgeoisie, before leading to certain measures of reforms contained in a timid social policy developed towards the end of the century, including the legal recognition of trade unions in 1884, the legal regulation of friendly societies, and the adoption of legislation in 1898 dealing specifically with compensation for accidents at work.

The brutal conflict between opposing social classes explains both the revolutionary tendency implanted in the heart of the French working class and the long delay before the introduction of social insurance, first in 1930 as a system of compulsory protection for wage earners, and then progressively extended, from 1945 to 1946 onwards, to the entire population under the title of social security.

In order to understand the evolution of social insurance, it is helpful first to outline the social conditions of the mid-nineteenth century, the period when people began to look to intervention by the state. The situation can be characterised by three principal elements: the hell of working-class existence, the search for an escape from that existence and the spread of ideas.

The Hell of Working-Class Existence

It is impossible to convey in a few lines the hell in which the working class lived at the beginning of the industrial revolution. According to Villermé, who conducted an official enquiry[1] at the end of the 1830s, this consisted essentially in the hours and conditions of work, the insufficiency of wages and the unhealthy state of housing and work place.

Hours and Conditions of Work

In manufacturing industry and weaving, the working day was about 15 hours, to which one or two hours were frequently added for meal breaks. To these 15 hours must be added also the journey time for workers living at a distance from their place of work. These slave-like conditions induced a dehumanization of the individual and a propensity to alcoholism.

Workers laboured in unhealthy workshops, where the air was often unbreathable and hygiene and organization non-existent. Villermé relates how, in a silk sorting shop at Nimes with four furnaces, he saw a hunchbacked old woman and three young girls—two of them deformed—serving as motors to turn the winders. The work of winding trams and carrying reels was reserved for children and needed hardly any skill except that of paying attention, but it required them to remain standing for 16–18 hours a day in a closed room unable to change place or stance. Villermé remarks:

> It is not piece work, but a form of torture; it is inflicted on children from 6
> to 8 years old, undernourished, ill-clothed, obliged to set out at 5 a.m. to

cover the long distance to the workshops and travel the same distance home in the evening. It results in an excessively high rate of infant mortality.

Insufficiency and Insecurity of Wages

Wages were so low that a worker could not even feed his family: women and children were compelled to work in the factories in order to contribute to their subsistence. According to Villermé, workers had to be content with bare necessities and live on three or four sous' worth of bread and three or four sous' worth of potatoes a day. The undernourishment of working families led to rickets and early death.

Achille Pénot, who undertook statistical research on the difference between mortality rates of the well-to-do and the poor in Mulhouse, established that the average expectation of life at birth, in 1827, was around 29 years for the children of merchants and the well-to-do but only 2 years for children in the cotton industry. He notes that the misery was such that 'the majority of workers regard the death of their children with indifference and sometimes even with joy'.[2]

Insecurity of earnings often went hand in hand with insufficiency. Competition among workers lowered the level of wages and unemployment meant total loss, leading to the complete ruin of those affected.

Insanitary Housing and High Rents

On top of the unhealthy and interminable work and permanent undernourishment, was the crowding of workers into housing which lacked all comfort. Villermé reports that in Lille and the North, which was already one of the major French industrial centres, nearly 400 000 workers lived 'without education, without provision for sickness or old age, brutalised by debauchery, worn out by labouring in the factories, crowded into dark cellars or garrets where they are exposed to all the rigours of winter. . . . Many are prey to hereditary diseases.'

The concentration of the working population around the factories led to speculation in rents which, in the words of E. Buret, 'increased in step with the workers' misery'.[3]

Thus, at all levels, the living conditions of the working class grew worse as the small cottage industries disappeared and were replaced by large manufacturing establishments. This might involve the ending of all personal ties, with the employer retreating behind the internal disciplinary rules of the company; it meant also that the exploitation of the workers became anonymous and was intensified. There is considerable literature dealing with the condition of the working class in this period.[4]

THE SEARCH FOR A WAY OUT

The working class was never resigned to the exploitation to which it was subject. From the beginning it looked for means to escape from or to fight exploitation, in order to improve its living conditions. The history of the first half of the nineteenth century is filled with revolts, borne sometimes of despair,[5] often leading to much bloodshed as in the case of the revolt of the silk-weavers of Lyons in 1831, the massacre of rue Transnonain in Paris in 1834 and the shooting in June 1848.

In this struggle for survival, the working class kept its own forms of organization secret—the journeymen's guilds and the benefit and resistance societies—and put all its weight behind a vain effort to achieve involvement by the State in providing social welfare.

The Journeymen

The abolition of the *corporations* and especially the prohibition of associations following the Revolution of 1789,[6] left worker and employer facing each other in a relationship of inequality without any system of social protection. In an initial sentimental reaction, the isolated working class turned to the past, seeking to re-establish the ancient corporatist structures, especially through the guilds of journeymen.[7]

The possibility of becoming one's own master one day and thus achieving independence, was tried as a way out for the working class. But the journeymen system, as it was re-established in the nineteenth century, was only a backward looking and individualistic form of resistance to capitalist exploitation.

After seeing the futility in most cases of individual solutions, the workers gradually became aware that they formed a separate class of person, bound by a community of interest, and that they therefore needed to organize and fight together in order to resist capitalist exploitation.

Benefit and Resistance Societies

Benefit and resistance societies were the first specific form of working-class organization. They were generally suppressed, however, and even when tolerated in the form of friendly societies, they were placed directly under the control of the police. Worker solidarity and resistance could virtually only develop and organize in secret.[8] These more or less clandestine societies were at times tolerated according to political circumstances; they inspired many worker uprisings and fostered the development of working class consciousness. They were the origin of friendly societies and trade unionism in France.

The Problem of the State's Involvement in Social Welfare

According to the prevailing view at the time, the state was unable to intervene, especially in the field of social welfare, without infringing the principle of the autonomy of the individual will. This sacrosanct principle was scarcely ever breached before 1850 except by the law of 22 March 1841 which sought to prohibit the employment in factories of children under 8 years of age, in order to avoid the premature destruction of the work force needed for the development of industry.

The 1848 Revolution was the first attempt to put a coherent social programme into practice, influenced by the ideas of Utopian socialism: proclamation of the right to work, which found practical expression in the opening of national workshops to give work to the unemployed; restriction of the working day to 10 hours for adults; recognition of freedom of association; condemnation of *marchandage,* that is to say speculation in labour; abolition of paying employment offices and the creation of a so-called Luxembourg commission which formed an embryonic Ministry of Labour. This brief experience of a social republic came to a premature end in the bloodshed of June 1848 and the return to conservative liberalism left the problem of intervention by the state in the field of social welfare completely unresolved.

THE SPREAD OF IDEAS

Liberal thought was unmoved by the misery of the working class, either attributing it to vice and laziness of the workers themselves or considering it to be, if not a necessary evil, at least an inevitable concomitant of industrial development. Honoré de Balzac, for example, practically ignores the proletariat of the time in his historical fresco *La Comédie Humaine* and Eugène Süe, in *Mystères de Paris*, treats them as the dregs of society.

Only socialist ideas, emerging in a more or less confused fashion, sought to humanize relations between capital and labour or to question the capitalist system itself.

Liberal Thought

Liberal thought was deeply wedded to the principle of the autonomy of the individual will and was hostile, *a priori*, to any notion of obligation on the part of the state with regard to the social protection of industrial workers. Even the provision of public assistance by the state was regarded as a purely moral duty, charitable works being in their view the province of private charitable foundations, particularly religious bodies.

The best statement of liberal ideas on social problems in the middle of the nineteenth century is the report of the commission on public assistance and social provision written by Thiers in 1850,[9] who writes as follows concerning the involvement of the State:

> What does it mean, if not that the principle of an obligation resting on the state inevitably leads the latter to exceed its proper functions? The undertakings towards those assisted can only be performed by the use of public funds or by a statutory obligation being put upon certain categories of persons to contribute to the financing of the system. Let us ignore for a moment the second of these two alternatives, which infringes the liberty of persons and the right of property. Even if the State intends to fulfil its obligations by means of public funds it exceeds its rights, since the public wealth is nothing other than that part of the wealth of the citizens of which the state is the trustee in carrying out works of general benefit such as the defence of the nation's independence or the maintenance of public order. Indeed, one can go further, and say that this public wealth, made up of monies belonging to other people, comes from the contributions of both rich and poor and more from the poor because of their greater number. And we repeat that it is not to ensure that the state gives less or gives little that we are setting these limits, but in order to safeguard the public wealth which belongs to the poor even more than to the rich, to maintain for all the obligation to work, and to prevent the vices of idleness which if widespread easily become dangerous and even atrocious.

In other words, as seen through liberal eyes, the state exceeds its function and violates the basic principles of civilized society when it seeks to use public funds to bring about a redistribution of resources.

Socialist Thought

The ideas of utopian socialism scarcely influenced the working class. The events of June 1848 destroyed many illusions. Nevertheless, it was in this period that the three elements of post-utopian socialist ideology, which later had such a profound influence on the French labour movement, began to take shape. These three elements can be stated[10] as follows:

1. the reformist element, which, under the influence of Proudhon, sought to reform the state and society by decentralizing government and aimed at collaboration among social classes to improve the lot of the working class;
2. the revolutionary element, which, under the influence of Marx and Engels,[11] aimed at a take-over of the state by the working class by means of the dictatorship of the proletariat in order to put an end to capitalist exploitation through the disappearance of social classes; and
3. the anarchist element, which, under the influence of Bakunin, sought the immediate destruction of the state as the principal obstacle to the social emancipation of the workers.

It is noticeable that all the currents, both of liberal and of socialist thought, can be placed according to their attitude to the role of the state in the field of social welfare. This role, whether passive or active, was and remains the decisive factor in the evolution of social insurance in France.

It is necessary, however, to make a distinction between two periods during this development: the first period runs from 1850 to 1930 and covers the transition from the principle of the autonomy of the will to that of legal obligation with regard to social welfare, and the second runs from 1930 to the present day and covers the period from the introduction of social insurance to the adoption of a general system of social security.

FROM THE AUTONOMY OF THE INDIVIDUAL WILL TO LEGAL OBLIGATION IN SOCIAL WELFARE (1850–1930)

Throughout the various political regimes of this period, liberal thought, as it was essentially opposed to social insurance, long held back the introduction of such a system, but was forced eventually to make concessions and finally to admit the principle itself in the face of the rise of socialist ideas and socially conscious Christianity. Similarly, French law shifted gradually from its embodiment of the principle of freedom of the individual in social matters to that of subsidized freedom, and arrived finally at a system based on legal obligation.

This period is consequently dominated by private initiatives: friendly societies; institutions established by employers for their employees; and charitable foundations; with the state intervening only with great caution in order to support and control these initiatives. The first statutes dealing with public assistance, friendly societies, compensation for accidents at work and pension funds appear only at the end of the nineteenth century.

After recalling briefly the political background to this period of French history, we consider first the private initiatives and the attitude of the state respectively, then assess the social gains made before the First World War and finally outline the debate, after the war, on social insurance which came into force on 1 July 1930.

THE POLITICAL BACKGROUND

During this period we have, in succession, the Second Republic, the Second Empire, the Commune of Paris and the Third Republic, the last named marking the point at which democracy arrived and took root in France.

The Second Republic (1848–1852)

The 1848 Revolution came after a long period of growth of republican ideas and an economic and moral crisis which undermined the July monarchy. The proclamation of the Republic raised the hopes of the working class.

Spurred on by the social fervour which marked the beginning of the Revolution, the authorities made a number of concessions to the working class: for example, they proclaimed the right to work; established freedom of association; set up a government commission for workers known as the Luxembourg Commission. But the conservatives still hoped secretly to sabotage the effects of these measures as soon as possible. This in fact occurred during June 1848 when a social Republic gave way to a conservative Republic.

The latter left hardly a mark in the field of social welfare other than the law of 18 June 1850, establishing a national pension fund guaranteed by the state, to which we shall return later.

The Second Empire (1852–1870)

Immediately after the events of June 1848 George Sand stated prophetically: 'I do not believe in the existence of a republic which starts by killing the proletariat.' In fact, the Republic did not long survive the election of Louis Bonaparte as President, for after the coup d'état of 2 December 1851, he became the Emperor Napoleon III. The Second Empire began, as the Second Republic had ended, by the taking of action against the workers' societies, which had gone underground, by instituting, in a law of 22 June 1854, a general requirement that workers carry a police identity card and by exercising political control over friendly societies.

During the Second Empire, France experienced an economic revolution marked by a growth of productivity, increased production and a fall in costs, with a parallel growth in the size of the working class as new sections of the population were deprived of their individual means of production, combined with periodic unemployment and a concentration of workers in fewer and larger enterprises. All these events unsettled the life of the workers and accentuated their insecurity, for the nominal rise in wages, when it occurred, was not translated into an increase in purchasing power. This led, especially at the beginning of the 1860s, to important strikes.

At this time Napoleon III began to experience difficulties with the political forces which had kept him in power. So he sought support from the working class. Once the author of *The Extinction of Pauperism*, he now agreed to several concessions, in particular:

1. the abolition, in 1864, of the delict of *coalition* (unlawful combination) from which it followed that trade union activity would be tolerated; and
2. the repeal, in 1868, of Article 1781 of the Code Civil which provided that in any proceedings concerning wages, the master should be believed upon his affirmation.

However, the Second Empire collapsed in the Franco-Prussian war of 1870, before imperial action in relation to social welfare provision could be taken.

The Commune of Paris (1871)

Though its days were short (18 March to 28 May 1871), the Commune of Paris had a profound effect on the area with which we are concerned. It was a popular outburst against the capitulation by the Thiers Government to Bismarck's troops who had besieged Paris for several months.

Inspired by socialist ideology, the Commune proclaimed its intention of putting into practice one by one, all the social reforms which the workers had for so long demanded: in particular, free, lay, universal education; the rights of assembly and association; the absolute freedom of the press; the freedom of every citizen and the availability to the municipality of police, armed force, health and statistical services, and so on.

This programme would have undermined the basis of bourgeois society and it brought about an alliance between Thiers, who had taken refuge at Versailles, and Bismarck, by which the Versailles troops were to liquidate the Commune in 'a bloody butchery' under the benevolent eye of the besiegers. Tens of thousands of communards, or suspected communards, were killed in street battles, shot down in particular at Versailles and at the Mur des Fédérés, deported to New Caledonia, or interned in Satory camp.

The worker movement was leaderless and bled white and needed several years to re-establish itself. At the same time, social reformers among the conservatives began to consider how best to contain the working class and thus spare the bourgeoisie the need for periodic slaughter of the workers. The social reformers, who were generally those who had been won over to the social doctrines of the Church,[12] took the view that, faced with the inevitable rise of the working class under the pressure of the industrialisation in the country, the politics of the sabre must sooner or later give way to a policy of compromise and social peace.

The Third Republic (from 1870)

Immediately after the Commune of Paris, France remained deeply divided between monarchists and republicans. The idea of democracy was finally implanted, however, by the consolidation of the Republic in 1875. Political democracy has been a fertile source particularly of internal conflicts which have divided public opinion: for example, the crisis caused by *boulangisme*; the Dreyfus affair; and the separation of Church and State. Social democracy on the other hand had still to be discovered.

Certainly democracy allowed workers' trade unions and socialist ideas to reappear, but these were enfeebled and disunited. The Confédération générale du travail was not established until 1895 and the various socialist movements were not united until 1905.

Nevertheless, the socialists and the social reformers finally succeeded, at the end of the nineteenth century, in putting through a number of social reforms which fulfilled popular demand and at the same time satisfied the needs of developing industry and commerce: public education; trade associations; legal provision for public assistance; compensation for accidents at work; friendly societies; freedom of association; pensions for industrial and agricultural workers and so on.

Thus at the time when, under the influence of Bismarck, Germany was setting up a system of social insurance to cut the ground from under the feet of the German socialist movement, France, because of the consequences of the destruction of the Commune of Paris, had different political preoccupations. This explains, at least partially, why the introduction of social insurance came so late and so slowly to France, and, in contrast to Germany, was preceded by private initiative and not action by the state.

PRIVATE INITIATIVE

For practically the whole of the nineteenth century, the relief of poverty, and social welfare were left exclusively to private initiative; friendly societies; welfare institutions established by employers; or private insurance. In addition to the traditional charitable works of the Catholic Church, which had continued since the Middle Ages, the contribution of social Christianity which, with the theory of the just wage, led to the creation of family allowances must also be recognized.

Friendly Societies

Originating in the benefit and resistance societies, friendly societies aimed to use the funds at their disposal to protect workers, deprived by definition of any asset other than their labour, against the risks of life: illness; accident; disability; unemployment etc. The cost of benefits was spread among the membership as a whole. In spite of their undeniable advantages such as a spirit of solidarity, benevolent management not seeking to make a profit at the workers' expense, and a profound respect for the autonomy of the individual will (since membership remained voluntary), friendly societies were long regarded with suspicion because of their working class origins.

Initially, benefit societies fell foul of the provisions of Article 291 of the Criminal Code promulgated in 1810 which forbade every association of more than twenty persons. These provisions were enhanced by a law of 18 April 1834, which added that the prohibition applied even when the association was divided into sections each containing a smaller number. This more or less compelled the benefit societies to operate in secret. There were, nevertheless, periods when they were tolerated, as political circumstances changed, and in 1845 there were at least 262 such societies in Paris with a total of 23 000 members.

The 1848 Revolution repealed Article 291 of the Criminal Code and benefit societies found themselves freed from preliminary formalities, but not for long. A law of 15 July 1850 placed several restrictions upon their operations, restrictions which were added to by a decree of 26 March 1852 which laid down the first general regulations governing such societies.

In particular this decree of 1852 provided that

1. the formation of a benefit society was a matter for the mayor and the parish priest in each commune where its usefulness had been agreed by the prefect;
2. the president of the society had to be apointed by the President of the Republic, or in effect by the Emperor to be;
3. the rules of the society had to be submitted to the Ministry of the Interior for approval; and

4. all funds in excess of a certain sum had to be deposited with the State Deposit and Consignment Bank.

Societies could only have the objects of providing temporary assistance to members who were sick, injured or disabled and of paying funeral expenses. They were authorized to set up pension funds by a decree of 26 April 1856. In return for the restrictions thus imposed upon them, they enjoyed certain advantages: free premises at the expense of the commune, exemption from registration and stamp duties and others.

At the end of the Second Empire there were 3879 approved societies and 1509 free societies with a total membership of 825 000.

On 27 October 1870 the government of national defense decreed that the presidents of benefit societies should in future be elected by the members, but it was not until 1 April 1898 that a statute gave all friendly societies their independence.[13]

Welfare Institutions Established by Employers

During the second half of the nineteenth century, larger employers set up their own pension and welfare institutions. They hoped to stabilize the workforce entitled to benefit by providing a pension guaranteed by the employer that would encourage the workers to remain in his employment; in addition they hoped to dissuade workers from suing employers in reliance on Article 1382 of the Code Civil by providing assistance in the event of illness or accident. This 'guarantee of the future' further allowed workers, who were generally of country origin, to break their ties with rural activities and thus be more at the disposal of their employer.

Employers were following the example of the state as employer, which, by a law of 8 June 1853, had made budget provision for the pensions of public servants. From then on, there existed autonomous pension funds in the various ministries subsidized by the state.

Pension and welfare funds were first set up by employers whose workers were particularly exposed to danger, as in mining, or where the work called for great regularity, as in the railways. In the heavy metal industry the *Comité des Forges,* founded in 1888, divided its members between two institutions: the union mutual insurance fund for the ironworks of France, against accidents at work, in 1891 and the employers' pension fund for the ironworks of France in 1894.[14]

According to an enquiry[15] undertaken by the Labour Office of the Ministry of Commerce in 1898, the industrial enterprises which were covered by a works' pension fund fell into two categories. On the one hand, those where the workers were entitled to draw on the national old age pension fund, either by virtue of an obligation implied in their contract of employment, or by virtue of a voluntary institution financed by contributions from employers and employees or by employers' contributions alone; altogether, in seventy-two establishments employing 40 491 workers, 25 128 workers held certificates of entitlement (62 per cent of the total workforce). On the other hand, those having an independent pension fund or participating in a fund covering more than one enterprise; only large establishments fell into this group, and in 135 establishments employing around 86 000 people, 74 000 had pension rights.[16]

Works' pension funds were not without problems. The size of the fund was generally a function of the risks of the business and the workers often forfeited their rights if they left their employment voluntarily or were dismissed. They had no preferential claims in the event of the business becoming insolvent.

Certainly, when dealing with these autonomous pension funds, which operated without juristic personality, tribunals emphasized the existence of a legal contract binding the parties. They assumed the right, where necessary, to enforce the agreement or to annul illegal terms,[17] but it was still necessary for the legislature to intervene in order to remedy abuses.

Two laws were passed to this end. One of 27 December 1890 provided that in the event of wrongful dismissal a worker should have a right to damages taking account of deductions or payments made towards a retirement pension and conversely that the worker could lose the benefit of his payments in the absence of a wrongful dismissal. A law of 27 December 1895 sought to make all sums paid to welfare institutions in the form of employers' contributions or workers' contributions, which had not been used in accordance with the rules, recoverable for the benefit of the workers and employees, in the event of the employer becoming bankrupt or insolvent, or on the closure of the establishment, or transfer of the business. A corresponding lien was created over all the property, movable and immovable, of the owner of the business. The law was never put into practice, however.

In order to overcome the resistance of recalcitrant employers, the legislature had to create a system of compulsory old age insurance.

Private Insurance

Private insurance was slow to become normal practice because of the moral reservations raised by the fact that a person could insure against the consequences of his own fault, which was for long considered to be unnatural. It was seen originally, moreover, as an encouragement to irresponsibility and as increasing risk, rather than as a means of making good loss suffered by oneself or by another.

In the field of social welfare, private insurance scarcely began to develop until the second half of the nineteenth century when life insurance, insurance against the risks of road traffic (horse-drawn vehicles) and, after the law of 9 April 1898, insurance against accidents at work began. After this law, employers took out private insurance to cover their workers against the risks of accidents at work or to cover their own liability. Other types of insurance, such as life insurance and accident insurance apart from accidents at work, drew their clients from the well-to-do and had scarcely any impact on the working class.

The Contribution of Social Christianity

The encyclical *Rerum novarum,* published in 1891 by Pope Leo XIII, advanced the theory of the 'just wage', according to which a wage is not just merely by being determined by contract, but only if it is sufficient to provide a living for a sober and honest worker and his family. From this came the novel idea of paying an additional amount, over and above the normal wage, to the worker with dependent children.

Followers of Social Catholicism took up this idea and sought to put it into practice, thereby separating themselves both from liberal thought, which saw the institution of a family salary as an advance of collectivism, and from working class traditions which feared the introduction of competition between unmarried workers and those with dependants.

Some Christian employers took this path from the end of the nineteenth century, and were followed later by others who saw the creation of special allowances for workers with families as a means, above all, of postponing general wage increases.

However that may be, a new type of welfare payment was created which gradually became of general application, helped by demographic considerations.[18]

THE ATTITUDE OF THE STATE

In the field of social welfare the state remained, throughout this period ideologically faithful to the principles of liberalism. Faced with the rise of socialist ideology, however, it was compelled, in practice, to take direct action in relation to the private institutions in order to retain political control over them, to limit abuses or to fill in gaps.

The attitude of the state was not rigid but became open to change, moving from support for private initiative to acceptance of the creation of obligations for the state and for individuals.

Support of Private Initiatives

The policy of supporting private initiatives was carried out, not without reservation, at two levels: the legislative and the financial.

Legislative Support

As has already been pointed out, legislative support occurred principally in the fields of benefit societies and of pensions, in both cases respecting the autonomy of the individual will. The state did not create individual obligations, but was content to encourage private initiative by the creation, to this end, of tax exemptions, and supporting administrative institutions. For example, the *rapporteur* M. Benoît d'Azy of the law of 18 June 1850, which set up the national pension fund guaranteed by the state, expressed its aims in these terms:

> To improve the lot of the poorer classes, to create for them a kind of property, of great value but easy to acquire nevertheless by economy and thrift, to develop that feeling of order which follows from having confidence in the future, to give all classes an interest in maintaining the social fabric, in which the fortune of each one is involved: this is the aim of the law before you.[19]

However, legislative support was not enough. In order to be able to save, to give up present consumption for the sake of future consumption, one needs an income in excess of the absolute minimum for survival. The workers just did not have any hope of saving, for their wages scarcely enabled them to survive in misery. Contrary to the intention of the legislature in 1850, the national pension fund attracted only the custom of the well-to-do, apart from businesses using it to set up pension funds for their employees. It was thus necessary to climb a step higher.

Financial Support

With the aim throughout of encouraging the poorer sections of the population to make provision for their own welfare, the state gradually turned to a policy of financial support for private institutions. The decree of 26 March 1852, mentioned above, provided some assistance for benefit societies through the communes and by means of tax exemptions. But useful though they were, these aids and exemptions were not enough to fulfil the need.

The problem became one of the choice between a system of state subsidies, and the creation of compulsory social insurance on the lines of the solution adopted in Germany by Bismarck. Always imbued with the principle of the autonomy of the individual will, France chose, by the law of 31 December 1895, which sought to encourage voluntary provision, a voluntary system subsidized by the state,[20] as also did the majority of the countries of Europe.

If such a system afforded an opportunity, at a political level, for discriminating between good and bad welfare organizations, it did not yield the social results hoped for. Voluntary welfare provision was practised above all by the middle classes, and was entirely neglected by the humbler wage earners who would have derived most benefit from it. State subsidies for voluntary welfare provision thus in general favoured the middle classes whose standard of living was highest, and served only to accentuate social inequalities.

In an effort to resolve ever-present social difficulties, the state had to resign itself, from the end of the nineteenth century, to the creation of legal obligations.

The Creation of Legal Obligations

The state finally acted, albeit in piecemeal fashion, to create a system of legal obligations, alongside the voluntary system, which fell on employers and employees.

The Obligation of the State

For a long time, the state had tried to avoid any social obligations, even in relation to public assistance. Thus, until the law of 14 July 1905, public assistance was the responsibility of local government — the communes and the departments. Obligatory assistance applied only to abandoned children and the insane, who were the responsibility of the communes (law of 5 April 1884 on the organization of the powers of the communes), and to the indigent sick (law on free medical aid of 15 July 1893).

The law of 14 July 1905 provided a system of compulsory assistance for the aged above 70 years, who were without means and unable to support themselves by working. In addition to admission to a hospital or home, the law provided for the possibility of domiciliary assistance. The cost was to be shared ultimately between the communes and the state.

The passage of this law through the legislature was the occasion of a lively debate between the proponents of the two extreme views: the liberals, on the one hand, who rejected any legal obligation on the part of the state with regard to public assistance, and those, on the other hand, who wanted to go further than the traditional forms of public assistance and establish in favour of the poor a right based on the principle of social solidarity.

The Comte de Lanjuinais, in the course of the parliamentary debates,[21] clearly set out the liberal conception of the State:

In a truly free country the role of the state should be limited as closely as possible to the functions for which it was created, that is to say to ensure external and internal peace. The rest does not fall within its province, and it is my view in particular that all the problems of public assistance would be resolved in a much more satisfactory manner, and at the same time much less onerously, if the matter were left entirely to the local government authorities, in other words to the communes and departments, and above all to the initiative of associations and private individuals.

This conception of the liberal state was already obsolete. The separation of Church and state compelled the latter to fight the Church on its traditional ground by setting up, within the field of charitable works, a right to public assistance and by participating in the financing of it.

The Employers' Obligation

The law of 9 April 1898 on compensation for accidents at work, substituted the concept of occupational risk for that of fault on the part of the employer or his supervisors. Employers responded to this change in the nature, if not the extent, of their responsibility by insuring with private insurance companies.

The debate on the employers' obligation concentrated more particularly on the institution of a compulsory system of workers' pensions. Following the traditional liberal view, employers were profoundly hostile to this proposal and preferred to retain the voluntary system of works' pensions. They argued that smaller businesses would not be able to meet the cost of compulsory insurance.

However the social doctrines of the Church began to have an effect on some employers and to weaken the liberals enough for them to change their position. There is the well-known example of the Mulhouse businessman, Jean Dolfuss, who declared that he could not understand how an employer could insure his stock against the risk of fire but not insure his workers against sickness, accident and old age.

In 1910, after long parliamentary debate, pensions for industrial and agricultural workers were finally introduced. Even if this institution experienced difficulties subsequently, the principle of an obligatory employers' contribution in the matter of welfare provision, had been admitted. In reality, this principle brought about a division of a worker's pay into a wage paid directly to him, and a wage paid indirectly on his behalf to a welfare institution, in the form of an employer's contribution.

The Employee's Obligation

Liberals were also opposed from the beginning to any obligation being put on workers with regard to welfare provision, arguing that any such obligation would infringe the liberty of man and the right of property. Since each person should be free to manage his own property as he chose and to make his fortune by thrift, the obligation to contribute to a welfare organization could only condemn the workers to remain among the ranks of wage earners.

This approach was neatly summarized by a conservative deputy from Paris, Denys Cochin,[22] in the debates on the first plan for compulsory workers' pensions

'If you place the worker in the position of being obliged to put his savings into your pension fund, you deprive him of alternatives which he might have preferred. In the country he would buy a field, a house, cattle; the urban worker would buy tools or a small business. He can thus become an employer himself.' (Hear! Hear! to the right, and on various other benches) 'You will keep him in the ranks of the wage earners by requiring the exclusive use of his small capital and imposing one single method of investment upon him. Gentlemen, the flaw in your plan is that you divide the population into two classes, and separate them into two camps, wage earners and employers. In actual fact the two camps overlap and the two classes intermingle. You will search in vain for the thrifty worker on your list of pensioners; he has become an employer, a bourgeois, without telling you and without needing you.'

However, this theoretical opposition accorded less and less with reality. The vast majority of workers received wages so low that they were not in a position to save anything at all; and an obligation to contribute to works' pension funds had in many cases already been imposed upon workers by their employers.

Certainly, on this last point there was criticism based on the distinction between a contractual obligation which could be imposed by an employer, and a general legal obligation which the state had no power to impose. But the contradiction was so striking and the room for manoeuvre so small, that the liberals had to yield to the passage of the law of 5 April 1910, setting up the pension scheme for industrial and agricultural workers, with contributions shared between employers and workers. However, they still had the intention of torpedoing it on a future occasion, as we shall see later.

Progress up to the First World War

The First World War had a traumatic effect both on the human level and on the evolution of ideas. It is thus useful to examine the situation in France with regard to public assistance and social welfare provision on the eve of the war.

Public Assistance

For centuries, charity had been more or less the exclusive province of the Church, with the secular authorities in the form of feudal lord, King or the modern state having no obligation except that of defending society against 'asocial' individuals, hence the laws against vagrancy and begging.[23] Until the end of the nineteenth century, public assistance was seen as an instrument for the protection of society and was included in the arsenal of police measures. Moreover, administration of the system came under the Ministry of the Interior, as the ministry responsible for the maintenance of order and public security.

In 1889, at a meeting in Paris of an international congress on public assistance, the following principles were adopted:

1. that the provision of public assistance should be obligatory for municipal authorities;
2. that assistance should be given in the territorial unit closest to the recipient, that is to say in the place where he lived at the time, with the state simply providing funds; and
3. that public assistance, provided solely to individuals without resources and

unable to work, is additional to all other forms of aid, particularly family allowances.

From 1893, these principles were put into practice in France in the major legislation on public assistance enacted by the Third Republic.[24]

Free Medical Aid

The law of 15 July 1893 on free medical aid was the first major French statute dealing with public assistance. Under its provisions, a list was to be drawn up annually in each commune naming those indigent sick who had received free domiciliary treatment or hospital care.

Hospital were reimbursed for the first time in respect of the cost of treating those without means. They began to lose the character of public assistance institutions and became care institutions instead.

For its part the commune was confirmed in the role of principal provider of public assistance, even though the cost was borne also by the department and the State.

Public Assistance for the Aged, the Infirm and the Incurably Sick

The law of 15 July 1905 introduced two forms of public assistance for the aged, the infirm and the incurably sick, with no distinction between these three categories of persons. These were admission to a home, or, failing that, a pension the rate of which varied with the cost of living in the commune; this was probably the earliest version of the notion of subsistence level for incomes.

The law also set up special commissions to deal with disputed claims to benefit.[25]

Public Assistance in Relation to Children

The industrial revolution which brought about the dislocation of families and plunged them into destitution and misery had already led the state to take direct action to deal with the problem by appointing a body of inspectors of children in receipt of public assistance (1871), and by forfeiture of paternal rights (1889). But the law of 27 June 1904 went much further by establishing a departmental children's service, with the costs being met by contributions from all three levels of government: commune, department and state.

Furthermore, this law laid down new rules concerning the neglect of children and entrusted the guardianship of wards of the state to the prefect. In a spirit of moral severity with regard to defaulting families, it was established that the state could in future not merely make good the absence of the parents, but if necessary protect a child against its parents. Brutal solutions were not rejected, and the law provided for the breaking of family ties and for the whereabouts of the child to be kept secret.

Welfare in relation to children has always remained, since then, separate from other forms of public assistance since the problems do not arise in the same terms.

The Impact of the Statutes on Public Assistance

The legislation as a whole had considerable influence, in the absence of other social measures, and in spite of certain administrative reservations. Since the

Ministry of the Interior was fully occupied with questions of public order, responsibility for public assistance was transferred to the Ministry of Labour which was created at the beginning of the twentieth century.

In 1906, more than 1.32 million individuals received assistance, principally in the working-class departments in the north of the country.[26]

Compensation for Accidents at Work

The introduction and spread of mechanization in industry led to a great increase in the number of accidents at work and added to workers' insecurity. The classical approach to civil liability, founded on the notion of fault, rarely allowed the victims of accidents at work to recover damages. To succeed in recovering damages from his employer the victim had to prove a causal link between the accident and his employment, the extent of the damage suffered and the fact that the accident occurred by reason of fault on the part of the employer. In the majority of cases, even if in law all these conditions were satisfied, the victims of accidents at work did not have the means to pursue their claims in the courts.

The gradual result of this was the growth of an army of men crippled at work, deprived of all or part of their means of subsistence, who formed, in the expression used at the time, the human waste of industry; their plight called for special treatment. This was a particularly difficult matter, since it involved a head-on collision with the classical principles of civil liability. The following were the principal stages of the development of the law.

The Failure of the National Insurance Fund against Accidents at Work

In 1868 a national insurance fund against accidents at work was set up to encourage employers and workers to insure individually. It did not meet with the success its promoters hoped for, either with employers or with workers. In general, smaller employers had nothing to do with it and only some large concerns insured their workers or themselves against claims by workers suffering accidents at work. This failure prompted several attempts by parliament and government to make insurance against accidents at work compulsory, but they came up against the full power of conservative liberalism in the Senate.

The Parliamentary Marathon

The first proposal for legislation was made in 1880 by a former worker, the Paris deputy Martin Nadaud,[27] who, at the time of the Commune of Paris had retired to his native region in disagreement with the Commune. His proposal followed, or was inspired by, the German legislation of 1871 with regard to railways, in that it sought to establish a presumption of employer liability for accidents at work.

This proposal was not adopted, but it was followed by several others which, under the influence of the German law of 1886 and the debates preceding it, were based on the principle of occupational risk coupled with compulsory insurance and statutory compensation in lieu of civil law claims.

These various propositions gave rise to interminable parliamentary debate. In the end, the proposal that insurance against accidents at work should be compulsory was unable to pass the Senate. The compromise reached in 1898 between the followers of the theory of occupational risk, and the followers of the traditional theory of fault as a basis for liability, excluded *a priori* any idea of compulsory insurance.

The Attitude of Lawyers

Seeing the impossible situation facing victims of accidents at work, some eminent lawyers looked for ways of adapting the techniques of civil liability to the needs of this special situation. Two theories were advanced which found acceptance eventually, though in areas other than that of accidents at work.

The contractual theory. By virtue of this, every contract of employment contains an implied term, derived from the employer's control over the employee, which is the essential characteristic of the contract; the employer exercising this authority has a corresponding obligation to guarantee the safety of his employee. This theory amounted to a reversal of the burden of proof. If the employer is bound to see to the safety of his employees, any employee who suffers an accident can successfully claim damages unless the employer can show *force majeure*, inevitable accident or contributory negligence.[28]

The theory established a presumption of liability against the employer. It was adopted by legislation in Switzerland from 1881 and enjoyed some success in the Belgian courts.[29] In France, it was rejected by the courts which stood firm by the view thus expressed in one decision:[30] 'Article 1710 (of the Code Civil) . . . which governs contracts for work and labour, imposes no obligation on the employer other than to pay the worker the agreed price.'

This theory was nevertheless adopted — much later — by the Cour de Cassation, which in 1911 finally recognized the existence of an obligation to ensure safety — but in contracts of carriage;[31] the law of 1898 had in the meantime enshrined the theory of occupational risk as the basis of the law governing accidents at work.

The objective theory. By this theory, liability need not be based solely on fault, but can equally be based on risk. The proponents of this theory relied on Article 1384-1 of the Code Civil which provides: 'A person is liable not only for damage which he causes by his own acts, but also for that caused by the acts of others for whom he is responsible or by things which he has in his control.'[31bis]

Previously this text had been interpreted simply as a transitional measure introducing the special provisions of Articles 1385 and 1386 of the Code Civil dealing with liability for animals and for dilapidated buildings respectively.

It was in Belgium (where Article 1384 applied as in France) that the 'discovery' was made that it was no longer incumbent upon the victims of accidents at work to prove fault on the part of the employer, but for the latter to show the absence of fault in the management and supervision of the things of which he was owner.[32] This interpretation of Article 1384 as establishing a presumption of fault for the employer to rebut was, however, only adopted by the Belgian Cour de Cassation several decades later.[33]

In France it was the Conseil d'Etat which proved receptive to the objective theory and, by a decision in 1895,[34] opened the way to liability for accidents at work being based upon the idea of occupational risk, while the Cour de Cassation maintained its former position in complete disregard of the change in public opinion.[35]

When the interpretation of the law of 9 April 1898 was settled the debate as to the theoretical basis of liability was concluded.

The Compromise Embodied in the Law of 9 April 1898

The passing of the law of 9 April 1898 on compensation for accidents at work was the result of a compromise based on the following points: (i) the abandonment of any idea of compulsory insurance contrary to the principle of the autonomy of the will of the individual; (ii) the introduction of a statutory compensation scheme founded on the idea of occupational risk; and (iii) an increase in the compensation where the conduct of the employer in carrying on the operation in question amounts to 'inexcusable fault'.

It was the introduction of this concept of 'inexcusable fault' into the parliamentary debates which had smoothed the passage of the legislation in 1898. It had the great merit of allowing the proponents of the fault theory to avoid capitulation, while at the same time enabling the adherents of the risk theory to achieve their main objective. The compromise was easier to arrive at as the concept of inexcusable fault was obscure.

It took the courts almost half a century to define inexcusable fault as

fault of exceptional gravity, requiring a voluntary act or omission in circumstances in which the defendant should have been aware of the danger and which do not provide any kind of justification; it is distinguished from the deliberate infliction of injury only by the absence of an intention to cause harm.[36]

It is clear therefore that intentional harm remained outside the scope of the legislation on accidents at work and continued to be a matter of civil liability.

This compromise represented a considerable improvement at the time in the remedies available to the victims of accidents at work. By contrast with Germany, which had enacted social insurance legislation in 1886, France had simply legislated on the question of employers' liability for accidents at work.

Subsequent Developments

The protection of the law of 1898, which originally applied only to industrial workers, was gradually extended, as work and transport became more mechanized, to agricultural workers, for accidents arising from the use of motorized machines (1899) and to all workers in commercial undertakings (1906) and forestry (1914); it was also made available, on a voluntary basis, to undertakings of any other kind which chose to submit to it.

Employers did not delay in taking out private insurance against the consequences of accidents which their workers might suffer in the course of employment. However, the insurance companies, anxious to derive maximum profit, systematically contested the nature of all accidents at work, putting the worker to the proof of the causal connection between his employment and the accident needed to obtain compensation for his injuries.

In view of the large element of chance as to whether the worker could establish this point, and also faced with manifest abuses, the courts finally recognized a presumption in favour of the victim that an accident at work arose out of his employment.[37] It thus became necessary for the employer, or his insurance company, to establish the absence of such causal connection. This presumption still applies at the present day.

Friendly Societies

For a number of years the Third Republic was not willing to accept the demands of the friendly societies. The war of 1870 and the communalist movement of 1871, together with the political opposition of the old benefit societies approved under the Second Empire, brought any initiative in favour of friendly societies to a halt. The situation changed, however, from the end of the nineteenth century.

The Granting of Free Status

The first proposal for legislation on friendly societies was presented to Parliament in 1881. It was only 17 years and many debates later that the societies were granted free status in preference to the establishment of a compulsory system of social insurance. The voluntary nature of the societies was fully in accord with the principle of the autonomy of the individual will, in which the Third Republic was steeped.

The law of 1 April 1898, granted friendly societies a broad measure of independence, permitting them to be formed without prior authorization, provided only that a copy of the rules was lodged with the administration. This relaxation of supervision was not made without some reservations, however, but the authorities considered that after all the trouble which had been caused, the societies would more readily be reconciled to the new regime if the latter showed itself to be liberal in its treatment of them. These hopes were not misplaced. A law of 4 July 1900, extended the friendly society concept to the economic risks of agriculture: accidents (whether in the course of work or not), hail, fire and death of livestock.

The Conquest by the Middle Classes

From the passing of the law of 1 April 1898, friendly societies experienced considerable growth in membership, from 1.4 million in 1890 (in itself almost double the figure at the end of the Second Empire) to 1.9 million in 1898, and to 3.75 million in 1905, finally reaching 5.3 million in 1914.

However, the societies drew the bulk of their membership from the middle classes, who had overcome their opposition to the idea of friendly societies, tradesmen, craftsmen, smallholders, small businessmen and the like, to the point at which they became one of the essential elements in the movement. Under this pressure the societies broke with their origins as an instrument of working class resistance to oppression and sank into an ideology of employer-paternalism and class-collaboration.

This change had been foreseen. In the course of the parliamentary debate on the law of 1898, one of the bill's staunchest supporters, Senator Lourties, declared that the law 'will have the effect of creating a new class of small capitalists through long-term saving, and of broadening the bases of social harmony'.[38] President Emile Loubet, in a speech to representatives of the friendly societies on 30 October 1904, described the societies' success in these terms.[39]

You are the practical expression of republican fraternity. In all our societies, large or small, rich or poor, we see those upon whom fortune has smiled giving their time, their efforts and their financial support to their less fortunate fellow citizens, uniting and mingling with them in fruitful and intimate collaboration; there is no more comforting sight than this . . .

Napoleon III had expressed the same idea, though with a different purpose in mind:[40]

As I understand them, benefit societies have the precious advantage of bringing together different classes of society, of putting an end to the envy which can exist between them, of neutralising the results of misery to a large extent by making the rich man, through the superfluity of his fortune, and the worker, through his savings, work together voluntarily in an institution where the industrious worker finds advice and support. This offers an example which different communities should emulate; it reconciles the classes and uplifts the individual.

The triumph of this ideology had the fatal consequence, however, of leading to a split between the friendly societies and the trade union movement.

The Split between the Friendly Societies and the Trade Unions

Faced with this change in the character of friendly societies, workers began to have reservations about them since they no longer felt at home in them. The mistrust of the working class remained for a long time, as the following extract from the report of a meeting of friendly societies at Lyons in 1923, published in the newspaper *Le Peuple,* the organ of the Confédération Général du Travail indicates:[41]

The national federation? A collection of much decorated gentlemen looking for a few extra gewgaws in the round of official ceremonies. The various federations of diferent categories? Breeding grounds for people wanting to be elected to Parliament. At Lyons we studied the nine hundred to a thousand delegates present, and arrived at the following remarkable conclusion: at least three quarters of them did not themselves make use of friendly societies. Apart from the members of the opposition — which does not yet include everbody! — the participants were employers, tradesmen, doctors, lawyers. . . . Who can say what people such as these are doing in friendly societies? Better not look for the causes of their 'devotion' for fear of finding that the reasons do not have anything to do with altruism. Great is the disregard of the aspirations of the working class shown by these social bourgeois, who are allied on more than one side with the employers and their family allowances.

In fact, although the Third Republic drew a number of its most prominent figures from the friendly societies, workers tended rather to join the trade union movement, unions have been legally recognized since the law of 21 March 1884 and organized chiefly within the Confédération Générale du Travail (CGT) which was established in 1895.[42]

The mistrust of the working class was not really allayed until the establishment in 1945–1946 of works' committees; by promoting the creation of works' benefit societies, they gave rise to a new form of workers' friendly society within the friendly society movement at large.

Pensions for Industrial and Agricultural Workers

As emphasized above, pensions based on works' pension funds were uncertain, since they depended on the goodwill of the employer. In view of this shortcoming, the legislature, in 1910 stepped in to establish a compulsory system of pensions for industrial and agricultural workers. This system was not well received either by employers or workers and was a failure.

The Shortcomings of Works' Pension Funds

Following the insolvency in 1883 of the Voulte-Bessèges mining company, where workers lost savings to the value of 1.7 million francs which had been deducted from their wages, and the insolvency, in the same period, of the Comptoir d'Escompte (a secondary bank) where 1.4 million francs paid by the employees in return for future benefits disappeared, the legislature had to act to clean up the situation.

The first legislative efforts were directed particularly at the mining industry and the railways since these two areas required a stability of the workforce and a level of work discipline greater than elsewhere. The statutes were:

1. A law of 27 December 1890, providing that deductions from wages or sums paid by the worker as retirement pension contributions should be taken into account in the calculation of compensation for wrongful dismissal; and that railway companies had to submit the rules of their pension and benefit funds for ministerial approval.[43]
2. A law of 29 June 1894, on mineworkers' pensions;
3. A law of 27 December 1895, providing for the recovery for the benefit of workers and employees of sums paid to social welfare institutions which had not been used in accordance with the rules of the institution, in the event of bankruptcy or insolvency of the employer, or the closure or transfer of the business.

These measures proved inadequate and, from the beginning of the twentieth century, the legislature had to turn to the establishment of a compulsory system.

The Establishment of a Compulsory System of Pensions

In addition to the uncertain nature of the pensions provided and the disquiet aroused by the management of works' pension funds, there was a third reason for establishing a compulsory system of pensions: outside the mining industry and the railways, works' pension funds only applied to a very small minority of workers.

A bill seeking to introduce a compulsory system of workers' pensions was debated in Parliament in 1901 but it came to grief on the principle of compulsory employees' and employers' contributions which clashed with the freedom of saving espoused by the friendly societies. The viewpoint of the opponents of such an obligation, which would make it impossible to choose between different forms of welfare provision, was clearly expressed by Deputy J. Drake in these terms:[44]

I ask myself, then, what right does the state have to say to the worker: 'You are going to save in this way, or in that.' Should saving not be free? Does not every worker, every labourer in our country have from birth, so to speak, the right to use as he wishes what he has earned and what he has been able to save by his labour? Is there not for every worker, whether in the country or in the town, a special form of saving which attracts him more or less? In the country he tries to buy a plot of land or a house; in the town he tries to save working capital which will sooner or later make a small businessman or a small tradesman out of him.

The trade union movement for its part totally rejected the principle of workers' contributions, and preferred a state pension scheme financed by taxation.

Notwithstanding the opposition, a law on pensions for industrial and agricultural workers was eventually passed on 5 April 1910. It was based on the principle of capitalization and of contributions by both employees and employers. However this factor made it a particularly vulnerable price of legislation.

Rejection of the System by the People

The 1910 pensions law was not successful. In the first place, it encountered both strong resistance among workers, for whom the formality of a contribution card revived memories of the old police workers' identity card, and hostility among certain employers who were unwilling to deduct contributions from wages; the courts ruled that employers could not deduct the contributions except upon presentation of the annual contribution card and were thus relieved of any criminal liability for failing to make deductions.[45] Secondly, the system of capitalization adopted under the law led to its downfall because of inflation: contributions paid in gold francs were converted to pensions paid in devalued currency, and legislation was required from time to time to increase the amounts of pension payments.

Family Allowances.

Family allowances, deriving from the ideas of social Christianity, are based on the notion of a family wage supplement. This idea arose from the convergence of two other arguments: that the family needed protection against the dangers to which individualism exposes it, since without stable families a balanced society is impossible; and that of the just wage, as defined in the Encyclical Rerum Novarum in 1891. Neither of these arguments formed part of socialist ideology or of working class tradition, since they were seen as a source of division between workers.

Christian employers, and others who followed them, set up among themselves special funds to equalize financial burdens and remove the risk of discrimination between employees. Payments made out of these funds nevertheless retained all the characteristics of payments by the employer and were designed to help workers' families and at the same time to improve and control the workforce. Payments in respect of young children were made contingent upon older children of the same family, if any, being employed in the same business or industrial consortium. Illegitimate children were generally excluded. For example, Article II of the rules of the Rouen employers' fund provided.[46] 'The employee having no legal right to an allowance, it may be withdrawn in the event of misuse of the allowance or of neglect of his children. The consent of the employer must however be obtained for the withdrawal of an allowance.'

Managers of these funds were in practice simply agents of the employers, who had the sole control over them, but they gave to family wage supplements, not being paid directly by the employer, the character of family allowances.

THE POST-WAR DEBATE ON SOCIAL INSURANCE

Wars, like economic crises, upset established patterns and make society aware of unfilled social needs. In the period after the First World War several factors worked in favour of the establishment in France of a system of social insurance on the lines of the Bismarck system which would guarantee those covered chiefly against the risks of sickness and old age. However, the debate continued for more than a decade. The law on social insurance was passed in 1920. Even then it encountered such opposition that it was shelved and only came into force on 1 July 1930.

The Social and Political Context

Among the factors favouring the introduction of social insurance one can point first to the very slight impact of the friendly societies on the working class and the failure of the law of 1910 on pensions for industrial and agricultural workers, where the level of pensions was very low and the number of contributors declined continually after the war;[47] secondly, to the return of Alsace and Lorraine, where workers continued to enjoy the benefit of the German system, which remained in force, and were better protected against social risks than workers in the rest of France.

Moreover, though some hard-core liberals saw social insurance as the essential cause of Germany's defeat,[48] others did not hesitate to take the view that, on the contrary, social legislation was one of the factors which 'helped to save Germany from the Spartacists, or in other words from Bolshevik Communism, in the post-war revolutionary turmoil of 1918–1919'.[49]

The various bills introduced on this subject encountered much opposition, sometimes of a political nature, but more generally corporatist.

The Corporatist Opposition

Apart from the political opposition of the revolutionary wing of the trade union movement,[50] which saw the introduction of social insurance as the establishment of a system for integrating the working class into the capitalist system, the opposition of the various pressure groups such as agriculture, the friendly societies, the trade unions, employers and the medical profession, was largely corporatist in nature.

The trade union movement, or at any rate the majority of trade unionists, opposed the principle of a workers' contribution, as in 1910; but it also considered the problem of the organization of social insurance funds, arguing that there should be parity of representation for employers and workers, and calling for a system of distribution, as opposed to capitalization, in order to avoid the damaging effects of inflation. The friendly societies, with their long experience of social welfare, sought to consolidate their position by obtaining the management of the social insurance scheme for themselves. Employers wanted to retain control of the pension and sickness benefit funds which they had set up and to minimize the financial burden upon themselves. Farmers fought for a lower rate of contributions than commerce and industry. The medical profession, finally, held fast to the concept of a free profession and rejected any move to give doctors the status of public servants through involvement in social insurance.[51]

Concessions had to be made to each of the above groups in order to make the social insurance scheme generally acceptable, and in the end it was restricted to the risks of sickness, maternity, disability, old age and death. Compensation for accidents at work thus continued to be governed by the law of 9 April 1898, and family allowances continued to be a matter for employers, and not the state.

The Exclusion of Unemployment Insurance

In 1925 the question arose of introducing unemployment insurance in order that those without work, whose contributions were no longer being paid, should not be deprived of their rights in respect of old age and sickness insurance. However, the proposal was vigorously resisted and fell into oblivion. M. Colson repeated Jacques Rueff's arguments[52] against it: 'To-day, even in England, if not officially, at least in private conversation, everyone acknowledges that the true cause of the crisis, of the considerable reduction in exports and of the difficulty of defending the home market in insurance against unemployment.'

While admitting that assistance for the unemployed might be necessary in some cases, the same writer nevertheless considered that it was

> essential, in the interest of workers themselves, as well as that of industry and the public purse, that this assistance should never become a right which might encourage idleness, or a refusal to accept economic conditions to which all men must adapt; for this reason it is absolutely necessary not to call it insurance.[53]

This deep-rooted opposition to unemployment insurance was maintained in France until the signature of the national collective agreement of 31 December 1958, which introduced unemployment insurance within the framework of social security and, seen from another perspective, sought to maintain the spectre of unemployment at a time of full employment in order to hold down wages.

Be that as it may, the passing of the law on the social insurance meant that a decisive step had been taken: the substitution of a legal obligation for the autonomy of the individual will in the field of social welfare.

FROM THE INTRODUCTION OF SOCIAL INSURANCE TO THE GENERALIZATION OF SOCIAL SECURITY
(1930 to the present day)

The introduction of compulsory social insurance came late in France by comparison with Germany. At the very moment when it came into force, the economic crisis of 1929–1930 was already undermining the system by plunging new strata of society beyond the working class into insecurity and want, a situation made even worse by the Second World War.

During the Nazi occupation, the Beveridge Report found a favourable echo among the political forces of the French Resistance, both inside France (the programme of the Conseil National de la Résistance) and abroad (the Free French in London under General De Gaulle).

The French plan for a social security scheme to be introduced after liberation, under the auspices of the Fourth Republic, was inspired by Beveridge; but it did not propose a clean break with the past, since it aimed to integrate the old system into new forms of organization and a new perspective with a view to extending social protection against the risks of life to the entire French population. However, once the upsurge of national resistance to Fascism had passed, existing social forces rapidly retreated into earlier class positions, or sometimes corporatist positions, and the social security plans ran into many obstacles, being accepted in their entirety only by wage-earners.

Nevertheless, the Fifth Republic was compelled to consider the introduction of social security, though it had little support among employers, since it had become indispensable for increasing the pace of industrialization of the country and creating large units of production. Alongside the general scheme for employees in commerce and industry which constituted the pilot scheme for social security, various other autonomous or supplementary schemes appeared over the years in response to economic and social upheavals and gave new impetus to the policy of a single, generalized social security scheme.

In this second part we consider in turn the original legislation on social insurance, the French social security plan, the development of social security under the Fourth Republic and the options open to the Fifth Republic in the field of social security.

The Original Social Insurance Legislation

Following the pattern of Bismarck's system, the social insurance scheme was essentially an insurance of the labour of the working class. However, although it did not include compensation for accidents at work, which continued to be a matter of employer's liability, it did co-exist with a system of family allowances which became compulsory in 1932.[54]

The Field of Application

The protection of social insurance only extended compulsorily to employees in industry and commerce whose wages fell below a certain amount, known as the ceiling of participation, which fixed a threshold of respectability separating the employee from the working class. Higher paid managerial staff thus retained the option of accepting or declining the protection given by the scheme against the risks of sickness, maternity, disability, old age and death, as their personal interests required.

With regard to retirement pensions, the law provided for a pension from the age of 60, and after 30 years in the scheme, equal to 40 percent of average earnings resulting from the compulsory insurance contributions made after the age of 16; the scheme was based on a mixture of capitalization and distribution.

Administrative Organization

The insured had a free choice of insurer, the latter being obliged to cover the whole range of social risks envisaged by the legislation. Special departmental insurance funds were set up by the government to which those insured belonged who had either elected to be insured with it or who had expressed no alternative choice of insurer.

The possibility of choosing one's own insurer led to a rapid growth in such institutions promoted by trade unions, employers, the friendly societies and even religious bodies and meant an enormous duplication of effort. The number of such social insurance institutions reached 727. The friendly societies had 176 of them and also ran 86 of the departmental social insurance funds.

Financial Arrangements

The financing of the social insurance scheme was secured by a contribution equal to 8 percent of earnings divided equally, 4 percent being paid by the employer, and 4 percent by the employee. The contribution was deducted at source and paid directly by the employer to the relevant institution. In order to obtain payment of benefits the insured had to prove, if necessary, that the employer had paid the contributions. This was uncomfortable for employees, placing them at the mercy of the employer.

Doctors' Remuneration

In view of the refusal by the medical profession to accept payment of fees by the insurance institutions, for fear of being dragged into an employee–employer relation, a compromise was found. Doctors remained free to accept or refuse patients under the scheme, but acceptance involved an undertaking to abide by the fees fixed by the social insurance institutions, so that the patients would be reimbursed on the basis of the level of fees actually paid. This system soon deteriorated with the refusal of the institutions to revise the level of fees. Doctors left the scheme as the cost of living increased, and the insured had to pay the bills.

The Legislation on Family Allowances

Family allowances had been progressively extended after the First World War, through special funds set up by employers. The problem arose of making the system one of general application for the benefit of all employees, so as to remove existing disparities. This was the aim of the law of 11 March 1932, which set up a compulsory system of family allowances alongside the social insurance scheme. Thereafter, family allowances, though conceived as a family wage supplement, continued to maintain their independence in relation to wages because of the respective effect of: (i) their extension in 1939, on demographic grounds, to self-employed workers, which meant that the test of being engaged in a trade or profession was substituted for that of being an employee as the basis of entitlement; and (ii) their continuation notwithstanding loss of wages due to accident at work, sickness, death, unemployment or maternity.

The existence side by side of three different schemes — accidents at work, social insurance and family allowance — the multitude of organizations having the same purpose and the collapse of the scale of fees for doctors were all arguments, at a technical level, for moving towards a unification of the social insurance system. This was the intention of the French social security plan for after the Second World War.

THE FRENCH SOCIAL SECURITY PLAN

The Conseil National de la Résistance launched the idea, in its social and economic programme, of 'a complete plan of social security, designed to secure the means of existence for all French men and women whenever they are incapable of providing such means for themselves by working, and administered by representatives of the insured and the state'. The foundations of the French social security plan were thus laid. It was for the government to complete the work after the Liberation. Pierre Laroque, who was the moving force behind the realization of the plan, saw in it the combination of three different policies:[55] (i) an economic policy of full employment; (ii) a policy of health care and medical organization which enabled disease to be fought initially by prevention and then by treatment in the best possible conditions; a policy which was naturally complemented by the provision of technical equipment to prevent accidents at work and occupational diseases; and (iii) a policy of redistribution of incomes aimed at modifying the division of wealth which results from the blind play of economic forces, in order to adapt the resources of each individual and each family to their respective needs, taking account of all the circumstances which could affect the development of those resources.

This programme gave the social security scheme its fundamental unity. But, because of the social and economic situation at the time, the full realization of the plan could only be contemplated as a long-term measure. Would it not then have been better to have done what was possible and necessary to do and in particular to establish an institution capable of putting the programme into practice by stages? These were the issues in the political debate which had a profound influence upon the establishment of French social security.[56]

The General Ideas Underlying the Scheme

The general ideas upon which the French social security plan is based may be summarized as follows.

1. To protect the entire population against the social risks of life and to ensure for each person an income at least sufficient for subsistence through the working of the principle of national solidarity, which necessarily implies a redistribution of income.
2. To unify the diverse institutions and occupational schemes concerned with social insurance within the framework of a general social security institution, so as to equalize costs and benefits on a national basis.
3. To entrust the management of the unified social security institution to representatives of the insured and of the state.

To the extent that these ideas might harm particular interests or established positions they crystallized the opposition to them and resulted in a political compromise which actually brought about the fragmentation of the social security plan.

The Political Compromise

At an early stage, the ideological conflict was polarized at the political and trade union level with two dominant tendencies being in contention, one favouring the unification and centralization of social security so that the security of the individual should be based on the support of the entire population (the French Communist Party, the Socialist Party and the Confédération Générale du Travail (CGT)), and the other attached to the principle of the autonomy of social security organizations and to their management directly by those representatives of the insured judged most able to defend the particular interests of their constituents (the Mouvement Républicain Populaire (MRP), the Confédération française des travailleurs chrétiens (CFTC), the friendly societies and self-employed workers).

In reality each of the two solutions proposed had advantages and disadvantages. The first solution increased the risk of a rapid development towards a public service and a take-over by the state of the social security system, but had the advantage of being able to give practical expression to the principle of national solidarity between individuals. The second had the advantage of management being in close touch with the insured, but the disadvantage of preserving social inequality between individuals who were at the mercy of economic imbalances arising between socio-occupational groups.

This conflict revived an old and never-ending debate between socialist ideology and the sentimental, sometimes opportunist, attachment to individualist principles, but it was cut short by a political compromise which has left its mark on the French social security system even to-day: the unification of contributions and benefits on a national level for the general employees' scheme and independent managment by regional and primary institutions. This compromise was shown by subsequent events not to be totally viable, for the state, taking advantage of the inevitable financial imbalance between the different independent institutions, acted swiftly to create financial equality on a national level and gradually to impose its own supervision of the whole social security system.

The Reactions of Particular Groups

As soon as the principle of the independence of management was admitted, various socio-occupational groups demanded to take advantage of it, either to escape altogether from compulsory affiliation and to create their own independent institutions as it suited them, or to create specific or supplementary institutions in order to obtain superior benefits or retain existing advantages.

The Self-employed

Self-employed workers, being utterly opposed to the whole idea of solidarity, because of the spirit of competition which inspires them, refused to join the general social security scheme. Nevertheless, they accepted the benefit of family allowances and the estasblishment from 1948 onwards of independent old age insurance schemes more or less divided according to socio-occupational groups, and merely refused to accept sickness and maternity insurance and compensation for occupational accidents. They thought at the time that they had sufficient resources at their disposal to meet these risks individually. However, developments in medicine and the cost of health care, plus their own impoverishment as a result of the concentration of the means of production and trade, soon dashed their hopes.

Managerial Staff

In 1928–1930, the majority of managerial staff had shunned social insurance out of contempt for the idea of public assistance, but they changed their position in the light of experience. They considered that they suffered an unfair disadvantage under the general social security scheme, which, because of the ceiling on earnings taken into account for contributions, did not enable them to draw retirement pensions related to the level of their own salaries, so they demanded a supplementary pension scheme. The government referred them to their employers and, after a damaging strike, the national collective agreement of 14 March 1947, was signed setting up a supplementary pension scheme for higher paid staff within the framework of the general social security scheme.

Supplementary pension schemes were later extended to other employees, by contrast with old age insurance, which deteriorated.

The Maintenance of Advantages Already Obtained

The categories of employees who already enjoyed superior social benefits, or who had the possibility of superior benefit, by a combination of the general social security scheme and their statutory or friendly society benefits, also obtained the right to maintain or to establish special schemes within the framework of the general scheme.[57] The special schemes, which had previously been much more favourable than the general scheme, now had to be compared with the total benefits obtained by other employees under the general scheme and under the welfare provisions of collective agreements. The difference between the two tended to become smaller and smaller.

These different attitudes rapidly led to the breaking up of the French social security plan; in practice it was reduced to the general scheme for employed workers, and very quickly became the object of hostility on the part of employers.

Employers' Hostility

At the time of the Liberation, employers had been weakened by the fact that a majority had collaborated with the Occupying Forces and they were not in a position to oppose the introduction of social security legislation. De Gaulle's words to the first delegation of employers he received after his return to France are often recalled: 'Gentlemen, I did not meet any of you in London.'

From 1947 onwards, however, thanks to the exclusion of Communist ministers from the government and the resulting changes in political alliances, employers extended their influence on the government and succeeded in implanting a latent source of decay in the general scheme from the beginning of the 1950s, namely the freezing of the earnings limit for contributions and consequently of benefit payments, reimbursement of medical fees at a derisory level failing renewal of agreements with the medical profession, reluctance on the part of employers to pay contributions, and laxity in the enforcement of employers' debts.

After giving up power, De Gaulle, speaking at Compiègne in March 1948, emphasized the necessity for 'an effective and lasting reduction of social expenditure, particularly by reforming the social insurance system'. He thereby became the focus for all the hopes of the opponents of social security upon his return to public life. The Fifth Republic came too late, however, to re-open fundamental aspects of the system which had then reached a point of no return. Changes in medicine meant that it now found crucial financial support in social security; in addition, that there existed a demand for social health care, even in sectors of the population previously opposed to the idea, in order to provide easier access to treatment, the cost of which had risen as it became more effective.

The Legislation

Faced with an ideological conflict which threatened to go on for ever at the political level, the government legislated by means of ordinances, a technique found more favourable to rapid reform than the classical parliamentary methods.

An ordinance of 4 October 1945, laid the foundations of a new social security system in these terms: 'There is established a social security organisation designed to guarantee workers and their families against risks of any kind which could reduce or take away their earning capacity, and to cover the costs of maternity and of the families supported by them.'

This system applied initially to workers employed in industry or commerce. In respect of the risks covered by social insurance[58] (which were the subject of a second ordinance of 19 October 1945) the system was intended to be progressively extended to other categories of workers. The working of the system was to be ensured by a network of social security offices, each able to deal with all parts of the scheme, the management of which largely followed the friendly societies' pattern, that is to say, management by the insured through their representatives.

A law of 22 May 1946, designed to make the system of general application, provided for social insurance to be compulsory for all French citizens resident in French territory. This principle was to be worked out in detailed provisions, made after consultation with organizations representing the different categories of people affected, and was also made conditional upon the recovery of the economy. However, the government did not wait, and a law of 13 September 1946, set 1 January 1947, as the commencing date for the old age insurance provisions which were to be extended to the whole active population.

Furthermore, a law of 22 August 1946, on family allowances, extended the benefit of the allowances to virtually the entire population, as part of a policy of promoting an increase in the birth-rate; it provided for a scale of family allowances, a one-wage allowance to enable mothers to remain at home, antenatal and maternity allowances.

Finally, a law of 30 October 1946, on the prevention of, and compensation for, accidents at work and occupational diseases, replaced the law of 9 April 1898, which had based employers' liability on the concept of occupational risk, by an insurance scheme for workers employed in industry and commerce, the management of which was placed under the general social security scheme.[59]

In the application of the ordinance of 4 October 1945, the general social security scheme was designed to ensure:

1. the protection of workers employed in industry and commerce against the burdens of bringing up a family and against the risks covered by social insurance, that is to say, sickness, maternity, disability, old age and death, as well as against occupational risks — accidents at work and occupational diseases;
2. the protection of self-employed workres in relation to social costs, but also with regard to the risks to be covered for employees, by social insurance when the proposals contained in the law of 22 May 1946, were put into practice.

Administrative unification did not, however, come about, since Article 17 of the ordinance of 4 October 1945, in fact allowed some special schemes to continue for the time being in the expectation that they would be absorbed later into the general scheme. It also preserved a special scheme for agriculture on a permanent basis as a concession to the farmers' insuperable opposition to the general scheme.

At the dawn of the Fourth Republic the social security system was characterized by the presence of two major schemes — the general scheme intended to encompass the entire active population apart from farmers and farmworkers, and the special scheme for agriculture. In the event, however, the system developed along different lines.

THE DEVELOPMENT OF SOCIAL SECURITY UNDER THE FOURTH REPUBLIC

The farmers' refusal to join the general scheme quickly convinced other self-employed people, such as tradesmen, businessmen, craftsmen and members of the professions, who feared that their contributions could be used to finance benefits paid to the employed. The general scheme found itself reduced to workers employed in commerce and industry, leaving aside the existence of special schemes. The special scheme for agriculture thus became, if not a magnet drawing other groups towards itself, at least a precedent for the creation of a network of autonomous or supplementary schemes within the framework of the general scheme.

The Reverses Suffered by the General Scheme

Though reduced to workers employed in industry and commerce, the general scheme nevertheless formed the centrepiece of the French social security system. However, notwithstanding an expansion of the scheme due to the extension of benefits to certain other categories of persons such as students,[60] professional servicemen and women,[61] self-employed authors,[62] and war disabled, war widows and war orphans,[63] the general scheme suffered serious reverses under the Fourth Republic.

The Failure of the Plan for a Single Institution

The ordinance of 4 October 1945, introduced the principle of having a single office within a particular district to administer the three branches of the general scheme, i.e. social insurance, accidents at work and family benefits. This arrangement reflected the unity of insurance based on a single contribution by employees[64] to cover the various social risks. It encountered opposition from those who wanted the scheme to be autonomous and who feared that the creation of a single institution would help to convert the general scheme into a public service. The autonomy of the family allowance offices from the social security offices was maintained provisionally by the law of 22 August 1946, which extended the system of family benefits, and was confirmed finally by the law of 21 February 1949. This autonomy can be explained by the fact that, in contrast to social security offices, family allowance offices had to pay benefits both to employed and to self-employed workers.

The structure of the general scheme then presented the following picture:

1. *family allowance offices* responsible for administering the payment of family benefits for employed and self-employed workers
2. *local social security offices* responsible for administering, separately, the social insurance scheme and the scheme covering accidents at work and occupational diseases for employed workers;
3. *regional social security offices* responsible for administering the services common to the local offices in their area, that is to say, essentially to organize the prevention of accidents at work and to set the contribution rates under that scheme and to ensure the payment of pensions and allowances.

These various offices operated as independent institutions and were directed by a board of management, set up on friendly society principles with three quarters of the members representing the insured, and the remaining quarter representing employers.[65] The members were elected by their fellow insured, or employers, as the case may be. The elected members coopted qualified persons to represent the employees of the office and the medical profession, so that all categories of persons with an interest in the management of the office should be represented on the board of management. Their independence was confined to the running of the office, however, with questions of social security contributions and benefits being for the government.

The Take-Over by the State

The state had the power to legislate on social security, but it was deprived of the management which had been entrusted to autonomous offices having the legal character of corporations under private law.[66] It seized on the opportunity to profit by the financial difficulties which appeared here and there because of unfavourable regional economic or demographic conditions, first by setting up a *national social security office,* in the form of a public administrative corporation, responsible for maintaining a financial balance between the various autonomous offices, and, secondly, by changing the control of the Minister for Social Security over the management of the autonomous offices from the original *a posteriori* system to one of *a priori* control, placing the offices under his control in the same way as juristic persons affected by a lack of legal capacity.[67] The policy of exercising increasingly tight control gradually led the state to assume a parallel power of management of the general scheme. This did not remain an isolated phenomenon, but subsequently affected all the social security schemes to a greater or lesser degree.

The Fall in Value of Social Security Benefits

The ordinance of 19 October 1945, established the principle of reimbursement of 80 percent of medical and associated expenses. Though the principle itself was not called into question it ran into difficulties which emptied it of its substance. To avoid falling again into the old error of a fixed scale of medical fees limiting the amount payable to the insured, a more flexible system was envisaged: in each department an agreement would be made between the regional social security office and the professional associations representing the doctors, fixing a scale of medical fees on the basis of a national classification of the various forms of treatment. These agreed scales, which could be revised periodically to take account of changes in the cost of living, were intended to govern the reimbursement of medical expenses under the social security scheme, though higher amounts could be authorized by reason of the eminence of the doctor, the means of the insured or other special circumstances. Where no departmental agreement had been concluded, the scheme only reimbursed medical expenses on the basis of an authorized scale set at a derisory level so as to apply pressure indirectly on the medical profession to conclude such agreements. This system worked very badly because, except in some especially disadvantaged rural areas, the departmental agreements once signed were never renewed and, in the great majority of cases, the insured were only reimbursed some 20 percent of their medical expenses instead of 80 percent.

Furthermore, the employers' hostility led to a stop being placed on the revision of the earnings limit for social security contributions, which in turn resulted in a stagnation of benefit levels, i.e. of the daily rates of payment during periods of temporary incapacity to work, and of old age and disability pensions. This situation led the ordinary workers to follow the example of higher-paid staff and accept the creation of supplementary pension schemes within the framework of the social security scheme.

A law of 26 July 1956 was needed to establish a National Solidarity Fund, financed out of taxation and having the object of paying a supplementary allowance to the aged or disabled who lacked sufficient resources for survival.

Moreover, the base wage taken for the calculation of family benefits had been fixed in 1946 by reference to the average wage of a labourer in the Paris heavy metal industry. The benefits were fixed as a percentage of the base wage and were thus automatically indexed to follow increases in wages. In 1947, however, a law was passed removing this indexation[68] and laying down that the base figure should be fixed by regulations, because of the financial difficulties resulting from the fact that the cost of sickness insurance was increasing more rapidly than had been foreseen in relation to earnings and earnings were at the time rising faster than prices. The base wage has constantly fallen in real terms since then and has dragged down with it the level of family benefits, which fell from 21.8 percent of GNP in 1948 to 9 percent in 1972.[69]

Nevertheless, in 1948, in return for the abolition of control of rents in new buildings,[70] which was aimed at promoting investment in the construction of residential accomodation, a lodging allowance was introduced, which came under the family allowance scheme, to allow less well-off beneficiaries to obtain better housing while maintaining the general high level of rents more easily. The policy of promoting an increased birth-rate thus went hand in hand with a policy of raising the standard of living. Some observers, however, saw in the introduction of the lodging allowance a device for taking funds from the family allowance institutions and investing them in land and buildings by passing them through the hands of beneficiaries.

The Survival of the Special Schemes

A decree of 8 June 1946, listed the special schemes whose independence was to be preserved,[71] but it envisaged their conversion into supplementary schemes which would maintain for their beneficiaries any advantages previously acquired which were more favourable than those provided under the general scheme. With rare exceptions, this conversion did not take place and some special schemes not covered by the decree were preserved.[72]

Among these different special schemes one finds a great diversity. Some are entirely self-contained and provide independent cover for the whole range of social risks; others are partial schemes in the sense that they only cover particular risks, with the beneficiaries being attached to the general scheme for cover against the other risks. Without embarking upon a detailed consideration of the benefits which were more favourable than those of the general scheme, one can mention:

1. the free medical treatment provided under some schemes, though with the condition that the treatment be given by approved practitioners;
2. the maintenance of remuneration, wholly or partially, in the case of illness or

accident, for periods of incapacity laid down in regulations governing the particular employment;
3. the right to retirement pension commencing between the ages of 50 and 60 years in special schemes, compared with the age of 65 in the general scheme.

These special advantages, generally of statutory origin and applying to workers in public services, were extended to a greater or lesser degree to the private sector within the framework of the general scheme by way of collective agreements on terms of employment or social security. Over the years, this has resulted in the growth of supplementary schemes and a corresponding erosion of the privileged position of the special schemes.

The Appearance of the Autonomous Supplementary Schemes

The failure of the proposals for general old age insurance finally led to a law of 17 January 1948, which introduced special old age insurance schemes for different categories of self-employed workers distributed among the following four autonomous organizations: (i) those engaged in industry and commerce; (ii) craftsmen; (iii) the professions; and (iv) those engaged in agriculture.

This solution gave satisfaction to the members of the groups concerned, who did not wish to be integrated into the general scheme for employed workers, but it led to the establishment of autonomous old age insurance schemes and reinforced the independence of the special scheme for agriculture, which henceforth was responsible for: (i) family allowances for those engaged in agriculture, whether self-employed or employees; (ii) social insurance for agricultural employees, which was based on the general scheme for workers employed in industry and commerce; and (iii) old age insurance for farmers.

Furthermore, the ordinance of 19 October 1945, had provided for the general scheme to apply to all employees irrespective of the level of earnings. This provision gave rise to much disquiet among engineers and other management staff anxious to preserve the pension advantages they had previously achieved by agreement and afraid that their inclusion in a compulsory social security scheme would leave them worse off because of the effect of the earnings limit for contributions upon the amount of old age pensions.

Several upheavals followed, including a strike by management staff, which ended in the signing of the collective agreement of 14 March 1947, on welfare and pensions for management staff and the creation, within the framework of the general scheme, of supplementary pension institutions falling under the General Association of Pension Institutions for Management Staff (Association générale des institutions de retraites des cadres: AGIRC).

The success achieved by management staff did not escape the notice of other employees who were disturbed at the failure to raise the earnings limit for social security contributions in the 1950s and the consequence reduction in value of old age pensions. The climate was favourable for the extension of supplementary pension schemes and such demands were made by supervisory staff, then by workers and all employees. The following action was taken.

1. In 1953 a special pension scheme was set up for supervisory staff in the heavy metal industry (Institution de retraite des chefs d'ateliers et assimilés de l'industrie des métaux: IRCACIM).

2. In 1955 a company-wide agreement was made by Renault establishing a supplementary pension scheme for workers in all its factories. This found a broad echo in other parts of the heavy metal industry and beyond.
3. In 1957, at the instigation of the Conseil National du Patronat Français (CNPF), a national union of employees' pension funds (Union nationale des Institutions de retraite des salariés: UNIRS) was established to facilitate the conclusion of collective agreements at national and company level on supplementary pensions.

Behind the supplementary pension institutions, which were managed by equal numbers of employers' and employees' representatives, the insurance companies appeared in the background, lured by the large sums involved, ready to offer their services and hoping to gain the market for themselves.[73]

The dream of the authors of the French social security plan of establishing a unified system for the whole population was finally shattered. Its place was taken by a mosaic of special autonomous or supplementary schemes alongside the general scheme, which still remained the essential core of the social security system. The system moved even further in this direction under the Fifth Republic.

THE OPTIONS OPEN TO THE FIFTH REPUBLIC IN THE FIELD OF SOCIAL SECURITY

The Fifth Republic soon realized that social security was an established feature of French life and that, like it or not, its existence had to be accepted. In fact, while setting up new institutions, an ordinance made a marked reduction in social security benefits from 1 January 1959: it raised the insured's quota, ended the reimbursement of the cost of thermal cures and introduced the rule that the first 3000 francs in each 6 months period had to be borne by the individual.[74] These measures were greatly resented by the aged and by the poorest families, who were deprived of reimbursements indispensible for their survival. The unpopularity of the 3000 francs rules led to its abolition from 1 July 1959, and reimbursement of the cost of thermal cures was also partially restored. During the spring of 1959 the fate of social security was thus moulded by public opinion.[75]

According to a well-established rule, as soon as a government finds it impossible to mount a frontal attack on a solidly based institution it seeks to convert the institution to serve its own ends. Social security was no exception. From 1960 onwards we begin to see the situation reversed. There was a considerable improvement in the reimbursement of medical fees, the earnings limit for contributions was linked to changes in the general earnings index, and sickness insurance was extended first to farmers and then to self-employed workers. At the same time as it extended the social security system, the state increased its power of control over the organizations responsible for administering the system, and increased the representation of employers at the expense of the representation of employees in the management of the general scheme. The concept of solidarity tended to be replaced by that of insurance, which was even introduced into the name of the institutions administering the general scheme.

After 1974 the question again arose of making social protection in relation to sickness, maternity, old age and family benefits available to all French men and women through the many existing social security schemes, but, contrary to the wish of the legislature, the extension only took place on an optional basis. Though the final excluded categories were permitted to belong to a social security scheme — categories such as French workers abroad, concubines, Catholic clergy, young people looking for their first job, prisoners, prostitutes and so on — the threefold aim of the legislation was not achieved, namely protection of all French men and women, harmonization of benefits among the various schemes and financial adjustments in the light of demographic changes affecting each scheme and the capacity of the members of the scheme to contribute.

In place of the French plan of 1945-1946 for a general social security scheme covering the entire population in unity and social equality there is a general scheme based on diversity and social inequality.

The Strengthening of Government Control of the Administration of Social Security

The Fifth Republic turned very quickly towards strengthening its power of control over the administration of the social security institutions. The reform of 12 May 1960, which was carried out by means of regulations, though in a field within the constitutional competence of the legislature in some respects,[76] modified the conditions under which directors were appointed, increased their powers at the expense of the board of management, and laid down requirements regarding the training and promotion of management personnel.

In 1967, using the pretext of the financial difficulties encountered by the general scheme, which were largely due to behind the scenes manipulations,[77] the government introduced further reforms to strengthen its control of the administration of the general scheme under the cover of achieving a financial balance between the different risks. This move was directly inspired by a report produced by the CNPF.[78] This reform, which, because of its unpopularity,[79] was enacted by ordinance[80] under powers given to the government for this purpose,[81] profoundly changed the structure of the general social security scheme under the cover of separating the risks and introducing parity of representation.

Changes in the Structure of the General Scheme

The separation of risks consisted in:

1. separating, in respect of finance and accounting, old age insurance from the other forms — sickness, maternity, disability and death — which had previously been run together under the heading, social insurance;[82]
2. breaking down the national social security office into the three following offices, in order to provide a structural base for the separation of risks:

(a) *the national sickness insurance office* which administers, separately, first sickness, maternity, disability and death insurance, and, secondly, the scheme for accidents at work; the local and regional offices continued, but received the title of sickness insurance offices in place of that of social security offices;
(b) *the national old age insurance office* which administers the old age scheme with the direct collaboration of the regional old age insurance office for Alsace and Lorraine[83] and, by delegation, of the regional sickness insurance offices; and
(c) *the national family allowances office* which administers the scheme for family benefits with the help of the local and regional family allowances offices;

3. creating a common treasury for the three national offices — the *Agence centrale des organismes de securité sociale* (ACOSS) at the head of the organizations for recovering social security and family allowance contributions (*Unions de recouvrement des cotisations de securité sociale et d'allocations familiales:* URSSAF);
4. substituting, for the national federation of social security organizations (Féd-ération nationale des organismes de securité sociale: FNOSS) and the national union of family allowances offices (Union nationale des caisses d'allocations familiales: UNCAF), a union of national social security offices (Union des caisses nationales de securité sociale: UCANSS) to safeguard the common interests of the national offices.

ACOSS and the three other national offices were accorded the legal status of public administrative corporations, which emphasizes the public nature of the administration of the general scheme, whereas the other offices, though placed under the direct authority of the national offices, retain their legal status as corporations of private law. This leads to an incredible legal tangle, with the authority of the national offices over the others being superimposed upon the exercise of control by the Minister of Social Security.

The Introduction of Parity of Representation

Parity of representation was the means of removing the majority enjoyed by representatives of the insured in the boards of management of the social security offices so as to give a preponderant influence to the Conseil National du Patronat Français.[84] Since this reform, boards of management are composed of eighteen members,[85] of whom nine represent employees' trade unions and nine represent employers' associations and, sometimes, the self-employed.

Whereas the CNPF enjoys a monopoly of employers representation, representation of employees is shared according to the following formula: CGT, three seats; CFDT, two seats; CFT-FO, two seats; CFTC, one seat; and CFC, one seat.[86] Members are no longer elected by the people they are to represent but are nominated by the most representative trade unions or employers' associations. They are appointed by the Minister for Social Security for a 4-year term and can be removed by him if they no longer satisfy the necessary conditions.

In addition, the boards of management contain, generally as consultative members, qualified persons to represent family associations, friendly societies, the medical and paramedical professions. Representation of the employees of the institutions has been entirely excluded, however.

The Extension of Compulsory Social Protection

The economic and social changes wrought by the acceleration of the process of industrialization of the country, and the resulting concentration of the means of production and trade, involving the disappearance of family farms, and the creation of large units of production and of large retail outlets in the towns, led the government to complete the social protection of the middle classes, in order to make these changes bearable for their potential victims and to move once again towards a system of compulsory protection for the entire population.

Sickness and Maternity Insurance for Self-employed Workers

Two important laws extended sickness and maternity insurance to self-employed workers. The law of 21 January 1961 established sickness, maternity and disability insurance for farmers (assurance maladie—Maternité et invalidité des exploitants agricoles: AMEXA). The beneficiaries of this law, farmers, family members working on the farm, partners in farming operations, holders of old age pensions under the special scheme for agriculture, spouses and dependent children, etc., must to this end join an organization of their choice, either the agricultural social benefit institution, an agricultural mutual insurance institution (under the 1900 friendly society law) or another friendly society, or any insurance organization specially recognized for this purpose.

The sickness insurance relates only to sickness properly so called, to the exclusion of accidents outside work, which, like occupational accidents, fall under a separate compulsory scheme for farmers. The maternity insurance guarantees the same benefits as are paid to employees with the exception of the daily allowance when unable to work. However, a fund for maternity leave in agriculture was set up in 1977, which enabled the cost of replacing a farmers's wife unable to work regularly on the farm because of maternity to be covered in part.[88]

The law of 12 July 1966, established the framework for sickness and maternity insurance for self-employed workers in industry and commerce, craftsmen and those engaged in the professions. At the time this law ran into a violent storm of protest from the groups affected. It had to be amended several times[89] in order to lighten the financial obligations and to bring the benefits into line with those of the general scheme for employees. This alignment is now practically complete, except for some minor risks.[90]

Non-agricultural self-employed workers do not have the benefit of any compulsory insurance scheme in relation to occupational accidents, which is a serious lacuna.

The Widening of Protection in Respect of Accidents at Work

First, the mechanization of agriculture led the legislature to improve the protection of farmworkers and farmers against farming accidents. Two laws were passed to deal with this.

The law of 26 December 1966, extended the effects of AMEXA and made insurance compulsory for farmers against accidents of any kind. This sort of insurance had, before this, been available only on an optional basis through agricultural mutual insurance institutions. From now on farmers were obliged to take out insurance with an AMEXA institution, either by contract or by membership depending upon the nature of the organizations, for themselves and for the other persons working under them on their holding—members of the family, partners, spouse etc.—covering them against accidents outside work, accidents at work and occupational diseases.

The law of 25 October 1972 extended the legislation on accidents at work in the general scheme to agricultural employees. Down to 1 January 1973, compensation for accidents suffered at work by agricultural employees was still based on the principles of the law of 9 April 1898. The rules of the general scheme now apply in their entirety to agricultural employees, with the addition of a few special provisions, such as a specific list of recognized occupational diseases and special rules on prevention.

Secondly, a law of 6 December 1976 strengthened the provisions on prevention of accidents in non-agricultural employments.[91] These provisions consist principally of: (a) an obligation on the employer to organize appropriate practical training in safety for his workers; (b) the insertion of safety rules in conditions and methods of work; (c) the extension of criminal liability for personal fault in the area of health and safety and the possible imposition of a safety plan upon the business;[92] and (d) virtually 100 percent compensation for the victim of an accident at work attributable to the inexcusable fault of the employer or his agent entrusted with powers of management, with compensation being given for loss of amenities of life.

If these measures are applied in practice in the way intended by the legislature, they should make a considerable improvement in the prevention of accidents at work.

The Diversification of Family Benefits

The Fifth Republic made certain innovations by introducing special family benefits for orphans, handicapped persons, single parents and others. However, these new benefits, like the family supplement which replaced the one-wage allowance, are subject to conditions as to the means of the family. Since the threshold is fixed in terms of available credits rather than actual needs, this greatly limits the number of potential beneficiaries.

At the same time as the range of benefits was being increased, the regular loss of purchasing power and the introduction of a means test have reduced family benefits to the level of public assistance. Thus these measures are inappropriate for the solution of any of the problems existing in France, whether those of social inequality or of the decline in the birth rate associated with the economic crisis.[93] However, from 1 January 1978 the right to family benefits no longer depends upon the claimant's having some trade, profession or occupation. This marks the final break with the origin of the institution as a family wage supplement.

Progress with Regard to the Generalization of Social Security

A law of 24 December 1974[94] provided for the introduction of a system of social protection common to all French men and women by 1 January 1978, at the latest, to cover the three branches of sickness and maternity insurance, old age insurance and family benefits. The principle became attenuated, however, in the course of the enactment of the implementing provisions and the process of generalization was at the end still not complete and was still characterized by social inequality both as regards rights to benefits and the sharing of the social burden.

Apart from requiring compulsory submission to the general social security scheme on the part of certain categories of persons who had previously been entirely excluded from social protection, such as young people looking for their first job, prisoners, and certain limited measures to increase the protection of the surviving spouse,[95] persons living together as man and wife[96] and others, the steps so far taken to make the scheme of general application have led mainly to the introduction of protection for those employed abroad, to a personal insurance which, contrary to all expectations, remained optional and to a special scheme in favour of the Catholic clergy, who had previously been opposed to social security.

If the most recent of the laws aimed at making social security generally applicable amounted to a new step forward, it did not completely achieve its objective, and there is reason to fear that because of the present crisis those who are unemployed and receive no compensation will be thrown back upon the optional personal insurance scheme, and, having no means to pay the contributions, will form a new army of people deprived of social protection.[97]

The Financial Choices

Financial instability is the price generally paid for having dynamic social institutions. Social security is no exception to this rule. In the area of social welfare, the predominant principle is that schemes should be financed by their beneficiaries. This principle is qualified at the political level, however, by the use of financial techniques with the object, in response to changes in social forces, either of coming to the aid of disadvantaged social categories, or conversely of throwing the main financial burden on to those social groups who are not the most prosperous. Four principal choices seem to have been made by the government.

The Principle of Financial Non-Participation by the State

With the exception of civil and military pensions for public servants[98] the state has never relied on the Budget to meet the cost of administering the social security system. The only forms of state intervention have been: the creation of certain special taxes, either to provide funds for the ancillary budget for agricultural social benefits (budget annexe des prestations sociales agricoles: BAPSA), or to contribute to the financing of the autonomous sickness, maternity, and old age insurance schemes for self-employed workers (extraordinary solidarity tax imposed upon large retail stores) and the additional tax on motor vehicle insurance premiums (to meet a fraction of the costs which road accidents impose upon the social security system); and the granting of subsidies to maintain the solvency of schemes which experience particular difficulty because of their demographic structure or the low level of contributions which those belonging to the scheme are able to pay.

These are the exceptional cases, however, and the normal rule is that the state aims to transfer its financial responsibility for social welfare on to the social security system, by making a compulsory financial set-off between the different schemes. In practice when a particular special tax measure proves to be productive, as happened with the vignette scheme for raising money for the National Solidarity Fund, it has been diverted into the state budget.

The Set-off Between Schemes

Originally piecemeal, the set-off between schemes has now been made legally obligatory.[99] It is designed to make the general scheme for employees meet the cost of the deficits incurred by the special schemes and also by the autonomous schemes for self-employed, on the basis of financial solidarity. Without going into technical details,[100] it may be pointed out that the set-off:

1. emphasizes the imbalance in demographic patterns between one scheme and another, caused by economic changes which are transforming French society; certain special schemes such as those for mines, the railways etc., and the autonomous schemes in agriculture and for self-employed workers are drained of their real substance because of the decline in their sector of the economy, or because of the industrialization of agriculture and the consequent exodus of workers to the towns, or because of the demise of small businesses and the crafts;

2. helps to meet the problem of the real contributive capacity of the self-employed, whose contributions are calculated on the basis of deemed earnings, using land registry or tax figures, which are generally lower than the figure for actual earnings, whereas employed persons contribute on the basis of their actual earnings, as declared by a third party.

Under these conditions, the compulsory set-off does not resolve the disparities existing between one scheme and another, but shifts them by pushing the financial burden of national solidarity on to the general scheme when it ought normally to be borne by the state budget.

The Shifting of the Contribution Share from the Employer on to the Worker

The shifting of the contribution share from the employer on to the worker has the avowed object of keeping down production costs to make French businesses more competitive in international markets by taking a higher proportion of the contribution in the form of direct deductions from wages. For example, on 1 August 1979, the worker's contribution was raised unilaterally by 1 percent of total earnings.[101] On 1 January 1980, it amounted to 10.2 percent, 4.7 percent being calculated within the earnings limit for contributions, and 5.5 percent being based on total earnings, as against the 6 percent ceiling when the social security scheme was first introduced.

Control of the Rising Cost of Health Care

As in all industrialized countries, the cost of health care tends to rise more rapidly than the gross national product. The government accordingly drew the conclusion that it was necessary to curb the amount spent on health care. Three particular aspects of this policy may be mentioned briefly.

First the medical profession is the determining factor in the cost of health care. Since the profession remains deeply attached to its independent status and to the principle of remuneration for each service provided, a system of national agreements has been in operation since 1971 to lay down at the national level scales of medical fees compatible with the working of the social security system, and at the same time to persuade the medical profession to exercise restraint and self-control in prescribing drugs. The operation of the national agreement follows the former departmental agreements in several respects, such as creating an individual pension, granting the right to charge higher fees in certain cases, and establishing of medico-social commissions. These provisions, which appear again in the various paramedical professions, have been completed by the introduction of a *numerus clausus* for admission to medical schools.

Secondly, hospital care places a heavy burden on the social security system, but is nevertheless indispensable for high quality health care and for the progress of medical science. Some relief has been found in the reduction of administrative costs and in more domiciliary care, but the possibilities of cut-back are very limited if the progress made in health care in the last 20 years is not to be put at risk.

Thirdly, the excessive use of drugs is due in large part to bad habits formed under the influence of advertising and of a market financially supported by social security. Some observers are beginning to ask if it would not be better, instead of reducing or stopping the reimbursement of certain types of drug, to go ahead with the nationalization of the pharmaceutical industry.

The Growth of Supplementary Institutions

As part of the social security system, supplementary institutions have grown considerably in the last 20 years, and some of them, though originating in collective agreements, now have a statutory basis.

Supplementary Pensions

An agreement made on 8 December 1961, aimed at extending supplementary pensions to all employees not in the category of management staff. To this end it established an association of supplementary pension schemes, the object of which was to coordinate the operation of the various institutions and make financial adjustments between them. A few occupations remained outside the scheme, and this led to the passing of the law of 29 December 1972, requiring all employees and former employees to belong to a supplementary pension institution.

Unemployment Insurance

Having been excluded from the social security scheme, unemployment was dealt with in a national agreement of 31 December 1958 concluded by the CNPF and several of the trade union confederations,[102] with the object of guaranteeing workers against the risk of involuntary loss of their employment by means of a system of contributions and benefits proportional to wages. The agreement set up unemployment insurance managed by institutions in which employers and employees were equally represented: the associations for employment in industry and commerce (Associations pour l'emploi dans l'industrie et le commerce: ASSEDIC) headed, at the national level, by the National Union for Employment in Industry and Commerce (Union nationale pour l'emploi dans l'industrie et le commerce: UNEDIC). The agreement was signed in a period of full employment, but had the aim, at least for the employers, of helping to form a labour reserve to keep down wages.

However, the rise in unemployment in the 1970s led to several amendments of this unemployment insurance scheme: first, an ordinance of 13 July 1967 harmonized the operation of public aid and unemployment insurance by establishing, through an agreement between the state and UNEDIC, a single organization to make both forms of payment — the ASSEDIC, in fact;[103] secondly, an agreement of 27 March 1972, introduced, as part of unemployment insurance, a guarantee of income equal to 70 percent of wages for employees dismissed after the age of 60 years;[104] and thirdly an agreement of 14 October 1974, guaranteed to employees dismissed on grounds of rationalization or recession the payment for 1 year of an amount equal to 90 percent of their former wages.

The system of benefits payable under the unemployment insurance scheme was remodelled with effect from 1 July 1979, by a law of 16 January 1979, and a national agreement of 16 March 1979, in order to mitigate certain inequalities, but without seriously affecting the underlying structure of payments. Public aid was, however, abolished and replaced by a global subsidy from the state for unemployment insurance.[105]

In 1978, of an average of 1 328 300 persons seeking employment, 276 210 received payments from public aid alone, and 389 740 received unemployment insurance benefit, either alone or in conjunction with public aid. Thus nearly one out of every two who were seeking employment drew some kind of benefit in respect of unemployment.

In addition to total unemployment, there is also a system of benefit for partial unemployment, under which an allowance is paid by the government, with supplementary payments sometimes being made under the terms of collective agreements.

Social Aid

A decree of 29 November 1953, replaced the expression 'public assistance' by that of 'social aid' and established a specialized public service, staffed, at the level of the communes or groups of communes, by the social aid bureaux. Unlike social security, social aid does not constitute a global system, but is broken down into distinct and independent forms of action, such as medical aid, aid for the aged, for the handicapped, for families, for children, and so forth. The granting of a particular form of aid is never permanent and claimants have to show details of their particular need and re-establish their need when required. To this extent the techniques of social aid have not broken completely with the practice of charity and public assistance.

An important trend was set by the law of 30 June 1975 which recast the social status of handicapped persons, placing them under the social security system, social action and social aid. The special education allowance and the allowance for handicapped adults have been brought into the family allowance system.

In general terms this legislation aims at making the handicapped the responsibility of society, a policy which raises complex problems going beyond the scope of this paper.

Social Action

Social Action is still an imprecise concept, the content of which is so varied and its forms so diverse that it is at times identical with social aid. If social aid can be defined as compulsory, specialized aid, social action remains discretionary and general in the sense that it can be available to the whole of a given population. Social action consists, as a general rule, in discretionary action by social institutions. A law of 30 June 1975, aims to give these institutions a legal status. For the purposes of this law social institutions are all public or private organizations whose principal objects include the following regular activities: carrying on, in collaboration with social workers and multidisciplinary teams, action of a social or medico-social nature, particularly the provision of information, prevention, investigation, guidance and support; and receiving and providing shelter for minors and adults requiring special protection and placing them with families.

In fact, leaving aside the social security institutions which have their own particular functions in relation to health and welfare, there are two categories of social institutions: public sector institutions, i.e. principally the social aid bureaux, which, in addition to making social aid payments, organize their own forms of social action at the level of the communes with regard to welfare, mutual aid, and social hygiene, as well as old people's homes, health education centres, child care homes, sheltered workshops, etc. run by public law corporations; and private sector institutions, a long list running from charitable foundations to the social work of friendly societies or works' committees, the definition of which is based on the concept of an undertaking, that is to say, on the requirement of a group of people and the use of funds, without necessarily excluding the object of making a profit.

It is thus the function of social action to innovate and to try out new forms of action which may subsequently be made compulsory as part of social aid or social security.

The Friendly Societies

With the extension of social security, it might have been thought that friendly societies would experience a decline since they were now reduced to covering the insured's share of the costs. However, the contrary has happened. There were more than 20 million friendly society members in France in 1975, against 13 million in 1964 and this trend seems to have continued since then. The friendly societies, in accordance with their objects, have succeeded in adapting to new circumstances by promoting free care and a higher standard of care thanks to a network of agreements with both public and private hospitals allowing payment by a third party and to the creation of health establishments, pharmacies owned by the societies and so on. Their success expresses above all the desire of the population for free health care without having to make an additional financial effort for this purpose.

Social Guarantees by Contract

Finally, we must add to the additional benefits those of a strictly contractual character since they are paid by the employer or by an insurance organization by virtue either of a collective agreement, such as one for the monthly payment of wages, or of a group insurance contract.

For a long time collective agreements provided for the payment by the employer of sums to compensate for loss of earnings by reason of holidays, or absence on account of sickness or family circumstances, as well as payments on dismissal or retirement. These guarantees were, however, generally reserved for management staff, technical employees, supervisors and foremen, i.e., for monthly paid staff, rather than those paid by the hour. In recent years collective agreements at company level, and then a national collective agreement of 10 December 1977, extended the principle of monthly payment of wages to hourly workers and thus conferred on them the benefits attached to monthly payment. This national agreement was made of general application by a law of 19 January 1978, which fixed the minimum rates of the payments.[106]

Group insurance contracts are generally made by supplementary pension institutions with insurance companies in order to provide, in return for a compulsory contribution, the benefit of supplementary cover against various risks, such as sickness, accident, death etc. This practice allows the insurance companies, who very often manage the funds of the supplementary pension institutions, to compete more or less fairly with the friendly societies. This type of contract is also used by employers, either to secure performance of their above-mentioned contractual obligations through a third party, or to guarantee their employees, and especially management staff, against particular risks, by providing additional compensation for accidents at work, payment of a lump sum on death etc.

The inadequacy of compulsory social security payments thus led to the creation of a parallel network of institutions and of supplementary social payments.

The Field of Action of the Insurance Companies

The insurance companies finally made the breakthrough into the field of social provision under the Fifth Republic. They had, of course, in practice retained their monopoly of life insurance, after the advent of social security, for the death insurance provided under the social security scheme was, and remains, limited to the grant of a modest lump sum[107] to the family of the deceased; they were also called upon, however, to play an active part in the administration of sickness and maternity insurance and the insurance against accidents at work and outside work for those engaged in agriculture, and sickness and maternity insurance for the self-employed outside agriculture.

Moreover, under the cover of group insurance contracts concluded with the supplementary pension offices and with employers, they sought to occupy the ground left free by social security and to compete with the friendly societies, where necessary, for the management for profit of a whole sector of social provision which they considered worthwhile.

There is thus a clear contradiction between the employers' revolt against the burden of social security contributions and their support for the creation of supplementary institutions and the profitable action of the insurance companies. In reality, this contradiction conceals either a shifting of the share of the social burden from businesses on to the individual, or the possibility for employers to make selective decisions at the level of supplementary payments and the persons to be benefited, which is an additional factor in producing social inequalities.

After the failure of the plan for unification of the system, social security runs the risk of suffering a degree of disintegration before the pendulum swings back again.

CONCLUSION: A CRITICAL VIEW

At the end of this account of the development of social provision from the beginning of the industrial revolution to the present day, we conclude by looking back over the path followed and looking forward to future trends after the present economic crisis.

THE FACTS

A compulsory system of social provision has had great difficulty in establishing itself in France. The bourgeoisie was long hostile to the creation of any legal obligation which might conflict with the autonomy of the individual will, a fact which explains why state intervention came so late in this area:

1898   employers' liability was based upon the concept of occupational risk with regard to compensation for accidents at work;
1910   the first legal obligation was introduced in connection with pensions for industrial and agricultural workers;
1930   compulsory social insurance came into force for employed workers.

Even when the question of making the social security system applicable to the entire population was placed on the agenda (1945–1946), the state continued to hold fast to two principles: respect for the wishes of socio-occupational groups in a spirit of social conservatism, and refusal to become financially involved so that it was merely a sort of manager of a fragmented social security system.

The State as Manager

In contrast with the concept of the social state which lies at the origin of social insurance in Germany, the state in France has always insisted, from the moment when intervention on its part became inevitable, on being no more than a manager of a compulsory system of social provision, limiting its role to legislation, regulation and control of the management of the system, and rejecting any financial obligation on its part, other than in exceptional circumstances. Thus, in the French tradition, the position adopted with regard to social provision consists, since an edict of Colbert in 1673 which established the first pension scheme for seamen,[108] in making potential beneficiaries pay for the scheme.

It is no accident, therefore, that, of all the Common Market countries, France is the one in which the state contributes least to the cost of social provision.[109] The conclusion to be drawn is that the state manages the social security system more or less directly, but finances it to the least possible extent.

The Fragmentation of Social Security

On the other hand, as we have seen, respect for the wishes of socio-occupational groups has ended in the breakdown of the plan for the unification of social security and has left in its place three major schemes corresponding to the principal components of French society.[110]

First the general scheme for employees in industry and commerce and others, which covers around 13 million people, plus a total of 4.5 million belonging to various other autonomous special schemes for employees, or schemes attached to the general scheme, among whom are 1.5 million public servants, 800 000 local government officers, 500 000 students, and 360 000 servicemen and women. Secondly the agricultural scheme which covers around 700 000 farmworkers and 2.1 million farmers. Thirdly the scheme for self-employed workers outside agriculture which covers 1.52 million people, consisting of 700 000 businessmen and tradesmen, 600 000 craftsmen and 220 000 members of the profession.

These major social security schemes, which have more or less split up into special, sectoral schemes, sometimes flanked by supplementary regimes which have themselves become legal, as in the case of old age and unemployment, do not cover every need, however. Some disparities and gaps remain. In this monumental social labyrinth, it is often the poorest who enjoy the least protection, while those who are better off gain most from the system.[111]

One may properly ask whether the result of this is, if not a redistribution of incomes in the wrong direction, at least a new source of social inequality, made worse by the current economic crisis.

THE CRISIS

Social security has not avoided the effects of the economic crisis which has been shaking the country for several years, and which has undermined the financial equilibrium of the system and may result in its dislocation.

The Repercussions of the Economic Crisis

Since 1975, the operation of the set-off between schemes on the basis of the demographic relationship between active and inactive schemes and of the real contributive capacity of those covered by the schemes has placed the main weight of the financial burden on the general scheme for employed workers. At a time of crisis, the slowing down in the rate of increase in earnings, the existence of a permanent pool of 1–1½ million unemployed, and the increase in employers' indebtedness deprive the general scheme of considerable resources. This results in a serious disturbance of its financial equilibrium.

Since the beginning of the crisis the government has reacted, one step at a time, preferring to raise the workers' contributions so as not to lessen the competitiveness of French businesses. However, the cutting of the purchasing power of wages, which helps to fuel the economic crisis by reducing domestic consumption, is on the way to reaching saturation point.

As the system becomes difficult to control at the financial level, some of those who are traditionally hostile to social security would like to solve the difficulties by breaking the system up and sating the appetites of the insurance companies which are lying in wait.

The Danger of Dislocation of the Social Security System

The government plan to introduce a three stage system of social protection, more or less on Common Market lines.[112]

1. *A public service* derived from public assistance, to guarantee for each individual basic health care and a minimum of welfare protection, having regard, where appropriate, to his personal means.
2. *A system based on collective agreements* administered on a basis of parity of representation with the collaboration of insurance companies and designed to provide supplementary payments so as to insure the labour force in its various socio-occupational groups.
3. *A free system* of individual protection, based entirely upon the principle of capitalization and managed, for profit, by insurance companies so as to attract private savings in the direction of an industrial over-concentration.

However, a system such as this very probably has more drawbacks than advantages, for it would undoubtedly lead to *a reduction in social payments,* under the cover of accrued individual responsibility, the full force of which would fall on the poorest categories of people, to *a permanent reduction in the value of old age pensions,* with the introduction of capitalization, because of the rate of interest being rendered negative by price inflation, and to *a destabilization of industrial society,* as the instrument of social regulation which it has acquired with such difficulty and patience begins to atrophy.

However that may be, social security is so firmly anchored in our way of life, and has become so indispensable for the development of modern societies that it would rise again from the ashes. It is to the future that we must now turn.

The Outlook for the Future

Social security has passed through two stages — insurance of the labour force in the Bismarckian sense and, in its more modern conception, protection of the entire population against the social risks of life — and is now, through all the changes to which every social institution is subject, about to reach a third stage — that of satisfying new human aspirations which are coming to maturity through the advance of science and the production of material goods. Among these it is possible to identify: *the right to life,* which raises complex questions of birth control, prevention of abortion and the adaptation of society to the increased human expectation of life; *the right to health*, which implies, not only that health care should be free[113] and that every person should have access to care of high quality, but also that negative attitudes to illness must be changed, such as prohibiting dismissal of a sick employee without first ensuring his means of existence, or preventing harassment through medical checks for non-therapeutic ends; *the right to well-being*, which implies improvement in conditions of work, in housing, in transport etc., and the prevention of accidents at work and on the roads — in a word, that the production of goods and services should be organized on a human scale based on the individual's creativity and need for contact with his fellow men.

If it does this, will not social security be returning to the conception of it contained in the Universal Declaration of Human Rights of 10 December 1948? It is right to remind ourselves of the terms of the Declaration, for, apart from its effect on the positive law of nations, this universal conception of social security is now part of human consciousness:

> Article 22: Everyone, as a member of society, has the right to social security and is entitled to the realization, through national effort and international co-operation and in accordance with the organisation and resources of each state, of the economic, social and cultural rights indispensable for his dignity and the free development of his personality.
> Article 25: 1. Everyone has the right to a standard of living adequate for the health and well-being of himself and of his family, including food, clothing, housing and medical care and necessary social services, and the right to security in the event of unemployment, sickness, disability, widowhood, old age or other lack of livelihood in circumstances beyond his control.
> 2. Motherhood and childhood are entitled to special care and assistance. All children, whether born in or out of wedlock, shall enjoy the same social protection.

GENERAL BIBLIOGRAPHY

E. Alfandari (1977). *Aide Sociale et Action Sociale (Social Aid and Social Action)*, 2nd edn, Dalloz, Paris.

M. Bouvier-Ajam (1969). *Histoire du Travail Depuis la Révolution (History of Labour Since the Revolution)*, LGDJ, Paris.

D. Ceccaldi (1957). *Histoire des Prestations Sociales en France (History of Social Benefits in France)*, UNCAF, Paris.

L. Chevalier (1958). *Classes Laborieuses et Classes Dangereuses à Paris Pendant la Première Moitié du XIX° Siècle. (Working classes and Dangerous Classes in Paris During the First Half of the Nineteenth Century)*, Plon, Paris.

E. Dolleans (1957). *Histoire du Mouvement Ouvrier (History of the Labour Movement)*, vol. I, *1830–1871*, A. Colin, Paris.

J. Doublet (1972). *Sécurité Sociale (Social Security)*, 5th edn, PUF, Paris.

J.J. Dupeyroux (1977). *Droit de la Sécurité Sociale (The Law of Social Security)*, 7th edn, Précis Dalloz, Paris.

P. Durand (1953). *La Politique Contemporaine de Sécurité Sociale (Contemporary Social Security Policy)*, Dalloz, Paris.

J. Fournier and N. Questiaux (1976). *Traité de Droit Social (Treatise of Social Law)*, Dalloz, Paris.

H.C. Galant (1955). *Histoire Politique de la Sécurité Social Française 1945–1952 (Political History of French Social Security 1945–1952)*, A. Colin, Paris.

X. Greffe (1976). *La Politique Sociale (Social Policy)*, PUF, Paris.

H. Hatzfeld (1971). *Du paupérisme à la Sécurité Sociale 1850–1940 (From Pauperism to Social Security 1850–1940)*. A. Colin, Paris.

P. Laroque (1953). *Refléxions sur le Problème Social (Reflections on the Social Question)*, ESF, Paris.

T. Laurent (1973). *La Mutualité Française et le Monde du Travail (French Friendly Societies and the World of Labour)*, Paris.

R. Lavielle (1964). *Histoire de la Mutualité Française (The History of Friendly Societies in France)*, Hachette, Paris.

F. Netter (1959). *La Sécurité Sociale et ses Principes (Social Security and its Principles)*, Sirey, Paris.

A. Rey (1925). *La Question des Assurances Sociales (The Question of Social Insurance)*, Paris.

Y. Saint-Jours (1980). *Le Droit de la Sécurité Sociale (The Law of Social Security)*, LGDJ, Paris.

R. Saleilles (1897). *Les Accidents du Travail et la Responsabilité Civile (Accidents at Work and Civil Liability)*, Paris.

R. Talmy (1962). *Histoire du Mouvement Familial en France 1896-1939 (History of the Family Movement in France 1896-1939)*, CAF.

Villermé (1840). *Tableau de l'État Physique et Moral des Ouvriers Employés dans les Manufactures de Soie, Coton et Laine (A Description of the Physical and Moral State of the Workers Employed in Silk, Cotton and Wool Mills)*, Renouard, Paris.

NOTES TO GENERAL OUTLINE

1   The Law Le Chapelier of 14-17 June 1791 followed the decree Allarde of 2-17 March 1791 which established the principle of freedom of labour as opposed to the system of *corporations*.

2   Law of 2 August 1868.

3   Law No. 74-1094 of 24 December 1974, concerning social security protection for all French persons.

NOTES TO MAIN TEXT

1   Villermé (1840). *Tableau de l'État Physique et Moral Des Ouvriers Employés dans les Manufactures de Soie, Coton et Laine (A Description of the Physical and Moral State of Workers Employed in Silk, Cotton and Wool Mills)*, Renouard, Paris.

2   Achille Pénot: *Discours sur Quelques Recherches de Statistiques Comparées Faites à Mulhouse (Discussion of Certain Comparative Statistical Research Done at Mulhouse)*, September 1848, Published by the author.

3   E. Buret (1840). *De la Misère des Classes Laborieuses en Angleterre et en France (The Misery of the Working Classes in England and France)*, Paulin, Paris.

4   See the authors cited by E. Dolléans (1957). *Histoire du Mouvement Ouvrier (History of the Labour Movement)*, vol. I, *1830-1871*, A. Colin, Paris.; M. Bouvier-Ajam (1969). *Histoire du Travail Depuis la Révolution (History of Labour since the Revolution)*, LGDJ, Paris.; and H. Hatzfeld (1971). *Du Paupérisme à la Sécurité Sociale 1850-1940 (From Pauperism to Social Security 1850-1940)*, A. Colin, Paris.

5   The slogan of the silk-weavers of Lyons testifies to this state of mind: 'To live in toil or to die in battle.'

6   Several texts to this effect may be cited: the decree Allarde of 2-17 March 1791, establishing the principle of freedom of labour as opposed to the *corporations* of the *ancien régime*; the Law Le Chapelier of 14-17 June 1791, rejecting any reconstitution of *corporations* and prohibiting workers and journeymen from forming associations to protect their alleged common interests, and finally the Penal Code of 1810 which made illegal every unauthorized combination of more than twenty persons.

7   See particularly Agricol Perguidier (1854). *Les Mémoires d'un Compagnon (The Recollections of a Journeyman)*, Geneva; re-published 1914 Rivière, Paris. P. Moreau (1843). *De la Réforme des Abus du Compagnonage à l'Amélioration du Sort des Travailleurs (Reform of the Abuses of the Journeyman System to Improve the Lot of Workers)*, Prévot, Paris. M. Gosset (1842). *Projet Tendant à Régénérer le Compagnonage sur le Tour de France Soumis a tous les Ouvriers (A Plan for Reviving the Journeyman System in France Addressed to all Workers)* published by the author, Paris.

8   See especially Louis Chevalier (1958). *Classes Laborieuses et Classes Dangereuses à Paris Pendant la Première Moitié du XIX° Siècle (Working Classes and Dangerous Classes in Paris During the First Half of the Nineteenth Century)*, Plon, Paris.

9   A. Thiers (1880). 'Rapport fait au nom de la commission de l'assistance' ('Report prepared in the name of the commission on public assistance') in *Discours Parlementaires de M. Thiers ('Thiers'*

Parliamentary Papers), part III published by M. Calmon; vol. VIII. Calman Lévy, Paris.

10 With the margin of approximation and accuracy inevitable in a generalized statement.

11 Marx and Engels published the Communist Manifesto in 1848.

12 This was the case in particular with the Comte Albert de Mun.

13 See R. Lavielle (1964). *Histoire de la Mutualité Française (The History of Friendly Societies in France)*, Hachette. T. Laurent (1973). *La Mutualité Française et le Monde du Travail (French Friendly Societies and the World of Labour)*, Paris.

14 See F. Netter (1963). 'Les retraites en France avant le XX° siècle' ('Pensions in France before the twentieth century'), *Droit Social, 358*; (1965). 'Les retraites en France au cours de la période 1895–1945 ('Pensions in France during the period 1895–1945') *Droit Social,* **448** and **514**.

15 Office du Travail (1898). *Les Caisses Patronales de Retraite des Établissements Industriels (Labour Office: Works' Pension Funds in Industrial Establishments)* Imprimerie nationale, Paris.

16 Pension funds could also have been set up in commercial and financial establishments, but these do not figure in the results of the enquiry.

17 Decision of the Cour de Cassation, 18 January 1872, cited by Netter in his study of pensions in France before the twentieth century (above, note 14).

18 See D. Ceccaldi (1957). *Histoire des Prestations Familiales en France (History of Family Allowances in France)*, UNCAF, Paris.

19. Legislate Assembly, 10 June 1850. Moniteur universel, 11 June 1850.

20 Léon Bourgeois, the apostle of solidarism, declared himself to be equally in favour of the subsidized voluntary system.

21 Chamber of Deputies, 15 June 1903: *Journal Officiel–Débats parlementaires*, 16 June 1903, p. 1974.

22 Chamber of Deputies, 25 June 1901 (2nd session): *Journal Officiel–Débats parlementaires*, 26 June 1901, p. 1568.

23 The provisions of the Criminal Code, which have never been repealed, clearly demonstrate this repressive approach: Article 269: 'Vagrancy is a delict'; Article 270: 'Vagrants or vagabonds are those who have neither a fixed abode nor means of subsistence and who follow no regular trade or profession'; Article 271: 'Vagrants or vagabonds who have been duly found to be such shall be punished by imprisonment for three to six months'.

24 J. Barthélemy (1910). L'effort charitable de la III° République' (The charitable effort of the Third Republic'), *Revue de droit public,* p. 334. Derouin, Gory and Worms (1914). *Traité d'Assistance Publique (Public Assistance),* 2 vols.

25 H. de Villeneuve and others (1811). *L'Assistance aux Vieillards, aux Infirmes et Autres Incurables (Public Assistance for the Aged, the Infirm and the Incurably Sick),* Paris.

26 Figures quoted by E. Alfandari (1977). *Aide Sociale, Action Sociale (Social Aid, Social Action),* Dalloz, 2nd edn., p. 9, Dalloz, Paris.

27 Martin-Nadaud (1880). *Débats parlementaires. Chambre des Députés,* no. 2680.

28 This theory had two enthusiastic adherents: in France; Sauzet (1883). 'Responsabilité des patrons envers les ouvriers' ('Employers' liability to their workers'), *Revue critique* **596** et seq.; and in Belgium Sainctelette (1884). *Responsabilité et Garantie (Liability and Guarantee),* p. 140, no. 13. Brussels.

29 See the decision of the Belgian Cour de Cassation, 8 January 1886 (Sirey 1886.5.25) While admitting that the contract of employment was the source of the employer's liability, the decision did, however, place upon the worker the burden of proving fault on the part of the employer.

30 Cour d'appel at Rennes, 20 March 1893 (Dalloz périodique 1893.2.256).

31 Cour cassation 21 novembre 1911. Dalloz 1913-1. 249 note Sarrut Sirey. 1912-1-73-note Lyon-Caen.

31bis And particularly Saleilles (1897). *Les Accidents du Travail et la Responsabilité Civile (Accidents at Work and Civil Liability),* Paris. Josserand (1897). *De la Responsabilité des Choses Inanimees (Liability for Inanimate things).*

32 See the submissions of deputy procureur Faidher adopted by the Brussels court in its decision of 31 May 1871 (Belgique judiciàire, 1871, col. 758). The judgment contains the following two clauses in particular:

Whereas it follows clearly from the text of Article 1384 of the Code Civil that the owner of a thing, even an inanimate thing, which he has under his control, is liable for damage caused by that thing,

Whereas if one looks to the spirit of this provision, one is convinced that this liability arises at the moment when damage results from the action of the thing, without more; and that it is in fact natural and logical that the owner of a thing, who has the right and the duty of supervision and management of it, should be legally presumed to be in a state of fault from the moment when this thing causes damage.

33   It was only in 1904 that the Belgian Cour de Cassation adopted the view put forward by deputy procureur Faidher and the Brussels court: Pasicrisie (1904) 246.

34   Conseil d'Etat, 21 June 1895. Cames. Recueil 509 (submissions by Romieu). Sirey 1897.3.33 (submissions by Romieu and note by Hauriou). Dalloz R. 1896.3.65 (submissions by Romieu).

35   Cour de Cassation, 16 June 1896. Dalloz périodique 1897.1.43 (note by Saleilles). Sirey 1897.1.17 (note by Esmein). The Cour de Cassation did not finally admit the presumption of liability against the person having control of a dangerous thing, based on Article 1384 (1) of the Code Civil until 1930, in the Jand'heur case (Full Court, 13.2.1930 with the submissions by Matter, Dalloz 1930.1.64, Gazette du Palais 1930.1.393).

36   Cour de Cassation, 15 July 1941 (Full Court). Dalloz critique 1941.117 (note by A. Rouast). La Semaine juridique 1941, 1705 (note by J. Mihura).

37   Cour de Cassation, 7 April 1921 (Full Court). Sirey 1922.1.81 (note by Sachet).

38   See Lavielle (1964). *Histoire de la Mutualité (History of the Friendly Societies)*, p. 55, Hachette.

39   Speech given at a banquet attended by 20 000 in the Galerie des Machines, a relic of the 1900 Exhibition, on the Champs de Mars.

40   Speech of Napoleon III, cited by Emile Laurent (1865). *Le Paupérisme et les Associations de Prévoyance (Pauperism and Welfare Associations)*, vol. I, p. 286, Paris.

41   Cited by A. Rey (1925). *La Question des Assurances Sociales (The Question of Social Insurance)*, p. 344, Paris.

42   Christian trade unionism only really began to develop with the formation of the Confédération française des traveailleurs chrétiens (CFTC) in 1919.

43   It was not until 1909, however, that a law was promulgated dealing with railway workers' pensions.

44   Chamber of Deputies, session of 10 June 1901. *Journal Officiel–Débats parlementaires*, 11 June 1901.

45   The number of contributors rose from 2.281 million in 1911 to 3.437 million in 1913, but fell to 1.798 million in 1920 and to 1.728 million in 1922.

46   R. Talmy (1962). *Histoire du Mouvement Familial en France, 1896–1939 (History of the Family Movement in France, 1896–1939)*, vol. II, p. 124, C.A.F.

47   The number of contributors rose from 2.281 million in 1911 to 3.437 million in 1913, but fell to 1.798 million in 1920 and to 1.728 million in 1922.

48   It is to one Dr Abramovitch that we owe the saying 'Germany lost the war because she damaged her nervous system by social insurance', though he himself attributes it to a Swill colleague. *Revue médico-sociale*, July–August 1929.

49   Paul Pic (1922). 'Le nouveau projet de loi sur les assurances sociales' ('The new social insurance Bill'), *Revue Politique et Parlementaire*, April, p. 174.

50   Particularly the Confédération générale du travail unitaire (CGTU) which sometimes called the social insurance law a fascist law.

51   It was at this time that the union movement gained a foothold in the medical profession to maintain its independent status.

52   A. Rueff (1925). 'Les variations du chômage en Angleterre' ('The variations of unemployment in England'), *Revue Politique et Parlementaire*, December. See also (1931) 'L'assurance chômage: cause du chômage permanent' ('Unemployment insurance-cause of permanent unemployment'), *Revue d'Économie Politique*.

53   C. Colson (1926). 'L'assurance contre le chômage' ('Insurance against unemployment'), *Revue Politique et Parlementaire*, April, p. 5.

54   Within the framework of the general scheme of social insurance special schemes were preserved for miners, seamen and others.

55   Pierre Laroque (1948). 'De l'assurance sociale à la sécurité sociale: l'expérience française' ('From social insurance to social security: the French experience'), *Revue Internationale du Travail*, no. 6, pp. 624–645.

56   See particularly Henry C. Galant (1955). 'Histoire politique de la sécurité sociale française 1945–1952' ('The political history of French social security 1945–1952'). *Cahiers de la Fondation Nationale des Sciences Politiques*, A. Colin.

57   There are around thirty special schemes at the present time, covering public servants, electricity and gas, railways, Paris transport, notaries' clerks, Rhine boatmen etc.

58   I.e., in the event, sickness, maternity, disability, old age and death.

59   On the other hand, the law of 9 April 1898, continued to apply to workers employed in agriculture until the passing of the law of 25 October 1972.

60   Law of 23 September 1948.

61   Law of 17 April 1949.

62   Law of 21 July 1949.
63   Law of 29 April 1954.
64   There are no contributions paid by employees except in relation to social insurance. Employers alone pay contributions in respect of accidents at work, since these continue to be their financial responsibility, as well as the family allowances contributions because of their origin as wage supplements.
65   The composition of the boards of management of the family allowance offices was necessarily different: 50 percent employees, 25 percent employers, 25 percent self-employed.
66   The social security offices are in effect considered as private organizations entrusted with the provision of a public service since the decision of the Conseil d'Etat of 13 May 1938. Dalloz 1939.3.65 (note by Pepy).
67   See particularly: J. Moitrier (1973). 'La tutelle sur les organismes de sécurité sociale' ('The control of social security organizations') *Droit Social* p. 186. H. Delabre and M. Lombardot (1971). 'Réflexion sur la tutelle administrative' ('Reflections on administrative control') *Revue française des Affaires Sociales*, no. 1.
68   Law of 25 June 1947.
69   See Evelyne Sullerot (1978). 'La démographie en France: bilan et perspectives' ('Demography in France: the present balance and future outlook') *Report to the Economic and Social Council. La documentation française.*
70   Law of 1 September 1948, which also dealt with rents in old buildings.
71   Under Article 17 of the ordinance of 4 October 1945, special schemes applied particularly to the following: public servants, workers employed by the state, officers of communes and departments, seamen, miners, railways, electricity and gas, water, the Banque de France, the opera, the comic opera, and the Comédie Française.
72   E.g., the special schemes for notaries' clerks, the Crédit Foncier, the Paris Chamber of Commerce etc.
73   In fact originally the majority of supplementary pension institutions had their headquarters in the offices of insurance companies who 'looked after' them.
74   Ordinance no. 58.1374 of 30 December 1958.
75   The unions did not fail to mobilize public opinion for this purpose.
76   Under Article 34 of the Constitution of 1958, the fundamental principles of social security fall within the exclusive competence of the legislature.
77   These manipulations consisted in charging items against the social security scheme which it should not have borne in order to relieve the State budget. See on this the Grégoire Report, published in 1976.
78   This report is better known as the Pichetti Report.
79   The structural reform was accompanied by a reduction in benefits and an increase in contributions.
80   Ordinances no. 67-706 to 709 of 21 August 1967, ratified by the law no. 68-698 of 31 July, 1968. Ratification should normally have occurred within 6 months.
81   Law of 22 June 1967.
82   The financial management of the scheme for accidents at work and of the family allowances scheme had already been separated from social insurance.
83   The existence of this one regional office is explained by the special scheme covering the three departments of Haut-Rhin, Bas-Rhin, and Moselle.
84   This influence has been exerted, as a general rule, by an alliance of the CNPF with one or other of the reforming unions.
85   The number is sometimes doubled, depending on the importance of the social security office.
86   Except in Alsace and Lorraine where the relationship between the CFDT and the CGT is reversed.
87   Family members mean ascendants, descendants, brothers, sisters and relations of the same degree by marriage of the head of the farm or his spouse, above the age of 16 years, who are living on the farm and working on it otherwise than as employees.
88   Article 1106-4-1 of the Code Rural.
89   Particularly by the ordinance of 27 September 1967, and the laws of 6 January 1970, and 27 December 1973.
90   Decree of 26 July 1977.
91   Y. Saint-Jours (1977). *Prévention et Responsabilité en Matière d'Accidents du Travail (Prevention and Liability with Regard to Accidents at Work)* (Commentary on the law of December 6, 1976), chron. p. 185, Dalloz, Paris. Nicole Catalá and J.C. Soyer (1977). 'La loi du 6 décembre 1976 relative au développement de la prévention des accidents du travail' ('The law of December 6, 1976, and the development of the prevention of accidents at work'), *La semaine Juridique* doct. 1.1. 2868.

92 See the Tribunal Correctionnel at Nevers, 24 January 1978, noted by Y. Saint-Jours, with regard to the imposition of a safety plan on the business. *Droit Social* (1979), p. 49.

93 The number of births was 875 000 in 1972 but has fallen under the impact of the economic crisis of 1973–1974 to less than 750 000 since 1975.

94 Law no. 74-1094 of 24 December 1974, which also introduces a set-off between the schemes based on compulsory social security. See also the law no. 75.574 of 4 July 1975, aimed at the generalization of social security.

95 Law no. 77-768 of 12 July 1977.

96 Loi no. 78-2 du 2 janvier 1978-art. 13.

97 There is currently a bill to this effect under consideration.

98 Pensions for public servants have been financed by the budget since a law of 9 June 1853.

99 Law no. 74.1094 of 24 December 1974 and the implementing decree no 75.773 of 21 August 1975.

100 See on this: J.F. Chadelat (1978). 'La compensation' ('The set-off') *Droit Social*, special number, p. 85.

101 Decrees no. 79-650 to 653 of 30 July 1979.

102 The CGT was not an original signatory of this agreement, but acceded to it subsequently.

103 This ordinance also extended benefit for total unemployment to non-titular officers of public administrative services.

104 Exceptionally, until 31 March 1981, employees who resign after the age of 60 can benefit from this guarantee of resources.

105 For a more detailed account the reader should refer to the UNEDIC circular no. 78-25 of 22 June 1979.

106 See Claude Desset (1978). 'Application et contenu de la loi sur la mensualisation' ('Application and content of the law on monthly payment of wages') *Revue pratique de Droit Social* p. 319.

107 Equal to 3-months' wages within the earnings limit for contributions.

108 The edict introduced 'half pay' (which was the name first given to retirement pensions) in order to keep seamen at the disposal of the service; the royal regulation of 23 September 1673 established a reserve fund for this purpose to deduct 6 deniers per pound of the pay of officers and all grades of seamen employed in the service of the King.

109 The figure for 1980 is 16.2 percent compared with 17.6 percent for the Netherlands, 20.8 percent for Belgium, 21.8 percent for Italy, 25.2 percent for Germany, 33.2 percent for Luxembourg, 41.7 percent for the United Kingdom, 62.3 percent for Ireland and 82.4 percent for Denmark, according to the projections in the European social budget.

110 These approximate figures are for 1978 and refer to active contributors and not potential beneficiaries; the figure for the latter, taking all schemes together, is around 54.05 million compared with 21.83 million contributors.

111 This phenomenon is known as the 'Mathieu effect': see Hermann Deleeck (1979). 'L'effet Mathieu' ('The Mathieu effect'), *Droit Social*, p. 375.

112 See J.J. Dupeyroux (1966). *Evolution et Tendances des Systémes de Sécurité Sociale des Pays Membres des Communautés Européenes et de la Grande-Bretagne (Development and Trends in the Social Security Systems of the Member Countries of the European Communities and Great Britain)*, Luxembourg. (A report commissioned by the European Coal and Steel Community).

113 The principle of free health care has not yet been established in France, except in certain special situations: accidents at work, maternity, insurance and long-term illnesses.

GREAT BRITAIN
by A.I. Ogus

INTRODUCTION

Social insurance was not introduced into Britain until 30 years after Bismarck's pioneering legislation, and the scheme which did emerge was different in significant respects from the German model. Progressively thereafter as it was extended and, eventually, reformulated, the British approach began increasingly to resemble continental equivalents.

In this study we trace the history of social insurance from its origins in the middle of the nineteenth century. In order to facilitate comparison with the German experience, the first section covers the period up to 1881, the date of Bismarck's legislation. We consider here the social, economic, political and philosophical background to such steps as were taken, public, voluntary and charitable, for the relief of poverty, and we essay some conclusions on why there was, at this time, no movement to introduce social insurance in Britain. In the second section (1881–1911), we then see how ideological and political developments combined to produce a number of different forms of legislative intervention designed to confer some protection against the major social hazards. The last of these was social insurance, and we attempt to explain why and how this method was finally adopted as the primary instrument of social welfare.

The third section then describes the evolution of social insurance from the National Insurance Act of 1911 to the legislation now in force. We see how, against the background of social and economic events, the schemes covering unemployment, health and pensions were formulated and extended. We then concentrate on Sir William Beveridge's rationalization of the social insurance principle, his proposals to consolidate and unify, and (to a lesser extent) modify existing schemes, and the legislation which implemented his recommendations. For reasons on which we elaborate, this legislation failed in its objectives, and we trace how increasing awareness of the limitations of the Beveridge approach forced governments in the 1960s and 1970s fundamentally to alter the structure of social insurance.

The section concludes with an extended analysis of the principles of social insurance as they have evolved from 1911 to the present day: we deal in turn with

*I am very grateful to Miss Lorraine Spence for her energy and enthusiasm in the typing of the manuscript.

social risks and the conditions of entitlement, the population covered by the scheme, the basis on which benefits are calculated, and the methods of financing, administration and adjudication.

In the concluding section, we provide a general perspective on the various functions of social insurance, drawing on the material which has been expounded in the main body of the report. We focus here on the legal and theoretical character of social insurance as a compromise between individualist and collectivist notions of welfare, and between private and public legal structures. We speculate on the economic function of the system as an instrument for the efficient allocation of resources, and for the redistribution of wealth. We also allude to its sociological role, as an endorsement of currently held social values, and as a means of constraining individual and bureaucratic behaviour.

HISTORICAL SUMMARY

There follows a historical summary of the main legislative developments in social security provision generally and social insurance in particular.

SOCIAL SECURITY PROVISION GENERALLY

Poor Law _

1834 *Poor Law Amendment Act.* The traditional form of relief for paupers was centralized. It was based on the principle of 'less eligibility': the welfare offered was not to exceed the standards enjoyed by the lowest paid workers. The able-bodied were confined to the workhouse; the aged and infirm were granted outdoor relief.

1852 *Poor Law Outdoor Relief Regulation Order.* In exceptional cases the workhouse condition for the able-bodied was replaced by a 'labour test': outdoor relief was granted in return for the execution of work obligations.

1911 *Relief Regulation Order.* The principles governing poor-law relief outside the workhouse were consolidated.

Industrial Accidents and Diseases

1880 *Employers Liability Act.* The circumstances in which a worker injured in the course of his employment could sue his employer were extended: where the accident resulted from the negligence of another employee entrusted with the supervision of work, the employer could no longer rely on the defence of 'common employment'.

1897 *Workmen's Compensation Act.* A workman suffering injury from specified employment was entitled to recover compensation from his employer without proof of neligence. Analogous provision was made for dependants in cases of death.

1906 *Workmen's Compensation Act.* The 1897 scheme was extended to cover industrial diseases and most of those occupations hitherto excluded.

Unemployment

1902 *Labour Bureaux (London) Act.* The metropolitan local authority was permitted to establish labour bureaux at which unemployed workmen could register.

1905   *Unemployed Workmen Act.* A national measure which enabled funds to be used by local authorities to assist unemployed persons to emigrate or move to another area, to provide temporary work, or to find more permanent employment.

1909   *Labour Exchanges Act.* A national system of labour exchanges, administered by the Board of Trade, was established.

1916   *National Insurance (Part II) (Munition Workers) Act.* From 1918, an unemployment donation was paid to ex-members of HM Forces who had failed to find work on their discharge from service.

1920   *Unemployed (Relief Works) Act.* Government departments and local authorities were given powers to acquire land and to spend funds on the setting up of work for unemployed persons.

1931   *Unemployment Insurance (National Economy) (No. 2) Order.* For those unemployed who failed to satisfy the continuity of contributions for the insurance benefit a new system of transitional payments was established. The payments, financed from general taxation, were subject to a means test administered by Public Assistance Authorities. Initial establishment in the insurance scheme was also required.

1934   *Unemployment Act.* Unemployment insurance was finally severed from unemployment assistance. A new body, the Unemployment Assistance Board, was established to determine entitlement to the latter, which was to be payable to all able-bodied unemployed persons below pensionable age whose resources (including those of other members of the household) were below a level prescribed by regulations.

1941   *Determination of Needs Act.* The household needs test under the unemployment assistance scheme was replaced by one based on the individual personal and family dependants' needs.

Sickness and Invalidity

1867   *Metropolitan Poor Law Act.* The Metropolitan Asylums Board was established. One of its functions was to organise the care and treatment of the sick poor.

1907   *Education (Administrative Provisions) Act.* Local education authorities were required to provide for the medical inspection of children.

1920   *Blind Persons Act.* The age of entitlement to the non-contributory old age pension was reduced to 50 for blind persons.

1946   *National Health Service Act.* A comprehensive health service, financed mainly from general taxation (though partly also from the national insurance fund) was introduced under which medical services and medicaments were made freely available to all. This replaced, *inter alia*, the system of medical benefits payable under the pre-war national health insurance scheme.

1970   *National Insurance Act.* A non-contributory attendance allowance was introduced for very severely disabled persons requiring attendance or supervision.

1975   *Social Security Benefits Act.* Two new non-contributory benefits were introduced to assist the long-term disabled: an invalidity pension, payable to those who could not satisfy the contribution conditions of the insurance benefit; and an invalid care allowance for persons who gave up full-time work to care for a severely disabled relative.

1975   *Social Security Pensions Act*. A non-contributory mobility allowance was introduced for persons unable, or virtually unable, to walk.

1977   *Non-Contributory Invalidity Pension (Amendment) Regulations*. Entitlement to the non-contributory invalidity pension was extended to women incapable of performing normal household duties.

Old Age

1908   *Old Age Pensions Act*. Pensions, financed from general taxation, were payable to persons aged 70 and above, whose means did not exceed a certain amount.

1940   *Old Age and Widows' Pensions Act*. Part II provided for supplementation of widows' and old age pensions through a needs test administered as under the unemployment assistance scheme by the Unemployment Assistance Board.

1970   *National Insurance Act*. A non-contributory pension became payable to those over pensionable age and who had retired but who were not covered by the post-war national insurance scheme.

1971   *National Insurance Act*. A non-contributory pension was introduced for all persons over 80 years not entitled to any other category of pension.

War Pensions

1915   *Ministry of Pensions Act*. A Ministry of Pensions was established to administer war pensions, which were however payable at the discretion of the Crown as part of the royal prerogative.

1919   *War Pensions (Administrative Provisions) Act*. A legal right to war pensions was introduced.

Family Endowment

1945   *Family Allowances Act*. Family allowances became payable to all families with two or more children under 16 years old.

1956   *Family Allowances and National Insurance Act*. The allowances were extended to children under 18 years receiving full-time education or in an apprenticeship.

1975   *Child Benefit Act*. Family allowances were replaced by child benefit which was also payable for the first child in a family. The benefit was eventually also to replace child tax allowances. Higher rates were granted for the children of a single parent family.

Social Assistance

1948   *National Assistance Act*. The Poor Law was abolished. Unemployment assistance and the means-tested supplementary allowance for widows and the aged were replaced by national assistance which was administered by the National Assistance Board and which was payable (broadly) to all those not in full-time work whose resources were insufficient to meet the statutorily prescribed requirements.

1966   *Ministry of Social Security Act*. National assistance was replaced by supplementary benefits payable as of *right* to those who formerly would have been entitled to national assistance. The functions of the National Assistance Board were transferred to the Ministry of Social Security and the Supplementary Benefits Commission.

1970 *Family Income Supplements Act*. A new non-contributory benefit was introduced to be paid to a family whose head was in full-time work but whose income was less than a prescribed level.

Social Insurance

1911 *National Insurance Act*. Two independently administered national insurance schemes were introduced. Part I established the health scheme under which there was compulsory insurance for (with some exceptions) all employed manual workers between 16 and 70, and other employed persons earning less than a prescribed amount. It provided for medical treatment and appliances and for flat-rate financial benefits for sickness, disablement and maternity. The scheme was mainly administered by independent approved societies (which were allowed to pay benefits above the national minimum). Part II established the unemployment scheme under which flat-rate benefits were payable for a maximum period of 15 weeks of unemployment in 1 year. It covered only workers in seven industries and was administered by the Board of Trade.

1920 *Unemployment Insurance Act*. The unemployment scheme was extended (with some exceptions, notably agriculture, domestic service and public service) to all manual workers and to other employees earning less than a prescribed amount.

1921 *Unemployment Insurance Act*. A special uncovenanted benefit became payable, at the discretion of the authorities, to those already established in the scheme but unable to satisfy the contribution conditions.

1921 *Unemployed Workers' Dependants Act*. Additions to the flat-rate unemployment benefit became payable to those with dependent spouses and children.

1925 *Widows', Orphans', and Old Age Contributory Pensions Act*. The health insurance scheme was extended to cover, (i) widows' pensions, payable on the husband's contributions, with additional allowances for children under 16, (ii) orphans' pensions payable to guardians for orphan children of insured persons or widows, and (iii) old age pensions, payable between the ages of 65 (insured women 60) and 70, when entitlement was transferred to the non-contributory pension but without a means test. Those not compulsorily insured under the health scheme could make contributions to the pensions scheme on a voluntary basis. It was administered by the Ministry of Health.

1927 *Unemployment Insurance Act*. The 'uncovenanted' benefit was replaced by 'transitional' benefit to which the claimant who satisfied the special conditions was entitled as of right.

1931 *Unemployment Insurance (National Economy) (No. 2) Order*. Transitional benefits were abolished and replaced by transitional 'payments', granted subject to a means test administered by public assistance authorities.

1934 *Unemployment Act*. The distinction between unemployment *insurance*, payable as of right to those who satisfied the contribution conditions, and unemployment *assistance*, payable subject to a means-test and to residual discretionary powers in the authorities to those not entitled to the insurance benefit, was consolidated by the separation both legally and administratively of the two schemes.

1936   *Unemployment Insurance (Agriculture) Act.* The unemployment scheme was extended to agriculture, though it was governed by special provisions.

1946   *National Insurance Act.* Following the Beveridge Report, the national insurance schemes were integrated into a single system administered by the Ministry of National Insurance. Of the many other modifications made, the most significant were: (i) extension of compulsory insurance to all members of the population of working age but with categorization into employed persons, self-employed persons, non-earners, and married women; (ii) additional benefits payable for maternity (interruption of earnings), and funeral expenses; (iii) replacement of medical benefits by the national health service; (iv) abolition of the approved societies, and the administration of sickness benefit assumed by the Ministry of National Insurance; (v) old age pensions replaced by retirement pensions — between the ages of 65 (women 60) and 70 (women 65) the claimant must have retired from full-time work; (vi) widows' benefit payable, after a short initial period, only if the claimant had children to care for or if she had reached a prescribed age; (viii) orphans' pension replaced by guardian's allowance.

1946   *National Insurance (Industrial Injuries) Act.* The workmen's compensation legislation was repealed and replaced by a new national insurance scheme for industrial accidents and diseases, funded independently of the general scheme. Benefits were payable for injury (short term, flat-rate), disablement (long term, with additions for lost or reduced earning capacity) and death (widows and other dependants). Only employees were covered, but there were no contribution conditions to be satisfied.

1957   *National Insurance Act.* A new benefit, the child's special allowance, became payable to a woman on the death of a former husband who had been maintaining a child or children in the care of that woman.

1959   *National Insurance Act.* A graduated pensions scheme was introduced for employees under which earnings-related retirement benefits became payable on the basis of earnings-related contributions. Contracting-out was permitted if the employee enjoyed rights under an occupational scheme at least as generous as those available under the state scheme.

1966   *National Insurance Act.* An earnings-related supplement became payable with the short-term benefits for unemployment, sickness, maternity and death.

1970   *National Insurance Act.* A new benefit, the invalidity allowance, was introduced for those incapable of work for a substantial period. The dependency additions to long-term benefits were also raised to a level substantially higher than those paid with short-term benefits.

1973   *Social Security Act.* The separate industrial injury fund was abolished. Henceforth, the industrial injury benefits were to be financed from the general national insurance fund.

1974   *National Insurance Act.* Parliament imposed on the administrators the duty to up-rate certain benefits in line with inflationary increases.

1975   *Social Security Act.* The flat-rate contribution system was replaced by one which was earnings-related; the self-employed paid on the basis of their taxable profits. Collection of contributions was integrated with income-tax collection.

1975   *Social Security Pensions Act.* A new earnings-related pension scheme was introduced for retirement, invalidity and death (widows' pensions). While employees participating in an approved occupational scheme were subject to a reduced contribution liability, such persons would nevertheless benefit from the state scheme's guarantee against inflation. The special rules under which married women earners paid reduced contributions and received reduced benefits were abolished. For pension purposes, persons spending part of their working life caring for children or relatives were granted special dispensations.

SOCIAL WELFARE FROM THE MID-NINETEENTH CENTURY

GENERAL BACKGROUND

Industrial Revolution and Socio-economic Developments

The background to the perceived need for institutionalized social welfare in the second half of the nineteenth century must be located first in the social, demographic, technological and economic changes which constituted what has conventionally been referred to as the Industrial Revolution.[a1] Why these changes took place in England before other European countries is a much disputed question:[a2] it is argued typically that the necessary spirit of innovation and entrepreneurial qualities resulted from a combination of the Protestant ethic, the strength of the individualist doctrine, a stable constitutional and legal system, and an open social structure which allowed for upward mobility.[a3]

In a narrow sense industrialization meant mechanization, itself the result of the astonishing degree of innovation in technology at the end of the eighteenth century; but in a broader sense it touched almost every area of social and economic life. Capital had to be made available and more freely transferable; hence the importance of the growth in banking and other financial enterprises. Labour had to be attracted from the land to the factory floor. The larger units resulting necessitated new forms of human organization: within individual enterprises this involved new forms of discipline to comply with the needs of the machine, the authority of the master, and the demands of the impersonal market forces. The results in terms of productivity were impressive: it has been estimated that the gross national product in England quadrupled in the course of the nineteenth century.[a4] But our chief concern here must be with the other side of the cost-benefit analysis: the social consequences of increased production and urbanization which provoked new attitudes and new efforts in social welfare.

Social Consequences of Industrialization

In the first place, there was a rapid expansion of the population.[a5] Paradoxically this was both a cause and a consequence of industrialization: the increased population promoted economic change, since it affected demand for the products of industry; and economic change led to even greater population growth in urban areas as a result of improved employment prospects and enlarged social contacts.

Larger families meant more mouths to feed and bodies to clothe. The supply of the appropriate commodities might be available to match the demand, but the more serious question was whether the distribution of wealth was such as to enable the labourer to afford them. Economic historians have been involved in a bitter dispute over the 'standard of living' question. [a6] No doubt there was a general rise in living standards, but the generally accepted view is that it was accompanied by a considerable shift in income distribution towards the rich. One reason for this was that the price of food rose higher than that of manufactured goods, and the poorer sections of the community spent proportionately more of their income on food. [a7]

Rapid urbanization gave rise to overcrowding in the towns; wretched housing conditions, squalor, degradation and disease. [a8] There was, perhaps, no other social condition in the nineteenth century which gave rise to so much concern, presumably because it had such an immediate impact on all members of society. It could be seen and smelt; moreover it was linked, perhaps rightly, with moral degradation: crime, prostitution, and drunkenness all flourished among the slums of the great cities.

Sickness, disability, and death resulted not only from general environmental factors but also more directly from inadequate working conditions. Child labour was not unknown before the Industrial Revolution but low standards of wages made it a widespread phenomenon in the early nineteenth century, and the discipline necessary for factory work as well as long hours, created an intolerable burden. [a9] Employers were slow to react to the dangers arising from the work: unfenced machinery was responsible for frequent physical injuries, and high temperature and humidity for respiratory diseases. [a10]

Ideologies

The social and economic changes and the conditions to which they gave rise must be viewed in the light of the political and economic philosophy which accompanied them and to a certain extent induced them. This period saw the emergence of a substantial and coherent body of writing, generally referred to as 'political economy'. [a11] Economic growth as the main constituent in human happiness was seen as the primary goal, and for Adam Smith that could be achieved by leaving all to pursue their own self-interest, uninhibited by state intervention:

> Every individual is continually exerting himself to find out the most advantageous employment for whatever capital he can command. It is his own advantage indeed and not that of society which he has in view. But the study of his own advantage naturally or rather necessarily leads him to prefer that employment which is of most advantage to society. [a12]

The free-market model of the economy was refined and elaborated by, among others, Ricardo and Senior. [a13] The implications for social welfare were clear: the individual as a free and rational human being should through his own efforts seek the maximization of his desires. The prevailing ideology of the first half of the nineteenth century was epitomized in the Report of the Poor Law Commission of 1834. [a14] Haunted by the alarming analysis of Malthus, who had seen the growth of population to have been a direct consequence of the overgenerous system of poor relief involved in the Speenhamland system, and concerned more with the existence of poverty rather than its causes, the Commission considered that the administration of poor relief had been too lax. Parish allowances in the form of relief of wages and additional payments for children had a demoralizing effect on the poor; they were encouraged to live at the community's expense and to produce children for whom they could not provide. The 'impotent poor', a category unable to act as rational maximizers, were to be given some relief, although at the barest minimum; the able-bodied, on the other hand, were to be deterred from idleness. The famous principle of 'less eligibility' was established: poor relief was only to be available to those whose want was clearly demonstrated by their acceptance of the rigours of the workhouse, the conditions of which were designed to be less attractive than the living circumstances of the lowest paid workers.

Collectivist Movements

To what extent were these individualist ideologies countered by collectivist movements? Emerging from the savage repression at the end of the eighteenth century (when the revolutionary excesses of the French were seen as a threat), the trade unions grew steadily in importance.[a15] The repeal of the Combination Laws in 1824 provoked a large number of strikes and in the following year their powers were restricted. Their activities were tolerated rather than encouraged, and as the Tolpuddle prosecutions of 1834[a16] were to reveal, militancy was to be quickly denounced and suppressed. Ambitious schemes for national cooperative movements to challenge the entire economic system were abandoned in favour of more modest and unco-ordinated growth in some of the key industries, the aim being to ensure collective bargaining. The proportion of the working population involved was still small and the one popular movement of the period, Chartism, though representing a spontaneous protest against the worst effects of industrialization, was too diverse in its membership, and insufficiently aggressive in its methods, to achieve any success.[a17] Some of its disappointed leaders turned to socialism, but this was not to gain any hold on the public attention until the 1880s.

Legal Framework

The importance of the legal system in its underlying support of individualist capitalism is still insufficiently understood by social and economic historians.[a18] Arguably the peculiar features of the legal framework in England played a considerable part both in providing the facilities for the rapid industrialization of the nineteenth century, and (in comparison with Germany for example) in delaying the introduction of centralized social insurance until the twentieth century.[a19] In the first place, there was a striking community of interests and sharing of ideology between the political economists and the practising lawyers, notably the judiciary.[a20] Perhaps at no other time in English legal history were current ideas in social philosophy so readily assimilated and even expounded by the judges. The second crucial element, and one peculiar to the anglo-saxon systems, was the primacy of the customary, or common law. This manifested itself in two different senses. On the one hand, judge-made law was seen as somewhat akin to natural law, superior in status and in content to Parliamentary law.[a21] Of course, due recognition and effect had to be given to statutes, but they were interpreted restrictively, as unwanted interventions on judicial power. On the other hand, within the judge-made law itself, the body of law emanating from the common law courts, with its emphasis on the strictness of property and contract rights, was to prevail more than previously over 'equity', the body of law emanating from the Court of Chancery, where the emphasis was more on individualized justice and the protection of the weaker members of the community.[a22] The nineteenth century saw the elaboration of the classical law of contract, transactions freely entered into by individuals to be enforced without regard to the 'fairness' of their content, and the development of assignable property rights, unencumbered by feudal and other fetters.[a23] The contribution of this law to capitalist enterprise can hardly be exaggerated and it was aided by an extension of juristic ideas into corporate personality (the evolution of company law[a24]) and negotiable instruments.[a25] Significantly, tort law, which was seen as a burden on economic enterprise, was much slower to develop. The doctrine of 'common employment', according to which a worker was deemed to 'accept the risk' of injuries caused by the fault of a fellow worker, and which was laid down in 1826, epitomizes the attitude.[a26]

The strength of private law, upholding the free-market system, is of course to be contrasted with the weakness of public law. While efficacious remedies had been devised by the judiciary to protect individuals against abuses of government power,[a27] these may be seen essentially as a complement of the common law efforts to protect freedom of action and of enterprise. Public law, in the sense of the direction of commerce and social activity in the furtherance of welfare ideals, was hindered by the paucity of the legal concepts to embrace such provisions and the lack of administrative machinery to enforce them.[a28] Centralized bureaucracy hardly existed; the machinery for such regulatory controls as did exist had to be accommodated within the framework of local government, where commercial interests predominated.

State Intervention and Social Legislation

Limits of Laissez-faire

The individualist philosophy, advocating self-help, and condemning state intervention ('letting alone should be the general practice, every departure from it, unless required by some great good, is a certain evil'[a29]) was neither absolute, nor so generally accepted, as some writers would have us believe. Important social legislation was passed in the first half of the nineteenth century. Our first task, then, is to see how this form of state intervention was to be reconciled with the prevailing social and economic philosophy.[a30]

Undoubtedly it is a mistake to identify the highly influential utilitarianism of Bentham and J.S. Mill completely with *laissez-faire*. The pursuit of the greatest happiness for the greatest number, to be achieved through the exercise of individual liberty, could only succeed if it were to take place within the context of a harmonious and orderly society, and this could be assured only by the state. If Adam Smith had rather blithely visualized a natural harmony of interests resulting from the free interplay of market forces, Bentham saw the need, in certain circumstances, to create, by intervention, an artificial harmony. There was, in other words, a minimum of good order and decency of living which only the state could preserve.[a31] Such an attitude could be used to justify not only the criminal law, and the public enforcement of property rights, but also the administration of the Poor Law, the advancement of education and, within certain limits, the safeguard of public health.

It may be, too, that we have to recognize an almost inevitable discrepancy between ideology and social reality.[32] Theoreticians, having 'discovered' the tenets of economic science, and being unable to verify them by empirical means, would understandably elaborate on them in a world insulated from the horrors of the industrial slums and the mines and factories.

While it would be wrong to minimize the role played by genuine philanthropists such as Shaftesbury in the control of working conditions,[33] it must be appreciated also that much of the effort behind the legislation shortly to be described was motivated by a conviction that the productivity of the working force would be improved if their health and lives were to be protected. As Franklin had observed, 'public health was public wealth'.[34] The Children's Employment Commission, for example, saw reform as necessary in the interests of the future of the working force, and in the preservation of morality and public order.[35]

Process of State Intervention

It has been surmised that, whatever the motivation, ideological or pragmatic, for the intervention, the process by which government first took cognizance of an evil and then sought to remedy it normally took the following form.[36] First came the revelation of an evil which was found to be intolerable and which, perhaps rashly, it was assumed could simply be eradicated by legislation in the appropriate form. At the second stage, it was appreciated that without an administrative machinery to enforce the legislative prohibition, the measure was useless. Legislation replacing the first would, therefore, provide for some form of inspectorate. While in theory this might be adequate, in practice there was insufficient expertise over the nature of the problem, and the means of controlling it. Therefore there would emerge a body of professionals familiar with the problems and the creation of a centralized agency to supervise the localized inspectorate. Finally, as scientific aids were introduced and overspecific regulation became too cumbersome, new legislation would confer a high degree of discretion on those administering the system, thus diverting the law-creation role from Parliament to the specialized agency within the executive.

Areas of Social Legislation

It would be tedious, and irrelevant to the purpose of this study, to catalogue the types of legislation which proceeded according to this model.[37] Suffice it to state that the main areas of intervention were in public health and housing, conditions of employment for children and women, and safety in factories. Two points of general significance can be made regarding these measures. First, they necessarily gave rise to new forms of regulatory controls and bureaucratic structures; as such they served as a model for the social security measures introduced at the beginning of the twentieth century. Secondly, although the new concepts of public law were being employed to confer welfare or protection on the weaker members of the community, in legal terms the recipients of the welfare benefitted only indirectly. They were not granted 'rights' which could be enforced in the courts.[38] Nor was there, at this time, any question of redistributing wealth by the most direct method of granting financial assistance. As will emerge from the next section, outside the harsh regime of the Poor Law, poverty was not a sufficient ground by itself to justify aid on a centralized, institutionalized basis.

RELIEF OF POVERTY

Extent of Poverty

It is almost impossible to apply an objective criterion to determine how much poverty exists in a society at any given time. 'Poverty' is a relative concept, dependent on the aggregate resources of society at a particular time, and how those resources are distributed amongst the various classes of that society.[a39] It is, therefore, difficult to estimate how much poverty existed in Britain during the middle of the nineteenth century. One helpful, though fallible, guide may be provided by the number of persons in receipt of relief under the Poor Law. Even here there are obstacles: the administrators of the system seemed more concerned to record the amount spent on relief rather than the numbers in receipt of it.[a40] Nevertheless some figures do emerge. In 1834 there was an estimated 1.26 million paupers on relief, some 9 percent of the population; the figures declined to about 1 million in 1870 (4.6 percent of the population).[a41]

Causes of Poverty

The popular myth, consistent with the individualist and self-help ideology, was that poverty resulted from idleness and intemperance. The political economists held that overgenerous welfare was an incentive to pauperism with the resulting burden on the community. The view is faithfully reflected in the 1834 Poor Law Report. Independent labourers 'are under the strongest inducements to quit the less eligible class of labourers and enter the more eligible class of paupers. . . . Every penny bestowed that tends to render the condition of the pauper more eligible than that of the independent labourer, is a bounty on indolence and vice.'[a42] To modern eyes, it is astonishing how little was understood about the problems of unemployment, underemployment and irregular employment. Yet clearly inadequate or irregular earnings must have been a major cause of poverty. The statistics reveal that in the early 1840s about 20 percent of able-bodied persons in receipt of poor relief were being aided because of 'insufficient wages',[a43] and the rate of pauperism tended to be highest in occupations where casual labour predominated.[a44] Large family size was also a typical cause, as was sickness. In the 1840s 40–50 percent of those in receipt of outdoor relief under the Poor Law were sick or maimed as the result of an accident.[a45] If the illness or accident resulted in death, family poverty was even more likely (widows constituted 17–20 percent of able-bodied recipients of outdoor relief).[a46] It is difficult to determine whether the aged, as a group, featured significantly amongst the paupers, since statistics were not related to age until the end of the century. Subject to this qualification, what emerged for those who were concerned to confront reality, rather than ideological hypothesis, was that poverty, far from being a moral failing, resulted predominantly from those social hazards against which modern systems of social insurance seek to offer protection.

Centralized Relief of Poverty: the Poor Law

References have already been made to the Poor Law and its administration. Constituting, as it did, the only centralized form of relief of poverty existing during this period, it now requires a more detailed description. The 'new' Poor Law, which dated from 1834, and which implemented the recommendations of the Poor Law Commission (whose views, as we have seen, were very largely influenced by the political economists), was based on three principles. The first rested on the naive assumption that anyone fit for work could find it and therefore assure for himself and his family an adequate standard of living. Individuals were therefore divided into the 'able-bodied', who would be granted relief only if they accepted it within the rigours of the workhouse, and the 'aged and infirm' who might be granted outdoor relief. [a47] The second which determined the form of relief to be available in the workhouse was grounded in deterrence. Relief was to be so unattractive that an individual to be willing to accept it would have to be completely devoid of assistance from other sources. [a48] The corollary to this was the third principle, that of 'less eligibility': to preserve work incentives, the conditions of support were not to exceed the standard of living enjoyed by the lowest paid workers. [a49] Behind these principles we may note an important distinction. The concern was to provide relief for 'paupers' rather than the 'poor': the latter were of no concern to the system as such; its principles came into play only when the impoverished individual was also destitute. One final aspect of the 1834 reforms deserves attention: the chaotic localized administration which had previously existed was replaced by a centralized, national system. No longer was it to be left to local units to treat the destitute as they thought best; instead a central body was to lay down detailed rules and ensure that they were carried out. [a50] The change was significant in two respects: it sought to apply a 'rational' approach uniformly and efficiently throughout the country, thus registering a faith in Utilitarian ideas; secondly, it established a pattern of bureaucratic control which was to serve as a model for much subsequent legislation.

The expectations of the Poor Law reformers were not all to be fulfilled in practice, and in many respects, the system turned out to be a failure. The notion of uniform criteria of eligibility was almost impossible to sustain. How were local officials to determine what was the living standard of the lowest paid worker? [a51] Moreover, very few guidelines were laid down on the standard outdoor relief to be offered to the 'impotent poor': standards therefore varied from one part of the country to another, and even within regions. [a52] The Poor Law Commission had anticipated, in line with the political economists, that one effect of their policy would be a rise in industrial wages, thus creating an even clearer distinction between the workers and the destitute. This did not occur; particularly in the rural areas, the earnings of labourers remained stubbornly low. [a53] In industrial areas the problem was made even more acute by the irregularities of employment. The workhouse test was based on the premise that anybody able to work could find it, but in many areas this was clearly not always the case. [a54] The principles of eligibility were therefore adapted: in some areas the 'workhouse test' was replaced by the 'labour test'. Outdoor relief was permitted for the able-bodied in return for the performing of some work, e.g. stone-breaking. [a55] The horrors of the workhouse and this form of forced labour, as faithfully recorded in the literature of the period, were exacerbated by the problem of stigma. If, according to the middle-class ideology of the time, poverty itself was the result of personal failure, then the actual receipt of poor-law relief, and the characterization as a pauper, was even more degrading. De Tocqueville wrote, 'in every country it is unfortunate not to be rich; in England it is a horrible misfortune to be poor'. [a56]

Alternative Forms of Relief

One of the paradoxes of British Victorian society was that while constantly reaffirming its faith in individualism and self-help, at the same time it indulged in a massive amount of philanthropy.[a57] It was estimated that in 1861 there were some 640 charities in London alone, half of which had been established during the century and as many as 144 in the decade since 1850.[a58] The income of these charities (about £2½ million) exceeded the amount spent by the Poor Law authorities in the city. Many of the charities were Church inspired, and can be seen as part of the inter-denominational struggle; others were connected with the Temperance movement. But the motivation for the upsurge in philanthropy had deeper roots. One explanation might be that it was a reaction to the fear of social revolution. As one writer has alleged, 'in order to prevent an assault upon the whole basis of society and the division of wealth within it, men were prepared, almost as an insurance against social revolution, to siphon off some of their wealth for use by those in need'.[a59] No doubt there was a considerable amount of charity which sprang from genuine concern for the plight of others – a primary Christian virtue; but in modern psychological terms, it could also be explained as providing a release from guilt feelings engendered by the inequitable distribution of wealth.[a60]

It could hardly be said that the charities represented an *efficient* mode of conferring welfare, in the Utilitarian sense of that word. There was much duplication of effort and a great deal of wasteful rivalry. There was little in the way of coherent scientific investigation of social need.[a61] To solve these problems a Charity Organization Society was established in 1869.[a62] Its aims were to rationalize the charitable effort within London by coordinating the most important groups involved. More significant, perhaps, was its concern to formulate and execute scientific methods of social casework, an enterprise which can be seen as the forerunner of modern social services. In the light of the paradox described above, it is not perhaps surprising that while adopting progressive methods for the location and satisfaction of need, the Society also expounded the reactionary, self-help, social philosophy. It conceived one of its important functions to be the education and reform of the beneficiaries of charitable assistance.[a63]

More easily to be located within the framework of the individualist ideology was the notion of welfare resulting from personal thrift. Protection against the hazards of illness, old age and death was properly to be achieved through voluntary saving, whether on an individual or collective basis. So strong was this feeling, that it was used as an argument against the public provision of financial assistance for these risks well into the twentieth century. For example, the political economist Nassau Senior argued that 'old age is so much the general lot of human nature that it would strike too much into the providential habits of the poor to make anything like a regular and systematic provision for it.'[a64]

The development of voluntary savings through the friendly societies, trade unions and insurance companies, is one of the most thoroughly investigated areas of nineteenth century social history.[a65] Friendly societies, by which the more affluent workers would seek mutual protection against sickness and to support survivors on death, had existed for some time.[a66] Their considerable expansion in the nineteenth century (what Beveridge described as 'as natural a by-product of industrialization as was the smoke of the factories'[a67]) prompted the legislature to grant them special legal status. By the 1870s, membership totalled some one and a quarter millions, with funds totalling some £7 million.[a68] It should not, however, be assumed that they covered the bulk of the working population: with their discipline, their ceremonial and pageantry, they rather represented the cultural identity of the more prosperous sections of the working class. While all this activity was heartily encouraged by governments, it was nevertheless thought necessary to have some form of regulation to ensure that the societies were not to abuse their financial power. Limits were placed on the amounts which could be insured and, in some instances, paid out by way of benefit; the types of investment which a fund could make were controlled; accounts had to be certified by an actuary and submitted for centralized scrutiny.[a69]

Analogous functions were performed by the trade unions, but, of course, in their case, mutual welfare was only one part of a much more considerable whole which centred on the general improvement of members' working conditions and pay. They were, perhaps, most concerned with those risks which were not covered by friendly societies, and one very serious gap was unemployment pay. In actuarial terms, this was a difficult risk to handle, and even trade union coverage was slow to emerge, but by 1880 they were some interesting examples of primitive forms of unemployment insurance.[a70]

One of the most widespread phenomena in Victorian society, and one which had a major influence not only on the voluntary modes of welfare here under discussion but also on the development of social insurance, was the fear and humiliation of a pauper's funeral. A commentator in 1912 wrote:

> so great is the desire to escape the final disgrace of a pauper's grave, and so keen is the army of insurance agents, that there is scarcely a household or tenement in the land which cannot boast of one or more petty burial-money policies. I have found them even in sweating dens where a penny an hour is hardly earned by unremitting labour.[a71]

We should, however, draw a distinction between two different forms of funeral insurance. The first were taken out with small, local burial societies, which in many respects were similar to the friendly societies. They were examples of cooperative welfare organized by the more affluent workers: they were under the control of their members who thus could ensure that administrative costs were kept to a minimum.[a72] Very different was the position of the large collection societies which were run on a commercial basis by insurance companies.[a73] Their clientele was predominantly from the poorest sections of the community and they were controlled by their own officials. There are frequent references in the literature to the almost clichéd picture of the insurance collector marching through the slums of industrial cities extorting premiums which very often the worker could not afford to pay.[a74] There were, moreover, forms of exploitation which were manifest on the face of a company's records, the scrutiny of which by governments could hardly be avoided. The administrative costs were very high, amounting in some cases to as high as 40–50 percent of the benefits paid.[a75] There was also a high proportion of so-called abortive insurance, that is where policies lapsed before they could mature, and on which there was no refund. This was hardly surprising, considering that many families had overcommitted themselves financially. Finally there were many instances of small companies breaking up, leaving the policyholders without the benefit for which they had paid.

The efforts to legislate on these matters were generally unsuccessful, at least during the period under review. For example, in 1868 Lord Lichfield introduced a bill which, if passed, would have given policyholders some security against lapse. It was vigorously opposed by the insurance companies, financing their campaign with their policyholders money.[a76] The recommendations of a Royal Commission established in the 1870s to investigate the matter[a77] were partially implemented, but with limited success, and in the 1880s and later industrial assurance, as it had, rather inappropriately, become known continued to be a major problem.

CONCLUSION: WHY NO BISMARCK IN BRITAIN?

The 1881 legislation of Bismarck had no exact parallel in Britain. Indeed, social insurance was not introduced here for another 30 years. Nor, as the following section will reveal, can one find in the 1880s (with the possible exception of compensation for work accidents) any decisive and major legislative changes in social welfare policy which mirror the German experience. Why the development of social insurance should have occurred so relatively late in Britain is a speculative matter which will require further consideration in due course.[a78] Nevertheless, as a reflection on some of the key issues raised in the preceding discussion, some tentative suggestions should now be made. The first reason may have been the enduring strength of the individualist ideology in Britain: the leading political economists from Adam Smith to Ricardo continued to exert an almost decisive influence on political and economic thought throughout the nineteenth century. Secondly, and as a counterpoint to this, collectivist political movements were slower to develop in Britain than in Continental Europe. As some compensation for this, there was, thirdly, the rapid expansion of private and voluntary collective welfare (through the friendly societies for example), which because of their widespread coverage of the more affluent workers, may have blunted the sharpness of the demand for centralized and universal schemes. Fourthly, the voluntary, decentralized, form of social welfare was strengthened by a legal system which continued to accord primacy to property and reciprocity as manifested in contract law. The fifth reason combines the other four: the notion of the supremacy of the state responsibility, the collective good, and of a bureaucracy ready to impose it on the population at large was alien to the British liberal and democratic tradition. The lack of enthusiasm for the German model is exemplified by the view expressed in *The Times* in June 1889.[a79]

> Natural as free individual development is to the English in their island home, equally necessary is for Germany a rigid, centralised, all pervading state control . . . how exceptionally is Germany fitted to be the scene of this great philanthropic experiment. Nowhere is the ponderous, plodding, incorruptible bureaucracy so effective and cheap. . . . Self-help and spontaneous growth are better suited to Englishmen but [we are] ready to believe and willing to hope, that state initiative and socialistic science and self-conscious statesmanship may be adapted to other circumstances and other habits . . . the German is accustomed to official control, official delays and police supervision from the cradle to the grave . . . whereas . . . self-help and spontaneous growth are better suited to Englishmen.

THE ORIGINS OF SOCIAL INSURANCE 1881-1911

INTRODUCTION

The absence of anything akin to Bismarck's pioneering legislation should not give rise to an inference that the situation was static in Britain. The last two decades of the nineteenth century witnessed a serious questioning of, and substantial challenges to, traditional social policy, and in retrospect these developments can be seen to be crucial for the Liberal welfare reforms of the period 1906 to 1914, and in particular the introduction of social insurance in 1911. In this section we shall examine the changes in ideology, the growth of more radical political movements, the individuals, institutions and international contacts, all of which played a part in the sequence of events which eventually led to the 1911 reform. After an account of some alternative social security measures, there follows an analysis of the background to the National Insurance Act 1911.

IDEOLOGICAL AND POLITICAL DEVELOPMENTS

The Growth of Social Science

If the force of the *laissez-faire* philosophy adumbrated by the political economists was to be stemmed, one effective method might be to show (or attempt to show) that the assumptions on which the theories were based did not accord with social reality, or alternatively that the consequences of individualist capitalism were not conducive to states of social welfare which the proponents predicted. We have suggested above that much of the theory was pure abstract reasoning which was not combined with any attempt to discover the facts of social life.[a80] The second half of the nineteenth century witnessed a major breakthrough in a form of social science which was based on empirical studies rather than on pure speculation.[a81] It had been one of Malthus' ambitions 'to prepare some of the most important rules of political economy for practical application by a frequent reference to experience'.[a82] The Statistical Society was founded in the 1830s in response to such aims, and much of its work was concerned with the gathering of data concerned with the condition of the poor.[a83] Within the schools, churches, workhouses, and prisons, field-work was undertaken to ascertain both the causes and effects of social conditions. In a scientific sense, these early studies were often of a dubious character: the collection, analysis and interpretation of the data were obviously highly coloured by the opinions of the researchers, which led to understandable scepticism and controversy.[a84] It was only in the later decades of the century that efforts were made towards the 'purer' use of statistical methods. In theoretical terms, the aim was for the recognition of a new inductive 'science', what was later to be known as 'sociology',[a85] and at the time was seen as superceding political economy.[a86] In 1887 Charles Booth wrote:

> the *a priori* reasoning of political economy, orthodox and unorthodox alike, fails from want of reality. At its base are a series of assumptions very imperfectly connected with the observed facts of life. We need to begin with a true picture of the modern industrial organism, the interchange of service, the exercise of faculty, the demands and satisfaction of desire.[a87]

The epistemological problems from which later generations of sociologists suffered were but barely perceived at this stage: the confident assumptions were that scientific endeavours could be directly employed in the social policy process for the amelioration of social problems. [a88] Whatever theoretical doubts may exist as to the nature of their reasoning, the enormous influence of their research on poverty went a long way to justify those assumptions.

Two figures stand out amongst those who adopted the new empirical approach and who revealed the facts about poverty which were to have such a marked influence on the appreciation of the need to take some alleviating measures outside the Poor Law. In 1887, Booth undertook a survey of the living conditions of the working class in London. [a89] His principal finding was that over 30 percent of the population had an income below that which he considered adequate for their support. [a90] The importance lay not only in this finding, which was in sharp contrast to estimates of poverty derived from statistics of those in receipt of poor relief (in 1887 this amounted to only 2.9 percent of the population[a91]), but also in his method of measurement. His definition of poverty, described by his biographer as 'perhaps the most striking single contribution to the social sciences', [a92] was based on objective criteria as to needs and was calculated at something between 18 and 21 shillings a week for the average family. [a93] This approach was to serve as the model for future legislation, for example the flat-rate subsistence benefit in the National Insurance scheme, and the means tests employed in the unemployment assistance, national assistance and supplementary benefit schemes.

Ten years later Benjamin Seebohm Rowntree conducted a similar survey in York which confirmed Booth's findings: he produced an estimate of 28 percent of the population without adequate income support. [a94] Rowntree's research was an advance on that of Booth in three different respects. First, the objective definition of poverty was rendered more precise: it was based on detailed physiological data (particularly nutritional needs) and it emerged at the exact figure of 21s 8d a week for a family of two adults and three children. [a95] Secondly, his efforts were directed also to the causes of poverty. He drew a distinction between *primary* poverty, the result of insufficiency of resources for basic human needs, and *secondary* poverty, the result of imprudent management of resources. [a96] The latter revealed that some of the poverty would not have existed if individuals had been trained to spend their income in a more efficient way. Thirdly, he saw poverty as a dynamic process, occurring in time, rather than as a static condition. He sought to relate indigence to cycles of unemployment and ill health. [a97]

The birth of sociology was accompanied by less radical, albeit substantial and important, developments in economic theory. [a98] While some of this took place within the field of abstract theory (the micro-analysis of value, price, production and distribution), there were also considerable developments in the use of statistical data. The significance of this latter work for our purposes was twofold. The growth in knowledge of demographic phenomena could help to counter Malthusian arguments employed to defend the Poor Law approach to welfare. [a99] Secondly, the study of crises of cyclical and other fluctuations in productivity and employment provided (at last) some sure basis for disarming the widely held conviction that unemployment was almost wholly a result of moral laxity. [b1]

New Ideologies

The causal connection between the revelations of the social scientists and the social welfare reforms of the 1906–1914 period was obvious, if not direct. Much greater controversy surrounds the relationship between those reforms and the changes in ideology and the political climate which occurred at the end of the nineteenth century.[b2]

There were a number of intellectual movements which, to a greater or lesser extent, sought to advocate collectivist ideals, in opposition to the individualist tradition. The first was a direct descendant of the Utilitarians. J. S. Mill in his later years began to appreciate that *laissez-faire* doctrines had not succeeded in alleviating the most serious instances of social evil and was drawn to argue for a greater degree of collectivist intervention. He attempted to reconcile this with the main tenets of Utilitarianism by arguing that the notion of pleasure, which on the orthodox interpretation was to be maximized on an individual basis, should be extended to include the welfare of persons other than the actor. Mill wrote

> As between his own happiness and that of others utilitarianism requires him to be as strictly impartial as a disinterested and benevolent spectator. . . . To do as you would be done by, and to love your neighbour as yourself, constitute the ideal perfection of utilitarian morality . . . laws and social arrangements should pace the happiness, or . . . the interest, of every individual, as nearly as possible in harmony with the interest of the whole.[b3]

As commentators have pointed out,[b4] we can find in Mill's reasoning a critical link between the individualism of the political economists and the more overt socialist doctrines. Since the middle of the century socialist doctrine had manifested itself in the works of various individuals and groups, without ever constituting a major political force in the community at large.[b5] *The Communist Manifesto* of Marx and Engels may have drawn on their work in England, but its publication made surprisingly little impact.[b6] 'Marx himself', observes one historian, 'was known rather as a learned German political exile than as the leader of any clearly-marked Socialist movement.'[b7] Yet there were undoubted affinities with home-grown doctrines. Robert Owen had evolved a philosophy whereby cooperatives would replace capitalists in the structure of production and society as a whole.[b8] From this sprang the Cooperative Movement which grew in strength as the century progressed but which soon abandoned its initial ideological thrust in favour of an honest but unadventurous commercial enterprise. As such it had little difficulty in winning general public approval for its insistence on working-class thrift and self-help.[b9] The socialist ideal passed, if anywhere, to the Christian Socialists: they stressed its ethical character; they preached the fellowship of man which they considered to be thwarted by competitive capitalism. Their essentially moderate approach manifested itself in their opposition to militant trade unionism: the Utopia was to be achieved by reconciling the classes, not by class war.[b10]

The Social Democratic Movement which had gained a foothold in continental Europe was slow to gain acceptance in Britain. The trade unions, anxious to gain respectability through legal recognition, withdrew from the International. Marx commented that they had 'offered up the principle of Trade Unionism on the altar of middle-class legitimisation'.[b11] It was only in the last two decades of the century that the pendulum swung again towards socialism. In 1881 under the influence of Henry George (arguing for the nationalization of land) and Henry Hyndman (who sought to publicize *Das Kapital*), an association was established which in 1883 called itself the Social Democratic Federation.[b12] Its programme included not only nationalization but also State-aided schemes of working-class housing, universal free education, and the public provision of work for the unemployed. Internal strife robbed the movement of its strength; it had forsaken parliamentary action in favour of more direct political action, and eventually it pinned its faith on the activities of the trade unions.

A diametrically opposed strategy was adopted by another group of Socialists, the so-called Fabians.[b13] This group, founded in 1884, and numbering among its early members Bernard Shaw and Sydney Webb, was intellectual in character. Its doctrines evolved from the later writings of J. S. Mill, rather than Marx. The Utilitarian aim of the 'greatest happiness for the greatest number' could best be achieved, they argued, by state intervention, and state control of the means of production. Through Parliamentary action it was hoped to convert the State into an instrument of public welfare. It visualized socialism as arising through a natural and gradual development of British institutions rather than by revolutionary pressure. The Fabian Group was never strong in its terms of membership — in 1900 it embraced only 850 individuals[b14] — but the quality of its publications,[b15] and the political acumen and renown of its leaders, ensured for it a significant role in the debates leading up to the welfare reforms of the early twentieth century. The exact nature of its contribution to the establishment of social insurance is the subject of some historical debate.[b16] The latest opinion is that 'no major political development can be attributed with certainty to Fabian influence; but few similar groups, so small and so much outside the established centres of power, can have exercised as great and as varied an influence in minor but not unimportant ways'.[b17]

Liberal Individualism

The ideologies described above were not, of course, representative of political opinions as a whole at the end of the nineteenth century. They constituted rather a new polar force which allowed for a gentle swing in the general political climate, away from the harsher forms of individualism. The introduction of social insurance in 1911, along with other welfare reforms of the period, was, in immediate terms, an achievement of the Liberal Party and it is in liberal doctrine that we must now attempt to find the roots of this legislation.

One explanation, at one time popular with historians, was to be located in the phenomenon of 'social imperialism'.[b18] Shortly described, this was a reaction to the decadence of late Victorian Britain: a loss of confidence in the classical material aims expressed itself not only in the extension of the Empire but also in a concern for the security of the ruling classes. It would be impossible to defend the Empire without a secure social base in Britain. Modern historians have tended to discount this theory, except in so far as it can be reconciled with what they consider to be the primary concern of the ruling classes, that of national efficiency.[b19] Even more pronounced than in earlier generations[b20] was the feeling that industrial prosperity could be maintained only by a healthy and relatively content working force. The notion was strengthened not only by the research of Booth and Rowntree but also by studies which had been undertaken on the health of recruits to the armed forces.[b21] Moreover, the argument rendered social reform much more palatable to commercial interests within the Liberal Party. It is not without significance that in 1906 the Liberal-dominated Birmingham Chamber of Commerce called for the introduction of a Bismarckian scheme of social insurance.[b22]

Undoubtedly, this was accompanied by some change of attitudes towards poverty, itself partially the result of the social surveys described above. The view that *all* cases of poverty resulted from moral failings had been undermined, and instead there was seen to be a distinction between the 'deserving poor' whose predicament lay in forces beyond their control and the 'undeserving poor', the idle and the unemployable. [b23] It was in the interests of society generally to protect the first category from being 'infected' by the latter; as such it was legitimate to introduce social insurance, while at the same time retaining the deterrence of the Poor Law.

Within the ranks of the younger Liberal politicians, at the turn of the century, there was a marked shift in ideology. [b24] They were influenced, perhaps, by new contributions to social philosophy which stressed the organic relationship between the state and individuals, in opposition to the view of the political economists that centralized intervention was an unwonted imposition on the liberty of the individual freely to pursue his own welfare. [b25] The implication of this shift was a concept of social justice, in which the different elements in the social organism might better cohere with a measure of redistribution of resources.

Popular Movements

There is much speculation and disagreement among historians as to the role of popular, working-class movements in the process of the liberal welfare reforms. [b26] On one, extreme view, the working-classes, in contrast to their German counterparts, did not want reform. Thus Pelling has suggested that the activity of Parliament in the period 1906–1914 'was by no means welcomed by members of the working class, was indeed undertaken over the critical hostility of many of them, perhaps most of them'. [b27] He bases his opinion on their apparent hostility to state institutions and to the fact that the trade union movement appeared to be more concerned with its own power and status than with social reform. The second view accepts that this might have been true of unorganized labour but it did not apply to the leaders of the working-class movements. [b28] It is clear that the newly born Labour Party and the Trades Union Congress advocated far-reaching reform in the social welfare field, including free education for all, old age pensions, assistance for the unemployed, the abolition of the Poor Law and even a comprehensive health service. Nevertheless, it has been doubted whether such a programme had a substantial effect on the political elite. [b29] Historians of this opinion point to the fact that the limited social changes involved in the reforms were, for reasons explained above, already within the compass of the traditional political parties, and on this view their implementation can be explained by the desire to attract electoral popularity.

The difficulties of diagnosing historical causes are epitomized by the question of popular manifestations. Some have drawn significance from the violent demonstrations of the unemployed which took place in 1886–7, [b30] arguing that they were directly responsible for the decision at that time to relax the conditions for outdoor Poor Law relief, [b31] and less immediately for the measures taken in the early years of the next century to abate unemployment. [b32] While these events certainly brought the plight of the unemployed more to public attention, it has been doubted whether they had any pronounced effect on the policymakers. They were seen by the major political parties as problems of public order rather than of social conditions; 'they revealed not the strength but the weakness of unconstitutional pressure'.[b33]

INSTITUTIONAL INFLUENCES

One of the important results of more recent historical studies of this period has been the recognition of the role played by institutional influences in the struggle for reform.[b34] There were, of course, some pressure groups in existence which wholeheartedly supported increased state intervention. In 1899 Charles Booth published a pamphlet, arguing for a universal old age pension,[b35] and under its influence a National Committee of Organized Labour on Old Age Pensions was established.[b36] For the next 9 years it sponsored a programme for the introduction of a universal scheme, a campaign which culminated in the Old Age Pensions Act of 1908. It was accompanied by parallel, if more sectionalized, pressure from the Women's Industrial Council, which argued that the problems of intermittent employment and low pay meant that few women were able to save enough to maintain themselves in old age.[b37] Opposition to reform came from other institutions which were primarily concerned to preserve commercial interests in existing decentralized welfare schemes. Chief amongst these were the Friendly Societies and the insurance companies.[b38]

A second type of influence was exerted by those working within the civil service, at both national and local levels. The growth in bureacracy in the nineteenth century had given rise to a new power basis within government.[b39] The leading administrators played a crucial role not only in the formulation of legislative schemes, but also in the policy debate which preceded them. There was no obvious consensus of social values amongst them. One group which very actively supported the reforms had typically worked with the unemployed and poor before entering government service – Beveridge himself was a prime example.[b40] Not unexpectedly there were others, particularly in the Treasury, who attempted to water down proposals on the grounds of cost.[b41]

In a sense too the administrative failings of some institutions facilitated the reform process. The nineteenth-century system of social services was organized predominantly on a local basis. The financing was cumbersome and ill-disciplined. To the social reasons for national welfare schemes was added, therefore, the growing recognition that the financial problems could be solved only by centralized control.[b42]

INFLUENCE OF FOREIGN EXPERIMENTS

In the introduction to the second edition of his *Law and Public Opinion in England during the Nineteenth Century* Dicey wrote the following.

Englishmen have rarely been directly and consciously influenced by the example of foreign countries. English political or social movements have been influenced far less by logical argument than by the logic of facts, and of acts observable in England. English collectivism and socialism owes its peculiar development in England mainly to the success of English trade unionism, but every part of the world is by means of railways and electric telegraph being brought nearer to each other. It may therefore be taken for granted that the progress of socialistic legislation and the trial of socialistic experiments in English colonies, such as the Australian Commonwealth, or in the United States, or even in an utterly foreign country, such as France, have promoted the growth of collectivism in England.[b43]

This passage has been quoted at length because it is revealing about British attitudes to foreign experiences in several respects. First, it constitutes, in its tone, an unhappy example of English insularity, which coming from an eminent jurist would not be altogether surprising if at the same time he had not been the leading exponent of private international law.[b44] Secondly, in its mistaken identity of the English political and administrative system with pragmatism (as opposed to 'logical argument') it manifests the typical ideological bias of the individualists. Dicey completely fails to appreciate the influence of political economy theory on nineteenth-century political life. He assumes that non-interventionist policies responded in some way to 'the logic of facts', when, as we have sought to show, the *laissez-faire* ideology began to crumble when the empirical sciences began to indicate its failings. Thirdly, the grudging recognition that foreign experiments in social legislation may have had some influence on the English policymaker comes closer to the truth but even here there is some historical distortion. The implication that the collectivist measures stemmed from a combination of trade unionism and foreign experience, both of them 'alien' to the English tradition, ignores the effect of the various movements, individuals and groups whose activities have been described in the preceding sections. Moreover the foreign experiments in social welfare, particularly the Bismarckian legislation (which Dicey incomprehensibly fails to mention), were relied on in the campaign for reform not because they constituted some alien ideology but because they provided a concrete example of how ideas perceived at home could be put into practice.

The reference to, and growing importance of, studies in foreign social legislation is understandable in the context of the political and intellectual climate at the turn of the century. The results of scholarship and scientific endeavours were now being freely exchanged; there was an increase of interest in how societies, at a similar stage of development, coped with common problems. Indeed, by the end of the nineteenth century it had become general practice for committees and other agencies investigating particular problems to seek contributions from experts in foreign systems.[b45] There was also a sense of international rivalry. If a foreign power, especially Germany, had taken major steps forward in social welfare, and there was some suspicion that this had promoted social solidarity and national efficiency, then there was at least a *prima facie* case for Britain proceeding in the same direction.[b46]

It may be impossible to attribute specific developments to foreign influences, but certainly the amount of information acquired on social welfare (especially social insurance) measures was considerable. Already in the 1840s reference had been made to continental systems of protection against work accidents.[b47] Surprisingly little notice was taken of the Bismarck legislation of 1881–1883, though this is, perhaps, because at that time there was no real interest in social insurance.[b48] Significantly, when reference to foreign experience again appears in contemporary accounts of debates, it is concerned with the Danish and New Zealand non-contributory old age pension schemes.[b49] A talk given in London in 1898 by the Agent General of New Zealand was used by Booth and others to launch the campaign for a similar scheme in Britain.[b50] The fact that the example had been set by a British colony added weight to its importance.[b51]

In 1905 the Board of Trade published a report entitled 'Agencies and Methods for Dealing with Unemployment in Certain Foreign Countries',[b52] and Beveridge visited Germany in that year to study the system of labour exchanges in operation there.[b53] His scheme, much influenced by his German experience, was implemented by legislation in 1908.[b54] During this period, too, the idea of social insurance had been adopted by several groups. By this time, knowledge of the Bismarck legislation had become widespread: it had been the subject of several books and articles.[b55] The non-contributory, means-tested approach was still considered the most appropriate for the aged and so interest centred on the health scheme. In 1908 Lloyd George went to Germany to study it and was very impressed by what he saw.[b56] The health section of the National Insurance Act 1911 was to a significant extent inspired by the German model, though there were important differences.[b57] In 1912 Lloyd George was to observe that Germany was the

> pioneer of National Insurance. . . . Its success is now triumphant, unquestioned alike by employers and employees. It was from Germany that we who were privileged to be associated with the application of the principle to the United Kingdom found our first inspiration, and it is with her experience before us that we feel confident of the future.[b58]

The original German scheme did not cover unemployment and the advocates of social insurance covering this risk had to look elsewhere. Some foreign experiments in this field were studied but were not found to be too promising.[b59] The compulsory scheme established in St Gall had failed through a combination of bad risks and maladministration. The influences on the unemployment aspects of the National Insurance Act 1911 were rather the successful voluntary schemes operating in Cologne and Ghent.[b60]

Alternative Approaches to Social Risks

Introduction

One of the explanations for the relatively late adoption of the social insurance principle in Britain may lie in the belief current at the turn of the century that other interventionist measures were, or would be, adequate to cope with the social risks recognized as giving rise to hardship. We shall examine, in this section, reforms undertaken in relation to work accidents, old age, and unemployment, as well as minor amendments to the Poor Law.

Work Accidents and Diseases

We have already alluded to the major problem of work accidents and diseases which was one of the results of industrialization.[b61] As regards accident prevention, steps had already been taken through the Factory legislation to impose safety precautions on employers.[b62] While some might have questioned the efficacy of these measures—the Factory Inspectorate was only partially successful in securing compliance with the statutory safety precautions[b63]—it was the inability of the injured workman (or his family in the case of death) to recover compensation which manifested itself as the greatest evil. For reasons already proffered, [b64] the common law, with its notorious doctrine of common employment and its insistence that the worker prove affirmatively personal fault against his employer, proved to be quite inadequate for this task. [b65] Indeed, until 1846 no action at all lay on the death of an individual. [b66]

The clamour for reform started with the miners and was then taken up by the trade unions generally. [b67] A Parliamentary Bill of 1876 which proposed the total abolition of the doctrine of common employment was withdrawn on the government's promise to establish a Select Committee to inquire into the matter. Its recommendation, a minor curtailing of the doctrine, [b68] was hardly even a palliative to the reformers, and the Bill was reintroduced in the next session. Without government backing it could not succeed, but by this time accident compensation had become a popular, and indeed an election issue. In 1880 legislation was at last passed, [b69] but unlike most of the public health measures of this period, it did not proceed from thorough investigation or rational appraisal of the problem. It was rather a temporary, compromise solution. In 1906 Winston Churchill was to write that it 'had not originated in the great departments of the State and was, both in principle and in drafting, an amateurish suggestion which might, indeed, sound very plausible and accommodating; but which had not been clearly thought out in a scientific spirit with the advantages of official information'. [b70]

Shortly described, the Employers Liability Act abrogated the defence of common employment in five specified situations where the workers suffered injury as the result of the negligence of someone who was the 'alter ego' of the employer, i.e. directly supervised the work. This was hardly a major advance: the employee had to fit his case squarely within one of the five prescribed situations, and the looseness of the statutory language did not make this easy. [b71] Aided by restrictive judicial interpretations, [b72] recalcitrant employers were thus able to avoid its most beneficial effects. Moreover, as the price for 'extending' their liability, the industrial interests had succeeded in persuading Parliament to limit the amount of compensation payable by amending common law principles of quantification: a limit was fixed at the estimated earnings of the worker for the three years preceding the injury. [b73] In defiance of the spirit of the legislation, the judiciary declared it legal for a worker to contract-out of the Act, by agreeing with his employer not to claim compensation under it. [b74] The unreality of this individualist approach was underlined by the fact that very many injured workmen found themselves dismissed when they pressed claims against their employer. [b75] Finally, the right to recover was circumscribed by technicalities unknown to the common law. Proceedings had to be taken within a very short time and were even then maintainable only if certain provisions as to notice had been complied with. [b76] The failure of the Act materially to improve the injured workman's position was amply demonstrated by the reported fact that in 1893 the amount paid by way of damages through the courts did not exceed £8000. [b77]

Not surprisingly, the campaign for reform was not abated. A Select Committee reporting in 1886 on the workings of the Act had little to offer in the way of major recommendations, [b78] but it did suggest that contracting-out should not be permitted unless it were for 'valuable consideration', which might include contribution by the employer to a workman's insurance fund. [b79] This might have signalled a more general investigation of the possibility of introducing a national accident insurance scheme along the lines already existing in Germany — at this time, of course, in Britain only voluntary schemes existed, and then only among the more affluent workers.[b80] In fact, the notion of a social insurance scheme was hardly entertained at all, and it has been suggested that the major reason for this was the antipathy of the trade unions to the idea.[b81] The latter were more concerned to bring home to the employer his responsibility for work accidents and a compulsory insurance scheme would weaken this.[b82]

Pressure was mounted therefore for a more complete regime of responsibility by the employer. Both political parties promised to introduce legislation along these lines. The first major step was the introduction of a Bill in 1893 which would have had the effect of rendering the employer liable for any accident which resulted from the negligence of anyone in his service, except, of course, that of the injured employee himself; moreover, contracting-out would no longer constitute a defence. In the view of many, these proposals did not go far enough: Joseph Chamberlain opposed the Bill on the ground that it did not overcome the hurdle of proving that the accident resulted from someone's fault. In the course of the debates, he said that 'no amendment to the law relating to employers' liability will be final or satisfactory which does not provide compensation to workmen for all injuries sustained in the ordinary course of their employment and not caused by their own acts or defaults'.[b83] Faced with this attack, as well as opposition from employers who wished to see the principles of contracting-out preserved, the government withdrew the Bill. The political issue was now, whether a no-fault principle should be admitted. The slogan, 'A compensation Act for workmen, irrespective of cause of accident' was widely heard in the election campaign of 1895[b84] and indeed formed the basis of the new Conservative Government's Bill in 1897. Notwithstanding opposition from industrial interests[b85] the measure became law. As noted by a Committee reviewing the matter some years later the reform constituted 'a revolution in the branch of law which concerns the relationship between employer and workman. . . . It set up an entirely new doctrine and provided rights and imposed obligations which nowhere fitted into the existing scheme of jurisprudence.'[b86]

Section 1 of the Workmen's Compensation Act 1897 stated concisely and simply the 'revolutionary' principle: 'if in any employment to which the Act applies personal injury by accident arising out of and in the course of the employment is caused to a workman his employer . . . shall be liable to pay compensation'. The limitations of this right should not, however, be lost sight of. It only applied to specified employments (though these included work on the railways, in factories, mines and building sites).[b87] Contracting-out was permitted but only on the condition that the workman concerned was a member of an accident compensation scheme which was 'on the whole not less favourable to the general body of workmen and their dependants' than the provisions of the 1897 Act.[b88] For the purposes of our present study, the most important limitation was the amount of compensation payable: an injured workman was entitled only to one half of his average weekly earnings to a maximum of £1.[b89] Though this was in no sense an insurance scheme, nevertheless the principle of compensation was that the worker's loss should be shared between himself and his employer, a notion true also of the social insurance schemes introduced some 13 years later.

At a later stage in this study, we shall examine the deficiencies of the workmen's compensation which in due course led to its being superseded by social insurance.[b90] Our concern at this stage is to relate the developments to the scheme which took place in the early years of the twentieth century, and to consider its significance on the earliest form of social insurance introduced in 1911.

Already, in 1904, the new scheme was subjected to comprehensive scrutiny by a government committee,[b91] and as a result of its recommendations, in 1906 the Workmens' Compensation Act was extended and modified.[b92] The Committee expressed cautious approval of the scheme in general, though it felt that it had given rise to excessive litigation,[b93] and had not operated as an incentive for safety.[b94] Two major gaps in the coverage of the scheme were exposed and were largely rectified by the 1906 Act. Instead of limiting liability to specified employments, the latter extended it to all occupations except a few (e.g. armed forces, non-manual labour earning more than £250 a year, and casual workers).[b95] The result was to increase coverage from 7.25 million to 15 million individuals.[b96] Secondly, and even more important in terms of principle, the new Act extended to diseases as well as accidents.[b97] This was a controversial reform, for the 1904 Committee, while recognizing the importance of work-related sickness, had considered it too impracticable to come within the workmens' compensation scheme: it would have preferred some system of sickness insurance.[b98] The solution found (and indeed preserved in subsequent industrial injuries schemes) was to prescribe certain diseases in relation to certain occupations, and to treat such diseases incurred while employed in the appropriate occupations as if they were 'injuries'.[b99]

Based as it was on the notion of the employer's individual liability, workmen's compensation would seem to be an instrument of private law (albeit a radical one) which was far removed from the idea of social insurance. Yet there were several aspects to it which heralded the path (in Britain) to this institution and thus justify the space devoted to it here. In the first place, the 1897 Act was the first major scheme to provide financial compensation against a social hazard; it also revealed that state intervention (if not centralization) was necessary to remedy defects in the conventional private law. Secondly, the principles of compensation it adopted foreshadowed those which were to be current under social insurance, as regards both the notion of the employer and employee 'sharing' the loss and the statutory maximum. Thirdly, the 1906 Act by extending the scheme to industrial diseases had admitted a condition which, for all practical purposes, was beyond the scope of the private law to remedy: because of the difficulties of proof and the lapse of time between the contraction of a disease and its manifestation, some centralized machinery became necessary, thus anticipating sickness insurance. Fourthly, the shortcomings of the scheme, as already appreciated in its early years, pointed the way to the alternative strategy based on a new legal relationship between the individual and the state. These shortcomings were: (a) the amount of litigation (and therefore personal and administrative costs) which resulted from the employee being obliged to proceed personally against his employer;[c1] (b) the fact that, being a personal claim, the employer could compromise it out of court, with the result, in practice, often of forcing the employee to accept inadequate compensation;[c2] (c) the risk that an employer might become insolvent, thus depriving the employee of any remedy.[c3] Indeed, in recognizing the dangers of this last hazard, the 1904 Committee realised that the only realistic way of dealing with it would involve some step towards a national insurance scheme. It concluded its report with these prophetic words.

Many witnesses have suggested that some system of national insurance should be established which would relieve the employers from all personal liability except that of providing the necessary funds. . . . It may be that the State should establish or regulate a system of insurance which would provide an opportunity for every employer and for every workman complete security. . . . It may be that ultimately some form of compulsion might be adopted requiring all employers to insure their workmen in some association under state regulations. . . . These and similar questions are probably in prospect. But it would be premature and beyond our commission to discuss them. We can only indicate that, beneficial as we believe the legislation of 1897 to have been on the whole, we do not think that it can be regarded otherwise than as a step in the direction of a more comprehensive system.[c4]

Old Age

One of the results of the more scientific approach to investigating poverty which emerged during the second half of the nineteenth century was the awareness that it was widespread among the aged. Booth, in particular, had found it to be the most frequent single cause of poverty, amounting to about one-third of all cases.[c5] Reliance on the Poor Law was the typical fate of these persons, for while voluntary pension schemes existed among trade union and friendly society members, these tended to concentrate on sickness rather than old age and in any event involved only a small proportion of the population.[c6] The question of how best to deal with the problem was the subject of a prolonged and strenuous debate in the last two decades of the nineteenth century and the first decade of the twentieth.[c7]

The Bismarck legislation indicated that social insurance might be a viable solution. Three years earlier a clergyman, Canon Blackley, had published proposals along similar if less ambitious lines: every working man between 18 and 21 would contribute to a fund, managed but not subsidized by the state, which would pay out benefits to those unable to work through sickness and to those over age 70.[c8] Neither the Bismarck scheme nor the Blackley proposals won much support, a failure which was attributable to a number of causes. First, there were the remnants of the individualist, self-help ideology which manifested themselves particularly in the report of a governmental committee which examined Blackley's proposals in 1885–1887. It objected to any state scheme which would involve the compulsory adherence of the population: this would necessarily extend the power of the state over the individual which was harmful to 'the self-taught habits of the thrift and self-help which prevail among the working classes to a considerable extent'.[c9] The Charity Organization Society expressed similar fears.[c10] The Friendly Societies understandably saw in the proposals a threat to their own privileged position in providing relief for old age.[c11] Less predictably, the trade unions were ambivalent. While the more powerful associations of skilled workers found the idea appealing, they did not see how it could operate in relation to casual and female workers.[c12] There was, finally, the practical issue of time scale. An insurance scheme would do nothing to help those already too old to work, and successive governments recognized that electoral popularity would be achieved only by some more immediate steps to alleviate the plight of the aged.[c13]

The alternative to an insurance scheme was clearly some form of non-contributory pension. This was widely supported by the labour movement in the 1890s: it could be seen as the state's reward for the years of working effort; it would cover casual and female workers; it would have an immediate effect. [c14] In 1899 a National Committee of Organized Labour for the Promotion of Old Age Pensions was established: [c15] it argued vociferously for a non-contributory scheme, such as had already been introduced in Denmark (1891) and New Zealand (1898). The campaign did not immediately come to fruition. A Royal Commission on the Aged Poor had in 1895 produced a most negative report. [c16] The majority had found that the number of aged poor was declining: a pension scheme was thus unnecessary, though the Poor Law might treat this group with greater consideration. At the time this seemed to imply that the matter was dead as a political issue: but under pressure from Joseph Chamberlain (who had accepted government office) and perhaps also public opinion, the government decided a year later to set up another committee to re-examine the question. [c17] The terms of reference of this second committee were, however, carefully drawn so as to exclude consideration of a non-contributory pension scheme, and not surprisingly it reported negatively on contributory schemes.

Chamberlain and other advocates of pensions within government pressed on notwithstanding this setback, and, unbelievably, a third committee was appointed in 1899, but this time under the chairmanship of Henry Chaplin, a known sympathizer with the pension movement. At last a solid legislative proposal emerged: [c18] a non-contributory scheme under which 5s per week would be paid to those over 65 years where the Poor Law Board of Guardians had determined that the claimant, (a) had an income of less than 10s a week, and (b) was not of 'bad character', i.e. had not been in prison or in receipt of poor relief within 20 years of the claim, and had 'endeavoured to the best of his ability . . . to make provision for himself and those immediately dependent on him'. [c19] The scheme would be funded partly out of the poor rates and partly from the Exchequer. The means- and character-test were of the utmost significance; it meant that the scheme was far from being a universal one, and it reaffirmed the traditional poor law distinction between the 'deserving' and 'undeserving' poor. [c20]

Even so, there was substantial delay before the proposal reached the statute book, primarily because of the outbreak of the Boer War, but also because of opposition from the Treasury. [c21] The Liberal electoral victory of 1906, with a large number of 'new' Liberal Radicals pressing for implementation finally forced the Government to act. Notwithstanding powerful arguments for a contributory scheme from Beveridge who had studied the German system, [c22] the Old Age Pensions Act of 1908 substantially followed the 1899 proposals. The chief modifications were: that entitlement should begin only at age 70 and a reduced pension, on a sliding scale from 1s to 5s a week for those with income between 8s and 12s a week. The character test was made more specific. An applicant must not have received poor relief after January 1908, must not have been imprisoned for any offence including drunkenness during the 10 years preceding the claim, was not an alien or the wife of an alien, and was able to satisfy the authorities that he had not been guilty of 'habitual' failure to work according to his ability, opportunity, or need, for his own maintenance or that of his legal relatives. [c23] In the words of one historian, 'it was a pension for the very old, the very poor and the very respectable'. [c24] As such, it was wholly alien to any notion of social insurance and yet, as with workmen's compensation, it can be seen as another tentative and halting step on the road to the 1911 reform. Here, for the first time, was a system of financial aid for a social hazard funded from general resources, administered centrally and independent of the stigmatizing poor law. Moreover, in legal terms, it was pioneering in its efforts to formulate a statutory means-test (something which had never been attempted under the Poor Law) which contained precise rules for computing income and capital[c25] and, more important for the national insurance scheme, a structure for the determination of claims, including the right of appeal against adverse decisions.[c26] These provisions thus had the effect of establishing for the first time in British legal history a *right* to financial assistance which existed in public law.[c27]

Unemployment

We have already indicated that moral attitudes to unemployment had begun to change.[c28] This went hand in hand with a more scientific analysis of the problem. Until the end of the nineteenth century unemployment was little understood. While it had become recognized that the phenomenon was not merely the result of personal failings and had its origin in economic causes, the method of dealing with it was based on certain misconceptions. In the 1880s, it was appreciated that the poor law was not an appropriate solution for those who were 'genuinely' unemployed, but state initiative was limited to the notion of 'tiding-over' such persons until ordinary work was again available. This was achieved by the provision of municipal relief work.[c29] The fallacy in this approach was its failure to recognize the difference between underemployment and unemployment.[c30] Unemployment was not simply a matter of a man losing his regular work during times of depression and other trade fluctuations; if it were, then no doubt the 'tiding-over' principle might be regarded as a reasonable, if often insufficient, prescription. It also contained, especially at this time, a large amount of underemployment, that is, where for a particular trade or industry there were reserve or casual workers who had no regular employment, but who found work when there happened to be a sufficient demand for it. This was the more fundamental problem, for the labour market was insufficiently organized for such people to be in the appropriate location, or equipped with the appropriate skills. Paradoxically, they rather than the unemployed (using that term in its strict sense) availed themselves of the opportunities provided by municipal relief work, a measure which, of course, did nothing to abate the fundamental problem.

Such were the perceptions of those like Beveridge, who examined unemployment in the first years of this century.[c31] In the circumstances, it is not surprising that the brunt of their early initiatives were directed, not towards providing a more coherent and rational system of relief to 'tide-over' the unemployed — arguably this could be done in any event by voluntary collective action through the trade unions — but rather to tackling the problem of underemployment at its roots by establishing state controls over the labour market. The institution regarded as having the potential to achieve this was the labour exchange. Beveridge examined the device in some foreign systems, notably Germany, and was so impressed by what he saw that for several years labour exchanges became his '*idée fixe*'.[c32] The institution was not completely unknown in Britain: 'Distress Committees' had been created at a local level to investigate need arising from unemployment, and where possible to provide work — the up-dated version of the municipal relief works.[c33] They were also given power to establish labour exchanges and to arrange for emigration. These measures were not a success: there were not the necessary funds available to make the placement of the unemployed anything more than rudimentary. It still partook of the old ideology of 'tiding-over' and it did nothing to attack the basic problem of underemployment, except perhaps in the very limited sense that it revealed that much more robust measures were necessary. So strong was this evidence that the otherwise backward-looking Majority of the Royal Commission on the Poor Law joined with the Minority in urging the establishment of Labour Exchanges. [c34] The Liberal Party adopted the notion in its programme for reform and a national system of exchanges was created by legislation in 1908. [c35] Once this step had been taken, the next logical step was to examine again the issue of relief, with the possibility that this too might be organized on a national basis.

The Poor Law

Among alternatives to social insurance, the Poor Law was, of course, the most traditional and also the most general in its coverage. With its repressive form of deterrence, and, in cultural terms, its highly stigmatizing effects, it was regarded by many as incompatible with the new spirit of collectivism which had inspired the reforms outlined above. Criticism of the Poor Law system was not, of course, confined to its ideology: its methods and failings were subjected to increased study. [c36] An unwillingness to place excessive burdens on ratepayers had led, in many areas, to a 'lumping together' of all the poor, whatever the cause of the poverty, and whatever their needs. [c37] The first demand was, therefore, for specialist treatment of the different categories of pauper. One group which suffered particularly from this aggregate approach was the sick: the Poor Law medical officers operating both inside and outside the workhouse were badly paid and often unskilled. [c38] The conditions in London were especially disquieting, [c39] and some alleviation had resulted from the Metropolitan Poor Act of 1867 which provided for the creation of separate institutions for the infirm poor in London and also for dispensaries to administer outdoor medical aid. The movement was taken a step further by the Medical Relief Disqualification Removal Act 1885 which abolished the electoral disqualification of those in receipt of medical relief.

The treatment of the unemployed constituted a greater problem. The 1834 principle of 'less eligibility'[c40] implied a harsh policy of deterrence but was this still appropriate in the light of the growing recognition of the distinction between the work-shy and the genuine unemployed? The problem was brought to a head by the crisis in the Lancashire cotton industry in the 1860s: many labourers were thrown out of work and the Poor Law administrators realized that the normal machinery was unsuitable. [c41] Local boards of guardians were instructed to apply less rigorous criteria in the restriction of outdoor relief. Paradoxically this was followed by a reversal of policy towards a more stringent application of the regulations limiting outdoor relief. [c42] The results were predictable: the unemployed, confronted by the degradation and stigma of the workhouse, fell back on relief from other sources, notably charity.

The obvious anachronisms of the Poor Law as well as its failures to provide a humane and constructive solution to the many problems of poverty raised, in the early years of the twentieth century, some fundamental questions concerning its future: in the light of the far-reaching social welfare measures already taken, could the institution of the Poor Law be rationalized as the only appropriate means of dealing with residual poverty? Could the system be improved? Or should it be abolished, and replaced by something of a very different nature? To answer these questions, the Conservative Government in 1905 appointed a Royal Commission, the first major review of the Poor Law since 1834. This body certainly represented expertise on the subject. It included not only bureaucrats who had been administering the Poor Law but also influential members of the Charity Organization Society, as well as more radical opinion, such as Charles Booth and Beatrice Webb.[c43] The inquiry was a detailed and prolonged one—the evidence filled forty-seven volumes.

Given the great variance of ideology of its members, it was inevitable that the Commission would be unable to produce a unanimous report. It was, perhaps, surprising that so much common ground did emerge between the Majority Report[c44] (which as an oversimplification may be said to have reflected the views of the administrators) and the Minority Report[c45] (which was drafted by Beatrice and Sidney Webb). The Majority were prepared to concede that the existing system was no longer an appropriate method of dealing with poverty. They referred to 'modifications and developments in our industrial system which cannot be ignored, and their products and wreckage, when either out of employment or in distress, require a treatment more elastic and varied than the simple method which, eighty years ago, was sufficient to cope with able-bodied pauperism'.[c46] Like the Minority, and in stark contrast to the 1834 Commission, they concentrated many of their recommendations on preventive and curative measures: a national system of labour exchanges, raising of industrial health standards, extension of technical education. Even more important, perhaps, they were prepared (if somewhat reluctantly[c47]) to see abandoned the ideology of relief based on 'less eligibility' and replace it by a programme of 'treatment' which would differ according to the circumstances of the individual: the creation of special public services for the care of the old, the sick, children, and the able-bodied unemployed.

On the other hand, there were some fundamental differences between the two Reports. The first related to the relationship between state and voluntary action: the Majority saw the latter as the *primary* source of welfare and was to be encouraged by making public assistance less attractive.[c48] This vestige of *laissez-faire* was anathema to the Minority who argued that it was only through a rational and coherent structure of state intervention that the proper degree of welfare could be attained.[c49] They also rejected the implicit discrimination which would result between the poor who could subsist through voluntary action and those who would have to rely on state aid. The second difference was not unrelated to the first and perhaps reflected the more idealistic aims of the Minority. They conceived that if the system of public assistance were established on a sound and comprehensive basis the problem of pauperism would disappear and there would be no need to provide facilities for the residual poor.[c50] The Majority's conception of Public Assistance would never have been so comprehensive as to eliminate this residual category, and they proposed the establishment of some Destitution Authority to distribute appropriate relief.[c51] The debate clearly goes to the heart of the question of social services and is beyond the scope of this work.[c52] Our task here must be to assess the significance of the Reports in the evolution of social insurance. We shall refer, in turn, to some general and then some specific aspects of the Commission's proposals.

Four general considerations deserve to be mentioned. First, there was formal recognition of the fact that the poor were not a single group for whom a general system of relief was appropriate: poverty was rather the consequence of a number of social risks which were to be sharply differentiated. Secondly, in so far as individual liberty was an insufficient guarantee of individual welfare, collectivist solutions were inevitable, though there were obvious differences as to how far such collectivist action should go. Thirdly, attention was clearly focussed on prevention and the social provision of benefits in kind rather than on financial relief. In this respect, social welfare measures involving financial benefits, including social insurance, were complementary to the main thrust of state intervention. Fourthly (and perhaps this was only to repeat a theme emerging from the 1834 Report) national rather than local administration was essential.

It will be at once apparent that while these general sentiments are compatible with social insurance, they are by no means logically connected with it, and indeed the Reports provided very little direct encouragement for the idea. They were, of course, concerned with the financial plight of those who for one reason or another were unable to earn, but the emphasis continued to be very much on *voluntary* systems of insurance with the state performing only a subordinate role. Thus, in relation to unemployment, both the Majority [c53] and Minority [c54] Reports supported the idea of building on existing trade union schemes but with some financial contribution from the Exchequer. A compulsory scheme for all employees and employers was regarded as neither 'practicable nor desirable': the burden of supporting casual and irregular labour, in particular, would have been too great. [c55] So also while the idea of invalidity insurance was found to be appealing, attention was directed to facilitating wider and more generous coverage by the Friendly Societies. [c56] As regards the aged, the difficulties in a contributory scheme formulated by previous committees [c57] were regarded as conclusive of the issue. [c58]

THE ADVENT OF NATIONAL INSURANCE

As will be clear from previous discussion, the notion of social insurance was by no means a novelty in Britain. Knowledge of foreign, particularly German, experience had accumulated and there had been Canon Blackley's bold, if ill-received, plan. In a previous section, we have attempted to speculate on why, in comparison with, for example, Germany, the introduction of social insurance was so long delayed. In this section we shall attempt to explain how and why the introduction took place in 1911.

The Royal Commission on the Poor Law had been set up in the last days of the Conservative administration of 1905. This was no mere coincidence. The commercial and other interests represented in that party mainly adhered to traditional views on the methods of alleviating distress caused by social hazards and it was hoped that a more efficient poor-law system as a residual form of relief combined with other measures on old age and unemployment, already described, would be sufficient. [c59] The new Liberal administration came to power with other ideas and ideals. Whether or not these were forced on them by political pressure from below, by influential pressure groups, or by a more conscious reaction to changing attitudes to social welfare is a major and controversial historical issue. [c60] The tone was already set in 1906. Lloyd George spoke of 'a new order coming from the people in this country . . . a quiet, but certain, revolution',[61] and in another speech he enunicated the principle of social justice which was to form the inspiration of the coming reforms: 'the law which protects those men in the enjoyment of their great possessions should, first of all, see that those whose labour alone produces that wealth are amply protected with their families from actual need, where they are unable to purchase necessaries owing to circumstances over which they have no control'.[62] At about the same time, Churchill commented on 'the whole tendency of civilisation . . . towards the multiplication of the collective functions of society'.[63]

Indeed, quite apart from those measures already mentioned and national insurance, the period 1906 to 1914 witnessed a major series of welfare reforms, to a greater or lesser extent inspired by redistributionary aims.[64] There were important measures on working conditions,[65] school meals,[66] medical services for children,[67] minimum wages for certain industries[68] and housing.[69] In order to appreciate the reasons for the inclusion of national insurance among these reforms, we must be careful to distinguish between the appeal of the general notion of social insurance, and the particular areas of unemployment and sickness covered by the original legislation.

If, as an oversimplification, we can characterize the two polar views of welfare as individualist and collectivist, the former based on the maximization of individual utility through the exploitation of free market forces, combined with the legal protection of property rights and contractual expectations, the latter involving a unilateral transfer of resources from one section of the community to another through state intervention,[70] it is not difficult to understand why, in the early years of the twentieth century, the notion of social insurance represented such a satisfactory compromise between these two extremes.[71] It maintained, in a somewhat modified form, the exchange or reciprocal basis to social welfare: it was based on past performance in employment, and on financial contributions from the individual himself; benefit could thus be justified as having been 'earned'. In legal terms, it gave rise to something akin to a contractual right. In moral, cultural terms, it incorporated the traditional puritan, capitalist virtues of thrift and foresight.

In these respects, then, it was compatible, if not totally consistent, with traditional values. In certain other respects, it marked a significant advance towards collectivist values, and for this reason is regarded by some as the cornerstone of the modern welfare state.[72] First, it involved a new kind of interference in industrial relations. Hitherto, the employment relationship had been seen as giving rise to a simple, legal form of reciprocal obligations: the employee worked, in return for which the employer paid him wages. Now, the contributions paid both by the employer and the employee for some *future* contingency, meant that the relationship gave effect to *long-term* consequences. The famous English jurist Maine had described, to the end of the nineteenth century, the evolution of the legal identity of the individual from 'status to contract'.[73] Here we begin to see the beginning of the reverse process, from 'contract to status'. Secondly, social insurance gave rise to a new form of relationship between the individual and the state. This, almost contractual, relationship might be significant in that it meant, or should have meant, that the right to welfare existed independently of the political whims of particular government. Of course, as will emerge, particularly in the early stages, this concept was weakened not only by the obvious difference between social and commercial insurance (the broad pooling of risks and the lack of a precise actuarial base to the financing) but also because, especially in relation to unemployment, the insurance technique proved to be inadequate in coverage. Thirdly, the financing and administration of the scheme would require new notions of collective responsibility. Here also the 'pooling of risks' notion was crucial. More valid in relation to sickness, than to unemployment insurance, the existence of universal and compulsory insurance would necessarily involve the covering of 'bad' as well as 'good' risks in a way which could hardly be reflected in different contribution ratings. The consequence was some limited form of redistribution between those less susceptible to the particular hazards covered and those more at risk. The exact extent of such redistribution must await detailed consideration of the particular schemes; we must now proceed to examine how these general considerations were brought to bear on the particular problems of sickness and unemployment.

For years evidence had been accumulating on sickness being a major cause of poverty.[74] It has also become increasingly apparent that the treatment of the sick within the traditional poor law structure was anachronistic. The principle of less eligibility, it will be recalled,[75] required that the position of a recipient should not be more favourable than that of wage-earners. This often became impossible to apply to the sick, for large numbers of earners could not afford appropriate medical treatment, and such treatment had to be available within the context of poor law facilities.[76] Outside the poor law, there was no 'system' of medical care, but rather a number of unco-ordinated and overlapping institutions. The typical working-class neighbourhood might have a provident dispensary, operated on a commercial basis by a group of doctors, or by a charity, or (more rarely) by a friendly society.[77] These were complemented by individual doctors working either by themselves, or else in conjunction with a friendly society or trade union. In terms of hospitals, the poor had to rely on so-called 'voluntary hospitals' (those run by charity) or else the poor-law infirmaries. As regards the protection of the earner against lost income, the position was not much brighter. True there existed the friendly societies and other forms of voluntary insurance[78] but, not unreasonably, they could hardly provide comprehensive coverage: only one-half of the working population were insured for sickness, and that did not often cover all an individual's needs.[79] In short, medical and financial provision for the sick was either inadequate, or, in so far as it involved the poor law, stigmatizing.

Lloyd George, perhaps the most powerful protagonist of the Liberal welfare reforms, was drawn to social insurance as the best solution for some of these problems. In categorical terms, he felt that the state ought to assist in making 'provisions against the accidents of life which bring so much undeserved poverty to hundreds of thousands of homes, accidents which are quite inevitable such as the death of the breadwinner or his premature breakdown in health'.[80] The cost of the noncontributory old age pension scheme[81] made it obvious that any comprehensive scheme could not be financed from general taxation: insurance, with contributions from employers and employees, was the obvious method. The resolve was strengthened by his short visit to Germany. He was very impressed by what he saw in that country, and instituted a more detailed study of it by his officials.[82]

It was one thing to proffer rational argument for a sickness insurance scheme; it was quite another thing to render it politically acceptable, and the years 1909 to

1911 witnessed a considerable struggle between the Liberal Government determined to introduce some form of the German model and those pressure groups who had a vested interest in the more traditional, voluntary, welfare schemes. [c83] In the first place, there was the medical profession. Now, this group was by no means satisfied with existing arrangements. Those under contract with Friendly Societies felt exploited by being underpaid and overstretched. At the same time, they were naturally wholly opposed to the notion of a national salaried service (as proposed by, *inter alia*, the Webbs [c84]), which would involve bureaucratic control and inhibit the freedom of the patient to choose his doctor. The compromise was not, however, difficult to envisage. A medical service was to be organized by a new institution ('Insurance Committees') with some degree of independence from central government; patients were allowed to choose their own doctors; the service provided by doctors who wished to join the scheme was free but it extended only to what a general practitioner could be expected normally to do — it did not include specialized services, dental or opthalmic treatment, nor hospitalization. Perhaps the major omission was the lack of coverage for the dependants of insured persons.

The second wave of opposition came not unnaturally from the Friendly Societies for whom any state scheme would constitute direct competition. The solution to this clash of interests was ingenious if, in the long term, not wholly satisfactory. Under the proposed scheme, the Friendly Societies would play no part in the supervision of medical care — their record in this regard, particularly in their handling of doctors, was not a distinguished one. Instead, they would have a substantial role in the provision of cash benefits. Those that satisfied certain conditions would become 'Approved Societies': each contributor would then become a member of a society of his choice, that society receiving the relevant proportion of the contribution from the State, and being responsible for the payment of benefits. But, provided that a minimum was exceeded, the amount of benefit was for the Society to decide. The intention was, of course, to preserve some element of voluntary insurance, though the principle was not extended so far as to permit variation in contributions.

Here were the basic elements in the scheme (further details will be given in a subsequent section), and its implementation in Part I of the National Insurance Act 1911 was, in the light of the radical changes it brought about and of the political opposition which had to be overcome, little short of a triumph for Lloyd George. One observer, at the time, hailed it as 'the greatest scheme of social reconstruction ever yet attempted'. [c85]

The unemployment insurance scheme, introduced contemporaneously as Part II of the 1911 Act, was less extensive in its coverage and yet, perhaps, an even greater achievement as, unlike the sickness scheme, it could not be modelled on any major foreign experience. It must not be assumed from the fact that these two substantial reforms were effected in one piece of legislation that they were conceived, much less implemented, as a unity. Both in its planning and its institution, the unemployment scheme was very different from that for sickness. Whereas it would be difficult to estimate whether sickness or unemployment was the more significant cause of poverty, it was clear that as a potential insurable risk unemployment was much more problematic. This was not just because scientific analysis of it as a phenomenon was so recent; [c86] it was also because it had major economic implications not present in sickness. Unlike the latter it did not strike haphazardly but rather resulted from management of the economy, and trade cycles generally. Its impact differed considerably according to the industry concerned and while the healthy subsidizing the sick was unexceptionable in policy terms, the arguments for 'healthy' industries subsidizing 'sick' industries were obviously less appealing. National unemployment insurance was not seriously considered in Britain until 1907 and, significantly, only then as part of an overall strategy towards unemployment, which included the institution of labour exchanges. [c87] In the light of these considerations, it was not surprising that the Board of Trade was responsible both for the scheme, and its eventual administration. [c88] The influential individuals there were Beveridge, who had worked in a London East End settlement, [c89] and Llewellyn Smith, who had been a member of Charles Booth's survey team. [c90]

The campaign for unemployment insurance did not encounter the major political opposition which Lloyd George had faced in relation to sickness, simply because there were no major vested interests which were threatened. Yet, in the initial period of debate, support for the alternative traditional approach of voluntary insurance administered by the trade unions and subsidized by the Exchequer was widespread, not least in the Reports of the Poor Law Commission. [c91] In this sense, of course, unemployment insurance was by no means novel: indeed in 1908 1059 unions, with nearly 2.5 million members, paid some kind of unemployment benefit. [c92] But the shortcomings were manifest. Those covered were the privileged elite of skilled and highly paid workmen — outside this group unemployment insurance hardly existed. [c93] The nature and amount of benefit varied and while, where depressions and labour markets were localized, it operated to encourage mobility, it could hardly have an effect on national trade cycles. Moreover, with contributions being made solely by employees, it ignored the interests and responsibilities of industrialists. As Churchill wrote in 1908: 'Unemployment is primarily a question for employers . . . their responsibility is undoubted, their cooperation indispensable'. [c94] It has been suggested, too, that the proponents of the national, compulsory, scheme were fearful of the growth in trade-union power, which they saw as implicit in a more expanded version of the traditional model. [c95]

Once the principle of a compulsory state scheme had been accepted, the next fundamental problem was that of coverage. The inference drawn from the failure of the only foreign experience, that of St Gall, [c96] was that a compulsory and comprehensive scheme was doomed, primarily because of actuarial difficulties: it was impossible to calculate the risk of unemployment, particularly in certain industries. [c97] These arguments proved to be conclusive in relation to any plan for a fully comprehensive scheme, and Llewellyn Smith thus concentrated on a compromise plan: compulsory insurance for all workers in certain industries including ship building, engineering and construction. These trades were liable mainly to seasonal fluctuations and fell midway between those which had a relatively stable employment record (and for whom the need was, therefore, less pressing) and those where unemployment was typically more chronic (and therefore difficult to handle). It followed that while the concept of state unemployment insurance might have been novel (in comparison with sickness insurance), the first scheme, in terms of its coverage, was quite tentative. In the words of Gilbert, 'in effect the planners of the world's first compulsory state unemployment insurance programme loaded their actuarial calculations and narrowed their risk in every possible way'. [c98]

If the requirement of employers' contributions could be justified in terms of their participation in the administration of the scheme, in the general improvement and discipline of the work force, it nevertheless also produced demands for safeguards against malingering. The answer came in the form not only of benefits set deliberately low — a vestige here of the Poor Law less eligibility principle — but also by limiting their duration and by rules imposing disqualification for voluntary leaving, misconduct, and refusal to seek alternative employment. Moreover, so as to limit the degree of subsidy provided by enterprises with good employment records, it was decided to provide refunds to employers who kept men regularly at work and to workmen who by the age of 60 had drawn less in benefit than they had paid in contributions. Needless to say, the fear that unemployment benefit might be used as a form of strike pay was countered by widely-drawn provisions disentitling those involved in trade disputes.[c99]

THE DEVELOPMENT OF SOCIAL INSURANCE FROM 1911

GENERAL BACKGROUND

Developments Between the Wars
First World War

No sooner had the liberal welfare programme been put into effect, than the Great War broke out, an event which produced changes in economic and social influences on a scale never before experienced.[d1] Unlike previous military engagements, this necessarily involved almost the whole population: conscription and the full-time employment of a large section of the population (especially women[d2]) who had not previously been regularly active in the labour market provide the most obvious evidence. The war effort could be financed only through a much greater burden of taxation, and this inevitably involved some narrowing of the huge gap between rich and poor.[d3] State control of the economy reached unknown levels which might, in the eyes of some, have led to a more permanent departure from the traditional decentralized form of economic planning. As R. H. Tawney observed,

> the period of war economy accelerated the demise of the individualist, competitive phase of British capitalism. It stimulated organisation and combination among manufacturers; advertised rationalisation; strengthened the demand for tariffs; and encouraged . . . the settlement of wages and working conditions by national rather than by local agreements.[d4]

All these factors raised the question whether, once peace had been restored, the apparatus of the state could be deployed to solve the equally acute, if less bloody, social problems of a mature industrial society.

Economic Recovery and Subsequent Crisis

Any hope of maintaining a broad level of centralized control of the economy was to be disappointed. Manufacturers, in particular, demanded a speedy return to prewar conditions and in the period 1919 to 1921 almost all wartime controls were abolished, and, spurred on by the prospect of high profits, there was a sudden and massive bout of speculative investment.[d5] These 'boom' conditions lasted for a very short time: already in 1920 heavy inflation set in; large concerns had become top-heavy; ill-judged investment began to take its toll. International trade had hardly recovered to create a sufficient foreign demand for products. Faced with an incipient depression, the policymaker was able to offer by way of response little other than orthodox economic wisdom: the ordinary interplay of market forces would produce automatic readjustment — the difficulties at the time were merely the continuing consequences of war and a return to 'normalcy' was simply a matter of time. [d6] Whether or not politicians and economists must take the major responsibility for the interwar depression is a much disputed issue. [d7] Certainly, they cannot be blamed for the legacies of former industrial structure, the excessive commitment to outmoded technology and industry and the lack of adaptation to new sources of energy and management techniques. On the other hand, there was a clear lack of strategy in dealing with ills, and the effects of the over-pragmatic approach were mainly to fall on the weaker sections of the community. Certainly, the very high levels of unemployment (in 1921, 22 percent of the insured population were out of work and in the early 1930s the figure was nearly as high[d8]), dominated social welfare policy during this period. While the emphasis might have been on the almost impossible demands made on unemployment insurance[d9] and the inevitable resort to alternative, means-tested forms of welfare, [d10] other aspects of the welfare system were not immune from its impact. All parts of the national insurance structure were, of course, obstructed by difficulties caused by the discontinuities in employment. Moreover, pre-Keynesian constraints on public spending and inadequate resources in the Insurance Funds meant that benefits could be paid at an absolute minimum level only.

Political Activism

We have already seen how the First World War involved the whole population to a hitherto unparalleled extent. Did this imply a social cohesion which overrode the principal class and wealth differences? The majority would probably answer that it did not, and in this respect the First World War differed significantly from that of the Second.[d11] There remained profound and often passionate differences of political opinion, and from this climate emerged the new strength of the Labour Party, with socialism (including common ownership of the means of production) as its basic creed. [d12] The party now offered itself seriously for government for the first time and was soon to replace the Liberals as the main alternative to conservatism. The trade union movement, not unexpectedly, grew at equivalent pace: membership rose from 4 million in 1914 to 8 million in 1920. [d13] Very radical opinion was rarely in evidence and both the labour and trade union movements were to see the Russian revolution as hindering the appeal to moderate opinion rather than fuelling the fires of discontent. Manifestation by means of strikes, while reaching significant levels in 1921 and again in the General Strike of 1926, tended to be construed as undermining the 'constitutional' and 'legitimate' pursuit of working class ideals by the Labour Party in Parliament.

A Divided Nation

Whether successive governments were concerned more to stem the tide of agitation outside Parliament, or rather to placate opinion which could express it itself through the ballot box (the franchise had been extended to all men and all women aged 30 in 1918[d14]), the labour movement was of such undeniable force that its claims could not be ignored. The failures of social policy of the inter-war period in no sense resulted from an attempt to flout collectivist ideology but rather stemmed from a sense of impotence in the face of the seemingly overwhelming economic forces. Even though governments may have been well intentioned, failure was still failure. For those who suffered under the Depression, failure was accentuated by the fact that its effects were not evenly distributed. The brunt of mass unemployment was felt in those regions of declining industries and declining communities, [d15] for example the North of England and Wales. Other regions, notably the Midlands and the South-East benefitted from new industries and increases in population. It was in this sense that it was possible to speak of a 'divided nation'[d16] one part enjoying relative prosperity, the other experiencing hardship and distress. Social insurance, and the other welfare measures of the period, may have mitigated the worst effects, but they could do nothing to alter the basic economic structure from which the evil resulted.

General Developments in Social Insurance

It will be our task in the next section to consider in detail developments in the legal principles of social insurance. Our concern here is to relate, at a general level, the major features of social insurance to the background already described.

Unemployment. While the period under review witnessed some major extensions to the scope of unemployment insurance—the categories of employment covered were much enlarged particularly in 1920[d17] and additions to the flat-rate benefit were paid for dependants from 1921[d18]—it was dominated by the unprecedented levels of unemployment which brought the insurance system very near to breaking point. A variety of devices was employed to supplement the conventional entitlement contributory benefit when it failed either because the period of unemployment exceeded that covered by the legislation or because the individual was unable to maintain a sufficient contributions record. As a temporary measure, it was first of all conceded that benefit might be paid in advance of contributions on the assumption that in the long run such contributions would in fact be made. [d19] An 'uncovenanted benefit' was introduced in 1921 (later known as 'extended' or 'transitional' benefit). [d20] This was payable at the discretion of the Minister and involved some investigation of means. As an outright deviation from the insurance principle this was condemned by a Committee reporting in 1927, [d21] but the continuing economic difficulties meant that the aim of returning to standard insurance principles could never be realized. Indeed in 1933 the number of claimants to the means-tested benefit exceeded those in receipt of insurance benefit. [d22] The whole question was reviewed by a Royal Commission in 1930–1932, [d23] and its recommendations established on a permanent basis the structure which, subject to minor modifications, has remained ever since. A clear distinction was drawn between insurance benefits, available for a limited duration to those satisfying the contribution requirements, and unemployment relief, a form of assistance administered by a special body and involving a means-test not only of the claimant himself, but also of all members of his household. [d24]

Health. In contrast the structure of National Health Insurance established by the 1911 Act underwent very little change during the interwar years. For no obvious reason, apart from finance, the scheme was never extended to cover dependants. The persistent problem of unemployment meant that special arrangements had to be made for those unable to maintain their contribution records. The chief modification was to extend the period of entitlement[d25] and because this placed an almost intolerable strain on the finances of the Approved Societies who administered the scheme, eventually a public Arrears Fund was set up to help out those societies in major difficulties.[d26]

Old Age Pensions. The change in social philosophy from means-tested, noncontributory old age pensions (under the 1908 Act) to the coverage of this social risk under the national insurance scheme (by legislation in 1925[d27]) was clearly a major one. On the one hand, it reflected a change in social attitudes towards social insurance which had taken place in a decade or so.[d28] This was clearly crucial, for in comparison with the short-term risks of unemployment and sickness (at least as covered by legislation at that time), the long-term nature of contributory old-age pensions involved a degree of financial and administrative commitment of quite a different dimension. On the other hand, it was clearly not appropriate to rely substantially on the non-contributory approach. Since the beginning of the century the number of people approaching old age had nearly doubled, and existing outlay on the 1908 scheme already exceeded £25 million.[d29] Two main questions were left to be resolved. First, how should the national insurance scheme relate to the means-tested benefits available to those aged 70 or more? Secondly, should the new system be integrated with unemployment insurance, with health insurance, or with neither? The answer to the first question was that for those aged between 65 and 70 only a contributory pension would be payable, but it would no longer be means-tested. As regards the second question, the scheme was to be combined with existing health insurance. There had been a campaign for linking all forms of social insurance in a single scheme;[d30] however, the administration of unemployment benefit involved the employment exchanges, and that of sickness benefit the approved societies. The most practical compromise seemed to be to link the new pension scheme with health insurance.

Widows and Orphans. Whereas the old age scheme in one sense added to existing provisions, there was nothing available in the public sector to protect widows and orphans from the rigour of the poor law. Any opposition from the industrial assurance companies had by this time been sufficiently diluted[d31] and the innovation could conveniently be seen as an adjunct to the old-age scheme. The 1925 Act thus added both risks to the liabilities of the health-insurance fund. As regards widows, one matter of controversy was whether those without dependent children should be entitled. There was understandable opposition from trade unionists (especially women members) to the notion of the insurance fund being available to those who were able to earn their own keep.[d32] For reasons which have yet to be fully explained, the government of the day ignored what was apparently the public sentiment on the question, and extended the new benefit to all widows of contributors, regardless of age, and whether or not she cared for children.[d33]

Beveridge and the Welfare State

Preconditions for Welfare State

It is against the background of the pre-war developments that the significance of Beveridge and the ideology of the 'welfare state' can be understood. The notion of adequate protection against social risks was, of course, nothing new: it had been a central tenet in Fabian socialism.[d34] The impact of the Beveridge Report was considerable and its achievement both in rationalizing existing systems of social security and integrating them into a coherent whole must not be underestimated. But there was little which was truly original or radical in the notion of a comprehensive programme of social insurance covering the major risks and paying benefits at a subsistence level; it was a logical extension and culmination of a programme which began in 1911. Indeed, in many respects, as we shall see, it can be said that Beveridge proclaimed a liberal individualist ideology which was not to accord with the realities of the second half of the twentieth century. The key to the political appeal of the Beveridge Report and the, at least temporary, success of the legislation which implemented it is to be found not in the substantive proposals on social insurance but rather on the more radical commitments to which they were appended. There were three such commitments: full employment, family endowment and the national health service.[d35]

It follows from what was said above that social security, unaccompanied by more fundamental economic and social policies, was likely to achieve little. In the words of George, 'social security benefits for controllable risks are only meaningful if a serious attempt is made by the government to abolish or reduce these risks'.[d36] The pursuit of a policy of 'full employment' was clearly one such attempt.[d37] It had its source in the Keynesian revolution in economic thought, the notion that the problem of unemployment could be solved by a greater degree of government planning which would be based on stimulating additional demand for goods and labour.[d38] It found its fullest expression in the White Paper 'Employment Policy', published in 1944.[d39] There was a government commitment to 'the maintenance of a high and stable level of employment'[d40] and the means for securing this were outlined: in the short term a substantial degree of control of production to speed reconstruction after the war; in the long term, control of capital expenditure and the creation of incentives for the proper distribution of industry and mobility of labour; public spending to stimulate demand where depression was threatened and training facilities to redeploy the work force. The relevance of all this to the Beveridge programme for social insurance may be seen in his observation that

> the probable and possible effects of the Plan for Social Security in stabilising the demand for labour are among its advantages. . . . But . . . they are subsidiary measures only; they do not touch the main problem of maintaining employment. For that other measures are needed. Unless such measures are prepared and can be effective, much that might otherwise be gained through the Plan for Social Security will be wasted.[d41]

The principle of family endowment played a less prominent role in policy debates during this period, yet in retrospect can be seen as equally significant. Family endowment, to be achieved either through the tax system (the set-off against taxable income according to the size of the family) or through an independent financial benefit (in Britain family allowances, later child benefit) involved state support for the family, and necessarily some degree of redistribution, in the most direct form. These forms of financial provision can fit but uneasily into a system of social insurance for the existence of children is hardly to be regarded as a 'social risk'.[d42] Moreover, it was, and still is,[d43] regarded as the primary instrument for dealing with poverty: it is not means-tested and therefore avoids problems of dependence and stigma; it is available whether or not the head of the family is employed, and therefore cannot involve work incentive problems. During the inter-war years the movement for family endowment, in contrast to those in other European countries was slow to grow. It stemmed from the Family Endowment Society and the influence of its leader, Eleanor Rathbone who in 1924 published an important tract, arguing in utilitarian terms that society as a whole benefitted when children were well fed and clothed.[d44] The force of its arguments became even more penetrating when supported by hard evidence of family poverty. The indefatigable Rowntree repeated his earlier inquiries into social conditions in York, and found the key factor of poverty to be family size, when combined either with unemployment or low wages. He estimated that about one-third of the working-class population was living below his definition of poverty.[d45] The findings were confirmed by a survey carried out in Bristol in 1937: one-fifth of working-class children were regarded as being inadequately fed.[d46]. The major theme in the campaign for family allowances, then, was redistribution and the need for a healthy working population in the future. A minor theme, but one stressed in Beveridge's Report,[d47] was to stimulate the birth-rate which had been falling steadily in the 1930s.[d48]

The third commitment which complemented the Beveridge plan of social insurance was the introduction of a national health *service*, thus replacing the system of national health *insurance*, dating originally from the 1911 Act. Now, with perhaps an excusable degree of exaggeration, Professor Gilbert writes,

> for most people before the war, social reform means Part I of the National Insurance Act. . . . Through the wage-earner, it touched five-sixths of the families of the United Kingdom, bringing them into contact with the national government in an unprecedented way. It began the transformation of relations between British citizens and the State.[d49]

In a similar way, it might be said that in the post-Second World War period it was the National Health Service which, for most people, represented the Welfare State. The transition in conviction from health care being based on the social insurance principle, and financed predominantly by contributions, to a system of universal provision financed by general taxation was therefore crucial both as regards the foundations of the modern welfare state and in the recognition of the limits of social insurance.

The perceived need for this fundamental change resulted from growing dissatisfaction with several aspects of the medical-care dimension of the national health insurance system.[d50] As we have seen, Lloyd George was compelled by political pressure, to compromise the theory of social insurance by combining a national system of contributions and minimum benefits with administration by the independent approved societies which were also free to fix the level of benefits above the minimum as they felt appropriate. In the eyes of some, particularly on the left of the political spectrum, this was, from the beginning, seriously to undermine the welfare potential of the system. The approved societies were understandably more concerned with the protection of their own members than with the functioning of the system as a whole.[d51] Competition between the societies was seen to create inefficiency of administration in the form of wasteful overlaps rather than to lead to better benefits for the contributors. In so far as it did give rise to major differences in the level and type of benefits offered, this was felt to be inconsistent with the theory of social insurance. [d52] The areas of medical care omitted from the scheme were notoriously broad; they included hospital treatment and consultation with specialists. This patchwork approach necessarily meant that there was no co-ordinated state approach to the provision of medical services generally: there were gaps and overlaps between state and local services, facilities maintained by the approved societies and voluntary (including charitable) agencies. [d53] More seriously still, there were no obligations on the societies to provide medical care for the dependants of contributors. It was this consideration which above all prompted the British authorities to diverge from the orthodox continental approach to social insurance. The need for medical care applied to all members of society whether or not they were in gainful employment. So long as social insurance was based on the protection of the employed earner, it was the appropriate form of protection against loss of, or interruption to, earnings, but not for indemnifying expenses which had nothing to do with earning power. The notion of a universal health service financed from general taxation [d54] gained further impetus during the Second World War from the ideal of social solidarity which wartime conditions had fostered: all members of the community were seen as playing a part in the national effort, whether or not they were contributors to the national insurance schemes.

The Beveridge Restatement and Rationalization

Arguably, therefore, the most important features of the 'Welfare State' ideology which gained currency during the 1930s and 1940s were unconnected with social insurance and formed only an ancillary part to the Beveridge Plan. What then was the significance of the Beveridge Report; in what sense did it advance or change existing notions of social insurance?

In the first place, the Report was a reaffirmation of the primacy of social insurance as the means of protecting individuals against social risks. The reciprocal model of welfare, with its emphasis on people earning the right to benefits through their contributions, [d55] was central to Beveridge's philosophy: 'benefit in return for contributions, rather than free allowances from the State, is what the people of Britain desire'. [d56] This naturally was reinforced by his antipathy towards, and popular dislike of, means-tested unilateral welfare which the prewar insufficiencies of unemployment insurance had rendered such a common phenomenon: there was, he said, 'resentment at a provision which appears to penalise what people have come to regard as the duty and pleasure of thrift, of putting pennies away for a rainy day'. [d57]

Secondly, it involved a rationalization of social insurance methods. For the first time in the history of British social policy, a comprehensive overview of social risks and the methods of meeting them had been attempted. The methods and objectives were subjected to critical scrutiny and what emerged was a framework of principles emanating from certain explicit values and assumptions. If the assumptions were correct and if the methods were to be applied consistently, then the goal of 'freedom from want' could be achieved. The plan comprised six fundamental principles. [d58]

Flat Rate of Subsistence Benefit. The notion familiar to continental systems of social insurance of earnings-related benefit was alien to the British tradition and also to the Beveridge philosophy. In this important respect the collectivist nature of social insurance was to be reconciled with what were seen as the virtues of liberal individualism: the individual should have the freedom to make provision for himself above the national minimum subsistence level.

> Social security must be achieved by cooperation between the State and the individual. . . . The State in organising security should not stifle incentive, opportunity, responsibility; in establishing a national minimum, it should leave room and encouragement for voluntary action by each individual to provide more than that minimum for himself and his family. [d59]

This first principle was, of course, already implicit in existing national insurance legislation, and it was to admit of exception only as regards the industrial injuries scheme. [d60]

Flat Rate of Contribution. The same is true of the second principle: the compulsory contribution of each insured person (and his employer) is flat rate, irrespective of means. Social insurance was not to be used as an instrument for the redistribution of resources, which would have been the case if earnings-related contributions had been combined with flat-rate benefits. Beveridge indulged in rhetoric to support this approach. Taxation according to capacity, he argued, 'involves a departure from existing practice, for which there is neither need nor justification and which conflicts with the wishes and feelings of British democracy. . . . Contributions means that in their capacity as possible recipients of benefits the poorer man and the richer man are treated alike'. [d61] There was, however, *some* form of redistribution in the limited sense that those less susceptible to risk were subsidizing those more vulnerable. The unwillingness to recommend any form of premium-rating of contributions (Beveridge did argue for such a system in relation only to industrial injuries but this did not prove to be acceptable[d62]) meant that particular industries were not to bear the appropriate cost of, for example, unemployment and accidents which their activities engendered. The social arguments for risk-pooling were thus seen to prevail over the economic arguments of price-distortion and cost-abatement incentives. [d63]

Unification of Administrative Responsibility. This third principle would constitute a major advance on previous arrangements. The pre-war national insurance schemes had been established at different times and with different administrative aims. The task was now, in the interests of efficiency, to have a single fund, to which individuals would make a composite (generally weekly) contribution; and a single office would be available to receive claims for all types of benefit. [d64]

Adequacy of Benefit. If the comprehensive network of social insurance was to achieve its goal of freedom from want, then clearly the benefit paid must be adequate. It followed that the flat-rate benefit would have to be based on a careful assessment of need. In particular, regard was to be had to family size. Time added another dimension to adequacy: the pre-war experience of chronic unemployment had shown only too clearly the dangers of too brief a period of entitlement.

Comprehensiveness. In terms of the immediate appeal of the plan, both in Britain and abroad, it was perhaps this principle which made the greatest impact. The idea was that all members of the population—not merely employed persons—should be covered against all the major social risks. In practice this would mean the inclusion of certain risks hitherto omitted, notably maternity and funeral expenses, and also the substitution of social insurance for individual employers' liability with regard to work accidents. As regards the population included, it would involve extending compulsory insurance to groups hitherto excluded, notably the self-employed. While the universality of coverage is rightly regarded as one of the hallmarks of British social insurance, the contrasts with foreign systems and indeed British pre-war systems should not be exaggerated. The great majority of those not active economically received protection as dependants of an earner, and those not so dependent (e.g. those on a private income and students) could be offered protection only for a limited number of purposes.

Classification. The sixth principle hardly exists in its own right but is rather a qualification to other principles. While the latter, as they stood, envisaged a unified treatment of the population as regards benefits, contributions and coverage, it was nevertheless necessary to take account of basic differences in the needs and activities of employees, the self-employed, housewives, and those not gainfully employed.

The Failure of the Beveridge Model of Social Insurance

The Beveridge Report aroused a degree of popular interest never before experienced with a Government publication.[d65] Rightly or wrongly, it was seen as heralding a new age in the social protection of the citizen. The Government White Paper which followed[d66] endorsed the underlying principles though they did deviate on certain detailed proposals.[d67] The national insurance legislation, together with the measures on national assistance, family allowances and the national health service, then established the structure Beveridge had envisaged for British social security.[d68] While the early years of the new era did not pass without difficulty, particularly in the financial sphere,[d69] this was considered to be unexceptional: Britain was, after all, engaged in the slow process of economic recovery from the war effort. Such was the confidence in the success of the new Welfare State that in 1950 the Labour Government went to the country with an election manifesto claiming that it had 'ensured full employment and fair shares of the necessities of life' and that 'destitution had been banished'[d70] and the latest in the series of Rowntree surveys in York apparently supported the claim.[d71] This revealed a decline in the poverty of the working-class population from 31 percent in 1936 to 3 percent in 1950; of this reduction, 20 percent was alleged to have resulted from the recent welfare legislation.[d72]

The complacency engendered by these findings was soon to be replaced by the growing realization that, far from achieving its objectives, the social security system with the Beveridge model of social insurance as its basis had failed in several significant respects. It is the existence of this failure, its causes and its consequences, in terms of replacement by a new model of social insurance that now fall to be examined.

Social Administration: A New Social Science?

Awareness of the inadequacies of the national insurance system is closely linked with the growth of 'social administration' as a social science. Under the inspired leadership of its pioneer, Richard Titmuss,[d73] a movement sprang up in the

1950s, operating mainly within the universities, whose primary concern was the positive and normative analysis of welfare provision in contemporary society.[474] Having no methodology of its own, it employed as appropriate the techniques of sociology, history and economics. Its impact was immense: as one writer has observed, 'this "outburst" of analysis can be paralleled with the work of Booth and Rowntree sixty years earlier. The complacency and the belief that poverty was a "non-problem" was shattered and it is apparent that the results had a considerable amount of influence on policy makers'.[475]

The Meaning of 'Poverty'

Clearly, the claim of this group to have 'rediscovered poverty' begged the question of what was meant by 'poverty'. To challenge the findings of the 1950 York Survey,[476] it might have been sufficient to question its methodology: the sample had been drawn unscientifically; there were anomalies in the definition of poverty adopted; most importantly, it was far from clear that York was representative of the country at large.[477] But in fact the criticisms of the new school went far deeper. They argued that the notion of poverty which had been adopted in earlier surveys, which subsequently was taken as governing entitlement to the means-tested benefits (unemployment assistance later national assistance) and which involved a list of consumption necessities,[478] was no longer appropriate. Not only did it imply that 'poor working-class people should and could live as social scientists and administrators think they should live'[479] but it ignored the fundamental fact that poverty was relative to the resources and general standard of living of a particular society at a particular time.[480] Poverty in the latter sense, therefore, referred to the general issues of wealth distribution, and to the power which arose from advantages in wealth.[481]

Poverty Rediscovered

Even on more traditional definitions, the studies in the 1950s and 1960s revealed that there were unexpectedly large numbers of families and individuals living below the officially recognized poverty line. A 1957 study found that one-third of retired people were entitled to national assistance, though through disinclination to apply or other reasons, were not all in receipt of it.[482] Family poverty was also a major subject of inquiry. In 1955 it was estimated that one household in ten was living at a standard less than 40 percent above the national assistance rates. It had been assumed that such poverty was to be associated normally with unemployment, retirement or disablement, but in fact in one-third of these households the head was working full-time.[483] In the 1960s and 1970s attention was focussed on two other groups: the disabled and single-parent families.

Chronically Sick and Disabled. A major government survey of handicapped and impaired persons was undertaken in 1968/9.[484] It provided an estimate of 1.1 million handicapped people. Many of these people were above retirement age and in receipt of the national insurance retirement pension and some were in hospital or other institutions. Of the 390 000 adults aged under 65 living in private households and handicapped in terms of self-care, about 250 000 received some form of insurance benefit, though not necessarily because of their disablement. The crucial remainder of 140 000 did not receive a benefit either because they did not come within a contingency covered by an existing scheme, or because they had not paid the necessary contributions. [485] The two most important categories here were housewives (who were not insured) and the congenitally disabled who would (but for their disability) have been the family breadwinner. Moreover, even for those who did succeed in establishing title to the insurance benefits, the amount payable often proved to be inadequate — the fundamental principle of Beveridge, that all victims of social risks should receive the same flat-rate benefit, subject to modification only according to the number of family dependants, failed to take account of the financial problems faced particularly by the severely disabled.

Single-parent Families. The single-parent condition was a social risk which was only dimly perceived by Beveridge. [486] He had flirted with the idea of an insurance benefit which would be paid for a temporary period following the breakdown of a marriage. The proposal was rapidly disposed of in the government White Paper which followed the Report. [487] This was not a risk which a social insurance scheme could embrace: administratively (and *sub silentio* politically) it was not feasible, particularly as it would involve some investigation into the cause of the breakdown. The matter was not resurrected until survey work showed that the group was particularly vulnerable in financial terms; the expectation that the erstwhile husband, or in the case of unmarried mothers the putative father, would provide the necessary maintenance was unrealistic as regards low-wage earners and those out of work. [488] At the same time, the number of single-parent families rose dramatically in the 1960s: in 1971 it was estimated that there were 620 000 such families (with over a million children), [489] and of these some 250 000 were in receipt of the means-tested supplementary benefit. [490] Moreover, in an effort to relieve the public purse, the Supplementary Benefits Commission had in many cases exerted undue pressure on the claimant to take legal proceedings against the 'liable relative', i.e. the person under a statutory obligation to maintain the woman and her children. [491]

The Adequacy of Benefits and Occupational Schemes

The findings of poverty outlined above, in particular the substantial proportion of national insurance beneficiaries who had to augment their income by resort to national assistance (subsequently supplementary benefit), demonstrated beyond question the failure of the system to implement Beveridge's principle of adequacy of benefit. The reasons for this failure may be summarized as follows. First, the actuarial calculations which had related expenditure on benefits to the level of contributions proved to be inaccurate. This was mainly because the post-war government had, for political reasons, been unwilling to endorse Beveridge's suggestion that full entitlement to retirement pension should arise only when the insurance fund had had 20 years to accumulate the necessary money. [492] Secondly, the situation could not be remedied by increasing the rate of employee contributions for under the flat-rate system these had to be set at a level which the lowest paid could afford. [493] Thirdly, there were limits to which the fund could be boosted by contributions from the Exchequer (and thus financed from general taxation) without seriously undermining the very nature of social insurance — in fact this contribution was raised from 11.9 percent in 1955 to nearly 20 percent in 1959. [494] Finally, that aspect of the Beveridge philosophy which had anticipated and encouraged voluntary methods of securing an income above the national insurance minimum could be said to have achieved but partial success. Now, there can be no doubt that, aided by tax incentives,[d95] occupational coverage against principally retirement and death, but also sickness, increased massively in the post-war period. In 1936 about 1.8 million people were members of such schemes. By 1951 the figure had risen to 6.3 million, by 1956 to 8 million and by 1967 to 12 million.[d96] But these figures themselves, as well as the more refined analysis which resulted from studies during the 1950s and 1960s[d97], reveal a marked degree of social divisiveness, such that those arguing from the Left could speak of the 'two nations in old age'.[d98] The problem was that while the more affluent worker, typically in the civil service or 'white-collar' employment, could normally look forward to retirement in which there would be a comparatively small drop in his living standards, the typical manual worker benefitted from no such superannuation scheme and had to fall back on a combination of the flat-rate, but inadequate national insurance retirement pension and (means-tested) national assistance.

Political Influences

Social facts do not exist in a vacuum. In order for them to influence governments and the legislature they must be not only communicated but also harnessed to political forces. We have already seen how the failures of the post-war social security system were investigated and published by a new breed of social scientists. It is now necessary to consider how these revelations were used by political groups who advocated legislative change. Three different facets must be distinguished.

First, during the two decades from 1955 to 1975 social security policy, particularly as it affected retirement pensions, played an important part in debate within the conventional political arena, that is to say between the Labour and Conservative Parties.[d99] The plight of the aged, as revealed above, and the fact that as a group this section of the electorate was always increasing, were not irrelevant considerations. While both major parties were in agreement that some fundamental changes to the Beveridge-inspired national insurance legislation were necessary, their different ideologies suggested different solutions. Conservative emphasis on individual freedom and responsibility as manifested in voluntary, non-centralized welfare resulted in a preference for private occupational coverage, though they also recognized the need for some improvement in residual welfare to be provided by the state.[e1] Their concern to maintain work incentives and their tolerance of means-tested approaches to welfare also led them to introduce Family Income Supplement, as an aid for lower-paid workers.[e2] In contrast the Labour Party stressed the primacy of collective welfare, which in this context was used to justify both an adaptation of the social insurance principle to accommodate a substantial degree of earnings-related protection and new levels of commitment to non-contributory, but also non-means-tested, benefits for the vulnerable sections of the community for whom national insurance protection was either unavailable or manifestly insufficient.[e3]

The second strand of political influence was relatively new to the British political scene, at least in size and impact. The 1960s and 1970s saw a massive growth in pressure groups representing different sections of the disadvantaged population. The phenomenon of such groups generally has attracted much attention from political scientists,[e4] but there has not been much specific study of the way in which they have affected policy decisions within the particular field of British social security. [e5] While naturally identifying themselves more with the ideologies on the left of the political spectrum, these groups have on the whole sought to be regarded as independent of party politics. [e6] They have benefitted from a greater readiness on the part of government to indulge in formal consultation during the policymaking stage. [e7] The pioneer in the social security area was, and to some extent still is, the Child Poverty Action Group, founded in 1965, and initially relying heavily for its membership and its publications on those active within the social administration discipline. [e8] While its name implies primary concern for child and family welfare, this group has concerned itself with poverty and welfare generally: its example has been followed by associations representing among others the disabled, [e9] the aged[e10] and single parents. [e11] Activities and political strategy vary; the majority favour an approach based on the communication of information to governments and the public at large and, where funds allow, often engage in the gathering of information on a more or less scientific basis. [e12] One group, on the other hand, which purports to represent recipients of supplementary benefit, indulges in more militant activity, arguing that fundamental change can be achieved only through a process of confrontation. [e13]

This last group effectively overlaps between the second and third category of political influences. The combination of the political parties and the pressure groups (including trade unions), it may be argued, achieved a form of consensus or compromise which resulted in the legislation passed in the period 1970 to 1975, described in outline below. One writer thus alleges that as a phenomenon which is common to affluent industrial societies, the British working class 'is satisfied with the capitalist system . . . has lost most of its drive to change the system substantially through peaceful or violent means . . . has enjoyed its newly gained relative affluence and its only desire is to increase it'. [e14] Whether such a degree of consensus in fact exists, and perhaps more pertinently, whether it will continue to exist in the economic climate of the 1980s are both controversial issues. Nevertheless, it may plausibly be contended that it has created frustration and hostility to the existing institutional framework in those of the radical Left who believe that social security as at present constituted does little to rectify the fundamental inequalities within contemporary society and in fact sustains rather than undermines the fabric of the capitalist economy. [e15]

Reconstruction of Social Insurance

Given the manifest failure of the 1946 national insurance legislation to fulfil the expectations which Beveridge and the post-war government had of it, the problem remained either to supplement it by additional welfare measures, or to modify it to remedy the deficiencies, or to engage in a strategy which would involve both. This last alternative was in fact adopted and the discussion will be divided accordingly.

Alternative Welfare Measures

Clearly there were certain aspects of the failure for which social insurance even in a different form could not, either for theoretical or for pragmatic reasons, provide the answer. The general problem of family poverty was regarded as one such area, and it led to a strenuous campaign conducted by the Child Poverty Action Group and others for a substantial degree of family endowment on a non-contributory basis.[e16] The Conservatives' response was the establishment of a new means-tested benefit to help families whose head was in full-time work but whose earnings were low.[e17] In 1975 the Labour Government replaced family allowances (the real value of which had declined over the years and which were payable only for the second child and subsequent children in a family) by child benefit which covered also the first child in a family. The amount was a substantial increase on the allowance previously paid but this was partly because it was intended to replace child income tax allowances.[e18] Single-parent families were to receive slightly more generous treatment under the child benefit scheme,[e19] but this was a paltry concession in comparison with the unimplemented recommendation of a powerful committee that such persons should receive a substantial non-contributory maintenance allowance.[e20]

As regards the seriously disabled, between 1970 and 1975 governments introduced a series of measures in recognition of the fact that national insurance was typically inadequate in relation both to coverage and to amount.[e21] Non-contributory allowances became payable to those who were substantially immobile,[e22] or who required constant attendance.[e23] In the latter case, the member of the family in attendance might himself or herself claim an independent non-contributory benefit if he/she would otherwise have been in full-time employment.[e24] Finally, there was introduced a non-contributory invalidity pension for the long-term disabled who were unable to claim the national insurance benefit.[e25] This was to be payable, most importantly, to housewives who were substantially incapable of performing normal household duties.[e26]

These measures may have had the effect of relieving some from the necessity of applying for the means-tested residual supplementary benefit, but such an improvement was at best marginal, and until the modifications to the national insurance scheme (particularly as regards the earnings-related elements payable to long-term beneficiaries) were fully to be realized, this unpopular form of welfare was to remain central to British social security: as recently as 1978 there were still 5 million people dependent on this benefit.[e27] Clearly, Beveridge's hope and expectation that the need for this type of financial aid would gradually 'wither away' had proved to be totally unrealistic. In the circumstances governments have taken steps to make the means-tested system somewhat more palatable. In 1966 its name was changed from 'national assistance' (which for many evoked memories of the much disliked unemployment assistance scheme operating between the wars[e28]) to 'supplementary benefit'[e29] and some effort was made to render its administration closer to that of national insurance. In particular, the legislation was to confirm that a claimant who satisfied the appropriate conditions had a 'right' to benefit rather than a mere expectation.[e30] Much later, attention was focussed on the demonstrably unsatisfactory features of the appeals structure in this area of social security[e31] and here too some integration with the national insurance tribunal system was effected.[e32]

Earnings-related Social Insurance

Rethinking about the nature and structure of social insurance, made necessary by the failure of the 1946 legislation to prevent substantial reliance on means-tested welfare, was concentrated almost exclusively on the desirability of abandoning the flat-rate contributions and benefits principle. As regards the financing of the system, it became clear by the late 1950s that the only politically acceptable method of re-establishing the National Insurance Fund on a sound basis consistent with social insurance principles was to introduce some form of earnings-related contributions. As regards benefits, the earnings-related principle accorded well with the Conservative ideology whereby welfare would reflect the price put by the market on an individual's contribution to the economy, though care had to be taken not to undermine the individual's own responsibility for higher levels of welfare, to be achieved through voluntary provision, particularly occupational pensions. [e33] While socialist doctrine was hard to reconcile with the notion of preserving the wage structure once an individual was no longer working, this argument could be overridden by the more pragmatic consideration that an earnings-related social insurance system would be extending to all that which was already available to the more affluent in the private sphere. [e34]

Implementation of the new strategy was, however, far from easy, and indeed took some 20 years before it was completely endorsed by legislation. The first step was the introduction (by the Conservative Government) of graduated pensions in 1959. [e35] Contributions were payable on a small band of earnings (between £9 and £15 per week), and to retirement pension only small earnings-related additions were to be paid. Employees who could show that they participated in an occupational scheme with benefits at least as generous were allowed to contract out. This first step in the direction of the continental model of social insurance was almost a complete failure, and even at the time was described by its opponents as being a 'Pensions Swindle'. [e36] Its motivation primarily had been the rescuing of the National Insurance Fund from deficit; benefits payable were a poor return for the money contributed, and, perhaps most seriously of all, they would not be revised to take account of inflation. [e37]

Already during the 1950s, when in opposition, the Labour Party had evolved an alternative strategy, that of 'national superannuation': [e38] a charge on the employee of 3 percent of his earnings, which together with contributions of 5 percent from his employer and another 2 percent from the state would ensure 10 percent of weekly earnings. This would enable pensions to be paid on a generous level and would also enable account to be taken of inflation. Although the Labour Party was returned to government in 1964 the attempt to translate this proposal into legislation did not occur until 1969 [e39] and before it could pass through Parliament, the Labour Party lost office. Meanwhile, a further step along the road had been taken: in 1966 earnings-related supplements became available to those in receipt of the short-term unemployment and sickness benefits. [e40] This was financed by a further earnings-related contribution from employees and employers, though in this case no contracting-out was permitted.

Conservative opposition to the Labour superannuation programme centred on the fact that it would permit only of partial contracting-out and, because the state scheme would have been a 'good buy' in comparison with what was offered in the private market, [e41] they feared that occupational welfare (and of course the interests of insurance companies and others) would suffer. Hence in their own proposals which reached the statute book in 1973, [e42] the Conservatives offered a package under which the state was to offer only a minimum, rather ungenerous earnings-related 'reserve' pension, to those whose occupational coverage was insufficient. This scheme would have come into effect in 1975 but by that time the Conservatives had in their turn lost office and the incoming Labour Government immediately repealed the legislation and replaced it with yet another version.

The main differences of this final scheme which came into effect in 1977[c43] was that the relationship between state and occupational coverage would be more that of 'equal partnership'. For those who did not contract out, the state would offer a substantial earnings-related element based on the best 20 years of the beneficiary's working life. The new scheme contained the further advantages that it would include invalids and widows, would offer state protection against inflation (even to those contracting-out), and would assist women who had been only partially active in the labour market by taking account of years spent at home with 'domestic responsibilities'.[c44]

THE PRINCIPLES OF SOCIAL INSURANCE

In this section we provide an account of the principles of social insurance as they developed in Britain from the initial schemes in 1911 to those actually in force at the time of writing. The subject matter is divided into the following categories. (1) risks covered and conditions of entitlement; (2) individuals insured; (3) benefits payable; (4) financing; (5) administration; (6) adjudication.

Risks Covered and Conditions of Entitlement

Unemployment

Unemployment was, with sickness, the first social risk to be the subject of social insurance in Britain.[c45] The conditions of entitlement have given rise to some of the most complex law under the social security system:[c46] many of the problems have arisen from technical considerations; the structure of entitlement has for the most part remained unaltered.

Unemployed. The claimant had first to establish that he was 'unemployed': the legislative formulation may have differed[c47] but it was left to the adjudicating authorities to determine whether a person was not pursuing an occupation from which he was entitled to remuneration.[c48] Nevertheless some regulation was required for persons who were only partially unemployed in the sense either that their work was seasonal or that they were working only short-time. As regards the latter, it was never a feature of the British system that the contract of employment had to be terminated, so that claims to the fund could be made by those who as a result of economic conditions had been 'laid-off' by their employers.[c49] This situation has given rise to immense difficulties in the formulation of entitlement and also to the administration of claims:[c50] suffice it, by way of summary, to indicate that a special condition had to be inserted whereby a person could claim benefit only for those days in a week when he would normally work.[c51] Special rules were also required for seasonal workers for it was deemed to be generally inappropriate for them to receive benefit during those parts of the year when they would not normally work.[c52] It was a delicate question, too, whether a claimant should be disentitled if he received from his employer some money by way of compensation on dismissal or redundancy, a phenomenon which has become increasingly common in recent years and, under certain legislation,[c53] compulsory. The solution eventually adopted, though not without difficulty, was to disentitle a claimant for a period during which he received from his employer money which was regarded as in lieu of wages (e.g. damages for wrongful or unfair dismissal[c54]) but this was not to cover other forms of compensation, e.g. redundancy.[c55]

Waiting-periods. Under British legislation a claimant has never been entitled from the first day of unemployment but rather has had to serve a number of 'waiting days': the reasons generally given are that an individual normally has resources sufficient to cope for a short period and that the administrative costs of administering benefit for short spells of unemployment are disporportionately high. [e56] The actual period of non-entitlement has been changed on several occasions: initially set at 1 week, [e57] it was twice reduced to 3 days [e58] only to return to 6 days shortly thereafter, [e59] until the 3-day period was finally established beyond recall in 1937. [e60] From 1946 [e61] a claimant who was unemployed for 2 weeks was entitled to a retrospective payment for those 3 days, but this was repealed in 1971 on grounds of cost. [e62] Important to the practical impact of this principle have been the rules under which closely related spells of unemployment can be linked together so that the waiting-days need not be repeated. [e63]

Availability. It has always been an essential element in the control of claims that the applicant should hold himself out as available to be engaged on full-time employment. As will be seen, [e64] the same notion lies behind some of the disqualification provisions. The 1911 National Insurance Act followed shortly after the establishment of public employment exchanges and it was natural for the latter to be incorporated administratively into the insurance scheme: from that time onwards a necessary condition of entitlement has been to register the fact of unemployment at the employment exchange. [e65] But while the case for authorizing the exchange staff to administer the scheme was almost self-evident, the formulation of the legal principle by which the genuineness of the claimant's availability for employment was to be tested was a matter for delicate judgment. Under the original Act, the claimant had to prove that he was 'capable of work but unable to obtain suitable employment', and the notion of 'suitable employment' was given some specific content. [e66] A vacancy resulting from a trade dispute was not suitable — clearly unemployment insurance was not to be used as an excuse for employing 'blacking' labour. Further, he was not expected to take up an offer of employment on terms less favourable than those which obtained in his usual occupation (thus recognizing the principle that the unemployed should not be forced to accept a lower standard of living than that to which they were accustomed) or than those generally prevailing for the particular occupation in the district (thus ensuring that the collective bargaining process should not be undermined by engaging cheaper labour). These provisions which in effect conferred on a worker a 'property right' in his pre-unemployment earnings status were (during the period of chronic unemployment) regarded as too generous and in 1927 a qualification was introduced which enabled the authorities to regard as 'suitable', employment of a lower grade or on less favourable terms than that which had been habitual for the claimant. [e67] As modified, these criteria still apply. [e68] During the 1920s, another step was taken to reinforce these controls: legislation introduced the requirement that the claimant must prove that he was 'genuinely seeking whole-time employment but unable to obtain such employment'. [e69] Applied first to uncovenanted benefit, and then extended to covenanted benefit, [e70] this implied that the claimant must show that he had been looking around for work actively even where none was available. As such it was bitterly attacked by the trade union movement and was abolished in 1930. [e71]

At the same time, the question of whether a claimant had not availed himself of reasonable opportunities for suitable employment was thought to be better incorporated as a ground of disqualification (for a maximum period of 6 weeks)[e72] rather than as a ground for total disentitlement and the 'capable of work but unable to obtain suitable employment' condition was replaced by the simple formula that the applicant be 'capable of and available for work'.[e73] This, as re-enacted under the 1946 legislation,[e74] was construed to mean whether there was a reasonable prospect of his obtaining the work for which he *held* himself available,[e75] and clearly the more restrictive the conditions which the claimant placed on his own availability, the less effective would be the control.[e76] The regulations were, therefore, altered effectively requiring the claimant to show that the restrictions on his availability were reasonable.[e77] With this accumulating body of legal controls, and with the substantial degree of discretion which they conferred on the administering authorities, it might have been assumed that the problem of ensuring genuine availability for work had been solved. But in recent years (as the level of unemployment has again grown), governments have been concerned with certain categories of persons who claim unemployment benefit, and register for employment, when in practice there are clearly no opportunities for them. The two categories who were regarded as not 'genuinely' available for work in this sense were: persons aged between 60 and 65 who had retired prematurely (and were generally in receipt of an occupational pension); and students during university vacations. Attempts were made to alter the availability conditions as regards such persons, but these were resisted on the ground that such steps would constitute a substantial and unjustified interference with the basic principles of insurance.[e78]

Disqualification for Voluntary Unemployment. A corollary of the availability principle was that a claimant should be disqualified, if only for a temporary period, where his loss of employment or his failure to find alternative work was the result of his own failings. This notion has translated itself into three different grounds for disqualification. The first is where the claimant voluntarily left his employment without just cause. The provision inserted in the 1911 Act[e79] has remained unchanged since:[e80] of course it confers considerable discretion on the administrators and adjudicators in determining what is 'just cause' in the individual case.[e81] Secondly, a claimant has been disqualified where the unemployment resulted from his 'misconduct'. The principle and the language used has also remained unchanged,[e82] though the vagueness of the notion of 'misconduct' has led to some dissatisfaction. In the early years, it caused some embarrassment as it had to be explained to some women claimants that it did not refer to their moral behaviour![e83] And though a Royal Commission, reporting in 1932, felt that some more precise formula was desirable, it could offer nothing constructive by way of alternative.[e84] The third ground of disqualification, arising where the claimant unreasonably refuses an offer or fails to take the appropriate steps to obtain employment which is suitable for him, developed out of the availability principle. Originally, there was no explicit provision to cover these contingencies: they were treated merely as conclusive evidence of the claimant's failure to satisfy the availability condition. The fact that that led to total disentitlement, rather than disqualification was an anomaly which was rectified by the legislature in 1930:[e85] refusal of, or failure to apply for suitable employment henceforth became an independent ground for disqualification and with minor modifications has remained unchanged since.[e86]

Trade Disputes Disqualification. That unemployment benefit should not be available to those participating in a strike is readily conceded by almost everyone. The aim must have been to formulate the disqualification in terms which fasten on those who are actively involved and therefore in a sense are 'responsible' for their loss of employment, but logically this would lead to the authorities adjudicating on the merits of the dispute and this is regarded as undesirable on political grounds and at any rate impracticable.[e87] Indeed, official government policy has always been that the social insurance authorities should remain neutral in industrial relations.[e88] The result has been that the legislative provisions have had, not always successfully, to run a middle course between enabling insurance funds to be used to support industrial action and depriving of benefit those who lose their employment as the result of a dispute in which they were, in no sense, involved. The history of the British provisions shows a gradual shift away from pronounced heavy emphasis on avoiding the first evil to a greater awareness of the second evil.[e89] Thus under the original 1911 Act, a workman who lost his employment because of a trade dispute at his place of work was disqualified from benefit so long as the stoppage lasted even though he was not himself involved in the dispute.[e90] The traditional justification for this seemingly harsh rule is that there is presumed to be 'a common bond of mutual interest and loyalty . . . between workers at one place of employment which enables them to be distinguished from other workers'.[e91] As applied to a small family firm this rationalization may have been attractive, but as applied to major industrial enterprises it was clearly artificial. This was revealed, in particular, by an incident occurring in 1919.[e92] There was a strike by moulders working in iron foundries, and those working with them were laid-off for 4 months but were disqualified from benefit, even though they played no part in the dispute and were not affected by its resolution. Those engaged on similar work but on different premises and who were also laid-off were not disqualified. Trade union discontent prompted the government to appoint a committee to review the trade dispute provisions, but it could not agree on a change.[e93] Eventually in 1924, a new clause was inserted in the legislation which relieved from disqualification those who were neither participating in, financing, directly interested in the dispute, nor belonged to a grade or class the members of which were participating in, financing or directly interested in the dispute.[e94] In 1926 members of a class of colliery workers throughout the country were disqualified because other members of the same class in one particular district belonged to a union which was financing the dispute.[e95] Following another committee report,[e96] the rule was amended so that membership of the 'grade or class' was relevant only if the employees worked at the same place.[e97]

There the matter rested until the 1965–1968 Royal Commission on Trade Unions critically re-examined the law.[e98] It was highly critical of the width of the disqualification provisions, arguing that an individual was not involved in a dispute merely because he was in some way financing it (for which membership of the relevant union sufficed[e99]), and that the traditional 'common bond of mutual interest and loyalty' argument was unrealistic and could not justify disqualification merely because the claimant belonged to 'a grade or class' of workers who were involved. In 1975 the recommendations of the Commission were implemented by legislation and under current law, the employee escapes disqualification if he can prove that 'he is not participating in or directly interested in the trade dispute which caused the stoppage of work'.[f1]

Medical Care

From 1911 until 1946 social insurance covered certain aspects of medical care; thereafter it was replaced by the National Health Service, providing free (or almost free[f2]) facilities to all, financed from general taxation.[f3] The peculiar character of the national health insurance scheme which represented a compromise between compulsory social insurance and voluntary private insurance[f4] gave rise to a distinction between 'medical benefits' to which a contributor had a guaranteed entitlement and 'additional benefits', entitlement to which was dependent on the rules of Approved Society to which he belonged and the resources it had available. As regards the first category, the legislation simply referred to 'adequate medical treatment and attendance from the medical practitioners with whom arrangements are . . . made';[f5] and this was to include 'the provision of proper and sufficient medicines and of the prescribed medical and surgical appliances'.[f6] This gave rise to no problem as regards medicines and appliances: it was left to the discretion of the insured person's doctor what should be prescribed. But the types of services included was given a very restrictive interpretation by those administering the scheme: it was confined to 'all proper and necessary medical services other than those involving the application of special skill and experience of a degree or kind which general practitioners as a class cannot be expected to possess'.[f7] It followed that specialists' or consultants' fees as well as hospital services were not covered. Notwithstanding a recommendation of a Royal Commission that extension to the scope of medical benefit was 'urgently desirable',[f8] no substantial change was made. With the exception of tuberculosis,[f9] for which the local health authorities assumed responsibility, and nursing which was administered by voluntary social service, all other aspects of medical care came under the category of 'additional benefits', most importantly dental and ophthalmic treatment, treatment in hospitals and convalescent homes, and treatment and attendance in respect of maternity.[f10] The unsatisfactory nature of the distinction between 'medical' and 'additional' benefits, with its uncertainty and arbitrariness in coverage, was one reason, among several others, why this part of National Health Insurance was dismantled and replaced by the National Health Service.[f11]

Sickness and Invalidity: Income Loss

The 1911 Act also covered the risk of income loss arising from sickness and invalidity and this was the only part of the National Health Insurance scheme to survive into modern legislation.

Incapacity for Work. The basic condition for benefit has remained unchanged since its original formulation: the claimant must be 'incapable of work by reason of some specific disease or bodily or mental disablement'.[f12] If this test were applied absolutely literally it would exclude a large proportion of claims, for there are many conditions of disablement which prevent the claimant from doing his normal work but which nevertheless do not render him incapable of undertaking *some* kind of remunerative work. The difficulty was recognized already in 1914 and it was, presumably, only that the authorities did not construe the provisions literally that delayed amendment of the law until 1973. In that year, the type of work of which the claimant must be incapable was limited to 'work which [he] can reasonably be expected to do'.[f13] In practice, the authorities generally regard it as reasonable for the claimant not to undertake work different from his usual occupation for the first 6 months of incapacity; thereafter inquiries will be made as to his fitness for any kind of work.[14] Under the 1946 legislation and subsequently, the process of medical certification was restructured[15] and at the same time provision was made to protect the entitlement of those who were not, strictly speaking, incapable of work but who, either because they suffered from an infectious disease or because working would prejudice their health, were recommended by their doctor not to work.[16] It should be noted that, in contrast to the rules on unemployment benefit[17] the definition of incapacity takes no account of whether the claimant receives remuneration from his employer (e.g. sick pay), or indeed, compensation for lost wages from any other source.[18] As a result it is left to the employer (or the other source) to modify the private arrangements to take account of sickness benefit. It is only very recently that the government has announced its intention of remedying this unsatisfactory state of affairs, probably by relieving the insurance fund of liability for short spells of incapacity.[19]

Waiting Days. The traditional period of 3 waiting days has always been applied to sickness benefit,[20] and unlike unemployment benefit was not raised to 6 days in the interwar period. Under 1946 and subsequent legislation the rules on sickness and unemployment benefit, including waiting days and periods of interruption of employment,[21] have been harmonized.[22]

Disqualification. As with unemployment, rules have always existed to disqualify claimants whose incapacity results from their own conduct. Under pre-1946 legislation, the position was complicated because, subject to certain limitations, the Approved Societies could lay down their own 'rules of behaviour' with which claimants were bound to comply.[23] One difficult problem was the extent to which a beneficiary could be forced to undergo medical treatment. A compromise had to be struck between the undesirability of interfering with a fundamental personal liberty not to receive vaccination or undergo an operation (especially where the latter might involve serious risks) and concern that a person should not be maintained by the insurance fund in circumstances where his capacity for work could be restored by remedial treatment. The solution reached in 1911 was that an Approved Society could not disqualify from benefit a claimant who had refused 'to submit to a surgical operation, or vaccination, or innoculation of any kind, unless such refusal in the case of a surgical operation of a minor character is considered . . . unreasonable'.[24] This principle is still incorporated in the law, though since the abolition of the Approved Societies, it now constitutes an exception to the general rule that failure without good cause to attend for, or submit to, medical treatment may justify disqualification.[25]

As regards other rules of behaviour, they covered a wide variety of different situations. One Approved Society, for example, had power to refuse benefit if a medical condition was the result of 'fighting, wrestling, using weapons, drunkenness, indecent or disorderly conduct, venereal disease'.[26] The modern legislation simply provides as a ground for disqualification: first incapacity resulting from the claimant's own 'misconduct', leaving it to the authorities to determine the meaning of this word, though it does explicitly exclude venereal disease from the provision;[27] and, secondly, a failure to refrain from behaviour 'calculated to retard his recovery'.[28] Mention should also be made of provisions attempting to maintain the efficacy of administrative procedures. Thus under threat of disqualification, a claimant must attend for a medical examination, answer reasonable enquiries made of him by the authorities, and not be absent from his place of residence without indicating where he may be located. [29]

Maternity

As we have seen, the medical care involved in confinement and maternity was covered by the national health insurance only to the extent that an individual's Approved Society included it among its 'additional benefits'. [30] The introduction of the national health service, of course, removed the matter from the concern of social insurance. As regards financial benefits payable to the mother, a distinction must be drawn between the maternity grant, a lump sum intended to idemnify her against expenditure occasioned by confinement, and the maternity allowance, intended to compensate for income lost on giving up employment as a result of pregancy and confinement.

Maternity Grant. This was payable under the 1911 National Health Insurance scheme to the wife or widow of an insured person. [31] As such, it has a place in the history of British social insurance for being the first benefit paid directly to the relative of an insured person. A woman, married or unmarried, who was herself insured was also, of course, entitled, and in her case could accumulate it with sickness benefit, payable for lost earnings. [32] Although the maternity benefit was not intended directly to compensate the mother for any loss of earnings, nevertheless it was considered to be an appropriate device to alleviate pressure on her to return to work after the birth earlier than was advisable in the interests either of her own or her child's health. A provision was thus inserted in the legislation obliging the Approved Societies to lay down a rule which required the woman to abstain from remunerative work during a period of 4 weeks after her confinement. [33] With the introduction of the maternity allowance in 1946, this rule became redundant and was repealed. At the same time Beveridge considered that the maternity grant, designed to cover expenses at the confinement, should be supplemented by another benefit, payable to those not entitled to the earnings-replacement allowance, to help with domestic expenses subsequent to the birth. [34] The proposal was implemented [35] but it was soon found to be administratively inconvenient to differentiate between confinement and post-confinement expenditure and in 1953 the new benefit was abolished; [36] thereafter the grant was considered to cover both types of expenditure. One other major change took place during this period. The grant had been criticized for not distinguishing between home and hospital confinements: on economic grounds it was thought appropriate to encourage more mothers to have their children at home, thus relieving the National Health Service of some of the costs. [37] To meet this criticism, an additional grant for home confinements was paid from 1953 [38] to 1964, when this too was abolished. [39] Changes in hospital maternity practice had reduced the normal confinement from 10 days to 3 days and as a result mothers confined in hospital had to meet about the same expenses as those confined at home. [40]

Maternity Allowance. The income-replacement benefit was introduced, following Beveridge's recommendations, [41] by the 1946 legislation. [42] It can be seen as complementing family allowances in encouraging population growth, [43] particularly from women already active in the labour market, and also as an incentive for such women to cease work for a medically appropriate period before and after confinement.[44] This latter consideration is the basis for the principle that the allowance is awarded for 18 weeks, commencing with the eleventh week before the expected time of confinement.[45] The grounds for disqualification from sickness benefit also apply here.[46] As with that benefit, entitlement is not affected by receipt of payments from a claimant's employer, but the value of the benefit *is* deducted from maternity pay which the employer is bound, under employment legislation, to confer.[47]

Old Age and Retirement

A means-tested, non-contributory, pension had been payable to persons aged 70 and more since 1908.[48] Income maintenance for aged persons was added to the social insurance system in 1925. A pension became payable to a male insured person on reaching 65 and to a female insured person at 60.[49] A married contributor might also claim a dependency allowance for his wife if she was also aged 65 or more.[50] The latter condition was thought to be an unnecessarily stringent one: a man in receipt of unemployment benefit before reaching 65 was entitled to an addition for his wife; when transferred to retirement pension he would lose that addition unless she was also 65. In 1940 the age of 60 was applied to women whether they claimed on their own contributions or as the wife of an insured person.[51]

This system of old age pensions, as developed between the wars, was typical of those existing elsewhere and posed few legal problems. However, following Beveridge's review of the provisions and the substantial increase to the number of persons insured, which resulted from his recommendations, it was thought to be impossible to award pensions to all those in the relevant age groups (65 for men and 60 for women) at an adequate level.[52] For the first 5 years following the attainment of the pensionable age, therefore, the basis of entitlement was changed to one of retirement. A man between 65 and 70, and a woman between 60 and 65 would be entitled only if he/she had retired from regular employment.[53] In order to preserve equity as between those who retired at the earlier age and those who stayed at work, and to incorporate work incentives, the 1946 legislation provided for an increment which would be earned during the period of 5 years and which would be added to the pension when eventually payable.[54] These peculiar characteristics of the British system — they seem to be almost unique among social security programmes[55] — have been maintained to the present day and have given rise to legal difficulties in determining the fact of retirement.[56] Of course someone wholly inactive is retired, but the legislation has given a much broader scope to the notion, so that persons working occasionally or for trivial earnings might not be excluded.[57] However, the pension of those who are thus treated as retired even though they may do some work are subject nevertheless to a reduction for earnings above a certain amount and accruing either to the pensioner himself, or, if a dependency allowance is claimed for her, his spouse.[58] When first introduced, this 'earnings rule' involved a pound for pound reduction above the prescribed level of earnings.[59] This was thought to undermine work incentives so much that in 1956 a band of earnings within which there was a reduction of only 50 percent of earnings was introduced.[60]

Much controversy and criticism has surrounded the earnings rule[61] and yet often, it would seem to be misdirected.[62] So long as pensions in Britain are based on retirement rather than the mere attainment of pensionable age, the principle would be considerably undermined if not complemented by an earnings rule — concern for work incentives should logically, therefore, be directed against the retirement condition itself. Secondly, it is sometimes argued that the rule interferes with the insurance principle: an insured person has contributed during his life and should be entitled, on reaching pensionable age, to his return unaffected by his working or financial situation thereafter. But this begs the question as to the risk which is the subject of insurance; under the British system contributions are being made not for *old age* pensions, but rather for *retirement* pensions. Paradoxically, while the principle of retirement has remained unchallenged in post-war legislation, hostility to the earnings rule has resulted first in governments setting increasingly genuine limits,[63] and eventually in the present government committing itself to the future abolition of the rule.[64] Whether changes will also take place on the ages at which individuals may draw retirement pension is also in question. While regard might be had primarily to the cost implications,[65] nevertheless future governments will have to contend with powerful arguments based either on hostility to the sex discrimination implicit in the present arrangements[66] or on general employment opportunities in an increasingly technological age.[67]

Death: Widowhood

It has been written on the history of British provision for widowhood that 'no part of our social security has shown such a consistent pattern of political failure as this'.[68] The difficulties have arisen mainly from the necessity of deciding to what extent a widow should be expected to work on the death of her spouse, but account has also to be taken of public sympathy aroused by the plight of widowhood. Lloyd George had hoped to include widows' pensions in his national insurance scheme of 1911 but was thwarted by opposition from the industrial assurance companies who saw in his proposals a threat to their vested interests in this form of protection.[69] By 1925, this opposition had weakened and it was convenient to include this social risk with the new scheme of old age pensions. The principal issues to be resolved under this, and subsequent, legislation may be categorized as follows.

Age and Existence of Dependent Children. If it be accepted that for social and/or economic reasons a widow should be entitled to receive a pension only during such periods as it was unreasonable to make herself available for work, then clearly the crucial considerations were: first, the time which it would normally take her to adjust to her new circumstances; secondly, her age; and thirdly, whether or not she had dependent children to care for. As regards the first, it was for a long time a principle under British law that pension at a relatively generous level should be payable for the first 3 months of widowhood, whatever the widow's circumstances,[70] and in 1966 the period was extended to 6 months.[71] Policy on the second and third considerations has hardly been consistent over the years. Notwithstanding some hostility to the payment of an indefinite pension to childless persons,[72] the legislature in 1925 rashly accepted the principle of a pension for life (or until remarriage) to all widows of insured persons regardless of age and family commitments.[73] The result was far from satisfactory: the uniform flat-rate benefit meant that childless recipients were relatively well off, while those with families to support suffered some hardship. Beveridge was trenchant in his criticism of existing provisions: 'there is no reason why a childless widow should get a pension for life; if she is able to work, she should work'. [174] He proposed to deprive widows of their pensions after 13 weeks unless they had children to care for. [175] So to remove rights already established by legislation was to prove to be politically unacceptable, and the government while accepting in substance his objections watered down his proposals in one significant respect: after reaching a certain age it was not to be assumed that a widow (particularly if she had not previously worked) would be able easily to find remunerated work. [176] Under the 1946 legislation, therefore, entitlement to the pension was to be maintained if the claimant was over 50 when her husband died, or was over 40 when she ceased to have dependent children to care for. [177] The structure of entitlement thus established remained substantially intact thereafter, though some modifications to it were made. The difference betwen the age condition of 40, for widowed mothers, and that of 50 for other widows was hard to justify, [178] and in 1956 the '50 years' age test was applied to both categories. [179] Another objection was that too many financial consequences depended on the exact age of the widow when her husband died or when her children ceased to be dependent. The compromise solution was the introduction, in 1970, of a sliding scale of pensions for those aged between 40 and 50 on the relevant date. [180]

Duration of Marriage. The widow's benefit is derived not, of course, from her own contributions to the insurance fund, but from those of her husband. Theoretically, therefore, a marriage taking place a few hours before death would be sufficient to ground entitlement. This might be considered to be an undesirable result, the more so if the pension is seen as a return for the widow's contribution to the insured person's household over a number of years. Under the original 1925 legislation the problem was avoided by requiring that the contributor and the claimant were married when the scheme was established or that the marriage had subsisted for 3 years before the death. [181] With the revision of the scheme in 1946, the principle was retained but only in relation to the pensions payable to widows over 50, or over 40 when family commitments had ceased, and in these cases the requisite period was extended to 10 years of marriage. [182] In 1956 the period was reduced again to 3 years, [183] and finally in 1970 the requirement that a marriage be subsisting for a certain time was abolished altogether. [184]

Remarriage and Cohabitation. It was an unexceptional principle that a widow's pension should cease on remarriage, and legislation has so provided since its inception. [185] Consistent with that, it must be appropriate that 'marriage-like' relationships should be treated no differently, and disqualification on the ground of cohabitation has also always featured among the provisions. [186] The rule has been criticized more on the problems to which it has given rise (difficulties of adjudication, invasions on a woman's privacy) than on the basic rationale of the rule itself, and subject to a technical reformulation of the definition of cohabitation, [187] it has remained at the heart of this and other social security measures. [188]

Earnings. Another delicate policy question has been whether deductions from the pension should be made on account of the widow's earnings. Unlike retirement pensions, there has been no requirement that the widow be inactive in the labour market. On the other hand, the assumption of the pension payable after the initial period has been that family commitments or age make it unreasonable to expect the widow to work. Not surprisingly, in the light of Beveridge's philosophy, [89] an earnings rule was introduced in 1946 for recipients of benefit in these circumstances. [90] Even more than with retirement pensions, the rule was continually attacked and it was abolished in 1964. [91]

Death: Other Consequences

A death in the family may give rise to financial losses other than that of the widow's maintenance, and it is convenient to group together here a number of other provisions.

Widowers. The stereotype of the husband being the breadwinner and the wife staying at home to care for house and children together with the notion that social insurance is aimed primarily at income maintenance has retarded any real concern for the plight of the widower: perhaps it is assumed that he can without difficulty obtain for himself a substitute spouse! [92] Apart from a limited exception under the industrial injuries scheme, [93] British social insurance has never allowed for a widower's benefit. With the growing movement against sex discrimination, the matter has been given some consideration recently [94] but hitherto the only concession made is that a widower may, in certain circumstances, rely on his deceased wife's contributions for the purposes of invalidity or retirement pension. [95]

Death of Divorced Father. For reasons already given, [96] the breakdown of marriage has never been regarded as a risk for which social insurance can offer protection. A feature of the British scheme which comes closest to that situation is the benefit, called child's special allowance, which a woman, whose marriage has been terminated by divorce and who has since been receiving payments from her former husband for the maintenance of her children, may be paid on this death. In truth, the policy-maker has been less concerned with the fact that marriage has broken down than with the analogy of widow's benefit, payable where the claimant has dependent children to care for. [97] The desirability of extending national insurance in this direction was recognized by the Royal Commission on Marriage and Divorce, reporting in 1956. [98] This body, however, considered that the benefit should not be paid if the divorce resulted from the woman's own 'misconduct'. With its overtones of the (now repealed) divorce law, this condition was hardly in keeping with general social insurance principles and did not prove acceptable to the National Insurance Advisory Committee when it studied the proposal. [99] The benefit was introduced by legislation in 1957, [81] the conditions of entitlement being that the marriage in question had been terminated by divorce, or had been annulled, and that the former husband, who had contributed to the insurance fund, had been maintaining the child or children. [82] As with widow's benefits the allowance ceases on remarriage or cohabitation. [83]

Orphans. It was consistent with the introduction of widow's pensions in 1925 that regard should also be had to the situation where both parents of a child had died. Thus the Act conferred on a guardian or other person caring for the child a pension for so long as the child was under 14 or receiving education at school.[g4] For this purpose regard was had to the contributions of either of the child's deceased parents. Following the reformulation of social insurance in 1946, it was considered that this was no longer the best way of dealing with the problem of orphanhood.[g5] It was not infrequent that an orphan's parents had disappeared or that neither had contributed to the insurance fund. Moreover, it was a proper concern of the state to provide financial incentives to someone to look after a child who lacked parental support, whether or not its natural parents had been contributors to social insurance. This social risk was, therefore, removed from the national insurance scheme: orphans' pension was abolished and replaced by a non-contributory allowance payable to the guardian where either both parents were dead, or one was dead and the other could not be traced.[g6]

Funeral Expenses. Though in financial terms the impact of funeral expenses may be relatively small compared with other social hazards, nevertheless this cost has played a not insignificant role in social policy. The desire to protect a family against the humiliation of a pauper's funeral was an important cultural phenomenon in the industrial revolution and in part accounts for the rapid expansion of friendly societies, burial societies, and particularly industrial assurance in the nineteenth century.[g7] While there was considerable evidence of exploitation and even malpractice in the commercial protection offered,[g8] it was not until Beveridge's powerful advocacy[g9] that the government felt able to resist the pressure exerted by the private insurance companies and introduce a benefit into the social insurance system. This occurred in 1946, in the form of a lump sum payable on the death of a contributor, or a member of his family.[g10] The benefit was to be claimed by any person who 'reasonably incurred or reasonably intends to incur' the funeral expenses.[g11] This method of conferring payment proved to be almost totally misconceived, since the administrative costs of determining who was to have priority in claiming benefit and whether the expenses were 'reasonably incurred' were proportionally very high.[g12] In 1957, the rules were radically altered so that the benefit constituted an asset of the deceased which formed part of his estate on death and was therefore paid automatically to his personal representatives.[g13] The connection with actual funeral expenses has thus been considerably weakened and this, together with the fact that governments have been reluctant to raise the benefit in line with inflation, means that under modern law it is little more than a small subsidy by social security contributors to the estate of deceased persons.[g14]

Industrial Injuries and Diseases. We have already described how until 1946 provision was made outside social insurance for the victims of industrial accidents and diseases and the shortcomings to which the private law system of workmen's compensation gave rise.[g15] Criticisms reached a high point in the late 1930s.[g16] A Royal Commission established in 1938 to investigate the matter curtailed its inquiries on the outbreak of war and its task was assumed by Beveridge as part of his overall survey of social security. His conclusions were that the many problems[g17] could be solved only by the replacement of the private law basis by a social insurance scheme but that the special nature of this form of hazard suggested that it should be independent of the general national insurance system.[g18] The latter followed from his arguments that the principles of financing the general scheme were inappropriate to industrial risks (in particular account should be taken of safety incentives[19]) and, less convincingly,[20] that benefits paid should be more generous than those available to other sick and disabled persons.[21] Whatever the merit of these arguments, the consequent necessity of distinguishing between disability conditions which result from employment risks and those arising from other causes has given rise to an immensely complex body of law.[22]

Employment Risk. For the most part, the definitions of employment risk marking out the boundaries of the new scheme were borrowed from the previous workmen's compensation law. First, a distinction was drawn between injuries caused by 'accidents' and diseases. The former arose when the claimant's condition resulted from an event or series of events; the latter resulted from an insidious process.[23] The distinction was crucial, for the victim of a disease could succeed only if it was prescribed by the authorities in relation to his occupation, and if the presumption that it had developed as a result of employment in that occupation was not rebutted.[24] British law has never adopted the EEC Recommendation[25] that the victim of an unprescribed disease should succeed if he were able to establish a causal connection between the disease and his employment.[26] Secondly, benefit was payable for the consequences of an accident only if it arose 'out of and in the course of employment'.[27] This classic formulation, perhaps the most notorious in the whole of social security law,[28] has been responsible for vast numbers of disputed claims and reported cases.[29] As an oversimplification it may be said that the claimant must in principle show not only that the accident took place during his hours of work and at his place of work, but also that it arose out of his working activities rather than from extraneous circumstances. In order, however, to alleviate the claimant's task in satisfying these two conditions, both have been weakened by statutory exceptions. As regards the time and place of work, an exception (though not nearly as generous as those made in some foreign systems[30]) was made in 1946 to cover journeys to and from work where undertaken under arrangements with the employer.[31] The second condition, that of causal connection between the work and the accident, has been so undermined by exceptions that in practice it is much less important than it once was. Under the 1946 Act, a claimant benefitted from a presumption that if an accident arose 'in the course of employment' it also arose 'out of that employment':[32] in other words, it was for the authorities to show that there was not a sufficient causal connection between the accident and the employee's activities. Even so, a number of decisions showed that this presumption was by no means difficult to rebut,[33] and in 1961, following trade union pressure, a new provision was added, classifying as employment risks accidents caused by 'another person's misconduct, skylarking or negligence, or by the behaviour or presence of an animal . . . or . . . caused by or consists in the employed earner being struck by any object or by lightning'.[34] This combined with other provisions which protect the employee if he were acting in an emergency[35] or if, notwithstanding a contravention of his employer's instructions, he acted in the latter's interests,[36] has considerably eased the claimant's burden.

Other Conditions for Short-term Benefit. To establish title to the short-term benefit, payable for the first 6 months, the claimant must in addition prove that the injury resulting from the accident, or the prescribed disease, has resulted in incapacity for work.[37] The test here and the disqualification provisions to which he is subject are exactly the same as those imposed in relation to sickness benefit[38] and require no further comment.

Other Conditions for Long-term Benefit and Special Allowances. The principles governing entitlement to the long-term benefit, payable once the period for the short-term injury benefit has elapsed, are very different. In the first place, for the basic disablement benefit, it is not necessary that the claimant be incapable of work; all that is required is that he has suffered a loss of physical or mental faculty (as a result of the accident or disease) which is more than trivial.[39] Thus, in sharp contrast to sickness and invalidity benefits payable in non-industrial cases, the basis of the award is not that of income-maintenance *per se* but rather compensation for general financial and non-financial losses. The principle was perhaps explicable in the context of the government's general approach to social insurance in 1946. The concern that benefit should be based on need rather than earnings loss was conveniently met by the notion, drawn from the war pension scheme, that compensation could be assessed according to the degree of disablement.[40] Under the 1946 Act it had to be shown that the loss of faculty was likely to be permanent or substantial.[41] That requirement was abolished in 1953;[42] it had constituted a severe obstacle for a large range of employees who had sustained only minor injuries, and for such persons the administrative cost of applying the formula was not justified in the light of the relatively small amounts of money paid out by way of compensation.[43]

The post-war government's notion of compensation according to need proved to be unacceptable politically.[44] Under the workmen's compensation scheme, awards had been based on earnings loss and trade unions were unwilling for the principle to be abandoned. The 1946 legislation therefore provided for the addition to disablement benefit of either of two allowances: the unemployability supplement, where the claimant is incapable of work and likely to remain so permanently;[45] and the special hardship allowance for those only partially incapacitated and based on the difference in earnings between the claimant's pre-accident and post-accident occupation.[46] The latter allowance is the only example within British social security law of a benefit being paid for partial, as opposed to total, earning incapacity. The legislative formulation is a complex one and has given rise to severe problems in its administration.[47]

There are, finally, three additional allowances payable to the severely disabled: the hospital treatment allowance entitles those receiving treatment as an in-patient in a hospital for disabilities caused by the accident or disease to receive a maximum disablement benefit, if they were otherwise not entitled to it;[48] the constant attendance allowance is paid to those 'to a substantial extent dependent on [constant] attendance for the necessities of life';[49] and the exceptionally severe disablement allowance, introduced in 1966,[50] confers additional resources on those already in receipt of maximum disablement benefit and whose entitlement to the constant attendance allowance is likely to be permanent.[51]

Other Conditions for Death Benefit. The benefits payable under the industrial scheme to widows and others depend, of course, on proof that the death resulted from the industrial injury or disease.[52] The more generous treatment of industrial victims compared with others manifests itself also here. There are three advantages which the dependents of a deceased person enjoy which are not present in the nonindustrial death benefits. First, for widows who are not expected to make themselves available for work, because they have no children to care for, or are not sufficiently old,[853] a pension is payable which, though not as great as that received by widows expected to stay at home, is not insubstantial.[854] Secondly, a widower may claim benefit, provided that he was, at the time of death, being maintained by his deceased wife, and is permanently incapable of self-support.[855] Thirdly, there is provision also for other dependent adults, including parents, relatives, and women caring for the deceased's child.[856] In these cases, however, the amount payable has not been raised since 1946 and has a trivial value today. In the circumstances, it has recently been recommended that the rights of these categories of dependant should be abolished.[857]

Individuals Insured

Before the Second World War there were, effectively, two independent social insurance schemes: that for unemployment, and that which covered health and widows', old age and orphans' pensions. In 1946 these schemes were amalgamated but a separate scheme for industrial injuries was created. Discussion of the scope of the schemes in terms of the population covered is divided accordingly.

Unemployment Insurance

The incidence of unemployment being difficult to predict, and the fact that the British scheme of 1911 was innovatory in international terms, naturally led its creators to a cautious view of which section of the employed population was to be covered. Seven trades were included (building, construction of works, shipbuilding, engineering, construction of vehicles, iron-founding and certain kinds of sawmilling).[858] These industries had in common that they were liable to cyclical or seasonal unemployment rather than chronic unemployment or underemployment.[859] Protection in the form of insurance was therefore not only desirable but also manageable. Contributing employees (of which there were about 2.75 million) had to be 16 years or older.[860] In 1916, to assist in the war effort, the government was given power under legislation to extend the scheme to any trade or industry in which substantial amounts of munition work were being carried out.[861] There were few industries which were not, in some way, involved in munitions but only about 1.5 million workers were added.[862] The great leap forward was taken in 1920 by which time the principle of unemployment insurance had become almost universally recognized as being desirable. Now *all* persons employed under a contract of service or apprenticeship were covered[863] but subject to certain exceptions. The most important of these were: agricultural workers, those in domestic service, members of the armed forces and of the civil service, teachers and others in non-manual employment earning more than £250 a year.[864] Further, particular trades or industries could, under an arrangement with the Ministry of Labour, contract-out of the scheme, but only if they offered equal or better protection to their workers.[865] The numbers insured rose dramatically to 11 million. Changes made subsequent to 1920 were mainly technical rather than substantial but the following should be noted. Financial considerations prompted suspension of the power to contract out in 1921[866] and its abolition in 1927. [67] The minimum age requirement was harmonized with the school-leaving age. [68] Finally, after much discussion [69] agriculture was added to the scheme, though under special conditions. [70]

Health and Pensions Insurance

The scope of Part One of the 1911 Act which dealt with health insurance was quite different from that of unemployment insurance. This was truly a 'national' scheme, which embraced with certain exceptions all manual workers employed under a contract of service, together with non-manual employees whose income did not exceed £160 per annum. [71] Moreover, it also enabled persons outside these categories voluntarily to insure, provided that they were engaged in some regular occupation on the earnings of which they were substantially dependent for their livelihood, but which did not exceed £160 per annum. [72] Those exempt from the provisions were most importantly members of the armed forces and of the civil service, teachers, railway workers and casual workers. [73] When, in 1925, national insurance was extended to provide pensions for widows, old age and orphans, the simple device was adopted of combining the new scheme with that already in existence and no differences as regards the insured population were made. [74]

Post-1946 National Insurance

The 1946 legislation, broadly implementing the Beveridge Report, not only unified the two schemes described above but also wrought fundamental changes in their scope. The argument of 'pooling all social risks' was used by Beveridge as a justification for abolishing those categories of employed persons hitherto exempt. [75] All persons, employed under a contract of service, subject only to some marginal exceptions, [76] were to be insured for all benefit purposes. [77] More radically, it was also decided to include for all purposes except unemployment benefit (the administration of which would be impracticable for this group [78]) self-employed persons. [79] Many of these, it was said, were poorer than many employed under contract and were just as much in need of protection against sickness and old age as any other group in society. [80] These two groups, categorized as Class I and Class II respectively, formed the bulk of the population and would provide effective coverage for many others who were family dependants of contributors. But the principle of universality was not to stop even here. There was yet another category of independent persons, to be called Class III, who though they were not gainfully occupied, nevertheless would need provision for retirement, funeral expenses, and perhaps maternity grant. [81] Typically included were unmarried women engaged in unremunerated domestic work, those retiring early under an occupational pension scheme, and persons living off a private income. It remains to mention the exceptions to this principle of universality. First, a special status was granted to married women. They fitted badly into Beveridge's notion of compulsory insurance of independent persons: the family was to be treated as a single unit. Even if a wife was an earner, her position was different from that of a single woman, in that employment might be interrupted or abandoned for childbirth and (so it was regarded at that time) her earnings were typically 'a means, not of subsistence but of a standard of living above subsistence'. [82] The solution adopted was to confer on a married woman earner the choice to contribute in her own right, or to opt out and rely on her husband's contributions for retirement pension and maternity grant.[83] Secondly, certain categories were exempted from paying contributions primarily because they could not afford to do so: the sick and unemployed; full-time students; and persons on low incomes.[84] However, it did not follow that they were always deprived of protection; for certain limited purposes, contributions were credited.[85]

These principles remained fundamentally unaltered until the change to earnings-related benefits took place. The ill-fated graduated retirement scheme of 1959 applied only to employed persons, and even these could opt out if their employer provided occupational coverage at least as beneficial as the state benefit.[86] More fundamental changes, however, took place in 1975, when earnings-related contributions became general, and when they became substantially assimilated with income-tax payments. Classes I and II remained the same, though to the category of employed persons was added the rather anomalous group of so-called 'office-holders', i.e. those working in the public service but not under a contract of employment.[87] Class III, as provided for under the 1946 legislation, was abolished.[88] It was no longer thought worthwhile to make special provision and collect small contributions from the limited numbers involved, and for a similar reason an even larger number were exempt under the low-earners provisions.[89] Instead there was introduced a facility for the payment, by non-contributors and others with deficient contribution records, of voluntary contributions.[90] The married woman's option of contracting-out was also abolished, though those who had already exercised this option need only pay contributions on a reduced basis.[91] The reform reflected, of course, major changes in the social and economic status of married women,[92] and was accompanied by the (in international terms) radical innovation of crediting contributions to persons of either sex who had spent some part of their working life discharging domestic responsibilities.[93]

Industrial Injuries Insurance

The 1946 industrial injuries insurance scheme covered fundamentally those employed persons categorized as Class I in the non-industrial scheme. There were, however, two differences: first, those on low earnings were included in the industrial scheme; secondly, under that scheme there were no contribution conditions for the payment of benefit — an employee was insured from the first day of his employment.[94] In 1975 the industrial scheme was amalgamated with the general scheme but the scope of the coverage provided for industrial accidents and diseases remains unaltered.[95]

Benefits Payable

In this section we consider the evolution of the principles upon which benefit has been calculated. Perhaps on no other matter have such radical changes occurred within the history of British social insurance. Discussion will be structured according to the method of calculation.

Flat-rate Benefits

The main feature which distinguished continental systems of social insurance from their British counterparts, at least until recently, was the heavy concentration of the latter on the principle of flat-rate benefit paid on the basis of assumed need rather than in relation to the individual's earning loss. The principle was first enshrined in the unemployment and sickness schemes of 1911[g96] and was consistent with the view at that time that social insurance was to provide nothing more than a 'life-belt' for survival during periods of temporary interruption of work.[g97] The conclusion of the International Labour Office that 'only the system of benefit varying with wages can secure that the sick person will be relieved in proportion to his resources and standard of living'[g98] was conveniently ignored. The British policy was both to preserve work incentives and to encourage voluntary provision for welfare above the minimum.[g99] Indeed, this latter notion was reflected in the sickness scheme under which the Approved Society which the individual contributor had selected to administer his insurance might offer additional benefit above the legislatively prescribed amount.[h1] The basis of assumed needs implicit in this amount was duly invoked to justify paying smaller sums to women and to young persons, though such individuals also paid less by way of contributions.[h2] On the other hand, the principle was applied neither uniformly nor consistently. This is demonstrated not only by the fact that, as will be seen, dependency allowances were introduced haphazardly but by the very marked inconsistency between the rates payable to individuals under the various schemes. For example in 1925, the ordinary benefit payable to men was for unemployment 18s,[h3] for sickness 15s,[h4] for old age 10s,[h5] and for long-term disablement 7s 6d.[h6]

Such arbitrary discrepancies were anathema to Beveridge and, on the basis of need, he sought to rationalize uniform rates of flat-rate benefit on the following arguments:[h7] first, as between unemployment and disability the needs of the latter were, if anything greater than those of the former, but in the light of the fact that voluntary provision was more readily available for sickness than for unemployment, equality of benefit was desirable; secondly, as between short-term and long-term disability, again contrary to existing practice, *prima facie* it was the latter who required greater financial assistance, though this was counterbalanced by the expectation that over a substantial period individuals might more easily adjust to lower standards of living; thirdly, as between retirement and short-term contingencies, it was to be assumed that the strict subsistence needs of the aged were probably slightly less, but the difference was not great and the advantage of avoiding any reduction when an individual was transferred from a sickness or unemployment benefit to a retirement pension was considerable. However, consistent with existing practice, Beveridge did favour a reduced benefit for younger persons and married women,[h8] and he considered that the immediate problems of widowhood justified a benefit 50 percent higher than others for the initial period of 13 weeks.[h9] These notions were, in general, endorsed by the post-war government[h10] and were implemented by the 1946 legislation.[h11] Benefits awarded to victims of industrial accidents and diseases were, however, more generous (the short-term injury benefit was 73 percent higher than sickness benefit[h12]). Though Beveridge attempted to justify this on a rational social policy basis,[h13] it is clear that political pressures and the fact that awards under the superseded workmen's compensation scheme had been earnings-related were more influential.[h14]

Three developments occurring since 1946 deserve our attention. The first two relate to the growing awareness that the needs of long-term beneficiaries, particularly if they are disabled, are more acute than those of persons only temporarily off work.[h15] In 1971 a new allowance was introduced for invalids the amount of which increased proportionately to the length of time the claimant had been unable to work.[h16] In the period 1973/5, there was a general tendency to raise the level of flat-rate pensions payable to retired persons, widows and invalids above the level of short-term benefits.[h17] The third development arose from concern that, with inflation reaching new heights in the 1970s, social insurance beneficiaries should be given a legislative guarantee that the real value of awards should not decline. Such a guarantee was forthcoming in 1975: short-term benefits were to be maintained in line with rises in prices, while long-term benefits should keep pace with prices, or earnings, whichever was more favourable to the beneficiary.[h18] The latter was subsequently thought to be too generous and the principle of relating up-rating of both types of benefit to prices has now been adopted.[h19] There are, however, two exceptions to this requirement. First, it does not apply to lump-sum awards for funeral and maternity expenses.[h20] These have been allowed to dwindle in value, and the efforts of pressure groups and others to reverse government policy have so far been unsuccessful.[h21] Secondly, the authorities are given some flexibility as regards the relationship between different types of benefit.[h22] If, in view of changing views on social priorities, governments wish to give preference to some beneficiaries rather than others, this may be taken into account in the up-rating process. The device has been used, for example, to whittle away the differential between industrial and non-industrial benefits, which is much harder to justify than it once was.[h23]

Dependency Additions

To be consistent with the needs approach to social insurance, it is, of course, highly appropriate that additions should be made to the standard flat-rate benefit, according to the size of the claimant's family. Prior to 1946, the policy of governments on this issue was surprisingly arbitrary. Dependency allowances were added to the unemployment scheme in 1921 on a temporary basis to relieve 'winter hardships',[h24] but in the following year were made permanent.[h25] As regards health insurance, they were never obligatory, though an Approved Society might pay them as an 'additional benefit'.[h26] Under the contributory pensions scheme, introduced in 1925, child allowances were payable to a widow,[h27] and an old age pensioner could claim for his wife, provided that she too had exceeded pensionable age.[h28] As part of this rationalization of needs-based social insurance, Beveridge naturally recommended that dependency additions be payed at a uniform rate to all recipients of income-maintenance benefits.[h29] Those qualifying for allowances were children[h30] and wives,[h31] women caring for claimant's children,[h32] but not husbands unless they were incapable of self-support.[h33] Other adult relatives might also qualify, provided they were being wholly maintained by the claimant.[h34] The introduction of earnings-related supplements for short-term benefits appropriately hindered further growth of the dependency principle, but as the new principle was not applied to long-term beneficiaries until the late 1970s, dependency increases to retirement, invalidity and widow's pensions were, from 1971, substantially higher than those payable with short-term benefits.[h35]

Degree of Disablement

Again, if social policy were to be consistent in its perception of need, it would, for the purpose of sickness and disability benefits, distinguish according to the gravity of the claimant's condition. Within the social insurance field, however, the principle has been recognized only for the purpose of the long-term disablement benefit payable under the industrial injuries scheme. Here, following a determination of the degree of disablement by medical authorities, benefit is varied on a percentage basis: lump-sums for assessments up to 19 percent and pensions for assessments of 20–100 percent. [h36] While, particularly within recent years, [h37] there has been increased awareness of the desirability of distinguishing between the needs of various types of disabled persons, effort has been concentrated on doing so outside social insurance, through the non-contributory provision, for attendance and mobility. [h38]

Earnings-Related Benefits

The needs approach to social insurance had its most ardent advocate in Beveridge. He abhorred the earnings-related principle both because he considered that individuals in similar circumstances should be treated alike and because provision above the subsistence minimum should be a matter for individual initiative. [h39] For reasons which have been explained elsewhere, [h40] this philosophy was not successful and during the period 1959–1975 earnings-related benefits were introduced. It is necessary here only to describe the methods adopted to achieve this end.

Graduated Retirement Benefit. The first scheme, introduced in 1959, conferred a weekly addition of 6d (now 2 ½ p) to the retirement pension for each 'unit' paid by way of contributions. [h41] A unit was £7.50 in the case of a man and £9 for a woman, [h42] the difference representing the fact that the latter is entitled to her benefit 5 years earlier than the man. Under this scheme, therefore, the amount received was entirely dependent on how much had been contributed and this close actuarial link also meant that no account was to be taken of inflation. [h43] Its inadequacies as an attempt at serious earnings-related provision have been faithfully recorded. [h44]

Earnings-Related Supplements to Short-Term Benefits. These were introduced for unemployment and sickness benefit, and the short-term widow's benefit in 1966 [h45] and were extended to maternity allowances in 1975. [h46] They are not payable for more than 6 months of any one period of interruption of employment. [h47] As originally conceived, they entitled the claimant to one-third of what he had earned, between £9 and £30, to a maximum supplement of £7. [h48] As average earnings increased substantially in the late 1960s and 1970s these limits became almost wholly unrealistic and under current legislation to that figure another 15 percent is added of earnings between £30 and a maximum figure which is revised yearly, and which is used as the ceiling on earnings beyond which contributions are not calculated. [h49] To preserve work incentives in the light of the fact that earnings-related supplements may be aggregated with dependency allowances, there is a further limit so that the total of benefit received does not exceed 85 percent of the claimant's previous earnings. [h50] While these provisions, as now revised, may seem to be quite generous, it should be pointed out that the base of earnings on which the calculations are made is derived from a period between 9 and 21 months prior to the date of claim, and in times of rapid inflation, this depresses the real value of the supplement.

Earnings-Related Components in Long-Term Pensions. The principle upon which the earnings-related components under the new pension scheme are calculated is very different. When fully in force it will provide a return of 25 percent of a person's average earnings between a lower limit (that figure below which contributions are not paid) and a ceiling of seven times that level. [h51] The pension is built up from the inception of the scheme in 1978 at an annual rate of 1.25 percent of those earnings, [h52] so that the full 25 percent will, at the earliest, be paid to an individual in 1998. To preserve equity as between non-manual workers, who typically reach their earnings peak just before retirement and manual workers, where this typically occurs earlier in their working lives, the legislation allows for the best 20 years of earnings (on the basis of which the claimant contributed to the new scheme) to be taken into account. [h53] Inflation-proofing is effected by the process of an annual revision of the amount of earnings on which the claimant contributed. [h54]

Financing

In this section, we consider a number of issues related to the financing of social insurance: the extent of risk-relating; the principles and methods of flat-rate and earnings-related contributions; supplementation by general taxation; the management of finance; and the relationship between contributions and benefits.

Risk-Related Contributions

The general principles of insurance assume some degree of relating the risks attached to individuals or categories of individuals to the financial charges made of them. [h55] In economic terms, this is seen as desirable since otherwise enterprises and individuals are 'externalizing' their costs, and the prices charged for their goods or services do not truly reflect the cost of production. [h56] Social insurance differs significantly from private insurance in that it almost completely avoids relating contributions to risks. [h57] The principle received its most explicit justification in the Beveridge Report: 'it has been found to accord best with the sentiments of the British people that in insurance organised by the community by use of compulsory powers each individual should stand in on the same terms; none should claim to pay less because he is healthier or has more regular employment'. [h58] This has become the general theme in the British systems; but it was not always the case. Our task here is to describe the exceptions to the principle of equal-pooling, which have existed in the history of the British legislation.

Unemployment Insurance. Acknowledgement of risk variation took a number of forms in the pre-1946 unemployment scheme. Originally, only employees in the 'safer' industries were covered. [h59] Subsequently, even when the scheme had become comprehensive, those enterprises with particular low unemployment were allowed to adopt their own scheme and, with the approval of the Minister of Labour, opt out of National Insurance. [h60] The particular problems of agriculture resulted in it not being admitted in the scheme until 1936 and even then was subject to special rates of contribution and benefit. [h61] Public employment was generally excluded either because the risk of unemployment was not a real one, or because redundancy provision was already provided. [h62] However, the most blatant risk-related measure adopted under the original 1911 Act, that employers of men who by the age of 60 had paid more by way of contribution than they had received by way of benefit were entitled to a refund,[h63] was very quickly abandoned.[h64]

Health Insurance. The adjustment of premium to risk was more marked in the health scheme which was, in any event, more comprehensive in its coverage. The system under which individuals were insured with an Approved society which could pay benefits above the minimum,[h65] naturally encouraged workers in healthier occupations or with a better sickness record to group themselves together in special societies so that they might reap the advantage in the form of additional benefits.[h66] Moreover, under the general legislation itself, low rates of contribution were paid, and even lower rates of benefit were received, by women, on the ground that they were 'poor risks'.[h67]

Post-1946 Insurance. The Beveridge principle of pooling of risks in a comprehensive social insurance system was implemented by the legislation and almost all the special categorization recognized before (and described above) was abolished.[h68] Beveridge was prepared to admit of exceptions only where the 'separation of risks serves a social purpose'.[h69] He gave the example of 'adjusting premiums of risks, in order to give a stimulus for avoidance of danger, as in the case of industrial accident and diseases', and he made specific recommendations along such lines,[h70] but this was rejected by the post-war government for the purpose of the new industrial injuries scheme, mainly on the ground of high administrative costs.[h71] The matter remains a controversial one, but the principle of equal contributions still prevails.[h72] Some form of risk-relating can be seen in the way contributors have been classified under the national insurance scheme,[h73] but the categories exist mainly for administrative reasons. There have, however, been some minor exceptions to the general principle: for the purposes of unemployment benefit, seasonal workers must satisfy special conditions;[h74] and members of the armed forces, who are effectively free of the risk of earnings loss, pay a slightly smaller contribution.[h75] As has been explained,[h76] the special position of married women has been substantially abolished by the 1975 legislation.

Flat-Rate Contributions

Two principles dominated British social insurance, at least until recently: contributions to be made by employer and employee; and both to be flat-rated rather than earnings related. Though economists and others may have argued about the consequences of charging employers and employees respectively,[h77] the first principle has rarely been challenged. Beveridge defended the practice of exacting contributions from employers on the grounds that social insurance provision should be reflected in the cost of production, and that it was desirable in the interests of administration and labour relations that employers should participate.[h78] More realistically, one might add that a tax on employers is a relatively easy way of raising revenue.[h79] The second principle, of flat-rate contributions, was easy to reconcile with liberal individualist philosophy: contributions varied according to capacity to pay would involve substantial redistribution from the richer to the poorer workers.[h80] It also conveniently reflected the notion of social solidarity: 'in their capacity as possible recipients of benefits the poorer man and the richer man are treated alike'.[h81] However, the corollary of the principle was that contributions had to be fixed at a level which the lowest paid workers could afford.[h82] As a consequence, unless the contributions of the employer and those from the Exchequer were to be at a disproportionately higher level, this would inevitably constrain the level at which benefits could be paid, and this was perhaps the main reason for the failure of the National Insurance system in the 1950s and for the replacement of the flat-rate basis by earnings-related contributions. [h83] As regards the relationship between the employee's and the employer's contribution, the pattern has generally been to aim at equality, but this has by no means been consistently followed. Initially under the 1911 health scheme, the employee paid more than the employer, [h84] and for certain periods, the reverse was the case in respect of unemployment insurance. [h85] In addition, an exemption which applied to a low wage earner did not relieve his employer of liability. [h86] For the purpose of the 1946 reforms, a new approach was taken: the ratio of employee/employer contribution was 55 percent/45 percent. [h87] This was rationalized by Beveridge on the grounds that the scheme introduced new benefits with which the employer has no obvious concern, and that profit-making enterprises would invariably contribute more to the Exchequer subsidy, because of their higher tax liabilities. [h88] On the other hand, for the industrial injury scheme, the intimate involvement of the employer and the extent of his liability under the superseded workmen's compensation scheme, suggested that he pay a larger proportion. Beveridge considered that this should be greater than the employee's portion, [h89] but the government preferred to equalize the burden. [h90] Under the general insurance scheme, a self-employed person paid more than an employed person, but not as much as the combined employee/employer contribution, [h91] because he was not entitled to unemployment benefit. This pattern was maintained for some time, though in the period 1957–1965, the employer's contribution was allowed to drag behind that paid by employees. [h92]

Earnings-Related Contributions

The shift in the financing of social insurance from flat-rate to earnings-related contributions has already been the subject of discussion; [h93] it remains here to consider the precise methods adopted. The 1959 graduated retirement benefit scheme provided that both employees and employers should pay 4.5 percent on a band of earnings between £9 and £15 per week [h94] — the band chosen was to straddle conveniently average earnings at that time. [h95] This was a stop-gap measure: it supplemented the ordinary flat-rate contributions, and was in any event payable only by those employees who decided not to opt out. The whole structure was fundamentally altered under the 1975 legislation; now all contributions were to be earnings-related. As such, it was convenient to harmonize the provisions with income tax legislation, the single, but significant, difference being that for social insurance purposes there was an upper earnings limit, above which no contributions were payable. [h96] Self-employed earners were also liable on this basis, and in their case it was convenient to apply taxation methods to their profits. As regards employed earners, the exact proportion of earnings to be paid by themselves and by their employers was left to be determined for each year by the Social Services Secretary, [h97] but in sharp contrast to Beveridge's position stated above, [h98] the employer's contribution (at the time of writing 10 percent of earnings between the lower and upper limits) is substantially higher than that of his employee (6.5 percent). [h99] These amounts are both reduced by 2.5 percent if the employment in question has been contracted-out of the new pensions scheme. [i1]

Contributions from General Taxation

From the very beginning of National Insurance there has always been a contribution from the Exchequer for the simple reason that otherwise those from employer and employee, particularly if calculated on the flat-rate basis, would be insufficient to pay benefits at an adequate level.[i2] On the other hand, too large an element from general taxation is thought seriously to undermine the social insurance principle.[i3] For a time, between the wars, it was readily accepted that the Exchequer should contribute one-third, and therefore equal to that of the other two sources, employer and employee.[i4] This high figure was, however, necessary in the light of the massive amount of unemployment existing at that time. Moreover, increases in the liability of the insurance funds, and the rate of debt which resulted, necessitated the Exchequer making loans and block grants.[i5] Notwithstanding recommendations by Beveridge to the contrary,[i6] this practice was to some extent preserved by the 1946 legislation, for the government required the extra finance to implement their policy of paying full benefit immediately to new entrants to the insurance scheme.[i7] Legally, this was effected by enabling an Exchequer supplement to be paid to the contributions of each individual who entered the scheme later than 16 years (the age on which actuarial contributions had been based).[i8] Subsequently, the government was enabled to pay from general taxation into the national insurance funds, sums equal to one-quarter of employees' and employers' contributions, and one-third of the self-employed's contributions, subject to an overall maximum.[i9] However, the time at which such supplementary contributions were to be made was left to the discretion of the Treasury,[i10] and the policy was to resort to this device for the purpose only of meeting the deficit between the income and expenditure of the fund. The degree of Exchequer contribution thus was to depend on a combination of several factors, including the size of the recipient population and general economic considerations, and it varied from, for example, 6 percent in 1950 to 20 percent in 1960.[i11] Under legislation currently in force, discretion as to time and mode of payment is maintained but a precise figure of 18 percent of all other contributions has been set.[i12]

Management of Finance

It is of the essence of private insurance that premiums must be actuarially related to the benefits payable, in so far as this is possible. A social security system can, on the other hand, through the government's power to raise taxation at any time, function on a 'pay-as-you-go' basis, whereby at any one time benefits are financed from current contributions. The merits of the two alternative approaches are the subject of lively discussion in the economics literature.[i13] Our concern is to relate how British social insurance has vacillated between the two extremes. It was implicit in the 1911 unemployement and health schemes that contributions were actuarially related to benefits.[i14] Of course the lack of adequate data and the difficulties, particularly as regards unemployment, of assessing future contingencies[i15] meant that strict adherence to the principle was impossible. The actuarial notions allowed for the setting off of good years against bad by accumulating surpluses in the insurance fund.[i16] In 1920 the unemployment fund was riding high with a reserve of £22 million.[i17] But were liabilities persistently to exceed expectations, then the actuarial principle was in serious danger. The experience in the 1920s and 1930s revealed this only too clearly. The basis of calculations had been an unemployment rate of 4 percent:[118] this was subsequently altered to 6 percent,[119] but between 1920 and 1940 the over-all rate never fell below 10 percent.[120] To a limited extent, the government was prepared to meet the short-fall through current contributions, but the actuarial principle was not to be abandoned lightly: the solution adopted was to maintain, and even to narrow,[121] insurance entitlement, and to provide further relief, financed from general taxation and administered through a means-test, outside the insurance system.[122] The actuarial basis was firmly reasserted in the Beveridge Report.[123] Estimates were made on the likely liabilities of the new fund for the first 20 years, and contribution and benefit rates were set accordingly. There was, moreover, legislative provision made for periodical reviews by the Government Actuary who was to 'report . . . on the financial conditions of the National Insurance Fund and the adequacy or otherwise of the contributions payable . . . to support the benefits payable'.[124] The apparent security of this financial basis was to prove illusory. Already in 1946, the post-war government refused to heed Beveridge's advice that full entitlement to retirement pensions for new entrants should be postponed for 20 years,[125] and, as we have seen, resort was had to general taxation to meet the deficit.[126] Other developments had an even greater impact on the actuarial principle: the number of persons, particularly the aged, dependent on the fund was underestimated and no allowance was made for inflation.[127] Inevitably, as benefits had constantly to be revised to keep pace with rising prices, the 'pay-as-you-go' approach began to prevail. Eventually, the government was forced formally to recognize it as the basis of future strategy. While the Conservative administration of 1971 had blanched at the prospect of inflation-proofing social insurance: 'pensions on a pay-as-you-go basis would simply force the percentage rates of contribution to rise higher and higher to meet the emerging cost which . . . would be to solve the present financial problem by creating an even bigger one for the future',[128] the succeeding Labour government was prepared to commit itself to the notion of 'a gradually increasing transfer of income . . . from the economically active section of the community to those who have retired'.[129] Technically, the 'pay-as-you-go' strategy is implemented by the process of notionally revising each year the value of each individual's contributions.[130] On the other hand, the lessons of the over-ambitious pensions strategy of 1946 having been learned, the new scheme attempts to avoid the pitfalls of too sudden and too large a transfer by building up to full entitlement to the earnings-related (and inflation-proofed) pension over a period of 25 years.[131]

Relating Entitlement to Contributions

Under conventional private insurance principles, a person is covered against the nominated risks from the moment the policy comes into effect, normally the date of the contract. Conversely endowment policies under, for example, life insurance, are seen as providing benefits in return for contributions actually made. Some parts of the social insurance systems are modelled on the first approach; some are modelled on the second; but the majority of benefits occupy a midway position, whereby, though benefits are not in any real sense a return on individual contributions made, nevertheless the claimant must establish a substantial and almost continuous participation in the scheme. The discussion is divided accordingly.

Minimum Contribution Requirements. The first approach is highly exceptional. It has found complete acceptance only in the industrial injuries scheme, under which an employee is entitled as from the first date of employment, without having to satisfy any contribution conditions.[132] Indeed, consistent with this, in 1973 independent national insurance industrial injuries contributions were abolished[133] and today an individual's entitlement rests on the fact that he is classified as an employed earner contributor to the general insurance fund.[134] The special position of industrial injuries is explicable on historical grounds: the 1946 scheme replaced a private law system under which the injured workman could sue his employer from his first day of employment.[135]

During the 1920s, the inability of many to satisfy the ordinary contribution requirements for unemployment benefit forced the government to adopt a compromising stance:[136] an individual in these circumstances was entitled to an 'uncovenanted benefit',[137] later known as 'extended'[138] or 'transitional'[139] benefit, but payable at a lower rate than the standard insurance benefit and only after an investigation of the claimant's means.[140] At first, this was rationalized as benefit paid in advance of contributions, on the assumption that they would eventually be paid.[141] Following an appraisal of the whole system of unemployment relief by a Royal Commission,[142] these fictions were abandoned and a distinction was drawn between unemployment benefit, for the purposes of which the conventional contributions requirements continued to apply, and unemployment assistance, a means-tested benefit financed by general taxation, and administered independently of the insurance authorities.[143]

There are, finally, two benefits payable under modern law, for which the contribution conditions are almost nominal: the death grant[144] and child's special allowance.[145] The first of these, payable as a partial indemnity for funeral expenses, is seen more as a 'bonus' under the insurance scheme, and does not depend on any link between it and the deceased person.[146] The latter, payable to a woman whose ex-husband was maintaining her child before his death, covers a very small section of the population.[147]

Endowment Approach. The endowment approach does not feature in traditional British social insurance for the simple reason that it conflicts with the basic premise of a pooling of social risks, combined with flat-rate benefits. Its presence in the new pensions scheme represents an acknowledgement of the failure of Beveridge's assumption that individuals would make voluntary provision for their old age above the flat-rate minimum. Thus the earnings-related component, first under the graduated retirement benefit scheme,[148] and subsequently under the 1975 pension scheme,[149] is in substance a form of compulsory saving rather than protection against a risk which might or might not occur. As such, it is wholly dependent on the amount which the claimant contributed, subject only, in the case of the 1975 scheme, to an element of inflation-proofing, financed by contributors at the time of payment.[150]

Substantial Contribution Requirements. The third, and most frequently encountered, approach is to demand of the claimant some substantial participation in the insurance scheme, while not basing the amount of benefit on the number of contributions. The conditions imposed may be said to reflect the desire to 'reward' those who have worked regularly and for a substantial proportion of their working lives, and to preserve equity as between persons in different social and economic circumstances.[151] The exact formulae adopted have changed substantially since the introduction of social insurance. At first glance, it is perhaps surprising that the conditions have become much more stringent over the years. For unemployment benefit, for example, until 1924 only twelve contributions needed to have been made.[152] From that date, the requirement was raised to thirty contributions in the last 2 years before the claim,[153] and after 1946 this figure had risen to fifty in the last year.[154] In part these changes reflect the fact that the amount and duration of benefit had increased, but in another sense the comparison is not a real one, for the pre-war tests took account of the difficulties of maintaining contributions through illness or unemployment, while from 1946 the requirement was of contributions actually paid or *credited*, and a system of credits was introduced for those unable to pay.[155] The crediting facilities represent one of the complexities of the modern law; but there are others. The rather rudimentary pre-war single test of participation in the scheme has been replaced by a dual condition which has regard to the claimant's contributory record for the purposes of determining sufficiency in terms both of initial establishment in the scheme and of consistency over a period of time.[156] For the former purpose, 6 months' contributions actually paid are essential; for the latter purpose, the claimant must have paid or been credited with forty-eight (subsequently fifty) weekly contributions in the last complete year before the claim.[157] Appropriately enough, there has always been a major distinction between the contribution requirements of short-term and long-term benefits, particularly where, as with retirement, the risk is one which should arise naturally in relation to most contributors. Thus under the pre-war health and pension schemes, twenty-six contributions were necessary for the short-term sickness benefit and 104 for the long-term disablement,[158] while for the contributory pension a claimant had normally to show, in addition to 104 contributions, that on reaching pensionable age he had been continuously insured for 5 years and that he had averaged thirty-nine contributions in each of the last three of those years.[159] Under modern legislation, a claimant for retirement pension must show (for initial establishment) one year's contributions actually paid, plus (for consistency) for each of not less than 90 percent of the years of his working life, fifty-two weekly contributions either paid or credited.[160] There are, of course, a large number of technical rules concerning *inter alia*, the reduction of benefit for incomplete contribution records, the aggregation of different classes of contributions, and the use of one person's contributions (e.g. a husband's) for another person's benefits (e.g. a wife's).[161]

Administration

One theme governs the history of the administration of British social insurance, that of increasing integration and centralization.

Uncoordinated Administration

The establishment of different insurance schemes at different times and for different purposes naturally led to a lack of coordination. Moreover, the compromise character of the health scheme which attempted to combine the virtues of a state system, providing minimum benefits, with those of private insurance, allowing for additional benefits above the minimum, resulted in a considerable degree of decentralization. Administration was fundamentally in the hands of the 'Approved Societies', such friendly societies, trade unions, insurance and collecting societies which satisfied two conditions: they were not carried on for profit, and they were subject to the absolute control of their members. [162] Approval had to be sought from the National Health Insurance Commissioners, who also performed the function of overviewing the system as a whole. [163] Each insured person enrolled with the society of his choice, which nevertheless, within certain limits, had power to refuse him membership. [164] It also formulated its own rules and regulations governing the payment of benefits, [165] though these too were subject to some overriding statutory conditions. [166] This system of administration was the subject of severe criticism during the interwar period: [167] the ideal of freedom of choice, both as to membership of an Approved Society and as regards medical treatment, proved in many cases to be unreal; the societies were unable to promote general measures of sickness prevention and improved treatment, because their competitive and disintegrated system of administration made this impracticable; such a decentralized structure with inevitable overlaps and inefficiencies was very costly. Nevertheless, with a few minor changes, including the transfer of central supervision from the Insurance Commissioners to the Ministry of Health, [168] this framework of administration remained intact until 1946, and its scope was extended in 1925 to govern also the contributory pension scheme. [169]

Unemployment insurance was more centralized. The employment exchanges administered the payment of benefit and the controls of voluntary unemployment, but they were under the supervision of the Board of Trade. [170] In 1920 the latter's powers were transferred to the newly established Ministry of Labour. [171] When, during the periods of chronic unemployment, individuals claiming uncovenanted benefits were subjected to means tests, it was clear that some additional institution was necessary to investigate each claimant's resources, and rather than employ the stigmatizing Poor Law authorities the government established Public Assistance Committees for the purpose. [172] Following a review by the Royal Commission and rationalization of unemployment relief into the dual system of insurance and assistance, administration was conferred, respectively, on the Unemployment Insurance Statutory Committee and the Unemployment Assistance Board. [173] Both of these were to be independent of ministerial control; the aim had been to remove some of the contentious issues from the political arena. [174] But the consequence was that neither body was accountable to Parliament, and yet the latter was, of course, responsible for effecting any changes in the law. The members of the two bodies were appointed by the Minister of Labour and in practice were equally divided between employers and trade unionists. [175]

Unification of Administration

The third of Beveridge's six fundamental principles of social insurance was the 'unification of administrative responsibility'. [176] The two existing schemes, unemployment and health and pensions, were to be amalgamated into a single national insurance system. The Approved Societies were abolished; Beveridge would also have preferred a single government department to be responsible for all social security benefits, including the means-tested national assistance (the successor to unemployment assistance). [177] This was rejected by the government; the insurance benefits, including the new industrial injuries scheme, were to be separately administered from war pensions (governed by the Minister of Pensions),[178] from the National Health Service (the responsibility of the Minister of Health)[179] and from National Assistance (administered like its predecessor by an independent National Assistance Board).[180] The new Ministry of National Insurance was instituted in 1944: originally it was to have been called the 'Ministry of Social Insurance' but the nomenclature was abandoned to preserve continuity with the pre-war schemes and also, apparently, because the phrase 'social insurance' was used in Germany![181]

Most of the changes taking place since 1946 have been of a cosmetic rather than of substantial character. In 1953 the Ministries of National Insurance and Pensions were merged,[182] and in 1966 at last Beveridge's wish for an integrated Ministry of Social Security was fulfilled.[183] The major impetus for this reform resulted from the patent fact that national assistance, far from withering away as Beveridge had hoped, was to remain as a source of welfare of paramount importance. As such, it was felt desirable to attempt to remove the stigma in administration which was thought to arise from the continuity between the pre-war Unemployment Assistance Board and the post-war National Assistance Board. It would be more convenient also for persons who were in receipt of both insurance and assistance benefits. Thus the Ministry of Social Security was to administer all social security benefits including supplementary benefit,[184] though as regards the latter an independent Supplementary Benefits Commission was to be responsible for adjudicating on claims, and, subject to legislative prescription, for formulating general policies to guide officers in exercising discretionary powers.[185] A final step in amalgamation was taken in 1968: the separate Ministries of Health and Social Security were combined in a new Department of Health and Social Security.[186]

Consultative Bodies

The vision of social insurance as in some way implying 'social solidarity' could not be realized fully if all policy decisions relating to it were taken by bureaucrats, or their political masters, at some remove from contributors and beneficiaries. At various stages in its history, therefore, efforts have been made to draw on the collective wisdom of the community through the establishment of advisory and consultative bodies. Under the health scheme it was envisaged that the Approved Societies, which were supposed to be constituted on a democratic basis,[187] could effectively perform this function. As has been seen, an effort was made in the 1930s for the policymaking role in the unemployment schemes to be assumed by bodies independent of government and representing employers and trade unions. On the 1946 re-establishment of national insurance, on an integrated basis, the consultative ideal was taken much further. First, there were to be national standing advisory bodies to deal with general policy issues arising under the general[188] and industrial schemes,[189] as well as to review subordinate legislation, to ensure that they were compatible with parliamentary legislation.[190] Both of these bodies contributed substantially to the development of social insurance law in the post-war period.[191] Secondly, at a 'grass roots' level, there were local advisory committees to deal with such matters as the location of offices, publicity on benefits, and also, where appropriate, the resolution of individual problems.[192] The bodies were abolished in 1971,[193] allegedly because, by that time, local managers and their staff were sufficiently experienced in their area to handle such questions themselves.[194] Such an attitude was hardly consistent with more general tendencies to establish consumer 'watchdogs', but nothing has been done yet to replace them. Indeed, the Conservative administration, elected in 1979, has recently announced its intention of curtailing the powers of other advisory bodies, mainly to save on public expenditure.[195]

Adjudication

The concern here has been to accommodate two principles which have often been seen as conflicting: that a claim to a social insurance benefit should be subjected to a process of adjudication (including a right of appeal against an adverse decision) which is impartial and which in other respects conforms to the tenets of natural justice; that procedures should be, on the whole, inexpensive, informal and speedy.

Pre-War Procedures

From the beginnings of the social insurance systems, the second of the two principles has been seen as a justification for avoiding, where possible, resort to the ordinary courts. In this respect, the amount and expense of litigation under the Workmen's Compensation legislation provided an example of what could go wrong.[196] In fact, the procedure established for unemployment insurance was to provide the model for much of what was to follow. Claims to benefit were decided in the first instance by Board of Trade (subsequently Ministry of Labour) 'insurance officers',[197] of which there was one at each employment exchange. A dissatisfied claimant could appeal against his decision to a locally constituted 'Court of Referees', comprising a Chairman, appointed by the Board of Trade, one person representing employers, and one representing workers.[198] From the decision of that body a further appeal lay to an 'Umpire' whose decision on the matter was 'final and conclusive'.[199] It should be noted that the jurisdiction of these bodies did not cover all matters capable of giving rise to disputes. So-called 'insurance' questions, e.g. whether an individual was under an obligation to insure, and if so, in what category, were determined, from 1920, by officials within the Ministry of Labour.[j1]

The procedure under the health scheme was somewhat similar, though here account had to be taken of the fact that, unlike unemployment insurance, the typical dispute would not be between a claimant and the bureaucracy, but rather between a member of an Approved Society and the Society, and this relationship was more of a contractual nature. In principle, such disputes were to be resolved by the Minister of Health, though he had power (which he normally exercised) of appointing referees to hear and adjudicate on the dispute.[j2] Such persons were selected from a body of practising lawyers and where the issue involved required expert medical opinion, a qualified medical practitioner was appointed as an assessor.[j3] A similar approach was taken on contributory pensions disputes.[j4] One difference between, on the one hand, the unemployment procedure, and on the other, the health and pensions systems, should be noted: the Umpire's decisions were reported, and there was established, therefore, a body of case-law on the most important issues.[j5]

National Insurance Tribunals

Beveridge was impressed by the workings of the adjudicators in the pre-war unemployment scheme and recommended an analogous procedure for disputes under the 1946 legislation.[j6] Classification and contribution matters were reserved for the Minister,[j7] presumably because they are considered to be more 'administrative' in character, though the matter has never been rationalized.[j8] Almost all other questions were to be determined by the insurance officer,[j9] then, on appeal, by a local, national insurance appeal tribunal, with a similar composition to the former Court of Referees,[j10] with final resort to the National Insurance Commissioner, a barrister of at least 10 years standing.[j11] Normally a Commissioner sits individually, but cases involving important matters of principle may be decided by a Tribunal of three Commissioners.[j12] Many decisions are reported, and the most interesting of these are published by Her Majesty's Stationery Office.[j13] The national insurance authorities serve similar functions for industrial injury disputes, though where these involve medical issues, appeals have to be made to a two-tier system of medical tribunals.[j14] Concern about the quality of decision-making in the latter led, in 1959, to the creation of a right of appeal, on point of law only, from the higher medical tribunal to the National Insurance Commissioner.[j15] Subject to certain technical changes, these procedures have remained unaltered since. As such, they have been kept totally independent of adjudication of claims to national assistance, later supplementary benefit.[j16] The appeal machinery here has proved to be highly controversial and, on general opinion, unsatisfactory.[j17] As a result, the government has very recently instituted a reform whereby the National Insurance Commissioner will hear appeals from the local supplementary benefit appeal tribunals.[j18]

Review by the Ordinary Courts

In contrast to typical European legal systems, British administrative tribunals are kept wholly distinct from the ordinary court system and there is no 'Supreme Administrative Court' which has power to review the decisions of these tribunals.[j19] Nevertheless, the ordinary courts do have certain powers to quash the decisions of inferior bodies where, for example, they exceed their jurisdiction, contravene the principles of natural justice, or make a patent mistake of law.[j20] For a long time, it was thought that this procedure could not be applied to the decisions of the national insurance tribunals, as the legislation provided that these should be 'final'.[j21] In the 1950s it was determined at last that the 'finality' clause did not preclude judicial review,[j22] and since then there have been a number of successful applications to the ordinary courts.[j23] However, it has been insisted that if the application for review rests on an alleged mistaken interpretation of the legislation, as opposed to an excess of jurisdiction or breach of natural justice, there must be 'a clear error of law appearing on the face of the decision before the courts will intervene'; otherwise the manifest intention of the legislature to avoid litigation in the ordinary courts would be circumvented.[j24] Nevertheless, at the time of writing, there is a legislative proposal for a general right of appeal on a point of law from the National Insurance Commissioner,[j25] and it remains to be seen whether this will prove to be acceptable to Parliament and, if so, under what conditions the right might be exercised.

CONCLUSIONS

Theoretical and Legal Character of Social Insurance[j26]

In socio-economic terms, social insurance can be regarded as a compromise between liberal individualist and collectivist ideologies of welfare.[j27] As such, in legal terms, it also straddles notions of entitlement derived respectively from private and public law. The individualist approach rests on a *reciprocal* or *exchange* system.[28] The notion here is of a relationship which is essentially contractual in character: an individual is entitled to welfare only if in some sense he has 'earned' it, either through his labour or through financial payments made to a fund. In political and economic terms this arrangement implies that the individual does not find himself in a state of dependence on the group or organization which confers the welfare. In legal terms, this is mirrored by a recognition that, should the conditions for the reciprocal transfer be satisified, he has an unqualified *right* to welfare. In the analysis which follows, the reciprocal system will be represented by a horizontal continuous line.

Fund ⟵——————⟶ Individual

The alternative collectivist approach gives rise to a *unilateral* system of welfare. Here there is no form of contractual relationship between the transferor and the transferee. The typical consequences are that the individual recipient of welfare is in a state of dependence *vis-à-vis* the transferor, the latter may impose stringent conditions for the conferring of assistance and the individual has no legal right to welfare. Such a system will be represented by a vertical line which, because of the weaknesses of the legal relationship, is punctuated.

Fund

Individual

Until the second half of the nineteenth century it was accepted dogma that personal and social welfare was primarily to be achieved through the market system.[29] Utility was to be maximized through an exchange process: surplus value was created by the bartering of assets, whether capital or labour. While risk was conceived at one time to be an inevitable feature of the capitalist economy, it became apparent that the exchange process could itself be used to provide forms of economic security, hence the growth of private insurance and later, cooperative mutual assistance.[30] The legal bases of these forms of welfare are property (the possession of resources from which the exchange process is possible) and contract (the exchange process itself). It is true that in a minority of cases it was accepted that the risk was so clearly caused by someone other than the individual who was a victim of it that the cost of the risk should be borne by its creator. This form of transfer was achieved by the law of tort and also (in a diluted form) by workmen's compensation.[31] The area of social risks covered by the tort mechanism was necessarily small and as a generalization it may still be posited that the primary form of social welfare throughout the nineteenth century coincided with the *exchange* system.

Of course a substantial proportion of the community had not the means to avail themselves of the exchange system, and some residual form of welfare had to exist. This clearly had to take the form of the *unilateral* system, the transferors being at this stage the individual's family, a charitable organization,[j32] or the publicly financed poor law.[j33] The consequences were, of course, that the poorer sections of society had no legal right to welfare, that they survived only through a state of dependence and, at least as regards the poor law, were subject to a strategy of repression and stigma which was thought necessary to discourage idleness.

This structure of social welfare which existed in Britain at the end of the nineteenth century may be represented in diagramatic form.

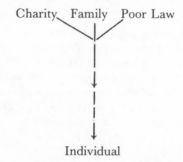

Charity   Family   Poor Law

Insurance Companies

Friendly Societies   Individual

The recognition at the end of the nineteenth century and the first decade of the twentieth century that poverty resulted not so much from personal moral failings as from external economic or natural hazards,[j34] and that the unimpeded operation of market forces was, as a means of assuring welfare, neither just (in distributional terms) nor humane (*pace* the degradation and humiliation of the poor law) nor politically astute (the socialist movements represented a threat to the established order), nor even economically sound (the labour force would produce more efficiently if protected against the major social and economic hazards), prompted a reappraisal of the role of the state in the administration of welfare. The potential of the *unilateral* system to provide the solution was limited: the poor law approach was too oppressive; an extension of the means-tested non-contributory benefit which in 1908 had been created for those over 70 years[j35] was neither economically nor politically feasible. The solution was sought in the concept of social insurance. It maintained in a somewhat modified form the *exchange* basis of social welfare: it was based on past performance in the labour market and benefit could thus be justified as having been 'earned'; it incorporated the traditional Puritan and capitalist virtues of thrift and individualism; it gave rise to legal, contractual rights to benefit, thus avoiding the notions of charity or means-tested assistance associated with the unilateral model.

The identification of the national insurance scheme (as it was introduced in 1911) with the *exchange* model must not, of course, be exaggerated. It departed from that model in two important respects. First, the premiums payable were not calculated according to risk, and so there was some redistribution of resources which could not be justified in purely economic terms. Secondly, the contractual aspect of the scheme was weakened by the fact that insurance was compulsory not voluntary. Yet it is important to appreciate that the modification necessary here is only a limited one. This is because benefit under the national insurance scheme was payable only on a minimum 'survival' basis, so that an individual was left free to take responsibility for his own welfare above that level.

As the following diagram reveals, the structure of social welfare as it existed at the time Beveridge wrote his report in 1942 was a complex one. It comprised two forms of the *exchange* system — the minimum covered by the social insurance scheme and any surplus by private transactions — with the *unilateral* system providing a safety net for those for whom the insurance approach was unavailable or insufficient.

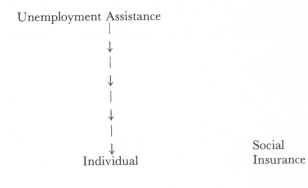

The legal implications of these welfare strategies now require some elaboration. The two outstanding traditional characteristics of the Anglo-Saxon systems have been the strength of customary law (and hence the importance of the judiciary) at least until the twentieth century[j36] and, though this is less marked in those countries which were formerly colonies, an antipathy to broad legislative generalizations, of a type which are to be found typically in codes and constitutions in Romano-Germanic systems.[j37]

The primacy of common law (the customary aspect of legal institutions) may have been in decline in the twentieth century but it remained as the residual source of law when legislation was incomplete or uncertain as well as a criterion of social and economic justice which judges could employ in their interpretation of statutory systems. As such, with its emphasis on liberal individualism and property, it was antipathetic to the socialization implicit in social insurance. The conception of statute law as an intrusion upon the common law also meant that the legislature was slow to use legislation as an instrument for statements of general principles or objectives.[j38] There was no question, in Britain, of establishing a constitutional framework for the operation of 'Sozialstaat': statute law was always more specific, even pragmatic. Finally, and perhaps most important, public law as the institution is known in continental Europe was slow to develop in Britain.[j39] It took some time before the state was recognized as an entity different from other members of the community, as something other than a *primus inter pares*. The second half of the nineteenth century had of course been a great period of public law and regulation but, with minor exceptions, it had not been necessary to create a system of public law rights, for the legislation had, typically, not conferred on individuals, rights which were enforceable against the State.

Four consequences may arguably be attributed to these special features of the British legal system. First, though perhaps this is too speculative, it may be said that the strength of the common law and its focus on private property, was to some extent responsible for the delay in the introduction of social insurance (some 30 years after the Bismarck legislation). Secondly, when social insurance was introduced, it was inevitable that the exchange or contractual basis should be emphasized. Thirdly, the inadequacies of the unilateral approach (poor law and unemployment assistance) were felt all the more acutely, as they could not be construed as giving rise to *rights* in the individual beneficiary. Fourthly, the social insurance legislation (and social security generally) was not conceived as being part of the 'ordinary law of the land': it pertained to the 'administration'; it was of little concern to the legal profession; and their participation in the system, its adjudicatory processes and its policy formulation was discouraged.[40]

While, arguably, the influences of traditional legal thought and practice still persist, they have to some extent at least been countered by dynamic new developments. First, the legal character of welfare provision has been strengthened, particularly in relation to unilateral transfers: discretionary elements have been reduced and legal entitlement is now formulated in terms of 'rights'.[41] Secondly, there has been a sudden upsurge of interest in social welfare shown by lawyers, both practising and academic;[42] groups have been formed whose main function is to assist the poorer sections of the community in their social security applications and appeals.[43] Thirdly, within social policy itself, there has been a marked development towards providing new benefits which are neither contributory nor means-tested, particularly to cover family and disability needs.[44] This may reveal that the legal system is beginning to contemplate new conceptions of rights which are no longer dependent on the possession and transfer of assets.[45] Whether or not we are moving consistently towards a new model of social welfare which may be visually represented thus,

State

Individual

is, however, doubtful so long as social insurance remains as the core of the social security system.

Role of Social Insurance in Welfare State

In this section, we attempt to draw some conclusions as to the economic and sociological significance of social insurance. Space does not allow for any rigorous analysis and we shall confine our attention to three substantial issues: to what extent can social insurance be regarded as an instrument for effecting an efficient allocation of resources within society? To what extent is it to be seen rather as a device for the redistribution of income and wealth from the richer to the poorer sections of the community? To what extent does it attempt to endorse currently held social values as regards the family, sexual equality and work and leisure?

Efficient Allocation of Resources

Economists typically analyse the effects of institutions in terms of a model which has regard to aggregate social welfare.[46] In terms of this reasoning, social arrangements are 'optimal' or 'efficient' when no individual can be made better off without at least one other becoming worse off.[47] While, on some interpretations it has a limited application to many social policy issues, because it is impossible to make interpersonal comparisons of welfare (how do we compare the utility of £1 to Bill with that of £1 to Bob?),[48] others are prepared to argue that if we can make some individuals better off and at the same time compensate those who would otherwise be made worse off, then such an arrangement can be regarded as more efficient than if no such transfers were to take place.[49]

This form of reasoning can be applied to social insurance from two different perspectives. From a narrower perspective, we can regard social insurance as a method of reallocating resources on the occurrence of particular social risks. Such risks as unemployment and disability, it may be argued, are costs which are incurred from certain activities and enterprises but which are then 'externalized' to those working within the enterprise (or their families), and are therefore not reflected in the prices which are charged for the products (i.e. goods or services) of that enterprise.[50] The existence of an externality means that such an arrangement is not socially efficient: the price that is being paid for the goods or services does not reflect its true costs and therefore they are being overproduced. If then we could ensure that through, for example, social insurance contributions the enterprise was bearing its proper burden of unemployment and disability, we would be making net gains in social welfare. It is very difficult, however, to reconcile this reasoning with the system of social insurance which has existed in Britain (or indeed elsewhere) for the very simple reason that, as has been seen,[51] with only some very minor exceptions, contributions have not been related to risk.

On a somewhat broader perspective, we may hold nevertheless that it is socially efficient to deprive some sections of the community of the ability to earn their livelihood through working because they are too old, or they are physically incapable of performing the job satisfactorily, or because advances in technology, and changes in demand, render it necessary for them to shift from one occupation to another, with an inevitable period of unemployment in between. In social terms, the cost of maintaining such persons in employment outweighs the benefit to them, in the form of wages, and to socety in the form of output. To achieve the improvement in aggregate welfare which would result from depriving them of work and wages, we should nevertheless, attempt to avoid making them worse off by compensating them, according to the principle described above. It is not too difficult to rationalize much of social insurance along these lines; indeed, these very arguments were used in 1966 as a justification for the introduction of earnings-related supplements for unemployment benefit.[52] On the other hand, the system of compensation, so envisaged, is far from perfect since British social insurance has never committed itself wholeheartedly to an earnings-replacement principle—to a certain extent it still fosters the Beveridge ideal of basing benefit on need—and in any event, the insurance basis of the system means that in part at least the individual is himself financing the compensation.

Redistribution of Income and Wealth

The form of economic reasoning to which we have so far referred does not purport to take account of income differences. The extent to which, quite independent of resource-allocation objectives, income and wealth should be redistributed from the richer to the poorer sections of the community depends on the assumption of certain moral or political values which lie outside the parameter of the economists' endeavours. Nevertheless, it is clear that the 'Welfare State' as a whole, comprising all social services and social security measures, is largely concerned with the redistribution of resources.[j53] What is more problematical is the degree to which, within the social services network, the social insurance system pursues such objectives. First, the fact that, in general, higher income groups are less prone to the short-term risks of unemployment and sickness,[j54] may provide some limited degree of progressive redistribution. Secondly, however, so long as contributions and benefits were both assessed on flat-rate basis (entirely the case before 1959 and substantially true also for the period 1959 to 1975) redistribution was, if anything, regressive, since the contribution constituted a higher proportion of the low-paid worker's income than that of the higher-paid's earnings.[j55] The current position is difficult to assess since while earnings-related contributions are used to finance benefits which provide a slightly higher earnings-replacement for the lower paid, and there is thus some *prima facie* evidence of progressive redistribution, nevertheless there is a ceiling on earnings beyond which contributions are not exacted.[j56]

Endorsement of Social Values

It can hardly be the case that the primary objective of social insurance is to endorse certain social values, but arguably the principles should be formulated in such a way as not to be inconsistent with such values. As regards the family, the system appears to adopt an equivocal position.[j57] On the one hand, social insurance law has regard for some, but by no means all, purposes to natural as opposed to legal family relationships: thus dependency additions may be claimed for illegitimate children and, in some circumstances, for women in a marriage-like relationship.[j58] On the other hand, such women have no entitlement to a widow's pension and cannot rely on the man's contributions for the purposes of their own retirement pension. Moreover, the traditional concern of British social insurance with need rather than income-replacement can be seen as reinforcing intra-family relationships even though these may not always be of a 'legal' character.

Social security law was deliberately excluded from the operation of the sex discrimination legislation and it remains an area where there are significant differences between the treatment of men and women.[j59] The model which still dominates social policy thinking is that of the wife doing the housework and caring for the children while the husband is the breadwinner. The model is reflected not only in the unexceptionable fact that the non-earning housewife had a reduced role in the insurance system but also, more critically, in the fact that even where she is an earner she has not the same insurance status as her husband. She may rely on his contributions for the purposes of widow's and retirement pension, and also for additions to other benefits, but subject to exceptional circumstances, he has no reciprocal entitlement based on her contributions.[j60] Certain significant developments towards equalization have, however, taken place during recent years. A widower may now to some extent base his entitlement to retirement or invalidity pension on his deceased wife's contributions;[j61] the married woman earner's ability to opt out of the system has been abolished;[j62] and, perhaps most important of all, years spent in domestic responsibilities (whether by a woman or a man) may now count for the purposes of pensions entitlement.[j63]

The concern to preserve work incentives has always played a fundamental role in social insurance law. This objective is reflected in such provisions as the medical criteria of incapacity for work[j64] and the controls imposed against voluntary unemployment.[j65] It may be seen also in the conscious effort not to set benefit at a level which would mean that a claimant would be better off not working.[j66]

Social Insurance as Instrument of Social Control

The shift from voluntary, individualized welfare to compulsory, collective welfare of which social insurance is an important, if also imperfect,[j67] example implies a degree of subservience of insured people, and beneficiaries in particular, to the authority of the state, and in practice its bureaucracy.[j68] Even, it should be noted, where legislation confers a certain amount of freedom, as with retirement pensions, to opt for occupational rather than state coverage, legally the private scheme must conform to certain centralized standards.[j69] We have already seen how the change from a private law relationship based on contract to a public law relationship between citizen and state posed considerable problems for a legal system whose perception of 'rights' in such an area was hesitant and often hostile.[j70] We have seen also how efforts have been made to rectify this weakness and how the legal relationship between individuals and bureaucracy has been strengthened.[j71] What remains to be told is the extent to which the existence of social insurance and the administrative structure which supports it imposes constraints on individual behaviour. In many respects social insurance shares features in common with other social services; in other respects, its 'reciprocal' character acts as a restraint on the abuse of power by the authorities.

The identity of social insurance as a social service involves a number of control mechanisms. In an institutional sense, social insurance is a system of rules and regulations demanding obedience from both administrators and those whom they administer.[j72] Claims and payments can be made only according to highly precise instructions, and within carefully prescribed time limits,[j73] deviation from which, while not always fatal, creates at least delays and uncertainties. The bureaucratic structures also tend to be impersonal, dehumanized methods of communication; the language used is formal, often opaque.[j74] Administrators typically have a monopoly of knowledge and expertise over the subject-matter of welfare provisions, thus leading to a state of dependence in the claimant and often an inability to assert his claim by adversarial encounters.[j75] The imbalance of power is relevant not only to the application of rules but also to their limitations. No set of rules can ever determine conclusively and exhaustively all circumstances which may arise; nor can they control precisely how they are to be administered. The 'open-texture' of rules therefore unavoidably confers on officials facilities for expressing their own social and cultural biases, even where these conflict with the spirit of the legislation, if not its letter. Research in the social administration field has uncovered such biases being shown towards the employed ('workshy'),[j76] and single parents ('parasites').[j77]

To some extent, social insurance avoids many of these dangers. Pinker writes that 'the status of a recipient may be enhanced when what he receives is recognised as being a restitution for earlier service, or a compensation for disservice previously suffered'.[178] The reciprocal character of the system, the notion of a return for contributions made and of a reward for past service, places insurance beneficiaries among the elite of the social services clientele. This is manifested in a number of forms. Discretion is limited in favour of rights; benefits are paid in cash (thus conferring some freedom of choice) rather than kind; claims are (with the exception of unemployment benefit) made by post instead of in person; the initiative for the payment of certain benefits, e.g. retirement pensions, is taken by the authorities instead of the claimant; the tribunal system encourages an adversarial, rather than an inquisitional, procedure.

In 1942 Beveridge looked forward to 'the development of State insurance as a new type of human institution, differing both from the former methods of preventing or alleviating distress and from voluntary insurance'.[179] Whether its character as a compromise between exchange and welfare, between private and public law, and between sufficiency and the bare minimum, has solved the many problems which have beset it must be left to the judgment of others. Whether it will prove adequate to meet the future demands of social and economic change must remain even more speculative.

POSTSCRIPT 1981

The above text was completed at the end of 1979. Since then very major changes have been wrought in the British social security system by a Conservative administration whose primary economic concern has been the revitalization of the economy and the control of inflation. Its monetarist policies have involved very sharp cuts in public expenditure and its efforts to boost productivity have focused on tax cuts (though in real terms only for those in the upper income range) and on a more vigorous attack on social-security abuse. These policies, combined with the worldwide economic recession, have led to substantial increases in unemployment. The number out of work is the largest since the interwar period and (in mid-1981) is fast approaching 3 million. The cumulative strain on the social security system has been severe: increases in the number of claimants have coincided with reductions in welfare expenditure.

Savings in the social security budget are being made by a variety of methods. The real value of the short-term insurance benefits for unemployment, sickness, maternity and industrial injury was not maintained in 1980–1981; they were increased by 5 percent less than the rise in the cost of living. This necessitated legislative amendment to the up-rating obligations imposed on government and, as such, may be regarded as a departure from one of the fundamental principles of social insurance. However, it was overshadowed by an even more drastic policy reversal. We have seen in these pages how the introduction in 1966 of earnings-related supplements to the short-term benefits constituted perhaps the most important step away from the Beveridge notion of needs-related provision to the Bismarckian concept of earnings-related indemnity. These supplements were reduced in value by 5 percent in 1981 and will be abolished altogether in 1982. By way of partial justification for this severe cut, the government argued that it was to anticipate two structural reforms in social security benefits which it was hoped to implement in the next few years.

The first such reform would involve rendering all short-term benefits subject to income tax. Quite independent of any macro-economic objectives, this measure could be defended on the distributional argument that it would remove an inequity between those who had worked continuously for a fiscal year and those whose earnings had been interrupted for part of that period. Nevertheless there is a widespread fear that the government will treat the reform as another means to reduce spending on social welfare, for, as yet, it has given no commitment that it will redeploy the revenue derived from the taxation to social-security beneficiaries.

The second proposed structural reform can similarly be regarded either as a relatively uncontroversial rationalization of existing provisions or as an excuse for further reductions in the level of welfare. We have seen earlier how the British system has hitherto failed to achieve an integration between social security provision for short-term sickness and private occupational coverage, mainly through sick-pay agreements. The government now proposes to adopt something akin to the German arrangements whereby responsibility for income-maintenance during short periods of incapacity for work is transferred from social insurance to the employer. Undoubtedly, this should involve a substantial saving in administrative expenditure (though of course a heavier administrative burden would fall on employers). But if the government holds to its provisional views on the minimum which employers will be bound to pay to sick employees, this will be substantially less than that to which (with earnings-related supplement) they are currently entitled.

The history of social insurance since the Second World War revealed how the system had failed to provide an adequate level of income maintenance for its beneficiaries and how many were forced to resort to the means-tested supplementary benefit. Notwithstanding the reforms carried out in the 1970s, particularly the new pensions scheme and additional aid for the disabled, there were still (in 1981) some 8 million individuals dependent in whole or in part on supplementary benefits. With the growth in unemployment as well as the reduction in benefits following the recent public expenditure cuts, this number is likely to increase. Faced with the evident fact that this form of social welfare was likely to remain for the foreseeable future as an integral part of the social security system (and not, as Beveridge had hoped, to wither away), the last two administrations have perceived the need to review and restructure the legislative framework. Perhaps the main objective of the reforms, which were carried out in 1980–1981, was substantially to reduce the amount of discretion exercised by officials. This was achieved through the replacement of the broad legislative powers by very detailed regulations. The greater 'legal' character of entitlement was underlined by the introduction of a right of appeal on questions of law from the supplementary benefit appeal tribunals to the Social Security (formerly National Insurance) Commissioners. The latter, as we have seen, have played a very important role in the development of social insurance law and it may be anticipated that they will have a similar impact on supplementary benefit law. The government hopes that these reforms will reduce the administrative costs of the system particularly by rendering the law more certain. On the other hand, the very complexity of the new regulations is likely to increase the number of legal issues which arise from claims and in any event it must render the system incomprehensible to a large proportion of claimants.

BIBLIOGRAPHY

BOOKS

A. Atkinson, Poverty in Britain and the Reform of Social Security (1969)
W. Beveridge, Full Employment in a Free Society (1944)
W. Beveridge, Unemployment, A Problem of Industry (1909)
R. Brown, The Management of Welfare (1975)
M. Bruce, The Coming of the Welfare State (4th edn.-1968)
D. Bull, Family Poverty (2nd edn.-1976)
E. Bruns, British Unemployment Programs 1920–1939 (1970)
H. Calvert, Social Security Law (2nd edn.-1978)
S. & E. Checkland, The Poor Law Report of 1834 (1974)
L. Chiozza Money, Insurance versus Poverty (1912)
M. Cooper, Social Policy: A Survey of Recent Developments (1973)
K. de Schweinitz, England's Road to Social Security (1961)
A. Forder, Concepts in Social Administration (1974)
D. Fraser, The Evolution of the British Welfare State (1973)
J. Fulbrook, Administrative Justice and the Unemployed (1978)
V. George, Social Security, Beveridge and After (1968)
V. George, Social Security and Society (1973)
V. George and P. Wilding, Ideology and Social Welfare (1976)
B. Gilbert, The Evolution of National Insurance in Great Britain (1966)
B. Gilbert, British Social Policy 1914–1939 (1970)
P. Gosden, Self-Help; Voluntary Associations in 19th Century Britain (1973)
P. Hall, H. Land, R. Parker & A. Webb, Choice and Conflict in Social Policy (1975)
J. Harris, Unemployment and Politics (1972)
J. Harris, William Beveridge (1977)
J. Hay, The Origins of the Liberal Welfare Reforms 1906–1914 (1975)
B. Jordan, Poor Parents (1974)
P. Kaim-Caudle, Comparative Social Policy and Social Security (1973)
J. Kincaid, Poverty and Equality in Britain (1973)
G. King, The Ministry of Pensions and National Insurance (1958)
A. Lesser, The Law of National Health Insurance (1939)
H. Levy, National Health Insurance (1944)
T. Lynes, Pensions Rights and Wrongs (1963)
L. McClements, The Economics of Social Security (1978)
T. Marshall, Social Policy in the Twentieth Century (4th edn.-1975)
R. Micklethwait, The National Insurance Commissioners (1976)
A. Ogus & E. Barendt, Law of Social Security (1978)
M. Partington & J. Jowell, Welfare Law and Policy (1978)
R. Pinker, Social Theory and Social Policy (1971)
J. Richardson, Economic and Financial Aspects of Social Security (1960)
D. Roberts, Victorian Origins of the British Welfare State (1960)
M. Rose, The Relief of Poverty 1834–1914 (1972)
A. Seebohm Rowntree, Poverty, A Study of Town Life (1901)
P. Smith, Industrial Injuries Benefits (1978)
P. Thane, The Origins of British Social Policy (1978)
V. Tillyard, Unemployment Insurance in Great Britain 1911–1948 (1949)
R. Titmuss, Commitment to Welfare (2nd edn.-1976)
R. Titmuss, Income Distribution and Social Change (1962)
R. Titmuss, Social Policy (1974)
P. Townsend, Poverty in the United Kingdom (1979)
P. Townsend, The Concept of Poverty (1970)
J. Walley, Social Security: Another British Failure? (1972)
S. & B. Webb, English Poor Law History, Part II (1929)
A. Wilson & H. Levy, Industrial Assurance (1937)
A. Wilson & H. Levy, Workmen's Compensation (1939)
T. Wilson, Pensions, Inflation and Growth (1974)

REPORTS AND GOVERNMENT PAPERS

Royal Commission on the Poor Laws and Relief of Distress (1909), Cd. 4499.
Royal Commission on National Health Insurance (1926), Cmd. 2596.
Committee of Inquiry into the Workings of Unemployment Insurance (1927) (Blanesburgh Report).
Royal Commission on Unemployment Insurance: Interim Report (1931); Cmd. 3872; Final Report (1932), Cmd. 4185
Social Insurance and Allied Services (1942), Cmd. 6464 (Beveridge Report)
Social Insurance Part I (1944), Cmd. 6550.
Social Insurance Part II, Workmen's Compensation (1944), Cmd. 6551.
Provision for Old Age (1958), Cmnd. 638.
Earnings-Related Short-Term Benefits (1966), Cmnd. 4755.
National Superannuation and Social Insurance (1969), Cmnd. 3883.
Strategy for Pensions (1971), Cmnd. 4755.
Social Security Provision for Chronically Sick and Disabled People 1973–4 H.C. 176.
Better Pensions (1974), Cmnd. 5713.
Committee on One-Parent Families (Finer Report) (1974), Cmnd. 5629.
Royal Commission on Civil Liability and Compensation for Personal Injury (1978), Cmnd. 7054 (Pearson Report)

NOTES

a1 See generally T. Ashton (1948). *The Industrial Revolution 1760–1830.*
a2 Cf. H. Perkin (1969). *The Origins of Modern English Society 1780–1880*, ch. 3.
a3 M.W. Flinn (1966). *Origins of the Industrial Revolution*; R.M. Hartwell (ed.) (1967). *The Causes of the Industrial Revolution in England*, chs. 7–8.
a4 P. Deane and W.A. Cole (1962). *British Economic Growth 1688–1959*, p. 282.
a5 It rose from 9 million in 1801, to approximately 14 million (1831) to approximately 18 million (1851): M. Bruce, *The Coming of the Welfare State* (4th edn), p. 58.
a6 See, especially, E.J. Hobsbawm and R.M. Hartwell, 'The Standard of Living in the Industrial Revolution: A Discussion' *Econ. Hist. R.* 16, 119.
a7 Perkin, above n. a2, p. 140.
a8 See, especially, the *Chadwick Report on the Sanitary Conditions of the Labouring Population of Great Britain 1842* (reprinted with introduction by M. Flinn 1965), and W.M. Grazer (1950). *History of English Public Health 1834–1939.*
a9 See *First Report of the Commission on Employment of Children in Factories (1842).*
a10 A Wilson and H. Levy (1939). *Workmen's Compensation*, vol. 1, pp. 8–23.
a11 See A.W. Coats (ed.) (1971). *The Classical Economists and Economic Policy.*
a12 *An Inquiry into the Nature and Causes of the Wealth of Nations* (Everyman Edition), vol. 1, p. 398.
a13 Coats, above n. a11, chs. 1–2.
a14 Ed. S.G. Checkland and E.O.A. Checkland (ed.) (1974). *The Poor Law Report of 1834*; see further *infra* p. 62.
a15 H. Pelling (1963). *A History of British Trade Unionism.*
a16 T.U.C. (1934). *The Martyrs of Tolpuddle 1834–1934.*
a17 A. Briggs (ed.) (1962). *Chartist Studies.*
a18 A major exception was R.H. Tawney (1926). *Religion and the Rise of Capitalism.* See also, more recently, E.P. Thompson (1975). *Whigs and Hunters.* Legal historians have at last shown signs of grappling with the realtionship between law and economic history; though the major work is still American: M. Horwitz (1977). *The Transformation of American Law 1780–1860*; M. Tigar and M. Levy (1978). *Law and the Rise of Capitalism.* For English legal history see now P.S. Atiyah (1979). *The Rise and Fall of the Freedom of Contract.*
a19 A.I. Ogus, 'Conditions in the Formation and Development of Social Insurance: Legal Development and Legal History', in H. Zacher (ed.) (1979). *Bedingungen für die Entstehung und Entwicklung von Sozialversicherung.*
a20 Atiyah, above n. a18, pp. 369–383.
a21 A. Harding (1966). *A Social History of English Law*, pp. 355–358.
a22 Atiyah, above n. a18, pp. 388–397.
a23 Ibid., especially pp. 348–408.
a24 T. Hadden, *Company Law and Capitalism* (2nd edn), ch. 1.

a25 J. Holden (1955). *History of Negotiable Instruments in English Law.*
a26 *Priestley* v. *Fowler* (1937) 3 M. & W. 1, on which see Howells 26 M.L.R. 367.
a27 A.V. Dicey, *Introduction to the Study of the Law of the Constitution* (10th edn) Part II.
a28 See G. Sawyer (1965). *Law in Society*, ch. 8, for the problems of reconciling traditional legal concepts with social control. On administrative machinery see O. MacDonagh (1977). *Early Victorian Government.*
a29 J.S. Mill (1970; ed. D. Winch). *Principles of Political Economy*, p. 314.
a30 There is considerable literature on this problem. The classic exposition of A.V. Dicey (1914). *Law and Public Opinion in England in the Nineteenth Century* (2nd edn) has been vigorously attacked by modern historians: see A.J. Taylor (1972). *Laissez Faire and State Intervention in Nineteenth Century Britain* with bibliography.
a31 J. Bentham (1970; ed. J.H. Burns and H.L.A. Hart) *An Introduction to the Principles of Morals and Legislation,* pp. 196–201. See also H. Scott-Gordon in ed. Coats, above n. a11, ch. 7.
a32 W.L. Burn (1964). *The Age of Equipoise*, pp. 135–136.
a33 G.F.A. Best (1964). *Lord Shaftesbury.*
a34 Quoted in the *Second Report of the Royal Sanitary Commission* (1871).
a35 See, especially, its *First Report on Employment in the Mines* (1842).
a36 O. MacDonagh, 'The Nineteenth Century Revolution in Government: A Reappraisal' Historical J. **1**, 52.
a37 For comprehensive treatment see, e.g., Bruce, above n. 5.
a38 Cf. H.W. Jones, 'The Rule of Law in the Welfare State' *Col. L.R.* **58**, 143.
a39 P. Townsend, 'The Meaning of Poverty' *Br. J. Sociology* **13**, 210.
a40 M. Rose (1972). *The Relief of Poverty 1834–1914*, pp. 13–15.
a41 Ibid., Appendix A.
a42 Above n. a14, pp. 335, 375.
a43 M. Rose, 'The Allowance System under the New Poor Law' Hist. Rev. **19**, Ec. 608.
a44 Rose, above n. a40, p. 18.
a45 Ibid.
a46 Ibid., p. 19.
a47 Above n. a14, pp. 114–116.
a48 Ibid., p. 334.
a49 Ibid., pp. 335–336.
a50 Ibid., pp. 398–414.
a51 Bruce, above n. a5, pp. 103–104.
a52 K. de Schweinitz (1961 edn). *England's Road to Social Security*, p. 139.
a53 N.C. Edsall (1971). *The Anti-Poor Law Movement 1834–44*, pp. 35–44.
a54 Ibid., pp. 58–72.
a55 See Outdoor Labour Test Order 1842.
a56 *Voyages en Angleterre* (1835), p. 90.
a57 B. Kirkman Grey (1908). *Philanthropy and the State.*
a58 D. Fraser (1973). *The Evolution of the British Welfare State*, pp. 115–116.
a59 Ibid., p. 117.
a60 B. Harrison, 'Philanthropy and the Victorians' Victorian Studies **9**, 360.
a61 A.F. Young and E.T. Ashton (1956). *British Social Work in the Nineteenth Century*, pp. 92–95.
a62 C.L. Mowat (1961). *The Charity Organization Society 1869–1913, Its Ideas and Work.*
a63 Ibid., ch. 4.
a64 Quoted in Bruce, above n. a5, p. 110.
a65 See, for example, P.H.J.H. Gosden (1961). *The Friendly Societies in England 1815–1875;* (1973). *Self-Help, Voluntary Associations in Nineteenth-Century Britain.*
a66 Ibid., ch. 1.
a67 *Voluntary Action* (1948), p. 55.
a68 Gosden, *Self-Help*, above n. a65, pp. 39–40.
a69 Ibid., pp. 64–76.
a70 J. Harris (1972). *Unemployment and Politics*, pp. 296–297.
a71 L.G. Chiozza Money (1912). *Insurance versus Poverty*, p. 10.
a72 Gosden, *Self-Help*, above n. a65, pp. 115–119.
a73 Ibid., pp. 119–132.
a74 See, for example, the remarks of Gladstone, cited ibid., p. 126.
a75 *Social Insurance and Allied Services*, (1942) Cmd. 6404 (Beveridge Report), p. 259.
a76 Gosden, *Self-Help*, above n. a65, pp. 133–134.

a77   Royal Commission appointed to inquire into Friendly and Benefit Building Societies, Four
      Reports, 1871–1874.
a78   Pp. 183–184, 232–236.
a79   Quoted by P. Thane, 'Non-Contributory versus Insurance Pensions 1878–1908' in P. Thane
      (ed.) (1978). *The Origins of British Social Policy*, p. 88.
a80   Above, p. 160.
a81   P. Abrams (1968). *The Origins of British Sociology*, chs. 2–3.
a82   Quoted by Abrams, ibid., p. 14.
a83   Ibid., pp. 16–18.
a84   Ibid., pp. 20–23.
a85   G. Duncan Mitchell (1968). *A Hundred Years of Sociology*, especially ch. 10.
a86   Abrams, above n. a81, p. 80.
a87   *Journal of Royal Statistical Society* 50, 376.
a88   Abrams, above n. a81, ch. 4.
a89   The findings were first published in 'The Inhabitants of Tower Hamlets . . .', *Journal of Royal
      Statistical Society* 50, 326; 'The Conditions and Occupations of the People of East London and
      Hackney 1887' *Journal of Royal Statistical Society* 51, 276. This led to the general inquiry, the
      results of which were published in seventeen volumes entitled *The Life and Labour of the People in
      London* (1902–4). On his life and work, see especially T.S. and M.B. Simey, (1960). *Charles
      Booth, Social Scientist.*
a90   *Life and Labour of the People in London*, vol. ii, p. 21.
a91   Rose, above n. a41, *loc. cit.*
a92   Simey, above n. a89, p. 88.
a93   *Life and Labour of the People in London*, vol. i, p. 133.
a94   S. Rowntree, (1901). *Poverty, A Study of Town Life*, p. 150. On his life and work, see A. Briggs
      (1961). *Seebohm Rowntree.*
a95   *Poverty, A Study of Town Life*, p. 161.
a96   Ibid., p. 164.
a97   Ibid., pp. 166–170.
a98   T.W. Hutchison (1953). *A Review of Economic Doctrines 1870–1929*, especially ch. 25.
a99   Ibid., p. 13.
 b1   Ibid., ch. 22 and see W. Beveridge (1909). *Unemployment, A Problem of Industry*, ch. 1.
 b2   See, generally, J.R. Hay (1975). *The Origins of the Liberal Welfare Reforms 1906–1914.*
 b3   M. Warnock (ed.) (1962). *Utilitarianism* (Fontana edn), pp. 268–269.
 b4   H. Perkin (1969). *The Origins of Modern English Society 1780–1880*, p. 324. A.V. Dicey (1914).
      in *Law and Public Opinion in England*, pp. 430–431, doubted whether the reasoning was consis-
      tent with Utilitarian principles.
 b5   See, generally, G.D.H. Cole, *A Short History of the British Working-Class Movement 1789–1947*,
      Part II; E. Halevy (1951). *A History of the English People in the 19th Century*, vol., 4 pp. 250–272;
      (1951), vol. 5 (2nd edn) ch. 2.
 b6   Halevy, ibid., (vol. 4, pp. 203–4; for arguments to the contrary, see E.J. Hobsbawm (1964).
      Labouring Men, ch. 13.
 b7   Cole, above n. b5, p. 193.
 b8   M. Beer (1953 edn). *A History of British Socialism*, vol. i, pp. 174–175.
 b9   Cole, above n. b5, pp. 155–160.
b10   'Christian Socialism is but the holy water with which the priest consecrates the heartburnings
      of the aristocrate', K. Marx and F. Engels (1930, ed. D. Ryazonoff). *The Communist Manifesto*,
      p. 56. For the history of the movement, see Halevy, above n. b5, vol. 4, pp. 258–272.
b11   Quoted in Cole, above n. b5, p. 195.
b12   Hobsbawm, above n. b6, ch. 12.
b13   A.M. MacBriar (1962). *Fabian Socialism and English Politics 1884–1918.*
b14   Cole, above n. b5, p. 289.
b15   The *Fabian Essays*, edited by G.B. Shaw were published in 1889; they were followed by a long
      series of *Fabian Tracts*. Many important works (e.g. those by Sidney and Beatrice Webb) were
      published independently.
b16   See, for example, Hobsbawm, above n. b6, ch. 14.
b17   MacBriar, above n. b13, p. 349.
b18   Halevy, above n. b5, vol. 5, pp. 18–22; B. Semmell (1960). *Imperialism and Social Reform.*
b19   B. Gilbert (1966). *The Evolution of National Insurance in Great Britain*, pp. 59–61; G.R. Searle
      (1971). *The Quest for National Efficiency.*

b20 Cf. above p. 160.
b21 Maj-Gen. Sir F. Maurice (1903). 'National Health: A Soldier's Study', Contemporary Review **83**, pp. 41–56; A White (1901). *Efficiency and the Empire.*
b22 Hay, above n. b2, p. 32.
b23 K. de Schweinitz (1961 edn). *England's Road to Social Security*, pp. 179–183.
b24 H.V. Emy (1973). *Liberals, Radicals and Social Politics 1892–1914.*
b25 E.g. J.A. Hobson (1909). *The Industrial System*; L.T. Hobhouse (1911). *Liberalism*; see generally Emy, op. cit., ch. 4.
b26 Hay, above n. b2, pp. 25–29.
b27 H. Pelling (1968). *Popular Politics and Society in Late Victorian Britain*, p. 2, and generally ch. 1.
b28 A. Marwick, 'The Labour Party and the Welfare State in Britain 1900–48' *Am. Hist. Rev.* **73**, 380.
b29 Emy, above n. b24, pp. 157–169.
b30 See Gilbert, above n. b19, pp. 32–39.
b31 Ibid., p. 38.
b32 K.D. Brown, 'Conflict in Early British Welfare Policy' *J. of Modern History* **43**, 615.
b33 Harris, above n. a70, p. 56.
b34 Hay, above n. b2, pp. 38–42.
b35 *Old Age Pensions and the Aged Poor.*
b36 Gilbert, above n. b19, pp. 193–196.
b37 Thane, above n. a79, pp. 91–92.
b38 See generally Gilbert, above n. b19; also below, pp. 185 and 210.
b39 E.W. Cohen (1941, reprinted 1965). *The Growth of the British Civil Service 1780–1939*; D. Roberts (1960). *Victorian Origins of the British Welfare State.*
b40 See J. Harris (1977). *William Beveridge*, ch. 3.
b41 M. Wright 'Treasury Control 1854–1914' in G. Sutherland (ed.) (1972). *Studies in the Growth of Nineteenth-Century Government.*
b42 Hay, above n. b2, pp. 40–41.
b43 (1914), p. lxv.
b44 See *Conflict of Laws* (1st edn, 1896).
b45 Cf. MacDonagh, above p. 160, n. a36.
b46 Halevy (1951). *History of the English People in the Nineteenth Century*, vol. v, (2nd edn), pp. 139–145.
b47 See H.S. Tremenhere's submission to the *Report on the Explosion of Darnley Colliery* (1849), p. 7 and his *Report on Mining Inspection in Germany* (1849).
b48 Cf. the extract from *The Times* reproduced above, p. 165, and Thane, above, no. a79, loc. cit.
b49 F.H. Stead (1910). *How Old Age Pensions Began to Be*, pp. 11–14.
b50 Gilbert, above n. b19, pp. 188–192.
b51 Though Australia and New Zealand escaped both the weight of the *laissez-faire* tradition and the size of the social problems of the 'mother country': Thane above n. a79, p. 19.
b52 (1905) Cd. 2304.
b53 Harris, above n. b40, pp. 134–136 and W.H. Beveridge, 'Public Labour Exchanges in Germany', Economic J., **18**, 69, pp. 1–18. The system in Luxembourg had been investigated in 1894: J. Harris (1972). *Unemployment and Politics 1886–1914*, p. 281.
b54 Labour Exchanges Act. See further below pp. 179–180.
b55 W.H. Dawson (1891). *Bismarck and State Socialism*; B.W. Wells (1891). 'Compulsory Insurance In Germany' *Political Science Q.* 6, 35; W.H. Dawson (1912). *Social Insurance in Germany; A.* Ashley (1912). *The Social Policy of Bismarck.*
b56 H.N. Bunbury (ed.) (1957). *Lloyd George's Ambulance Wagon: The Memoirs of W.J. Braithwaite 1911-1912.*
b57 Ashley, above n. b55, pp. 71–76.
b58 Introduction to L.G. Chiozza-Money, (1912). *Insurance versus Poverty*, p. viii.
b59 See, especially, Beveridge's submission to the Royal Commission on the Poor Laws (1910). 'Insurance Against Unemployment in Foreign Countries; Cd. 5068, Appendix XXI.
b60 Harris, above n. b53, pp. 298–302.
b61 Above, p. 161.
b62 Particularly the Factory Act of 1844: see, generally, J.T. Ward (1962). *The Factory Movement 1830-1855.*
b63 P. Bartrip and P. Fenn (1980). 'Safety at Work: the Enforcement Policy of the Early Factory Inspectorate' *Public Administration* 58, 87.

b64   Above, p. 158-9.
b65   P. Bartrip (1978). 'Injured at Work: The Employer's Liability' *New Society*; D.G. Hanes (1968). *The First British Workmen's Compensation Act 1897*, ch. 1.
b66   On the Latin maxim *'actio personalis moritur cum persona'*. See W. Holdsworth (1923). *History of English Law* (3rd edn), vol. III, pp. 331-336, 576-583. Reform was effected by the Fatal Accidents Act 1846.
b67   A. Wilson and H. Levy (1939). *Workmen's Compensation*, vol. I, pp. 31-33.
b68   Report from the Select Committee on Employers' Liability for Injuries to their Servants (1876) H.C. 372.
b69   Employers Liability Act 1880.
b70   W.S. Churchill (1907). *Lord Randolph Churchill*, pp. 110-111.
b71   Hanes, above n. b65, p. 21.
b72   E.g. *Kiddle* v. *Lovett* (1885) 16 Q.B.D. 605. For the details of the Act and its interpretation see H. Slesser and A. Henderson (1924). *Industrial Law*, pp. 46-53.
b73   Above n. b69, s.3.
b74   *Griffiths* v. *Earl of Dudley* (1882) 9 Q.B.D. 357.
b75   Wilson and Levy, above n. b67, p. 51.
b76   Above n. b69, s.4.
b77   Hanes, above n. b65, p. 25.
b78   Report of Select Committee on the Employer's Liability Act 1880 (1886) H.C. 192.
b79   Ibid, p. 33.
b80   cf. above p. 164.
b81   Wilson and Levy, above n. b67, pp. 53-54.
b82   In 1889 an anonymous trade union secretary wrote: 'the feeling that [the workmen] have had all along is that neither insurance nor compensation as they may be in themselves, will ever meet their position unless the personal responsibility rests upon the employer', *Westminster Review*, p. 500.
b83   8 H.C. Deb., col. 1961.
b84   G. Howell (1902). *Labour Legislation, Labour Movements and Labour Leaders*, p. 430.
b85   See Wilson and Levy, above n. b67, pp. 67-70.
b86   Report of Departmental Committee on Workmen's Compensation (1920), Cmd. 816, p. 7.
b87   S. 7(1).
b88   S. 3.
b89   Sch. I. In the case of death, compensation was limited to a lump sum not exceeding £300.
b90   Below pp. 213-4.
b91   Report of the Departmental Committee on Compensation for Injuries to Workmen (1904), Cd. 2208.
b92   Workmen's Compensation Act 1906.
b93   Above n. b91, pp. 13-21.
b94   Ibid., pp. 22-23. The Committee considered that the British legislation compared unfavourably in this respect with the German insurance scheme: ibid., p. 33, and see Memorandum on Foreign and Colonial Laws relating to Compensation for Workmen, in vol. III.
b95   Above n. b92, ss. 1, 7, 9.
b96   Wilson and Levy, above n. b67, p. 102.
b97   Above n. b92, s. 8.
b98   Above n. b91, p. 45. The problem of industrial diseases had been appreciated since the middle of the nineteenth century, (see Wilson and Levy, above n. b67, pp. 104-105) but this was the first measure to alleviate the need for compensation arising from it.
b99   Above n. b92, Sched. III. The Secretary of State was given power to add other diseases by subordinate legislation: s. 8(7).
c1   Above n. b93.
c2   Cf. Chiozza-Money, above n. b58, p. 53.
c3   See 1904 Report, above n. b91, p. 37, and Wilson and Levy, above n. b67, pp. 89-91.
c4   Above n. b91, pp. 123-124.
c5   C. Booth, 'Enumeration and Classification of Paupers and State Pensions for the Aged' J. of Statistical Society, **54**, 610, 637.
c6   Cf. above pp. 163-4.
c7   See P. Thane (1978). 'Non-Contributory versus Insurance Pensions 1878-1908' in P. Thane (ed.), *The Origins of British Social Policy*; Gilbert, above n. b19, ch. 4.
c8   W.L. Blackley, 'National Insurance: A Cheap, Practical, and Popular Means of Abolishing Poor Rates' *Nineteenth Century*, **4**, pp. 834-857.

c9 *Report of Select Committee on National Provident Insurance* (1887). H.C. 257.
c10 Charity Organization Society (1879). *Friendly Societies and the Limits of State Aid and Control in Industrial Insurance.*
c11 Gilbert, above n. b19, pp. 162–180; though see Thane, above n. c7, pp. 92–95, for the view that the friendly societies were by no means unanimous in their opposition.
c12 Ibid., pp. 91–92.
c13 See e.g. Booth, above n. c5.
c14 Thane, above n. c7, p. 95.
c15 B.B. Gilbert (1966). *The Evolution of National Insurance in Great Britain*, pp. 193–196.
c16 C. 7684.
c17 *Report of Departmental Committee on Old Age Pensions* (1898) C. 8911.
c18 *Report of the Select Committee on Aged Deserving Poor* (1899) H.C. 296.
c19 Ibid., para. 56.
c20 Gilbert, above n. c15, p. 195: he asserts that in consequence the proposal was 'not an old age pension'.
c21 Thane, above n. c7, p. 98.
c22 J. Harris (1977). *William Beveridge*, pp. 100–103.
c23 S. 3.
c24 Thane, above n. c7, pp. 103–104.
c25 Old Age Pensions Act 1908, s. 4.
c26 Ibid., s. 7, which, however, enunciated that the decision of the appeal tribunal should be conclusive, thus excluding access to the ordinary courts: see *Murphy* v. *R.* [1911] A.C. 401.
c27 See *King* v. *Local Government Board* [1910] 2 I.R. 440.
c28 Above p. 167.
c29 J. Harris (1972). *Unemployment and Politics 1886–1914*, pp. 73–80.
c30 M. Bruce (1968). *The Coming of the Welfare State* (4th edn), pp. 182–183.
c31 J. Harris (1977). *William Beveridge*, ch. 6. His published monograph, (1909). *Unemployment: A Problem of Industry*, became the standard work on the subject. Other analyses were published by J.A. Hobson (1906). *The Problem of the Unemployed*; P. Alden (1905). *The Unemployed: A National Question.*
c32 W. Beveridge, 'Labour Exchanges and the Unemployed' Econ. J. **17**, (Mar. 1907), pp. 66–81; 'Public Labour Exchanges in Germany' Econ. J. **18**, (Mar. 1908), pp. 1–18 (reprinted as Appendix A in *Unemployment: A Problem in Industry*, above n. c31.
c33 Unemployed Workmen Act 1905.
c34 *Report of the Royal Commission on the Poor Laws and Relief of Distress* (1909), Cd. 4499 (Majority Report), Part VI, ch. 4.
c35 Labour Exchanges Act 1908. For details see Gilbert, above n. c15, pp. 261–265.
c36 Cf. Sir G. Nicholls and T. Mackay (1898–9). *A History of the English Poor Law* (3 vols); G.R. Sims (1889). *How the Poor Live*; H. Bosanquet (1896). *Rich and Poor*. See also above pp. 166–167.
c37 M. Rose (1972). *The Relief of Poverty 1834–1914*, pp. 37–38.
c38 Above n. 34, pp. 293–296.
c39 T. Archer (1865). *The Pauper, the Thief and the Convict.*
c40 Above p. 162.
c41 W. Henderson (1934). *The Lancashire Cotton Famine 1861–65.*
c42 K. de Schweinitz (1943). *England's Road to Social Security*, ch. 15.
c43 See on the origins and composition S. Webb and B. Webb (1929). *English Poor Law History* Part 2, pp. 470–471.
c44 Above n. c34.
c45 *Report of the Royal Commission on the Poor Laws and Relief of Distress* (1909), Cd. 4499 (Separate Report).
c46 Above n. c34, p. 359.
c47 Thus they thought that the general mixed workhouse 'may act as a deterrent in the case of the aged and inform to whom it might legitimately be a refuge': Ibid., p. 140.
c48 Above n. c34, p. 632.
c49 Above n. c45, ch. 12.
c50 Ibid., pp. 1214–1215.
c51 Above n. c34, pp. 604–607.
c52 Cf. T. Marshall (1975). *Social Policy in the Twentieth Century* (4th edn), pp. 50–52.
c53 Above n. c34, pp. 415–421.

c54 Above n. c45, pp. 1199–1201.
c55 Above n. c34, pp. 415–417.
c56 Ibid., pp. 528–530.
c57 See above p. 178.
c58 Above n. c34, pp. 164–167.
c59 Harris, above n. c29, p. 247.
c60 J. Hay (1975). *The Origins of the Liberal Welfare Reforms 1906–1914*, (with bibliography).
c61 D. Lloyd George (1929). *Slings and Arrows* (collection of speeches), p. 5.
c62 Ibid., p. 8.
c63 W. Churchill (1909). *Liberalism and the Social Problem*, p. 80.
c64 Bruce, above n. c30, ch. 5; D. Fraser (1973). *The Evolution of the British Welfare State*, ch. 7.
c65 Coal Mines Regulation Act 1908.
c66 Provision of Meals Act 1906.
c67 Education (Administrative Provisions) Act 1907.
c68 Trade Boards Act 1909.
c69 Housing, Town Planning etc. Act 1909.
c70 Cf. A. Ogus, 'Conditions in the Formation and Development of Social Insurance', in H. Zacher (ed) (1979). *Bedingungen für die Entstehung und Entwicklung von Socialversicherung.*
c71 V. George (1973). *Social Security and Society*, pp. 17–19; R. Pinker (1971). *Social Theory and Social Policy*, pp. 141–144.
c72 E.g. De Schweinitz, above n. c42, pp. 208–209.
c73 H. Maine (1906, ed. F. Pollock). *Ancient Law*, p. 170.
c74 Above p. 167.
c75 Above p. 180.
c76 Fraser, above n. c64, pp. 147–148.
c77 Gilbert, above n. c15, pp. 304–306.
c78 Cf. above pp. 163–164.
c79 Bruce, above n. c30, p. 214.
c80 Quoted in Fraser, above n. c64, p. 150.
c81 £8 million instead of the expected £6.5 million: ibid.
c82 Gilbert, above n. c15, pp. 291–293. The visit was originally intended for the study of the German old age pension scheme.
c83 Gilbert, above n. c15, chs. 6–7.
c84 Above n. 45, pp. 886–889.
c85 J. Garvin, quoted in Bruce, above n. c30, p. 218.
c86 Cf. above p. 179.
c87 Harris, above n. c29, ch. 6; on labour exchanges, see above pp. 179–180.
c88 For another view see J. Fulbrook (1978). *Administrative Justice and the Unemployed*, p. 127.
c89 Harris, ch. 3.
c90 Fulbrook, above n. c88, p. 128.
c91 Above p. 182.
c92 Tables on Rules and Expenditure of Trade Unions in respect of Unemployment Benefit (1911), Cd. 5703.
c93 Harris, above n. c29, p. 298.
c94 Quoted ibid., pp. 303–304.
c95 Fulbrook, above n. c88, p. 129.
c96 See, for example, Beveridge's evidence to Royal Commission on Poor Laws, Minutes of Evidence, Appendix XXI (K), (1910) Cd. 5068.
c97 See the submission to the Royal Commission of three actuaries: Statistics relating to England and Wales, Part XVI (1911) Cd. 5077.
c98 B. Gilbert (1970). *British Social Policy 1914–1939*, p. 53.
c99 See further below p. 205.
d1 A. Taylor (1970). *English History 1914–1945* (Penguin edition), pp. 25–26.
d2 A. Milward (1970). *The Economic Effects of the World Wars on Britain*, p. 31.
d3 Ibid., p. 18.
d4 'The Abolition of Economic Controls 1918–1921' Econ. His. Rev. **13**, 1, p. 8.
d5 C. Mowat (1955). *Britain Between the Wars 1918–1940*, pp. 25–28.
d6 B. Alford (1972). *Depression or Recovery? British Economic Growth 1918–1939.*
d7 Cf. D. Aldcroft (1970). *The Inter-War Economy: Britain 1919–1939*; Alford, above n. d6; R. Sayers (1967). *A History of Economic Change in England, 1880–1939.*

d8   E. Burns (1941). *British Unemployment Programs 1920–1938*, p. 35.
d9   Below pp. 189, 225–226.
d10 Below p. 227.
d11 Taylor, above n. d1, pp. 224–228.
d12 G. Cole (1948). *History of the Labour Party from 1914.*
d13 Mowat, above n. d5, p. 19.
d14 Representation of the People Act 1918.
d15 W. Beveridge (1944). *Full Employment in a Free Society*, p. 73.
d16 M. Bruce (1968). *The Coming of the Welfare State* (4th edn), pp. 234–236.
d17 UIA 1920, below p. 216.
d18 Unemployment Workers' Dependants (Temporary Provisions) Act 1921, below, p. 000.
d19 UIA 1920, s. 8(4).
d20 For details see E. Burns (1941). *British Unemployment Programs 1920–1938.*
d21 *Report of the Unemployment Insurance Committee* ('Blanesburgh' Committee).
d22 A. Ogus and E. Barendt (1978). *Law of Social Security*, p. 80.
d23 Royal Commission on Unemployment Insurance (1931). *Interim Report*, Cmnd. 3872; (1932). *Final Report*, Cmnd. 4185.
d24 Cf. Burns, above n. d20, Part IV, and J. Fulbrook, above n. c88, pp. 159–170.
d25 Especially NHIA 1928.
d26 See the Arrears Regulations S.R.& O. 1937 No. 1023.
d27 WOOCPA 1925.
d28 Bruce, above n. c30, pp. 247–248.
d29 Ibid., p. 246.
d30 See, for example, W. Beveridge (1924). *Insurance For All and Everything*; Walley (1972). *Social Security: Another British Failure?* pp. 52–54.
d31 Gilbert, above n. c98, pp. 246–251.
d32 Walley, above n. d30, p. 63.
d33 Above n. 27, s. 3.
d34 Above p. 169.
d35 *Social Insurance and Allied Services* (1942). Cmnd. 6404, para. 301.
d36 V. George (1973). *Social Security and Society*, p. 20.
d37 Cf. Beveridge, above n. d15.
d38 W. Barber (1967). *A History of Economic Thought*, ch. 8.
d39 Cmnd. 6527.
d40 Ibid., para. 3.
d41 Above n. 35, para. 443.
d42 Though Beveridge did, at one time, flirt with the idea that 'children are a contingency for which all men should prepare by contributions to an insurance fund': ibid., para. 415 and see J. Harris (1977). *William Beveridge*, pp. 343–346.
d43 E.g. Sir J. Walley, in D. Bull (ed.) (1972). *Family Poverty* (2nd edn), ch. 9; F. Field and P. Townsend (1975). *A Social Contract for Families.*
d44 E. Rathbone (1924). *The Disinherited Family.*
d45 S. Rowntree (1937). *The Human Needs of Labour.*
d46 H. Tout (1938). *The Standard of Living in Bristol*, p. 28.
d47 Above n. 35, para. 413.
d48 Mowat, above n. d5, pp. 517–518.
d49 Gilbert, above n. c98, p. 255.
d50 See, especially, the White Paper (1944). *A National Health Service*, Cmd. 6502; *Report of Royal Commission on National Health Insurance* (1926) Cmd. 2596; H. Levy (1944). *National Health Insurance.*
d51 Royal Commission Report (Minutes), above n. d50, p. 327.
d52 Levy, above n. d50, ch. 27; though the majority of the Royal Commission did not adopt this perspective: above n. d50, para. 251.
d53 Ibid., para. 81; Levy, above n. d50, ch. 12.
d54 It should be noted, however, that there has always been a minor contribution to the financing of the National Health Service from the National Insurance Fund.
d55 Cf. above, pp. 183–184.
d56 Above n. 35, para. 21.
d57 Ibid.
d58 Ibid., paras. 303–309.

d59 Ibid., para. 9.
d60 Cf. below, p. 215. Beveridge's attempt to justify the different treatment of the industrially in-
      jured, (above n. 35, paras. 80–86) hardly stand up to sustained argument: Ogus and Barendt,
      above n. d22, pp. 264–265 and the references cited there.
d61 Para. 273.
d62 He recommended a special charge on high-risk industries: paras. 88–92. This was rejected in
      the Government White Paper (1944). *Social Insurance Part II, Workmen's Compensation*, Cmd.
      6551, para. 23(iii). *The Report of the Committee on Safety and Health at Work* (1972), Cmd. 5034,
      paras. 428–430 thought that the matter should be reconsidered, but the *Royal Commission on
      Civil Liability and Compensation for Personal Injury* (1978), with one dissentient, reaffirmed the
      traditional principle: Cmnd. 7054-I, paras. 898–905, 940–948.
d63 In addition to the discussions cited in the last note, see E. Burns (1956). *Social Security and
      Public Policy*, pp. 165–171; T. Rejda (1976). *Social Insurance and Economic Security*, pp. 383–390.
d64 The only exception was to be the separate fund for industrial injuries, but in 1973 this was
      amalgamated with the (general) National Insurance Fund: SSA 1973, s. 94.
d65 See Harris, above n. d42, pp. 420–421.
d66 *Social Insurance Part I* (1944), Cmd. 6550 and *Social Insurance Part II, Workmen's Compensation*,
      above n. d62.
d67 The differences included the following: (a) unemployment benefit should not be of unlimited
      duration; (b) the full rate of retirement pension to be paid immediately rather than 20 years
      from the inception of the scheme; (c) no benefits for marriage, on the breakdown of marriage
      or partial incapacity allowances for the blind.
d68 Family Allowances Act 1945, NIA 1946, NIIIA 1946, National Health Service Act 1946, Na-
      tional Assistance Act 1948.
d69 V. George (1968). *Social Security, Beveridge and After*, pp. 51–52.
d70 Quoted in D. Bull (ed.) (1972). *Family Poverty* (2nd edn), p. 13.
d71 B. Seebohm Rowntree and G. Lavers (1951). *Poverty and the Welfare State*.
d72 Ibid., p. 51.
d73 For a review of his work and contributions see D. Reisman (1977) *Richard Titmuss. Welfare
      and Society*.
d74 R. Titmuss (1976). *Commitment to Welfare* (2nd edn), chs. 1–4; H. Heisler (1977). *Foundations of
      Social Administration*.
d75 A. Maynard (1973). in M. Cooper (ed.), *Social Policy: A Survey of Recent Developments*, p. 188.
d76 Above n. 71.
d77 See P. Townsend, 'Poverty Ten Years After Beveridge' *Political and Economic Planning*, **19**, 344,
      pp. 36–39.
d78 This had been the basis of the Rowntree Studies, and of the Beveridge guidelines for means-
      tested national assistance: above n. d35, paras. 217–232.
d79 P. Townsend, 'Measuring Poverty' *Br. J. Sociology*, **5**, 130, p. 136.
d80 Ibid. See also Townsend 'The Meaning of Poverty' *Br. J. Sociology*, **13**, 210, and (1970). *The
      Concept of Poverty*.
d81 See, for example, J. Kincaid (1973). *Poverty and Equality in Britain*.
d82 P. Townsend (1957). *The Family Life of Old People*. See also D. Cole and J. Utting (1962). *The
      Economic Circumstances of Old People*.
d83 Abel-Smith and P. Townsend (1965). *The Poor and the Poorest*. See also A. Atkinson (1969).
      Poverty in Britain and the Reform of Social Security.
d84 OPCS Survey, (1971). *Handicapped and Impaired in Britain*, vol. 1, (1971). *Work and Housing of
      Impaired Persons in Great Britain*, vol. 2, (1972). *Income and Entitlement to Supplementary Benefit of
      Impaired People in Great Britain*, vol. 3.
d85 See also P. Townsend (1967). *The Disabled in Society*; S. Sainsbury (1970). *Registered as Dis-
      abled*.
d86 Above n. 35, para. 347.
d87 Above n. 66, para. 118.
d88 Report of the Committee on One-Parent Families ('Finer Report') (1974), Cmnd. 5629.
d89 Ibid., Appendix 4.
d90 Ibid., Appendix 9.
d91 Ibid., paras. 4.191–4.202.
d92 Maynard, above n. d75, p. 185.
d93 George, above n. d69, pp. 51–52.
d94 Maynard, above n. d75, pp. 185–186.

d95 Kincaid, above n. d81, pp. 149–155.

d96 *Occupational Pensions Schemes*, Surveys of Government Actuary 1958 and 1968.

d97 E.g. R. Titmuss (1962). *Income Distribution and Social Change*, ch. 7; Ministry of Pensions and National Insurance (1966). *Financial and Other Circumstances of Retirement Pensioners*.

d98 See, for example, Labour Party (1957). *National Superannuation: Labour's Policy for Security in Old Age*, pp. 13–16.

d99 V. George (1973). *Social Security and Society*, pp. 32–36.

e1 White Paper (1971). *Strategy for Pensions*, Cmnd. 4755, and see A. Seldon (1957). *Pensions in a Free Society*.

e2 Family Income Supplement Act 1970.

e3 White Paper (1969). *National Superannuation and Social Insurance*, Cmnd. 3883.

e4 E.g. G. Moodie and G. Studdert-Kennedy (1970). *Opinions, Publics and Pressure Groups*; P. Hall, H. Land, R. Parker, and A. Webb (1975). *Change, Choice and Conflict in Social Policy*; G. Wootten (1978). *Pressure Politics in Contemporary Britain*.

e5 Though see F. Field, 'A Pressure Group for the Poor' in Bull, above n. d70, ch. 12.

e6 Hall, Land, Parker, and Webb, above n. e4, pp. 94–95.

e7 R. Brown (1975). *The Management of Welfare*, pp. 59–64, 192–199.

e8 Field, above n. e5.

e9 Perhaps the most important is the Disablement Income Group; but there are very many others who (rather loosely) co-ordinate their activities under the Disability Alliance.

e10 Age Concern.

e11 The Gingerbread Group.

e12 Field, above n. e5, pp. 149–151.

e13 The Claimants Union: see Brown, above n. e7, p. 92 and Kincaid, above n. d81, pp. 244–246.

e14 George, above n. d99, p. 29.

e15 Kincaid, above n. d81; B. Jordan (1974). *Poor Parents*.

e16 Bull, above n. d70.

e17 Family Income Supplement Act 1970: see Ogus and Barendt, above n. d22, ch. 13.

e18 Child Benefit Act 1975: see Ogus and Barendt, ibid., ch. 11.

e19 Typically they have received £1 more per child.

e20 Finer Committee Report, above n. d88.

e21 See generally *Report on Social Security Provision for Chronically Sick and Disabled People 1973–4* H.C. 276, and A. Ogus and E. Barendt (1978). *Law of Social Security*, pp. 140–145, 167–187.

e22 SSPA 1975, s. 22.

e23 National Insurance (Old Persons', and Widows' and Attendance Allowance) Act 1970, s. 4.

e24 Social Security Benefits Act 1975, s. 7.

e25 Ibid., s. 6.

e26 Although this measure was included in the 1975 Act, it was not payable until 1977, and since that time the principles of entitlement have been controversial: see, for example, M. Richards, 'A Study of the Non-Contributory Invalidity Pension for Married Women' J.S.W.L. (1978–79), 77.

e27 White Paper (1979). *Reform of the Supplementary Benefits Scheme*, Cmnd. 7773.

e28 Above p. 189.

e29 Ministry of Social Security Act 1966.

e30 Ibid., s. 14.

e31 See, especially, M. Adler and A. Bradley (1975). *Justice, Discretion and Poverty* and K. Bell (1975). *Research Study on Supplementary Benefit Appeal Tribunals, Review of Main Findings*.

e32 SSA 1979.

e33 George, above n. 99, p. 32.

e34 Ibid.

e35 NIA 1959, based on the White Paper (1958). *Provision for Old Age*, Cmnd. 638.

e36 Mr. Richard Crossman in the House of Commons, 27 January 1959.

e37 See T. Lynes (1963). *Pensions Rights and Wrongs*, and Walley (1972). *Social Security: Another British Failure?* ch. 11.

e38 Above n. 98.

e39 National Superannuation and Social Insurance Bill 1969, based on the White Paper, above n. e3.

e40 NIA 1966, based on the White Paper (1966). *Earnings-Related Short-Term Benefits*, Cmnd. 2887.

e41 Maynard, above n. d75, p. 189.

e42   SSA 1973, based on the White Paper (1971). *Strategy for Pensions*, Cmnd. 4755.

e43   Introduced by SSPA 1975, based on the White Paper (1974). *Better Pensions*, Cmnd. 5713.

e44   See further, below pp. 238–239.

e45   NIA 1911, Part Two.

e46   Thus H. Calvert (1978) in *Social Security Law* (2nd edn) devotes over half of his analysis of social insurance law to unemployment benefit.

e47   In pre-war legislation, the claimant had to be 'continuously unemployed' (NIA 1911, s. 86(2)); under modern legislation, entitlement is based on a 'day of unemployment' (e.g. SSA 1975, s. 14(1) (a)).

e48   Though the legislation has allowed for the disregard of subsidiary work for trivial remuneration: e.g. UIA 1920, s. 7(2) (a), see now S.I. 1975/546, Reg. 7(1) (h).

e49   See generally Ogus and Barendt, above n. e21, pp. 92–104 and Calvert, above n. e46, pp. 62–108.

e50   Cf. A. Ogus, 'Unemployment Benefit for Workers on Short-Time' *I.L.J.*, 4, 12.

e51   The problem was first tackled by regulations made in 1931 (S.R.&O. 1931 No. 818), following the *Interim Report of the Royal Commission on Unemployment Insurance*, Cmd. 3872. Following reformulation in 1948 (S.I. 1948/1277), the matter was examined by the National Insurance Advisory Committee (*Report on the Question of Very Short Spells of Unemployment* (1955) Cmnd. 9609). The legislative changes made (NIA 1957, s. 4(1)) may have solved some technical problems but they greatly added to the complexity of the law. In 1966 an effort was made to transfer the burden of very short spells of employment onto the employer (see NIA 1966, s. 2) but both employers and trade unions do not appear to have responded to this initiative.

e52   See the 1931 Regulations, above n. e51. The matter has been referred three times to the National Insurance Advisory Committee: (1948–9), H.C. 202; (1952), Cmd. 8558; (1978), Cmnd. 6991 and the rules have been subject to frequent challenge and modification.

e53   E.g. Redundancy Payments Act 1965; Industrial Relations Act 1971; Employment Protection Act 1975.

e54   The first measure was UIA (No. 2) 1924, s.1(4). Subsequent regulation has attempted (not always with success) to cover different forms of severance pay: S.I. 1948/1277; S.I. 1966/1049; S.I. 1971/807.

e55   See, especially, *R.* v. *National Insurance Commissioner, ex parte Stratton* [1979] Q.B. 361.

e56   See, for example, *NIAC Report on Very Short Spells of Unemployment*, above n. e51.

e57   NIA 1911, Sch. 7.

e58   UIA 1920, Sch. 2; UIA (No. 2) 1924, Sch. 7.

e59   UIA (No. 2) 1921, S. 3(3); UIA 1925, s.3.

e60   S.R.& O. 1937 No. 194.

e61   NIA 1946, s.11(1).

e62   SSA 1971, s.7(1).

e63   The rules have been changed several times: see, for example, UIA 1920, S. 7(2) (b); UIA 1939, s.3; NIA 1946, s.11(2) (c), which as reenacted still represents the law.

e64   Below p. 204.

e65   See, for example, S.R.& O. 1912, p. 1002.

e66   NIA 1911, s.86(3) and proviso.

e67   UIA 1927, s.5(2) (ii), following a recommendation of a Committee of Inquiry into the workings of Unemployment Insurance ('Blanesburgh Committee') published by Ministry of Labour 1927.

e68   SSA 1975, s.20(4), as to which see Ogus and Barendt, above n. e21, pp. 117–120 and Calvert, above n. e46, pp. 192–198.

e69   UIA 1921, s.3(3) (b).

e70   UIA (No. 2) 1924, s.1(3) (d): it was approved by the Blanesburgh Committee, above n. e67.

e71   UIA 1930, s.4.

e72   Below n. e86.

e73   UIA 1930, s.6.

e74   NIA 1946, s.11(2) (a) (i).

e75   See, for example, *R(U) 12/52*.

e76   See NIAC Report on the Availability Question (1953), Cmd. 8894.

e77   S.I. 1955/143, now S.I. 1975/564, Reg. 7(1) (a). See Ogus and Barendt, above n. e21, pp. 106–108 and Calvert, above n. e46, pp. 113–118.

e78   See NIAC Reports on the Question of Conditions for Unemployment Benefit for Occupational Pensioners (1968), Cmnd. 3545, and the Draft Regulations (for students) (1978), Cmnd. 6976.

e79   NIA 1911, s.87(2).
e80   Now SSA 1975, s.20(1) (a).
e81   See Ogus and Barendt, above n. e21, pp. 114–115 and Calvert, above n. e46, pp. 188–190.
e82   NIA 1911, S.87(2); now SSA 1975, s.20(1) (a).
e83   V. Tillyard (1949). *Unemployment Insurance in Great Britain 1911–1948*, pp. 24–25.
e84   Final Report (1932), Cmd. 4185, para. 443. For a modern analysis of the circumstances which may constitute 'misconduct', see *R(U) 2/77*.
e85   UIA 1930, s.4, implementing a recommendation of the Committee on Procedure and Evidence for the Determination of Claims for Unemployment Insurance Benefit (1929), Cmd. 3415.
e86   There are actually four independent grounds of disqualification, all of them variations on the same theme; SSA 1975, s.20(1) (b)-(e). For the meaning of 'suitable employment' see above p. 203.
e87   Sir John Simon, Solicitor General, introducing to Parliament the 1911 National Insurance Bill, 31 H.C. Deb., col. 1729. See also *Report of the Royal Commission on Trade Unions and Employers Associations* (1968), Cmnd. 3623, paras. 993–994.
e88   See the Memorandum of the Ministry of Social Security to the Royal Commission (ibid.), *Minutes of Evidence*, p. 2310.
e89   See, generally, M. Hickling (1975). *Labour Disputes and Unemployment Insurance Benefits in Canada and England.*
e90   NIA 1911, s.87(1).
e91   Ministry of Social Security Memorandum, above n. e88, p. 2312.
e92   Hickling, above n. e89, p. 18.
e93   Ibid., p. 19.
e94   UIA (No. 2), s.4(1).
e95   See Report of Blanesburgh Committee, above n. e67, paras. 135–138.
e96   Ibid., paras. 135–140.
e97   UIA 1927, s.6.
e98   Above n. 87, para. 953–993.
e99   See, e.g., *R(U) 15/55*.
f1   SSA 1975, s.19(1)(a), as amended by Employment Protection Act 1975, s.111(1).
f2   Charges (though not related to cost) have been imposed on a number of items and services and the phenomenon has increased within recent years: see M. Ryan (1973). in M. Cooper (ed.) *Social Policy: A Survey of Recent Developments*, pp. 118–124.
f3   National Health Service Act 1946 and see above, p. 192.
f4   Cf. above pp. 184–185.
f5   NIA 1911, s.15(2).
f6   Ibid., s.15(5).
f7   S.R.& O. 1930 No. 523.
f8   Report of Royal Commission on National Health Insurance (1926), Cmd. 2596, paras. 261 and Conclusion (11).
f9   This was originally covered by the insurance scheme as a separate 'sanatorium benefit' (NIA 1911, s.8(1)(b)) but was transferred to the public service by NHIA 1920, s.4 and Public Health (Tuberculosis) Act 1921.
f10   See H. Levy (1944). *National Health Insurance*, pp. 96–97.
f11   Ibid., and Royal Commission Report, above n. f8.
f12   NIA 1911, s.8(1)(c); SSA 1975, s.17(1)(a)(ii).
f13   National Insurance and Supplementary Benefit Act 1973, s.5(1), now SSA 1975, s.17(1)(a).
f14   *R(S) 2/78.*
f15   See further below p. 232.
f16   S.I. 1948/1277, Reg. 3. For modifications to the rule and guidelines to its interpretation, see *R(S) 2/79.*
f17   Above p. 202.
f18   Cf. Ogus and Barendt, above n. e21, pp. 148–149.
f19   See the article on a 'confidential' Cabinet committee report in the *Guardian*, 3 December 1979.
f20   NIA 1911, s.8(1)(c); SSA 1975, s.14(3).
f21   Above p. 203.
f22   See now SSA 1975, ss.14(3) and 17(1)(d).

f23 NIA 1911, s.14(2). Subsequently, the Ministry of Health issued a Model Code of Rules which
     was in practice adopted by most societies: for details, see A. Lesser (1939). *The Law of National
     Health Insurance*, pp. 1108–1109.
f24 NIA 1911, s.14(2)(e).
f25 S.I. 1975/564, Reg. 12(1)(c).
f26 See Reported Decision No. XIII on Appeals and Applications under NHIA 1936, s.163.
f27 S.I. 1975/564, Reg. 12(1)(a).
f28 Ibid., Reg. 12(1)(d)(i).
f29 Ibid., Reg. 12(1)(b) and 12(1)(d).
f30 Cf. above p. 206.
f31 NIA 1911, s.8(1)(e).
f32 Ibid., s.8(6).
f33 NHIA 1936, s.58(2).
f34 *Social Insurance and Allied Services* (1942), Cmd. 6464, para. 341.
f35 NIA 1946, s.14(1).
f36 NIA 1953, s.1, following a recommendation in the NIAC Report on Maternity Benefits
     (1952), Cmd. 8446.
f37 Ibid., paras. 22–35.
f38 NIA 1953, s.4.
f39 NIA 1964, s.1(4).
f40 See V. George (1968). *Social Security: Beveridge and After*, p. 130.
f41 Above n. f34, *loc. cit.*
f42 NIA 1946, s.15, now SSA 1975, s.22.
f43 Cf. above p. 192.
f44 Beveridge, above n. f34, *loc. cit.*
f45 SSA 1975, s.22(1)(a), and S.I. 1975/553, Reg. 4(1).
f46 SSA 1975, s.22(9), and S.I. 1975/553, Reg. 9. For discussion see above pp. 207–208.
f47 Employment Protection Act 1975, s.37.
f48 Old Age Pensions Act 1908, above p. 178.
f49 WOOCPA 1925, s.1(1)(c).
f50 Ibid.
f51 Old Age and Widows' Pensions Act 1940, s.1(1).
f52 Above n. f34, para. 133–136. Even with this modification, Beveridge doubted whether the
     fund would be able to finance benefits at an appropriate level immediately and recommended
     a gradual increase in the amount of pension over a period of 20 years. One of the reasons for
     the financial difficulties experienced by the national insurance system was the failure of the
     post-war government to implement this idea: above p. 197.
f53 NIA 1946, s.20(1)(a); now SSA 1975, ss.28(1) and 29.
f54 NIA 1946, s.20(4); now SSA 1975, s. 28, as amended by SSPA 1975, Sch. 1, and SSMPA
     1977, s.3(1)(b). See generally A. Ogus and E. Barendt (1978). *Law of Social Security*, pp.
     219–221 and H. Calvert (1978). *Social Security Law* (2nd edn), pp. 288–290.
f55 Cf. P. Kaim-Caudle (1973). *Comparative Social Policy and Social Security*, ch. 6.
f56 Ogus and Barendt, above n. f54, pp. 201–211; Calvert, above n. f54, pp. 271–285.
f57 NIA 1946, s.20(2); now SSA 1975, s.27(3).
f58 NIA 1946, s.20(5); now SSA 1975, s. 30, as amended by SSPA 1975, s.11 and SSMPA 1977,
     s.5(2). For history and general discussion see, e.g., NIAC Report on the Earnings Limit for
     Retirement Pensioners (1966), Cmnd. 3197.
f59 NIA 1946, s.20(5).
f60 NIA 1956, s.1, implementing a proposal in the NIAC Report (1955), Cmd. 9752.
f61 See, for example, Conservative Political Centre (1976). *An End to the Earnings Rule?*
f62 Cf. Ogus and Barendt, above n. f54, pp. 216–217.
f63 Between 1974 and 1977 the limit was raised from £13 to £40.
f64 Cf. Report on the Earning Rule 1978 H.C. 697.
f65 See DHSS Memorandum (1976). *Pension Age*, para. 22.
f66 See Equal Opportunities Commission (1976). *Sex Equality and the Pension Age*.
f67 Cf. V. George (1973). *Social Security and Society*, pp. 109–114.
f68 J. Walley (1972). *Social Security: Another British Failure?* p. 249.
f69 B. Gilbert (1966). *Evolution of National Insurance in Great Britain*, pp. 326–343.
f70 WOOCPA 1925, s.1(a); NIA 1946, s.17(2)(a).
f71 NIA 1966, s.4(3), now SSA 1975, s.24(2).

f72 Walley, above n. f68, pp. 63–64.
f73 Above n. f70.
f74 Above n. f34, para. 153.
f75 Ibid., para. 346.
f76 White Paper (1944). *Social Insurance Part I*, Cmd. 6550, para. 121.
f77 NIA 1946, ss. 17–18. Also where she was incapable of self-support: ibid., s.18(3). Widows not qualifying under any of these provisions were nevertheless entitled to a small non-contributory pension.
f78 See NIAC Report on the Question of Widow's Benefits (1956), Cmd. 9684, para. 45.
f79 FANIA 1956, s.2(5).
f80 NIA 1970, s.2.
f81 WOOCPA 1925, s.3(1).
f82 NIA 1946, s.17(1)(c).
f83 FANIA 1956, s. 2(2), following a NIAC recommendations, above n. f78.
f84 NIA 1970, s.3.
f85 WOOCPA 1925, s.3(2); NIA 1946, s.17(2); SSA 1975, s.26(3).
f86 WOOCPA 1925, s.21(1). NIA 1946 and SSA 1975 ibid., *loc. cit.*
f87 From 'cohabiting with a man as his wife' to 'living together as husband and wife': SSMPA 1977, s.14(7).
f88 For general discussion and criticisms, see Ogus and Barendt, above n. f54, pp. 404–408.
f89 Above n. 74.
f90 NIA 1946, s.17(3).
f91 NIA 1964, s.1(5)
f92 Cf. K. Clarke and A. Ogus, 'What is a Wife Worth?' *Br. J. Law and Society*, 5, 1.
f93 Below p. 216.
f94 E.g. *Report of the Committee on One-Parent Families* (1974), Cmnd. 5629, pp. 349–350.
f95 SSPA 1975, s.8.
f96 Above p. 197.
f97 Above pp. 210–211.
f98 (1956), Cmd. 9678, paras. 714–716.
f99 *Report on the Question of Dependency Provisions* (1956), Cmd. 9855, paras. 72–73.
g1   NIA 1957, s.5.
g2   See now SSA 1975, s. 31.
g3   Ibid., proviso. For other details see Ogus and Barendt, above n. f54, pp. 240–242.
g4   WOOCPA 1925, ss.1(1)(b) and 1(2).
g5   See NIAC Report 1948, H.C. 165, paras. 8–13.
g6   NIA 1946, s.19, now SSA 1975, s.38. The principles adopted are, however, problematic and complex: see Ogus and Barendt, above n. 54, pp. 256–263.
g7   See A. Wilson and H. Levy (1937). *Industrial Assurance.*
g8   Between 1872 and 1933 the matter was investigated by three different government commissions: see Ogus and Barendt, above n. f54, p. 243, n. 5.
g9   Above n. f34, paras. 157–160 and Appendix D.
g10 NIA 1946, s.22.
g11 Ibid., s.22(1)(a).
g12 NIAC *Report on the Death Grant Question* (1956), Cmnd. 33.
g13 NIA 1957, s.7, now SSA 1975, s.32.
g14 Ogus and Barendt, above n. f54, p. 246; Calvert, above n. f54, pp. 247–248.
g15 Above pp. 176–177.
g16 See, especially, A. Wilson and H. Levy (1939). *Workmen's Compensation.*
g17 Summarized above n. 34, para. 79,
g18 Ibid., paras. 80–105.
g19 Ibid., paras. 86–89.
g20 See Ogus and Barendt, above n. f54, pp. 264–266, and the references there cited.
g21 Above n. 34, paras. 81–83.
g22 See Ogus and Barendt, above n. f54, ch. 8, and P. Smith (1978). *Industrial Injuries Benefits.*
g23 Ogus and Barendt, ibid., pp. 273–276; Smith, ibid., pp. 16–21.
g24 NIIIA 1946, s.55 and S.I. 1948/1371; now SSA 1975, s.76 and S.I. 1975/1537, as amended.
g25 Rec. 2188/62.
g26 The Royal Commission on Civil Liability and Compensation for Personal Injury ('Pearson Commission') (1978) Cmnd. 7054, paras. 880–887, has however recommended its adoption.

g27 NIIIA 1946, s.7(1); now SSA 1975, s.50(1).
g28 On its interpretation under the workmen's compensation, it was said that 'no other form of words has ever given rise to such a body of litigation': Departmental Committee Report on Workmen's Compensation (1920), Cmd. 816, para. 29.
g29 Ogus and Barendt, above n. f54, pp. 276-293; Smith, above n. g22, pp. 24-45.
g30 See Pearson Commission, above n. g26, paras. 858-868. They recommend that, as in several foreign systems, coverage should be extended to all journeys to and from work.
g31 NIIIA 1946, s.9; now SSA 1975, s.53(1).
g32 NIIIA 1946, s.7(4); now SSA 1975, s.50(3).
g33 E.g. *R. v. National Insurance (Industrial Injuries) Commissioner, ex parte Richardson* [1958] 1 W.L.R. 851.
g34 FANIA 1956, s.2; now SSA 1975, s.55(1).
g35 NIIIA 1946, s.10; now SSA 1975, s.54.
g36 NIIIA 1946, s.8; now SSA 1975, s.52.
g37 NIIIA 1946, s.11(1); now SSA 1975, s.56(1).
g38 Above pp. 206-207.
g39 SSA 1975, s.57(1): 'trivial' here means less than 1 percent on the assessment of disablement, cf. below, p. 221.
g40 See White Paper (1944). *Social Insurance Part II, Workmen's Compensation*, Cmd. 6551, para. 29, rejecting Beveridge's recommendation (*Social Insurance and Allied Services* (1942) Cmd. 6404, para. 332) that an earnings-related pension should be awarded. For war pensions generally, see Ogus and Barendt, above n. f54, ch. 9.
g41 NIIIA 1946, s.12(1)(a): 'substantial' meant 20 percent or more disablement.
g42 NIIIA 1953, s.3.
g43 See, e.g. *R(I) 35/51.*
g44 Ogus and Barendt, above n. f54, pp. 303-304.
g45 NIIIA 1946, s.13; now SSA 1975, s.58.
g46 NIIIA 1946, s.14; now SSA 1975, s.60.
g47 Cf. Ogus and Barendt, above n. f54, pp. 318-331 and Pearson Commission, above n. g26, paras. 810-821 and Annex 6. The Commission recommended that the whole matter be reconsidered by the government in the light of European experience.
g48 NIIIA 1946, s.16; now SSA 1975, s.62.
g49 NIIIA 1946, s.15; now SSA 1975, s.61.
g50 NIA 1966, s.6, following the recommendations of the McCorguodale Committee on the Assessment of Disablement (1965), Cmnd. 2847.
g51 SSA 1975, s.63.
g52 NIIIA 1946, s.7(1)(c); now SSA 1975, s.50(2)(c).
g53 See above, p. 211.
g54 NIIIA 1946, s.19(3); now SSA 1975, s.68(3).
g55 NIIIA 1946, s.20; now SSA 1975, s.69.
g56 NIIIA 1946, ss. 22-24; now SSA 1975, ss. 71-73. For details see A. Ogus and E. Barendt (1978). *Law of Social Security*, pp. 347-349.
g57 Pearson Commission, above, n. g26, paras. 849-850.
g58 NIA 1911, Sch. 6.
g59 Cf. above p. 179.
g60 NIA 1911, s.107(1).
g61 National Insurance (Part II) (Munitions Workers) Act 1916.
g62 J. Fulbrook (1978). *Administrative Justice and the Unemployed*, p. 149.
g63 UIA 1920, Sch. 7, Part I.
g64 Ibid., Part II.
g65 Ibid. s.18.
g66 UIA (No. 2) 1921, s.5.
g67 UIA 1927, s.11.
g68 UIA 1934, s.1.
g69 See Report of Unemployment Insurance Statutory Committee to Minister of Labour, 1934.
g70 UIA (Agriculture) 1936. For details, see J. Clarke (1946). *Social Administration* (4th edn), pp. 597-602.
g71 NIA 1911, s.1 and Sch. 1.
g72 Ibid., s.2.
g73 Ibid., Sch. 1, Part II.

g74 WOOCPA 1925.
g75 Supra n. 40, paras. 149–152.
g76 See S.I. 1948/1425, Sch. 1, Part III, now S.I. 1975/528, Sch. 1, Part III (as amended). The notion of a 'contract of service' is by no means always easy to apply: sometimes an occupation is classified by the Secretary of State under his regulatory powers; there is, independently of this, a large body of case-law on the subject - see Ogus and Barendt, above n. f56, pp. 48–53.
g77 NIA 1946, s.1(2)(a); now SSA 1975, s.1(2).
g78 'The income of a farmer, a shopkeeper or a business manager may come at any time; how busy or how active he is on a particular day is largely within his own control': Beveridge, above n. g40, para. 122.
g79 NIA 1946, s.1(2)(b); now SSA 1975, s.1(2).
g80 Beveridge, above n. g40, para. 118.
g81 NIA 1946, s.1(2)(c). See Beveridge, above n. g40, para. 317.
g82 Ibid., para. 108.
g83 NIA 1946, s.59 and see V. George (1968). Social Security: Beveridge and After, pp. 19–22.
g84 NIA 1946, s.5.
g85 Ibid. For details see S.I. 1948/1417.
g86 NIA 1959, Part II.
g87 SSA 1975, s.2(1)(a).
g88 SSA 1973, s.1.
g89 SSA 1975, s.4(2)(b).
g90 SSA 1975, s.8. See Ogus and Barendt, above n. f56, pp. 61–62.
g91 SSPA 1975, s.3. For details see Ogus and Barendt, above n. f56, pp. 66–68.
g92 Cf. K. Clarke and A. Ogus, 'What is a Wife Worth?' Br. J. Law and Society 5, 1.
g93 SSPA 1975, s.19(3).
g94 NIIIA 1946.
g95 SSA 1973, s.94.
g96 NIA 1911, Sch. 4 and 7.
g97 M. Bruce (1968). The Coming of the Welfare State, (4th edn), p. 198.
g98 I.L.O. (1936). The International Labour Organization and Social Insurance, p. 49.
g99 Cf. above p. 194.
h1   NIA 1911, Sch. 4, Part II and see Report of the Royal Commission on National Health Insurance (1926), Cmd. 2596, paras. 301–303.
h2   NIA 1911, Sch. 2 and 4.
h3   UIA (No. 2) 1924, Sch. 1.
h4   NHIA 1924, s.13(2).
h5   WOOCPA 1925, s.1(1)(c).
h6   NHIA 1924, s.13(2).
h7   Above n. g40, para. 123.
h8   Ibid., paras. 367–368.
h9   Ibid., para. 153.
h10 White Paper (1944). Social Insurance Part I, Cmd. 6550.
h11 NIA 1946, Sch. 2.
h12 Ibid., and NIIIA 1946.
h13 Above n. g40, paras. 81–83.
h14 Cf. above p. 177.
h15 Research undertaken during the 1950s revealed that a substantial proportion of long-term national insurance beneficiaries had to resort to the means-tested national assistance: above pp. 196–197.
h16 NIA 1971, s.3. For details see Ogus and Barendt, above n. f56, pp. 164, and 166–167.
h17 E.g. National Insurance and Supplementary Benefit Act 1973, Sch. 1. For the most recent figures, see S.I. 1980/1245.
h18 SSA 1975, s.125.
h19 SSMPA 1977, s.7.
h20 SSA 1975, s.125(1). Under SSA 1979, s.13, there is a duty to 'review' the amounts payable but not to revise them!
h21 See, for example, the private members Social Security (Maternity Grant) Bill 1979 which did not receive government support.
h22 SSA 1975, s.126(4).
h23 The differential has been reduced from 73 percent (above n. h12) to 12 percent.

h24 Unemployed Workers Dependants' (Temporary Provisions) Act 1921.
h25 UIA 1922, s.1.
h26 Cf. above p. 193. A recommendation of the 1924 Royal Commission, above n. h1, paras. 314–326, for the introduction of dependency allowances was not implemented.
h27 WOOCPA 1925, s.1(1)(a).
h28 Ibid., s.1(1)(c).
h29 Above n. g40, para. 325.
h30 NIA 1946, s.23; now SSA 1975, ss. 41–43.
h31 NIA 1946, s.24(1); now SSA 1975, ss.44(1) and 45(1). The earnings of the wife must not exceed a prescribed amount.
h32 NIA 1946, s.24(2)(c); now SSA 1975, s.44(3)(c).
h33 NIA 1946, s.24(2)(a); now SSA 1975, s.44(3)(a).
h34 NIA 1946, s.24(2)(b); now SSA 1975, s.44(3)(b). But this is not claimable as an addition to retirement pension.
h35 NIA 1971, Sch. 2, Part II.
h36 NIIIA 1946, s.12; now SSA 1975, s.57. For details and discussion, see Ogus and Barendt, above n. f56, pp. 308–314.
h37 See, e.g., Report on Social Security Provision for Chronically Sick and Disabled People, 1973-4 H.C. 276.
h38 Above p. 200.
h39 Above n. g40, para. 302. See also, above p. 194.
h40 Above pp. 197–198.
h41 NIA 1959, s.4(2).
h42 Ibid., s.4(3).
h43 As a belated gesture, the government has recently assumed power to up-rate these benefits, which otherwise are (today) of an almost derisory amount.
h44 Above p. 201.
h45 NIA 1966, s.2.
h46 SSA 1975, s.22(4). Prior to that mothers were entitled to claim the supplement as sickness benefit (as also today are industrial injury beneficiaries).
h47 NIA 1966, s.2(3); now SSA 1975, s.14(7).
h48 NIA 1966, s.2(4)(a).
h49 SSA 1975, Sch. 6, Part II.
h50 Ibid., para. 3. The shortfall of 15 percent is explicable on the ground that benefit, unlike the earnings on which it is based, is not taxable.
h51 SSPA 1975, s.6.
h52 Ibid.
h53 Ibid., s.6(2).
h54 Ibid., s.21(3).
h55 R. Titmuss (1974). Social Policy, ch. 7.
h56 G. Calabresi (1965). The Costs of Accidents, ch. 6.
h57 J. Richardson (1960). Economic and Financial Aspects of Social Security, pp. 145–146.
h58 Social Insurance and Allied Services (1942), Cmd. 6404, para. 26.
h59 Above p. 216.
h60 Ibid.
h61 Above p. 217.
h62 Above p. 216.
h63 NIA 1911, s.94.
h64 It was abolished by UIA 1920, s.25.
h65 Above p. 185.
h66 See Report of the Royal Commission on National Health Insurance, above n. h1, para. 253.
h67 H. Land (1976), in ed. D. Barker and H. Allen (eds) Sexual Divisions in Society, p. 109.
h68 Above pp. 216–217.
h69 Above n. h58, para. 26.
h70 Ibid. and paras. 86–89.
h71 White Paper (1944). Social Insurance, Part II, Workmen's Compensation, Cmd. 6551, para. 23.
h72 See A. Ogus and E. Barendt (1978). Law of Social Security, pp. 267–268, and the references there cited.
h73 Above p. 217.
h74 Above p. 202.

h75 S.I. 1949/875; now S.I. 1975/492, Reg. 109, as amended.
h76 Above p. 218.
h77 L. McClements (1978). *The Economics of Social Security*, ch. 4, and the references cited in Ogus and Barendt, above n. h72, p. 28, n. 11.
h78 Above n. h58, para. 276.
h79 George, above n. g83, p. 48.
h80 Above p. 194.
h81 Beveridge, above n. 58, para. 273.
h82 For more detailed consideration of how the contribution was assessed see ibid., paras. 283–286.
h83 Above pp. 197–198.
h84 NIA 1911, Sch. 2.
h85 E.g. UIA (No. 2) 1921, s.2; UIA 1925, s.4. The principle of equality of contribution was reaffirmed by the Royal Commission on Unemployment Insurance (1932). *Final Report*, Cmnd. 4185.
h86 UIA 1920, s.5(7).
h87 NIA 1946, Sch. 1.
h88 Above n. h58, paras. 277–278.
h89 Ibid., paras. 289–291. The employer's burden was subsequently to be marginally greater than that of the employee: NIIIA 1965, Sch. 2.
h90 White Paper, above n. h71, and NIIIA 1946, Sch. 2.
h91 NIA 1946, Sch. 1.
h92 V. George (1968). *Social Security: Beveridge and After*, p. 51.
h93 Above pp. 200–202.
h94 NIA 1959, s.1.
h95 Cf. George, above n. h92, p. 54.
h96 SSA 1975, s.4(6). The figure is revised every year to take account of inflation. In 1980 it is £8300 per year.
h97 SSA 1975, s.122.
h98 Above n. h89.
h99 S.I. 1977/2180. The figures in this instrument are confused by the fact that the employer's rate includes a 2 percent surcharge for ordinary taxation purposes.
i1   SSA 1975, s.4(6).
i2   In the debates on the 1911 Act, Mr. W. Churchill said that state supplementation was necessary 'to make it just worth while for the superior workman to pool his luck with his comrades', quoted by M. Bruce (1968). *The Coming of the Welfare State* (4th edn), p. 198.
i3   Cf. Beveridge, above n. h58, para. 273.
i4   E.g. NIA 1911, s.85(6); UIA 1929, s.1.
i5   E.g. UIA 1921, s.5; UIA (No. 2) 1930; UIA (No. 3) 1930; UIA (No. 4) 1930. Conversely, for a period, the economic crisis was used as a justification for reducing the Exchequer's standard regular contributions to the fund: Economy (Miscellaneous Provisions) Act 1926, s.8.
i6   Above n. h58, paras. 241–243.
i7   Above, p. 197.
i8   NIA 1946, s.2(3)(b).
i9   NIA 1965, s.7(1).
i10 Ibid., s.7(2).
i11 George, above n. h92, p. 61.
i12 SSA 1975, s.1(5).
i13 Richardson, above n. h57, ch. 5; T. Wilson (1974). *Pensions, Inflation and Growth*, pp. 34–52; T. Rejda (1976). *Social Insurance and Economic Security*, ch. 7.
i14 J. Cohen (1921). *Insurance Against Unemployment*, p. 206.
i15 See the remarks of Mr. T. Ackland, the Government Actuary, cited ibid.
i16 Richardson, above n. h57, p. 70.
i17 Bruce, above n. i2, p. 199.
i18 Ibid., p. 241.
i19 Report of the Committee on Unemployment Insurance (1927).
i20 Bruce, above n. h18, *loc. cit.*
i21 Cf. above p. 203.
i22 Above p. 189.
i23 Above n. h58, paras. 265–271 and Appendix A, Memorandum by the Government Actuary.

i24 NIA 1946, s.39(1)(a). See, to similar effect, NIIIA 1946, s.59(1)(a).
i25 Above n. i6.
i26 Above p. 225.
i27 George, above n. h92, pp. 69–71.
i28 White Paper (1971). *Strategy for Pensions*,Cmnd. 4755, para. 4.
i29 White Paper (1974). *Better Pensions*, Cmnd. 5713, para. 83.
i30 Above p. 222.
i31 Ibid.
i32 Above p. 218.
i33 SSA 1973, s.94.
i34 Cf. above p. 218.
i35 Workmen's Compensation Act 1897.
i36 See, generally, E. Burns (1942). *British Unemployment Programs 1920–1937*.
i37 UIA 1921, s.3(1).
i38 UIA (No. 2), 1924, s.1(3).
i39 UIA 1927, s.14.
i40 See, generally, J. Fulbrook (1978). *Administrative Justice and the Unemployed*, pp. 154–159.
i41 See UIA 1920, s.8(4).
i42 *Final Report* (1932), Cmd. 4185.
i43 Unemployment Act 1934, and see Fulbrook, above n. i40, pp. 159–170.
i44 SSA 1975, Sch. 3, para. 7.
i45 Ibid., para. 6.
i46 A wide range of persons might have satisfied the contribution conditions: see A. Ogus and E. Barendt (1978). *Law of Social Security*, pp. 244–245.
i47 In 1976 only 677 women were given the allowance: DHSS Social Security Statistics 1976, Table 9.35.
i48 Above p. 221.
i49 Above p. 222.
i50 Ibid.
i51 Cf. Beveridge, above n. h58, para. 127; NIAC Report on the Question of Contribution Conditions and Credits Provisions (1956), Cmd. 9854.
i52 UIA 1920, s.7(1) (i).
i53 UIA (No. 2) 1924, s.3(1).
i54 NIA 1946, Sch. 3, para. 1.
i55 NIA 1946, s.5, and S.I. 1948/1417. For the current law, see Ogus and Barendt, above n. i46, pp. 72–75.
i56 Ibid., pp. 71–72.
i57 Above n. i54, and for current law, SSA 1975, Sch. 3, paras. 1–4.
i58 NHIA 1936, s.46.
i59 WOOCPA 1936, s.9.
i60 SSA 1975, Sch. 3, para. 5 (as amended).
i61 See Ogus and Barendt, above n. i46, pp. 75–76.
i62 NIA 1911, s.23.
i63 Ibid., ss. 57–58.
i64 Ibid., s.13.
i65 Ibid., s.14.
i66 Ibid., ss.15–19.
i67 See, for example, H. Levy (1944). *National Health Insurance: A Critical Study*, especially pp. 211–265.
i68 Ministry of Health Act 1919, s.3(1)(b).
i69 WOOCPA 1925.
i70 NIA 1911, ss. 88 and 91.
i71 UIA 1920, s.47(1)(d).
i72 S.R.& O. 1931, So. 876.
i73 Unemployment Act 1934, ss. 17 and 35. See, generally, Fulbrook, above n. i40, pp. 162–167.
i74 See *Final Report of the Royal Commission on Unemployment Insurance* (1932), Cmd. 4185.
i75 Fulbrook, above n. i40, p. 162.
i76 *Social Insurance and Allied Services* (1942), Cmd. 6404, para. 306.
i77 Ibid., paras. 44–47.
i78 This had been established by the Ministry of Pensions Act 1916.

i79 National Health Service Act 1946.
i80 National Assistance Act 1948.
i81 Ogus and Barendt, above n. i46, p. 572.
i82 517 H.C. Deb., col. 267. It did not require legislation.
i83 Ministry of Social Security Act 1966.
i84 Ibid., s.2.
i85 Ibid., s.3. The exact demarcation of functions between the Commission and the Ministry of
     Social Security (later the Department of Health and Social Security) has always been prob-
     lematic: cf. Ogus and Barendt, above n. i46, pp. 577–578; R. Brown (1975). *The Management
     of Welfare*, pp. 90–91.
i86 S.I. 1968/1699.
i87 Cf., above p. 185.
i88 The National Insurance Advisory Body (NIAC), NIA 1946, s.41.
i89 The Industrial Injuries Advisory Council (IIAC), NIIIA 1946, s.61.
i90 See NIA 1946, s.77, and NIIIA 1946, s.61(2). The statutory obligations of consultation have,
     however, been weakened: see now SSA 1975, s.139(1). One of the important functions of
     IIAC has also been to consider additions to the list of prescribed diseases: G. King (1958). *The
     Ministry of Pensions and National Insurance*, p. 120.
i91 Ogus and Barendt, above n. i46, pp. 580–585.
i92 NIA 1946, s.42.
i93 SSA 1971, s.9.
i94 See remarks of Sir K. Joseph, Standing Committee E Debates on Social Security Bill 1971,
     cols. 461–464.
i95 Cf. Social Security Bill 1980.
i96 See A. Wilson and H. Levy (1939). *Workmen's Compensation*.
i97 NIA 1911, s.88.
i98 Ibid., and s.90.
i99 Ibid., s.88.
j1   UIA 1920, s.10.
j2   NHIA 1920, s.9. Consistent with the 'contractual' nature of the scheme, certain disputes
     could be decided by arbitration procedures: S.R.& O. 1930, No. 523.
j3   Ibid.
j4   WOOCPA 1925, s.29.
j5   See, e.g., H. Emmerson and E. Lascelles (1928). *Guide to the Unemployment Insurance Acts*.
j6   Above n. 76, para. 394.
j7   NIA 1946, s.43(3), now SSA 1975, ss. 93 and 95 (as amended). There is a right of appeal, on
     a point of law, to the High Court: SSA 1975, s.94.
j8   Cf. Ogus and Barendt, above n. i46, pp. 623–624.
j9   S.I. 1948/1144, Reg. 10; see now SSA 1975, ss. 98–99.
j10 S.I. 1948/1144, Reg. 8; see now SSA 1975, s. 100 and Sch. 10.
j11 NIA 1946, s.43(3)(c), now SSA 1975, s.101 and Sch. 10. In 1979, solicitors were also eligible
     for appointment: SSA 1979, s.9.
j12 S.I. 1948/1144, Reg. 16(5); see now SSA 1975, s.116.
j13 See, generally, R. Micklethwait (1976). *The National Insurance Commissioners*.
j14 NIIIA 1946, ss.38–41. See, generally, Ogus and Barendt, above n. i46, pp. 635–640.
     Anomalously, some entitlement issues are determined by the Minister, from whose decision
     there is no appeal: ibid., pp. 333–335.
j15 FANIA 1959, s.2, now SSA 1975, s.112.
j16 On which see Ogus and Barendt, above n. i46, pp. 649–659.
j17 Above p. 200 and the references there cited.
j18 SSA 1979, s.6.
j19 See, generally, R. Wraith and P. Hutchesson (1973). *Administrative Tribunals*.
j20 See, generally, S. de Smith (1974). *Judicial Review of Administrative Actions* (3rd edn).
j21 Cf. *R.* v. *National Insurance Commissioner, ex parte Timmis* [1955] 1 Q.B. 139, 147.
j22 *R.* v. *Medical Appeal Tribunal, ex parte Gilmore* [1957] 1 Q.B. 574.
j23 Cf. Ogus and Barendt, above n. i46, pp. 645–647.
j24 *Per* Roskill L.J., *R.* v. *National Insurance Commissioner, ex parte Michael* [1976] 1 W.L.R. 109,
     116.
j25 Social Security Bill 1980, Cl. 14.
j26 This section is derived substantially from A. Ogus (1979). 'Conditions in the Formation and

Development of Social Insurance: Legal Development and Legal History', in H. Zacher
(ed.) (1979). *Bedingungen für die Entstehung und Entwicklung von Sozialversicherung*, pp. 337–348.

j27 Cf. V. George and P. Wilding (1976). *Ideology and Social Welfare*; Ogus and Barendt, above n.
i46, pp. 2–7.

j28 Cf. R. Titmuss (1947). *Commitment to Welfare* (2nd edn), pp. 21–22; R. Pinker (1971). *Social
Theory and Social Policy*, ch. 4; R. Pruger, 'Social Policy: Unilateral Transfer or Reciprocal Exchange' *J. Social Policy* **2**, 289.

j29 Above pp. 157–158.

j30 Above pp. 163–165.

j31 Above pp. 173–175.

j32 Above p. 162.

j33 Above pp. 161–162, 180–182.

j34 Above pp. 166–167.

j35 Above p. 178.

j36 F. Lawson (1951). *The Rational Strength of English Law*, ch. 1.

j37 W. Dale (1977). *Legislative Drafting: A New Approach*.

j38 R. David and J. Brierley (1978). *Major Legal Systems in the World Today* (2nd edn), p. 363.

j39 Cf. L. Scarman (1975). *English Law: The New Dimension*.

j40 Ibid., Part III; H. Street (1968). *Justice in the Welfare State*, ch. 1; and see above pp. 231–232.

j41 Cf. above p. 200.

j42 See M. Partington and J. Jowell (eds) (1979). *Welfare Law and Policy*.

j43 Ibid., chs. 16–17.

j44 Above pp. 199–200.

j45 Cf. C. Reich, 'The New Property' *Yale L.J.* **73**, 733.

j46 See, for example, A. Culyer (1973). *The Economics of Social Policy*, ch. 2.

j47 Ibid., pp. 22–25.

j48 L. McClements (1978). *The Economics of Social Security*, pp. 45–46.

j49 See, for example, D. Winch (1971). *Analytical Welfare Economics*, pp. 143–150.

j50 Culyer, above n. j46, pp. 25–30.

j51 Above pp. 222–223.

j52 *National Economic Development Council Report on Conditions Favourable to Growth* (1963), paras.
50–52.

j53 McClements, above n. j48, ch. 4.

j54 Ibid., p. 141.

j55 J. Kincaid (1973). *Poverty and Equality in Britain*, pp. 88–90.

j56 McClements, above n. j48, p. 34.

j57 A. Ogus and E. Barendt (1978). *Law of Social Security*, pp. 8–9.

j58 Above p. 220.

j59 H. Land (1976). in D. Barker and H. Allen (ed.) (1976). *Sexual Divisions and Society*, pp.
108–132; K. Clarke and A. Ogus, "What is a Wife Worth?' *Br. J. Law and Society* **5**, 1.

j60 Cf. above p. 212.

j61 Ibid.

j62 Above, pp. 217–218.

j63 Above p. 218.

j64 Above pp. 206–207.

j65 Above p. 204.

j66 See, e.g., above p. 201. Though the policy is not very effectively implemented; see the
literature on the so-called 'poverty trap', e.g., D. Howell (1976). *Why Work?*

j67 Cf. above p. 234.

j68 See, for example, Pinker, above n. j28, ch. 4; A. Forder (1974). *Concepts in Social Administration*, ch. 6.

j69 Above p. 201.

j70 Above pp. 158–159, 233–235.

j71 Above pp. 200, 232.

j72 Forder, above n. j68, pp. 101–104.

j73 Ogus and Barendt, above n. j57, pp. 587–618.

j74 For an excellent survey of the problem in Canada, and attempts to solve it, see Law Reform
Commission of Canada (1977). *Unemployment Insurance Benefits*, pp. 237–258.

j75 Forder, above n. j68, pp. 103–104.

j76 A. Sinfield (1970). in P. Townsend (ed.) *The Concept of Poverty*, ch. 13.

j77 D. Marsden (1969). *Mothers Alone.*
j78 Above n. j28, p. 170.
j79 *Social Insurance and Allied Services* (1942), Cmd. 6404, para. 26.

ABBREVIATIONS

Conventional abbreviations have been adopted for law reports, and reports of National Insurance Commissioners. The following have also been employed for social insurance legislation.

FANIA	Family Allowances and National Insurance Act
NHIA	National Health Insurance Act
NIA	National Insurance Act
NIIIA	National Insurance (Industrial Injuries) Act
SSA	Social Security Act
SSMPA	Social Security (Miscellaneous Provisions) Act
SSPA	Social Security Pensions Act
UIA	Unemployment Insurance Act
WOOCPA	Widows', Orphans', and Old Age Contributory Pensions Act

AUSTRIA

by Herbert Hofmeister

THE TERM 'SOCIAL INSURANCE' IN AUSTRIA

The main part of this work will show how Austria has developed a social security system, partly modelled on the German pattern and partly self-styled and original, which places Austria, a comparatively small country since 1918, among the leading 'social welfare states' in the world today.[1]

Before going into greater detail about the social value of social insurance, it is necessary to mention briefly the usual definition of the term[2] in Austria, with special reference to the jurisprudence of the Constitutional Court (Verfassungsgerichtshof). According to the 'objective historical' interpretation, as applied in the administration of justice by the Austrian Constitutional Court, the 'type of social insurance established in 1925' is the basis of the facts and competence of the 'social insurance system'. In the light of this interpretation, 'social insurance' represents a particular form of security to eliminate or alleviate dangers which threaten the economic existence of man (and not just of certain sectors of the pouplation). It also has the following characteristics: (a) in general, a gainful occupation is required for compulsory insurance; (b) there need not be an actuarial but rather a 'functional' link between contributions and benefits; and (c) to a certain extent, subsidizing social insurance with public funds is typical; however, public financing *per se* would not be compatible with the usual concept of 'social insurance' in Austria.

THE PRINCIPLE OF COMPULSORY INSURANCE; THE INSURED

The principle of compulsory insurance has been fundamental to Austrian social insurance ever since it began. Following the German model,[3] individual groups of gainfully employed persons were subject to compulsory insurance depending on their need for protection. Industrial workers formed the 'nucleus' which was gradually expanded by other groups of employed persons (railway staff, agricultural and forestry workers etc.). Austrian law has long been characterized by extensive uniformity of treatment for the insured in the individual branches, particularly due to the linkage of compulsory insurance in accident insurance with standards of sickness insurance. Over the last few years practically all gainfully employed persons and their dependants have been included in the protective sphere of social insurance both in Austria and Germany. Thus, not only have the

265

two systems of social law which were already closely and historically linked grown even closer together, but they have also become similar to those systems based on the principle of domicile. For example, on average, in 1978, 99.1 percent of the total population (averaging 7 508 000) were entitled to benefits from sickness insurance; some of the insured paid contributions and others were covered as co-insured dependants. Insurance coverage is similarly comprehensive in accident and pension insurance.[4] Nevertheless, like the German system, Austrian social insurance still has some gaps, for example inadequate social protection of people just starting work, of housewives who are not gainfully employed and of those disabled from birth.[5] Furthermore, great progress has been made in adjusting the level of social insurance benefits for the self-employed to that of the employed; however, this process is not yet complete. The question of a widowers' pension is still awaiting a solution in keeping with the spirit of reform of family law.[6]

THE CURRENT STATUS OF SOCIAL INSURANCE LEGISLATION

After 1945 (on account of the 'SozialversicherungsÜberleitungsgesetz'—SV-ÜG—the Provisional Law on Social Insurance), the German provisions for employed persons continued to apply initially. Special social insurance laws were only brought into force for two professional groups, civil servants and notaries. Social insurance law (sickness and accident insurance) is currently regulated by the B-KUVG ('BeamtenKranken- und Unfallversicherungsgesetz'—Law on Sickness and Accident Insurance for Civil Servants) of 1967 and by the NVG ('Notarversicherungsgesetz'—Law on Insurance for Notaries) of 1972. The latter provides only for pension insurance for notaries, including certain risks covered by accident insurance.

In 1955 the ASVG ('Allgemeine Sozialversicherungsgesetz'—General Social Insurance Law) was passed for the largest group of insured persons, the employed (workers, employees and miners). This law covered all branches of social insurance except unemployment insurance. It also provided for accident insurance for the self-employed both in trades and in agriculture and forestry. Special insurance laws have been passed for these two groups since then; these are the GSVG ('Gesetz betreffend die gewerbliche Sozialversicherung'—Law on Social Insurance for Tradespeople) of 1978 and the BSVG ('Bauernsozialversicherungsgesetz'—Law on Social Insurance for Farmers) of 1978. The latter provides for sickness, accident and pension insurance for farmers and the former regulates only sickness and pension insurance for tradespeople while accident insurance for them is still provided within the framework of the ASVG. In 1978, closely linked with the GSVG, the Law on Social Insurance for free-lance self-employed persons was also passed.

Apart from the single law governing unemployment insurance for all insured persons,[7] Austrian social insurance law is currently spread over five laws: the ASVG, GSVG, BSVG, B-KUVG and the NVG. Thus, compared with the past, the legal content has been concentrated considerably. Nevertheless, considering the frequent amendments, summarizing the whole of social insurance law in a single law would appear to be desirable.[8] Austrian social insurance law has been documented by law since 1976; this is intended to help those institutions that create or prepare laws to handle this difficult subject matter — which is as complex now as ever — more easily.

ORGANIZATION OF AUSTRIAN SOCIAL INSURANCE INSTITUTIONS

Self-administration

It has always been uncontested in Austrian statute and case law that Austrian social insurance institutions should have administrative autonomy. Korinek[9] recently confirmed this doctrine.

Institutions

Altogether there are twenty-eight insurance institutions in Austria. Nineteen (nine regional and ten works' sickness insurances) only deal with sickness insurance. This figure is extremely low compared both with the number of schemes in Austria in the past and with the current situation in the Federal Republic of Germany (with some 1400 sickness insurances).[10] While, for example, insurance institutions are rigidly divided according to the relevant branch of insurance in the Federal Republic of Germany, there are five institutions in Austria which implement more than one branch of insurance.

Administrative Bodies of Social Insurance
Institutions: Their Composition and Competences

The social insurance institutions are composed of a general assembly, an executive board and a supervisory committee. Only the 'Versicherungsanstalt öffentlich Bediensteter' (Insurance Institution for Civil Servants) is organized differently; it does not have a general assembly. Further noteworthy administrative bodies are the 'Landesstellenausschüsse' (boards of the regional offices which only come into consideration if regional offices exist), pensions, old age pensions and rehabilitation committees. The rules on the proportion of employed persons and employers in the general assembly, the executive board or in the 'Landesstellenausschüsse' are extremely varied. Apart from tasks of a private business nature (establishing and running hospitals, outpatients' departments, etc.), the social insurance institutions issue general administrative acts (charter, regulations) as well as individual provisions by means of special rulings.

PROCEDURE IN SOCIAL INSURANCE LAW

One of the characteristics of procedure[11] in Austrian social insurance law is the coexistence of two types of procedure, i.e. procedure concerning benefits (particularly the establishment of a right to draw benefits and the reclaim of insurance benefits paid out by mistake) and procedure in administration (particularly the determination of compulsory insurance or entitlement to insurance, or compulsory contribution).

MAIN FEATURES OF ENTITLEMENT TO BENEFITS

Sickness Insurance

The range of sickness insurance benefits[12] (according to the ASVG) includes both benefits in kind (preventive medical examinations, hospital treatment, care for the sick at home, institutional care, dental treatment and dentures, the assistance of doctors and midwives during pregnancy, at and after delivery) and monetary benefits (sick pay, family assistance, daily allowances, etc.). From an economic point of view,[13] expenditure on care of the sick both at home and in institutions has taken first place since 1978 (27.1 percent of expenditure), followed by expenditure on medical treatment (25.7 percent) and medicines and other such requisites for treatment (13.2 percent). 'Sickness assistance' in the form of monetary benefits only accounted for 5.6 percent and maternity benefits for about 5 percent of the total expenditure. The insured or co-insured dependants are free to consult any doctor of their choice. Thus, they can consult a panel doctor, a non-panel doctor or a doctor employed by the insurance.

Sick pay is granted from the fourth to the forty-second day of inability to work due to illness at a rate of 50 percent — and from the forty-third day (up to a maximum of twenty-six weeks) at 60 percent — of the basis of assessment (the so-called 'Bemmessungsgrundlage'). There are provisions for possible increases both of the amount and the duration of benefits (up to 75 percent, and up to 52 weeks respectively). Further monetary benefits are family assistance and day allowances. According to the GSVG, sick pay, family assistance and day allowances are only granted within the framework of supplementary insurance. The same applies to monetary maternity benefits (weekly allowance and delivery grant). Benefits of this kind are entirely unknown to the BSVG; moves are currently being made to introduce them.

Austria has not been spared the worldwide problem of rising costs[14] in the health sector. Expenditure on sickness insurance rose by 102 percent and receipts by 97 percent between 1973 and 1978. However, one must remember that initially (1973) Austria had a relatively low level of costs compared, for example, with the Federal Republic of Germany (factor 83 compared with 100 in the Federal Republic of Germany).

Accident Insurance

The range of accident insurance benefits[15] also includes benefits in kind, namely treatment following an accident, the provision of auxiliary help and rehabilitation, as well as monetary benefits. The latter include both short-term benefits (family assistance and day allowances, etc.) and disability pensions. In 1978, expenditure on pensions[16] accounted for about half and on treatment following an accident about a quarter of total expenditure on accident insurance. Expenditure on treatment has been increasing at about double the yearly rate of expenditure on pensions. Compared with other countries, the benefits provided, particularly by the 'Allgemeine Unfallversicherungsanstalt' (General Accident Insurance),[17] in the field of treatment following accidents stand out because of their excellence. Accident insurance also provides pensions for surviving dependants and (as in pension insurance) an allowance for the helpless (Hilflosenzuschuss) amounting to half a full pension if the disabled person 'continually requires nursing and assistance' (§105 (a) ASVG).

Pension Insurance

In accordance with the ASVG, GSVG, BSVG and NVG, the range of pension insurance benefits includes the 'normal' old age pension (paid out at the age of 65 for men, 60 for women) and also, with the exception of the NVG, the 'early pension' (at the age of 60 for men, 55 for women) if insurance contributions have been paid over a long period, plus — only under the ASVG — early pensions for the unemployed (at the age of 60 for men, 55 for women) and miners' pay (at the age of 45) in miners' pension insurance. A claim to benefit also exists in cases of reduced working capacity; this is assessed according to different criteria amongst individual occupational groups. Among unskilled workers, disability is assessed according to the criterion of whether or not the person concerned can be employed elsewhere (known as 'Verweisbarkeit'). In the case of skilled and semi-skilled workers and of employees, however, disability is assessed according to the individual's 'serviceableness' in all jobs requiring similar training and knowledge. 'Job protection' (Berufsschutz) is more markedly developed for miners; less so for notaries, however, who come within the scope of insurance for the self-employed.

One of the special features of Austrian law with regard to pension assessment[19] — since the ASVG was passed — is that with the sole exception of the NVG, the pension level is not assessed according to the so-called 'Durchrechnungsprinzip' (principle of calculation based on a person's earnings during his/her entire working life) but according to the level of the last earned income (in some circumstances the level of income earned before the age of 45 or 55). This system aims at largely maintaining the pensioner's previous standard of living. At the same time it provides for a transfer of income from the young to the old (especially considering the allocation procedure — 'Umlageverfahren'). In order to ensure the pensioner a basic minimum, compensation allowances (Ausgleichszulagen) are also granted if the basis of assessment is too low and/or insurance contributions have not been paid for long enough. Such allowances bridge the gap between the pensioner's income and the standard rate which is published each year. Furthermore, pensions are partly automatically adjusted and partly indexed. The standard rates, maximum contribution limits etc. are also adapted each year to income developments; because of the method of assessment applied, there is a delay which is important economically.

THE ECONOMIC IMPORTANCE OF SOCIAL INSURANCE; PROVISION OF FUNDS; 'REDISTRIBUTION'

Statistical Data

Expenditure on social insurance in Austria is very high and — of continuously growing importance amongst the total sum of social benefits. According to recent figures (1978) expenditure of the social insurance institutions accounted for 14.73 percent of the gross national product and 45.6 percent of the federal budget. These percentages are even higher if one takes the receipts (mean) of social insurance as the basis (15.1 and 47.1 percent respectively).[20]

Raising of Funds

As will be seen in the main part of this work, Austrian legislation was strongly opposed to the financial participation of the state in social insurance, as Bismarck had proposed in Germany. Thus, from the very beginning both accident and sickness insurance were financed only by contributions from the insured and/or their employers. Originally, the contribution for accident insurance was shared in a ratio of 9 : 1 and for sickness insurance 2 : 3. These ratios have changed: nowadays the employers bear the whole cost of contributions for accident insurance (1.5 percent of the wage) while employers and the employed share equally the costs of contributions for sickness insurance. However, the principle of financing solely by contribution has remained unchanged, if one disregards special state assistance to structurally weaker social insurance institutions (particularly financial assistance to sickness and accident insurance of farmers according to § BSVG; cf. also §447(a), section 3 ASVG).

As far as the method of financing is concerned, the allocation procedure (Umlageverfahren), originally used only in sickness insurance, now applies to all three branches, i.e. to accident and pension insurance also. The level premium system (Kapitaldeckungsverfahren) failed, as will be seen, because of the inflation during the early 1920s and was not reintroduced after 1945 as the pensions and other monetary benefits had lost their economic relation to the contributions which had been paid in. As far as contribution rates are concerned, the proportion of gross wages of employed persons required for sickness, pension and unemployment insurance currently amounts to 13.95 percent for workers and agricultural workers and 13.2 percent for employees, i.e. the contributions lie within the limits of the maximum contribution level (Höchstbeitragsgrundlage).

In contrast to sickness and accident insurance, pension insurance is financed to a considerable degree by the state. There are very great differences among the groups of persons insured. The proportion of pension expenditure borne by the state in 1978 amounted, for example, to 86.8 percent for farmers' pension insurance, 73.1 percent for tradespeople, 50.9 percent for miners, 25.4 percent for railway staff and 21.1 percent for workers. The state did not contribute anything to pension insurance for employees or for notaries (for which no legal claim to state subsidies exists).[21]

The state subsidy to pension insurance schemes for the self-employed involves three types of benefit[22] which have different functions: (a) compensation for burdens which are extraneous to the insurance (especially maternity benefits, housing allowances and cost-of-living bonuses); (b) state contributions to pension insurance of the self-employed as equivalent of the non-existent employer contribution; and (c) the actual state liability in pension insurance which obliges the federal government to provide a contribution of the amount by which expenditure (currently raised to 100.5 percent) exceeds receipts. Redistribution at the expense of the employed only takes place with regard to those aspects of state subsidy mentioned under (a) and (c).

The 'Redistribution Effect'

Redistribution also takes place among the employed: on the one hand indirectly via the state subsidy and on the other hand directly via the compensation fund (Ausgleichsfonds) of the pension insurances. (The fund has existed since 1978 and provides for the transfer of funds from the pension insurance of the employees to that of the workers.) As a result, social insurance makes an extremely significant contribution to eliminating or reducing structural differences between the level of social benefits for individual occupational groups (or sections of the population). The extremely important redistribution between young and old has already been discussed in the context of eligibility for benefits.

HISTORICAL DEVELOPMENT

PART I: BACKGROUND

POLITICAL, CONSTITUTIONAL AND IDEOLOGICAL BACKGROUND

Introduction

The development of Austrian social insurance law[23] can only be correctly understood and explained by someone who has become acquainted with the constitutional development[24] of the Habsburg monarchy during the period under investigation. The major political upheaval of 1879 and the years that followed[25] is of particular importance in this respect. It is also necessary to discuss briefly constitutional development prior to 1879, as this helps to put the scope and significance of the political upheaval of 1879 and later years into proper perspective while providing a background for numerous precursors and alternatives to social insurance.

From 1815 until the March Revolution of 1848

Before 1848, unlike most of the other states in the German Confederation, the Austrian Empire was characterized by absolutism, as far as constitutional law was concerned.[26] Due to fear of revolutionary forces, major and minor policies alike were designed to preserve the status quo. This meant that by the early 1840s, major legislation of all kinds had virtually come to a standstill. The legislature's almost fatalistic attitude is most clearly reflected in the failure of all attempts to solve the most important social and economic problem of the age, namely the dissolution of landlordism and the nationalization of the magisterial rights incumbent upon the lords of the manors by the means of suspension of the property rights of these landlords.[27] Compared with this central legislative problem, all economic and social problems connected with the industrial labour force remained in the background from the start, not least because of the low level of industrialization in those countries which formed the Austrian Empire at that time. In some ways the mining industry is the only exception for it had — particularly in Bohemia — an old tradition of legislation on workers' protection and of social legislation (see p. 284) which continued to be effective during the period before 1848. It is also worth mentioning that the legislative apparatus of that period did pass the so-called 'Verpflegskosten-Normale' (maintenance norm), an imperial decree of 18 February 1837,[28] repeating the ruling established in the decree of the chancery court dated 4 May 1814; this provided rather modest protection for sick workers in industry. According to this decree (especially §12) factory owners were bound to pay for the board of workers or apprentices in public hospitals for one month. This ruling also applied to the employer in cases of illness which were not connected with the employed person's occupation; exceptions to this, however, were certain venereal diseases and illnesses connected with pregnancy.[29]

The 1848 Revolution in Austria

The year 1848 was a turning point in the constitutional development of the Austrian Empire.[30] Shortly after the March events, the Liberal demand for the introduction of a Ministry which would be answerable to the people was fulfilled.

This was soon followed by the issue of the so-called 'Pillersdorfschen Verfassung' (Pillersdorf Constitution—PGS 76, no. 49)[31] of 25 April 1848 in answer to demands for a 'constitution'. According to §31 of the voting regulations issued in this context, 'workers receiving a daily or weekly wage' were denied the active (and thus also the passive) right to vote (Imperial Charter of 8 May 1848, PGS no. 57). However, this restriction was lifted by a voting law amendment in June 1848[32] and with it a ruling on the right to vote was created—following the principles applied in the German Confederation. This voting law was more favourable for workers than any later Austrian rulings on the subject until the (re-)introduction of universal franchise in 1907.[34]

This is not the place to attempt a comprehensive appreciation of the 1848 Revolution.[35] However, it is surely interesting to note that the movement was led by the bourgeoisie, liberal-minded intellectuals and former leading representatives of the bureaucracy which had existed until then, whereas representatives of the peasantry and of the labour force were almost completely in the background as far as political power was concerned.

Rather like the Frankfurt Parliament in the 'Paulskirche', the Viennese and the Kremsier 'Reichstag' missed the chance of changing socio-economic conditions by passing immediately realizable single laws in keeping with the liberal spirit of the time, as they were (solely) concerned with the question of the constitution and of franchise. Considering the Viennese or Kremsier 'Reichstag' of 1848 did not even complete reforms which counted among the most urgent according to liberal legal thinking, then it is not surprising that the economic and social problems of the labour force were not even mentioned in 'Reichstag' debates—apart from a single exception—let alone solved satisfactorily. The only socio-political problem of the workers which was actually dealt with in the 'Reichstag'[36]—upon the motion of Hans Kudlich—was the mass unemployment both in Vienna and Bohemia which the workers thought was predominantly caused by increasing mechanization.

Neoabsolutism (1851-1860)

The 'Vereinspatent' (Charter on Associations) of 1852

Turning away from the principles laid down in the imposed constitution of 4 March 1849, the constitutional development from 1849–1851 finally culminated in the reintroduction of absolutism with the 'Sylvesterpatent' (New Year's Eve Charter) of 31 December 1851.[37] The era of neoabsolutism (or the Bach era) following the 'Sylvesterpatent' turned against liberal thought and the freedom of association which had been granted in the 'Vereinspatent' of 17 March 1849, RGB no. 171. According to this charter the 'system of concessions' which had applied to all associations until then was now only to apply to associations intent on making a profit.[38] Freedom to form political associations applied if the principle of registration was upheld. The 'Vereinspatent' of 26 November 1852, RGB no. 253, however, reintroduced the system of concessions for all types of associations. This ruling was in force until the 'Vereinsgesetz' (Law on Associations) was passed in 1867. The 'Vereinspatent' of 1852 continued to play an important role after 1867 (see below p. 287) with particular reference to association sickness insurances. This role was predominantly negative as the system of concessions made it difficult for workers to set up sickness and (also partly) pension insurance associations. The situation did not improve until the 'Arbeiter-Kranken-versicherungsgesetz' (Law on Workers' Sickness Insurance) of 30 March 1888, *RGB* no. 33, came into effect. In certain circumstances (§60 sections 1 and 2) a concession to form or re-form an association could only be denied for particular reasons (§60, section 3, lines 1 and 2).[39]

The 'Berggesetz' (Mining Act) of 1854

While the 'Vereinspatent' of 1852 clearly bore the antiliberal traits of neoab-solutism, two other laws of this era which are relevant, the 'Berggesetz' of 23 May 1854, *RGB* no. 146, and the 'Gewerbeordnung' (Trade Act) of 20 December 1859, *RGB* no. 227, show more progressive features. The first is one of the finest achievements of Austrian executive administration of the time, embodying a skilful compromise between the economically desirable freedom of the mine-owner on the one hand and the state's supervisory right on the other. The attempt by the authors of the 1854 'Berggesetz' to revive mining associations and to develop social protection for miners is of special interest for the history of social insurance law (see below p. 284).

The 'Gewerbeordnung' (Trade Act) of 1859

The 1859 'Gewerbeordnung' is even more marked by economic liberalism[40] than the 1854 'Berggesetz'. This liberalism gained in importance after Minister Tog-genburg entered the government (in 1855) and contrasted curiously with the general political line of neoabsolutism. The 1859 'Gewerbeordnung'[41] granted that very measure of economic freedom which later served as a guideline for art. 6 of the Basic Law of the State (Staatsgrundgesetz) on the citizens' common rights when constitutional conditions were reintroduced.

The basic liberal ideas of the 1859 'Gewerbeordnung' were by no means restricted to the act's central subject, namely the pursuit of a trade, but were also reflected in the rejection of price taxes (cf. 'Gewerbeordnung' §55) and in the principle of a free market. The provisions of the 'Gewerbeordnung' on workers' accident and sickness insurance will be discussed in detail later (below p. 285). At this point it is interesting to note that the liberal spirit of the 'Gewerbeordnung' also prevailed in these provisions; it was reflected in the principle of the voluntary establishment of relief funds (Unterstützungskassen) and in an 'individualistic' limitation of such institutions to the respective company. These two features jeopardized the success of the provisions concerned (§§85, 106 ff.) right from the beginning.[42]

Return to Constitutionalism 1859–1867,
the December Constitution of 1867

As far as constitutional law is concerned, the period from 1859 to 1867 is marked by two major developments: first the political estrangement of the two halves of the Austrian Empire — only of marginal importance here — culminating in the so-called 'Ausgleich' (the Austro-Hungarian Agreement) of 1867;[43] and secondly the gradual transition to constitutionalism, especially in the Cisleithan half of the Empire, i.e. situated on the Austrian side of the river Leitha.

The beginning was marked by the 'Oktober-Diplom' (charter) of 20 October 1860, *RGB* no. 226, followed by the 'Februar-Patent' (charter) of 26 February 1861, *RGB* no. 20. This process ended with the 1867 December Constitution. Its

five Basic State Laws (Staatsgrundgesetze) of 21 December 1867, *RGB* no.
141–145, formed the main constitutional basis of the 'kingdoms and provinces
represented in the imperial council (Reichsrat)' until the fall of the monarchy.
One of these laws, namely the 'Basic State Law on the Citizens' Rights', *RGB* no.
142, remained valid in Austria after 1918 — apart from art. 20 — and still provides
a useful catalogue of basic law.[44] Freedom of speech and association, guaranteed
to Austrian citizens in art. 12 and regulated by a new law on association, the
'Vereinsgesetz' of 15 November 1867, *RGB* no. 134, is of special significance for
the development of social insurance. The (politically minded) liberals,[45] composed largely of the upper middle class, of some bureaucrats and of a relatively
small but politically highly active group of aristocrats, were responsible for the
constitutionalization process which began in 1860/1 and was for the most part
completed in 1867.

The 'Oktoberdiplom', 'Februarpatent' and the December Constitution of 1867
represented a political compromise between the demands of these liberals and the
political wishes of the crown and propertied classes. This compromise[46] found expression from a constitutional point of view in the two chambers of the
'Reichsrat': the 'Herrenhaus' was conceived as an upper house which was partly
to 'absorb' the traditional upper class and to function as the 'extended arm of the
crown', while the lower house, known as the 'Abgeordnetenhaus' (House of
Delegates), used a so-called 'Kurienwahlsystem' (curia voting system)[47] combined with a census; this system also applied to the 'Landtage' (regional governments).

Because of the census and the 'Kurienwahlsystem' large sections of the population, in particular workers and small-scale tradespeople, were not represented at
all in the 'Reichsrat' for a long time; other groups (particularly farmers) were extremely underrepresented. It was not until after the upheavals of 1879, discussed
later, that moves were made towards universal and equal suffrage. This was first
brought in for small-scale tradespeople in the cities in 1882. The working population did not benefit from attempts to democratize electoral law for the
'Reichsrat'[48] until 1896 (to a very small extent) and 1907. This digression on the
development of electoral law is necessary to show clearly that the political role of
the labour force in Austria differed considerably from that in Germany. While
German workers could participate directly in parliamentary activities as early as
1867–1871 because of the ruling on franchise of the North German Confedera-
tion/German Reich,[49] which largely followed the principles of universal and
equal suffrage, their Austrian counterparts were still denied the vote when the
three basic laws on social insurance were created.

Political Activities of the Labour Force, 1867–1889

The political activities of the labour force[50] after 1867 consisted primarily of
single political demands, especially those for the introducion of universal and
equal suffrage, freedom of meeting and the repeal of the compulsory associations
(see below p. 287) stipulated in the 'Gewerbeordnung'. This applied in particular
to the 'Manifesto for the Austrian Labour Force' which was adopted unanimously
at the Vth Workers' Meeting (arbeitertag) of 10 May 1868 and to the so-called
'Hartung-Programm',[51] adopted at the Meeting of Workers' Delegates
(Arbeiterdelegiertentag) of 22 August 1868 and at the IXth Workers' Meeting of
30 August 1868.

Developments in 1870 were doubled-edged for workers: on the one hand a law came into force—on 7 April 1870, *RGB* no. 43—bringing the workers at least *de jure* the freedom of meeting they had sought for so long; on the other hand, numerous workers' associations (thirty-two in all) were dissolved in July 1870 because of their danger to the state following the Oberwinder-Scheu[52] trial for high treason. However, most of these associations were soon set up again (for example, the Viennese 'Arbeiter-Bildungsverein'—Workers' Education Association—on 30 November 1870). In 1872 there were some 130 special trades' or workers' educational associations in the Cisleithan half of the empire.[53]

After a short recovery phase, the labour movement again fell into serious crisis, mainly due to internal differences of opinion on the labour force's attitude to the liberal movement. While the group around Heinrich Oberwinder, that dominated at first, wanted to integrate workers into the liberal movement and thus form a link between the political endeavours of the middle classes and workers, Oberwinder's opponents (first Ludwig Neumayer and then Andreas Scheu in particular) spoke for a class-conscious workers' policy conceived as the nucleus of a movement 'of all those classes which are oppressed by capitalist interests' and based on the (German) Social Democratic Labour Party's Eisenach Programme of 7/9 August 1869.[54] The victory of the second of these policies was already apparent in the so-called Neudörfler Programme (adopted on 5 April 1874) which upon Scheu's proposal was closely linked to the Eisenach Programme.[55] Like this, the Neudörfler Programme demanded 'the abolition of modern private capital-oriented production methods'. In conformity with point 8 of the Eisenach Programme, point 7 of the Neudörfler Programme demanded the 'introduction of a standard working day, the restriction of female and abolition of child labour in factories and industrial workshops'. Going beyond the scope of the Eisenach Programme, it also demanded the 'introduction of independent factory inspectors and [the] abolition of competition to free workers by prison work'. Sickness and disability schemes were discussed just as little in the 'Wiener Neustädter Programm' as in the Eisenach Programme.

The programme[56] finally adopted at the 'Wiener Neustädter Arbeitertag' (from 13 to 15 August 1876) also continued along Scheu's lines rather than Oberwinder's. However it was clearly more moderate than the Neudörfler Programme both in form and content. This manifested itself particularly in the following words: 'Austria's workers will fight . . . on the basis of the existing constitution'. Furthermore, the 'Wiener Neustädter Programm' is characterized by its considerably greater treatment of socio-political questions, compared with the Neudörfler Programme. This may be connected with a certain readiness to reach a compromise, as expressed in the programme, *vis-à-vis* the existing state and economic system, particularly as a result of the difficult situation facing the labour force following the economic crisis of 1873 (see p. 282) and the fact that a parliamentary draft on the reform of the 'Gewerbeordnung' was under debate at that time (see below p. 287).

The following points[57] of the programme are of special interest with regard to social insurance:

1. Radical reform of the 'Gewerbeordnung' as follows: the abolition of any compulsion in trade organizations, the abolition of compulsory associations, of the compulsory relief funds so far proposed in the government draft, complete autonomy for all workers' relief and assistance funds. . . .

[This is followed by important demands concerning labour laws, especially the legal standardization of a 10-hour working day.]

3. A law establishing the employer's unconditional liability to pay damages for injuries to persons employed in his concern as soon as the employer is unable to prove that the worker's injury was his own fault. Damages should correspond to the injured party's loss of income and be extended to surviving dependants if death occurs due to injury. Litigation over the amount of damages ought to be settled in the civil court in the usual way.

4. A law to safeguard worker's health, particularly for occupations hazardous to health, which compels every employer to take all measures in their workshops designed to reduce or completely eliminate health risks at work. . . .'

The outcome of the 'Wiener Neustädter Programme' which unequivocally documents the up-grading of socio-political demands, as distinct from central political matters, was very disappointing: first, the 'tamest of all programmes' was forbidden by the government as a danger to the state and, secondly, it did not lead to the unification of the labour movement as hoped.[58] Influenced by the state of emergency[59] in Germany, radicalism increased from the end of the 1870s. The most important leaders among the radical swere Otto Most, who mainly acted from London, and Josef Peukert.[60] The 'radicals', who were sometimes in the majority (for example in Vienna and Graz) vis-à-vis the 'moderates' (Karl Kautsky, Karl Höger, and Josef Bardorf), aimed at 'the overthrow of the existing order' and thus rejected the inclusion of socio-political reforms in their political programme.[61]

The height of disputes between the 'radicals' and the 'moderates' came in 1883 and continued until 1887/8.[62] Thus, in the very years when Austrian social insurance laws were evolving, the Austrian labour movement was undergoing one of the most difficult tests of its history.

In addition to the split into radicals and moderates, the Anti-Socialist Law, brought in by the Taaffe Government on 20 January 1885 (see below) but not adopted by both houses of the 'Reichsrat' until the next legislative session, weakened the Austrian labour movement further and almost brought its activities to a standstill from 1884 to 1886.[63] Although this law was primarily considered a reaction to the terror acts of anarchistic elements among the radicals, the moderates also feared that their associations would be dissolved by the authorities and so they closed them down themselves (particularly in Vienna) in anticipation.[64] All these factors explain why the Austrian labour force was prevented from playing an active role either at parliamentary or at extra-parliamentary level in the preparatory work for the three main social insurance laws. The Austrian Social Democrats' view on workers' insurance legislation will be discussed later (see below p. 302).

The Hohenwart-Schäffle Government;
Eberhard Friedrich Schäffle's Socio-political Ideas

Following the December Constitution of 1867 the so-called 'Bürgerministerium' (government under the Minister-President Prince Carlos Auersperg, later under Duke Eduard von Taaffe), in which the German liberal element dominated, was in power.[65] In the course of disputes over the reform of electoral law for the 'Reichsrat', a split developed in the 'Bürgerministerium' which finally persuaded the Kaiser to put the business of government into the hands of a group whose policies largely deviated from the governmental course so far. This was the Hohenwart–Schäffle government. It was not in office long enough (5 February to 30 October 1871) to carry out any fundamental reforms but it is nevertheless of interest because of its significance for later developments. The Hohenwart–Schäffle ministry was characterized on the one hand by a strong federalistic trend (mainly represented by Hohenwart) which aimed particularly at a political settlement with the Czechs, and on the other hand by ardent socio-political commitment (linked with Schäffle).[66]

Albert Eberhard Friedrich Schäffle,[67] born in 1831, professor of national economics at Tübingen University from 1860 onwards, had outlined his major political and socio-political ideas in *Kapitalismus und Sozialismus (Capitalism and Socialism)* which was published in Tübingen (1870) shortly before his appointment as Austrian Minister of Trade and Agriculture. His central idea was to point to a feasible middle course between the extremes of a capitalistic production system and communism. With visionary foresight, he warned people against excessive speculation on the stock exchange which shortly afterwards ended in the Viennese stock exchange crash of 1873 (see below p. 282). Schäffle also recognized the political signs of the time earlier than others; this is particularly apparent from his advocacy of universal and equal suffrage.[68]

Schäffle's far-sightedness is of special interest to us with regard to his idea of social insurance. Schäffle was probably the first Austrian politician who openly advocated the idea of compulsory insurance (even if this was done within the framework of a scientific dissertation). His ideas were based on liberal thought; namely that 'communism' couched in its various forms of poor relief goes far more against 'the principle of personal responsibility and freedom' than enforcement of 'compulsory insurance' because poor relief tends to undermine the idea of self-help.[69]

Schäffle was not in office long enough to implement his ideas on reform which found favour among the most influential group of the labour force (Oberwinder: see p. 275 above). His ideas could have helped to bridge the gap between moderate liberal and social democratic ideas.

In anticipation of later developments, the period of the Hohenwart–Schäffle Government points to a feature that marked Austrian social policy most decisively until the First World War. After the failure of centrally oriented liberalism to overcome the economic and socio-political problems of the 1870s, particularly after the 1873 crisis, there was bound to be a trend after 1879 towards that very political alternative which had already been tried in 1871 at the time of the Hohenwart–Schäffle Government, namely the combination of federalistic elements prepared to renounce the domineering role of German speakers in the Cisleithan half of the 'Reich' (and thus in the 'Abgeordnetenhaus' of the 'Reichsrat') in order to realize the constitutional principle (art. 19 of the Basic State Law on the Citizens' Rights) of the 'equal status of nationalities' and socio-politically active groups. Because of this and the progress of democratization as the franchise gradually spread, social policy became fatally involved with the problem of nationalities,[70] which increasingly paralysed the 'Reichsrat' and prevented the smooth development of socio-political achievements in the 1880s.

We now discuss in more detail the late phase of political liberalism in Austria and the events leading up to the major turning point in 1879.

The Late Phase of Political Liberalism in Austria; Causes of the Political Turning Point of 1879

After the dismissal of the Hohenwart–Schäffle Government and the provisional government under Holzgethan, a liberal-centralistic government was appointed under Adolf Auersperg on 25 November 1871.[71] Thus, the alliance between the liberal middle class and the aristocracy, ever faithful to the constitution, was again confirmed in its governmental function.

While the tremendous economic boom of the early 1870s had led politically to a renewed rise of liberalism, the stock-exchange crash of 1873 was a heavy blow to liberalism. More details of the 1873 crash will be given later (see below p. 283). At this point, however, we consider the psychological repercussions[72] of the crash: on the one hand the liberal movement suffered a great loss of public confidence; on the other, the liberal camp was increasingly shaken from 1873 onwards by internal crises and splits due to perplexity over future courses of action.

The common cause for these setbacks was that since 1873, both among large sections of the public and among leading representatives of the liberal camp, doubts had begun to be expressed about the correctness of the central liberal thesis that the state should and could only intervene in the economy and society to remedy extreme abuses. Unrestricted freedom of economic activity had been shown in 1873 that could lead to serious national economic and social consequences which were difficult to eliminate afterwards. During the liberal era, laws were passed which provided some limitations to the economic and legal freedom of action of the individual: for example, the Law on Bonds (Pfandbriefgesetz) of 1874 and the Law on Profiteering (Wuchergesetz) of 1877 — only passed for Galicia and the Bukovina; the about-turn on the protective tariff question, discussed below, is also to be noted at this point.[74] Furthermore, the history of the reform of the Trade Act (Gewerbeordnung) (see below p. 287 and 291) also shows that many later achievements were already anticipated in liberal thought of the 1870s in both the labour and social law sector. K. Ebert[75] has demonstrated this in his writings on amendments to the Trade Act of 1883 and 1885. According to Ebert, Austrian liberals lacked neither ideas on social reform nor the necessary socio-political commitment during this period. The reason for the failure of liberal policy was that the liberals were not prepared to 'buy' socio-political progress with fundamental restrictions on freedom.[76] Despite the events of 1873, the faith in the self-regulating power of the freedom principle in the economy and society was still too strong. Consequently, tension led to hesitation which resulted either in a total absence of necessary legislative measures or in 'half-way' measures.

Moreover, on the eve of the 'Reichsrat' election of 1879 — which was to set the trend for later developments — there were grave internal differences of opinion in the liberal camp which led to a split in the liberal party coalition before the election even took place.[77] At the same time, the opposition attained a degree of unity unknown hitherto and formed the so-called 'Eiserne Ring' (Iron Ring), an alliance of German clericals (conservatives) with the Czechs and the Poles. When the newly elected delegates of the 'Abgeordnetenhaus' of the 'Reichsrat' assembled in October 1879, the Iron Ring had a majority, however slight and relatively unstable vis-à-vis the liberal parties.[78] Neither the Iron Ring as such, nor the partners of the alliance in it can be termed parties in the true sense of the word. The common and unifying factor in the Iron Ring was its anti-liberalism. This was reflected by the rejection of the centralistic tendencies by the Slav partners and the sharp opposition of the conservatives to the social and economic policies of the liberals.

The Conservatives' Ideas on Social Reform
(Ketteler, Liechtenstein, Vogelsang)

Conservative social policy[79] was based on the ideas of Wilhelm E. Ketteler, the Bishop of Mainz, who demanded state intervention for the protection of craftsmen and workers since 1869.[80] Ketteler believed that the liberal innovations (free trade, economic freedom, repeal of profiteering prohibition) presented a great danger for the middle class which was not equal to the competition of haute finance in the long term and threatened to sink into a subordinate position to 'capital'. With regard to the workers, Ketteler criticized the existing form of the employment contract which was conceived solely from an economic point of view. Ketteler wanted this to be replaced by the 'benevolent concern of Christian charity'. Ketteler's ideas were made known to a broader public in Austria[81] from the end of 1874 onwards; this was largely due to the work of Alois Liechtenstein.

The Catholic social movement in Austria reached a first climax at the Catholic Meeting (Katholikentag), held in Vienna in 1877, where Liechtenstein read a fundamental paper.[82] Like Ketteler, Liechtenstein opposed the 'limitless' freedom of trade introduced by liberalism which had paved the way for the 'survival of the fittest' at the cost of the middle classes. For the farming population, Liechtenstein demanded the return to pre-liberal debt restrictions for land, to the right of succession to undivided farm estates and to strict prohibition of profiteering.[83] Like Ketteler, he demanded in the workers' interest that a purely economic attitude to employment had to be overcome, especially by protective measures against the excessive pressure on wages which threatened the very existence of the labour force.[84] Liechtenstein did not reject the idea of state intervention[85] to implement these reforms. However, he believed that such intervention was only to mediate and create a balance between 'the individual classes of productive society'. Liechtenstein was of the opinion that autonomous trade associations[86] should be modelled in accordance with the pattern of Mediaeval society and were to be instrumental in policy-making. Consequently, he demanded the establishment of statutory trade associations (chambers) for farmers, small-scale tradespeople and workers.[87]

Liechtenstein's influence was considerably outclassed by that of Karl Freiherr von Vogelsang,[88] a baron and Conservative politician from Mecklenburg, who was particularly interested in social policy and had been editor-in-chief of the Österreichische Monatschrift für Gesellschaftswissenschaft und christliche Sozialreform (an Austrian monthly publication on social science and Christian social reform) since the beginning of 1879. Like Liechtenstein, Vogelsang also saw his ideal society shaped on the basis of Mediaeval Christian social order (the 'Stände'). However, while Liechtenstein had come to terms with the fact that industrial development had led to an irreversible split between the propertied classes and the workers and thus aimed at a social order adjusted to this situation, Vogelsang aimed at overcoming the divide between capital and labour. Accordingly he advocated the idea of partnership between employers and the employed. Moreover, he was for segregating farmers from the modern money and credit economy to prevent further debts being contracted and also to prevent the farmers' existence from being threatened.[89]

The ideas of the early Christian social reformers, steeped in ethics and put forward with untiring determination, are very important within the framework of the development of Austrian social policy—and this is even recognized by political opponents (such as Otto Bauer)[90]—as they presented for the first time the most urgent social questions to a broad public in an impressive way. As Hans Rosenberg[91] correctly points out, Christian social reformers greatly influenced the anti-Liberal movement in Austria, as in other parts of Europe, around 1880. This movement was not only particularly vehement but was also—in addition to Rosenberg's observation and in anticipation of our results—more straightforward than was, for example, the case in German social legislation.

In the 1880s Austrian social policy consisted of two closely linked elements: social insurance and worker protection. The latter were two components of one and the same socio-political programme. Christian social reformers who were concerned with the overall improvement of the workers' lot would have considered the postponement of worker protection, as opposed to social insurance—a feature of Bismarck's social legislation—an untenable inconsistency.

Compared with the undeniable influence of the Christian social reformers on the general course of Austrian social legislation of the 1880s, Liechtenstein's and Vogelsang's concrete proposals did not meet with much success. This applies not only to Vogelsang's proposals which were often utopic, but also to Liechtenstein's proposal—along with practical points on implementation—to establish up to date professional organizations.[92]

The development of the social insurance system shows that the (fundamentally accepted) idea of autonomy of the Austrian social insurance institutions seems far more restricted by the bureaucracy's rights to participate and intervene than was the case in the German Reich. A detailed analysis of the drafts of the social insurance laws, particularly of the drafts on the Accident Insurance Law of 1887/8, will demonstrate this.

The Role of Bureaucracy

As already mentioned, some Austrian bureaucrats were counted among the Liberals' most important supporters in the 1860s, 1870s and even later.[93] Cooperation between Liberals and bureaucrats was based particularly on their common centralistic and other attitudes, anchored in the tradition of Joseph II and directed against the feudal aristocracy. However, bureaucracy, committed to the socio-political elan so characteristic of the tradition of Joseph II, was initially sceptical about the extravagances of economic liberalism and later rejected it for the most part. Thus, 1879 was not such an important turning point for Austrian bureaucracy as one would imagine judging by the political scene. The intensification of social thinking met with approval in broad circles of civil servants while the idea of largely handing over powers to subordinate autonomous associations in line with the 'Subsidiaritätsprinzip' (subsidiary principle—i.e. provision of assistance when it is really necessary), as put forward by the Christian social reformers, was less popular.

The alterations which Emil Steinbach[94] made, compared with the German drafts on accident insurance legislation, are significant; even compared with the second German draft for Accident Insurance Law, the idea of associations formed by the trades was noticeably pushed into the background in relation to state influence. The reasons for this, which are tied up with the problem of nationalities, will be discussed again later.

SOCIO-ECONOMIC BACKGROUND

The Beginning of Industrialization in Austria and Its Social Repercussions

As a result of the dynamic economic policy of the era of enlightened absolutism (Maria Theresa, Joseph II) Austria[95] was among the first countries to follow the Industrial Revolution begun in England. From about 1775 onwards, large industrial concerns, especially textile industries, were established in the area that was then Austria. The main industrial centres lay partly on the plains to the south of Vienna and partly in Bohemia.[96]

Social malpractices, so characteristic of the initial phase of industrialization, developed immediately; of these, child labour was the worst. The negative aspects of child labour were recognized earlier in Austria than in other European states by the enlightened monarch, Joseph II; measures were introduced to combat them (with the 'Handbillet' of 20 November 1786).[97]

Socio-economic Development from 1815 until the March Revolution of 1848

The period from 1815 until 1848 is marked both by economic and socio-political stagnation, particularly from 1830 onwards. Statistics for 1850 show that Austria had clearly fallen behind the leading industrial states (Great Britain, the German states, France) with regard to industrial development.[98] Seen as a whole, socio-political standards were also lower than in the leading industrial states (particularly England) despite individual legislative successes[99] during this period.

Neoabsolutism

The era of neoabsolutism restored political and constitutional laws to their status before 1848 (see above p. 272). However, at the same time—contrary to the previous period of stagnation—the era of neoabsolutism was characterized by feverish activity in all legislative spheres.[100] The state's dynamic economic and financial policies deserve special attention: important elements of neoabsolute economic policy were in particular the implementation of the so-called 'Grundentlastung' (discharge of debts on ground) through which the comprehensive indemnity funds were channelled into the economy; furthermore, the Austrian Government made efforts (particularly Prince Felix Schwarzenberg, Karl von Bruck) to create a Central European economic area which resulted on the one hand in the abolition of the customs frontier with Hungary and on the other hand in the treaty with the German 'Zollverein' (customs union) in 1853.[101] The increased trade relations with Hungary and the German 'Zollverein', the expansive monetary policy of the Austrian National Bank, the liberal trade and industrial policy after Toggenburg came into office (see above p. 273) and the favourable economic situation in the whole of Europe made the economy of the 'Imperial State of Austria' (including Hungary) develop extremely well between

1851 and 1857. This development is reflected most clearly in the growth of steam-power, the spread of the railway network (trebled or doubled)[102] and the establishment of important industries.

The Depression, 1857–1866

For the first time the negative aspects of such an overheated economic boom also came to light. The consequences of boundless speculation on the stock exchange and excessive credit expansion became apparent earlier in Austria than in other European states. In the autumn of 1857, Austria was rocked by a serious economic crisis entailing a drop in share prices, a sharp decrease in industrial production and railway construction and — in many parts of the monarchy — mass unemployment.[103] The war in 1859 prolonged the crisis until 1866; during this period certain sectors of industry, for example the textile industry and iron production, suffered severe setbacks which were accompanied by mass unemployment.

Economic Recovery, 1867–1873

The year 1867 in Austria was not only marked by political (see above p. 274) but also by comprehensive economic consolidation. In the period that followed, the end of Plener's deflationary policy,[104] free-trade agreements between Austria and a large number of European and non-European states,[105] and also the abundant harvests from 1867 to 1871 contributed towards an economic boom placing that of 1850 in the shade. Industrial production and transportation expanded by leaps and bounds again from 1857 onwards; however, there was an even greater (relative) increase in share prices and in the number of newly founded joint-stock companies than there was in the production and foreign trade figures.

The 1873 Stock Exchange Crash and
its Socio-Economic Repercussions

The collapse of the stock exchange on 9 May 1873 ('Black Friday') which resulted in a large number of insolvencies put a sudden stop to those high-flying activities.[106] Once again the Austrian economy plunged into a depression lasting for about 7 years; in addition to the crash, the repercussions of the worldwide crisis emanating from America began to make themselves felt at the end of 1873. Corn prices fell rapidly from about 1875 onwards, further aggravating the crisis. During the economic boom, there had been a low level of unemployment among workers but the labour force had nevertheless suffered because of steep rises in prices of food and rents due to inflation.[107] In the years following 1873, the immense growth of unemployment was the main economic problem of the working classes. The negative experiences of both periods contributed towards the workers' attitudes; they were increasingly disinclined to accept Oberwinder's plan for cooperation and switched to a self-confident class policy (see above p. 275).[108]

Structure of the Austrian Economy (Particularly
the Level of Industrialization) around 1880

From an overall European point of view, Austria (composed of the kingdoms and countries represented in the 'Reichsrat') did not figure among the leading industrial states in Europe in 1880. The proportion of all Austria-Hungary's industrial production of the entire European production was less than half that of the German Reich in 1880 (8 percent as opposed to 16.6 percent).[109]

It is important to point out that industrial production was concentrated in a relatively small part of the state territory (particularly in Bohemia, the southern part of Lower Austria, the Rhine valley in Vorarlberg). Thus, the level of industrialization and the social problems connected with these areas were comparable with those of other European industrial states. Moreover, the boom from 1867 to 1873 as well as the subsequent depression were far more evident in Austria where industrialization was developing than in the leading industrial countries. These economic factors, in addition to the political and constitutional background (see above p. 278), led to an extraordinary increase in social differences at the end of the 1870s. This was to become of decisive significance for the political motivation towards social insurance legislation.

The Social Situation of the Labour Force around 1880

The very unfavourable social situation of people employed in trade and industry grew even worse in the 1870s. The pressure on wages increased enormously, particularly in industrial conurbations. This led to a drop in wages (up to 80 percent in extreme cases); moreover, food prices sometimes rose at an even higher rate.[110] Not only poor nutrition but also catastrophic living conditions were extremely damaging to the workers' health. Accidents at work and industrial diseases also posed a threat to the workers' health and economic existence. These two items will be discussed in connection with the relevant social insurance laws.

SPECIAL FEATURES OF THE LEGAL TRADITION

Civil Law

The main source of civil law at the time of the emergence of insurance laws for workers was (and still is) the 1811 'Allgemeine Bürgerliche Gesetzbuch' (Civil Code).[111] In anticipation of later social and political developments, the Civil Code is primarily oriented to the needs of the middle class. Thus, although there must have been enough illustrative material available when it was issued, the Civil code does not go into the problems of employment in industry. Quite apart from its overall inadequacy, the law on employment contracts, as provided in the Civil Code, is based on the concept of equality of the contractual partners, a concept which could not be applied to industrial employment contracts. The law of liability in the Civil Code was and is only applicable to accidents at work in rare cases (if the employer or one of his staff is at fault: §1315) because liability is restricted to damage caused by negligence; the onus of proof (§1296) rests with the damaged party. There are only the very modest beginnings in the Civil Code (§1310 and similar) of liability which is quite independent of fault. The Railway Liability Act (Eisenbahnhaftpflichtgesetz) of 5 March 1869, *RGB* no. 27,[112] took the first decisive step towards breaching the principle of fault or at least turning away from the Civil Code's rule on the onus of proof which was highly disadvantageous for the injured party. However, the idea of liability was not extended to cover the elements included in the Liability Law (Reichshaftpflichtgesetz) of 7

June 1871. The reasons for this development, deviating from that of the German Reich, will be discussed in more detail later.

Civil Law Procedure

The inadequacy of civil law procedure was mentioned several times during debates on accident insurance legislation (see below p. 294) as the reason why the further development of liability legislation was not likely to be successful.

PART 2: PRECURSORS AND BEGINNINGS

THE 'BRUDERLADEN' (MINING ASSOCIATIONS), ESPECIALLY
SINCE THE 'BERGGESETZ' (MINING ACT) OF 1854

On account of the high accident risk in the mining industry and the frequency of occupational diseases leading to disablement so-called 'Knappschaftskassen' (miners' funds) had already been established in the Middle Ages. They gave a miner or his dependants insurance protection in case of illness, accident, disability or death of a miner.[113]

Within the area that belonged to Austria until 1918 (i.e. kingdoms and countries represented in the 'Reichsrat') miners' funds had first been legally regulated in 1301 by the 'Kuttenberger Bergordnung' (Kuttenberg Mining Regulations).[114] Further mining regulations were issued in the sixteenth, seventeenth, and eighteenth centuries. Unlike the 'Gesellenladen' (journeymen's associations), the 'Bruderladen' for miners could continue their traditional function until the middle of the nineteenth century. The system of 'Bruderladen' had numerous gaps as many mine owners had waived their establishment. Moreover, the economic situation of the 'Bruderladen' was not generally satisfactory.[115]

With the Mining Act (Allgemeine Berggesetz) of 23 May 1854, *RGB* no. 146, passed during the era of neoabsolutism (cf. above p. 272; p. 281), an attempt was made to reform completely the 'Bruderladen'. From that date onwards, the tenth main part of the Mining Act (§§210–214) as well as §103 of the implementation regulations of the Mining Act (of 25 September 1854)[116] formed the legal basis of the 'Bruderladen'. The main concern of the 1854 Mining Act regarding the 'Bruderladen' was the standardization of compulsory establishment and membership. Thus, according to §210, section 2 of the Mining Act each mine owner was obliged 'either to arrange for the independent establishment of a "Bruderlade" at his works or to join with other mine owners — with the approval of the mining authorities — for this purpose'.

Nevertheless, the Mining Act did not bring about fundamental improvements to the 'Bruderladen'. The following factors in particular proved disadvantageous:

1. The weak wording on obligatory establishment resulted in numerous delays or even in complete 'non-performance'. The Mining Act had not provided for the possibility of such an association being set up by the power of the authorities if the mine owner defaulted.[117]
2. As the 'Bruderladen' were usually only established for one mine or for several mines belonging to the same owner, the number of persons exposed to the same risks was too small to be able to provide effective help when large-scale

mining accidents occurred. Use was rarely made of the alternative provided for in the Mining Act, of establishing district 'Bruderladen', although the implementation regulations (§103, section 5) stressed that it would be ideal to establish jointly 'Bruderladen' for several mines in one district.

3. The number of miners per 'Bruderlade' was usually very low. The lack of provisions in the Mining Act for the possibility of a miner transferring from one 'Bruderlade' to another proved a grave disadvantage. If a miner changed employer (either through choice or because of dismissal) he lost all his claims on the 'Bruderlade' and thus all the contributions he had paid in. This impeded workers' freedom of movement and resulted in excessive dependence on the respective mining concern.

4. Compulsory contributions were only standardized for the employed and not for the mine owners according to the Mining Act (§211).

5. In spite of management controls by mine overseers, in accordance with the implementation regulations, the economic situation of the majority of 'Bruderladen' was alarming. The reason for the poor economic situation was primarily due to the fact that the relationship, established by statute, between contributions and benefits had not been fixed according to actuarial principles but at the discretion of those concerned. The linkage between various branches of insurance (sickness, accident, and disability insurance) which was so characteristic of the 'Bruderladen' made it even more difficult to establish the right relationship between contributions and benefits.

Thus, the first attempts to reform the 'Bruderladen'—during the liberal era (cf. above p. 272; p. 278)—aimed primarily at disentangling the traditional linkage of the individual branches of insurance and especially at giving disability insurance a completely new organizational basis.

Factory and Trade Association Insurances in Accordance with the 1859 'Gewerbeordnung' (Trade Act)

Factory Sickness Schemes

The 1859 'Gewerbeordnung' (p. 273; p. 275) provided for two types of relief fund. First, §85 of the 'Gewerbeordung' stipulated:[118]

> If special welfare provisions for the relief of workers in case of accident or illness seem necessary because of the large number of persons employed or because of the nature of the work, the employer is bound either to set up an independent relief fund of this kind at his establishment—to which workers are to contribute—or to join an already existing scheme.

This regulation had similar defects to the relevant provisions of the 'Berggesetz' (Mining Act) passed some 5 years earlier to regulate the 'Bruderladen'.[119] Like the 'Berggesetz', the 'Gewerbeordnung' avoided laying down norms for employers' compulsory contributions to factory schemes. This rule also features a mixture of insurances (accident and sickness insurance) which is unfavourable both from an economic and actuarial point of view. Moreover, there is no clear ruling on the participation of the insured in the administration of the factory schemes. Furthermore, compulsion to establish factory insurance schemes was not as strongly expressed as in the case of the 'Bruderladen' as §85 of the

'Gewerbeordnung' stipulated compulsory establishment under certain circumstances only.

Trade Association Sickness Insurances

As an alternative, or to complement the factory schemes, the 1859 'Gewerbeordnung' also provided for the establishment of sickness insurance schemes based on trade associations that either already existed or were to be set up. These associations were compulsory amalgamations of employers and employed persons; the former became members *ipso iure* when they entered the trade while the latter also automatically 'belonged' to the trade association when they took up employment (§106 'Gewerbeordnung'). The aims of such compulsory associations, some of which were based on the old guilds while others were newly founded, were defined in general terms in §114 of the 'Gewerbeordnung': 'cultivation of a communal spirit', 'maintenance and improvement of professional honour', 'promotion of common interests of members'. Then a series of concrete tasks were listed which largely concern the relations between the owner of the business and his staff and the social problems of the latter.

Of particular interest is §114, section 2, lit(e) of the 'Gewerbeordnung', as 'the provision of help for sick journeymen either by establishing sickness insurance funds or by joining already existing schemes of this kind' is expressly named among the tasks of the compulsory trade associations. The level of compulsory contributions is uniformly regulated for all trades by §124 of the 'Gewerbeordnung': journeymen were not to contribute more than 3 percent of their wage, while contributions by the owner of the business were not to exceed half of the journeymen's contributions.[120] Moreover, the journeymen were to have due influence on the administration of the schemes.

There was no more to the (very vague) provisions of the 'Gewerbeordnung' regarding trade association insurance schemes. According to §128 of the 'Gewerbeordnung' (in concurrence with §213 of the Mining Act) more exact rulings on the level of contributions, on the mode of payment, on prerequisites and scope of benefits as well as the degree of participation of journeymen in the administration of the schemes were to be left to the statutes of the associations.

The relief funds planned in the 1859 'Gewerbeordnung' were not as successful as had been hoped. In 1879, the year of the great political 'turning point', there were 860 industrial relief funds altogether, of which only 116 were trade association schemes, in the whole area 'of the kingdoms and countries represented in the "Reichsrat"'.

One of the defects of the fund system was the undefined relationship between factory and trade association schemes. Thus, it could happen that some workers had to pay contributions both to the factory scheme at their place of work and to the trade association scheme of the relevant branch of industry. Furthermore, as already mentioned, the combination of accident and sickness insurance in factory schemes proved unsatisfactory and the funds' very limited financial resources caused problems in cases of mass accidents or widespread sickness. Moreover, the regulation on uniform contributions in §124 of the 'Gewerbeordnung', which took neither the size nor the type of business into account,[121] was largely rejected. Even one of the most central items of the 'Gewerbeordnung' was extremely controversial at the beginning of the 1870s, namely the question of compulsory contributions.

Towards Reform of the 'Gewerbeordnung' in the 1870s

Although little sympathy for compulsory membership was evident among various circles in the Ministry of Justice, the four drafts of the reform of the 'Gewerbeord-nung' (1872, 1875, 1877, 1879)[122] continued to advocate compulsory subscription. The 1877 draft even aimed at the establishment of disability insurances and schemes for widows and orphans without, however, extending compulsory membership beyond the sickness insurance schemes. The 1875 and 1877 drafts, which are in my view a convincing example of the Liberals' budding socio-political commitment in the late phase of their rule, brought about a decisive change, as they provided for the possibility of associations composed of employed persons only and thus took the workers' criticism of compulsory associations with employers into account. The 'Allgemeine preussische Gewerbeordnung' (Prussian Trade Act) of 1845[124] probably acted as example for the parallel existence of compulsory trade association insurances[123] and insurance schemes solely for the employed; the Prussian Trade Act was often quoted to defend compulsory subscription in the face of extreme liberal points of view.[125]

Seen as a whole, the Liberal drafts to reform the 'Gewerbeordnung', including the 1879 and 1880 drafts, bear witness to a remarkable attempt, first to reinforce the idea of compulsory trade associations for employers and the employed, including the (sickness) insurance system connected with this, by compulsory establishment and contribution by the employer — an idea which was only vaguely standardized in the 'Gewerbeordnung'; and secondly, to integrate voluntary relief funds into the system of trade insurance schemes in order to put an end to the parallel existence of two such systems which had arisen after 1867 (cf. below).

This project — based on the Prussian-German model — had as little success as attempts, made within the framework of reform of the 'Gewerbeordnung', to establish special employer liability for accidents at work. These attempts will be discussed in greater detail in the context of the 1887 Accident Insurance Law (see below).[126]

VOLUNTARY RELIEF FUNDS (AFTER 1867)

Although the December Constitution of 1867 did not provide any participation for the working class in policy-building (see above p. 274–276),[127] art. 12 of the Basic State Law on the citizens' general rights and the 1867 'Vereinsgesetz' (Law on Associations) created a certain basis for political, social and cultural activities outside parliament.[128] A further education society for printers in Vienna ('Fort-bildungsverein für Buchdrucker in Wien')[129] had been successfully established in 1864, based on the 1852 'Vereinspatent'. Numerous workers' organizations sprang up after the 'Vereinsgesetz' was passed (15 November 1867). This development was largely due to the fact that the 1867 'Vereinsgesetz' facilitated the establishment of associations as compared with the 1852 'Vereinspatent'.

The most important organization to be founded was undoubtedly the 'Wiener Arbeiter-Bildungsverein' (Viennese Workers' Education Society)[130] which started its activities at the beginning of December 1867 after the association's existence had been confirmed in accordance with §9 of the 'Vereinsgesetz' in November 1867.[131] When this organization was set up, there was an argument between followers of the Schulze-Delitzsch idea of self-help and those who eventually won and who—like Lassalle—advocated a link between workers' self-help and state assistance. The 'Wiener Arbeiter-Bildungsverein', followed by similar foundations in numerous places in the Cisleithan half of the 'Reich', was also intended by its founders and its first members from the start to be an institution to improve workers' economic position.[132] Thus, it was perfectly logical that the committee of the 'Wiener Arbeiter-Bildungsverein' should come forward as 'organizer and founder' of a General Workers' Sickness and Disability Insurance Scheme, established as an association in compliance with the 1867 'Vereinsgesetz' and which was linked closely at an organizational level with the 'Arbeiter-Bildungsverein' by operation of its statutes (§11).

An end was made to this liberal practice by decree of the Ministry of the Interior, 18 December 1882.[133] Benevolent associations whose statutes could 'give rise to the expectation that contributions establish a right to secure benefits from the association' were no longer to be treated according to the 1867 'Vereinsgesetz' but to the 1852 'Vereinspatent' as well as the so-called 'Versicherungsregulativ' (Insurance Regulation) of 18 August 1880, *RGB* no. 10. In spite of these setbacks, several insurances, such as the afore-mentioned scheme in Vienna, expanded considerably in the 1880s with regard to numbers of members and benefits (1880, 12 070 members; total benefits, approx. 110 000 fl.: 1887, 44 256 members; total benefits, approx. 403 000 fl.).[134]

From 1876, there was also a 'Verband der Arbeiter-Kranken- und Invaliden-Unterstützungsvereine innerhalb Osterreichs' (Federation of Workers' Sickness and Disability Benevolent Associations within Austria).[135] This did not have a reserve fund for the various schemes but was only to guarantee the provision of benefits to non-resident members.

The workers' insurance schemes founded on the basis of voluntary association undoubtedly contributed significantly to workers' material security, particularly in cases of sickness or accident, until compulsory sickness and accident insurance was introduced. Politicians with insight, particularly those who had learnt from the English example, such as J. M. Baernreither,[136] endeavoured to follow the activities of the labour force and to promote state assistance. This was realized much later with the 'Hilfskassengesetz' (Law on Relief Funds) which Baernreither drafted (see below pp. 299ff).[137]

PART 3: THE BEGINNINGS OF THE BASIC WORKERS' INSURANCE LAWS

POLITICAL BACKGROUND

Composition and Political Course of the Taaffe Government(s)

After the resignation of Stremayr's Liberal government following the elections in July 1879, Duke Eduard von Taaffe was appointed Minister-President; his position as Minister of the Interior was confirmed at the same time by Emperor Franz Joseph. Taaffe's[138] achievement in connection with social legislation was primarily the creation of a political framework; he actively supported competent politicians who specialized in social policy. Of these, Emil Steinbach was a dominant figure in the sphere of social insurance.

As far as the creation of a specific political framework is concerned, it is remarkable that Taaffe—who had already been Minister-President of a Liberal

Government first of all wanted to form a government in 1879 entirely of members of the 'Verfassungspartei' (Constitutional Party). However, the party rejected this.[139] In this situation Taaffe was compelled to turn to the Czechs, who had kept away from the 'Reichsrat' so far, the Poles and the Conservative/Federal groups (Hohenwart Club, *inter alia*) to obtain a majority.

In so doing, Taaffe took the grave step of including Alois Pražák, a (moderate) Old Czech, in the government, first as Minister without Portfolio, then from 1881 to 1887 as Head of the Ministry of Justice and then until 1892, as Minister without Portfolio.[140] Pražák had a key role in Taaffe's government, both with regard to general policies and to social insurance legislation. Pražák's importance in the history of social insurance legislation is explained by the fact that he was head of the Ministry of Justice, at a crucial time.

After the reshuffle in January 1881 Taaffe's 'coalition cabinet' became entirely 'right wing', i.e. composed of Conservative/Federal groups in the 'Reichsrat'. Thus, the Iron Ring's political autocracy was broken (see above pp. 278 and 279) and the decisive political framework for Austrian social insurance legislation in the 1880s was created.

If one considers the changed conditions in which Taaffe's cabinet took office, the role that social policy would play within the framework of Taaffe's overall political concept soon becomes clear. During the liberal era, both the ideas of centralistically oriented liberalism and German dominance — which was artificial because of the Czech policy of non-cooperation — in the 'Reichsrat' and in governments functioned to unify and govern elements in the Cisleithan half of the Empire. However, as early as 1879, Taaffe's regime professed its faith in the constitutional principle of the equality of all nationalities (art. 19 of the Basic State Law on the citizens' rights). Now a new 'clamp' had to be found for the centrifugal powers with their renewed strength which would be capable of preventing the monarchy from breaking up. It was clear to all members of Taaffe's government that the only way to hold the monarchy together was to master the 'social question' jointly with far-reaching socio-political legislation. Moreover, the belief in social policy was — in the long term — the only item which the various elements in Taaffe's government had in common, apart from their antipathy towards liberalism which held them together (cf. above).

The Emperor's Speech, 1879

It was not by chance that, in the Emperor's speech at the beginning of the Taaffe era, on 8 October 1879, in which the Emperor was most happy — by way of introduction — to welcome the Czechs again in the 'Abgeordnetenhaus' of the 'Reichsrat', comprehensive socio-political measures were announced which were generally designed to improve the lot of the 'man in the street' and to ensure support for the government among the broad mass of the population. Moreover, the Emperor's speech of 1879 reveals yet another political factor of significance for the creation of Austrian social legislation in the 1880s: namely Taaffe's close relationship with the monarch.[142]

It was now of decisive importance for Austrian social legislation that the new political framework, which Taaffe's government had created, should enable dynamic forces in the field of social policy, particularly the Christian social reformers (see above p. 280 for their theses), gradually to put their ideas on social reform into practice. Apart from Prince Alois Liechtenstein mentioned earlier,

Duke Egbert Belcredi[143] and Leon Ritter von Biliński deserve mention, at this point; as leading right-wing social politicians they were assigned the role of expert advisers in the appropriate board of the 'Reichsrat'.

Emil Steinbach's Role

In addition to those persons who were directly involved in the political debates on draft laws concerning accident and sickness insurance, special mention must already be made of a man whose influence was of the utmost importance: Emil Steinbach. His biographer (Alexander Spitzmüller)[144] writes:

> Once called to the Ministry of Justice by Glaser in 1874, he soon became the heart and soul of the legislative department and quickly passed through all stages of the hierarchy. In 1888 he was appointed head of the department. Recent history of the Austrian civil service cannot show a single case of an administrative officer developing such all-embracing activity and having such far-reaching influence as Steinbach in the Ministry of Justice.

Records prove that this is true. In spite of this comparatively subordinate position as departmental head or ministerial adviser, Steinbach was entrusted — and practically he alone — with the elaboration of drafts for workers' accident and workers' sickness insurance law. Moreover, he usually presented these personally in the Council of Ministers and sometimes even in the 'Abgeordnetenhaus' of the 'Reichsrat' as government representative.[145]

It is all the more important to point to Steinbach's ideas and socio-political aims. These certainly are linked with the ideas of the Christian social reformers but also have very individual features with regard to certain central points. These features are connected with Steinbach's high opinion of the bureaucratic element in both state and society and have influenced in no uncertain fashion the shaping of Austrian social insurance legislation.

SOCIO-POLITICAL ACTIVITIES BEFORE THE WORKERS' INSURANCE LAWS

The 'Linz Programme', 1882

Even before the Taaffe Government presented its first socio-political government bills in the 'Reichsrat', opposition groups took the initiative by drawing up programmes of concrete social reforms. One of these was the so-called 'Linz Programme'[146] of the German Nationals, published on 1 September 1882. It was drawn up by Georg Schönerer, Engelbert Pernerstorfer, Heinrich Friedjung and Viktor Adler[147] who later became leader of the Social Democratic Party.

The socio-political demands of this programme, which are of greatest interest here, are rightly ascribed to Viktor Adler. Section 8 of the 'Linz Programme' demands the nationalization of socially important industrial concerns and item 23 demands specifically 'the nationalization of insurances at the same time as the introduction of an old age and accident insurance'.

The Liberals' Proposal, 1882

On 5 December 1882, the Liberals ('Vereinigte deutsche Linke' — the United German Left), led by Johann von Chlumecky tabled a motion[148] according to which a thirty-six-strong board was to be formed by the 'Abgeordnetenhaus' to discuss socio-political questions. In this way, Liberals wanted to oppose the Taaffe Government's decision to postpone settling the social and legal position of the workers until a later phase of reform of the 'Gewerbeordnung'. Of course, such a venture was merely considered a 'political manoeuvre' by members of parliament who were politically close to the government.[149] The thirty-six-strong board was to deliberate on the basis of 'rules and directives' which were elaborated in detail in the proposal. The following measures were proposed, *inter alia*, for 'unskilled workers':

> the insurance of unskilled workers against sickness and other risks is to be effected (a) by introducing compulsory sickness insurance to support the sick for a fixed period; for this purpose, sickness insurance schemes, trade associations, factory and mining insurances or registered relief funds are to be established and financed by appropriate contributions by employers and employed; associations of such schemes are to be organized in order to guarantee the individual scheme's ability to provide benefits and to start other types of assistance; schemes are to be self-administered by members and under state supervision; (b) by introducing accident insurance on a cooperative basis whose scope goes beyond that of the liability principle in order to compensate for incapacity to work, caused by an accident, either for a longish period or for life, or to provide for surviving dependants, without collecting dues from the insured; schemes are to be self-administered by the associations concerned and under state supervision.

The Liberals were accordingly the first to advocate the introduction of compulsory sickness and accident insurance in the 'Reichsrat' and thus publicly admitted the inadequacy of previous attempts to overcome the problem of accidents at work by introducing general liability for employers.[150]

Amendments to the 'Gewerbeordnung' in 1883 and 1885

Social legislation between 1883 and 1885, which is now to be outlined briefly, was predominantly concerned with questions of labour protection.[151] Already on 15 December 1882 the government submitted a draft law on 'the employment of young workers and women, then on the number of working hours per day and a Sunday rest in the mining industry'; however, this bill did not become law until 21 June 1884.[152] The Law on the Appointment of Factory Inspectors had already been passed on 17 June 1883, *RGB* no. 117.[153]

The (second) amendment to the 'Gewerbeordnung' of 8 March 1885, *RGB* no. 22, was temporarily the highpoint of legislation on workers' protection. Modelled on legislation in England and Switzerland, which at that time had the highest socio-political standards, it was also based on the results of an enquiry which had been made in 1883 in consultation with representatives of the labour force.[154]

With the provisions of the second amendment to the 'Gewerbeordnung' Austrian legislation on workers' protection attained a considerable level, even when compared with the state of legislation in the German Reich at that time. Unlike Bismarck, Austrian social reformers—including those in the opposition—considered workers' protection a necessary element, indeed one of priority, of social policy (see above p. 280). This probably explains why the government did not give its full attention at first to the problems of precaution against social risks and thus to social insurance.

Efforts to reform trade association insurance schemes, made within the framework of the first amendment to the 'Gewerbeordnung' of 15 March 1883,

RGB no. 39 (§§121–121(h)), were crowned with legislative success although the government itself considered the reform merely as a temporary solution until the Law on Sickness Insurance was passed.[155] The provisions of the 1883 amendment to the 'Gewerbeordnung' on association sickness insurances continued largely along the lines of reform which had begun in the Liberal era — despite some changes of detail.

However, with its bill on accident insurance of the same year (4 December 1883)[153] the government took a new course; it proposed the introduction of statutory compulsory insurance modelled on Bismarck's government bills of 1881[157] and 1882.[158] Before examining the background to this vital decision, made in the bosom of the Taaffe Government at the end of 1882, and the preliminary work on the 1883 bill, a brief discussion of Bismarck's legislation on workers' insurance is needed.[159]

THE PIONEERING LEGISLATION ON WORKERS' INSURANCE
OF THE GERMAN REICH

The pioneering legislation on workers' insurance of the German Reich is inseparably linked with the political concept of the Chancellor of the German Reich from 1871–1890, Prince Otto von Bismarck.[160] Bismarck's main aim — at a time when the labour force was not yet politically organized — was to reintegrate workers into the state and thus to eliminate the process of alienation which had started because of the labour force's poor economic and social position. Bismarck was opposed to political repression of social democracy to which he himself attributed only limited importance.[161] The state's advocacy of safeguarding the material existence of the labour force seemed the only possibility to Bismarck of improving relations between the state and the workers both fundamentally and permanently.

Bismarck did not have the necessary political latitude to realize his reforms until he broke with the Liberals in 1878. In the speech from the throne of 12 February 1879,[162] following remarks on the Anti-Socialist Law, indication is made of possible socio-political bills. The speech from the throne of 15 February 1881[163] is even clearer and reads as follows: 'The cure (of social ills) is not exclusively to be found in the repression of Socialist excesses but also by positively promoting the well-being of the workers. In this respect welfare for persons unable to earn a living is of primary importance. . . .'

Then a plan to draft a law 'on accident insurance for workers' was announced; this was done on 8 March 1881.[164] This first draft of an accident insurance law is already marked by the typical features of Bismarck's social insurance legislation. (a) Statutory compulsory membership and contributions (§§1 and 13 of the draft.) Their standardization had two aims: complete integration of all persons to be insured — an actuarial feature — in the interest of the insurance's ability to provide benefits and realization of the idea of social cooperation between employers and the employed. In 1880 Bismarck stopped all further attempts at standardizing general liability for employers (in the form of absolute liability)[165] mainly because all rulings on civil law damages connected with accidents at work involved protracted lawsuits full of bitterness which threatened to worsen the social climate. Accident insurance with statutory membership and compulsory contributions (by both parties) promised social cooperation instead of the earlier confrontation. (b) State subsidy to the social insurances. Bismarck had the idea of a state subsidy to help towards financing social insurance right from the start. There were two reasons for this: first, Bismarck wanted to prevent overburdening national industries (particularly with regard to competitiveness with foreign firms); secondly, he wanted to give the insured (the workers) the feeling that the state had an active interest in their social problems. The first draft for an accident insurance law failed to realize this idea since state subsidy (amounting to one-third of the total contribution) was only provided for the lowest paid workers (§13, fig. 1).[166] (c) As far as the organization of insurance institutions was concerned, the first draft for an accident insurance law provided for a 'Reichsversicherungsanstalt' (Insurance Institution) which was to be established in line with centralistic and bureaucratic ideas. The possibility of including structural elements of cooperative associations is only mentioned marginally in the draft's 'substantiation' and is not stressed. Bismarck did not make compulsory trade associations, to which he attached far-reaching political expectations, an essential structural element of social insurance until after the failure of the first draft.

In clear contrast to the Austrian Liberals who had a positive attitude to social insurance on principle, the (liberal) Progress Party (Eugen Richter) in particular keenly fought against the first draft of the German Accident Insurance Law. However, this opposition was not responsible for the failure of the first bill but rather the deletion of the state subsidy at the Centre's instigation;[167] this was unacceptable to Bismarck.

After the reasons for establishing social insurance had been made clear to the deputies of the German 'Reichstag' upon Bismarck's initiative in the 'First Imperial Message on the Social Question'[168] of 17 November 1881 — the speech from the throne read on 27 April 1882[169] — the 'Second Imperial Message on the Social Question' read on 14 April 1883[170] and the speech from the throne of 22 November 1888[171] all had a similar purpose. The 'Draft of a Law on Sickness Insurance for Workers'[172] was presented in the 'Reichstag' by the government on 29 April 1882. According to this, compulsory insurance and contributions were also to apply to sickness insurance. The 'Ortskrankenkassen' (local sickness insurances) were to be the underwriters. Voluntary relief funds were to continue to exist; their members were exempted from compulsory subscription to local sickness insurances. Sickness insurance was to be completely financed by contributions of employers (one-third) and employed (two-thirds). As no provision was made for state subsidies to sickness insurance, the Sickness Insurance Law was the first of Bismarck's social insurance laws to gain a parliamentary majority. On 31 May 1883 the bill was adopted with a large majority (216 votes) against the votes of the Progress Party and of the Social Democrats (totalling 99) and made law on 15 June 1883. Already on 28 May 1885[173] the first Extension Law (Ausdegnungsgesetz) was passed; this subjected all people employed in the transport trade to compulsory insurance. The law of 5 May 1886[174] was even more important for, by adding certain modifications, it integrated farm and forestry workers into the sickness and accident insurance system.

The second draft[175] of an accident insurance law, submitted to the 'Reichstag' on 8 May 1882, proposed, as already mentioned, a completely new basis for organizing accident insurance. Instead of the 'Reichsversicherungsanstalt' planned in the first draft, trade associations were to be responsible for the insurance, under the supervision of 'higher administrative authorities' of the federal

states. However, as the second draft maintained the idea of compulsory insurance and Reich subsidies it once again did not gain a parliamentary majority.
The third draft,[176] submitted to the 'Reichstag' on 6 March 1884, maintained
compulsory insurance as well as the trade associations' own administration of
social insurance. The establishment of workers' committees (§§41–45) was new to
the draft. The most important variation from the first drafts was the renunciation
of the state subsidy; Bismarck had to give in on this point. In its place, a state
guarantee was given for the trade associations' efficiency and solvency.[177]
Without having to make fundamental cuts, the third draft of the Accident Insurance Law was approved by a clear majority on 27 June 1884, again opposed
by the Liberals and the Social Democrats, and came into force on 6 July 1884,
German RGB p. 69.

Old age and disability insurance completed Bismarck's social insurance legislation. On 22 November 1888 the bill which had already been adopted by the
Federal Council was submitted to the 'Reichstag'.[178] It proposed that all wage
earners in trade, industry and agriculture should receive an old age pension upon
completion of their 70th year of age. From an organizational point of view the
draft chose the compromise solution of 'Landesversicherungsanstalten' (insurances by the individual states); it provided for financing by equal contributions by employers, the employed and the state (i.e. one-third each); thus, for the
first time, Bismarck's demand for a standardized state subsidy was taken into account. On 24 May 1889 the Law on Old Age and Disability Insurance was
passed in the 'Reichstag' with a small majority. The Progress Party, the Social
Democrats and the majority of the Centre Party voted against it. On 22 June
1889, German *RGB* p. 97, the Law on Old Age and Disability Insurance came
into force.[179]

THE WORKERS' ACCIDENT INSURANCE LAW OF 28 DECEMBER 1887

Steinbach's Detailed Exposition

Plans for an accident insurance law were first mentioned in a meeting of the
Council of Ministers of 23 November 1882[180] when Pražák, Head of the
Ministry of Justice, announced he would be submitting a relevant draft to the
Council of Ministers shortly. In the Council of Ministers of 4 December 1882,[181]
a detailed exposition 'On the Question of Liability', drawn up by the departmen-
tal councillor in the Ministry of Justice, Emil Steinbach (cf. above p. 290) was
discussed under item III of the agenda ('Aspects to Consider for a Draft on
Liability in Cases of Accident in Industrial Undertakings').

To support his case, Steinbach quoted extensive sections of the substantiation
of the first German draft which showed how difficult it was for the injured worker
to provide proof of fault, how much bitterness lawsuits caused, and to what extent private insurances forced employers to take legal action against their
employed.[182] Criticism was also voiced that the 'unrestrictedness of judicial
discretion' regarding damages frequently resulted in unjustifiably high claims so
that the few who succeeded in proving fault stood out in even stronger contrast to
the majority of the injured parties.

If, Steinbach continued, one does not consider the confrontation of interests
but rather the harmonious cooperation of all parties concerned to be the purpose
of the desired statutory ruling, then such a purpose can 'only be achieved by the

participation of all concerned and by a general accident insurance law as had also been the aim of German legislation since 1881'.[183]

Debates of the Council of Ministers

According to the minutes of the Council of Ministers of 4 December 1882, Steinbach had the opportunity to present his detailed exposition 'On the Question of Liability' as well as the first draft, which he obviously elaborated himself, in the Council of Ministers. The ensuing discussion showed that the entire Council of Ministers with one exception (Falkenhayn, Minister of Agriculture) accepted the principle of compulsory insurance. There were, however, differences in details of procedure.

Falkenhayn held the view that accident insurance was not yet 'mature' for statutory regulation as the 'masses' had not yet shown any interest in it; the government ought to be 'pushed' rather than to take the initiative itself, otherwise it looked as if the workers had been made to wait for something to which they had been entitled for a long time. If reforms were wanted, these were to 'include disability pensions'. And as far as the system was concerned, he proposed using the existing 'Bruderladen' as a pattern and not the 'German legislator'.

The Council of Ministers then passed the following resolution:[184] 'The Council of Ministers hereby approves the principles of the Ministry of Justice and at the same time resolves that a draft bill is to be elaborated by the Ministries of Justice, Interior, Agriculture and Trade.' Bearing the objections and suggestions of the Council of Ministers in mind, Steinbach made amendments to his handwritten draft which were already taken into account in the first printed draft sent by Pražák to Taaffe on 14 January 1883. As a comparison — made later — will clearly show, this first draft was highly reminiscent of the second German draft and comprised forty-eight paragraphs.[185]

Using the first draft as a basis for discussion, a commission, composed of representatives of the Ministries of Justice, Agriculture, Trade and Finance, chaired by Kubin, head of department, debated the matter from 22 January 1883 for several days. Here again, Steinbach had the role of expert adviser. The discussions resulted in the second draft,[186] consisting of sixty paragraphs, which Pražák passed on to Taaffe on 19 February 1883. The major difference between the second and the first draft was that the mines were included again in the second draft, at the instigation of the majority of the commission. Steinbach had eliminated the mines from §1 of the first draft because of Falkenhayn's misgivings and in §2 had expressly exempted them from the impact of the law.

With regard to the benefits it is remarkable that the first draft (§6) not only mentioned a pension but also 'the costs of treatment'; however, these were not mentioned in the second draft (§7). Moreover, the question of the beginning of a claim to a pension was left open in the first draft, whereas in the second draft (§7, section 1) this was settled in accordance with the 5-week period which was later to become so controversial. In the case of complete incapacity to work the first draft (§6) provided for 66.6 percent of the previous wage and the second draft (§7) for 70 percent as pension.

Differing fundamentally from the second German draft, the first draft, like all later drafts, was based on the territorial system. Basically, an insurance institution was to be set up for each area with its own Chamber of Trade and Commerce at the location of these chambers. Thus, the principle of trade associations described in the second German draft was clearly rejected.

The accident insurance institutions were conceived from the start as self-administrative bodies; the institutions' executive boards were to consist of equal numbers of employers, employed and persons appointed by the Minister of the Interior (first draft, §9; second draft, §13). The idea of grouping industries together with similar accident risks was nevertheless taken into account, almost verbatim from the second German draft, only, however, to assess the level of contributions. Like the second German draft, the first two Austrian drafts assume the average level for the most dangerous industries to be 100 percent, that of others with lower percentages. Relying further on German legislation, the results of accident statistics should be applied, although these did not exist in Austria at that time.

With regard to contributions, the first draft (§13) provided for a graded fraction of income (depending on its level) between a minimum of 5 percent and a maximum of 40 percent. The second draft (§19), however, provided for only two levels (daily wage of over 1 fl., 25 percent; of less than 1 fl., 0 percent). No provisions were made for a state subsidy in either of these two early drafts nor in a later one.

The insured person's claim to damages towards a third party was 'to be transferred to the insurance institution in so far as the liability of the latter to provide damages is founded in law' (legal transfer of §48 of the first German draft; second German draft §118; Austrian draft §38; second Austrian draft §47).

If the insured (injured party) had caused the accident deliberately he was not entitled to claim damages from the insurance; the claims of surviving dependants, however, were not affected (first German draft §35; second German draft §82; first Austrian draft §6, last section; §7, penultimate section; second Austrian draft §7, last section; §9, last section).

In order to pursue a claim for damages which was not recognized by the insurance, §32 of the first Austrian draft provided for the establishment of arbitration courts at the insurance institutions' headquarters. Appeals could not be made against their verdicts. This contrasted with the second German draft which provided to a limited extent (in §91) the possibility of having recourse to ordinary legal action.

As already mentioned, provision was made in the Austrian drafts for a one-third representation of the insured on the executive boards of the insurances. Thus, overall the insured in Austria were in a more favourable position than their German counterparts. According to the German drafts, the insured only had a say in determining damages and in passing regulations on accident prevention (second German draft §§85–91; 73, no. 2).

Like the provisions of the second German draft, the supervision of the insurance institutions, according to the two Austrian drafts, was to be entrusted to political authorities headed by the Minister of the Interior (first draft, §39; second draft, §48; second German draft, §§39–41). One of the most important achievements of the third German draft, namely the 'Reichsversicherungsamt' (insurance office) designed primarily as a supervisory body and as an appeal court (third German draft §§87–91), was unknown to the second German draft and thus to the first two Austrian drafts. Despite numerous later proposals there is still no central court of appeal in the field of Austrian social insurance jurisdiction.

After this digression on the most important provisions of the first two Austrian drafts which anticipated the subsequent law to a considerable extent, let us return again to the history of the origin of the Accident Insurance Law. During the session of the Council of Ministers of 25 March 1883[187] there was a 'Special Debate on the Draft of an Accident Insurance Law for Workers and on the Introduction of Such a Bill', based on the second draft. Taaffe opened the debate remarking that the Minister of Agriculture had moved for the exclusion of miners from the law on accident insurance. Steinbach's reply was that this question had been 'considered doubtful . . . right from the start' in the mixed commission but that the majority had been for the inclusion of mines and saltworks 'as the "Bruderladen" do not provide such extensive insurance coverage as is envisaged by the present draft. Furthermore, in view of the German model and its propositions, it was thought questionable to exclude the most dangerous industries.' Pražák and Taaffe also spoke in favour of their inclusion; the majority, however, decided on the exclusion of mines and saltworks, mainly for tactical reasons, once Falkenhayn had declared 'that he had to insist on his demand regarding the mines and that the matter was a subject for the cabinet as far as he was concerned'. Then Taaffe also joined the majority with the remark, however, that 'he greatly regretted this particular exclusion', whereupon the necessary modifications were made to §§1 and 2 of the draft.

The First Government Bill; Deliberations in the Trade Board of the 'Abgeordnetenhaus'

As Minister Pražák was entrusted by the Council of Ministers with the introduction of the bill (third draft) in the 'Reichsrat' it fell to Steinbach to draw up the speech to the monarch. This draft[188] provides insight into Steinbach's attitude to basic questions of social insurance as well as to the German models. Steinbach's observations were later largely incorporated in a slightly modified and refined form in the 'Special Part' of the 'Explanatory Remarks' on the government bill.

As far as the range of people subject to compulsory insurance was concerned, Steinbach made it quite clear that he preferred the attitude expressed in the German drafts — i.e., the inclusion of miners as a matter of principle — and that he did not consider the opposition of the Minister of Agriculture justified. At the same time he defended the exclusion of workers in small-scale trades as a matter of principle, thus following the first two German drafts. There were three reasons for this: (a) because of the low level of risks at work compared with industry; (b) because of the technical difficulties of implementation, particularly as there was no statistical documentation available; and (c) as the inclusion of workers in small-scale trades would be linked with too great a financial burden on these trades. Steinbach also rejected the inclusion of farm workers for similar reasons; an additional argument was the ascertainable frequency of casual labour in this sector. Steinbach made out a case for the non-inclusion of persons employed with the railways and in shipping, mainly because of the employers' liability — independent of fault — introduced by law in 1869 (see above p. 276, *inter alia*).

Pražák could not fulfil the mandate of introducing the bill at first as the Kaiser (Franz Joseph I) refused to give his authority as required.[189] The assumption that Minister-President Taaffe urged the monarch, to whom he was close personally,[190] to act in this way may be well founded but cannot be proved. At all events, on 19 October 1883[191] the Council of Ministers once again had to debate the 'question of inclusion of miners and saltworkers in a draft of a law on accident insurance for workers'.

A reference (by Steinbach?) to a 'regulation of the German Law on Sickness Insurance for Workers' (passed on 15 June 1883), according to which persons insured with the miners' schemes (knappschaftskassen) were not subject to compulsory sickness insurance if such schemes provided adequate benefits (§74), finally saved the day and provided a solution. The assurance that an analogous regulation would be included in the Austrian Accident Insurance Law finally persuaded Falkenhayn to give in. On the following day the Council of Ministers adopted the draft (fourth draft) modified by Steinbach in three items in particular; inclusion of miners[192] and regulation of relations of the 'Bruderladen' with the accident insurance institutions; lowering of the maximum income which prevailed for compulsory insurance; lowering of the pension level in cases of complete incapacity to work from 70 percent to 60 percent.

Pražák once again requested his imperial majesty's permission to introduce the draft as a government bill and this was finally granted on 10 November 1883. On 7 December 1883[193] this first government bill[194] for the Accident Insurance Law was introduced in the 'Abgeordnetenhaus' and, after a first confrontation between Neuwirth, a Liberal member of parliament, and Steinbach, as government representative, during the first reading on 7 December 1883,[195] it was assigned to the Trade Board (chairman: Franz von Zallinger-Stillendorf; rapporteur: Prince Alois Liechtenstein). This board did not present its report until 24 February 1885[196] as the end of the parliamentary session intervened.

The Trade Board agreed (by a majority) with the government bill in all matters of principle and expressly welcomed the fact that the government 'was not letting itself be diverted by events in the German Reich[197] where accident insurance was to be built up [sic!] on a trade association basis'.

The Liberal minority of the Trade Board also presented a report, drawn up by Josef Neuwirth, on 24 February 1885. This report surpasses the 'majority report' in scope and also partly in thoroughness. More important than formal superiority, however, was the fact that Austrian Liberals had already openly and unequivocally advocated the idea of compulsory insurance with autonomous administration — under state supervision — for the institutions (cf. above p. 267) at the end of 1882, in contrast to the destructive campaign of the Progress Party in the German 'Reichstag'. Furthermore, Austrian Liberals confirmed their point of view and understandably even agreed with the rejection of state subsidies without any reservations. However, they did criticize dealing with accident insurance before sickness insurance as this entailed a special burden for the employer during the qualifying period.[199]

The minority also criticized what they considered to be too limited a range of persons subject to compulsory insurance. Referring to the statistics submitted to the German 'Reichstag', the exclusion of agricultural and forestry workers who did not work in machine-operated concerns was especially criticized. Moreover, the opinion was voiced that a law that only included about 1 million out of a total of 7 million workers in the Cisleithan half of the Reich in the insurance could not contribute to 'social reconciliation'. Suspicion was also clearly voiced that matter-of-fact criteria for determining the range of insured persons were of far-less decisive importance than the political wish to burden large-scale industry disproportionately compared with (small-scale) trades and the farmers.[200]

As far as the organization of the insurances was concerned, the minority preferred the model of trade associations as insurance institutions which had been accepted in Germany since the second draft for the Accident Insurance Law (cf. above p. 296). This may have been due to the Liberals' preference for the idea of cooperatives and to their dislike of federalistic tendencies such as were supported by the majority of the board. The minority group thought that optional establishment of trade associations, as envisaged by the majority, would be ineffective. As the parliamentary session came to an end, the draft of the Accident Insurance Law could not be debated in the Plenum.

Opinions Voiced by Economic Circles

In the period that followed, the draft became the subject of detailed debate in economic circles. Steinbach was informed of the results, partly by the Ministry of the Interior and partly by the Ministry of Trade. Steinbach also kept receiving reports through official channels on the progress of German social legislation. He also had comprehensive private sources of information.

Reorganization of the 'Reichsrat'; J.M. Baernreither

The newly convened 'Reichsrat' (22 September 1885) was characterized by a further power shift away from the Constitutional Party (Verfassungspartei) towards the right.[201] In the 'Herrenhaus' (upper house) the nomination of several peers led to the further strength of the right wing,[202] and in the 'Abgeordnetenhaus', the 'Fünfguldenmänner' (people who only have five guilders to tax were granted both an active and passive franchise for the first time.[203] Many prominent members of the liberal 'Verfassungspartei' had to leave parliament. At the beginning of this (tenth) 'Reichsrat' session, however, a Liberal delegate entered parliament who was not only soon to become the leading politician on social issues in his party but of the entire closing phase of the Habsburg monarchy: Joseph Maria Baernreither.[204]

Baernreither was born in Prague in 1845. After studying law and beginning his career as a judge, he was appointed district court assistant in 1874 in Reichenberg where he became acquainted with the living and working conditions of the German-Bohemian textile workers. In 1875 Baernreither was nominated to a post in the Viennese Ministry of Justice to work in the sphere of civil law proceedings. There he worked closely with Emil Steinbach.[205] In 1878, Baernreither was elected as member of the large estate owners' 'Kurie' (curia) into the Bohemian Diet (Landtag) and, in 1885, as representative of the large estate owners—who were faithful to the constitution—into the 'Abgeordnetenhaus' of the 'Reichsrat'.[206]

From 1880 onwards Baernreither studied the economic and social developments in England intensely. He was given many stimuli, largely by the German 'academic socialist', Lujo Brentano, as well as by the English Christian social politician, John Malcolm Ludlow.[207] Following Brentano's line of thought, Baernreither tried to show the reasons for the relatively minor response which Marxist doctrines had found in England at that time.[208] In his comprehensive paper on 'the English Workers' Societies and their Law', Tübingen 1886, Baernreither outlined the substance and development of English friendly societies, the cooperative voluntary workers' associations whose aim was practical self-help, particularly in the insurance sector. Baernreither attributed the success of the friendly societies especially to their voluntary and cooperative aspects.[209]

Obviously, experiences in England triggered off Baernreither's later attempts to provide Austrian relief funds with an up-to-date legal basis. However, as the debates on the Accident Insurance Law show, Baernreither was realistic enough to realize that voluntary insurance schemes in Austria could only be an integrated part of the social insurance system but could not alone provide an alternative for insuring risks.[210]

The Second Government Bill and Its Parliamentary Treatment

In the speech from the throne of 26 September 1885[211] planned social insurance legislation was only briefly mentioned: 'I hope that My government's bills on the insurance of the many workers against accidents and illnesses and that the regulation of conditions of the "Bruderladen" will meet with your approval.'

From an accident insurance point of view, the indication of a plan to reform the 'Bruderladen' was remarkable. Thus, the inclusion of miners in general accident insurance, so fraught with difficulties, seemed to have become superfluous.

At the end of November 1885[212] inter-ministerial discussions on the recent draft for the Accident Insurance Law took place in the Ministry of the Interior. On 19 and 21 January 1886[213] the Council of Ministers deliberated on the introduction of bill; shortly afterwards His imperial majesty's permission was requested and granted on 26 January 1886.

On 4 February the draft of the Accident Insurance Law (at the same time as the Sickness Insurance Law: see below p. 302) was introduced in the 'Abgeordnetenhaus'[214] and then passed on to the Trade Board for consideration. This time the majority of the board made only technical amendments. The minority, to which Baernreither belonged, largely repeated the objection it had raised in its report the year before; only the motion to prolong the qualifying period was dropped; otherwise a demand was made for the replacement of territorial organization with trade associations and the abolition of the employed person's contribution (against Baernreither's special vote). Moreover, a proposal for a resolution demanded the extension of accident insurance to cover workers in trade, agriculture and forestry who had been excluded so far.[215] It must first be stressed that when the general debate[216] of the 'Abgeordnetenhaus' opened on 20 May 1886, all the delegates agreed in principle on the central question, namely the necessity of accident insurance for workers. Unlike in the German 'Reichstag', Liberal groups did not oppose the basic idea of social insurance; even the autonomous administration of the insurance institutions was universally accepted. Moreover, all groups basically approved of extending compulsory insurance to other sectors (sickness, old age and disability insurance) but there were differences of opinion about timing.

Differences of opinion were far more deep-seated on the extension of compulsory insurance beyond the narrow circle of industrial workers. Taaffe's government and those social politicians who were close to it, Alois Liechtenstein and Emil Steinbach, were indeed fully aware that the circle of people subject to compulsory insurance would soon have to be extended. Nevertheless, it would be incorrect to believe that the basic limitation to industrial workers was merely an expedient solution, thoughtlessly taken over from the German system to avoid difficulties. Indeed there were ideological reasons for social insurance legislation to begin in industrial concerns: the Christian social reformers were utterly convinced that the misery among the workers and the threats to the trades of the middle class were ultimately due to the power and destructive influence of the high finance concentrated in industry.[217] Thus, from their point of view, reform had to start here not only for practical reasons but for the sake of social justice.

For equally understandable reasons, the Liberal opposition aimed at demonstrating the limitation of insurance to industrial workers as being adverse and even 'unjust'. It is particularly clear from the speech of the Liberal leader, Ernst von Plener,[218] that the Liberals' aim to extend compulsory insurance to all workers in trades, agriculture and forestry was ultimately tantamount to defending industrial progress in the face of small-scale industrial and agricultural counter-currents.

Based (presumably) on his experiences in England, Baernreither also defended the level premium system (Kapitaldeckungsverfahren) chosen by the government and spoke against the German allocation procedure (Umlageverfahren) supported by the minority of the Trade Board.[219] Heinrich Prade[220] also distinguished himself in the course of the general debate. On the one hand, he moved for the introduction of a bill on disability, widows' and orphans' pensions by the government and, on the other hand, he criticized the fact that the working class was not represented in parliament and thus could not participate in debates on accident insurance legislation.

In a special debate the Liberals again demanded the introduction of trade associations and the deletion of the workers' contribution, without success. On 5 June 1886 the bill was finally accepted at the third reading and passed to the 'Herrenhaus'.

The latter made some remarkable amendments of detail:[221] widowers incapable of working were included in the circle of persons entitled to claim; the previous reduction of claims by surviving dependants of a suicide was abolished; the possibility of the injured party making a claim against his employer, even in cases of gross negligence, was granted, and finally compulsory contribution was restricted to employed persons who earned more than 1 guilder per day. Thus, particularly workers in agriculture and forestry[222] (in so far as they counted among those who had to pay compulsory contributions at all) and less-well-paid workers in the textile industry[223] were freed from having to pay dues. The 'Abgeordnetenhaus' adopted all these amendments with exception of the last two,[224] whereupon the 'Herrenhaus'[225] was conciliatory and supported the decision of the 'Abgeordnetenhaus'.

As the decisions of both houses of the 'Reichsrat' tallied, his imperial majesty's sanction could be given to the bill on 28 December 1887.[226] The 'Law on Accident Insurance for Workers', published as RGB no. 1 of 1888, came into force 3 months later in accordance with §63, section 1. The Minister of the Interior[227] arranged for accident insurance to become effective on 1 November 1889 in accordance with §63, section 2.

In the period that followed, a total of eleven ministerial decrees[228] were issued on the implementation of the law. Three of these deserve mention: the ministerial decree of 22 January 1889, RGB no. 11, on the definition of districts and the determination of the headquarters for the insurance institutions; the ministerial decree of 24 January 1889, RGB no. 13, in which a model statute for accident insurance institutions was published, and the ministerial decree of 22 May 1889, RGB no. 76, on determining the percentages of classes of risk and on dividing industries subject to compulsory accident insurance into risk categories.[230]

The Attitude of Social Democratic Workers

As far as the attitude of the Social Democratic workers to the development of accident insurance legislation was concerned, it is important to repeat that the Social Democrats were not represented in parliament and were not even in a position to present a uniform party point of view outside parliament as the party was not united until the Hainfeld party conference in 1889.[231] Nevertheless, opinions existed which can be said to be representative of a majority of the Social Democratic labour force, particularly as these views were published in a weekly called *Gleichheit* which had been founded by Viktor Adler at the end of 1886 and is said to have acted as the mouthpiece of the unification movement.[232] Opinions were expressed in the form of a resolution passed at an association meeting of the 'Arbeiter-Kranken- und Invaliden-Unterstützungs-Vereine Österreichs' (Austrian Workers' Sickness and Disability Assistance Societies)[233] (cf. above p. 288) which took place in Linz on 13 and 14 June 1886, i.e. shortly after the special debate of the 'Abgeordnetenhaus'.

Neither this resolution nor the editorial comments of the *Gleichheit* expressed fundamental rejection of the idea of compulsory insurance.[234] Indeed, the number of people subject to compulsory insurance was generally considered too limited. The fact that particularly dangerous work (covered by German accident insurance legislation), such as roofing, stonemasonry and well building, as well as work in agriculture and forestry, were not subject to compulsory insurance was criticized in particular. As in the report of the minority of the Trade Board, the protest was voiced that only about one million out of a total of some 7 million workers were covered by the law.

As already mentioned, there was probably no central court of appeal in Austria similar to the German 'Reichsversicherungsamt' as Austrian law was based genetically on the second rather than on the third German draft.[235] Unfortunately, the danger of a lack of uniform jurisdiction, recognized at an early date by Social Democratic workers and numerous experts alike, soon became reality once the law was enforced. Later attempts to create a central court of appeal failed.[236]

THE WORKERS' SICKNESS INSURANCE LAW OF 30 MARCH 1888

The Government Bill

At the end of 1884,[237] the draft Steinbach had prepared for a law on sickness insurance was sent to the ministries that had participated in consultations on the acicdent insurance law and was subsequently used as the basis of inter-ministerial discussions. In 1885 a government bill for the sickness insurance law was introduced in the 'Reichsrat' for the first time;[238] however, it was not dealt with in parliament before the end of that session.

On 1 February 1886 the government introduced the bill again. It was not changed in essence.[239] Apart from individual modifications to §§1 and 2, the Austrian draft completely adopted the German Sickness Insurance Law of 15 June 1883 (see above p. 293) in spirit, content and structure.[240] Like the German law and the bills submitted earlier in the 'Reichsrat' on accident insurance law, the draft of the sickness insurance law gave priority to the principle of compulsory insurance.[241] According to the Austrian draft, industrial workers formed the main group of persons subject to compulsory insurance; however, as under German law, this group was far broader for sickness insurance than for accident insurance. It included 'workers and works' officials' who were employed: (a) 'in mines for specific minerals'; (b) 'in a concern specified in the "Gewerbeordnung" (Trade Act) or in another type of business run for profit'; and (c) 'with the railways and inland shipping companies'. Persons employed in ocean-going shipping were not subject to compulsory insurance, as was also the case under German law.[242]

The draft also provided for 'conditional' compulsory insurance following the idea of §2 of the German Sickness Insurance Law. According to §2 of the draft, the Minister of the Interior could make persons employed in agriculture and forestry subject to compulsory insurance — parallel to the 'statutory'[243] compulsory insurance in §2 of the German law.

The system of benefits planned in the draft followed that of the German law minutely. According to §6 of the draft 'at least' the following were to be granted (i.e. without prejudice to any 'statutory' increase):[244]

1. 'free medical treatment' etc. from the beginning of the illness;
2. further, in the case of incapacity to work, 'sick pay amounting to half of the usual local(!)[245] daily wage of a common day labourer' from the third day of illness;
3. in case of death, a death benefit amounting to 'twenty times the amount' of the above-mentioned daily wage.

The question of organization of sickness insurances was considered the 'main difficulty' in the 'remarks' on the draft. In this respect, the draft also followed two principles which had already been realized in the German law: administrative areas were to be kept considerably smaller than in the case of accident insurance to ensure effective control over the members of the schemes and to prevent illness from being stimulated; and the new system was to be linked to already existing institutions in the case of illness.

On condition that they could provide the minimum benefits stipulated in the future law, cooperative or association sickness insurance schemes (cf. above p. 286) and the miners' 'Bruderladen' (above p. 284) in particular were not subject to the new law (according to §§56 f.) and thus their members were free of compulsory insurance.[246] According to §58 the same procedure also applied to (free) society schemes, however, with a serious limitation: members of such schemes were only free of compulsory insurance if the society concerned had been established from the start in accordance with the 'Vereinspatent' of 26 November 1852 (cf. above p. 272) or had been reorganized later in accordance with this charter. In the spirit of administrative practice such as it had been since 1882 (cf. above p. 291) the view was expressed in the 'remarks' that only the 1852 'Vereinspatent', 'as opposed to the "Vereinsgesetz" of 15 November 1867, RGB no. 134, grants the state enough supervisory power to be able to leave the satisfactory execution of compulsory insurance up to those societies which are affected by this law'.

In addition to the three types of schemes which already existed, the draft intended the provision of newly organized works' sickness insurances and builders' and district sickness insurances[247] which were hitherto totally unknown in Austria.

Employer contributions were fixed uniformly at one-third of the total for all schemes (§§25, 46 of the Austrian draft), thus following the German law (§65) and continuing the rules provided within the framework of reform of the 'Gewerbeordnung' (cf. above p. 291). In the case of works' sickness insurances, employers were also bound to provide the supplementary benefits required[248] (§46 of the draft) as well as advances free of interest (§45, line 5). As far as administration of the schemes was concerned (see below) works' sickness insurances had one special feature: according to the statute the industrialist (employer) or his representative could be chairman of the general assembly.

The district sickness insurance schemes (Bezirkskrankenkassen) of the draft (§§11–39) copied the local sickness insurances (Ortskrankenkassen) of the German law (§§16–48). In contrast to the latter, however, it was not the communities but the district circuits which formed the territorial basis of these schemes, considered as 'supplementary organisms', to which all persons subject to compulsory insurance and not insured with one of the other schemes, as well as persons insured voluntarily, were to belong. Provisions were also made for the possibility of amalgamating several district sickness insurances to run communal hospitals (§37 of the draft; §47 of the German law).

The sickness insurance institutions were to be organized as self-administrative bodies like the accident insurance institutions. At least two-thirds of the members of the general assembly and of the executive board were to be members of the scheme (the insured) and a maximum of one-third was to be composed of employers. The political authorities of first instance (known as 'Bezirkshauptmannschaften') acted as supervisory authorities; the political regional authorities and the Ministry of the Interior were responsible for further appeals (draft §18).

Debates in the 'Abgeordnetenhaus'

The draft of the Sickness Insurance Law was also passed on to the Trade Board which submitted its comprehensive report, marked by social commitment and drawn up by Leon von Biliński,[249] on 25 May 1886. For one member of the Trade Board, J. M. Baernreither,[250] this provided an opportunity to voice two views that deviated both from the government bill and majority opinion. First, bearing the model of the English friendly societies in mind,[251] Baernreither criticized the fact that the government had given compulsory insurance membership priority instead of concentrating on the promotion of 'free' insurance schemes. Compulsory insurance continued to be given priority; however, Baernreither managed to push through a resolution in the Trade Board which requested the government to submit 'the draft of a law on relief funds as soon as possible'.[252] Baernreither, in his role as rapporteur of the minority, also spoke during the plenary discussions in favour of the free insurance schemes.[253] His second essential concern consisted in the inclusion of agricultural and forestry workers in sickness insurance. This demand was also put forward by a 'minority vote'.

The majority had adhered to the proposals of the government bill according to which the Minister of the Interior could order such inclusion after requesting the opinion of the Regional Cultural Councils (Landeskulturräte) and the Regional Boards (Landesausschüsse); the majority had only put the latter in place of the provincial diets (Landtage).[254]

Arguments on this complex of questions also dominated the debates in the 'Abgeordnetenhaus' during which[255] Baernreither moved to regulate the inclusion of agricultural and forestry workers by a special law which was to be valid throughout the Empire. Baernreither's federalistically minded opponent, Josef Kaizl,[256] however, considered special regional laws on the subject more appropriate.

Opinions of the Social Democratic Labour Force

While debates were still continuing in the 'Abgeordnetenhaus', on 12 February 1887, the Social Democratic publication, *Gleichheit,* commented on the draft of the Sickness Insurance Law. Once again it relied upon the resolution of the 'Verbandstag der Arbeiter-Kranken- und Invaliden-Unterstützungsvereine' of 13 and 14 June 1886 which in turn set forth in more detail the 'Principles' decided by the 'Wiener Verein' in March 1886. As in the case of accident insurance, the approval in principle of the idea of compulsory insurance coupled with the wish to extend compulsory insurance even further is much to the fore.

Once again the limited scope of the benefits was criticized, as was the restrictive attitude of the draft towards society schemes (Vereinskassen), while demands were made to eliminate or else not to introduce works' and builders' insurance schemes. A reserve amounting to 'twice the average yearly expenditure' (§27 of the draft and of the law) was also rejected. It is remarkable that this reserve only had to be half as large according to the German law (§32). The demand to establish a 'Reichsversicherungsamt' — already raised in connection with the Accident Insurance Law — was made once again.

On 13 August 1887, Viktor Adler[257] himself expressed the fears of the labour force linked with the Sickness Insurance Law in the *'Gleichheit'.* Adler said that Bismarck's social reform was not to be considered 'eyewash with intent'; even if one looked upon social reform as 'a serious if hopeless attempt to make the lot of the working man tolerable', it was impossible to overlook its other purpsoe, namely 'to paralyse any independence of the working class, if not to prevent it completely'.

Debates in the 'Herrenhaus'; Imperial Sanction

Following the Trade Board's conclusions and with hardly any amendments on the second and third readings, the 'Abgeordnetenhaus' accepted the draft of the Sickness Insurance Law on 29 March 1887.[258] The draft was then passed on to the 'Herrenhaus' which appointed a committee of fifteen men on 4 April 1887 to deliberate upon the law.[259] In their report of 30 April 1887,[260] approved by the plenum of the 'Herrenhaus' on 5 May 1887, provision was made in particular for the possibility of optional membership of agricultural and forestry workers (cf. §3, section 2 of the later law). Two details were also modified: limitation of insurances' compulsory payments to public hospitals to a period of treatment of 4 weeks — later §8, section 3 of the law; and the licensing of smaller works' insurance schemes if they could provide appropriate benefits — later §42, section 3 of the law.

When the draft was returned to the 'Abgeordnetenhaus' the dispute over competences flared up again. On 28 October the decision was made to combine the resolution adopted in accordance with Kaizl's proposal with that of the 'Herrenhaus'.[261] Later attempts, particularly by the Liberal, Anton von Hye, to give the state an opportunity to legislate to some degree on sickness insurance for agricultural and forestry workers failed.[262]

No attempt was made to include agricultural and forestry workers in sickness insurance for over 30 years (1921)[263] and even then the attempt failed again because of the question of competence. Prerequisites under constitutional law did not exist for nationwide statutory regulation of this matter until the rules on the powers of the B-VG came into force on 1 October 1925. These will be discussed in more detail later.

On 30 March 1888 the imperial sanction was given to the 'Law on Sickness Insurance for Workers' (*RGB* no. 33) which then came into force on 6 July 1888.[264] According to the ministerial decree of 14 July 1889, *RGB* no. 94, sickness insurance was to be effective as of 1 August 1889. Although parliament dealt with sickness insurance after accident insurance, the former was 3 months 'ahead' of accident insurance in the final phase.

First Amendments to Details

Before sickness insurance actually became effective, two amendments were made by the law of 4 April 1889, *RGB* no. 39. The first concerned the regulations on the 'reserve quota', vehemently contested by both the works' and the 'free' schemes alike, which were deleted upon the motion[265] of deputy Adolf Schwab and his followers (of 30 January 1889). The second one, added by the Trade Board,[266] provided for largely[267] exempting apprentices from compulsory sickness insurance. After these amendments of detail had been made, the Sickness Insurance Law remained unchanged and in force until 1907. The reform of the trade association sickness insurances in 1907 and the comprehensive reforms of 1917 will be discussed later.[268]

THE LAW ON RELIEF FUNDS (HILFSKASSENGESETZ) OF 16 JULY 1892

Evolution

As the 1892 Law on Relief Funds[269] is closely connected with sickness insurance legislation, the evolution of this law is to be discussed before turning to the 'Bruderladengesetz' which was actually passed at an earlier date.

While the Sickness Insurance Law was still being debated Baernreither introduced the draft of a Law on Relief Funds[270] for the first time on 25 February 1887. During the tenth session, the draft was debated in the 'Abgeordnetenhaus' and accepted in the second and third readings. As there was no more time for the draft to be passed in the 'Herrenhaus', Baernreither had to introduce the draft again on 13 April 1891. It was passed on to the Trade Board and accepted by the 'Abgeordnetenhaus' in the second and third readings.[271] Once the draft was accepted by the 'Herrenhaus' — without amendments — it was given imperial sanction on 16 July 1892, *RGB* no. 202.

Aims

The main aim of the law was to create a solid legal basis for the voluntary insurance association. The 'Hilfskassengesetz' provided 'free' insurance schemes with the possibility of gaining 'special rights' through registration (with the political, regional authority: §5) without referring to the 1852 'Vereinspatent'. The most important of these rights was the equal legal footing with society schemes in accordance with §60 of the Sickness Insurance Law (cf. §7, section 2) so that members of 'Hilfskassen' were not subject to compulsory sickness insurance (§7, section 3).

There were also secondary aims which Baernreither incorporated in §1 of the Austrian law, based on the English law on relief funds of 1875.[272] These were disability and old age assistance (§1, section 2, line 3), widows' and orphans' assistance (line 4) and the payment 'of a sum of money in favour of a third party (especially as marriage settlement or for fitting out a child) payable at a certain date'. This all-embracing aim, along with the inclusion of members' dependants in the range of persons entitled to benefits seemed to Baernreither the 'expression of the cooperative spirit which exists in English friendly societies' which he wanted to transfer to Austrian conditions.

Like the other registered sickness insurances, the registered 'Hilfskassen' were subject to state supervision according to §§19 and 20 of the Sickness Insurance Law (§35, last section). Unlike the Accident and Sickness Insurance Law, the draft of the 'Hilfskassengesetz' was welcomed in almost all its details by the labour force (*Gleichheit* of 2 April 1887). It was only regretted that such a law had not been passed 20 years earlier.

Repercussions

The practical success of the 'Hilfskassengesetz'[273] was very slight at first. The number of registered relief funds only rose from one (at the end of 1893) to thirty-five (at the end of 1897). One of the reasons for this failure is presumably the legislative error of 1892: thus, associations founded on the basis of the 1852 'Vereinspatent' continued to exist unchanged rather than being obliged to become registered relief funds.

It was not until the Trade Act Amendment (Gewerbeordnungsnovelle) of 23 February 1897, *RGB* no. 63, reflecting the active middle-class policy of the government of that time,[274] that this solution was chosen for Masters' Relief Funds and Masters' Sickness Insurances (Meisterunterstützungsund Meister-krankenkassen) — §115 a 'Gewerbeordnung'.[275] The masters' schemes could only be organized as registered relief funds from then on and not as societies as stipulated in the 1852 'Vereinspatent' or in the 1867 'Vereinsgesetz'. Thus they contributed considerably to the boom of the registered relief funds from 1898 onwards. Their number rose from 61 (at the end of 1898) to 199 (at the end of 1903); only 175 of these still functioned at the end of 1903. Seventy of these 199 funds had the right to be run as sickness insurances in accordance with §7 of the 'Hilfskassengesetz' by the end of 1903.[276] Sickness insurance was by far the dominant branch of insurance; only a few schemes provided for other forms of insurance. Disability and old age insurance, to which Baernreither attached so much importance, were of very subordinate significance. This can easily be seen from the funds' benefits.[277] As far as geographical distribution was concerned, Prague and Vienna were major centres for registered relief funds (1903: thirty-four in Vienna, eighty-two in Prague).[278]

THE 'BRUDERLADENGESETZ' OF 28 JULY 1889

Reform Plans of the Liberal Era

The defects of the 'Bruderladen' system, established in accordance with the 1854 'Berggesetz' (Miners' Act), have already been discussed (above p. 284). The disadvantages were that benefits were too low, there was no statutorily standardized compulsory contribution for mine owners, the economic situation was unfavourable and, finally, the organization of the 'Bruderladen' was poor as it was impossible for miners to transfer membership from one mine to another. The expert advisers' draft of a new Miners' Act (1876),[276] which had been made during the Liberal era, attempted to improve the situation of the 'Bruderladen' in §§138–157 with the following rulings: (i) far-reaching organizational separation of sickness insurances and pension associations; (ii) enlargement of the districts of the pension associations beyond the sphere of the works; and (iii) the standardization of a compulsory contribution by the owners of the works, amounting to half the worker's contribution.

After the failure of the 1876 draft, reform of the 'Bruderladen' did not become the object of political initiative again until 1882. On 9 March 1882 the deputy Josef Krofta proposed the amendment of the tenth chapter of the Miners' Act[281] concerning the 'Bruderladen', following unrest and bloodshed amongst the miners. His proposals corresponded with those of the 1876 draft.

Government Debates: Statistical Preliminaries

In government circles[282] there were grave disputes between the Minister of Agriculture concerned, Falkenhayn, and other members of the government during debates on the Accident Insurance Law (cf. above p. 295) with regard to the question of including miners in statutory accident insurance. It is clear from the government debates that the driving forces of social insurance legislation, Taaffe, Pražák and Steinbach, considered the inclusion of miners in the socio-political reform absolutely unavoidable. At the same time, a common phenomenon occurred, namely that it is more difficult to overcome older inadequate institutions than to establish a new institution which does not have to take any traditions into account. In spite of defects known to all, most of the mine owners thought the 'Bruderladen' adequate and, for example, in the 'Denkschrift der sämentlichen montanistischen Vereine Österreichs' (Memorandum of all Austrian Mining Societies)[283] at the beginning of 1884, it was stated that bringing the 'Bruderladen' up to the level of benefits of the Accident Insurance Law would entail an intolerable extra burden on Austrian mining (apparently an increase in production costs of 6.5–8 percent).

Falkenhayn, the Minister of Agriculture, originally had a similar attitude to the Association of Mining Societies, for he denied that the 'Bruderladen' needed reforming. However, in view of the dominant trend in Taaffe's government, Falkenhayn changed his tactics: so as to forestall the advocates of including miners in the Accident Insurance Law he took over leadership of a movement to reform the 'Bruderladen' himself.

The 1887 Government Bill and Its Treatment in Parliament

After an enquiry in 1885[284] Falkenhayn introduced a government bill[285] on 1 February 1887 'on the regulation of conditions of the "Bruderladen" which were or are still to be set up in accordance with the General Miners' Act'.

First, the Trade Board—commissioned to consider the bill by the 'Abgeordnetenhaus'—appointed Baernreither as spokesman.[286] At the beginning of 1887, Baernreither expounded his views, based on thorough studies of the 'Bruderladen' system, to the Board and handed it his report in the autumn of 1887.[287] This differed on two major items from the government bill, modelled on the draft of a new Miners' Act (1876) Baernreither proposed only assigning sickness insurance to the works' 'Bruderladen' while transferring all other branches of insurance to district 'Bruderladen'. Furthermore, Baernreither vehemently rejected the possibility of dissolving 'Bruderladen' in financial straits, which was considered the 'ultima ratio' in the government bill, and advocated state subsidies for the 'Bruderladen'. One of the most important basic ideas expressed in a book by Baernreither on English workers' societies is the connection between self-help and state assistance which, by the way, was even advocated by discerning mine owners with concrete reference to the 'Bruderladen'.

The majority of the Trade Board could neither adopt the idea of the compulsory introduction of district 'Bruderladen' nor that of the state subsidy—whether this was a matter of principle or due to the condition of state finances is open to question—and rejected Baernreither's proposals on 28 February 1888.[289] Thereupon Baernreither tendered his resignation; Biliński,[290] a Conservative delegate who was almost as eminent a social politician, was appointed spokesman in his place.

The draft elaborated by Biliński took no notice of the two amendments Baernreither had proposed but seen as a whole it represented a compromise between these and the government bill. In its final version, modified by the Board in the course of surveys[291] held from 20 to 22 March, on 26 April and on 12 May 1888, Biliński's draft was accepted by the Trade Board. It was then debated[292] in the 'Abgeordnetenhaus' on 22 February, 7 and 9 March 1889 and finally adopted[293] on 7 March in the second and on 9 March in the third reading with one major amendment regarding the regulation of reorganization. Based on an extremely thorough report[294] by a commission he had appointed for consultation purposes, the 'Herrenhaus' also accepted the bill without amendments.[295] Imperial sanction was granted on 28 July 1889, *RGB* no. 127. In order to implement the 'Bruderladengesetz' a decree was issued by the Ministry of Agriculture on 11 September 1889, *RGB* no. 148, and on 14 November 1890 the model charter[296] was published upon the order of the same Ministry.

The Essential Provisions of the 'Bruderladengesetz'

The essential provisions of the 'Bruderladengesetz' are now discussed briefly. If no indications are made to the contrary, these coincide with the proposals in Biliński's draft. According to §1 the 'Bruderladen' had to grant two types of assistance: '1. sickness or funeral benefits' and '2. compensation for the disabled, or for widows and orphans'. In order to fulfil this two-fold task from an organizational point of view (according to §2), each 'Bruderlade' was to 'set up a special administrative department (sickness scheme, compensation fund) which was to determine and to account separately for all receipts and expenditure required for its purposes'.

As far as the system of benefits was concerned, only the ruling on sickness benefits concurred with the bill at that time. According to §3, sickness benefits had to be at least as much as those laid down in the Sickness Insurance Law (§§6-8).[297] However, deviating from the principles of the government bill—at least for workers with somewhat higher wages—(§4) accident insurance of the 'Bruderladen', integrated in disability insurance, provided for considerably lower minimum values than the Accident Insurance Law.

A demand made by miners, and by many experts and politicians for a long time, was fulfilled in §7: when a member changed from one 'Bruderlade' to another, his share in the reserve of the compensation fund of the former 'Bruderlade' had to be transferred to the new one. Thus, miners were finally able to enjoy greater freedom of movement without economic disadvantages.

As far as the organizations of the 'Bruderladen' was concerned, the law (§§16 ff.) evolved in accordance with the government bill from the model of the works' sickness insurances. As in works' sickness insurances,[299] the works' owners could only have a maximum of one-third of the total number of votes both in the executive board and in the general assembly (§17, section 1; §18, section 2). The 'Bruderladengesetz' granted the works' owner the right to be chairman of the executive board (§17, section 2), while the right of chairmanship of the executive board of the works' sickness insurances was left to the charter in accordance with the Sickness Insurance Law.

The Question of Reorganization

As far as reorganizing passive 'Bruderladen' was concerned, the Trade Board subscribed to Baernreither's proposals as their disbandment was declared inadmissible. The following measures were planned to reorganize the 'Bruderladen': contributions were to be raised; claims were to be reduced up to half of the statutory minimum; employers' contributions were to be increased up to 2 percent of the wage, and compensation already provided was to be reduced (§§41 ff.). It soon became clear that these measures were either inadequate or politically unenforceable.

Legislation on the 'Bruderladen' was undoubtedly the most difficult part of workers' insurance legislation in the 1880s, both from an actuarial and a political point of view. It is important to note that the miners—admittedly as a continuation of the initial spirit of the provisions in the Miners' Act and in older regulations—received the most comprehensive insurance protection of all Austrian workers. This is all the more remarkable in view of the late date of old age insurance for the other workers in Austria. If mining in Austria, seen as part of the whole economy even before the loss of the Sudeten lands, did not play such a dominant role as in the German Reich, the number of members and benefits of the 'Bruderladen' taken together were noteworthy.

In spite of the undeniable progress which the 'Bruderladengesetz' brought compared with the previous legal state of affairs, it provoked mostly negative reactions among the miners.[300] Baernreither had recognized the situation correctly when he demanded state participation in the financing of the 'Bruderladen' (particularly of compensation insurance). From a psychological point of view, state subsidies would have been a type of reparation for the many years of inaction with which the (Liberal) state had faced the miners' problems. In the workers' eyes, the state was also responsible for the poor financial situation of the 'Bruderladen' as it had hesitated over standardizing compulsory contributions for employers for years and had left the fate of the 'Bruderladen' to the judgment of the mine owners. Thus, when the state refused to grant financial aid but made provisions for the contributions to be raised or compensation to be reduced to an even lower level than it was already, the miners were bound to be disgruntled.

There was also widespread and justified criticism of the fact that miners exposed to special risks were granted a pension in cases of accident which hardly reached the level stipulated in the Accident Insurance Law; moreover, the miners' compensation was graduated according to their length of service, even in cases of incapacity to work following an accident. The loss of entitlement to benefits from the sickness insurances of the 'Bruderladen' when employment ended also meant that miners were worse off than other workers.[301] Thus, in retrospect it is regrettable that Taaffe's, Pražák's and Steinbach's initial attempts to integrate [302] miners into the system of general workers' insurance failed and that Falkenhayn pushed thorugh his idea of reforming the 'Bruderladen'. Among the labour force, however, the above-mentioned endeavours to integrate miners remained very much alive and led — many decades later (see below p. 330) — to the abolition of the 'Bruderladen'.[303]

PART 4: DEVELOPMENT FROM 1893 TO 1918

A SURVEY OF SOCIAL INSURANCE LEGISLATION WITH REFERENCE
TO CONSTITUTIONAL, SOCIAL AND ECONOMIC DEVELOPMENT

On 2 February 1891 Minister-President Taaffe appointed Emil Steinbach, who had been his adviser for many years, Minister of Finance. For the first time a leading social politician was a member of the government.[304] Thanks to his extensive influence on Taaffe, partly noted with distrust by the political groupings of the 'Iron Ring', Steinbach can be deemed to have actually been responsible for most of the socio-political plans and schemes from 1891 to 1893. These include the first Extension Law to the Accident Insurance Law (see above p. 294) and plans to reform income tax.[305]

The following passage from the Emperor's speech from the throne of 11 April 1891 shows that the government was really prepared to continue social insurance legislation: 'The beneficial effects which the . . . law on accident insurance for workers has manifested, made it desirable to extend this law to other groups of people'.

This plan was not carried through under Taaffe as a bill on reforming voting rights,[306] drawn up with Steinbach, was their undoing. On 11 November 1893 the dismissal of the Taaffe Government was announced.

The 14 years in which Taaffe's government was in power was the last time in the eventful history of the Habsburg monarchy when it was possible to conduct parliamentary business smoothly over a longish period. Even at the beginning of the 11th session of the 'Reichsrat' (April 1891) there was evidence of increasing radicalism of the whole state apparatus, particularly, of the 'Abgeordnetenhaus' of the 'Reichsrat', from both a political and national point of view.[307] After Windischgrätz's coalition government and Kielmannsegg's temporary cabinet, the Polish Duke, Kasimir Badeni, was appointed Minister-President (18 August 1895). He tried to solve the problem of franchise by reducing the property qualification in the town and country community 'Kurie' and by introducing a fifth 'general' class of voters (law of 5 December 1896, *RGB* no. 226). If one disregards the fact that there was no female suffrage as a matter of principle, this law largely took the idea of universal suffrage into account,[308] however, at the cost of even greater inequality than had existed previously. Thus, the number of voters rose from about 1.7 to 5.3 million; however, the 5.3 million voters of the general voting class could only elect 72 of the 425 deputies in the 'Reichsrat'; of these about 3.6 million voters were only entitled to give their vote to provincial government. This explains why the Social Democrats only had fourteen seats in the 'Reichsrat' when it reopened on 29 March 1897. Prominent leaders of the workers, such as Viktor Adler, did not have a seat. Practically all the major industrial areas turned out to be Socialist strongholds, particularly the Sudeten regions, Galicia and Graz. There were no Social Democratic seats for Vienna or for Lower Austria where the Christian Social Party dominated.[309] This party had been founded in Vienna in 1891 after the papal encyclical 'Rerum novarum' had been issued and was largely successful because of the charisma of Karl Lueger.

The 1897 Trade Act Amendment with its provisions for masters' sickness insurances for the first time is an especially noteworthy piece of legislation of the Badeni era.[310] From a political point of view, the Badeni government was marked by radical measures against workers' organizations (the abolition of the Railway Workers' Benevolent Society in March 1897)[311] and by national interests. The Badeni Language Decrees[312] of 5 April 1897 triggered off serious intra- and extra-parliamentary conflicts which sometimes completely paralysed the 'Reichsrat' and finally led to Badeni's dismissal in November 1897. A series of shortlived governments followed (Gautsch, Franz Thun, Clary-Aldringen, and Wittek) whose activities continued to be overshadowed by national unrest and the controversy over the Law on Emergency Decrees (Notverordnungsrecht). The creation of two extremely important institutions for the further development of Austrian social policy, namely the 'Arbeitsstatistiche Amt' (Labour Statistics Office) and the 'Arbeitsbeirat' (Labour Advisory Board)[314] is due to the fact that the important social politician, Baernreither, was Minister of Commerce in the Thun Government for about 7 months (March to October 1898).[313]

Apart from questions of labour protection (initiatives for the introduction of the 9-hour shift in coal mines, 1901; and for protection for workers in cottage industries) the 'Arbeitsbeirat' was particularly concerned with appraising the social insurance reform programme submitted by Minister-President Körber (see below) in 1904. A committee was appointed by the 'Arbeitsbeirat' to debate the draft in a preparatory capacity from 1905–1907. Baernreither drew up the committee's report after Leo Verkauf,[315] a Social Democratic social politician, resigned.[316]

With the nomination of Ernest von Körber as Minister-President[317] (18 January 1900), Austria had for the first time a politician in a leading position who tried to bring government policy directly into line with the needs and demands of the population. In particular, Körber endeavoured to fill the old Austrian administration, from which he himself had come, with a social spirit and to modernize it. This applied especially to Körber's 'Programme for the Reform and Development of Workers' Insurance', submitted in the last year of his government.

Like the reform of workers' insurance, including the introduction of old age and disability insurance that had first been mentioned in the speech from the throne of 4 February 1901 (opening the 17th session),[318] most of Körber's other major reform projects (particularly the reform of administration) had not been implemented by the time he stepped down from his post on 30 December 1904. Nevertheless, the Körber Government must be given credit for advancing social insurance as its work paved the way for the epoch-making Pensions Insurance Law for Employees (see below p. 319).

After Körber's resignation, external events (the Russian Revolution in 1905 and attempts to introduce universal suffrage in Hungary) led to widespread agitation among the parties of the masses (especially the Social Democratic and the Christian Social parties) to introduce universal and equal suffrage. The hope — entertained by the monarch in particular, who had led the voting reform movement — that the introduction of universal and equal franchise would help to solve the problem of nationalities remained unfulfilled. On the contrary, conflicts in the 'Reichsrat' increased in bitterness, not least because of the decline of the Liberal element. The split of the cosmopolitan Social Democrat Party into three national clubs in 1910/11 was a particularly disturbing feature indicating the predominance of nationalism at that time.[319] Again the 'Reichsrat's' ability to function was severely handicapped. Like many other bills on social policy at that time, the reform of general workers' insurance (including the introduction of old age and disability insurance), announced in the speech from the throne of 19 June 1907[320] and the reform of miners' insurance, mentioned in the speech from the throne of 16 July 1911,[321] were not carried out.

In the spring of 1914 the Minister-President at that time, Count Karl Stürgkh, closed the session.[322] The 'Reichsrat' was not actually dissolved but after the outbreak of the First World War it was not convened again; this led Stürgkh to believe that he was justified in governing the country on the basis of so-called emergency decree law (Notverordnungsrecht). Thus, Austria was once again 'absolutistically and exclusively ruled and administered by its bureaucracy'.[323]

From a legislative point of view, some progress was made in the sphere of social insurance during this new era of absolutism. This especially concerned accident insurance for miners, pension insurance for employees (decrees of 7 April 1914, *RGB* no. 80 and of 25 June 1914, *RGB* no. 138) and sickness insurance (decree of 4 January 1917, *RGB* no. 6). Considerable progress was also made in other sections of social policy during the war years; for example, the beginnings of legislation on the sale of land and rents, measures concerning public health, youth welfare, welfare for the (war) disabled, and job placement.[324] The establishment of a Ministry of Social Welfare, instigated by Baernreither[325] in his capacity as Minister without Portfolio in the Clam-Martinic government (21 December 1916 to 23 June 1917), deserves special mention. In his speech before the Council of Ministers on 25 March 1917, Baernreither said that this ministry was to ensure 'the socio-political transition from war to peace' and it was already considered in a handwritten letter by his Highness Kaiser Karl, dated 1 June 1917. After the dismissal of the Clam-Martinic Government, the establishment of the Ministry of Social Welfare was approved by his imperial highness's handwritten letter of 7 October 1917 and the new Minister-President, Ernst von Seidler, was authorized to introduce the bill in the 'Reichsrat' which convened again on 30 May 1917. The law, sanctioned on 22 December 1917, *RGB* no. 499,[326] assigned the Ministry of Social Welfare matters of social insurance, including the registered society and cooperative sickness insurances (the latter in consideration of Viktor Adler's resolution on the subject). In place of J. M. Baernreither, as originally planned, Viktor Mataja, a Christian Socialist, was the first Minister of Social Welfare. In the last few days of the monarchy, he was replaced by Iganz Seipel, who later became Federal Chancellor. The publication in July 1918 of 'Guidelines for the Extension of Social Insurance' counted among the most significant achievements of Mataja's ministry. Of course, there was no longer any opportunity to carry out this project: on 30 October 1918 the German-speaking members of the 'Reichsrat' took account of the decline of the Habsburg monarchy by establishing the state of 'German-Austria' and on 12 November 1918 Austria was proclaimed a republic.[327]

The Social Democratic Party's attitude to social insurance is evident from the relevant passages of the programme adopted at the 'Hainfelder Einigungsparteitag', a party convention held from 30 December 1888 to 1

January 1889. This programme points to the party attitude to 'labour protection legislation and social reform'. Despite the extremely belligerent attitude of the resolution, it is remarkable that the criticism it expresses is predominantly directed at the principal motives and at the range of benefits, not at the basic idea of workers' insurance legislation. Furthermore, the whole resolution was obviously based on the fear that the enactment of social insurance legislation could result in less legislative activity in the field of labour protection.

The attitude of the 'Hainfelder Parteitag', which did not directly reject social insurance legislation but was marked by deep distrust of the motives behind it, was replaced by a pragmatic reform-oriented viewpoint at the convention of the entire Austrian Social Democratic Party in Vienna from 2 to 5 November 1901. According to the 'Viennese Programme',[329] of 1901: 'Workers' insurance is to be thoroughly reformed: it is to be completed by introducing a general old age and disability insurance as well as widows' and orphans' pensions, and to be organized uniformly with self-administration by the insured as a rule.' The fundamentally positive attitude of the Social Democrats to social insurance became even clearer when Körber's reform programme was published. However, the Social Democrats were critical of the government bills of 1908 and 1911 as these had included insurance for the self-employed in the reform project upon the insistance of the Christian Social Party.

Although questions of social insurance were not expressly mentioned in the first Christian Social Party programme, the so-called Schindler-Programme of 1891,[330] there is no doubt that the Christian Social Party had a positive view of social insurance legislation from the start. The Schindler Programme gave priority to legislative measures to protect the interests of trade and agriculture as opposed to legislation on workers' protection. This priority is understandable in view of the Christian Social voters' potential and the relatively limited successes of legislation on the protection of trade and agriculture under the Taaffe administration. Accordingly, Albert Gessmann, the Christian Social Minister of Labour in the Beck Government, demanded on principle the inclusion of the self-employed (small-scale industrialists, tradespeople and farmers) in old age insurance.[331] The government bill of 1911 took this demand into account.

The 'Arbeitsbeirat' had already adopted a resolution[332] proposed by the Christian Social Viktor Kienböck and by Eugen von Philippovich in its session of 9 December 1907. According to this, the extension of old age and disability insurance to small-scale industrialists and smallholders was declared desirable, while adding 'that it was not to stand in the way of workers' insurance coming into being'. As will be shown later, the problem of old age and disability insurance remained unsolved until the end of the monarchy and even later, both for the workers and for the self-employed.

There were three economic booms in Austria from the end of the 'Great Depression' in 1896 until 1913, the last year of peace, namely in 1898/9, 1906-1908 and—in a somewhat weaker form—1910 onwards, each interrupted by a short phase of economic slump. Then, in 1913, the Balkan crisis began to have noticeable repercussions on economic activities (e.g., sales difficulties in the metal and textile sectors).[333] Thanks to overall favourable economic developments the national income in the Cisleithan half of the empire grew in real terms by about 49 percent from 1901/3 to 1911/13.

In 1913 the *per capita* income in the Cisleithan half of the empire was about 50 percent lower than in Great Britain and 38 percent lower than in the German

Reich.[334] However, it is important to add that within the Cisleithan half of the empire there were great differences of average incomes in the individual crownlands. During the first decade of this century wages rose continually, in keeping with the favourable economic trend; however, the wage growth rates of individual sectors were extremely varied.[335]

Apart from the economic situation, the trade unions and collective bargaining played an important role in raising workers' wages. The Austrian trade union movement began to increase in the 1890s.[336] The first trades' union congress, held in Vienna from 24 to 27 December 1893, was of decisive importance for the development of socialist trade unions. Some years later Christian Social workers' associations also began to flourish; the first Christian Social labour meeting, at which the 'Programme of the Christian Social Labour Party' was adopted, as mentioned earlier, took place in Vienna on 5 January 1896.

The development of the state budget[337] is worth examining, especially in the context of the project to introduce general old age and disability insurance for which a state subsidy of 90 K per annum was planned for each eligible pensioner. The state budget expanded enormously between 1900 and 1913, both in expenditure and receipts.

Finally, a few words about Austria's economic situation during the First World War. Shortly after the war began, the state intervened in economic activity by standardizing maximum prices for foodstuffs, rents, etc. and by taking over supplies and regulating industrial production. By 1916 the official[338] aim of state economic policy was 'the transfer of increasingly large sectors of our economic life to the state of planned economy'. This was linked with overcoming traditional bureaucratic institutions of economic administration and with establishing a strictly organized and centralized apparatus (commission and general commission for war and interim economic affairs; a 'main board' acting as a 'parliament' for the economy).[339] Austria partly kept in step with developments in Germany in this respect and was partly ahead of Germany. According to J. Redlich[340] 'the ideology of so-called "Hyper-Etatismus" — a totally state-run society — was even more drastic in Austria during the war than in Germany'.[341]

THE DEVELOPMENT OF ACCIDENT INSURANCE

The Extension Law (Ausdehnungsgesetz) of 20 July 1894[342]

As indicated in a letter of the Ministry of the Interior, dated 9 March 1890,[343] Taaffe planned first of all to extend compulsory accident insurance to people working in the transport sector in particular (excluding, however, railways and shipping companies) with a decree based on §3, section 2 of the Accident Insurance Law. However, the Ministry of Justice advised against such a measure as it could have meant that 'the whole of agriculture and all the tradespeople would also be subject to compulsory accident insurance' and this 'was certainly not what the legislative body had intended'. Thus, it recommended passing an Extension Law. In Germany such a law had already been passed on 28 May 1885, *RGB* p. 159; the Austrian legislature followed the contents of the German law closely.

Initially some 150 000 persons were affected by the Extension Law; over 100 000 of these worked for the railways. Subsequently, the 'Berufs-genossenschaftliche Unfall-Versicherungs-Anstalt der österreichischen Eisen-bahnen'[344] (Austrian Railway Workers' Accident Insurance Institution), established shortly after the Accident Insurance Law came into force — the only cooperative accident insurance founded in accordance with §58 — attracted a large number of members. Thanks to article VII of the Extension Law, the pensions paid out by this institution for persons totally unable to work were well above those of the regional institutions both in percentages of the earned income (84 percent compared with 60 percent) and in absolute terms (1253 K as opposed to 421 K). This is all the more significant if one considers that the number of railway workers permanently unable to earn a living was extremely high in comparison with workers in other branches.[346]

Practical Experiences with the Accident Insurance Law; Jurisdiction in the Accident Insurance Sector

The 1887 Austrian Accident Insurance Law laid even greater stress on pension benefits than the German law. From 1891 to 1900 these rose from 1.7 to 13.4 million K, the latter figure accounting for 50 percent of insurance contributions.[347] The accident insurance institutions, however, had very few means of ensuring accident prevention. Moreover, the accident insurances had no influence whatsoever on the treatment of the injured. Both the jurisdiction of the administrative court and the accident insurances' own arbitral jurisdiction influenced practical activities decisively.

The jurisdiction of the arbitral courts became particularly important for the development of accident insurance law after 1894 because of the decline in legislative activity. Unfortunately, this jurisdiction was marked by a lack of uniformity as there was no central court of appeal and thus, frequently — and justifiably — the object of complaint among the workers. Nevertheless, this system led to some remarkable achievements.[348] Four major items were: (a) criteria of responsibility; (b) definition of a work or industrial accident; (c) definition of an accident on the way to or from work; (d) determination of the extent to which a person's ability to earn a living is reduced.

Criticism and Attempts at Reform; the Reform Draft of the Badeni Era; Accident Insurance in the Körber Programme

At the beginning of this century, Otto Stöger,[349] the expert on social insurance law, summarized the reactions of those involved in the rulings of the Accident Insurance Law:

> It is a remarkable phenomenon that the operation of the Accident Insurance Law over fifteen years has not succeeded in making the law popular nor has it proved satisfactory for a single group of those affected by it. . . . Instead of equalizing social differences, the law has indeed unleashed the dogs of war among the groups involved. . . . The insurance institutions — through no fault of their own — stand at the centre of these attacks and are publicly labelled the 'best hated' institutions.

This assessment is all the more significant as only a few years later it was confirmed in the regional accident insurances' appraisal[350] of the Körber Programme, albeit in less drastic terms.

At the end of 1895 the insurance advisory committee, helped by experts, held an enquiry at which amendments to the Accident Insurance Law were debated. Based on their proposals the draft of an Amendment Act was prepared in the

Ministry of the Interior in 1896, i.e. in the Badeni era, and was discussed in the Ministry of the Interior from 3 July 1896 onwards.[351] Although this draft was never dealt with in parliament, some of its trend-setting regulations merit our attention. There were in particular two new provisions in which the jurisprudence, still in its early stages, was taken up in connection with the definition of an accident at work and of pension assessment:

§1, last section (new): Accidents which occur at work are to be considered on a par with those which take place at home or in the course of other activities, which the insured person has been told to perform (apart from his usual occupation) by his employer or by a person authorized to do so by the latter, and also those accidents which occur on the way to or from the place of work.

§5, section 2 (new): The damage suffered by the injured is determined by·the degree of the remaining earning capacity, i.e. the capacity which corresponds to the person's condition—taking due consideration of his bodily and mental status after the accident, to perform a job of satisfactory earning capacity.

The 'Programme for the Reform and Development of Workers' Insurance',[352] submitted by the Körber Government at the end of 1904, provided for several noteworthy new rulings on accident insurance, partly in the first ('General Provisions') and partly in the fourth main section ('Accident Insurance'): the inclusion of additional sectors of small-scale trades- and craftsmen (for example, carpenters) in the group of people subject to compulsory insurance and the exclusion of people working in agriculture and forestry engineering workshops (§5); the introduction of the wage group system (six wage groups) for accident insurance (§§14, 138); the possibility of standardizing the compulsory payroll by decrees (§16); the possibility of raising pensions for the destitute one-and-a-half times (§139, section 3); (obligatory) compensation in cases of reduced ability to earn a living by less than one-fifth (§139, section 4);[354] the possibility granted to accident insurances of taking over treatment (§141, section 1); change from the level premium system (Kapitaldeckungssystem) to a 'quota system of insurance contributions depending on the wage scale' (§152);[354] finally, the establishment of a 'Supreme Court for Workers' Insurance' (§§223–226)—in keeping with Körber's political idea (see above) the latter was to be composed exclusively of bureaucratic elements (half each of judges and administrative officials) without the participation of representatives of the insurance institutions.[355]

Legislation in the Sphere of Accident Insurance until 1918

The imperial (emergency) decree of 7 April 1914, *RGB* no. 80,[356] took a step which Taaffe, Pražák, and Steinbach had planned as early as 1883 but which had failed because of Falkenhayn's opposition. It included miners in general accident insurance ·and was linked with considerable improvements to the benefits system.[357] While only a few compartments had been created within the 'Bruderladen' in 1889 so as to adapt miners' sickness insurance to the Sickness Insurance Law (cf. p. 309), more radical steps were now taken. As of 1 January 1915 accident insurance for miners was completely transferred from the 'Bruderladen' to the newly created 'Unfallversicherungsanstalt der Bergarbeiter'

(Miners' Accident Insurance) (§2). When the monarchy collapsed, this institution, which had been responsible for the entire Cisleithan half of the empire, lost its legal basis and its assets had to be distributed to the successor states in accordance with article 275 of the Peace Treaty of Saint Germain. The law of 10 December 1919, *StGB* no. 579, stipulated that miners' accident insurance was to be entrusted to the regional accident insurance institutions. While the establishment of a special miners' accident insurance was nothing but an episode, the emergency decree of 7 April 1914 was of lasting significance as for the first time the rulings on accidents on the way to and from work or the accident insurance's right to take over the treatment of an injured person from the sickness insurance — planned in draft much earlier — became law.

With the law of 21 August 1917, *RGB* no. 363 (3 amendment to the Accident Insurance Law) a regulation on accidents on the way to and from work was incorporated into the main law (§5, section 3) and any jobs commissioned by the employer outside the works were covered by the insurance (§5, section 1; cf. the 1896 draft). Moreover, one-and-a-half-fold pension incresaes in keeping with the Körber Programme now became law (§6, penultimate section); pensions for the totally disabled were raised from 60 percent to 66.6 percent and — in view of the inflation caused by the war — annual earnings counting for pension rights were also raised.[359] According to §12 of the emergency decree of 7 April 1914, the 10 percent contribution by the employed was abolished (§17).

THE DEVELOPMENT OF SICKNESS INSURANCE

Practical Experience with the Sickness Insurance Law; Administration of Justice in the Sphere of Sickness Insurance; Criticism and Attempts at Reform

As mentioned when discussing the early stages of the Sickness Insurance Law, sickness insurance was implemented by a large number of insurance institutions which varied greatly from one another both in size and structure. In 1901 there were altogether 2935 sickness insurances in the Cisleithan half of the empire. Of these, 564 were district,[360] 1322 works', 7 builders', 887 cooperative and 155 society sickness insurances. In the same year, an average of 2.5 million people were members of these insurances; this figure corresponded to about 9 percent of the population. In the decade from 1890 to 1900 sickness insurances' receipts rose from 24.7 to 47.2 million K and their expenditure from 22.7 to 45.6 million K. The financial situation of these insurances varied; about two-thirds of them ended the year with a running surplus and one-third with a deficit. This percentage was quoted quite uniformly by all types of insurance.[361]

As we see from a written enquiry in 1894 and from an enquiry[362] in 1897, as well as from the discussions of the 'First Austrian Sickness Insurance Meeting' (28 to 30 June 1896),[363] criticism of sickness insurances — both by the insured and by experts — was not only directed at the financial aspects just discussed but also at fundamental questions of law regarding organization and benefits and the scope of compulsory insurance.

The Körber Programme[364] basically extended compulsory sickness (and disability) insurance to all persons who were employed, as the enquiry had proposed. A large group of persons included for the first time, namely those 'persons subject to decrees for servants'[365] and apprentices, were only to be partly insured, i.e. they had only a claim to treatment but not to sick pay (§§26, 27). The wage group system—rejected by the enquiry—was also innovatory; this would have provided for a graduated sick pay (§27). The government bills of 1908 and 1911 largely followed along the lines of Körber's plans for reforming sickness insurance.[366]

Legislation on Sickness Insurance up to 1918

Salzburg was the only crownland to pass a 'Law on the Establishment of Community Sickness Relief Funds for Servants and Day Labourers in the Province of Salzburg' on 29 November 1888, *LGB* no. 40 (amended by the law of 6 December 1901, *LGB* no. 5/1902).

There was no further legislation on sickness insurance until the 1897 Amendment of the Trade Act which provided for the establishment of 'Meisterkrankenkassen' (sickness insurances for master craftsmen) (see below p. 346)[367] while at the same time creating the possibility of introducing compulsory insurance by means of a qualified majority resolution.

No major changes were made to the main law until the emergency decrees of 4 January 1917, *RGB* nos. 6 and 7, were passed. When the 'Reichsrat' reassembled, these were replaced by the laws of 20 November 1917, *RGB* no. 457, and of 3 December 1917, *RGB* no. 475 which largely had the same wording. Their provisions not only adjusted insurance benefits to the price level which had risen greatly because of inflation but also extended the range of benefits quite considerably, namely by prolonging the maximum period for receiving assistance from 20 to 26 weeks and by introducing maternity benefits (§6, line 3) and a nursing premium (§6, line 4). Moreover, based on the Körber Programme, the wage group system (with eleven wage groups) was introduced and even the demand, made in 1896, to include members of the family in sickness insurance was taken into account: the introduction of family insurance was left up to the insurance's statutes (§9a).

THE PENSIONS INSURANCE LAW FOR EMPLOYEES OF 16 DECEMBER 1906 AND ITS FIRST AMENDMENT OF 25 JUNE 1914

Background

While Austrian legislation on workers' insurance followed the German pattern with numerous detailed corrections, Austrian legislation for employees was far ahead of its German equivalent[368] to perform a social function of international importance.[369]

Unlike civil servants whose legal status had been characterized for a long time by a well developed old age and disability pension scheme, few privately employed persons were members of such schemes. Largely due to the initiative of Anton Blechschmidt,[370] the introduction of compulsory old age, disability and surviving dependants' insurance was demanded in two petitions to the 'Reichsrat' (the first of these in 1888) whereupon the 'Abgeordnetenhaus' invited the government on 26 March 1895[371] to introduce an appropriate bill soon afterwards. The government first gathered statistical data in 1896 on the 'Situation of Employees'; the results were published in 1898 and used as a basis for preliminary work on the bill[372] submitted in the 'Abgeordnetenhaus' on 21 May 1901. On 16 December 1906 (*RGB* no. 1/1907) the 'Law on Pensions Insurance of Employees in Private Concerns and in Some Public Services' was granted the imperial sanction.

Major Provisions

The definition of an 'employee' proved extremely difficult when drafting the government bill, particularly where commercial auxiliary staff were concerned. Therefore, no far-reaching precise definition was made. The wording of §1 ('subject to compulsory insurance and insured') chosen by the committee is remarkable both from a legal and a practical point of view for it not only gives expression to the principle of compulsory insurance but also to unlimited independence of registration.[373]

The benefits proposed in the government bill covered disability, old age and surviving dependants' pensions as well as unemployment assistance[374] which deserves a special mention as the forerunner of unemployment insurance, although dropped by the committee. Although appropriate proposals were made to the government there were neither plans for a state subsidy nor for the state's compensation of deficits.

Criticism and Attempts at Reform, Particularly the First Amendment, 1914

The 1906 Employees' Pension Insurance Law aroused criticism from all sides, similar to and perhaps even more than the Workers' Accident Insurance Law in its day.[375] The inadequacy of the minimum pensions was most criticized. On 22 May 1908 Stefan Licht, a deputy, had proposed an amendment to the law. This aimed at improving statutory benefits and at defining the term of 'employee'. From a legal technical point of view, it was finally agreed to enumerate demonstratively the characteristics which establish compulsory insurance as well as the characteristics of activities which exclude compulsory insurance. Moreover, the principle of independence of registration was largely dropped and a ruling made which can be considered the precursor of the present ASVG.[376]

On 22 January 1914[377] the 'Abgeordnetenhaus' accepted the bill which was then passed to the 'Herrenhaus'.[378] However, it was not dealt with as the 'Reichsrat' was adjourned. Nevertheless, the so-called First Amendment to the Pensions Insurance Law became law shortly afterwards with the imperial (emergency) decree of 25 June 1914, *RGB* no. 138. §1, 2–4 and 1(a) contain the transcript of the term 'employee' or of the expression 'predominantly mental services' which originated from the main law. This became exemplary for later legislation.

PROJECTS FOR A GENERAL DISABILITY AND OLD AGE INSURANCE

Parliamentary Activities Since 1891

On 16 April 1891, at the beginning of the eleventh session of the 'Reichsrat',[379] the German National Heinrich Prade repeated the motion he had tabled in May 1886 during debates on workers' accident insurance, namely to pass a law on old age and disability insurance for workers.[380] Thereupon the Trade Board (rapporteur: Gustav Gross) called upon the government to 'accelerate, if possible' the preliminary work on such a law.[381] From then on, draft bills on old age and disability insurance for workers, the privately employed (i.e. employees), agricultural and forestry workers, were a routine part of the agenda of the 'Abgeordnetenhaus'. Basically, all political and national groups agreed on the necessity of an old age and disability insurance for workers.

The 'Programme for the Reform and Development of Workers' Insurance' (see above p. 312), submitted by Körber at the end of 1904, was not the promised bill but from a practical point of view it went far beyond old age and disability insurance as all existing or planned branches of workers' insurance were summarized into a comprehensive work for the first time. As the plans of the Körber Programme for reforming accident and sickness insurance had already been discussed (above pp. 316–317), it is now only necessary to give a few details on old age and disability insurance.

The Körber Programme

According to the programme, all employed persons were subject to compulsory insurance. However, agricultural and forestry workers in particular were exempt from compulsory disability and old age insurance, in so far as these were not subject to the 'Servants' Regulations', as were (private) employees and persons over the age of 60.[382] In cases of incapacity to work,[383] a person was entitled to a disability pension after a qualifying period of 200 weeks and to an old age pension after 1200 weeks of contributions, if the insured person had already reached the age of 65. Both types of pension consisted of a basic and a progressive amount, depending on the respective wage bracket. Compensation was to be paid instead of pensions to surviving dependants. A standard state subsidy of 90 K was to be paid to the pensions.

The First 'Social Insurance' Projects of the Government Bills of 1908 and 1911

The 1908 government bill[384] extended the range of persons subject to compulsory disability and/or old age insurance quite considerably compared with Körber's Programme. All agricultural and forestry workers were now included under the heading of 'employed persons'. Moreover, an attempt was made — quite revolutionary at that time — to subject the self-employed with an annual income of less than 2400 K — i.e. particularly small-scale tradespeople and farmers as well as members of their families who help them out (more than occasionally) — to compulsory insurance, though the scope of such an attempt was extremely modest.

Nevertheless, one cannot overlook the fact that the combination of insurance for workers and for the self-employed, however justified the latter's wish for social security may have been, delayed the reform project from becoming law considerably, and against a background of adverse political circumstances (the 'Reichsrat' was not convened again after war broke out) contributed to its failure.[385]

The 1908 government bill was introduced both during the nineteenth and the twentieth session[386] of the 'Reichsrat' and assigned by the 'Abgeordnetenhaus' to the Social Insurance Board, subsequently[387] declared a permanent fixture (rapporteur: Karl Drexel of the Christian Social Party).[388] After long controversies, largely on matters of organization and of insurance for the self-employed, agreement was finally reached on all major issues in July 1914 in the Social Insurance Board and in the subcommittee it had appointed.[389] The outbreak of war shortly afterwards thwarted continuation of the reform project which would have provided about 10 million people — 6 million employed persons and about 4 million self-employed persons and members of their families who help out — with comprehensive protection against the most important social risks (not, however, against unemployment). In spite of its failure, the Körber Programme and the 1908 and 1911 bills deserve greater notice than they are usually given because of the numerous interesting rules they proposed.

The 'Governing Principles' for the Development of Social Insurance, 1918

In July 1918 the newly created Ministry for Social Welfare (Heinrich Mataja) published its 'Governing Principles for the Development of Social Insurance'[390] in which reform of the existing 'insurance for workers and employees', the introduction of 'disability and surviving dependants' insurance for workers', reform of the relief fund system and 'unemployment insurance for the future' were discussed as the most urgent items. Turning away from the pre-war projects, insurance for the self-employed was again excluded. Only old age insurance was to remain loosely connected with the workers' disability insurance but was not to be compulsory (borrowing from the 'Franco-Belgian system of basing qualifying periods for old age pensions on continuous voluntary payments'.)[391]

PART 5: DEVELOPMENT IN THE FIRST REPUBLIC (1918–1938)

SURVEY OF SOCIAL INSURANCE LEGISLATION
AGAINST A BACKGROUND OF CONSTITUTIONAL,
SOCIAL AND ECONOMIC DEVELOPMENTS

By 'Act of the Provisional National Assembly for German-Austria' of 30 October 1918, *StGB* no. 1, which must be considered as the foundation of the new state, two important decisions were made for the further development of social insurance legislation. One of these stipulated that existing social insurance laws as well as all other 'laws and institutions' were to remain 'valid until further notice'. According to the other decision, the Social Democratic politician, Ferdinand Hanusch, was appointed head of the 'State Office for Social Welfare' (Staatsamt für soziale Fürsorge), created by resolution of 30 October 1918. Even after the elections when the Social Democratic party gained the most votes and seats,[391] he remained head of the social department which had been renamed 'State Office for Social Administration' (Staatsamt für soziale Verwaltung) since its link with the health department by the law of 14 March 1919, *StGB* no. 180. From 21 November 1918 onwards he was assisted by Josef Resch, a Christian Social politician, as undersecretary of state who later became Federal Minister. Karl Renner was Chancellor and head of this coalition government.

After the collapse of the coalition on 10 June 1920, a cabinet was formed in accordance with the proportional representation system — mainly in order to complete the constitution — to which Hanusch belonged in his previous capacity.[394] On 1 October 1920 the Constituent National Assembly adopted the Federal Constitution Law (Bundes-Verfassungsgesetz — B-VG; BGB no. 1/1920) and at the same time the Interim Law on the Constitution (Verfassungs-Übergangsgesetz — V-ÜG; *BGB* no. 2/1920) according to which rules on matters of competence, laid down in the December Constitution of 1867, remained in force. (For more details see below in connection with the social insurance of agricultural and forestry workers: p. 329).

The elections (of 17 October 1920), held only a few weeks after the Law on the Federal Constitution and the Interim Law on the Constitution had been adopted, completely reversed the political situation. Now the Christian Social Party had the most votes and seats. Under these circumstances, the majority of leading politicians of both parties were no longer prepared to form a coalition government. The cabinet, based on proportional representation, collapsed on 20 October 1920 and with it Hanusch's activity came to an end.[395] From then on, until the party was forbidden in 1934, the Social Democrats were in opposition.

Josef Resch (28 September 1880 to 6 April 1939)[396] was also familiar with the workers' world, if only in the trade sector, in contrast to Hanusch. After his early beginnings in the glazier's trade, Resch became an official in the Accident Insurance Institution in Vienna and between 1920 and 1938 he was Federal Minister of Social Administration several times. After the war, food and coal supplies, increasing unemployment and particularly high budgetary deficits and subsequent inflation, figured prominently among economic and social problems.[397] As Max Lederer[398] rightly noted, the unfavourable economic situation which particularly affected the labour force meant that the socio-political reforms, introduced by Hanusch shortly after his appointment as Secretary of State, were expedited. Politicians were more prepared than ever before to take steps for greater labour protection which were linked either with no or very low financial consequences.

Next to the great progress of labour- and labour-constitutional laws, reforms of social insurance laws achieved in the Hanusch era were modest. This was not because Hanusch was unprepared to carry out reforms in this field, but because of major technical and financial difficulties with such reforms. Nevertheless, benefits of the sickness and accident insurance schemes were considerably improved and organizational improvements were made to the sickness insurance system (with the 'Kassenkonzentrationsgesetz' — Law on Insurance Concentration: see below p. 325). Moreover, the Law on Sickness Insurance for Civil Servants of 13 July 1920, *StGB* no. 311 (cf. below p. 325), and especially the Unemployment Insurance Act of 24 March 1920, *StGB* no. 153 (see below p. 326), which by international comparison was a considerable achievement, were important pioneering feats. The draft law on the introduction of workers' old age and disability insurance of 15 December 1920 (see below p. 326), based on a preliminary draft of September 1920, bears witness to even more comprehensive plans for reform.

1922 was marked by the Geneva reorganization measures,[399] begun by the Federal Chancellor, Ignaz Seipel, and by the first and increasing confrontations between the middle class block (Christian Social Party and pan-Germans) on the one hand and the Social Democrats on the other.

While currency devaluation reduced the number of unemployed in 1921 to less than 20 000, the number of unemployed rose steeply at the end of 1922 and the beginning of 1923, fell again in 1924 to the relatively low level of about 63 000 and then rose to almost 190 000 by 1928 (including old age pensioners).[400] The unfavourable employment situation around 1925 led to a considerable recovery of the Social Democratic Party. However, this suffered severe setbacks after the fire in the palace of justice (law courts) in 1927.[401]

The two Christian Social ministers in the government, Josef Resch and Richard Schmitz, were particularly concerned with the further improvement of workers' and employees' protection. Both the Employees' Law of 11 May 1921, *BGB* no. 292, and the improvement of factory inspection and industrial courts deserve special mention. As far as development of social insurance was concerned, the government bill of a law on disability insurance for workers and employees, December 1921, failed just like the bill Hanusch had introduced 1 year earlier. By contrast, independent bills on insurance for employees, workers and farm workers, introduced from 1925 onwards, were highly successful. However, for the latter only those parts on old age welfare, provided as a substitute for the old age pensions, were enforced because of the unfavourable economic situation. The year 1929 was marked by a final boom both from an economic and political point of view: the number of unemployed dropped temporarily to the level of 1924 and politically the parties worked together successfully to reform the constitution.[402]

Both the economic and political situation became more critical in the years to follow. By 1931 the number of unemployed had risen to about 250 000, by 1932 to 378 000 and by 1933 — at the height of the crisis — to about 400 000. The tense political situation led to the so-called 'Selbstausschaltung' (self-elimination) of the National Council in March 1933. This served the Federal Chancellor at the time, Engelbert Dollfuss, as a starting point for the transition to an authoritarian state ruled by the 'Stände' (the estates) which he had planned for quite a long time. When the Social Democratic insurrection of February 1934 had been quelled, this idea of the state was legally anchored in the May Constitution of 1934. After Dollfuss was murdered by National Socialist rebels in July 1934, the idea of an authoritarian state ruled by the 'Stände' was continued by his successor, Kurt Schuschnigg, until German troops marched into Austria on 13 March 1938 and until the 'Law on the Reunification of Austria with the German Reich' of the same date (*DRGB* I, p. 237) put an end to Austria's political independence (or, from a legal point of view, Austria's capacity to act).[403]

From an economic point of view the years 1934 to 1937 were marked by a slight improvement. However, the number of unemployed did not fall below a yearly average of 300 000. It was not until 1938 that the number of unemployed was reduced to about 100 000[404] within a short time due to politically motivated orders and other measures. The unfavourable economic situation at the beginning of the 1930s, resulting in a decline of the number of insured, led to plans to cut benefits in individual sectors of social insurance. Later a solution to economic problems was sought with far-reaching organizational changes and as comprehensive rulings as possible. Although this aim could not be achieved to a large extent, more details will be given on the 1935 GSVG, a major piece of legislation, at a later juncture. (see below p. 331)

(see below p. 331)

REFORMS AND REFORM PROJECTS OF THE HANUSCH ERA

Reform of the Insurance Organization[405]

As the radical demand to reduce the large number of insurances by introducing 'uniform insurances' had been voiced in the 'Guiding Principles' of the Mataja ministry, Hanusch tried at least to take a step in this direction by closing the 'small' insurances (with less than 1000 or 500 members) in accordance with the so-called 'Kassenkonzentrationsgestz' (Insurance Concentration Law) of 6 February 1919, *StGB* no. 86 (third amendment to the Sickness Insurance Law).

The Law of 13 July 1920 on Sickness Insurance for Civil Servants

Until 1920, civil servants depended on monetary assistance from their employers if they fell ill.[406] Such assistance was frequently inadequate and thus did not prevent the civil servant from becoming destitute if he or a member of his family was ill. As civil servants were entitled to their salary in case of illness, sick pay was not included in the range of benefits. This only covered help for the sick, maternity benefits and funeral allowances (§4). The 'free choice of doctor' (§6: 'The choice of doctor is left up to the individual') was introduced to Austrian law for the first time and must be stressed as particularly progressive.

The 'Krankenversicherungsanstalt der Staatsbediensteten' (Sickness Insurance of Civil Servants), the 'Krankenversicherungsanstalt der Bundesangestellten' (KVA — Sickness Insurance of State Employees) since 1921, was responsible for civil servants' sickness insurance. The law was promulgated again in an amended form as the 'Bundesangestellten-KVG' (BKVG — State Employees' Sickness Insurance Law) in 1937. The high standing of Austrian social insurance law was also evident when Austrian statutory sickness insurance, which was quite alien to German law, was integrated into German civil servant law and was not in fact altered.

The 1947 Social Insurance Interim Law (see below p. 337) reinstated the rule which dated back to 1920[407] and to Hanusch and Resch.

Introduction of Unemployment Insurance,[408] especially the Law of 24 March 1920

At the end of the nineteenth and beginning of the twentieth century trade unions catered largely for unemployment assistance (for their members). From the turn of the century the so-called 'Ghent system', which consisted in the promotion of such trade union activities by the state, community, etc., became widespread in some Scandinavian countries, in Belgium, France, Switzerland and in several German and Austrian towns (Graz, Liesing, and Atzgersforf).

The return of the army in the autumn of 1918 led to a rapid rise in unemployment, especially in Vienna (in May 1919 there were 180 000 unemployed in Austria, 130 000 in Vienna). This forced the government to act quickly. A meeting of representatives of both employers and the employed, chaired by Hanusch, was held at the beginning of November 1918; this resulted in the executive order on 'unemployment assistance' being issued on 6 November 1918, StGB no. 20.[409] This was to provide assistance, financed exclusively by the state, to all workers and employees who had paid compulsory contributions to sickness or pension insurances in cases of unemployment (despite the person's ability and willingness to work) without consideration of prior length of service and for an unlimited time.

The system of 'unemployment assistance' was in force for about 18 months (from 18 November 1918 until 8 May 1920); its social repercussions were generally extremely positive. However, there were also numerous abuses. There were especially objections of principle to a system of state assistance; these were finally taken into account by the law of 24 March 1920, StGB no. 153, on 'Unemployment Insurance' which also evolved during the Hanusch era.[410] It was particularly evident that the law was modelled on the principle of (workers') insurance from the equal division of the contribution between the employer, the employed and the state. (Later, in 1922, employers and employed each paid 40 percent.)

With the introduction of these new elements Austria was the first country after England to have state unemployment insurance. Statutory unemployment insurance with financial participation of the employer, the employed and the state had been introduced for several branches of industry in England. With the National Insurance Act of 1911/12[411] (Part 2). With the law of 20 March 1920 Austria was the first state to extend such a ruling to all employed persons (subject to compulsory sickness and/or pension insurance). The system of state unemployment insurance was later adopted in the German Reich (with the law of 16 July 1927, *RGB* I, p. 187, 320),[412] in Bulgaria, Ireland, Italy, Poland, in Soviet Russia and in some cantons of Switzerland.[413]

Nevertheless, the law of 20 March 1920 maintained certain features which were characteristic of the welfare system, for example, need as a legally definable prerequisite for eligibility (cf. §1, section 3 of the law as well as the executive order of 29 March 1920, *StGB* no. 160).

The further development of unemployment insurance was mainly influenced by the fact that — contrary to original expectations — unemployment became a permanent feature of life, though subject to periodical fluctuations. After the relatively favourable years from 1920 to the beginning of 1922, a deflationary crisis began at the end of 1922 following currency reform. As unemployment assistance for a maximum of 30 weeks — provided there was an absolute need — proved inadequate in this situation, 'emergency relief' was introduced by the law of 15 December 1922, *BGB* no. 924. This was initially financed from unemployment insurance funds and later by additional contributions from employers, the employed and the state. The average[414] number of unemployed rose from the middle of 1924 onwards (1926, 176 000) then fell slightly for a while (1928, 156 000) to reach exorbitant levels in the years following 1930 (1931, 253 000; 1932, 378 000; 1933, 408 000). The fact that an extremely high percentage of the unemployed drew on 'emergency relief' — and this figure grew as the depression continued — is just as important as the absolute figures themselves. (According to federal estimates for 1932, 98 000 drew emergency relief and 152 000 received unemployment assistance.)[415]

Moreover, one must bear in mind that a special old age pension had been introduced at the end of 1927 (with the Workers' Insurance Law; see below p. 328) for unemployed persons over the age of 60. Thus, the true unemployment figures were far higher. Because of these unfavourable circumstances, unemployment insurance became — as Max Lederer[416] says — increasingly like 'a type of poor relief'. The 1935 GSVG took this into account by combining unemployment and old age pensions financially (cf. below p. 331). However, in view of the continuing high unemployment, it was impossible to reorganize unemployment insurance financially before 1938.

REFORM OF WORKERS' AND EMPLOYEES' INSURANCE

Partial Improvements

Shortly after the end of the First World War, four important changes were made to accident insurance.[417] First, following §10 of the Decree on Accident Insurance for Miners of 7 April 1914, the right of other accident insurances also to take over treatment was now firmly established (§37 (a) UVG) with the fourth amendment to the Accident Insurance Law of 30 June 1919, *StGB* no. 399. Shortly afterwards the 'Wiener Anstalt' (Viennese Insurance) contacted Lorenz Böhler, the founder of modern accident surgery, to assign the treatment of fractures to him. Even if this first attempted project (1919/20) at a small accident

hospital failed, it does represent the beginnings of the unprecedented development of Austrian accident surgery, largely the result of the initiative of the accident insurances.[418]

Secondly, the accident insurances' financing system was greatly affected by inflation. Pensions had to be supplemented with cost-of-living bonuses, apportioned to concerns subject to compulsory accident insurance, in accordance with
numerous amendments to Accident Insurance Law.[419] Thus, there was a gradual
change from the level premium system to the allocation procedure which was
finally approved by the legislature[420] with the thirteenth amendment of 13 July
1923, *BGB* no. 414.

The seventeenth amendment to the Accident Insurance Law of 16 February
1928, *BGB* no. 50, was also significant as, according to this, certain occupational
illnesses — in so far as these reduced earning capacity by more than one-
third — ranked equally with accidents at work (defined more closely by the
decrees of 6 September 1928, *BGB* no. 237). The Accident Insurance Law was
republished, including all amendments made up to 1 January 1929, in the decree
of 9 March 1929, *BGB* no. 150 ('1929 Accident Insurance Law').

Apart from the reform of the insurance system (cf. above p. 324) and the inclusion of agricultural workers (below p. 329), it is important to note legislative
amendments made between 1919 and 1925 in the field of sickness insurance.
These attempted to adapt benefits and contributions to continually changing
monetary values.[421] As these measures frequently proved inadequate, provision
had to be made many times for state subsidies and advance payments by
employers to bridge financial gaps.

The Second and Third Amendments to the Pensions Insurance Law of 1906; the Idea of Classification of Social Insurance According to Professional Groups; the Employees' Insurance Law of 31 December 1926

The reform of employees' insurance began after the First World War with the
Pensions Insurance Law of 1906 (cf. above p. 319). The second amendment (law
of 23 July 1920, *StGB* no. 370) brought numerous improvements to benefits. Of
these, the allowance for the needy — already anchored in workers' accident insurance — as well as the extensive reduction of indemnification arrangements
(complete abolition of indemnification agreements; radical reduction of indemnification institutions) are especially noteworthy. The principle of registration independence ('Meldeunabhängigkeit'), considerably limited by the 1st amendment
(cf. above p. 320), was further restrained: once an insurance claim was made,
further applications were not effective, corresponding to the valid legal position.
Finally, it was remarkable that the second amendment included the life companion — if there was no widow entitled to benefits — in the range of persons entitled
to a pension (§4, line 2) while the law of 1926 restricted the companion's claim to
a compensation payment (§36, section 1, lit. (c)).[422] The third amendment, law
of 27 October 1921 *BGB* no. 594, took account of financing problems caused by
inflation of the employees' pension insurance by changing from the 'Anwart-
schaftsdeckungssystem' (full funding system) to the 'Aufwanddeckungsverfahren'
(an expense covering system).[423]

While the Employees' Pension Institution (only) prepared further reforms for
pensions insurance from the middle of 1922, the government took a new path

with the draft reform presented to the public on 12 June 1923[423] and the government bill — largely based on this — of 20 November 1923[425] (Minister Richard Schmitz). This was already outlined in the Employees' Law of 11 May 1921, *BGB* no. 292: instead of special laws for individual branches of insurance, as hitherto, social insurance was to be divided into professional categories[426] comprehending all branches of insurance. There were to be four groups:[427] (i) civil servants for which the 1920 Sickness Insurance Law (that was quite exhaustive for this sector) had been passed (cf. above, p. 324); (ii) employees; (iii) the industrial labour force; and (iv) agricultural and forestry workers (with optional inclusion of farmers).

In accordance with this goal, the 1923 government bill aimed at the codification of sickness, unemployment and pensions insurance for employees. The Board of Social Administration (of the National Council) added accident insurance later (in accordance with the official adviser's draft) so that finally all branches of social insurance were amalgamated in the law of 29 December 1926, *BGB* no. 388. Unemployment insurance for employees covered the same risks as unemployment insurance for workers.[428] The Social Democrats were originally against the idea of a comprehensive employees' insurance and supported the plans initiated by the Pensions Insurance Institution for pension insurance reform only (bill of 12 April 1923; Heinrich Allina)[429] but soon fell into line with the government at the beginning of 1926.[430]

The Workers' Insurance Law of 1st April 1927

Only a few days after the bill for the Law on Employees' Insurance (20 November 1923) had been introduced, the Chancellor, Iganz Seipel, announced in the National Council[431] that the government would introduce an analogous Workers' Insurance Law covering and settling all branches of social insurance uniformly in the near future.

Shortly afterwards, on 20 February 1924, the Social Democrat deputy, Smitka, and his party friends presented a bill[432] on disability, old age and surviving dependants' insurance for workers. This followed on from Hanusch's bill of December 1920, particularly with regard to financing (progressive supplements to income tax, *inter alia*). In accordance with Seipel's announcement, the government continued its programme of social insurance divided according to professional groups in one further way with the official adviser's draft of a law on workers' insurance and the government bill based on this of 10 November 1923[433] (Minister Josef Resch). After initial resistance from the opposition, a party agreement was reached in the autumn of 1926 and the Board for Social Administration was thus able to conclude its debates positively. On 1 April 1927, *BGB* no. 125, the 'Law on Sickness, Accident and Disability Insurance for Workers' (Workers' Insurance Law) was passed.

The Workers' Insurance Law could not be put into effect immediately (apart from the tenth section) because of the difficult economic situation. This was left, in art. III, section 2, to a decree which was to be passed if

(a) the number of persons receiving unemployment assistance (emergency aid) dropped to 100 000 on average in half a calendar year . . . and (b) if the overall economic situation improved due to a combination of increased foreign trade, growth of domestic consignments and progress in the field of agricultural production so that the extra burden of the Workers' Insurance Law on economy and public administration seems compensated.

As the increasingly critical economic situation soon made fulfillment of this 'prosperity clause' seem illusory,[434] the enactment of the Workers' Insurance Law was linked with the condition of relieving the economy with reforms in the public taxation system with the law of 12 July 1929, *BGB* no. 247. However, this way also proved impracticable because of the government's and state's lack of finance. Thus, the tenth section on 'old age pensions',[435] in accordance with art. III, section 1, in force as of 1 July 1927, remained the only practical item of progress linked with the Workers' Insurance Law. The old age pension was a permanent payment tantamount to reduced unemployment assistance (by about one-third)[436] and was for persons over the age of 60 (from the age of 65 also in addition to earnings from work which was subject to compulsory sickness insurance). Thus, persons who were still capable of working received prolonged emergency aid and persons who were incapable of working were now embraced by unemployment assistance.[437]

The number of old age pensioners was initially (October 1927) about 18 000 and rose to about 70 000 by 1932. In addition, under the law of 23 November 1927, *BGB* no. 338, there were some 1750 miners with claims to subsidies, about 4500 household helps (according to the law of 17 December 1928, *BGB* no. 356) and, some 23 000 land labourers (see below p. 330). Thus, the number of pensioners exceeded the 100 000 mark in 1932.[438]

Further development of workers' insurance will be discussed in the context of the 1935 GSVG (see below p. 331–332).

The Notaries' Insurance Law of 28 October 1926

This law (*BGB* no. 317) deserves attention as it is the first example[439] — still relevant today — of a combination of employees (the notaries' candidates) and independent persons (the notaries) into a single statutory compulsory insurance.[440] However, compulsory sickness, unemployment and accident insurance (for accident pensions) were restricted to the first-named group; the restriction of abstract pension calculation in the case of accident pensions as planned in the law was interesting (prerequisite of a reduction of earnings of at least one-tenth).[441] The 'Versicherungsanstalt des Notariats in Wien' (Notaries' Insurance in Vienna)[442] was responsible for all sections of notaries' insurance.

The Inclusion of Agricultural and Forestry Workers in Social Insurance, Particularly the Agricultural Labourers' Insurance Law of 18 July 1928[443]

Since the memorable dispute between Baernreither and Kaizl during the course of deliberations on the Sickness Insurance Law of 1888, hardly any progress had been made in the field of agricultural and forestry workers' social insurance until 1918. Compulsory accident insurance continued to be limited to workers in the agricultural and forestry machinery works. Only Salzburg had made use of the possibility of standardizing compulsory sickness insurance for land labourers (cf. above p. 319). Otherwise, these labourers had to make do with the employers' obligatory payment of costs for care and treatment for a limited period as well as the continued payment of their wages as laid down in the old servants' ordinances or in the farm labourers' decrees[444] passed in the various counties in 1921 and following years.

Thus, with the law of 21 October 1921, *BGB* 581 (seventh amendment to the KVG), an attempt was made to extend compulsory sickness insurance to persons working in agriculture who were not self-employed. In the case of smallholdings, members of the farmer's family were included. The farming population opposed such measures, particularly because of the last-mentioned item, and this opposition was taken into account with exemption regulations.[445]

As the regulations on jurisdiction of the 1920 B-VG were not yet in force (cf. above p. 322) because of §42 of the 1920 V-ÜG, but rather the obscure regulations of the 'Grundgesetz über die Reichsvertretung' (Basic Law) of 21 December 1867, *RGB* no. 141, on this matter, the Salzburg local government contested the seventh KVG amendment at the Constitutional Court — with success. In its judgment of 27 June 1924, G2/24/10,[446] the court was of the opinion that the enumeration of 'Reichsrat' powers in §11 of the Basic Law meant that social insurance law, not being part of 'legislation on civil law', fell under the jurisdiction of the 'Land' (province). After the Constitutional Court had declared in its judgment that the extremely dubious consequences of the abolition of the relevant law and the unsettled state of jurisdiction in general were regrettable, the seventh amendment to the KVG was partly adopted in the 'Länder' (with the exception of Salzburg and Upper Austria) as a county (or provincial) law or else new county laws were created. Finally, based on the V-ÜG amendment of 30 July 1925, *BGB* no. 269, §9, regulations on jurisdiction of articles 10–13 B-VG came into force as of 1 October 1925. From this moment, the county laws[447] just mentioned (according to §2 V-ÜG) were valid as federal laws.

While the law on insurance, both for employees and workers was being passed, demands were made for the inclusion of farm and forestry workers in social insurance. After two government bills[448] had been introduced the Farm Workers' Insurance Law was finally passed on 18 July 1928, *BGB* no. 235. Disability insurance for farm workers came into force just as little as for industrial workers. Here too old age pensions bridged the gap and became a permanent solution.

REFORM OF MINERS' SOCIAL INSURANCE[449]

From 1920 subsidies had to be paid to the miners' pensions (law of 16 April 1920, *StGB* no. 198) because of the depreciation in value of the currency. These were partly financed by levies — charged to the mining concerns — and partly by the miners' pension fund (financed through levies on imported coal etc.), set up in 1925. In line with the 1927 Workers' Insurance Law, the law of 23 November 1927, *BGB* no. 338, art. II (linked with the decree of 4 July 1928, *BGB* no. 172) stipulated that disabled miners over the age of 60 were to receive old age pensions instead of the pension allowances to which they were otherwise entitled. Thus, old and disabled miners were doubly provided for temporarily. As the miners' statutory contributions to the 'Bruderladen' had practically dwindled to nothing, but the government wanted to activate the financial participation of the insured, the 'Bruderladen' were closed down by decree of 21 July 1933, *BGB* no. 326,[450] and the pension insurance transferred to the miners' insurance fund established at the workers' accident insurance institution in Graz. Miners' sickness insurance was transferred to the regional sickness insurances and — very occasionally — to the works' sickness insurances. The 1935 GSVG finally put an end to the independent administration of the miners' pension insurance.

SOCIAL INSURANCE FOR THE TRADES[451]

The Masters' Sickness Insurance established in accordance with the Relief Fund Law of 1892 (cf. above p. 306) was considerably stimulated by the amendment to the Trade Act of 10 July 1928, *BGB* no. 189. This declared (in Art. XV) that the written approval of a two-thirds majority of the voters was sufficient to establish compulsory (sickness) insurance; previously a three-quarters majority had been required — in accordance with §115(c), section 1 of the Trade Act. This new rule led to the foundation of numerous insurances or to considerable expansion of the membership of already existing schemes.

THE LAW ON TRADESPEOPLE'S SOCIAL INSURANCE (GSVG) OF 30 MARCH 1935[452]

The unfavourable overall economic climate and particularly the steep rise in the number of unemployed and thus the sharp drop in the number of insured (1930, about 1 million; 1933, about 745 000 in workers' insurance)[453] plunged the whole Austrian social insurance system into grave crisis in 1930 and following years. Thus, in 1933, all branches of social insurance except employees' sickness insurance had deficits which took on menacing proportions in unemployment insurance and old age pension schemes (1933, deficits of 83.3 million and 14.3 million S).[454]

Robert Kerber, appointed Federal Minister for Social Administration in March 1933, intended to take the matter in hand with restrictive individual measures (cutting back benefits, increasing claim requirements) while maintaining the former system as a matter of principle. Indeed, in the sphere of unemployment assistance and emergency aid, measures of this kind were carried through with decrees.[455] When Kerber left the government (21 September 1933)

> the idea he had rejected won the upper hand, . . . namely making the social burden independent of aggregate wages and the number of employed as a function of the volume of production, for which Dr Dollfuss, the Federal Chancellor at that time, coined a readily remembered formula: 'The employment of workers must not be punished on the very next day with regulations on contributions.'

Based on this idea a draft was elaborated in 1934 under Minister Odo Neustädter-Stürmer which was to provide for a common social insurance fund for all branches of insurance. This fund was to be financed partly by insurance contributions and partly by surcharges on sales taxes. 'The government and employers were thus to be freed of any direct contribution to the costs of social insurance.'[456]

Although the government could only realize its plans on reforming the social insurance system to a modest extent, the whole reform movement bore fruit inasmuch as it brought about a far-reaching legislative amalgamation of all insurance branches—in the Federal Law on Social Insurance for Tradespeople (known as the 'GSVG') of 30 March 1935, *BGB* no. 107—and also a considerable concentration and simplification of the insurances' organization.

The putting into operation of workers' disability and old age insurance was, as already under the Workers' Insurance Law, subject to decree by the federal government; special reference was made to the future possibility of financing it from surpluses from unemployment insurance (§196).

In view of the identity of the insured in all sectors, a uniform social insurance contribution could be fixed for workers and employees amounting to 20 percent of the contribution basis (§80, section 2, lit. (a) and section 4, lit. (a)). Employer and employed were to share the burden of this contribution equally (section 6). The organization of the social insurance institutions was also subjected to a radical process of simplification.

PART 6: THE NATIONAL SOCIALIST ERA

SURVEY OF SOCIAL INSURANCE LEGISLATION AGAINST A BACKGROUND OF
POLITICAL EVENTS AND ECONOMIC DEVELOPMENTS[457]

According to Adolf Merkl's[458] and Ludwig Jedlicka's opinions[459] in particular, which are detailed, convincingly formulated and dominant[460] in Austrian literature on the subject, the 'Federal Constitutional Law . . . on the Reunification of Austria with the German Reich', *BGB* no. 75 as well as *DRGB* I, p. 237, passed by the Seyss-Inquart government on 13 March 1938, did not lead to annexation and thus to the disappearance of Austria as a subject of international law as this act was null and void legally as regards form and content, and could not be rectified by the plebiscite of 10 April 1938; only Austria's capacity to act under international law was eliminated during the occupation by German troops (so-called occupation theory).

According to the National Socialist rulers the 'reunification' had caused Austria's 'legal personality' to vanish. Initially, the ' "Land" of Austria', ruled by a 'Reichsstatthalter' (governor), formed an administrative and legal unit, subordinate to the supreme authorities of the Reich. There were, however, plans from the very beginning to destroy this unit and to bring Austrian administrative organization and Austrian law into line with the 'Altreich' (old 'Reich'). As far as administration was concerned, Austria began to be divided into 'Reichsgaue' (regions), directly answerable to Reich authorities in 1939. This process was complete by 1940 and Austria as an organizational unit had been destroyed.[462] 'Legal standardization' was also pushed through vehemently. Social insurance legislation was among those items dealt with immediately. With regard to efforts to standardize legislation, the 'Commissioner for the Reunification of Austria with the German Reich' was of decisive importance. This post had been created in April 1938. His representative for social insurance affairs, the chairman of the 'Reichsknappschaft' (Miners' Insurance of the Reich), Reinhard Jakob, was called to Vienna. One of the very first legislative measures, Art. VI of the decree of 26 March 1938, *DRGB* I, p. 335, stipulated that workers' pension insurance was to be applied in the ' "Land" of Austria' according to the legal principles of the Reich. Moreover, in 1938, decisive steps were taken to reorganize Austrian social insurance, partly with direct state subsidies, particularly for disability insurances, and partly indirectly as a result of the growing numbers of employed persons and the corresponding increase in the number of contributions being paid in.

While the number of unemployed[463] averaged over 300 000 in 1937, it dropped to about 100 000 in 1938 after the Germans had marched in. In 1939 unemployment as a mass phenomenon disappeared entirely; the majority of the unemployed were integrated in the labour market which was revived by the stimulation of armament production, the inflationary monetary policy and the great demand by German consumers for Austrian consumer goods. The rest were enlisted into the labour service to build roads — the 'Todt' organization.

The 'Law on the Standardization of the Law on Marriage and Divorce in Austria and in the Remainder of the Reich' of 6 July 1938, *DRGB* I, p. 807, was of special significance for the law on widows' pensions as for the first time it permitted Catholics to divorce in Austria. With the 'Decree on the Introduction [sic!] of Social Insurance to Austria'[464] of 22 December 1938, *DRGB* I, p. 1912, based on the 'Reunification Law' of 13 March 1938, the following German laws were brought into force in Austria as of 1 January 1939 (§1, section 1):

1. The 'Reichsversicherungsordnung' (insurance decree) of 19 July 1911, *DRGB* p. 509;
2. the Employees' Insurance Law of 28 May 1924, *DRGB* I, p. 563;
3. the 'Reichsknappschaftsgesetz' (Law on Miners' Provident Funds) of 1 July 1926, *DRGB* I, p. 369 and
4. the Law on Labour Exchanges of 16 July 1927, *DRGB* I, p. 187.

Although the title of the decree was meant to sound as if social insurance was something new, introduced by the Germans, some of its regulations point to a certain restraint *vis-à-vis* the Austrian achievements in the field of social insurance legislation prior to 1938. Thus, according to §2, section 1 or §12, compulsory insurance in line with Austrian law was to continue inasmuch 'as it goes beyond the scope of Reich law'. Furthermore, compulsory sickness insurance for pensioners of employees' or miners' insurance, quite unknown to German law, was to continue. In order to 'continue and complete' the decree of 22 December 1938 three more decrees were issued in 1939/40.

During the war numerous benefits were introduced in the sphere of social insurance, beginning with the War Measures Law of 15 January 1941, *DRGB* I, p. 34. These were granted to all insured persons[465] to promote the war effort of the entire population beyond the circle of those who actually participated in the war.

CHANGES REGARDING COMPULSORY INSURANCE, FINANCING AND BENEFITS

In cases where Austrian law had been more generous, sickness benefits remained at the same level as before (particularly regarding the duration of sickness benefits for up to 1 year: §149 GSVG 1935). At the same time, individual improvements were taken over from German law (more family sickness benefits; replacement of the 'district doctor system' in accordance with §105, section 3, GSVG 1935, by the 'free choice of doctor' — not limited to any particular district). In the field of accident insurance, the following improvements were introduced:

accident insurance institutions were bound to treat injured persons and to provide vocational aid (i.e. measures to re-establish or improve the capacity to
work). Moreover, accident prevention was upgraded to become the primary purpose of accident insurance.[466]

The most important innovation was undoubtedly the assimilation of the rules
of the 'Reichsversicherungsordnung' (§§1250, 1253, 1255 ff.) on disability, old
age and surviving dependants' pensions for workers which the first republic had
tried in vain to introduce. This step was of great psychological and political
significance and, of course, the National Socialist rulers were fully aware of this.
However, from an economic point of view it was less spectacular: disability, old
age and surviving dependants' pensions were initially hardly any higher than the
former old age pensions, at least for industrial workers, according to a comparison which Jakob made.[467] There was only a substantial difference for farm
and forestry workers who earned low wages. From a socio-economic point of
view the main improvement was that disability pensions were paid out before the
age of 60, in keeping with their function, unlike old age pensions. Furthermore,
pensions for surviving dependants were new.

Contributions and benefits of Austrian employees' pension insurance were
considerably higher than their German equivalents. By upgrading, an attempt
was made to prevent a drop in these levels *vis-à-vis* the former Austrian law.[468]
Moreover, social insurance benefits in practically all sectors were 'extensively
developed—especially during the last years of the war—due to the monetary
fluidity caused by the war and the German government's obvious intention of
winning over workers and employees so they would take an active part in the
wartime economy. . . .'[469]

ORGANIZATIONAL CHANGES

The basic organizational structure of the sickness insurances which had largely
been patterned on the German model with the 1888 law (cf. above p. 294) remained unchanged.

Changes in accident insurance were more radical. The clearly arranged
Austrian organization was replaced by a confusing diversity of trade associations
whose range of activities stretched partly across the whole Reich (including the
so-called 'Ostmark'—eastern province, i.e. Austria) and partly only across the
'Ostmark'. These trade associations were divided into two federations—for industrial and agricultural associations—whose headquarters were in the 'Altreich'
(the old 'Reich').

The most serious organizational change, however, was due to the fact that the
German social insurances were no longer self-administrative institutions since
the 'Law on the Structure of Social Insurance' of 5 July 1934, *DRGB* I, p. 577,
but were run according to the 'Führerprinzip' (The 'Führer' principle). This
meant that policy was determined completely by the responsible leader of the insurance, supported by an advisory council composed of representatives of both
the insured and their employers.[470]

There were also fundamental procedural changes: the traditional two-line
system of the Austrian social insurance procedural law was stopped by abolishing
the arbitration courts. According to German law,[471] the insurance and supreme
insurance offices as well as the 'Reichsversicherungsamt' (Reich Insurance Office) were responsible for 'award' and 'decision' procedures. This scheme was

largely applied to Austria (the 'Ostmark') also although insurance offices were not set up.[472]

PART 7: THE SECOND REPUBLIC (1945 UNTIL THE PRESENT)

SURVEY OF SOCIAL INSURANCE LEGISLATION AGAINST A BACKGROUND OF
CONSTITUTIONAL, SOCIAL AND ECONOMIC DEVELOPMENT

When the German Reich was defeated, Austria was occupied by allied forces and divided into four zones of occupation[473] in accordance with the First Control Agreement of 4 July 1945. Although the Second Control Agreement of 28 June 1946 recognized the authority of Austrian legislative and administrative bodies, Austria did not regain its full sovereignty until the 'State Treaty of Vienna' was concluded on 15 May 1955 and came into force on 27 July 1955, *BGB* no. 152.[474] The declaration of independence (proclamation of Austria's autonomy) of 27 April 1945, *StGB* no. 1, submitted by the three 'licensed parties',[475] namely the 'Sozialistische Partei Österreichs (the Austrian Socialist Party — SPÖ), the 'Österreichische Volkspartei' (Austrian People's Party — ÖVP) and the 'Kommunistische Partei Österreichs' (Austrian Communist Party — KPÖ), was of decisive importance for the constitutional development of the second republic. This proclamation especially outlined the re-establishment of the democratic republic of Austria 'in the spirit of the 1920 constitution' and entrusted the provisional government under Karl Renner — which had been appointed at the same time (*StGB* no. 2) — with legislative and executive powers. This government — not recognized by all four occupying powers until 20 October 1945 — reinstated the 1929 B-VG on 1 May 1945, *StGB* no. 4 (1945 V-ÜG). However, this law did not come into force until the National Council convened for the first time (19 December 1945). Beforehand, based on the so-called 'Vorläufige Verfassung' (provisional constitution) of 1 May 1945, *StGB* no. 5, the 'Rechtsüberleitungsgesetz' (act on transitional law) of the same date and the 'Behörden-Überleitungsgesetz' (transitional law on authorities) of 20 July 1945, *StGB* no. 94, had already been passed.

According to §2 of the 'Rechtsüberleitungsgesetz' all 'laws and decrees' passed for the republic of Austria after 13 March 1938 were 'temporarily valid as Austrian legal regulations' in so far as these did not fall under the rescinding clause of §1.[476] Thus, the social insurance law of the German Reich continued to apply temporarily as Austrian law.

The 'Behörden-Überleitungsgesetz' ordered the abolition of the (three) supreme insurance offices in §59 for the social insurance sector; it transferred their powers as supervisory authorities to the 'Staatsamt für soziale Verwaltung' (State Office for Social Administration) and their other tasks (especially decisions on questions of administration and benefits) to the 'Landeschauptmannschaften' (county boards of administration) or the magistracy in Vienna. Johann Böhm[477] (26 January 1886 to 13 May 1959) was head of the State Office for Social Administration. He later became the first chairman of the Central Federation of Social Insurances and of the Austrian Federation of Trade Unions.

Böhm was an outstanding representative of that group of politicians in both major democratic parties whose main aim was a practical policy in the spirit of social reconciliation while neglecting ideological contrasts. Leopold Kunschak was very much in the foreground as a social politician in the newly founded

Austrian People's Party (ÖVP) in the early years after the war.[478] The ruling on powers in the 'Behörden-Überleitungsgesetz' was only considered a provisional arrangement.[479] The real aim was to re-establish autonomous social insurance institutions; in preparation for this the insurances were run by 'provisional administrators'. For example, the 'provisional administrator' for the employees' insurance sector was appointed as early as 4 May 1945.[480] However, a largely permanent solution of the organizational questions was not brought about until the Social Insurance Transitional Law of 12 June 1947, BGB no. 142, was passed (reissued as the 'SV-ÜG 1953", BGB no. 99/153; more details below).

The legislation on material social insurance law, dealt with in more detail on pp. 337–340, was restricted initially to adjusting social insurance benefits to economic conditions in the post-war period (especially the Adjustment Law of 12 December 1946, BGB no. 13/1947). Later, new rulings, particularly in favour of women who were insured (lowering pensionable age etc.), attempts at standardizing workers' and employees' insurance and improvements in pension assessment were added. Finally, persons who were self-employed in trades were included in old age pension schemes for the first time (on the principle of welfare benefits) on account of the 'Handelskammer-Unterstützungsgesetz' (Chamber of Commerce Benefits Law) of 9 July 1953, BGB no. 115. At the same time, the first steps were taken towards replacing social insurance law of the German Reich with Austrian reforms, particularly with the first Social Insurance Reform Law of 3 April, BGB no. 86.

Furthermore, the Federal Ministry for Social Administration under Karl Maisel (from 20 December 1945 to 23 January 1956) prepared legal regulations for the individual branches of insurance—a plan, however, that was dropped after the draft of a General Accident Insurance Law failed, in favour of a project for a General Social Insurance Law (see below pp. 340–344).

The General Social Insurance Law (the 'ASVG') of 9 September 1955, BGB no. 189, is undoubtedly the most significant socio-political achievement of the 'Grand Coalition'. This alliance between the two major parties, entered for the first time after the elections on 25 November 1945 and frequently renewed, formed the political basis of Austrian federal governments from 20 December 1945 until the ÖVP assumed office on its own under Josef Klaus on 19 April 1966.[481] Apart from great success in foreign affairs, for example the State Treaty (see above), this 'Grand Coalition' takes particular credit for its firm stance against Communist agitation (particularly on the occasion of the October rising, 1950) and for the development of a system of 'Sozialpartnershcaft' (literally: social partners, referring to collective bargaining etc.) which is highly praised internationally and considered as a model (cf. especially the wage-price agreements and the 1962 Raab-Olah-Agreement).[482]

Indeed, Austria's decisive step towards being a 'social constitutional state of western style' was taken as early as 1945–1955, before the State Treaty, during the first decade of the 'Grand Coalition'.[483]

In its late phase, the negative aspects of the 'Grand Coalition' became obvious: government based on daily compromises made it increasingly difficult to tackle larger scale legislative projects and the political value of parliament was reduced—a delicate matter with regard to constitutional law.[484]

After Klaus's government had been in office for about 4 years, the National Council elections of 1 March 1970 resulted in a change in political conditions in favour of the Socialist Party as the newly elected chairman of the party, Bruno Kreisky, succeeded in winning over considerable numbers of voters from the liberal middle class.[485] As a return to the 'Grand Coalition' did not prove feasible, a Socialist minority government was formed. Since the 1971 elections the Socialist government has been supported by an absolute majority of votes and seats. Nevertheless, the 'Sozialpartnerschaft' which began during the coalition era has enjoyed continued significance and effectiveness. This factor is of fundamental importance for the further development of social insurance law.

The great progress in social insurance legislation in the second republic, to be discussed in detail, would not have been possible — at least not to the same extent — if the favourable economic climate[486] had not provided the material prerequisites.

National Socialist rule and war events had cost nearly 300 000 lives in Austria; 120 000 persons were war-disabled. In 1946 industrial production only amounted to 43.1 percent of pre-war production (1937) and the gross national product was only two-thirds of the 1937 level whic had been very low in any case. Soon the level of employment did actually exceed that of the pre-war figures (1947, 119.0 percent); however, this figure is deceptive because of many fictitious jobs.[487] In 1951 the number of registered unemployed averaged 129 000.

After the real national product had reached the last pre-war level (1937) in 1949 and even the best result of the first republic (1929) in 1950, the currency began to stabilize at the beginning of the 1950s. At the same time there was almost full employment. The years 1950 to 1975 were marked by a boom, unprecedented in Austrian economic history. Overall, the real gross national product rose '3.4-fold or on an average of 5 percent per annum'.[488] This growth rate was achieved again recently (1979) and even exceeded[489] after temporary setbacks (1978). However, the number of unemployed has risen slightly since 1973 (to about 2 percent); nevertheless, it has been 'among the lowest figures in the OECD area over the last few years'[490] while the total number of employed continues to rise at the same time.

The migratory trend — already obvious in the National Socialist era — among people employed in agriculture and forestry towards the 'secondary sector' (industry and processing trades) increased noticeably after 1951. While 27 percent of the working population worked in agriculture and forestry in 1934, this percentage fell to 22 percent in 1951 and to 11 percent in 1971.[491] However, this sector experienced far greater increases in productivity than industry.[492] Recent years have been particularly marked by the great expansion of the 'tertiary sector' (services) which accounted for 42.4 percent in 1978, thus overtaking the 'secondary sector' (41.9 percent). In 1978 only 13.8 percent of the working population were active in the 'primary sector'.[493]

THE SOCIAL INSURANCE TRANSITIONAL LAW
(SOZIALVERSICHERUNGS-ÜBERLEITUNGSGESETZ) OF 12 JUNE 1947

The continued effectiveness of German social insurance law, as stipulated by §2 of the 'Rechtsüberleitungsgesetz', had been considered a provisional arrangement from the outset. A return to social insurance law of the first republic could not be considered because of the many improvements to benefits in the meantime (particularly workers' disability and old age insurance and the development of maternity benefits).

The government's aim was far more 'the development of social insurance leading towards a people's insurance comprehending broad sectors of the population' during the renewal of the 'whole of social insurance law . . . from top to bottom'.⁴⁹⁴ However, it did not feel able for financial reasons to complete this aim straightaway. Thus, a 'provisional law' was created, the 'Sozialversicherungs-Überleitungsgesetz' of 12 June 1947, BGB no. 142. This was to prepare the organizational aspects of future reform; otherwise, it was limited to 'provisional regulations which could not be further postponed concerning benefits and contributions'.⁴⁹⁵ Despite this comparatively modest reform programme, preliminary debates on the draft laws took over one-and-a-half years. Deliberations centred particularly around the following three main questions: (i) the organization of accident and pension insurance institutions; (ii) the formation and composition of self-administrative bodies; and (iii) the financial participation of the state in pensions insurance.⁴⁹⁶

The Austrian People's Party and the Socialists held extremely different views on organization. While the former wanted to re-establish the institutions provided by the 1935 GSVG as well as a (workers') disability insurance, the latter aimed at 'as much concentration as possible . . . by setting up a single central insurance institution with the required establishments in the counties. . . .' In the course of inter-party discussions a decision was finally made to establish a total of seven insurance institutions for pensions and/or accident insurance (cf. §2, section 1 SV-ÜG: (i) General Accident Insurance Institution; (ii) Employees' Insurance Institution; (iii) General Disability Insurance Institution; (iv) Agricultural and Forestry Social Insurance Institution; (v) Austrian Railways' Insurance Institution; (vi) Miners' Insurance Institution; and (vii) Notaries' Insurance Institution). By contrast, sickness insurances were largely to follow on from existing institutions (§5); this meant particularly the renunciation of the re-establishment of independent sickness insurances for employees. Only the terms 'district sickness insurance' (Gebietskrankenkasse) and 'agricultural sickness insurance' (Landwirtschaftskrankenkasse), used in the first republic (GSVG 1935, LAVG 1928), were reintroduced.

The political parties agreed totally on the second central theme of the SV-ÜG, namely the 're-establishment of self-administration' including the arbitration court system. The 'Führerprinzip', established according to Reich law, was abolished and politicians fell back on the principles of Austrian social insurance law; upon the board's insistence not only executive and supervisory boards were planned but also general meetings in order to re-establish contact with the insured as soon as possible (§14, section 1).

The number of associations was reduced compared with earlier Austrian law: 'Apart from the Association of the Masters' Sickness Insurances, only the Central Association of Social Insurance Institutions (Hauptverband der Sozialversicherungsträger) to which all social insurances belong (the masters' sickness insurances via their association) was established' (cf. §9).

The idea of concentration was also followed when the arbitration courts were reintroduced: instead of establishing organizations according to the professions, arbitration courts 'for all social insurance institutions' were established in each federal state (§94); at the same time these were subdivided into 'departments' (§95).

No definite solution could be found to the question of financing pensions insurance. Only the government's commitment to make advance payments towards the contributions which it was to pay in future was standardized for the time being (§85, section 3, lit. (b)).

The Adaptation Laws, the Law on Supplementary Allowances and Others

Based on the law of 12 December 1946, *BGB* no. 13/1947, a total of six laws attempted to adapt social insurance benefits to the unstable economic conditions of the post-war period by increasing minimum pensions, bonuses etc. The last of this series of laws, dated 25 July 1951, *BGB* no. 189, led to an increase of benefits by 218 percent[497] since the end of 1946. The 'Zusatzrentengesetz' (Law on Supplementary Allowances) of 19 May 1949, *BGB* no. 115, also made an important contribution towards the improvement of benefits in employees' insurance. Finally, the law of 21 April 1948, *BGB* no. 80, lowered the retirement age for insured women to 60.

Approximation of Workers' Pensions to Employees' Pensions Insurance; the Reduction of War Preferences; 'Delevelling' of Pensions

The law of 19 May 1949, *BGB* no. 112, contributed considerably towards bringing workers' pensions into line with employees' pensions, particularly as it ordered basic amounts of workers' insurance to be raised to the level of employees' insurance.[498] The first Social Insurance Reform Law of 3 April 1952, *BGB* no. 86, departed from the 'permanent rights to benefits' which had been introduced during the war and had become a heavy burden on pensions insurance. However, it provided the possibility of paying up insurance contributions later if payments were interrupted resulting in a disruption of claims. Finally, the pensions scale was given a new basis in accordance with the idea of 'delevelling' by the law of 6 July 1954, *BGB* no. 151. This made it possible to reduce the considerable financial differences between one's working period and when drawing a pension.

Old Age Pensions for Tradespeople

In 1947 a Socialist motion and in 1948 a motion by the ÖVP demanded the establishment of comprehensive social insurance for all the self-employed.[499] Thereupon the National Council only approved a 'Unternehmerkrankenversicherungsgesetz' (Law on Sickness Insurance for Entrepreneurs) on 14 July 1950 which would have applied to tradespeople who were not already subject to compulsory sickness insurance by decree. However, the Federal Council lodged an objection so that the law was not passed. Several years later at least a small measure of success was gained with regard to old age pensions when the law 'on the old age assistance of the chambers of commerce' of 9 July 1953, *BGB* no. 115, was passed, although this provided only for extremely modest benefits.[500]

Others Laws

Many other laws concerning social insurance law were passed between 1945 and 1955. Of these, the following merit special mention: the 'Opferfürsorgegesetz' (Law on Victims' Pensions) of 4 July 1947, *BGB* no. 183, which regulated pensions of victims of the National Socialist persecution; the law of 8 July 1948, *BGB* no. 177, regulating social insurance matters when taking up employment in a public institution; and the law of 14 July 1949, *BGB* no. 196, on regulations on social insurance for railway workers in the field of public transport. The SV-ÜG was amended eight times, reissued in 1953 (*BGB* no. 99) as the 'SV-ÜG 1953' and then amended a further three times. The law of 3 April 1952, *BGB* no. 86, must be considered a first step towards the reform of social insurance law and led up to the era of the ASVG. This (first) Social Insurance Reform Law contained provisions on qualifying periods, the procurement and crediting of insurance periods in pensions insurance as well as on the insurance of persons who periodically work in agriculture and forestry.

THE 'ALLGEMEINE SOZIALVERSICHERUNGSGESETZ' (ASVG–GENERAL SOCIAL INSURANCE LAW) OF 9 SEPTEMBER 1955

History

Shortly after the SV-ÜG was passed (cf. above p. 337) the Ministry of Social Affairs submitted a draft of a General Sickness Insurance Law[501] on which the general association of social insurance institutions, established on 1 January 1948, issued a comprehensive report. At the same time this association had other far-reaching aims: as early as 1949 a board of experts was appointed to screen all legislative material and thus to create the basis for codifying social insurance law. It was soon generally accepted that the plan of the Ministry of Social Affairs gradually to replace German Reich law with Austrian partial reforms would take too much time. Thus, the draft of a second Social Insurance Reform Law, which was ready by the middle of 1952 and was to reform some insurance sectors such as the range of persons insured, the contribution system and procedure, did not become law.

Further development was based on the draft of a General Social Insurance Law which had been prepared gradually in 1953 and 1954 by the General Association of Social Insurances. This draft was in turn the basis of the draft prepared by experts of the Ministry of Social Affairs in 1954 and submitted for appraisal. As the opinions voiced in the course of the appraisal could not be reduced to a common denominator, an attempt was made to reach an agreement on the basis of inter-party negotiations of the coalition parties, including experts from the Ministry of Social Affairs, the General Association and representation of other interests. The dominant personalities of these inter-party negotiations held from 24 January to 6 September 1955 were Chancellor Julius Raab (Chairman) and Reinhard Kamitz (Minister of Finance) representing the ÖVP and Karl Maisel (Minister of Social Affairs) and Johann Böhm (Chairman of the Austrian Trade Union Congress) of the Socialist party. On 9 September 1955, only three days after these extremely intense negotiations, the ASVG was passed during a special parliamentary session.

Main Aims and Characteristics

The main aims and characteristics of this law, comprising a total of 546 paragraphs and divided into ten parts, are to be discussed briefly:

Summary of social insurance law adjusted to Austrian circumstances

The most obvious progressive measure which the ASVG brought for the 'sector of general social insurance' (see below) was to overcome the fragmentation of law and thus the lack of confidence in the law. It was clearly shown how bad this situation was by §1, section 1 of the SV-ÜG: 'all provisions inconsistent with the ASVG' were repealed. Moreover, sixteen social insurance laws of the second republic were expressly repealed. The summary of provisions which apply to all branches of insurance in a 'General (1st) Part' (§§1–115) was of major significance for the sake of clarity. To an even greater extent than the '1st book' of the 'Reichsversicherungsordnung', this 'General Part' fulfils more than just the function of a formal summary. It forms the legal basis of a 'General Social Insurance Law' whose main elements are the identity of the groups of insured in all branches of insurance, the use of sickness insurance institutions as an organizational basis for the whole of social insurance, uniform social insurance contributions and arbitration courts which all branches of insurance have in common.

Validity and organization of social insurance

The 'general social insurance' (§1) encompasses sickness, accident and pensions insurance with the exception of the 'special insurances' which include sickness insurance of government employees, sickness insurance for masters (at that time) and insurance for notaries (§2). Deviating from the principles of the 1935 GSVG (cf. above p. 331) unemployment insurance was not included in the system of 'general social insurance' by the ASVG. No major changes were made with regard to the circle of persons subject to compulsory insurance. There were two significant changes, with regard to so-called 'self-insurance': self-insurance ceased to exist in pensions insurance while it was made easier in sickness insurance for independent farmers and other persons who earned independently (§18).[502] The latter change was of major significance and the subject of much political debate. The organization of the insurances, modelled by the SV-ÜG, was not changed by the ASVG. However, some new terms were introduced: Pensions Insurance for Employees and Workers, Austrian Miners' Insurance.

Summary of benefits system in old age, disability and surviving
dependants' insurance into a pensions insurance with
approximation of the scope of benefits to the pension
law of civil servants; reform of pension assessment

The Pension Law for Workers and Employees, regulated in the ASVG and in force from 1 January 1956 onwards, was a new development as it deviated quite considerably from previous principles of pension calculation and from German law.[503] While the old system was based on the principle of equivalence of contributions and benefits, the new system aims at the equivalence of last wage with old age pension,[504] similar to the pension law of civil servants. Thus, the previous 'Durchrechnungsprinzip' (estimation of rates of increase in addition to basic amounts according to paid contributions) was replaced by a system of 'Bemessungsgrundlage' (basis of assessment), based either on average income[505] immediately before retirement (average contribution basis of the last five years of insurance before the calendar year in which the deadline falls: §238 ASVG) or on the average income earned at the height of a person's biological creativeness, i.e. until completion of his/her 45 year.

The basic amount, uniformly set at 30 percent, and the rate of increase are calculated from the more favourable of the two bases of assessment for the individual concerned. The progression of the rates of increase is remarkable as the length of the insurance period increases; this is to encourage the insured to claim benefits as late as possible. As far as eligibility for a claim is concerned, the ASVG (which only knew the 'general case of insurance' of §253 in its original version) demands that men have reached the age of 65 and women that of 60; it also demands the fulfilment of the qualifying period, one-third coverage with contributions, and — deviating from previous legislation — the non-existence of employment subject to compulsory insurance.[506] The most important innovation of the law on qualifying periods was the possibility of continuing to pay voluntary insurance contributions upon reaching the age of eligibility to establish the right to a claim or to increased benefits. The so-called 'Ausgleichszulage' (compensation allowance) was introduced (§§292 ff. ASVG)[507] for persons eligible for a claim whose pensions, however, did not reach the usual subsistence level as insurance contributions had not been paid long enough or because the level of assessment was very low.

While regulations on workers' and employees' old age insurance completely concurred (cf. §270 ASVG), a fundamental difference continued to exist for disability insurance between the definition of disability for workers' and employees' inability to work (§273); only the degree of decreased ability to work ('less than half') was adapted to the traditional rules of employees' insurance (cf. §225, section 1 as well as §273 ASVG).

In contrast to the far-reaching uniformity of employees' and workers' pension insurance, the miners' pensions insurance has many special rulings (cf. §§275 ff.) which cannot be discussed in detail here. Apart from reform of pensions insurance, there were also many individual improvements, such as the introduction of 'Wahlarzthilfe' (assistance for a doctor of one's choice) which enabled insured persons to consult non-panel doctors and to have the costs reimbursed by the sickness insurances (cf. §131, section 1, ASVG) and the inclusion of senior employees in sickness insurance (in keeping with the idea of solidarity).[508]

Procedural reforms

As far as procedural regulations were concerned, the ASVG largely followed the provisions of the SV-ÜG. However, certain regulations of the 'Allgemeine Verwaltungsverfahrensgesetz' (AVG — General Law on Administrative Procedure) which had been passed in the meantime (1950), *BGB* no. 172, were declared applicable (§357 ASVG) both in the field of administration and of benefits.

As the Constitutional Court had declared the legal move — as provided by §111 SV-ÜG — from the arbitration courts of the social insurance to the administrative court unconstitutional in its judgment of 15 June 1953, G 3/53, as it held that the former courts were 'real courts', more comprehensive changes were required in benefit litigation procedure. In order to show that the arbitration courts do not act as the appeal courts of the social insurance institutions and in order to continue to make it possible to check decisions by arbitration courts — considered necessary by everyone — the following solution (§§383 ff. ASVG) was chosen. To begin proceedings before an arbitration court a complaint must be lodged (§383); if the suit is filed early enough the insurance's decision is invalid (§384); the arbitration court is to make a decision on the claim (§391); in accordance with the provisions of §400 ASVG, appeals against judgments in cases of litigation concerning benefits are to be made at the 'Oberlandesgericht' (supreme court) in Vienna.[509]

Amendments to the ASVG

Since it was passed in 1955 the ASVG has been modified or completed by twenty-four 'amendments'. Further modifications or supplementary regulations were brought in with other laws; the most important of these was the 'Pensionsanpassungsgesetz' (PAG—Pensions Adjustment Law), *BGB* no. 96/1965. Some of these amendments aimed only at adapting the money amounts stipulated in the law to the new income and wage conditions; others contained important new provisions or occasionally even 'corrections' to the system. The major innovations were, briefly, as follows:[510]

1. Reorganization of the law on compensation allowances by separating it from welfare law; compulsory prescription charges.
3. Premature old age pensions in cases of unemployment.
4. Introduction of a fee for sickness (and dental treatment) certificates; fixing of a lump sum for paying off claims for compensation between the General Accident Insurance and the regional and works' sickness insurances as well as the Austrian Miners' Insurance.
6. Abolition of sickness (dental treatment) certificate fee.
8. Introduction of an equalization fund (Ausgleichsfond) for sickness insurances; solution of the long-established pensions problem; premature old age pensions in cases of a long insurance record; supplementary pensions for the severely disabled.
9. Inclusion of rehabilitation in the range of benefits of both accident and pension insurance; new definition of the state of 'disability' by adapting it to the definition of employees' disablement for workers in skilled and semi-skilled jobs; binding force of the sample regulations of the central association of social insurances; substitution of the term 'Rente (Rentner)' with 'Pension (Pensionist)' for pension (pensioner).

The 'Pensionsanpassungsgesetz' of 28 April 1965, *BGB* no. 96, made fundamental changes to the pension law of the ASVG and the GSPVG (cf. below, p. 346).[511] (Cf. §§108 (e)–108 (i) ASVG; 32 (a), (e), (f) GSPVG; as well as §§24–26 B-PVG since 1969.) During the 'rule' of the traditional system of static pension assessment, changing incomes and prices had to be taken into account with '*ad hoc* adjustments' which depended to a large degree on political chance, which in the long term made disadvantages for 'old pensioners' seem inevitable. The PAG stipulated that accident insurance pensions and old age insurance pensions were to be adjusted yearly to the respective wage levels. This adjustment was to be partly automatic and partly indexed. Automatic adjustment is used when assessing benefits of pension or accident insurance for the first time; the contributory bases relevant to the basis of assessment are automatically adjusted with an 'index figure'.[512]

Disability or old age pensions which are already drawn are (merely) indexed. The 'indexing factor' which has to be proposed by the 'Advisory Board for Pension Adjustments' (§108 (e) ASVG) and fixed by decree of the Minister of Social Affairs is fundamentally the same as the 'index figure'. However, deviations are possible, depending on the country's economic situation and on a possible (considerable) change in the 'quota of burdens'.[513]

18/19. Abolition of the former ruling on maximum duration of treatment in public hospitals; treatment of the sick is now to be granted according to §144, section 1 ASVG 'if and as long as the illness requires it'.

21. Introduction of full compulsory insurance for persons undergoing vocational training; extension of statutory claim to sick pay to seventy-eight weeks; conversion of the insured person's death benefit into a statutory minimum benefit.

23. Reform of continued voluntary insurance; cancellation of benefits upon marriage; transition to demonstrative listing of accident prevention measures.

29. Introduction of preventive medical examinations as a compulsory item of sickness insurances (effective as of 1 January 1974); bonus for old age pensions and introduction of compensation on old age pension deference (taken over from the GSPVG); incorporation of the agricultural sickness insurances in the regional sickness insurances; dissolution of the 'Land- und Forstwirtschaftliche Sozialversicherungsanstalt' (Agricultural and Forestry Social Insurance Institution); transfer of the accident and old age pension insurance of agricultural and forestry workers to the workers' pension insurance and to the general accidents insurance; transfer of accident insurance for self-employed farmers to the 'Sozialversicherungsanstalt der Bauern' (Farmers' Social Insurance) newly created as of 1 January 1974 (see below p. 347).

32.[514] Introduction of statutory accident insurance for schoolchildren and students; reform of rehabilitation; possibility of voluntary insurance in the sickness insurance; possibility of 'purchasing' time insured; uniform accident insurance contributions for workers and employees; uniform contribution rates in pension insurance for workers and employees; ruling on liquidity reserves in pensions insurance.

The 'Sozialversicherungs-Änderungsgesetz' (Social Insurance Amendment Law) of 29 December 1977, *BGB* no. 192,[515] which amended almost all social insurance laws, aimed at relieving the federal budget and at 'equalization' in favour of the workers' pension insurance which was structurally at a disadvantage.

For this purpose an additional contribution was introduced into pensions insurance; together with transfers of unemployment insurance this went to the newly established compensation fund of the pension insurances.[516] Furthermore, the maximum contribution basis in sickness insurance was raised to three-quarters of the maximum contribution basis of pension insurance in order to finance hospitals.

The thirty-third ASVG[517] amendment, passed within the framework of the 'Sozialrechts-Änderungsgesetz' (Social Law Amendment Act) of 16 December 1978, *BGB* no. 684, which at the same time also represented the first amendment to the new laws (GSVG, BSVG) in force as of 1 January 1979, provided, *inter alia*, for a continuation of insurance and self-insurance in pensions insurance at a cheaper rate for times when the insured bring up their children. It also provided for the later 'purchase' of such times and for further financial measures in favour of the workers' pension insurance.

FURTHER DEVELOPMENT OF SOCIAL INSURANCE FOR CIVIL SERVANTS
AND NOTARIES[518]

The law of 13 July 1920, *StGB* no. 311, reissued with *BGB* no. 94/1937, on sickness insurance for civil servants (cf. above p. 324) was put into force again with the 1947 SV-ÜG (cf. above p. 337), §1, section 2. However, the outdated regulations of this law proved inadequate, especially once the ASVG came into force. Thus, numerous improvements to sickness insurance had to be made circuitously via ASVG amendments.[519] Accident insurance did not exist for civil servants. If a civil servant was unable to work following an accident when on duty the relevant regulations of civil servant law provided for the addition of a 10-year service period to assess the pension. Financial compensation was not provided for civil servants who continued to be active. Medical treatment etc. of complaints arising from an accident while in service was assured by the Federal Employees' Sickness Insurance.

During the course of negotiations between the four trade unions of the civil service and the 'employers' (federal government and states) on the 1965 Pensions Law (PG), BGB no. 340, the trade unions demanded, inter alia, the introduction of 'accident insurance corresponding to the principles of the ASVG'. After lengthy disputes on the competence question between the Office of the Federal Chancellor and the Ministry of Social Affairs, the 'Beamten-Kranken- und Unfallversicherungsgestz' (B-KUVG — Law on Sickness and Accident Insurance for Civil Servants) of 31 May 1967, BGB no. 200, was finally passed. It was effective as of 1 July 1967. It contains a rule on sickness insurance adapted to the standard of the ASVG as well as a rule for the first time on accident insurance for civil servants. However, the latter has no maximum contribution basis and thus no maximum assessment basis and it does not provide for pensions for parents and brothers and sisters.[520] Moreover, pensions are not adjusted in accordance with the PAG (see p. 343 above) but in line with the automatic mechanism of the 1965 Pensions Law.

The B-KUVG is of major significance for the entire Austrian social insurance system as this law brought the last large professional group into the circle of people covered by accident insurance. The B-KUVG has been amended several times; the last (seventh) amendment[521] was made in 1978 and was closely linked with the 'Sozialrechts-Änderungsgesetz'. The 'Versicherungsanstalt öffentlicher Bediensteter' (BVA — Civil Servants' Insurance) in Vienna is responsible both for civil servants' sickness and accident insurance.

The 1926 Law on Notaries' Insurance (see above p. 329), reissued with BGB no. 2/1938, was put into force again[522] with the 1947 SV-ÜG, §1, section 3, apart from regulations on sickness and unemployment insurance which only affected the candidates to the notary profession. The 'Versicherungsanstalt des österreichischen Notariats' (Austrian Notaries' Insurance Institution) in Vienna became responsible for the remaining two spheres of notaries' insurance, namely accident and pensions insurance for notaries and candidates to the notary profession in accordance with §2, section 1, line 7 of the ASVG.

Notaries' social insurance law developed further on account of several amendments[523] from 1951 onwards and the special provisions of the ASVG (§§494-499). The 'Pensionsversicherung für das Notariat/Notarvericherungsgesetz 1972 (NVG)' (Pensions Insurance for Notaries/Notaries' Insurance Law of 1972) reformed both pensions insurance and accident insurance integrated in the former. The latter is extensively reduced.[524] The definition of the term 'disablement' in the NVG (§2, line 12) deserves special mention (in accordance with the legal situation so far); it excludes any possibility of referring an insured notary to another form of employment and thus notaries' insurance is an 'absolute professional insurance'.[525]

Further Development of Social Insurance for the Self-Employed in the Trades and Professions

Assistance granted in cases of need by the 'Handelskammer-Alters-unterstützungsfonds' (Old Age Assistance Fund of the Chamber of Com-merce—cf. above p. 336) had been considered a provisional measure from the start.[526] Thus, when the ASVG was passed, moves were initiated to introduce an old age pension scheme based on the insurance principle for the self-employed. First, a draft was submitted by the Ministry of Social Affairs in February 1956 aiming at introducing a pension insurance ruling for all the self-employed. Although the majority of representatives for the interests of the self-employed re-jected this, the federal government appointed a committee of ministers on 25 June 1957 to draft a government bill. Shortly afterwards a decision was made to provide special laws both for the self-employed in trades and industry and for those in agriculture and forestry. It was made possible—but left open to persons in the professions—to subscribe voluntarily to the future pensions insurance.

Once the main problem of the new law, namely that of providing contribu-tions, was solved—the state was to pay half the contributions out of the trade taxes—the 'Gewerbliche Selbständigen-Pensionsversicherungsgesetz' (GSPVG—Pensions Insurance Law for the Self-Employed) of 18 December 1957 was passed. It came into force on 1 January (contribution law) resp. 1 July 1958 (benefits law). Among the professions, accountants, dentists and journalists opted for inclusion in pension insurance according to the GSPVG although they had to bear the full cost of contributions in accordance with §18, section 1, lit. (b)—an inequality which was later rectified by the judgment of the Constitutional Court of 26 March 1960, G 10/59.

Although the GSPVG constituted a decisive step towards pension insurance for the self-employed in trade and industry and for members of the professions, the law in its original form was not exactly satisfactory in the following points: originally the pension level was extremely low, even for new pensions; no real ac-count was taken of the pension needs of the insured until the 'Pensionsan-passungsgesetz' (Pensions Adjustment Law) of 1965 was passed (cf. above p. 343). Overall, the average direct pension, expressed in index figures, rose from 100 in 1959 and 157 in 1965 to 667 in 1977. This increase in benefits is all the more remarkable as the number of insured in pensions (or social) insurance for the self-employed in trades was continually falling (1959, 220 000; end of 1977, 177 000).[527]

The 'Gewerbliche Selbständigen-Krankenversicherungsgesetz' (GSKVG—Sickness Insurance Law for the Self-Employed in Trade and In-dustry) of 14 July 1966, BGB no. 167, reformed sickness insurance of the self-employed (Meisterkrankenversicherung—Masters' Sickness Insurance). It adhered to the principle of voluntary subjection to compulsory sickness insurance by majority decision but standardized the statutory obligation to implement such a decision within a year.

The 'Gewerbliche Selbständigen-Krankenversicherungsgesetz' of 13 July 1971, BGB no. 287 (GSKVG 1971), replaced the corresponding law of 1966. Apart from numerous improvements to benefits the 1971 GSKVG provided in par-ticular for the amalgamation (carried out on 1 January 1974) of the insurance in-stitutions of the GSKVG and of the GSPVG to become the 'Sozialversicherungsanstalt der gewerblichen Wirtschaft' (Social Insurance of the Trades) with its main office in Vienna and with nine regional offices. As the ballot votes introduced by the 1971 GSKVG did not bring the desired result, the legislature decided on statutory compulsory sickness insurance (law of 29 December 1976) for all persons engaged in a trade and for pensioners with the fifth amendment to the GSKVG.[528] The development of social insurance for the self-employed in the trades reached a temporary climax with the law of 11 October 1978, *BGB* no. 560, on 'the social insurance of persons independently engaged in trades'.[529] This law is largely a summary of the provisions of the GSKVG and the GSPVG (currently in the version of the first amendment of 16 December 1978, *BGB* no. 684).[530] In addition to those groups of self-employed persons who were subject to the compulsory pension insurance of the GSPVG from the very beginning (see above), independent artists were soon subject to this insurance (1958), followed by veterinary surgeons in 1964 and managing partners of limited liability companies in 1978. The law on 'social insurance for the self-employed' of 30 November 1978, *BGB* no. 624,[532] now provides the possibility of also subjecting doctors, lawyers, (dispensing) chemists, and engineers, *inter alia,* to compulsory sickness and accident insurance.

FURTHER DEVELOPMENT OF SOCIAL INSURANCE FOR FARMERS[533]

When the ASVG was passed in 1955 there was a marked lack of social insurance protection for farm owners and their dependants. At that time, social insurance coverage extended only to statutory accident insurance as the regional governments of Vienna, Lower Austria and the Burgenland had already made use of the possibility of extending compulsory accident insurance to self-employed farmers and their dependants as provided in the 'Landarbeiterversicherungsgesetz' (Insurance Law for Farm Workers) of 18 July 1928 (cf. above p. 329) which also applied to forestry workers. Later the '6th Law on Amendments in Accident Insurance' of 9 March 1942, *DRGB* I, p. 107, in accordance with the new version of §537, line 1 of the 'Reichsversicherungsordnung' (effective from 1 January 1942 onwards) had declared that farmers in the remaining parts of Austria (the 'Ostmark' at that time) were also subject to compulsory insurance.[534] Self-employed farmers and their dependants — in so far as these were not employed by the farmer — were not subject, however, to compulsory sickness and disability insurance.[535]

At the end of 1955 the government was urged in a draft resolution to introduce a bill. However, as the draft prepared by the Ministry of Social Affairs did not meet with the approval of the representatives of the farmers' interests, the latter submitted a proposal in parliament via a motion by an ÖVP deputy which was discussed from June until November 1957 by a committee of ministers and which was then used as a basis for the 'Landwirtschaftliche Zuschussrentenversicherungsgesetz' (LZVG — Law on Agricultural Pension Allowances) of 18 December 1957, *BGB* no. 293. The 'Landwirtschaftliche Zuschussrentenversicherungsanstalt' (LZVA — Institution for Agricultural Pension Allowances) was responsible for administering this insurance. The group liable to compulsory insurance included the farmer and his children (including adopted children and step-children) and children-in-law if they mainly and continually work on the farm or in forestry. As its very title expresses, this insurance is not a full and adequate pensions insurance but consists only of cash allowances in addition to the farmer's share of property—usually in kind—upon his retirement. As material on the LZVG[536] shows, the fundamental idea of this law was based on three conditions: (a) constant work in agriculture and forestry; (b) guarantee of accomodation and full board by share of the property reserved for the farmer on his retirement; (c) lack of (other forms of) old age pensions for children working on farm.

Although the LZVG represented considerable progress, compared with the previous situation, as over 150 000 pensions paid out by the LZVA prove, it soon did not come up to socio-political expectations as the conditions on which the law was based increasingly gave way to new situations: the migration of the farming population to the secondary and tertiary sectors of employment, as discussed earlier (above p. 337), made the assumption of 'constant working' unjustifiable. This and growing specialization in agriculture made the traditional system of annuities upon the transfer of a farm to a descendant begin to collapse. In cases of tenant farmers or farmers without anyone to take the farm over, the system of annuities as a pension basis could not be applied.

In June 1967 proposals were made by the conference of chairmen of the Chambers of Agriculture to the Ministry of Social Affairs to reform the system of pension subsidies.[537] However, shortly afterwards a decision was made to introduce full pension insurance in the spirit of the GSPVG (see above p. 346); as a plan had been prepared within the ÖVP from July 1968 to July 1969 and used as a basis for the government bill, the 'Bauern-Pensionsversicherungsgesetz' (B-PVG—Farmers' Pension Insurance Law) was passed on 12 December 1969, *BGB* no. 28/1970; the law on benefits of the B-PVG came into force on 1 January 1971.

The 'Pensionsversicherungsanstalt der Bauern' (PVAB—Farmers' Pension Insurance Institution) succeeded the LZVA. As of 1 January 1974 this insurance institution fused with the 'Österreichische Bauernkrankenkasse' (ÖBKK—Austrian Farmers' Sickness Insurance) to form the 'Sozialversicherungsanstalt der Bauern' (SVAB—Farmers' Social Insurance Institution) with the second B-PVG amendment, *BGB* no. 33/1973, in connection with the twenty-ninth ASVG amendment (cf. p. 344 above). At the same time the SVAB became responsible for farmers' accident insurance.

The beginnings of obligatory sickness insurance for farmers were recognizable in the sickness insurance of subsidized pensioners which was to be provided according to the LZVG but was not possible for financial reasons. A motion introduced to the National Council on 17 February 1960 as well as a meeting held by representatives for the farmers' interests in the same year on the worrying health conditions of the farming population again pointed to the necessity of compulsory sickness insurance for farmers.[538] In the spring of 1961 the Ministry of Social Affairs submitted the draft of a Farmers' Sickness Insurance Law; this was revised, taking opinions of representatives of the farmers' interests into account, and presented to the Council of Ministers on 15 December 1963 whereupon it was subjected to rigorous examination.

When the farmers' four main demands[539] had been considered in the government bill, namely: (a) 'Subsidiarität' (subsidiary principle, i.e. assistance when self-help has failed) *vis-à-vis* other insurances, (b) federal administration; (c) governmental financial participation; and (d) extensive co-insurance of dependants, the 'Bauern-Krankenversicherungsgesetz' (B-KVG—Farmers' Sickness

Insurance Law), *BGB* no. 219, was passed on 7 July 1965. (The law on its benefits became effective as of 1 April 1966). The 'Krankenversicherungsanstalt der Bauern' (Farmers' Sickness Insurance Institution) whose title was changed to the 'Österreichische Bauernkrankenkasse' (ÖBKK—Austrian Farmers' Sickness Insurance) with the first amendment, *BGB* no. 256/1967, was responsible for underwriting this insurance. Farmers' sickness insurance did not develop satisfactorily from a financial point of view. While the paid-in contributions stagnated from time to time, due to a drop in the number of insured, expenditure rose by 120 percent from 1967 to 1975.[541]

Similar to social insurance law for persons engaged in the trades, social insurance law for farmers was only recently summarized in the law of 11 October 1978, *BGB* no. 559, on social insurance for the self-employed in agriculture and forestry ('Bauern-Sozialversicherungsgesetz'—BSVG—Farmers' Social Insurance Law). This was done by combining the provisions of the B-KVG and of the B-PVG as well as by including references to the ASVG, particularly with regard to general regulations and relevant accident insurance provisions. In the BSVG a move was made away from a system of insurance classes in sickness insurance and thus the entire farmers' social insurance law adapted itself along the lines of the GSVG, even in the law on contributions. At the moment the first amendment to the BSVG, *BGB* no. 684/1978, carried out within the framework of the 'Social Law Amendment Act', is in force.[542]

CONCLUDING REMARKS

The Initial Situation in Austria in the 1880s Compared With Other European States (Especially the German Reich)

Political and Ideological Situation of the Danube Monarchy (Cisleithan Half of the Empire)

Austria has a special status with regard to its territorial and political structure compared with the other states discussed in this collective volume. Austria, designated officially as 'the kingdoms and lands represented in the "Reichsrat"', when the first social insurance laws were passed, was a state of many ethnic groups.

This did not lead to any noticeable disadvantages for social legislation in general and social insurance legislation in particular. On the contrary, one of the major achievements of the Taaffe Government (1879–1893) was to succeed in making social policy the great common task of those countries united in the Cisleithan half of the empire and thus in creating an effective counterweight to the nationalist tendencies among supporters of Taaffe's government. Apart from the dispute over sickness insurance for agricultural and forestry workers (above p. 330), national differences remained largely in the background while developing the first social insurance laws.

After 1890, however, and especially after Taaffe's dismissal (1893), national differences of opinion gained the upper hand to such an extent that all spheres of legislation were affected. This explains why the flow of socio-political laws temporarily dwindled away to nothing between 1893 and 1900 (above p. 311). Somewhat calmer conditions did not prevail again until the Körber era (1900–1905). In Körber's major reform plan, social policy played an important role as an integrating element for the multiracial state, even if Körber's priority was clearly the reform of administration. Ever since the first elections carried out according to the principle of universal and equal franchise in 1907, social policy and especially social insurance (which now went beyond the scope of workers' insurance) has been in the foreground of parliamentary and other political activities. Parliamentarians and other experts of all the nations united in the Cisleithan half of the empire worked right up until the outbreak of the First World War towards the completion of an all-embracing social insurance legislation that would have covered a total of 10 million people (including 4 million self-employed people) in accident, sickness and pensions insurance (above p. 321).

Since the collapse of the Danube monarchy in October 1918 Austria is no longer a multiracial state but a federal state (with individual national minorities). Based on the provisions of the Federal Constitutional Law of 1 October 1920 concerning powers which did not come into force until 1925, 'social insurance' legislation and its execution are matters for the federal government (art. 10, section 1, line 11). From the start Austria had some remarkable political structures, both in 1880, and during the course of later development, which were of considerable significance for social insurance legislation: from 1860/1 to 1879 liberalism was the dominant political force in Austria, apart from the 'Hohenwart-Schäffle' intermezzo in 1871 (above p. 276–278). Although Austrian liberalism sometimes surpassed the urge for freedom of Prussia and of the German Reich in intensity (particularly during the last few years before the stock exchange crash of 1873), one cannot help but agree with Hans Rosenberg[543] who maintained that liberalism was not as deeply-seated socially in Austria as, for example, in Prussia. This proved to be the case in 1879 when slight shifts in the proportion of seats in parliament and the return of the Czechs to the 'Reichsrat' made Liberal rule totter and soon fall. Political and (to a limited extent) economic liberalism was routed earlier and more intensively in Austria than elsewhere. It was replaced by an extremely heterogeneous alliance of federalists and conservatives, the so-called 'Iron Ring'. The social idea as a national and ideological unifying factor filled the ideological vacuum which liberalism had left behind (above p. 279–280). It would, of course, be quite inappropriate to deny Austrian liberalism any socio-political commitment: for both the drafts of a new 'Gewerbeordnung' (Trade Act — with very extensive employer liability) and the plans to reform the 'Berggesetz' (Miners' Act) clearly indicate willingness to improve social conditions in favour of those who were socially weaker.

Later on, Austrian liberals proved more flexible in their attitudes towards compulsory insurance than, for example, the 'Freisinnigen' (free thinkers i.e. Liberals) of the German 'Reichstag'. Although the 1882 motion demanding the introduction of compulsory accident and sickness insurance for workers (above p. 290) is said to have at least been influenced by the fear of being politically 'run over' by the government's socio-political bills, the fundamentally positive attitude of the Austrian liberals towards applying 'compulsory insurance' in the interests of socially prejudiced groups is clearly contrasted with the rejection of compulsory insurance by liberal groups in other European countries.

As far as the ideological background of Taaffe's legislation on workers' insurance is concerned, it is important to note from the first that — if the negative aspects must be emphasized — it was far more marked by defensive attitudes towards liberalism than towards Social Democracy. This difference — which I consider fundamental — to Bismarck's social legislation is partly due to the fact that the Social Democrats had not formed themselves into a uniform political group by the beginning of the 1880s and also that they were not represented in parliament because of the curia voting system (with census), and partly due to the primarily anti-Liberal and secondly anti-Social Democratic line taken by Christian Social reformers.

There is no doubt that the latter set the trend for many items of the Taaffe Government's policy; after all, leading representatives of Christian Social reform (such as Liechtenstein and Belcredi) belonged to the 'Reichsrat' and assessed the government bills in the (Trade) Board responsible. The aims of these Christian Social reformers were socio-revolutionary in such an all-embracing way that social insurance legislation could only be attributed a secondary role as a means of relieving social ills.

The real task of social legislation was to re-establish the economic and social balance which — at least according to the Christian Social reformers' ideas that did not always conform with historical reality — had existed before liberalism had helped the dogma of freedom to victory by tearing apart most social and economic barriers. Thus, the primary task of economic and social policy was to re-establish or newly set up economic and social barriers of private autonomy. Thus, it is hardly surprising that economic and social legislation of the Taaffe Government (above p. 289–311) began with legislation on profiteering (1881), the introduction of proof of qualification in trade law (1883), and workers' protection measures (1885).

There was also a considerable difference between the people involved in social insurance legislation in the German Reich and in Austria. While Bismarck was a central figure of this legislation both ideologically and politically in Germany, Taaffe tended to remain in the background as the coordinator of government activity and as contact man between the government and the monarch, a role of great political importance. Beyond that, Taaffe, without being a great ideologist, was an honest believer in social reform which he knew how to combine with the requirements of the policies of the day with great skill. Emil Steinbach's role, extending beyond mere editing, was also very important to Taaffe and the responsible head of department (Pražák). Once again Steinbach's socio-political ideas, discussed in detail in the main part of this work (above p. 294), must be stressed here for they found their expression particularly in the organizational details of Austrian workers' insurance.

As far as the Austrian Social Democrats attitude to workers' insurance legislation from 1887 to 1889 is concerned, one must bear in mind the special political situation of the Austrian labour force at that time (above p. 302). In contrast to the situation in the German Reich, the labour force was not represented in parliament (the 'Reichsrat') because of the curia voting law and the census. Moreover, until the 'Einigungsparteitag' (Hainfeld convention of 1889) the Social Democrats were divided into two groups (moderates and radicals). However, although there were no 'official' parliamentary comments, the following basic attitude is apparent from articles in 'Gleichheit', edited by Viktor Adler who later became party chairman, and from later resolutions of the Hainfeld convention: the vast majority of Social Democrats considered the workers' protection legislation of the Taaffe Government to be inadequate in many individual points and it was criticized with regard to its treatment by the authorities; however, they welcomed the general trend. The Social Democrat's working class, however, initially rejected workers' insurance laws. It is striking that criticism was directed only to a small degree at the content of these laws (especially the level of benefits); instead the labour force was largely critical of what it considered to be the political motives behind the laws ('alms' for 'crippled workers'; the shift of the community welfare burden to the workers; an attempt at the political 'conversion' of the workers, etc.—above p. 305). Soon after the Social Democratic labour force was able to send deputies to the 'Reichsrat' for the first time (1897), there was a remarkable change of direction; the labour force began to approve in principle of the idea of social insurance linked with the demand to create old age and disability insurance. Taking this line, Viktor Adler agreed to support Körber's programme. Social Democrats were initially less in favour of the demand to extend the insurance for the employed to 'social insurance' which even embraced the self-employed. However, they changed their views on this point later.

The Socio-economic Situation of the Danube Monarchy;
Existing Social Welfare Institutions and Legal Protection

In contrast to the other countries discussed in this context, Austria was not one of the leading industrial nations of Europe when social insurance legislation began to be passed. However, in the relatively small area of state territory where industrial production was concentrated (Bohemia, southern part of Lower Austria, Rhine valley in Vorarlberg), social conditions corresponded to those of the leading industrial states. The 1873 stock exchange crash had particularly negative repercussions on the economic and social situation of industrial workers in Austria. The combination of increasing wage pressure and continually rising prices exacerbated the workers' economic and social position even more. Workers' housing and health conditions also reached on all time low by the late 1870s and early 1880s.

At the same time there was a marked lack of protection against social risks. With few exceptions (see below about the 'Bruderladen') workers exposed to accidents at work or occupational diseases only had recourse to civil law proceedings, i.e. the possibility of suing for damages in cases of injury due to the fault of the employer or of one of his staff. The recognition of a claim for damages usually failed because of the difficulties of proving fault (1296 ABGB). Mainly on account of this factor, the absolute liability of the railway companies was introduced in 1869 with the 'Eisenbahnhaftpflichtgesetz' (Railways Liability Act); this considerably increased the chances of successful recognition of claims for damages of passengers and railway workers injured in railway accidents (above p. 283). The 1871 'Reichshaftpflichtgesetz' (Liability Act) (§1) created a similar legal position for the German Reich; there was no absolute liability for mines, quarries and factories but only employer liability for *culpa in eligendo vel inspiciendo* with regard to his staff (§2), a ruling which hardly went beyond the legal position existing in Austria.

As in the German Reich, numerous attempts were made in Austria—as far back as the 'Liberal era'—to introduce general employer liability modelled on the idea of railways' liability. However, Bismarck put an end to such attempts in 1880 and soon afterwards Austria also dropped this project. The reason for this decision was primarily the negative repercussions on the social climate in industrial concerns (above p. 292) linked with the assertion of claims to damages against the employer. This was also the main reason given by the Austrian legislature (above p. 296), which took over some of the explanations of the second German bill verbatim, for introducing statutory accident insurance. The latter was a type of 'redemption' for the planned and—in the case of railways—for already existing employer liability. Of course, during the course of later developments this historical link receded increasingly into the background (see p. 335).

As far as sickness insurance was concerned, there existed at the time of the workers' insurance laws works' and trade associations' sickness insurances in accordance with the provisions of the 'Gewerbeordnung' and societies' sickness insurances in accordance with the provisions of the 'Vereinsgesetz' (above p. 286). All three types of already existing schemes—based on the German system—were integrated into compulsory sickness insurance. The societies' sickness insurances had to be established in accordance with the 1852 'Vereinspatent' if scheme subscription was to comply with compulsory insurance. The 1888 Sickness Insurance Law (above p. 302) slightly weakened the government's previous restrictive attitude towards societies' schemes (from about 1882 onwards) but nevertheless basically confirmed it. Undoubtedly the government's distrust of workers' societies played a significant role; the greater control of the whole insurance system was no doubt part and parcel of the anti-Liberal tendency of the Taaffe Government and thus a move to develop the chance of state control.

The legal basis of the societies' sickness insurances was not improved in accordance with their needs until the law on 'registered relief funds' was passed. This law was conceived by the major socio-politician of the later Liberal era, Baernreither, and was largely based on the English pattern. However, as societies' sickness insurances of the old pattern were allowed to continue, workers made only little use of the Law on Relief Funds (Hilfskassengesetz). 'Masters' sickness insurances', started in 1897, were the first institutions to make use of this new legal form to a larger extent (above p. 307). While numerous beginnings already existed in Austria in the sickness insurance sector even before the legislation of the 1880s—as, for example, in the German Reich—early signs of old age and disability insurance were (apart from schemes for civil servants) only in evidence in the miners' 'Bruderladen' (above p. 307) whose benefits were extremely varied and overall very low. It was indeed difficult for Taaffe's government to reform the existing 'Bruderladen' in a form corresponding to the other workers' insurance laws and at the same time to maintain or even improve old age and disability schemes which were so far denied to other workers (above p. 309). Falkenhayn, Minister of the department concerned, was strongly opposed to the reform of the 'Bruderladen' which explains why it did not count among the socio-political achievements of the Taaffe Government. It was not until 1914 and the years that followed that improvements were made to the system of benefits of the 'Bruderladen' and that accident insurance benefits caught up with those of other workers.

INDIVIDUAL AND TRENDSETTING FEATURES OF
AUSTRIAN SOCIAL INSURANCE LAW

The Insured

As in the German Reich, industrial workers in Austria formed the nucleus of persons subject to compulsory accident and sickness insurance (above pp. 315–319).

Undoubtedly the historical connection between the (planned) employer liability and the accident insurance which replaced it was only loosely decisive for this 'pioneering role' of industrial workers in Austria. Ideological and practical considerations, as already mentioned in part, also played a role.

Insurance for the self-employed began with sickness insurance, especially with the 1897 'Gewerbeordnungsnovelle' (Amendment to the Trade Act) which provided the possibility of establishing compulsory insurance by majority decision (above p. 319).

The Pensions Insurance Law for Employees (p. 319) was a pioneering feature in so far as, earlier than in Germany, employees were singled out as a special group; as such, they were the first after miners (and civil servants) to receive old age pensions. In spite of the difficulty of defining employees compared with other employed persons, the path chosen by the Austrian legislature in 1906 proved a trendsetter (for German legislation too).

The idea of a ruling as comprehensive as possible which would also establish the identity of those employed persons to be insured obligatorily was taken up again by the 1927 Employees' Insurance Law and the 1928 Workers' Insurance Law.

Since then the idea of the identity of the insured belongs to the main principles of the system of Austrian law in all three insurance sectors although old age and disability insurance for workers continued not to be realized. From 1921/5 onwards agricultural and forestry workers were subject to compulsory sickness insurance and from 1929 (including persons who were not in machine-operated concerns) were subject to compulsory accident insurance. (The regulations on old age and disability insurance did not come into force, like those of the industrial workers.) Miners have been totally integrated in insurance for employed persons since 1935. Some of the self-employed tradespeople were subject to compulsory insurance in the masters' sickness insurances; however, there has only been compulsory sickness insurance without any gaps since the fifth GSKVG amendment of 1976 (above p. 347). Voluntary membership of employers of concerns with inherent dangers in accident insurance had been possible for 1894 onwards; statutory compulsory insurance, however, has only existed since the 1955 ASVG.

After tentative beginnings (1954), some of which were based on the welfare principle, compulsory pensions insurance was also introduced for self-employed tradespeople by the 1957 GSPVG (above p. 346). In 1958 freelance artists and in 1964 veterinary surgeons decided to make use of the possibility of compulsory pensions insurance; since 1978 the inclusion of freelancers and the self-employed in all three branches of insurance has been regulated by a special law instigated by the individual professional representatives concerned.

Farmers in the eastern provinces (Vienna, Lower Austria and Burgenland) were subject compulsory accident insurance from 1929 onwards; in the other provinces this was not the case until 1942. Moreover, farmers are able to subscribe voluntarily to sickness insurance; about one-fifth of all farmers (farm owners or managers) made use of this in 1965. All Austrian farmers (farm workers) have been subject to the compulsory sickness insurance since 1965/6. The 'Zuschussrentenversicherungsgesetz' of 1957 was a first attempt at pensions insurance; proper pensions insurance for farmers has only existed since 1970/1 (above p. 348).

The creation of compulsory sickness insurance for civil servants in 1920 (Hanusch era) which was supplemented by compulsory accident insurance in 1967 counts among the pioneering achievements of Austrian social insurance legislation. In view of civil servants' legal position, there is no need for a social insurance ruling on their old age pension (above p. 344). Finally, notaries' insurance has existed since 1926 (details above on pp. 324, 345).

Legislative Practice

The three workers' insurance laws, namely the workers' sickness insurance law, the workers' accident insurance law and the 'Bruderladengesetz', formed the beginning of social legislation. At the beginning of this century Körber's Programme provided a comprehensive ruling on insurance for all employed persons (above p. 312); however, only the Employees' Pensions Law actually came into force. Continuing Körber's Programme the three government bills of 1908 and the years that followed moved towards a project on 'social insurance' (as opposed to merely 'workers' insurance') to include all the self-employed and employed. This project would have amalgamated all three types of insurance (sickness, accident and disability or old age insurance.)

In the first republic, legislative attempts were made to create laws in which all branches of insurance, including unemployment insurance, were regulated for the various professions and types of employment. The result was the Employees' Insurance Law of 1926, the Workers' Insurance Law of 1927 and the Agricultural and Forestry Workers' Insurance Law of 1928.

The 1935 GSVG is largely a summary of the above-mentioned laws; in other words — unlike the currently valid GSVG of 1978 — it codified social insurance for the employed (workers, employees and miners), including unemployment insurance.

At least as far as legislative technicalities were concerned, Austrian legislation had almost reached a higher level after the 1935 GSVG than the German legislation of the day according to which social insurance law was largely spread over four laws, namely the 'Reichsversicherungsordnung', the Employees' Insurance Law, the 'Reichsknappschaftsgesetz' (Law on Miners' Insurance) and the Law on Labour Offices and Unemployment Insurance. In 1938 German social insurance law was then enforced in Austria in the form of these four laws (above p. 333). Apart from unemployment insurance, reformed in 1949, and the reintroduction of Austrian social insurnace for civil servants and notaries, German legislation continued to apply in Austria until the ASVG came into force in 1956. The ASVG primarily regulates insurance for the employed (workers, employees, miners) for all branches of insurance except unemployment insurance (above p. 340). Insurance for the self-employed was only partly regulated at first (GSPVG, GSKVG, B-PVG, B-KVG). Now, however, there are provisions for self-employed tradespeople in the 1978 GSVG and for the farmers in the 1978 BSVG. These provisions largely imitate the pattern of the ASVG (above pp. 346–347). It has already been mentioned on p. 341 that among Austrian experts the summarization of the ASVG, GSVG and BSVG in a single all-embracing law is considered the ultimate aim of efforts so far to concentrate legislation. This would indeed mean that the bold Austrian reform plan of 1908 and later has been realized at a later date under greatly altered material conditions.

Covered Social Risks; Benefits

The following four sickness insurance cases were known to the original law: sickness, incapacity to work due to illness (not originally considered an independent case for insurance), maternity and death. According to the law in force these four cases of insurance are still of central significance. Since the 29th amendment to the ASVG (above p. 344) a threat to health has also become a case for insurance (preventive medical examinations, medical examinations of adolescents) as has the continued payment of wages since the 1974 'Entgeltfortzahlungsgesetz' (Law on the Continued Payment of Wages). As benefits (in kind) in case of sickness the original law provided free medical treatment, including medicines etc. from the beginning of illness onwards; the statutory minimum duration was fixed at 20 weeks and the maximum limit of a statutory extension at 52 weeks.

The time limit for normal cases was abolished (§134, section 1 ASVG) for the treatment of sickness (also in hospitals) with the nineteenth amendment to the ASVG (1967; above p. 343). A limitation (to a maximum period of 26 weeks) only applies to cases of illness occurring after the end of insurance (§134, section 3 ASVG). As to the treatment of the sick, it must be remarked that the 1920 B-KVG (above p. 325) for the first time established the 'free choice of doctors' in Austria; otherwise the district doctor system generally became obsolete when the German social insurance law was introduced. Then the ASVG made the transition to the so-called 'Wahlarztprinzip' (principle of a doctor of the insured person's own choice with reimbursement of costs for non-panel doctors). According to the original law (§6, section 2, line 6) a claim to sick pay could only be made if the insured person was unable to work due to illness of more than 3 days; however, if this condition was met, sick pay was provided from the first day of illness onwards. Since the 1935 GSVG (§151) sick pay is available from the fourth day onwards (provided illness occurs while the person is engaged in employment subject to compulsory insurance. The rulings in force of the ASVG and the GSVG (which only grants sick pay within the framework of additional insurance) concur with this; the statutory minimum duration is fixed at 26 weeks according to both laws and the upper limit of extension in accordance with the statutes is fixed at 78 weeks since the twenty-first ASVG amendment (1967) and 52 weeks according to the GSVG. The law provided for uniform sick pay for all insured amounting to 60 percent of the 'usual daily wage' of the respective court circuit. Although the system of wage brackets was only recommended by a minority of experts in the debates on reform at the end of the nineteenth century, this was already provided in Körber's Programme in 1904 (above p. 319). However, this system did not become part of the law until the second amendment of the KVG in 1917. The 1935 GSVG also adhered to the wage bracket system in order to determine insurance benefits in sickness insurance (§§146, 151, section 6) although this law determined contributions according to percentages of the contribution basis. The 'Reichsversicherungsordnung' left it to statute to fix the basic wage 'according ot real earnings or according to wage schedules' (§180, section 2). After the Second World War, sick pay was assessed according to wage schedule tables issued by the Federal Ministry for Social Administration. Since the ASVG has been passed sick pay is calculated according to the assessment basis; it amounts to 50 percent of the assessment basis from the fourth until the forty-second day of inability to work due to illness and 60 percent from the forty-third day onward. These percentages and times have not been amended since the

ASVG came into force. Statutory extended benefits up to 75 percent of the assessment basis (according to the ASVG) or 80 percent of the daily basis of contribution (according to the GSVG) are possible. The inclusion of members of the family in sickness insurance had been provided as a statutory extended benefit since the second amendment of the Sickness Insurance Law of 1917 (so-called family insurance). Family assistance (family treatment, maternity allowances) with the exception of death benefits did not belong to the sickness insurances' compulsory benefits until the 'Reich' law came into force in Austria. As far as maternity insurance is concerned, the original law provided for monetary benefits which were equivalent to sick pay 'for a period of at least four weeks after the birth' as well as for benefits in kind. Insurance coverage for maternity cases was considerably improved by the second amendment of the Sickness Insurance Law of 1917.

An accident at work justified a claim in accident insurance according to the original law of 1887; such an accident, however, was labelled a 'work-related accident subject to compulsory insurance'. Accidents on the way to and from work were put on a par with industrial accidents at an early date by the decisions of the arbitration courts; this equal treatment in legislation first appeared in a draft in 1896 (above p. 317); however, it did not become the subject of a legal ruling until the emergency decree of 7 April 1914 on accident insurance for miners and soon afterwards for all other persons insured against accidents with the third amendment to the Accident Insurance Law of 1917 (above p. 318). Since then, jurisdiction and—with some hesitation—also legislation has continually tried to extend accident insurance protection with regard to accidents on the way to and from work, most recently by including accidents which occur on the way to or from the place of work or training when the insured has had to attend to 'crucial personal need' (thirty-fourth amendment to the ASVG). Occupational illnesses were not recognized as a basis for a claim in the original law; this step was only completed with the 1927 Workers' Insurance Law—which did not come into force in this sector, of course—and with the seventeenth amendment of the Accident Insurance Law of 1928 (above p. 327). It is striking that the original Accident Insurance Law (1887) did not provide for obligatory benefits in kind of any sort. Towards the end of the nineteenth century (the Badeni era) a provision was included for the first time in a reform proposal, whereby accident insurance was at least entitled to take over treatment of an insured person who had had an accident; a provision of this kind did not become part of the law until 1914 when miners' statutory accident insurance was reformed. In 1917 it was incorporated into the whole of accident insurance. However, the treatment of injured persons—following an accident—did not become obligatory by law for the accident insurances until the 'Reichsversicherungsordnung' applied, i.e. from 1939 onwards. At the same time accident prevention became a primary task of accident insurance; even when deliberating on the Accident Insurance Law proposals were made in that direction.

Rehabilitation takes a special place among benefits in kind. This is also largely thanks to the 'Reichsversicherungsordnung', and to the so-called 'job provisions' (§§558, 558 f.) In contrast, the original law only provided monetary benefits, namely pensions for the disabled as well as widows', widowers', orphans' and parents' pensions if the insured person died.

Originally a claim was based on a reduction of earning capacity of over 5 percent; following the twelfth amendment to the Accident Insurance Law of 1923 (above p. 327) the possibility of agreeing on a lump-sum payment of the pension was created in cases of inability to work not exceeding one-sixth. The 1935 GSVG (§178) stipulated that a claim was justified on a reduction of ability to work of at least one-sixth or one-third (in the case of occupational illnesses). According to the current ruling, the injury caused by an accident at work must reduce working ability at least 20 percent for a period of at least three months (50 percent for occupational illnesses, schoolchildren and students).

According to the original law the waiting period was only 5 weeks; nowadays, in view of corresponding provisions in sickness insurance, this period usually lasts 26 weeks. The arithmetical basis of pensions assessment has remained largely unchanged (300 or 360 times the daily earnings; the daily maximum contribution basis). Under the original law the full pension was only 60 percent and then (from 1917 onwards) 66.6 percent of annual earnings (of the assessment basis). However, pensions can reach 80 percent with the addition of supplementary allowances for the severely disabled.

The idea of a so-called 'Hilflosenzuschuss' (allowance for the helpless) had first been voiced in 1896. However, this allowance did not become an obligatory benefit in accident insurance until the third amendment was made to the Accident Insurance Law; it was also included in (employees') pensions insurance from 1920 onwards. The allowance for the helpless is also granted within the framework of surviving dependants' pensions following the fifth amendment to the ASVG (1959). A few details regarding surviving dependants' pensions have been changed. However, these pensions are still largely granted in accordance with the principles of the original law; this applies especially to widowers' pension. Under the original law the maximum of all surviving dependants' pensions was not to exceed 50 percent of the annual earnings; this now amounts to 80 percent of the basis of assessment. Moreover, pensions for parents and brothers and sisters still exist; however, these only amount to 20 percent (once).

For a long time the miners were the only group in Austria who were entitled to a disability pension from compulsory insurance. The employees were the second group to receive pensions insurance in Austria (1906/7). Employees' pensions insurance was indeed very modest at first; later, however, following the first amendment in 1914 and the Employees' Pensions Insurance Law of 1926/7 and later laws, these pensions reached such a high level as regards both benefits and contributions that when German employees' insurance was introduced in 1938/9 a reduction in their level had to be obviated by higher ratings.

One of the major omissions of Austrian social insurance legislation was that workers' old age and disability insurance could not be realized despite efforts in this sphere when the original laws were created in 1887 and 1888. Körber's Programme (1904) contained remarkable plans for workers' disability insurance. Shortly afterwards a plan for comprehensive disability and old age insurance for both the employed and the self-employed was submitted in the framework of the 1908 government bill (above p. 321).

The 1927 Workers' Insurance Law (above p. 328) made legal provision for disability insurance for workers for the first time. However, its operation depended on the fulfilment of the 'prosperity clause'. A parallel situation existed for workers in agriculture and forestry following the 1928 Law on Agricultural Workers' Insurance (above p. 329). Despite a later easing of prerequisites, this situation was also maintained by the 1935 GSVG. Thus, up to 1938 both industrial and agricultural and forestry workers were to rely on old age welfare pensions.

The close economic link between the problem of unemployment and workers' disability insurance became completely clear when it was introduced in the wake of German legislation in 1938. In view of the sudden reduction of unemployment, financing workers' insurance required relatively little effort on the part of the government of the German Reich.

German pensions insurance remained largely valid until the ASVG came into force. This law provided an entirely new basis for the pension assessment of employed persons. It replaced the previous 'Durchrechnungsprinzip' (calculation principle) by a system of assessment based on last earnings (see above p. 334).

Furthermore, pensions insurance law was substantially completed with the introduction of equalization allowances by the ASVG. These are extremely important from a social point of view. Such allowances are welfare benefits for persons whose incomes are below the standard level (to provide a minimum existence.) This institution was also introduced to insurance for the self-employed (see below). Farmers' eligibility for such allowances depends, however, on a so-called 'fictitious share of property reserved by a farmer on his retirement' when assessing (other) income. This restriction is politically controversial at present.

The beginnings of pensions insurance for the self-employed in Austria were first evident in the 1908 government bill which provided for (extremely modest) old age pensions for tradespeople and farmers (above p. 321). Albert Gessmann, a Christian Social member of the Beck government, initiated this project. Soon after the Second World War the first efforts were made to introduce old age insurance for the self-employed. Initially, a preliminary stage was interpolated (with low insurance benefits and allowances of a welfare nature to some extent) both for the self-employed in trade and industry (with the 1953 Law on Old Age Pensions of the Chambers of Trade and Industry) and for the farmers (with the 1957 'Supplementary Pensions Insurance Law'). Later 'full' pensions insurance was introduced for these groups with the 1957 GSPVG and the 1969 B-PVG (above pp. 346, 349). Thus, the self-employed in trade and industry have had 'full' pensions insurance since 1 July 1958 and the farmers since 1 January 1971. Since the GSPVG and the B-PVG have been in force, efforts have been made to adapt extensively their provisions to the standards of pension law for the employed (the ASVG). Pension adjustment, regulated by the 1965 law (PAG) and applied for ASVG, GSVG and BSVG pensions, is an important element of Austrian pension insurance law. Both 'automatic' adjustment used for the new assessment of pensions and 'indexed' adjustment of already existing pensions (cf. above p. 343) are designed to adapt pensions to the respective economic conditions, independently of political imponderables.

Financing

The question of a state subsidy played a decisive role in debates on German workers' insurance laws. This was not the case in Austria during preliminary work and parliamentary treatment of the accident or sickness insurance law for two reasons; first, the government was itself of the opinion that in view of the condition of the state budget, the state could not be burdened further (cf. above pp. 278 and 320); and secondly, Taafe's government did not consider financial state assistance of such great ideological value as Bismarck had done (cf. above p. 294). Even the state advance provided to finance expenditure the first year was not based on any legal obligation on the request of Dunajewski, Minister of Finance at the time. Thus, accident and sickness insurance was financed from the start exclusively by contributions in Austria, in keeping with the solution which corresponding German legislation had chosen. A state guarantee — such as was provided by the German Accident Insurance Law in the form of a 'Reichsgarantie' — that the trade associations could provide benefits was also unknown to the original Austrian laws. With regard to contributions, the original law provided for a division of contributions between the employers and the employed in a ratio of nine to one. In practice, many employers did not deduct the contribution of the employed.

Compulsory payment of contributions by the employed was no longer included in the emergency decree on accident insurance for miners of 1914. Compulsory contributions were then eliminated for all other persons insured against accidents with the third amendment to the Accident Insurance Law of 1917.

Originally, the employer's contribution to accident insurance was not uniform for all concerns but graded according to classes of danger in keeping with the original character of accident insurance as compulsory insurance for workers in particularly dangerous industries. The decree connected with the original law provided for twelve classes of danger (danger percentages: from 5 percent to 100 percent); later two further sub-classes were added (A: 1 percent and 2 percent; B: 3 percent and 4 percent). The 1935 GSVG finally put an end to this division into danger classes. The thirty-second ASVG amendment (1977) introduced a uniform accident insurance contribution for workers and employees which is currently (since 1979) 1.5 percent of the contribution basis and as usual is paid exclusively by the employer. The original law had a maximum contribution basis in accident insurance which, however, was set extremely high with 1200 guilders. The maximum contribution basis in accident insurance currently used in Austria is identical with that in pensions and unemployment insurance; in recent years it has greatly increased because of wage developments (it trebled from 1965 to 1978; last order for an extraordinary increase by the thirty-second amendment to the ASVG).[544]

The original law provided for a form of ruling on contributions to sickness insurance which continued to apply in Austria until relatively recently (if one disregards the ruling of the 1935 GSVG which was valid for a short time and the rulings of the National Socialist era). The law provided for a maximum framework (3 percent to meet the statutory minimum requirement: §26) within which insurances were entitled to set contribution levels with their own charter. A change took place in Austria only relatively recently: contribution rates are now fixed by legal rulings which no longer give the insurances' charters any latitude.

As no law on workers' disability insurance existed, the question of financing pensions insurance could be posed only in connection with the newly regulated (1889) old age assistance of the 'Bruderladen'. As the financial situation of the 'bruderladen' was extremely unfavourable, the Liberal deputy, Baernreither, proposed reorganizing 'Bruderladen' in dire straits by providing state subsidies rather than closing them down (as the government bill had put forward as the *ultima ratio*). Unfortunately, parliament did not support this proposal. The refusal of a state subsidy resulted in the miners being at a disadvantage compared with other industrial workers (until 1914) with regard to benefits in other branches of insurance (accident and sickness insurance). At the same time loans were taken out to help reorganize the 'Bruderladen'; employers and employed then had to pay contributions to pay off the loans. Furthermore, the level of the pensions was barely above the statutory minimum. Whereas the government stubbornly rejected state subsidies in the 1880s, the necessity of state financial participation was usually more or less clearly indicated in numerous later proposals to introduce old age and disability insurance for workers. The 1904 Körber Programme provided for extremely far-reaching financing of old age and disability insurance by the state. Furthermore, state participation was also planned in the government bills of 1908 and later; this would have consisted of the payment of uniform allowances to pensioners amounting to 90 K. Pension insurance for employees, however, started in 1906, was to survive without state financial assistance.

A new era of financing in the social insurance system began when contributions and funds required as cover rapidly lost their value in the early 1920s due to the inflation. In order to ensure that benefits would be provided to some extent, the state had to step into the breach on several occasions with advance payments; these, however, were collected again from employers and employed by means of an allocation procedure (Umlageverfahren). The first case of actual state financing in Austria occurred when unemployment assistance was provided entirely out of state funds from November 1918 until May 1920 (cf. above p. 325). The Unemployment Insurance Law, issued in March 1920, reduced state financing to one-third of the expenditure. The state share was further reduced by later laws at the expense of the contributions of the employers and the employed. While pension insurance was also entirely financed by contributions, based on the 1926/7 reform (above p. 328), everyone concerned realized that the planned introduction of old age and disability insurance for workers (as well as for agricultural and forestry workers) would not be possible without a state subsidy. Opinions varied only on the extent to which tax moneys were to be used (cf. Hanusch's motion of December 1920: above p. 320). The 1927 Workers' Insurance Law finally opted for a compromise: it was financed by contributions and by a 'subsidy from public funds' (§119) at a fixed rate.

At the same time as the introduction of old age and disability insurance the system of state assistance to pensions insurance was adopted by virtue of National Socialist legislation (cf. above p. 333 and 334). This system was partly regulated by the 'Reichsversicherungsordnung' and partly by later German laws (1934 'Aufbaugesetz' — Reconstruction Act; 1937 'Ausbaugesetz' — Extension Law). It consisted

1. in the provision of the necessary funds for the basic amounts (§§1268, section 2; 1272, section 1 'Reichsversicherungsordnung');
2. in an annual amount (from the 'Reich') of 204 million RM which was increased by a further 16 million when Austria was annexed (§25 of the insurance decree on the introduction of social insurance to the province of Austria);
3. in contributions to the increases;
4. in the guarantee by the Reich, newly introduced by the 'Ausbaugesetz'. According to prevailing law part of the amount required for old age pensions was also to be financed by funds from the Reich (§23 of the insurance decree).

In 1956 the currently valid system of financing the ASVG came into force: the state has to pay a contribution of that amount for which 110 percent of the expenditure for pensions exceed the receipts (101.5 percent from 1971 onwards and 100.5 percent since 1978). The state obligation to pay fixed subsidies, temporarily introduced, has not existed since 1969. As discussed on pp. 307–311 the state is not only liable for deficits but is also bound to provide compensation for benefits which are not covered by insurance (particularly equalization allowances).

According to the 1906 Employees' Pension Insurance Law contributions were divided for the lower income brackets in a ratio of two to one; for the higher income brackets contribution payments were shared equally. The 1926 Employees' Insurance Law made this equal division between the employers and the employed apply to all wage brackets; however, a contribution limit was set — in favour of the employed — at 15 percent of 'his earnings'. Employers and employed currently share the costs of contributions equally in pensions insurance for the employed. In pension insurance for the self-employed, the state takes the place of the employer by doubling the contribution (see p. 346).

Until and including 1977, federal contributions to pensions insurance rose steadily both in absolute terms and in relation to the other revenues. Excluding compensation for benefits which are not covered by insurance as well as reserve funds, federal contributions reached a record 29.49 percent in the whole of pensions insurance in 1977; numerous measures were introduced with the 1977 Social Insurance Amendment Law which succeeded in reducing this to about 22 percent in 1978.[545]

The Organization

The organization of the Austrian social insurance institutions deviates considerably, particularly in accident insurance, from Bismarck's model workers' insurance legislation. The dominant organizational principle was the 'territorial principle', anchored in the original law of 1887 (§9), according to which an accident insurance was 'usually' to be established for each of the crownlands of the Cisleithan half of the empire. However, as the Minister of the Interior frequently made use of his power to amalgamate several crownlands to form one district, only seven 'territorial' accident insurances were established (in Prague, Vienna, Salzburg, Graz, Brno, Lvov, and Trieste).

The reasons for this were, first, that the ethnic structure of the Cisleithan half of the empire created a completely different situation for insurance organization from that of Germany. A single trade association organization to cover concerns in related branches of all the crownlands would have faced great difficulties — from a language point of view alone. Moreover, it was of significance that Taaffe's government was largely supported by federally oriented political forces. Thus, this government was in favour of linking the organization to the division of the crownlands while the 'centralistically' minded Liberals preferred the trade association principle. With regard to the internal organization of the territorial accident insurances, one must stress that on Steinbach's proposal, despite the principle of self-administration being recognized, bureaucracy had a marked influence on the administration of the accident insurance institutions which went beyond the right of the state to supervise.

The organization of Austrian sickness insurance concurs largely with German law. Austrian law used the existing insurances (works', cooperative and society insurance) and in addition created district sickness insurances like the German local sickness insurances. Up to the end of the First World War the types of sickness insurances in Austria were as diverse as in the German Reich and indeed as is still the case in the Federal Republic of Germany today. There were, for example, about 3000 sickness insurances in the Cisleithan half of the empire in 1900. The concentration process did not begin until after the First World War (in the Hanusch era). This process was continued later in the first republic for reasons of economy (cf. above pp. 322–324). The system was further simplified in the National Socialist era when employees' and workers' (regional) sickness insurances were combined. In the 1920s the organization of social insurance institutions began to be influenced by the principle of social 'Stände' (estates) (cf. above p. 330).

The 1947 SV-ÜG which is still the basis of organization of Austrian social insurance today largely followed the lines of organization of the old Austrian empire. The 'Allgemeine Unfallversicherungsanstalt' (General Accident Insurance) — specialized in one branch of insurance — for both workers and employees was newly established; otherwise the link between workers' and employees' insurance in the regional (previously: local) sickness insurances was maintained.

It is difficult to interpret[546] the development according to the significance of the one or the other principle of classification. In the sphere of insurance for the employed, various groups have undoubtedly grown closer to one another since the 1930s (namely workers in trade and industry, agricultural and forestry workers and employees) if one ignores the traditional separation of pensions insurance for workers and for employees. Thus, pensions insurance aside, classifications are predominantly organized according to insurance branches. The situation is different for insurance of the self-employed, as already discussed; here the group of insured persons plays the dominant role.

One cannot deny that the social insurances have been self-administrative bodies ever since they were founded by the original laws of the 1880s or else reorganized (the 'bruderladen'), even if certain reservations are justified with regard to the apointment by the Minister of the Interior (later: of Social Affairs) for accident insurance as well as to the relatively strong position of the entrepreneur (factory owners, etc.) in works' sickness insurances and 'Bruderladen'.

The period following 1934 (GSVG 1935), was characterized by the limitation of the principle of self-administration and from 1938 to 1945 this was entirely displaced by the 'Führerprinzip' (above pp. 333 and 334). When re-establishing self-administration under the 1947 SV-ÜG, rules prior to 1934 were resumed (especially regarding regional sickness insurances); in some sectors the influence of the insured was further increased,[547] namely in agricultural sickness insurances and pensions insurances. In the social insurance institutions for the self-employed established in the 1950s the administrative bodies were and are exclusively composed of the insured.

Wannagat's[548] view that social insurance is one of the oldest forms of 'Sozialpartnerschaft' (cooperation between management and labour) also applies to the historical development in Austria. This is of increased importance partly because of the high standing of the 'Sozialpartnerschaft' in the second republic and partly—from a historical point of view—because of the late date when the majority of the labour force in Austria obtained voting rights.

Accident Insurance

As in the German Reich the (Workers') Accident Insurance Law paved the way for a social insurance system. Accident insurance has changed fundamentally[549] since the original law in three ways: first with regard to the events which lead to a claim. Already at an early stage the term 'Betriebsunfall' (accident at work) was extended by the judicature particularly by including accidents on the way to and from work among such accidents. This extension process was continued later on a legal basis and is still being carried on today. Thus, 'accidents at work' became decreasingly linked with the risks incurred in a particular industrial concern. Correspondingly the idea of 'redemption' of the employer's liability by the social accident insurance applies to an ever smaller number of cases. Possible additional extensions are the inclusion of household accidents as well as accidents occurring during sport and other leisure activities. Secondly, with regard to persons covered by accident insurance: following the change from the 'insurance of a concern to that of people', the group of persons subject to compulsory accident insurance was initially enlarged to that of people subject to compulsory sickness insurance, then groups were included where there was no linkage to their employment (for example, lifesavers, volunteers in catastrophes, schoolchildren and students); the inclusion of further groups (housewives who are not gainfully employed, *inter alia*) is currently the subject of political discussion. Thirdly, with regard to the duties of accident insurance: although expenditure for pensions accounts for about half the total expenditure of the accident insurances, accident prevention, treatment and other benefits in kind have come very much into the foreground. In this respect also accident insurance has grown away from its original purpose, namely the replacement of employer liability.

In view of this change one may ask whether and to what extent the historical subsitution of employer liability by accident insurance is still relevant; first, with regard to further expansion projects which are more loosely linked with concrete employment conditions and, secondly, as nowadays claims for damages (especially compensation for pain and suffering) are discussed despite accident insurance.

In accord with Friedrich Steinbach,[550] I believe that the trend towards extending accident insurance to more people and areas is to be welcomed. Steinbach, however, rightly demands that the inclusion of private spheres of life must be covered by means of personal insurance.

The ultimate aim of this legislation was, indeed, to avoid or reduce social tensions particularly by avoiding court action between employers and the employed. The very dispute on the delineation of accidents at work and other accidents is just as distasteful as any liability trials would be, even if the insurance—and not the employer—now opposes the insured. Equalization of such fundamental differences would undoubtedly constitute social progress.

When assessing the degree of reduction of working capacity it would be appropriate also to consider[551] the injured person's concrete earning capacity before the accident while adhering to the principle of abstract calculation of damages.

Sickness Insurance

The development of sickness insurance as portrayed on pp. 318–319 is marked on the one hand by an increasing shift away from monetary benefits to benefits in kind, as is also the case in the Federal Republic of Germany and the other states dealt with in this context, whereby over the last few years payments to hospitals and other such institutions have risen out of proportion (above p. 344) and are expected to rise further as reductions of benefits can hardly be envisaged in this sector and economizing by rationalization is only possible to a limited degree. On the other hand there was at least a slight decrease of the trend towards rising costs of drugs and medicines about 2 years ago and even a (temporary) fall in costs. Moreover, development in Austria is also marked by the advance of the 'Finalprinzip' (principle of finality, i. e. a purpose-oriented approach) as opposed to the causal principle.

In relation to the few 'relics' of the causal principle, the principle of finality has been greatly upgraded recently with the inclusion of preventive medicine in the scope of the sickness insurances' work (medical examinations of adolescents and of healthy adults). 'Meaures to strengthen health' (accommodation in rest and recuperation homes) are of increasing importance; such measures are, however, currently still voluntary benefits on the part of the sickness insurances.

The question of financing sickness insurance has also been given a specific character by the rapidly rising proportion of benefits paid out to hospitals: the major problem in this context is that of financing hospitals;[552] the financial position of the insurances depends on the management or non-management of this problem.

Pensions Insurance

Despite the urgency of the financing question, one must not forget that certain structural elements of Austrian pensions insurance require critical re-examination. This applies in particular to the Austrian pensions assessment system (above p. 341) as well as to the rulings on pension adjusting and indexing (see above p. 343 on the PAG). There are doubts concerning the former as to whether the remedy of a 5-year assessment period (10 years for the self-employed) at the end of a person's working life does justice to the principle of contribution adequacy as well as to the socio-political aims of pension law. It seems particularly questionable that the Austrian assessment system urges the insured—far more than a system based on the 'Durchrechnungsprinzip'—to aim at paying as high contributions as possible during the last few years of their working life, thereby the transition from working life to retirement—fraught with manifold problems—can be even more abrupt than it would otherwise have been.

The Austrian system of pensions adjustment has undoubtedly been successful in so far as its main aim, the 'emancipation' of pensions adjustment from political imponderables, was achieved. As far as the parallel existence of automatic and indexed pensions adjustment is concerned (above p. 343), however, later legislative amendments of the assessment of index figure calculation lead one to conclude that a uniform solution in favour of indexing would have been preferable.[553] In this way the delay in pensions indexing arising from the adjustment system could be prevented from being too extreme, particularly in times of great wage and price level changes—which may yet be imminent; the collapse of the entire pensions adjustment system could also be prevented.

NOTES

1   For more details see Richard Novak (1979) in: *Allgemeines Verwaltungsrecht* (Festgabe für W. Antoniolli), 64 pp.; Raoul F. Kneucker, p. 515.

2   Cf. Theodor Tomandl (ed.) (1979). *System des österr. Sozialversicherungsrechts*, section 0.2.1. (Tomandl) with bibliographic references (cited henceforth as *"System"*).

3   Cf. Detlev Zöllner in this volume; also Joachim Umlauf (1980). *Die deutsche Arbeiterschutzgesetzgebung*, 79 pp.

4   Bericht über die soziale Lage 1978 (Sozialbericht), 1979, 84 pp.; according to the 'Handbuch der österr. Sozialversicherung' for 1979, 13 pp., 99.3 percent were covered by sickness insurance (without double insurance this figure amounted to about 96 percent); about 5 million were covered by accident insurance and 2.78 million by pension insurance (At an employment level of 2.8 million).

5   See Eike v. Hippel (1979). 'Grundfragen der sozialen Sicherheit' (= *Recht und Staat 492/493*), 56 pp.

6   See Helmut Koziol-Rudolf Welser (1979). *Grundriss des bürgerlichen Rechts II*, 5th edn, 168 pp.

7   See Tomandl (1974). *Grundriss des österr. Sozialrechts*, 182 pp.

8   Peter Widler (1977). *Soziale Sicherheit (SozSi)*, 241 pp.

9   *System*, part 4.1.3 a.E.

10 Zöllner in this volume.

11 *System*, part 6 (Peter Oberndorfer).

12 *System*, part 2.2. (Martin Binder).

13 *Sozialbericht 1978*, 105. Also HdBSV 1979, 36.

14 Alfred Radner (1979). *SozSi* 107 pp.

15 *System*, part 2.3. (Tomandl).

16 *Sozialbericht 1978*, 107 (table 10).

17 See (the most recent) annual report (Jahresbericht), 1977, 29 pp., and Wolfgang Krösl (1979) in: *90 Jahre soziale Unfallversicherung in Österreich*, 42 pp. and Friedrich Steinbach (1979). *Die gesetzliche Unfallversicherung in Österreich* passim.

18 *System* 2.4. (Hellmut Teschner).

19 *System* 2.4.4.1. (Teschner); Reinhold Melas, Hans Gabler, Friedrich Steinbach, Othmar Rodler, and Ernst Bakule, (1955). *SozSi* 331 pp.

20 *Sozialbericht 1978*, 57, 91, 104; also *HdBSV* 1979, 32, according to which the provisional percentages are 15.0 and 47.5 respectively and are dropping slightly compared with the federal budget; on method see Norbert Geldner, *Die soziale Sicherheit im Wirtschaftskreislauf*, 35 pp.

21 *Sozialbericht 1978*, 93 pp.; also Karl Muhr (1979). *SozSi* 204 pp.

22 *System Abschnitt* 0.5.2. (Tomandl). The load ratio of the diverse old-age insurance institutions indicated in the following cf. in *Sozialbericht* 1978, 199.

23 There is no comprehensive portrayal available; see Ludwig Brügel's *Soziale Gesetzgebung in Österreich von 1848 bis 1919;* on the history of Austrian social law until 1918; see Friedrich Steinbach's *Die gesetzliche Unfallversicherung in Österreich*, 1979; see also in: *90 Jahre soziale Unfallversicherung in Österreich*, 7 pp.; see Eduard Stark, 60 pp. and Wolf D. Mostböck, 82 pp.; see Ernst Bruckmüller, Roman Sandgruber, and Hannes Stekl, 'Soziale Sicherheit im Nachziehverfahren' (= *Geschichte und Sozialkunde*, 3), 1978 on the inclusion of farmers, farm labourers, tradespeople, domestic staff in Austrian social insurance; see also the following work written in the framework of the project of the Institut für Wirtschafts- und Sozialgeschichte, Vienna University (Prof. Michael Mitterauer), devoted to the history of Austrian social insurance and welfare: Andreas Baryli (1977). *Die Sonder-Sozialversicherung der Angestellten in Österreich bis 1938*, phil. Diss., Wien; also Dieter Stiefel (1979) 'Arbeitslosigkeit. Soziale, politische und wirtschaftliche Auswirkungen am Beispiel Österreichs 1918 bis 1938' (= *Schriften zur Wirtschaftsund Sozialgeschichte*, 31), Cf. also the historical sections in Adolf Menzel's *Die Arbeiterversicherung nach österr. Recht, 1893*, 12 pp.; Max Lederer (1932) *Grundriss des österr. Sozialrechts*, 2nd edn, 13 pp.; 426 pp.; Ernst Legat, Stefan Grabner (1963). *Sozialversicherungsrecht*, 1 p.; Tomandl, *Grundriss*, 16 pp., also Werner Ogris (1975). in: *Die Habsburgermonarchie 1848–1918*, vol. II, 630 pp.; also the publication of the central association of Austrian social insurances, *Soziale Sicherheit*, in which good historical essays frequently appear; reference will be made to recent contributions where appropriate.

24 See in particular Edmund Bernatzik, *Die österr. Verfassungsgesetze*, 2nd edn, 1911; Gustav Kolmer (1902–1914) *Parlament und Verfassung in Österreich*, volumes I–VIII; Richard Charmatz (1912) *Österreichs innere Geschichte von 1848 bis 1907*, 2nd penultimate edn; from recent literature

cf. Hermann Baltl (1979) *Österr. Rechstgeschichte*, 4th edn; Wilhelm Brauneder and Friedrich Lachmayer (1980); *Österr. Verfassungsgeschichte*, 2nd edn; Ernst C. Hellbling (1974); *Österr. Verfassungsgeschichte*, 2nd edn; also *Die Habsburgermonarchie 1848–1918*, Vol. II, 1975; see also Walter Goldinger and Adam Wandruszka in: (1974, reprint 1977). *Geschichte der Republik Österreich*, 15 pp.; lately Robert Walter and Heinz Mayer (1978). *Grundriss des österr. Bundesverfassungsrechts*, 2nd edn, 4 pp.

25 Pp. 278–279.
26 More details in: Brauneder and Lachmayer, *Verfassungsgeschichte*, 90 pp.
27 Ogris, *Rechtsentwicklung*, 619.
28 Sammlung d. Gesetze f. d. Ehzt. *Österr. unter der Enns XIX (1837)* 70 pp. (Nr.g35); cf. also Kurt Ebert (1975). 'Die Anfänge der modernen Sozialpolitik in Österreich' (= *Studien zur Geschichte der österr. ungarischen Monarchie*, 15), 102 p.; most recent Martin Binder (1980). 'Das Zusammenspeil arbeits- und sozialrechtlicher Leistungsansprüche . . .' (= *Wiener Beiträge zum Arbeits- und Sozialrecht*, 12), 51; Josef Pinter, (1951), *SozSi* 191 pp.
29 Ebert, *Sozialpolitik*, 103.
30 See Brauneder and Lachmayer, *Verfassungsgeschichte*, 79, on the official designation of Austria from 1804 onwards.
31 Bernatzik, *Verfassungsgesetze*, 101.
32 Brauneder and Lachmayer, *Verfassungsgeschichte*, 126.
33 Cf. Ernst Rudolf Huber, *Deutsche Verfassungsgeschichte seit 1789, Dokumente*, I, p. 274.
34 P. 312.
35 On the role of the workers in the 1848 revolution see Brügel, *Soziale Gesetzgebung*, 29 ff.; Hans Hautmann and Rudolf Kropf, (1974). 'Die österr. Arbeiterbewegung vom Vormärz bis 1945' (= *Schriftenreihe des Ludwig-Botlzmann-Instituts . . .*, 4), 31 pp.; Ebert, *Anfänge*, 17.
36 Ogris, *Rechtsentwicklung*, 648 pp.
37 Bernatzik, *Verfassungsgesetze*, 208 pp.
38 Ogris, *Rechtsentwicklung*, 647.
39 Cf. p. 301.
40 Ogris, *Rechtsentwicklung*, 648 pp.; cf. also Heinrich Waentig (1898). *Gewerbliche Mittelstandspolitik*, 47 pp.
41 Ogris, *Rechsentwicklung*, 650; Waentig.
42 More details on p. 285.
43 Bernatzik, *Verfassungsgesetze*, 223; Brauneder and Lachmayer, *Verfassungsgeschichte*, 179; on the economic aspects of the 'Ausgleich' see Herbert Hofmeister, *Rechtliche Aspekte der Industrialisierung in der österr.-ungarischen Monarchie*.
44 Cf. art. 159 of the BVG of 1 October 1920, *BGB* no. 1.
45 See Georg Franz (1955). *Liberalismus*, 131 pp., on the social background of the Liberal movement in Austria (with reservations).
46 See Josef Redlich (1926). *Das österr. Staats- und Reichsproblem*, II, which is still indispensable today.
47 See §§6 and 7 of the '(Staats-) Grundgesetz über die Reichsvertretung' of 21 December 1867, *RGB* no. 141; later law of 2 December 1873, *RGB* no. 40.
48 Survey in Brauneder and Lachmayer, *Verfassungsgeschichte*, 159 p.
49 Ernst Rudolf Huber (1964). *Dokumente zur deutschen Verfassungsgeschichte*, II, 243 pp.
50 Ludwig Brügel (1922). *Geschichte der österr. Sozialdemokratie*, Vol. II and III, and Leo Verkauf (1906). *Zur Geschichte des Arbeiterrechts in Österreich*, 5–25; also Steiner, *Arbeiterbewegung;* Hautmann-Kropf, *Arbeiterbewegung*. Also Gustav Otruba (1980). in: *Österreichs Sozialstrukturen in historischer Sicht*, Erich Zöllner (ed.), 123 pp.
51 Berchtold, *Parteiprogramme*, 109 and 111.
52 Steiner, *Arbeiterbewegung* 28.
53 See *ÖStWB*, I, 302 (Leo Verkauf); see also the figures for 1873 in Herbert Steiner (1964). *Die Arbeiterbewegung Österreichs 1867–1889*, 74.
54 Cf. Steiner, *Arbeiterbewegung*, 60 pp.; the Eisenacher Programm, cf. Berchtold, *Parteiprogramme* p. 123.
55 Berchtold, *Parteiprogramme*, p. 115.
56 Berchtold, *Parteiprogramme*, p. 119; Steiner, *Arbeiterbewegung*, 125 pp.
57 Cf. pp. 285 and 287.
58 Cf. *ÖStWB*, I, 302 (Leo Verkauf).
59 Cf. Huber, *Dt. Verfassungsgeschichte*, IV, 1153 pp. and notes 154, 161.
60 Cf. Steiner, *Arbeiterbewegung*, 155 pp.; Berchtold, *Parteiprogramme*, 18 pp.

61   In 1882 the radicals supported the moderates' demand for social legislation and workers' protection but were against the demand for democratic voting rights: Steiner, *Arbeiterbewegung*, 202.

62   Brügel, *Sozialdemokratie*, III; Steiner, *Arbeiterbewegung*, 241 pp.

63   Steiner, *Arbeiterbewegung*, 244 pp.; Brügel, *Sozialdemokratie*, III, 249 pp.

64   Steiner; cf. also Verkauf, *Arbeiterrecht*, 8.

65   Cf. Friedrich Walter and Adam Wandruzska (1972). *Österr. Verfassungsund Verwaltungsgeschichte von 1500–1955*, 237 pp.

66   Walter and Wandruszka, *Österr. Verfassungs- und Verwaltungsgeschichte*, 242 pp.

67   Constant v. Wurzbach, *Biographisches Lexikon des Kaiserthums Österreich* . . . , vol. 29, 54 pp.

68   Cf. Alexander Novotny, in: *Die Habsburgermonarchie*, I. 83.

69   *Kapitalismus und Socialismus*, 703, the following quotation: 702.

70   See Brügel, *Soziale Gesetzgebung*, 78; of the vast selection of literature on the problem of nationalities in the Habsburg monarchy I recommend the analysis in Joseph Redlich (1925). *Österr. Regierung und Verwaltung im Weltkriege*, 39 pp.

71   See Walter and Wandruszka, *Österr. Verfassungs- und Verwaltungsgeschichte*, 245 pp.

72   See Hans Rosenberg (1967). *Grosse Depression und Bismarckzeit*, 51 pp.; also Herbert Matis (1972). *Österreichs Wirtschaft 1848–1913*, 260 pp.

73   Law of 19 July 1877, *RGB* 66; on more recent legislation on profiteering see Justus Wilhelm Hedemann (1910). *Fortschritte des Zivilrechts im 19. Jh.*, I, 132 pp.

74   See Matis, *Österreichs Wirtschaft*, 371 pp.

75   See in particular the summary in: *Sozialpolitik*, 251.

76   Cf. Schäffle's early advocacy of compulsory insurance, pp. 276–277.

77   Kolmer, 3.

78   Kolmer, 12.

79   Cf. Ebert, *Sozialpolitik*, 22 pp.; Alois Brusatti (1962). *Geschichte der Sozialpolitik in Dokumenten*, 29 pp.; Gerhard Silberbauer (1966). *Österreichs Katholiken und die Arbeiterfrage*, 61 pp.; Ernst Hanisch (1975). *Konservatives und revolutionäres Denken*.

80   Wilhelm E. Ketteler (1911). *Schriften. Chosen and edited by Johannes Mumbauer*, III 161. See also the publication of 1864: *Die Arbeiterfrage und das Christentum* (extract in Brusatti, *Geschichte*, 174 pp.).

81   Cf. Ebert, *Sozialpolitik*, p. 25; for Liechtenstein see Erika Weinzierl and Fischer, *Neue österr. Biographie (NÖB)* 14, 96 pp.

82   *Die soziale Frage* . . . , 1877.

83   See also Ebert, *Sozialpolitik*, p. 26; on the legal situation at the time see Hofmeister in: *Bericht über den 12. österr. Historikertag*, 147 pp.

84   See p. 283.

85   Ebert, *Sozialpolitik*, 28, note 82.

86   Waentig, *Mittelstandspolitik*, 110.

87   Legally based representation for workers (and employees) in Austria was not established until the law of 26 February 1920, *StGB* no. 100, came into force (Hanusch era); agricultural chambers (for the farmers) were founded later (based on provincial law).

88   Johann Christoph Allmayer-Beck (1962). *Vogelsang. Vom Feudalismus zur Volksbewegung;* Silberbauer, *Österreichs Katholiken*, 61 pp.; Wiard v. Klopp (ed.) (1938). *Die sozialen Lehren des Frhrn. v. Vogelsang*, 2nd edn.

89   See in particular: *Die Notwendigkeit einer neuen Grundentlastung*, 1880

90   See Brusatti, *Geschichte der Sozialpolitik*, 31.

91   See Ebert, *Sozialpolitik*, 253; not least in view of the misleading title, this characteristic of Bismarck's social policy in Joachim Umlauf's 'Die deutsche Arbeiterschutzgesetzgebung' (meaning legislation on workers' insurance) 1880–1890, should have been discussed in greater detail.

92   Cf. Silberbauer, *Österreichs Katholiken*, p. 63.

93   Franz, *Liberalismus*, 142 pp.

94   More detail on pp. 290 and 294.

95   I.e. the kingdoms and countries which were later represented in the 'Reichsrat'.

96   Matis, *Österreichs Wirtschaft*, 22 pp.

97   Ebert, *Sozialpolitik*, 48 (and the study of Ludwig Mises), also Theo Mayer-Maly (1977). *Zs.f. Arbeits- und Sozialrecht (ZAS)* 3 pp.

98   Matis, *Österreichs Wirtschaft*, 23 pp.

99   More detail in Ebert, *Sozialpolitik*, p. 51.

100   This is excellently documented in Carl Joseph v. Czoernig (1858). *Österreichs Neugestaltung*.

101   *RGB* no. 207/1853: Matis, *Österreichs Wirtschaft*, 87.

102 Matis, p. 91.
103 Matis, p. 95.
104 Matis, p. 141.
105 Matis, p. 150.
106 Matis, p. 260.
107 Steiner, *Arbeiterbewegung*, 78 pp.
108 Steiner, 82; Berchtold, *Parteiprogramme*, 14 pp.
109 Nachum Th. Gross (1973). *Die Habsburgermonarchie 1848–1918*, I, 20.
110 Steiner, *Arbeiterbewegung*, 165pp. The social conditions of the labour force were also frequently discussed in Anton Tschörner (1879). 'Die materielle Lage des Arbeiterstandes in Österreich', in: *Monatsschrift für Gesellschaft, Wissenschaft und christliche Sozialreform*, 284 pp. and Karl Freiherr von Vogelsang (1883). in: *Monatsschrift für christliche Sozialreform*, 561 pp., and 1884, 1 pp.; cf. also Theodorf Wollschack, (pseud.: T.W. Teiffen), *Das soziale Elend und die besitzenden Klassen in Österreich, 1894*. The social conditions of the labour force were also discussed in *Gleichheit*.
111 See Franz Wieacker (1967). *Privatrechtsgeschichte der Neuzeit*, 2nd edn, 335 pp. and Gerhard Wesenberg and Gunter Wesener (1976). *Neuere deutsche Privatrechtsgeschichte*, 3rd edn, 149 ff.; also 'Forschungsband Franz v. Zeiller', Walter Selb and Herbert Hofmeister (ed.), 1980. Cf. for labour legislation Werner Ogris, *Die Rechtsentwicklung in Zisleithanien 1848–1918*, 632 pp. (cf. studies by Theo Mayer-Maly and Kurt Eberts).
112 Ogris, 600.
113 Georg Wannagat (1965). *Lehrbuch des Sozialversicherungsrechts*, I, p. 45, for Austria: Otto Stöger, *Art. Bruderladen, ÖStWB*, I 645 pp.
114 Cf. Ernst C. Hellbling, *Österr. Verfassungs- und Verwaltungsgeschichte*, 2nd edn, p. 181; Wannagat, 46.
115 Cf. Czoernig, *Österreichs Neugestaltung*, 584 pp.
116 Decree of the Ministry of Justice of 13 December 1857, Z. 20256.
117 Menzel; *Arbeitversicherung*, 17.
118 *ÖStWB*, I, 527 pp.; Menzel, *Arbeiterversicherung*, p. 18; Ebert, *Sozialpolitik*, 102 pp.
119 See literature in the above note as well as 'Entwurf einer Gewerbe-Ordnung sammt Motive', 1880 (= *StProtAH*, 9. *Sess., Beil*. Nr. 253), also 150 pp.
120 Menzel, *Arbeiterversicherung*, 19.
121 Cf. Menzel, *Arbeiterversicherung*, 18; Otto Stöger, 'Art. Arbeiterkrankenversicherung', in: *ÖStWB*, I, 227.
122 Ebert, *Sozialpolitik*, 105 pp.; Menzel, *Arbeiterversicherung*, 20 pp.
123 The 1875 draft even wanted to give trade associations the same status as societies; see Ebert, *Sozialpolitik*, 111.
124 Cf. Detlev Zöllner in this collection, above, p. 20.
125 Ebert, *Sozialpolitik*, 107.
126 Cf. Menzel, *Arbeiterversicherung*, 30.
127 See in particular the two standard works by Ludwig Brügel, *Geschichte der österr. Sozialdemokratie*, I (bis 1870); II (1870–78), always 1922; Steiner, *Arbeiterbewegung*, 3 pp.; Berchtold, *Parteiprogramme*, 12 pp.
128 See literature in above note as well as Leo Verkauf, Art. 'Organisation der Arbeiter', in: *ÖStWB*, I, 301 ff., also: *Zur Geschichte des Arbeiterrechtes in Österreich*, 1906.
129 Verkauf, *ÖStWB*, I, 301; Steiner, *Arbeiterbewegung*, 5.
130 Steiner, *Arbeiterbewegung*, p. 6.
131 Steiner speaks incorrectly of *Genehmigung* (approval).
132 Steiner, *Arbeiterbewegung*, 6.
133 Verkauf, 16.
134 Statutes, rules of procedure and order of the 'Arbeiter-, Kranken- und Invalidencasse' as well as of the 'Verband der Arbeiter-, Kranken- und Invaliden-Unterstützungs-Vereine Österreichs', 1888, 36 and 45.
135 Statutes printed in publication mentioned in note 134.
136 See p. 299.
137 This law has become particularly significant for the so-called 'Meisterkrankenkassen' of the self-employed in trades; p. 307.
138 Charmatz, *Österreichs innere Geschichte*, II, 10 pp.; Alois Czedik, *Zur Geschichte der k.k. österr. Ministerien 1861–1916*, I, 1917, 304 pp.; Wurzbach, *Biographisches Lexikon . . . 42*, 294 pp.; also Brügel, *Soziale Gesetzgebung*, 109 pp., 110 and Brügel (1922). *Geschichte der österr. Sozialdemokratie*, III, 16 pp. Recent literature cf. Walter and Wandruszka, *Österr. Verfassungs- und Ver-*

waltungsgeschichte, 248 p. as well as Kurt Ebert, *Sozialpolitik*, 30, and literature in note 91. Cf. Walter Knarr, *Das Ministerium des Grafen Taaffe und die soziale Frage;* Friedrich Lerch, *Die Konservativen und die österr. soziale Gesetzgebung in der Ära Taaffe.* Cf. also under note 154 on the attitude of the Taaffe Government to the Social Democratic labour force (emergency legislation).

139   Wurzbach, 296. Czedik, *Geschichte*, I, 304 ff.

140   Czedik, *Geschichte*, I 351 p.

141   In Kolmer, *Parlament und Verfassung*, III, 15 pp.

142   Hugo Hantsch, Graf Eduard Taaffe, in: *Gestalter der Geschicke Österreichs*, 447 pp.; Alexander Novotny, in: *Die Habsburgermonarchie*, I, 82.

143   Ebert, *Sozialpolitik*, 139; Silberbauer, *Österreichs Katholiken*, p. 76.

144   *Neue österreichische Biographie (NÖB)*, 1. Abt. II. vol., 1925, 48 pp.; see also Leo Wittmayer (1907); *Emil Steinbach als Sozialphilosoph;* cf. Czedik, *Geschichte*, I, 359 and Franz Klein (1907). *Allg. österr. Gerichts-Zeitung*, 345 pp.

145   See B/4, I on Steinbach's appointment in 1891 as Minister of Finance in the Taaffe Government and on his role in the failed voting reform project.

146   Cf. Berchtold, *Parteiprogramme*, p. 75.

147   Cf. Steiner, *Arbeiterbewegung*, 259 and literature in note 72. Also Berchtold, *Parteiprogramm* 21; Victor Adler: 'Victor Adler's Aufsätze, Reden und Briefe', V: 'Victor Adler über Fabrikinspektion, Sozialversicherung und Arbeiterkammern', 1925. As his collaboration in the 'Linz Programme' (1882) shows, Adler's main interest lay with social policy while he belonged to the German national movement. Schönerer's anti-Semitism made Adler (and Pernerstorfer) leave the German national movement, whereupon Adler joined the Social Democrats in 1886.

148   *StProtAH*, 9. Sess., Beil. Nr. 596.

149   Cf. Ebert, *Sozialpolitik*, 148 p.

150   More details on pp. 292, 294.

151   Ebert, *Sozialpolitik*, 162 pp.

152   *RGB* Nr. 115.

153   Brügel, *Soziale Gesetzgebung*, 134 pp.; Ebert, *Sozialpolitik*, 162 pp.

154   Brügel, *Soziale Gesetzgebung*, 137 pp.; Ebert, *Sozialpolitik*, 179 pp.; shortly afterwards the Taaffe Government followed the path taken by the German Anti-Socialist Law of 22 October 1878, *DRGB* p. 351 pp., with its emergency legislation. Two government decrees of 30 February 1884, *RGB* nos. 15 and 16, proclaimed a state of emergency for Vienna and the industrial areas around Vienna and ordered that courts with juries were no longer to be valid. As some of the (liberal) Left assented, the decrees met with the approval of the 'Reichsrat' in accordance with §11 of the law of 5 May 1869, *RGB* no. 66. On 20 January 1885 the government submitted a draft of an Anti-Socialist Law. However, this did not pass into law until it was reintroduced in a modified form in 1886 (imperial sanction on 25 June; *RGB* no. 98). The government application to prolong the law after 10 August 88 (the end of the Law's validity) was rejected by the 'Abgeordnetenhaus'; however, prolongation of the 1888 decree (until 31 July 1889) was approved. Viktor Adler, the Social Democratic Party leader, was a victim of the emergency legislation: he was sentenced by the Viennese Emergency Court on 27 June 1889 (cf. Kolmer, *Parlament und Verfassung*, III, 378 ff.; IV, 339 ff. sowie Brügel, Geschichte der österr. Sozialdemokratie, IV, 19 ff.). The Anti-Socialist Law in the German Reich finally expired on 30 September 1890, i.e. over a year after the state emergency had ended in Austria.

155   Ebert, *Sozialpolitik*, 157 (Belcredi's comments in this undoubtedly correspond to the government point of view).

156   *StProtAH*, 9. Sess., 10951, Beil. Nr. 783; Kolmer, *Parlament und Verfassung*, III 374.

157   See p. 292.

158   See p. 292.

159   See Detlev Zöllner, notes 223 ff. (and literature).

160   Ernst Rudolf Huber, *Deutsche Verfassungsgeschichte*, IV, 1191 pp.; Umlauf, *Arbeiterschutzgesetzgebung*, 44 pp.

161   Huber, 1192. See note 154 on the German Anti-Socialist Law.

162   Huber, 1197, note 12.

163   Huber, 1197.

164   Reports on *Verhandlungen des Reichstags*, 4. LP, IV. Sess., 1881, Vol. 3, Anlagen Nr. 41 (p. 222 pp.); Umlauf, *Arbeiterschutzgesetzbegung*, 51.

165   See Zöllner, note 311.

166   Employers paid two-thirds and the employed one-third of the contribution or (in the case of workers with high earnings) the contribution was shared equally (half and half).

167 Rejection of the bill by the Federal Council on 25 June 1881.
168 Huber, *Dokumente*, II, Nr. 260.
169 Huber, *Deutsche Verfassungsgeschichte*, III, 1199.
170 Huber, *Dokumente*, II, Nr. 263.
171 Huber, *Deutsche Verfassungsgeschichte*, III, 1202.
172 Sten. Berichte über die Verhandlungen des Reichstags, 5. LP, II. Sess., 1882/83, vol. 5, Anlage Nr. 14 (p. 124 pp.).
173 *DRGB* 1885, p. 159.
174 *DRGB* 1886, p. 132.
175 Ste. Berichte über die Verhandlungen des Reichstags, 5. LP., II. Sess., 1882/83, vol. 5, Anlage Nr. 19 (p. 173 pp.).
176 Sten. Berichte über die Verhandlungen des Reichstags, 5. LP., IV. Sess., 1884, vol. 3, Anlage Nr. 4 (p. 50 pp.).
177 Later §63 of the (German) Accident Insurance Law, *DRGB* p. 69/1884.
178 Sten. Berichte über die Verhandlungen des Reichstags, 7. LP., Sess. IV, 1888/89, vol. 1, Anlage Nr. 10 (p. 31 pp.).
179 The draft was accepted by the 'Reichstag' with 165 votes (and 145 votes against it); it was of decisive importance that fifteen deputies of the Centre Party approved the bill; Huber, *Verfassungsgeschichte*, III, 1204.
180 AVA, MRP 1882 (Karton 16), Nr. 92 (cf. note 230). Cf. Steinbach, *Unfallversicherung*, 16 pp.
181 AVA, MRP 1882 (Karton 16), Nr. 96.
182 The insurance usually made payment depend on the prior court establishment of a claim for compensation.
183 Already quoted in Ebert, *Sozialgesetzgebung*, 145, note 138.
184 There are no details about voting; as there is no mention of opposition Falkenhayn must have voted in favour or abstained from voting.
185 AVA, Justizministerium (JM), Karton 1448; the first draft exists in both a handwritten version (Steinbach's writing) and a printed version.
186 AVA, JM, Karton 1448, Beilage zu P. 2.
187 AVA, MRP 1883, Nr. 25. Cf. also Czedik, *Geschichte*, I 358.
188 AVA, JM, Karton 1448, Nr. 3 (Beilage zum Amtsvortrag vom 19.4.1883). Czedik, *Geschichte* I 330; also table in Matis, *Österreichs Wirtschaft*, 55. Kolmer, *Parlament und Verfassung*, III 374.
189 A note of the Minister-President of 12 September 1883 requested *inter alia* the bill's reconsideration and reintroduction in the 'Reichsrat'. The note continued: 'The exclusion of the miners prompted renewed consideration of the matter. . . .'
190 Cf. note 142.
191 AVA, MRP 1883, Karton 19, Nr. 61 and 62.
192 Cf. particularly §§1 and 2 and also the completely new provision of §13 according to which mines of certain minerals were not to be included in territorial accident insurance. However, if the benefits of the 'Bruderladen' were less than the rate provided by the accident insurance law, and if the employers did not provide at least equally high contributions to the 'Bruderlade', then the benefits and/or contributions had 'to be raised to designated minimum amounts' 1 year after the law came into force at the latest.
193 *StProtAH*, 9. Sess., 10951.
194 *StProtAH*, 9. Sess., Beil. Nr. 783.
195 Neuwirth especially criticized the employer contribution provided in the government bill, whereupon Steinbach advocated the ethical aspect of co-responsibility of the insured; *StProtAH*, 9. Sess., 10971 pp.; Kolmer, *Parlament und Verfassung*, III 374.
196 *StProtAh*, 9. Sess., Beil. Nr. 1091; unchanged *StProtAH*, 10. Sess., Beil. Nr. 75.
197 Cf. p. 292. The Trade Board obviously already had the third draft of the German Accident Insurance in mind; this catered for the trade association principle to an extreme degree while the second draft had still known professional societies as an alternative — a compromise between the trade association and the territorial principle.
198 Cf. note 196.
199 The employer (entrepreneur) was to provide the costs of board and treatment during the first four weeks after an accident 'if appropriate welfare measures have not been taken by the community or by the existing sickness insurances in good time or if the injured person is poor'.
200 This is not the primary aim but a subsidiary aspect of worker's insurance legislation in the 1880s which was not unwelcome for the Taaffe Government.
201 Kolmer, *Parlament und Verfassung*, IV 1 ff.

202 Kolmer, 5.
203 Law of 4 October 1882, *RGB* no. 142; see also p. 274 at note 48.
204 Harald Bachmann (1977). *Hoseph Maria Baernreither (1845–1925)*, with a detailed survey of literature on p. 13.
205 Bachmann, 16.
206 Baernreither owned the estate of Lünz/West Bohemia where he prepared the bills — with Franz Klein in the summer of 1894 — for the permanent board which deliberated on laws (Bachmann, 40. p.).
207 Bachmann, 17 p.
208 Baernreither, *Arbeiterverbände*, 18.
209 Baernreither, 448.
210 Cf. Baernreither's views in connection with the so-called 'Hilfskassengesetz' p. 306.
211 *StProtAH*, 10. Sess., Beil. Nr. 1; Kolmer, *Parlament und Verfassung*, IV, 6 ff.
212 See Taaffe's letter to Pražák with the invitation of Steinbach to the first session on 25 November 1885: AVA, JM, Karton 1448, Nr. 25.
213 Cf. the official address of 22 January 1886 'on the introduction of the bill regarding workers' accident insurance': AVA, JM, Karton 1448, Nr. 38, as well as the (second) government bill, no. 39. The question of including workers employed in mines for certain minerals was left open; the law only expresses 'that this insurance should be regulated by a special law'. The reason for this was the 'urgent wish of the Minister of Agriculture to solve this question with a special draft (on regulating the conditions of the "Bruderladen")'.
214 On 4 February 1886 (eighteenth session); cf. *StProtAH*, 10. Sess., 548; die Regierungsvorlage (E 5): *StProtAH*, 10. Sess., Beil. Nr. 75.
215 *StProtAH*, 10. Sess., Beil. Nr. 148, p. 53.
216 *StProtAH*, 10. Sess., p. 2485–2615.
217 Cf. p. 279.
218 *StProtAH*, 20 Sess., 2808 ff.; Plener vgl. Czedik, *Geschichte*, I 210; Charmatz, *Österreichs innere Geschichte*, II 26 f. *StProtAH*, 10. Sess., 2557 ff.; cf. Ebert, *Sozialpolitik*, 223 ff.
219 *StProtAH*, 10. Sess., 2505 ff.
220 *StProtAH*, 10. Sess. 2485 ff. (application: 2496; Beil. Nr. 188). Cf. Ebert, *Sozialpolitik*, 206 ff.
221 *StProtAH*, 10. Sess., Beil. Nr. 107.
222 The average daily wage was about 50 K; in some crownlands (Galicia and others) the average wage was lower.
223 Average daily wage about 80 K.
224 *StProtAH*, 10. Sess., Beil. Nr. 381.
225 *StProtAH*, 10. Sess., Beil. Nr. 195.
226 AVA, JM, Karton 1448, Nr. 54. In a (handwritten) 'Mémoire' Steinbach proposed postponing the imperial sanction of the Accident Insurance Law until the end of negotiations on the Sickness Insurance Law and advised ensuring that 'sickness insurance does not come into force later than accident insurance'. Pražák nevertheless met Taaffe's request of 2 November 1887 and applied for imperial sanction (official address of 22 December).
227 Decree of 14 June 1889, *RGB* no. 95 (see previous note for reasons why accident insurance came into force later).
228 See *ÖstWB*, I, 263 p., Pkt. II, 3.
229 Printed in: 'Gesetze und Verordnungen betreffend die Unfallversicherung der Arbeiter' (= *Österr. Gesetze mit Erläuterungen aus den Materialien,* 58), Leo Geller, (ed.), 1897, 155 ff.; 165 ff.; 224 ff. (revised version).
230 A few years later two sub-classes (A: 1 and 2; B 3 and 4 percent) were added to the original danger classes (I-XII; 5–100 percent).
231 Ludwig Brügel, *Geschichte*, III, passim; Steiner, *Arbeiterbewegung*, 282 ff.; Berchtold, *Österr. Parteiprogramme*, 22 f.; 137 ff.
232 Details in Steiner, *Arbeiterbewegung*, 261 ff.
233 Cf. Steinbach, *Unfallversicherung* 44 ff.
234 Steinbach, *Unfallversicherung*, 50.
235 While the second draft (§91) declared the decision of the arbitration court final and only provided for the possibility of civil court procedures by way of exception, the third draft (§63) — which finally became law — provided for appeal to the 'Reichsversicherungsamt' (§§87 ff.).
236 In the 'Mémoire' of 22 December 1887 Steinbach said that he did not recommend introducing a 'Reichsversicherungsamt' following the German pattern as 'such large organizations are not advisable'. See AVA, JM, Karton 1450, Nr. 76 on later attempts to introduce a higher instance

for accident arbitration courts.

237 AVA, JM, Karon 1448, Nr. 15 (dated 21 November 1884).

238 *StProtAH*, 9. Sess., Beil. Nr. 1052.

239 *StProtAH*, 10. Sess., Beil. Nr. 84.

240 The extremely brief 'Remarks' on the draft of the Sickness Insurance Law conform far less with the substantiation of the German draft than was the case of the bills for the Accident Insurance Law (Gemeinden und 'weitere Kommunalverbände').

241 §1, section 1.

242 §1, III. Persons employed in inland shiping had been included in compulsory insurance by the 'Ausdehnungsgesetz' of 28 May 1885, *DRGB* p. 159.

243 According to the DKVG territorial self-administrative bodies (communities and 'other communal bodies') — and not bureaucratic institutions — were responsible for carrying out compulsory insurance under §1.

244 Cf. §10, section 3, DKVG.

245 §6, section 2, line 2; while the level of accident insurance pensions was based on the concrete wages of the insured, the relevant 'usual local daily wages' were fixed for the level of contributions and benefits of the KVG by the political authority of first instance, divided according to sexes or types of workers (unskilled workers, workers, foremen, or similar); more details in *ÖStWB*, i, 234.

246 At the end of 1900 (when the first exact statistical data were available) there were separate sickness insurance departments in 185 'Bruderladen'; cf. *ÖStWB*, i, 655 and p. 307.

247 The latter soon developed to the dominant type of scheme (in 1900: over 1 million members of a total of 2.5 million members of all schemes) while the builders' sickness insurances played a subordinate role (a maximum of about 3500 members).

248 In so far as the statutory minimum benefits could not be provided, although the contributions were 3 percent 'of the usual local or average daily wage or of the real earnings'.

249 Cf. *ÖBL*, i, 84 f. and Ebert, *Sozialpolitik*, 186 ff. Menzel, *Arbeiterversicherung*, 36.

250 See text at note 204.

251 See at note 208.

252 *StProtAH*, 10. Sess., 4314; Beil. Nr. 336.

253 Further development, see p. 306.

254 *StProtAH*, 10. Sess., Beil. Nr. 185.

255 *StProtAH*, 10. Sess., 4232.

256 The young Czech Joseph Kaizl and Baernreither belonged later (1898) to the same government (Duke Franz Thun); the national differences soon forced Baernreither to resign. Bachmann, *Baernreither*, 42 ff.

257 Also in Viktor Adlers essays, speeches and letters, 5. Heft, 147 ff.

258 Cf. *StProtAH*, 10. Sess., Beil. Nr. 359.

259 *StProtAH*, 10. Sess., 388.

260 *StProtAH*, 10. Sess., Beil. Nr. 143.

261 Cf. §3 of the KVG.

262 Hye only wanted to assign the ruling on compulsory insurance for workers in agriculture and forestry to the 'Landtage' on one condition, namely that all 'regulations which are considered necessary and are part of Reich legislation according to the constitution, are to be presented to the "Reichsrat" for a decision'.

263 P. 329.

264 Cf. Max Mandl's publication of the KVG, of the 'Hilfskassengesetz' (VI), of the relevant decrees and model statutes in the series: *Österreichische Gesetze mit Erläuterungen aus der Rechtsprechung, Einzelausgaben*, Heft 39, 1894.

265 *StProtAH*, 10. Sess., Beil. Nr. 732.

266 *StProtAH*, 11. Sess., Beil. Nr. 753.

267 Namely in cases where treatment had not been provided for in the master's own scheme but in the hospital.

268 P. 318.

269 Cf. Otto Stöger (2nd edn by Wimbersky), Art. 'Hilfskassen', *ÖStWB*, ii, 851 ff.

270 *StProtAH*, 10. Sess., 4314; Beil. Nr. 336.

271 *StProtAH*, 10. Sess., Beil. Nr. 9; Beil. Nr. 129; 471. *RGB* Nr. 110.

272 Cf. Baernreither, *Die englischen Arbeiterverbände*, 314 ff.; by comparison, the German 'Hilfskassengesetz' of 7 April 1876, *RGB* p. 125, was only of very minor significance as a pattern for Baernreither's relief fund model.

273 Cf. *ÖStWB*, ii, 857 ff.
274 Cf. *ÖStWB*, ii, 456, Waentig, *Mittelstandspolitik*, 472 ff.; Sandgruber, in: *Soziale Sicherheit im Nachziehverfahren*, 138 ff.
275 Compared with the previous legal position it was now also possible to make membership of master's sickness insurances compulsory with a three-quarters majority in the general assembly (§115 a GeWO). Cf. Sandgruber, 144 on the discussion which led to this new ruling. See p. 331 on later development.
276 *ÖStWB*, ii, 858.
277 In 1903 benefits provided by all registered relief funds amounted to almost 1.5 million K, the sum of all disability and old age pensions, however, only 1600 K: *ÖStWB*, ii, 858.
278 *ÖStWB*, ii, 858.
279 Cf. p. 284.
280 Cf. *ÖStWB*, i, 646 ff.
281 *StProtAH*, 10. Sess., 7316; Beil. Nr. 484; see the vivid portrayal of conditions in the Austrian mining industry in *Gleichheit*, 2 July 1887, 3 f.
282 AVA, MRP, 1882, Nr. 96; 1883, Nr. 25.
283 Cf. p. 297.
284 See also Menzel, *Arbeiterversicherung*, 38 ff.; Lededed, *Grundriss*, 429, note 1.
285 *StProtAH*, 10. Sess.,; Beil. Nr. 300.
286 See p. 299.
287 *StProtAH*, 10 Sess. Beil Nr. 729; Brügel, *Soziale Gesetzgebung*, 149.
288 Bachmann, *Baernreither*, 32.
289 *StProtAH*, 10. Sess., Beil. Nr. 729; draft *Baernreither*, part C.
290 Leon Ritter von Bilìnski was professor of national economics in Lvov, (Galicia); see *ÖBL*, I, 84 f., Ebert, *Sozialpolitik*, 185 ff.
291 Cf. *StProtAH*, 10. Sess., Beil. Nr. 381.
292 *StProtAH*, 10. Sess., 10679–10705 bzw. 10906–10925.
293 *StProtAH*, 10. Sess., 10962.
294 *StProtAH*, 10. Sess., Beil. Nr. 381.
295 *StProtAH*, 10. Sess., 969.
296 Decree of the Ministry of Agriculture of 14 November 1890, line 16906, supplement no. 9 (printed in Max Mandl, law of 28 July 1889, 115 ff.).
297 The usual local daily wages were to be used as a basis and not the concrete wage of the insured; an average value was to be taken for works whose plants were in several districts.
298 There was no analogous ruling in sickness insurance.
299 See p. 302.
300 A good compilation of the objections raised by the labour force is to be found in Otto Stöger, *ÖStWB*, i, 658 f.
301 According to §13, line 3, KVG 'members of schemes who cannot pay contributions because of unemployment' continued to have 'membership and the right to benefits for at least six weeks'.
302 See p. 295.
303 Pp. 317 and 330.
304 See Kolmer, *Parlament und Verfassung*, v, 333 ff.; on the end of the Taaffe era. Charmatz, *Österreichs innere Geschichte*, ii, 71, 79 f.; Brügel, *Soziale Gesetzgebung*, 167 ff.
305 See Charmatz, *Österreichs innere Geschichte*, ii, 83; Matis, *Österreichs Wirtschaft*, 312; Spitzmüller, *NÖB*, 1 Abt., ii. vol., 58 f., on the tax reform introduced by Steinbach—but completed by Eugen Böhm-Bawerk (1896)—whose main feature was the introduction of an income tax with moderately progressive rates. See Matis, *Österreichs Wirtschaft*, 315 f.; Spitzmüller, 56 ff., on the 1892 currency reform (introduction of the gold standard) which is largely considered to be one of Steinbach's achievements.
306 Charmatz, *Österreichs innere Geschichte*, ii, 79 f.; Spitzmüller, 54 f.
307 Walter and Wandruszka, *Österr. Verfassungs- und Verwaltungsgeschichte*, 249 ff.; Brügel, *Soziale Gesetzgebung*, p. 170.
308 Limited by the 'Sesshaftigkeitsklausel' (domicile clause) of §9(a) of the law.
309 Cf. Berchtold, *Parteiprogramme*, p. 50; Silberbauer, *Österreichs Katholiken*, 121 ff.
310 See p. 319.
311 Cf. Charmatz, *Österreichs innere Geschichte*, ii, 118.
312 Berthold Sutter, *Die Badenischen Sprachenverordnungen of 1897*, i, 1960; ii, 1965.
313 Bachmann, *Baernreither*, 42 ff.
314 Bachmann, *Baernreither*, 44 ff.; Lederer, *Grundriss*, 24 ff.; *ÖStWB* I 314–318.

315 V. counted among the first fourteen Social Democratic deputies of 1897 ff. and as legal adviser of the association of cooperative sickness insurance schemes he was extremely familiar with the problems of workers' insurance; cf. Brügel, *Geschichte d. Sozialdemokratie*, IV, 308 f.

316 Baernreither, *Grundfragen der sozialen Versicherung*, 1908, VII.

317 Alfred Ableitinger (1973). *Ernest v. Koerber und das Verfassungsproblem im Jahre 1900*.

318 Kolmer, *Parlament und Verfassung*, VIII, 146 ff. Upon Koerber's and Lueger's invitation of the Seventh Meeting of International Workers' Insurance Congress took place in Vienna from 17-23 September 1905 (publication of the minutes, 2 vol., 1906).

319 Cf. Berchtold, *Parteiprogramme*, p. 28.

320 Brügel, *Soziale Gesetzgebung*, 225 ff.

321 See previous note.

322 See Redlich, *Österr. Regierung und Verwaltung im Weltkriege*, 127 ff.

323 Redlich, p. 80.

324 Redlich, 157 f.; Brügel, *Soziale Gesetzgebung*, 234 ff.

325 Lederer, *Grundriss*, p. 27; Bachmann, *Baernreither*, 163 f.; *HHStA*, Nachlass Baernreither, Karton 21, foll. 1253 ff.

326 See Lederer, *Grundriss*, p. 27 on the powers of the new ministry.

327 Redlich, *Regierung und Verwaltung*, 296 ff.; Brauneder and Lachmayer, *Österr. Verfassungsgeschichte*, 187 ff.; Walter and Mayer, *Grundriss* p. 18.

328 Berchtold, *Parteiprogramme*, 137 ff.; cf. Emmerich Talos (1976). *Zu den Anfängen der Sozialpolitik*, *Österr. Zs.f. Politikwiss.*, 5 145 ff.

329 Brügel, p. 344; Berchtold, *Parteiprogramme*, 145 ff.

330 Cf. Friedrich Funder, *Aufbruch zur christlichen Sozialreform*, 1953; also *Vom Gestern ins Heute*, 3rd edn, 1971, 75 ff.

331 'Die Sozialversicherung . . .', 23 ff.

332 Baernreither, *Grundfragen*, p. 2.

333 Matis, *Österreichs Wirtschaft*, 432 f.

334 Matis, p. 433.

335 Matis, *Österreichs Wirtschaft*, p. 436.

336 Leo Verkauf, *Geschichte des Arbeiterrechts*, 16 ff.; also *ÖStBW* I 304 ff.

337 Matis, *Österreichs Wirtschaft*, p. 55 (table 4).

338 Redlich, *Österreichs Regierung und Verwaltung*, 213 ff.

339 Redlich, 147 ff.

340 Redlich, p. 229.

341 Cf. decree of 29 November 1914, *RGB* no. 330, on allowing insurances under public law to use funds for extraordinary purposes during war.

342 *RGB* no. 168.

343 AVA, JM, Karton 1449, Nr. 119.

344 Without the adjective 'berufsgenossenschaftlich' from 1925 onwards; accident and sickness insurance of railway employees was summarized in the 'Versicherungsanstalt der österr. Eisenbahnen' by the 1947 SV-ÜG (B/7, II); see Steinbach, *Unfallversicherung*, 151 ff.

345 Figures for 1901; see *ÖStWB*, I, 288.

346 1901; 215 compared with 193 at all other institutions: *ÖStWB*, I, 288.

347 *ÖStWB*, I, 285.

348 See Friedrich Steinbach, *Unfallversicherung*, 74 ff., based on preparatory work by Elisabeth Kunst. Tomandl's 'Der Wegunfall in der österr. und dt. Unfallversicherung, in: *Grenzen der Leistungspflicht*, 137 (note 2) is inexact inasmuch as refusal of insurance protection for accidents on the way to or from work was common at first after the Accident Insurance Law came into force (until about 1894) but does not apply for the whole period up until 1911.

349 *ÖStWB*, I, 290 ff.

350 'Gutachten der territorialen Arbeiter-Unfallversicherungsanstalten über das Regierungsprogramm für die Reform und den Ausbau der Arbeiterversicherung', 1907, 1 ff.

351 AVA, JM, Karton 1450: the amendments to the Accident Insurance Law, proposed by the Insurance Board, were used as a basis of deliberations.

352 1904; also printed as an appendix to the *Gutachten* (mentioned in note 350) of the territorial workers' accident insurances. Cf. *StProtAG*, 17. Sess., 26215.

353 Cf. twelfth amendment to the Accident Insurance Law.

354 Cf. *Gutachten* (as note 350), 98.

355 Criticism in the *Gutachten*, 210 f.

356 See the law of 30 December 1917, *RGB* no. 523.

357 On differences see pp. 294 and 307.
358 See Kerber, *Kranken- und Unfallversicherung*, 38 (table) on later increases (by amendments IV ff.).
359 For origins of the law see Kerber, 37.
360 These were in seven associations.
361 When calculating these values the schemes' payments to the reserve fund were considered as liabilities (*ÖStWB*, I, 256).
362 See the records of the enquiry held by the Ministry of the Interior from 19 March to 21 May 1895 on the reform of the Sickness Insurance Law, 1897.
363 Record of the first Austrian Sickness Insurance Meeting of 28, 29 and 30 June 1896 (Vienna). Stöger has made a good compilation of the proposals brought forward within the framework of the enquiry and at the meeting, *ÖStWB*, I, 257 ff.
364 See §§2–6.
365 Hannes Stekl, 'Soziale Sicherheit für Hausgehilfen', in: *Soziale Sicherheit im Nachziehverfahren*, 174 ff., 204 f.
366 §§39 ff.
367 Sandgruber, in: *Soziale Sicherheit im Nachziehverfahren*, 146 f. See also 'StProt der Gewerbe-Enquête', 1893, 723 ff.
368 Wannagat (1965). *Lehrbuch des Sozialversicherungsrechts*, I, 77 ff. also Zöllner in this collection, point 416.
369 Robert Kerber (and Eugen Spann, and Artur Rudolph) (1929). *Das Angestelltenversicherungsgesetz*, I, 1 ff.; also Lederer, *Grundriss*, 25, 433 f.; Hans Schmitz (1951). *Die Angestelltenversicherung*, I, 1–22 (Entwicklung bis 1939); (1951). II, 1–37 (1939 bis ca. 1950). Cf. diss. quoted in note 23 by Andreas Baryli.
370 Cf. *ÖBL*, I, 92 f.
371 *StProtAH*, 11. Sess., 11080 f.
372 *StProtAH*, 17. Sess., Beil. Nr. 1476.
373 See Krejci im System, Pkt. 1.2.1.4. For another point of view see Schmitz, *Angesetlltenversicherung*, I, 3, who equates 'Meldeunabhängigkeit' (registration dependence) with the *ipso iure* principle.
374 §§14–16 of the government bill.
375 Kerber, *Angestelltenversicherungsgesetz*, 5 ff.
376 Cf. Schmitz, *Angestelltenversicherung*, I, 5. The ruling of the amended insurance for employees corresponded largely to today's ruling of §225, section 1, line 1, lit. (b). ASVG; according to lit. (a), however, this does not apply if the application for compulsory insurance takes place within six months of beginning work.
377 Board's report in *StProtAH*, 21. Sess., Beil. Nr. 2187; decision in the 198th session, *StProtAH*, 21. Sess., 9534.
378 Cf. *StProtAH*, 21. Sess., Beil. Nr. 219.
379 *StProtAH*, 11. Sess. Cf. Schönerer's and Fürnkranz's motion of 5.2.1884. Kolmer, *Parlament und Verfassung*, III 387.
380 Cf. Brügel, *Soziale Gesetzgebung*, 172.
381 One of the factors influencing these parliamentary activities was undoubtedly that in 1891 German old age and disability insurance came into force (see p. 292).
382 See §§3 and 4.
383 Baernreither, *Grundfragen der sozialen Versicherung*, p. 22.
384 *StProtAH*, 18. Sess., Beil. Nr. 1160.
385 See Sandgruber in: *Soziale Sicherheit im Nachziehverfahren*, 150 ff. This clearly shows that the idea of insurance of the self-employed or of a community of risks between the self-employed and the employed was not only opposed by the Social Democrats but also by circles from trade and industry — sometimes most vehemently. The community of risks between self-employed persons in the trades and in agriculture was rejected by the Social Democrats in particular. Basically the Christian Social party was quite alone in promoting the inclusion of the self-employed in a comprehensive 'social insurance'.
386 See Oberndorfer in *System*, 6 January 1.
387 Since June 1912.
388 Funder, *Von Gestern ins Heute*, p. 328.
389 Lederer, *Grundriss*, p. 25 and 439.
390 Heinrich Mataja (1877–1937) was the (first) Minister of Social Welfare (from 22 January 1917 to 27 October 1918); in the republic he was State Secretary of the Interior (1918/19) and later Foreign Minister (1924–1926).

391 Leitsätze, p. 23.
392 Brauneder and Lachmayer, *Österr. Verfassungsgeschichte*, p. 188. Walter and Mayer, *Grundriss*, p. 18. From 30 October 1918 onwards government power was 'double-tracked' as the Lammasch government, appointed on 27 October 1918, to which Ignaz Seipel belonged as Minister of Social Welfare, did not lose its legal basis until the decision on the form of government (with the Law on the Form of the State and of the Government, *StGB* no. 55) on 12 November 1918. See Lederer, *Grundriss*, p. 27, note 2.
393 The Social Democrats obtained 1.2 million votes (and 69 seats), the Christian Social Party 1.06 million (63), the German Nationals about 600 000 (25). The numbers of seats do not include the German-speaking Tyrol and southern Styria. See Berchtold, *Parteiprogramme*, p. 33 and 57; Funder, *Vom Gestern ins Heute*, 467 f.; Walter Goldinger, (1954, reprint in 1977). 'Der geschichtliche Ablauf der Ereignisse in Österreich 1918–1945', in: *Geschichte der Republik Österreich*, Heinrich Benedikt (ed.), 46 f. (also published under the title *Geschichte der Republik Österreich*, 1962).
394 Cf. Goldinger, 109 f.; Funder, *Vom Gestern ins Heute*, p. 194.
395 Goldinger, p. 110, 116 ff.; Funder, *Vom Gestern ins Heute*, 499 ff.
396 Cf. Silberbauer, *Österr. Katholiken*, 261 f.; Steinbach, *Unfallversicherung*, 98 f.
397 Cf. Friedrich Thalmann, in: *Geschichte der Republik Österreich*, 490 f.; Anton Kausel (1976). 'Österreichs Wirtschaft an der Schwelle zur Industrienation höherer Ordnung', in: *Wirtschaft und Politik. Festschrift für Fritz Klenner*, 192 f.
398 *Grundriss*, 28 f.
399 Thalman, 492 f.; Kausel, p. 192.
400 For the figures up to and including 1931 see Karl Forchheimer (Josef Hammerl, Franz Keller, and Josef Stangelberger) (ed.) (1932). 'Die Vorschriften über Arbeitslosenversicherung' (= *Die sozialpolitische Gesetzgebung in Österreich*, VI). The figures for 1932–1938 (see text after note 402) are in Thalmann, 497 ff.; this only takes the registered unemployed into account (cf. Kausel, p. 193 for the figure of 560 000 unemployed in 1933).
401 Goldinger, *Der geschichtliche Ablauf*, 152 ff.
402 Gernot Hasiba (1976). *Die zweite Bundes-Verfassungsnovelle von 1929*, Klaus Berchtold (ed.) (1979). *Die Verfassungsreform von 1929 (Dokumente und Materialien)*, 2 parts.
403 Cf. Walter and Mayer, *Grundriss*, p. 22; also note 459. On the Dollfuß-Schuschnigg-era cf. Brauneder and Lachmayer, *Verfassungsgeschichte*, 231 ff.; Walter and Mayer, *Grundriss*, 21 f.; Berchtold, *Parteiprogramme*, 36 ff.; 63 ff.
404 Thalmann, in: *Geschichte der Republik Österreich*, p. 500; see also Reinhard Jakob, *Neues Sozialversicherungsrecht in der Ostmark*, (1939?), p. 16.
405 Kerber, *Kranken- und Unfallversicherung*, p. 51; Lederer, *Grundriss*, p. 435, 530 p.; Josef Papouschek (1951). 'Die österr. Krankenversicherung', in: *SozSi*, 270 ff., 271.
406 Cf. Hugo Mehrer (1951). 'Die Krankenversicherung der Bundesangestellten', *SozSi* 275 pp.; Lederer, *Grundriss*, p. 436.
407 *StGB* Nr. 311; after numerous amendments: BKVG 1937, *BGB* Nr. 94.
408 Karl Forchheimer (ed.) (1923). 'Gesetze und Verordnungen über Arbeitslosenversicherung' (= *Die sozialpolitische Gesetzgebung in Österreich*, VI); Forchheimer, Josef Hammerl, Franz Keller, and Josef Stangelberger, *Die Vorschriften über Arbeitslosenversicherung* . . . (note 400); Josef Hammerl (1951). 'Die Arbeitslosenversicherung', *SozSi* 230 ff.; also Lederer, *Grundriss*, p. 28, 594 ff.; and Dieter Stiefel. *Arbeitslosigkeit* . . . (note 23).
409 Forchheimer, *Gesetze und Verordnungen*, 12 f.
410 See the draft law (prepared by Prof. Karl Pribram) in *StProtKonstNV*, Beil. Nr. 680; Forchheimer, *Gesetze und Verordnungen*, p. 16, note 1. Also during the last 2 years by way of exception; cf. §1, section 2 of the law and Forchheimer, *Gesetze und Verordnungen*, p. 17.
411 Cf. Lederer, *Grundriss*, p. 590; see also Antony I. Ogus in this collection.
412 The German 'Bundesrat' had drawn up guidelines for unemployment welfare as early as 1914. The decree on unemployment welfare of 13 November 1918, *DRGB*, I, p. 1305, was based on these. See Wannagat, *Lehrbuch*, I, 83 f. and Zöllner in this collection, Pkt. 434.
413 See Maurer on Switzerland (transition to insurance principle, influenced by a federal law of 1924); see Forchheimer etc., Vorschriften, 3, on other data. An unsuccessful attempt was made in St. Gallen as early as 1895 to introduce unemployment insurance.
414 Winter values are always worse. See note 400 on the calculation of figures in general. Good compilation of unemployment figures up to and including 1931 in Forchheimer etc., Vorschriften, 768 f.
415 As above note and numerous tables on the financial management of unemployment welfare up

to and including 1931 in Forchheimer etc., 770 ff.; also Lederer, *Grundriss*, p. 597 and 'Statistiken zur Arbeitslosenversicherung', I (1920–1929); II (1930).

416 Lederer, *Grundriss*.

417 Kerber, *Kranken- und Unfallversicherung*, 36 ff.; Steinbach, *Unfallversicherung*, 88 ff.; Lederer, *Grundriss*, 435 ff.

418 Steinbach, *Unfallversicherung* p. 97; Wolfgang Krösl, in: *90 Jahre soziale Unfallversicherung in Österreich*, 42 ff.

419 Survey in Kerber, *Kranken- und Unfallversicherung*, 38 f.

420 Kerber, *Kranken- und Unfallversicherung*, p. 38; Steinbach, *Unfallversicherung*, p. 92.

421 Cf. survey in Kerber, *Kranken- und Unfallversicherung*, 52 ff.

422 See Schmitz, *Angestelltenversicherung*, I, 8; also Wolfgang R. Mells in: *Festschrift Heinrich Demelius zum 80. Geburtstag*, 155 ff., 163. The reason given in the government bill for worsening the companion's position was in particular the avoidance of double provisions (see Kerber, *Angestelltenversicherungsgesetz*, I, 426).

423 Schmitz, *Angesetelltenversicherung*, I, 8.

424 Kerber, *Angestelltenversicherungsgesetz*, I, 32.

425 *StProtNR*, 2. GP, Beil. Nr. 21.

426 Thus Kerber, *Angestelltenversicherungsgesetz*, I, 34; Schmitz, *Angestelltenversicherung*, I, 9, talks of 'social categories' (instead of 'professional categories').

427 Schmitz, *Angestelltenversicherung*, I, 9.

428 At the same time as the Insurance Law for the Employed was passed, two resolutions were adopted unanimously by the National Council; these aimed at repealing the community of risks. See Kerber, *Angesetelltenversicherungsgesetz*, I, 102.

429 *StProtNR*, 2. GP, Beil. Nr. 1455.

430 Kerber, *Angestelltenversicherungsgesetz*, I, 35.

431 *StProtNR*, 2. GP, 15. Cf. Spalowsky, Drexel inter alia, *StProtNR*, 2. GP, 2.

432 *StProtNR*, 2. GP; reference in the explanatory remarks on the 1925 draft of the Workers' Insurance Law. Lederer, *Grundriss*, 34 ff.; 437 ff.; Robert Kerber (Fridrich Pernitza, and Artur Rudolph) (1936). *Die gewerbliche Sozialversicherung*, 306 f.; Robert Uhlir (1951). 'Die Invalidenversicherung', *SozSi* 241 ff.; W. Hubinger (1949). 'Die Entwicklung der Arbeiterversicherung, in: *VersRdSch* 296 ff.

433 *StProtNR*, 2. GP, Beil. Nr. 451.

434 Lederer, *Grundriss*, p. 36.

435 §§265 ff. Lederer, *Grundriss*, 554 ff.; Uhlir (1951). *SozSi* p. 242.

436 See §268 (twenty-fold of daily earnings).

437 Old age pensions were also available (according to §265, section 1, lit. (b)) for persons who were excluded from unemployment assistance or emergency aid 'only because of incapacity to work'. In all cases, eligibility was based on need (reference to the prerequisites for granting emergency aid).

438 Lederer, *Grundriss*, p. 557.

439 The first (however, no longer topical) example was sickness insurance for sailors; see p. 319.

440 Voluntary membership in a compulsory insurance for the employed was first made possible for the self-employed in the transport industry with the Accident Insurance Extension Law of 1894.

441 See §9 of the Notaries' Insurance Law of 1938, as it was on 1 January 1961, §9: 'If ability to carry out one's profession is reduced by more than 20 percent and if the reduction of income amounts to more than one tenth. . . .'"

442 See the Notaries' Insurance Law of 5 January 1938, *BGB* no. 2, mentioned in the above note. This was brought into force again in 1947 with §1, section 3 of the SV-ÜG. For information on the situation of notaries' insurance in the National Socialist era (notaries' insurance in Munich etc.) see Lorenz Linseder (ed.) (1948). *Das Sozialversicherungs-Überleitungsgesetz*, 17 and Kurt Wagner (ed.) (1961). *Das Notarversicherungsgesetz*, 3 ff. See also p. 000.

443 Lederer, *Grundriss*, p. 37, 439; Leopold Ehrenberger (1951). 'Die landund forstwirtschaftliche Sozialversicherung', *SozSi* 246 ff. and Bruckmüller, *Soziale Sicherheit im Nachziehverfahren*, 67 ff.

444 Adler (1930). *Das Angestellten- und Arbeiterrecht*, 763 ff.; see also Kerber, *Kranken- und Unfallversicherung*, p. 213.

445 Ehrenberger, p. 247.

446 *VfSZg*. Nr. 328. Printed in Kerber, *Kranken- und Unfallversicherung*, 213 ff.

447 Kerber, *Kranken- und Unfallversicherung*, 221 ff.

448 The first government bill of January 1927 only concerned sickness insurance; a bill regulating the other branches of insurance (apart from unemployment insurance) was not introduced until the autumn of 1927 (*StProtNR*, 2. GP, Beil. Nr. 15). See also Bruckmüller, p. 76.

449 Hans Unterreiner (1951). 'Der Bergmann—Pionier der sozialen Sicherheit', *SozSi*, 265 ff.; Kerber, *Die gewerbliche Sozialversicherung*, p. 329, 331.

450 After the so-called 'self-elimination' of the National Council on 4 March 1933 the government derived the right from the Enabling Act on the War Economy, *RGB* no. 307/1917, to pass decrees of the same standing as laws: Brauneder and Lachmayer, *Verfassungsgeschichte*, p. 232; Walter and Mayer, *Grundriss*, p. 21.

451 Franz Herzer (1951). 'Die Krankenversicherung der selbständig Erwerbstätigen', *SozSi*, 279 ff.; Sandgruber in: *Soziale Sicherheit im Nachziehverfahren*, p. 157.

452 Cf. Kerber (Pernitza, and Rudolph) (1936). *Die gewerbliche Sozialversicherung*, VIII ff.; Schmitz, *Angestelltenversicherung*, I, 21 f.; Legat and Grabner, *Sozialversicherungsrecht*, p. 5; Steinbach, *Unfallversicherung*, 124 ff.; and Gert Rudolf (1975). 'Die gewerbliche Sozialversicherung 1935, *SozSi*, 565 ff.

453 Kerber, *Gewerbliche Sozialversicherung*, V.

454 Kerber, VI.

455 Details in Kerber, *Gewerbliche Socialversicherung*, IX.

456 Kerber.

457 For information on the political and economic development in the National Socialist era see Helfried Pfeifer (1941). *Die Ostmark. Eingliederung und Neugestaltung;* Walter and Wandruszka, *Österr. Verfassungs- und Verwaltungsgeschichte*, 296 ff.; Goldinger, in: *Geschichte der Republik Österreich*, 273 ff.; Thalmann, 500 ff.; Brauneder and Lachmayer, *Verfassungsgeschichte*, 248 ff.; Ludwig Jedlicka (1963). Verfassungs- und Verwaltungsprobleme 1938-1955, in: *Die Entwicklung der Verfassung Österreichs*, 120 ff.; Anton Adalbert Klein (1968). 'Die österr. Länder während des Zweiten Weltkriegs', in: *Österreich—50 Jahre Republi*, 103 ff.; Gerhard Botz (1976). *Die Eingliederung Österreichs in das Deutsche Reich*, 2nd edn.

458 'Der anschluss Österreichs an das Deutsche Reich—eine Geschichts-legende', in: *Juristische Blätter* 1955, 439 ff.

459 *Verfassungs- und Verwaltungsprobleme*, p. 123.

460 Walter and Mayer, *Grundriss*, p. 22.

461 Jedlicka, *Verfassungs- und Verwaltungsprobleme* 123 f.

462 Cf. the law on changes of districts in Austria, 'Gesetz über Gebietsveränderungen im Lande Österreich', of 1 October 1938, *DRGB*, I, p. 1333 = *GblLÖ*, Nr. 443/1938.

463 Cf. Thalmann, in: *Geschichte der Republik Österreich*, 500 f.

464 Cf. Reinhard Jakob (1939). *Neues Sozialversicherungsrecht in Ostmark;* Wilhelm F. Funke (1939). *Verordnung über die Einführung der Sozialversicherung im Lande Österreich.*

465 This law replaced the ruling of the 1935 GSVG—self-administration in unemployment insurance was abolished and transferred to federal administration—however, it brought no fundamental changes to the legal situation; such a change (a turn away from the insurance principle) did not take place until the decree of 5 September 1939, *DRGB* I, p. 1674. The dominance of the insurance principle was not reinstated until the Unemployment Assistance Act of 15 May 1946, *BGB* no. 97. The federal law of 22 June 1949, *BGB* no. 184, forms the basis of current unemployment insurance law; this was reissued by the federal law of 1 July 1958, *BGB* no. 199 and again by the federal law of 1977/109; on this see Karl Dirschmied (1980). *Arbeitslosenversicherungsrecht.*

466 Steinbach, *Unfallversicherung*, p. 137.

467 Steinbach, 182 ff.

468 Report on the motives of the government bill on the 1947 SV-ÜG, *StProtNR*, 5. GP, Beil. Nr. 328.

469 According to §11, section 2 of the 'Decree on the Introduction of Social Insurance in Austria', the Austrian ruling on the division of contributions (§80, section 6, GSVG 1935) was to continue to apply.

470 Wannagat, *Lehrbuch*, I, 87; Zöllner in this collection, Pkt. 442; Schmitz, *Angestelltenversicherung*, II, 6 f.; Steinbach, *Unfallversicherung*, p. 138.

471 See especially §§405 ff.; 1637-1640; 1676-1678; 1727; 1772-1774; 1783-1787 RVO as well as §§132, 147 of the (German) AVG and 195 ff. of the 'Reichsknappschaftsgesetz'. According to §4 of the 'Decree on the Introduction . . .' more precise rulings on authorities and procedure were left up to the Minister of Labour with the consent of the 'Reichsminister' of the Interior; with the (first) 'Decree on the Implementation and Completion . . .' of 9 February 1939, *DRGB* I, p. 196, §4, the 'two track' Austrian system was upheld at first as the 'district prefects and the chief burgomasters' or else the provincial leaders and the lord mayor of Vienna were declared responsible for decision procedure while the Austrian arbitration courts were to continue to be responsible for award procedure. Almost complete assimilation to German social insurance pro-

cedural law followed with the second 'Decree on Implementation and Completion . . .' of 5 February 1940, *DRGB*, I, p. 270.

472   On the constitutional development of the second republic see Ludwig Adamovich (H. Spanner, and L.K. Adamovich) (1971). *Handbuch des österr. Verfassungsrechts*, 6th edn, 29 ff.; Ermacora, *Österr. Verfassungslehre*, I, 44 ff.; Walter and Mayer, *Grundriss*, 22 ff.; Brauneder and Lachmayer, *Österr. Verfassungsgeschichte*, 255 ff.; Goldinger, in: *Geschichte der Republik Österreich*, 284 ff.; Wandruszka, 481 ff.; Stephan Verosta, *Die geschichtliche Kontinuität des österr. Staates und seine europäische Funktion*, 573 ff., 608 ff.; Franz Nemschak (1951). 'Die österr. Wirtschaft seit Kriegsende', *SozSi* 213 ff.; Thalmann, in: *Geschichte der Republik Österreich*, 502 ff.; Kausel, in: *Festschr. Fritz Klenner*, 193 ff.; (1977–end 1979): OECD-Wirtschaftsberichte (German translation) Österreich, Februar 1980; see also 'Bericht über die soziale Lage 1978' (*Sozialbericht*), 1979, parts I (survey), II (Zur sozialen Lage) und IV (Beiträge der Interessenvertretungen).

473   Ermacora, *Verfassungslehre*, I 47.

474   Ermacora.

475   Walter and Mayer, *Grundriss*, 27 f.; of course the State Treaty of Vienna imposed certain obligations under international law (cf. Ermacora, *Österr. Verfassungslehre*, I, 49); however, these did not impinge on Austria's sovereignty.

476   'All laws and decrees passed after 13 March 1938 . . . , which are incompatible with the existence of a free and independent state of Austria or with the principles of a true democracy, which contradict the legal concept of the Austrian people or the typical mode of thought of National Socialism . . . are to be repealed.'

477   See obituary (twentieth anniversary) in *SozSi* 1979, p. 195.

478   See Wandruszka, in: *Geschichte der Republik Österreich*, p. 349:

> Based on the prestige of the old Christian Social labour leader Kunschak, whose inner opposition to the 'authoritarian' home defence course was not forgotten, younger Christian Social politicians were able in 1945 to begin to build up the ÖVP; interestingly the left wing of the 'Federation of Workers and Employees' initially had the leadership; later, however, this was taken over by the Farmers' Association with Fgl and finally by Raab's Association of Economic Interests (Wirtschaftsbund).

See also Berchtold, *Parteiprogramme*, 65 ff.

479   Steinbach, *Unfallversicherung*, p. 140.

480   Wilhelm Schmidt (1979). '70 Jahre Pensionsversicherung der Angestellten', *SozSi*, 52 ff., 57 f.

481   Cf. Berchtold, *Parteiprogramme*, p. 69; Erich Zöllner (1979). *Geschichte Österreichs*, 6th edn, 545 f.

482   Cf. Erich Zöllner, p. 543.

483   Ermacora, *Österr. Verfassungslehre*, I, 48.

484   Erich Zöllner, 541 ff.; Ermacora, I, 49 ff.

485   Zöllner, p. 548.

486   See literature in note 473.

487   Cf. Nemschak (1951). *SozSi*, p. 218.

488   Cf. Kausel, *Festschr. Klenner*, p. 194.

489   OECD Report, February 1980, 9.

490   OECD Report, 18. See also 'Arbeitsmarkt', 19.

491   Cf. Zöllner, *Geschichte Österreichs*, p. 553.

492   Kausel, p. 196.

493   *Sozialbericht*, 1978, p. 35.

494   Also the resolution of representatives of all insurances of 15 March 1946; cf. *SozSi*, 1955, p. 298.

495   See Linseder, *Sozialversicherung-Überleitungsgesetz* (note 442). The representatives of the insurances began their work on the draft of the SV-ÜG as early as July/August 1945. The first draft of the Federal Ministry of Social Administration was available at the end of 1945 (see *SozSi*, 1955, p. 298).

496   Linseder, *Sozialversicherungs-Überleitungsgesetz*, p. 7.

497   Schmidt (1979). *SozSi*, 58. A compilation of social insurance law norms before the ASVG came into force is to be found in Franz Skolnik (1952). *Sozialversicherungsrecht*, I: *Das rezipierte Reichsrecht*.

498   Cf. W. Hubinger (1949). *VersRdsch* 296 ff.; 300 ff.

499   *StProtNR*, 5. GP, 1641 (Agb. Kostroun u. Genoss.); previously motion by Raab *et al* (1946) to introduce old age and disability insurance for self-employed tradespeople; Sandgruber, *Soziale Sicherheit im Nachziehverfahren*, 161 ff., 162.

500   On the 'Sickness Insurance Law for Entrepreneurs' see *StProtNR*, 6, GP, 1073 ff. u. Beil. Nr. 200, *StProtBR*, 6. GP, 1077 f.; on 1953 law see *StProtNR*, 7. GP, 519 ff. and Beil. Nr. 134, and Sandgruber, p. 163.

501 Cf. Reinhold Melas, Hans Gabler, Friedrich Steinbach, Othmar Rodler, and Ernst Bakule (1955). 'Das Allgemeine Sozialversicherungsgesetz (ASVG)', *SozSi* 297 ff.; now also Friedrich Steinbach, *Unfallversicherung*, 144 ff. Cf. also *StProtNR*, 7. GP, 3589 ff., 3668.
502 According to the legal situation hitherto the possibility of self-insurance was only available to those self-employed persons who employed a maximum of two people. See *SozSi*, 1955, 312.
503 *SozSi*, 1955, 331 ff.; Teschner in *System* 2.4.4.; Tomandl, *Grundriss*, 109 ff. (Nr. 171).
504 The word 'Pension' (for pension) only replaced 'Rente' with the ninth ASVG amendment.
505 In pension insurance for the self-employed which is still to be discussed (see pp. 346 and 347) 'B 55' as opposed to 'B 45' forms the alternative to the general basis of assessment; furthermore, the assessment period of both assessment bases in insurance for the self-employed is 10 years (cf. §§122 f. GSVG; 113 f. BSVG).
506 See §94 ASVG as well as §§60 f. GSVG; 56 f. BSVG. Detailed discussion in *Teschner im System* 2.4.9.3. C.
507 §§292 ff. ASVG; 149 ff. GSVG; 140 ff. BSVG. See A VI 3 on character and method of calculation of the compensation allowance. Cf. Anton Hindhab (1977). 'Pensionsversicherungsanstalt der Arbeiter—ein Beispiel für den sozialen Wandel', *SozSi*, 525 ff. which shows interesting figures on this topic: in the middle of 1977 about every fourth worker pensioner drew a compensation allowance; at that time it accounted for 7.87 percent of the whole pension burden of pensions insurance for workers. At the end of 1978 the proportion of pensions with compensation allowances was 23.3 percent (tending to drop). The level of the compensation allowances averaged about S 1000 accounting for about 6.2 percent of total expenditure of pension insurance (*Sozialbericht* 1978, 89, 108).
508 Cf. on this and on further individual improvements: Festschrift '50 Jahre Ministerium für soziale Verwaltung 1918-1968', p. 40.
509 On ASVG procedural law see particularly Oberndorfer im System 6, on litigations concerning benefits 6.4. See also the comprehensive discussion of constitutional law problems of Austrian social insurance law; Otto Ladislav, Robert Walter, Karl Marschall, and Viktor Heller (1961). in: *Verhandlungen des 1. Österr. Juristentages*, I, 4. Teil: Sozialversicherungsrecht und Bundesverfassung.
510 Years of publication and *BGB* numbers of amendments mentioned in the text: (1.) 1956/266; (3.) 1957/294; (4.) 1958/293; (6.) 1960/87; (8.) 1960/294; (9); 1961/13 ex 1962; (18.) 1966/168; (19.) 1967/67; (21.) 1967/6 ex 1968; (23.) 1968/17 ex 1969; (29.) 1972/31 ex 1973; (32.) 1976/704; (33.) 1978/684. Instructive survey of the majority of amending laws in Egon Schäfer (1975). *SozSi*, 621 ff.
511 Karl Fürböck (1975). *SozSi*, 314 ff.
512 See Tomandl, *Grundriss*, 124 f. (Nr. 199); and in *System* 0.6; also pp. 269 and 365.
513 Tomandl in *System* 0.6.4.
514 Alois (1977). 'Dragaschnig *inter alia*', *SozSi*, 2 ff.
515 Alois (1978). 'Dragaschnig', *SozSi*, 53 ff.
516 Cf. Tomandl in *System* 0.5.3.
517 Walter Uhlenhut *et al.*, (1979). *SozSi*, 4 ff.; Egon Schäfer (1979). *VersRdsch* 52 ff. The thirty-fourth ASVG amendment of 4 December 1979, *BGB* no. 530, brought in the extension of accident insurance protection for the 'satisfaction of vital needs' (lunch etc.) (§175, section 2, line 7 ASVG); introduction of multiple insurance in pensions insurance for the self-employed; increase of the supplementary contribution in pensions insurance from 2 to 3 percent (§51 a ASVG); additional transfers to the equalization fund of the pensions insurances (§447 g ASVG).
518 Cf. Hellmut Teschner and Hermann Schneider (ed.) (1968). *Beamten- Kranken- und Unfallversicherungsgesetz* (mit Nachträgen); Kurt Wagner (ed.) (1961). *Das Notarversicherungsgesetz;* Kurt Wagner (1969). *Das österr. Notarversicherungsrecht*.
519 Cf. Franz Skolnik, Alfred Kudrnac, and Rudolf Olbrich (1966). *Sozialversicherungsrecht*, II. Teil/2, 607 ff.
520 Details in Tomandl, *Grundriss*, 71 (Nr. 99).
521 Cf. Egon Schäfer (1979). *SozSi*, 62.
522 Kurt Wagner, (1961). *Das Notarversicherungsgesetz*, 3 ff.
523 Kurt Wagner, *Das Notarversicherungsgesetz*, 63 ff.
524 Teschner in *System* 2.4.4.2.4.
525 Teschner in *System* 2.4.2. B.
526 Cf. Sandgruber, in: *Soziale Sicherheit im Nachziehverfahren*, 163 ff.; Martin Spitzauer (1978). 'Zum zwanzigjährigen Bestand des GSPVG, *SozSi*, 401 ff.
527 Spitzauer, 404.

528 *BGB* no. 7060 particularly §2, section 1.
529 Cf. Hellmut Teschner (ed.) (1979). *Gewerbliches Sozialversicherungsgesetz (GSVG)* . . . *samt Bundesgesetz über die Sozialversicherung freiberuflich selbständig Erwerbstätiger,* (mit Nachtrag 1980).
530 Cf. *SozSi,* 1979, 21 ff.
531 Federal law of 10 July 1958. *BGB* no. 157 on social insurance for artists.
532 Cf. note 529; see also Elisabeth Kainzbauer (1979). 'Bundesgesetz über die Sozialversicherung freiberuflich selbständig Erwerbstätiger', *SozSi,* 23 ff.
533 Ernst Bruckmüller, in: *Soziale Sicherheit* . . . *;* Karl Fürböck and Hellmut Teschner (1970). *Die Sozialversicherung der Bauern,* (mit Nachträgen, insbes. Text des BSVG); good survey of the development of farmers' sickness insurance in *SozSi* 1975, 556; Kainzbauer, (1979). *SozSi* 18, 23 ff.
534 Steinbach, *UInfallversicherung,* p. 139. After the ASVG came into force accident insurance for farmers was (partly) compulsory insurance in §8, section 1, line 3, lit. (b), now §3 BSVG.
535 Cf. Bruckmüller, p. 93.
536 *StProtNR,* 8. GP, Beil. Nr. 344; also the government bill on the B-PVG, *StProtNR,* 11. GP, Beil. Nr. 1411, and Fürböck and Teschner, *Sozialversicherung der Bauern* II: B-PVG, 1 ff.
537 Bruckmüller, in: *Soziale Sicherheit* . . . , p. 102.
538 Bruckmüller, 100 ff.
539 *SozSi,* 1975, p. 556.
540 This resulted in an exception from compulsory insurance in sickness and/or pension insurance if — based on other compulsory insurances — appropriate insurance protection existed already; cf. §5 BSVG; similarly §§4 f. GSVG. Now, however: introduction of multiple pensions insurance for the self-employed by the thirty-fourth ASVG amendment (cf. note 517).
541 *SozSi,* 1975, 556; this increase in expenditure ought to remain in the framework of cost development in the whole of sickness insurance; see Alfred Radner, (1979). *SozSi,* 107 ff.
542 Cf. Kainzbauer, (1979). *SozSi,* p. 18.
543 *Grosse Depression und Bismarckzeit,* 227 ff., 239; cf. analysis in the following text.
544 Cf. Dragaschnig *et al.* (1977). *SozSi* 2 ff.; Krejci in *System* 1.2.4.
545 Cf. Dragaschnig (1978). *SozSi,* 53 ff.; also p. 269. With the thirty-fourth ASVG amendment (see note 517) additional transfers to the equalization fund of the pensions insurances (§447 (g) ASVG) from funds of the accident and sickness insurance as well as the reserves for medical examinations for adolescents and adults were provided amounting to over 1000 million; moreover, the government contribution to the transfer fund of the sickness insurances (§§447 (a) ASVG) was stopped.
546 Cf. Korinek in *System* 4.1.2.; see also Rudolf Strasser and Kurt Hillinger, (1971). *Soziale Sicherung,* p. 30 (criticism of the 'lack of system' of the Austrian 'system' of social security).
547 See §19 SV-ÜG in Linseder (1948). *Das Sozialversicherungs-Überleitungsgesetz,* 56 f.
548 Die Selbstverwaltung in der Sozialversicherung, in: *Verhandlungen des deutschen Sozialgerichtsverbandes,* 9 ff.; see also Gerhard Weißenberg, (1973). *SozSi,* 117 and Korinek in *System* 4.1.3.C.
549 Tomandl (1977). *Das Leistungsrecht der österr. Unfallversicherung,* 1–6; Steinbach, *Unfallversicherung,* 158 ff.; numerous articles (Gottfried Winkler, Wolfgang Gitter, Theodor Tomandl) in: *Publikation 'Sozialversicherung: Grenzen der Leistungspflicht',* 1975, Tomandl (ed.); for Germany see Walter Bogs (1955). *Grundfragen des Rechts der sozialen Sicherheit und seiner Reform,* 35 ff.; also Eike v. Hippel (1979). 'Grundfragen der sozialen Sicherheit' (= *Recht und Staat,* **492/493**).
550 See above.
551 Tomandl in *System* 2.3.3. (note 12).
552 Cf. Radner (1979). *SozSi,* 107 ff.; see also p. 267.
553 See text after note 503 and Dieter Bös and Robert Holzmann, *Simulationsanalysen zur österr. Pensionsdynamik* (SBAK Wien, phil. hist. Kl., 304/3), 1976, 143 ff.; Tomandl in *System* 0.6.4. and my own explanations above p. 269 and p. 343 (note 511).

ABBREVIATIONS

ABGB	Allgemeine Bürgerliche Gesetzbuch (Civil Code)
art.	article
ASVG	Allgemeine Sozialversicherungsgesetz (General Social Insurance Law)
BGB	*Bundesgesetzblatt (Federal Law Gazette)*
B-KUVG	Beamten-Kranken und Unfallsversicherungsgesetz (Law on Sickness and Accident Insurance for Civil Servants)
BKVG	Bundesangestellten-Krankenversicherungsgesetz (State Employees' Sickness Insurance Law)

B-KVG	Bauern-Krankenversicherungsgesetz (Farmers' Sickness Insurance Law)
B-PVG	Bauern-Pensionsversicherungsgesetz (Farmers' Pension Insurance Law)
BSVG	Bauernsozialversicherungsgesetz (Law on Social Insurance for Farmers)
BVA	Versicherungsanstalt öffentlicher Bediensteter (Civil Servants' Insurance)
B-VG	Bundes-Verfassungsgesetz (Federal Constitution Law)
DRGB	*Deutsches Reichsgesetzblatt (Law Gazette of the German Reich)*
GeWO	Gewerbeordnung (Trade Act)
GSKVG	Gewerbliche Selbständigen-Krankenversicherungsgesetz (Sickness Insurance Law for the Self-employed in Trade and Industry)
GSPVG	Gewerbliche Selbständigen-Pensionsversicherungsgesetz (Pensions Insurance Law for the Self-Employed in Trade and Industry)
GSVG	Gesetz betreffend die gewerbliche Sozialversicherung (Law on Social Insurance for Tradespeople)
K	Krone
KPÖ	Kommunistische Partei Österreichs (Austrian Communist Party)
KVA	Krankenversicherungsanstalt der Bundesangestellten (Sickness Insurance of State Employees)
KVG	Krankenversicherung (Sickness Insurance)
LGB	*Landesgesetzblatt (Provincial Law Gazette)*
LZVA	Landwirtschaftliche Zuschussrentenversicherungsanstalt (Institution for Agricultural Pension Allowances)
LZVG	Landwirtschaftliche Zuschussrentenversicherungsgesetz (Law on Agricultural Pension Allowances)
NVG	Notarversicherungsgesetz (Law on Insurance for Notaries)
ÖBKK	Österreichische Bauernkrankenkasse (Austrian Farmers' Sickness Insurance)
ÖVP	Österreichische Volkspartei (Austrian People's Party)
PAG	Pensionsanpassungsgesetz (Pensions Adjustment Law)
PG	Pensionsgesetz (Pension Law)
PVAB	Pensionsversicherungsanstalt der Bauern (Farmers' Pension Insurance Institution)
RGB	*Reichsgesetzblatt (Law Gazette of the 'Reich')*
S	Schilling
SPÖ	Sozialistische Partei Österreichs (Austrian Socialist Party)
StGB	*Staatsgesetzblat (State Law Gazette)*
SVAB	Sozialversicherungsanstalt der Bauern (Farmers' Social Insurance Institution)
SV-ÜG	Sozialversicherungs-Überleitungsgesetz (Provisional Law on Social Insurance)
V-ÜG	Verfassungs-Überleitungsgesetz (Interim Law on the Constitution)

SWITZERLAND
by Alfred Maurer

The Country and its People

Switzerland is an industrial country of 41 288 sq. km. The area used for agriculture only accounts for 6.5 percent of the total and in 1970 only 7.2 percent of the gainfully employed worked in agriculture. The resident population was as follows: on 1 January 1979 6.29 million; 1950 4.7 million; 1910 3.7 million; 1880 2.8 million and 1850 2.3 million. The age index, i.e. the proportion of those 60 years or older as a percentage of the under-twenties was 53.7 percent in 1970; 46 percent in 1950; 32.1 percent in 1930; 22.9 percent in 1900 and 21.5 percent in 1860. It has more than doubled since the turn of the century. If one divides the resident population according to language groups, one finds the following figures per thousand for 1970 (the figures in brackets refer to 1880): German 649 (713), French 181 (214), Italian 119 (57), Rhaeto-Romanic 8 (14) and other languages 43 (2).[1] The official languages of Switzerland are German, French and Italian. Each text of the federal laws in these official languages ranks equally, which is important when interpreting the law. Apart from the three official languages Rhaeto-Romanic is also a national language (BV 116). Compact groups of the population speaking Rhaeto-Romanic are only to be found in the Grisons which is an especially interesting canton from a language point of view. Of its population (about 170 000) some 58 percent speak German, 24 percent Romanic and 16 percent Italian. Rhaeto-Romanic has no uniformly written literary language but is divided into different variants, so-called 'idioms', some of which deviate greatly from one another. Primary school books have to be printed in seven different languages in the Grisons, namely in five 'idioms', German, and Italian.

The Swiss Constitution

Organization and Legislative Power of the Federal State

Switzerland, officially named: Schweizerische Eidgenossenschaft; Confédération Suisse; Confederazione Svizzera, is a democratic federal state consisting of twenty-three cantons as member states. Three of these are subdivided into 'half' cantons. The federal constitution of 29 May 1874 has been revised and supplemented with over eighty partial amendments. According to the constitution, the federal government is only competent to legislate when the constitution empowers it to do so. Other legislative powers are left to the cantons (BV 3). The National Assembly (Bundesversammlung) — parliament and legislative power — consists of two sections (chambers or councils), the National Council (Nationalrat) whose members are elected by proportional representation and the State Council (Ständerat) for which each canton elects two deputies or one deputy in the case of a 'half' canton. Both chambers have equal competence. Thus, for example, federal laws can only be passed if both the National Council and the State Council give their assent. Differences between the two are settled by means of a statutory procedure designed for this very purpose. If agreement cannot be reached, the bill is dropped, but this is extremely rare.

For certain business both chambers confer together in order to make a decision as the United National Assembly (Vereinigte Bundesversammlung), chaired by the President of the National Council. In this way it elects the Federal Council (Bundesrat) — central government, executive power — which is composed of seven members (with a term of office of 4 years) and from these it chooses the Federal President each year who, however, is not the head of state but only the Chairman of the Federal Council.

Each member is head of a Department and thus of part of federal administration. The Department of the Interior, for example, is responsible for most branches of social insurance. One of its divisions, namely the Federal Office for Social Insurance (Bundesamt für Sozialversicherung), has a supervisory role, drafts bills for new social insurance laws or amendments and is the court of appeal in certain cases of complaints.

The United National Assembly also elects the Federal Law Court in Lausanne and the Federal Insurance Court (Eidg. Versicherungsgericht) in Lucerne. This acts as the federal court for social insurance as it represents the supreme judicial authority in the field of Swiss social insurance. While it was originally completely separate from the Federal Law Court, the legislature made the Insurance Court part of the Federal Law Court, although its organization has remained entirely independent, with an amendment of 20 December 1968 to the Federal Law on the Organization of Federal Administration of Justice. Its seat is still in Lucerne. The judges are elected separately by the National Assembly (cf. below, p. 395).

Constitutional Initiative and Referendum

The Swiss constitution can be completely or partially revised at any time. Total revision — the first since 1874 — has been started, though, its fate seems uncertain. It can be instigated by the people's suggestion (constitutional initiative or a petition for a referendum) or by proposal of the National Assembly. As to the first, the signatures of at least 100 000 voters are currently required.[2] An amendment to the constitution is only legally possible if it is accepted by a majority of the citizens taking part in the plebiscite (known as the 'Volksmehr') and also by a majority of the cantons (known as the 'Ständemehr'). The National Assembly decides in the majority of cases whether it will recommend to the people the acceptance or the rejection of a referendum. It frequently makes a counter-proposal of its own to a referendum. The people then have to vote on the referendum and on the National Assembly's counter-proposal.

Federal laws and certain other decrees which the National Council and the State Council have approved are subject to a facultative referendum. They must be submitted to the people for acceptance or rejection, if this is requested at the time by 50 000 voters. Only the majority of the plebiscite (Volksmehr) is decisive; a majority of the cantons (Ständemehr) is not needed. The Swiss constitution does not contain similar provisions relating to changes in statute law. This has often meant that voters have proposed rulings, which actually belong in statute law, by means of the constitutional initiative because statutory initiative does not exist.

As will be seen, both constitutional initiatives and referenda have played a significant role in the emergence and development of Swiss social insurance.

Cantonal Constitution

As a member state, each canton or 'half' canton has its own constitution; it has its own parliament which is usually known as the Cantonal Council (Kantonsrat) or Great Council (Grosser Rat), a government with its own administration and its own courts. Recourse is frequently made to the obligatory referendum for legislative purposes, otherwise to the facultative referendum. The Federal Court can test whether cantonal decrees violate federal law (cantonal law is subordinate to federal law). However, BV 113 §3 does not give the Federal Law Court the authority to examine 'the laws and legally binding decrees passed by the National Assembly, as well as the state contracts approved by it', to see that they are in line with the constitution and, if need be, to declare them inapplicable or even to quash them.

The Swiss Confederation: a Social Constitutional State

Adopting modern concepts of public law, Switzerland can be described as a constitutional state which has been democratically and socially developed to a high degree. According to BV 31 §1 the principle of free trade, i.e. a system of free enterprise, prevails; however, the government can limit this if the conditions described in BV 31bis §2-5 are met. There is no explicit social state clause in the federal constitution, corresponding approximately to Art. 20 and Art. 28 of the German Basic Law (Grundgesetz). Opinions differ on whether or not this belongs to its guiding principles today.[3] Nevertheless, Switzerland can clearly be characterized as a social and democratic constitutional state.[4]

OUTLINES OF SWISS SOCIAL INSURANCE ACCORDING TO THE LAWS IN FORCE

Definitions

Controversies

When writing a history of Swiss social insurance, it is expedient to begin by defining the term. It is particularly controversial in the following questions. Can a protective system be brought within the concept of social insurance when it is only financed by public funds as, for example, in the case of military insurance? Are insurance situations which are covered by an insurance policy under private law — particularly if this comes within the scope of the law on insurance contracts — to be excluded from social insurance? Are situations requiring social insurance only to be regarded as such which fall within the competence of the social insurance courts?[5]

Social Insurance – an Insurance Regulated by Public Law

In the last few years, opinion has consolidated that only insurance conditions established under public law properly belong to social insurance. The government has taken this into account by interpreting social insurance law as administrative law and thus as public law in the amendment of 20 December 1968 to the Federal Law on the Organization of Federal Administration of Justice, already mentioned: it integrated social insurance jurisdiction in federal administration jurisdiction.

It is incorrect to use insurance terminology which has developed within the framework of private insurance for public insurance without closer analysis.[6] This applies especially to financing. In private insurance several insurance companies compete with one another; they have to fix a price for their benefits or services, the premium, which they charge the insured person, as the companies are run in accordance with the principles of free enterprise. The state, however, can finance insurance situations in another way, i.e. wholly or partly by taxation. Thus, it seems appropriate to talk of public insurance if situations requiring such insurance are financed entirely or partly by contributions from the state. Situations requiring insurance already exist if certain questions are settled: the insured persons, the risks insured against, the insurance benefits. Thus, for a situation involving insurance to be held to exist at public law, contributions do not have to be paid by the interested persons as this type of financing is merely one model.[7] However, public insurance is only to be classified as social insurance if it covers so-called social risks. A list of these has been drawn up in accordance with various international agreements, for example, agreement no. 102 of the International Labour Organization of 28 June 1952, and is hardly controversial nowadays. Finally, social insurance only exists if the legislature expresses this by assigning it a branch of social insurance jurisdiction. By means of this formal characterisation, social insurance can clearly be differentiated from numerous related institutions such as compulsory accident, sickness and liability insurances etc. based on insurance contracts under private law.

Definition and Branches of Swiss Social Insurance

Swiss social insurance law can currently be described as that field of federal law 'which is designed to safeguard the whole population or certain sections of it against social risks by means of insurance conditions which function under public law and are subject to social insurance jurisdiction'.[8] According to this definition the following branches are to be attributed to Swiss social insurance: (a) sickness insurance according to the KUVG (i.e. 'Bundesgesetz über die Kranken- und Unfallversicherung' — Federal Law on Sickness and Accident Insurance); (b) compulsory accident insurance according to the KUVG; (c) AHV (i.e. 'Alters- und Hinterlassenenversicherung' — Old Age and Surviving Dependants' Insurance); (d) IV (i.e. 'Eidgenössische Invalidenversicherung' — Disability Insurance); (e) supplementary benefits to the AHV/IV; (f) income compensation; (g) unemployment insurance; (h) family allowances for farm workers and smallholders; (i) military insurance. This list outlines the field of law whose historical development is to be described in the following pages.

First of all, however, each of the above-mentioned branches of Swiss social insurance will be sketched, according to current laws. When and where necessary, existing or planned revisions will be mentioned.

Sickness and Accident Insurance According to the KUVG

The Federal Law on Sickness and Accident Insurance of 13 June 1911 (KUVG) is the oldest law on social insurance still in force. It lays down rules for both branches of insurance separately as they are completely differently conceived.

The first attempt at legislation failed: the so-called 'Lex Forrer' was rejected by the plebiscite of 20 May 1900. Its opponents had rejected state obligation in sickness insurance. The obligation of both branches was limited to employed persons which is why the bill clearly bore specific class traits. [8a]

Sickness Insurance [9]

As far as sickness insurance is concerned, the KUVG is largely a law on subsidies and promotion. A sickness insurance scheme that wants government subsidies can apply to the Federal Council for recognition. This is granted when the insurance institution has proved that it fulfils all the prescribed minimum requirements in the KUVG and in the implementation regulations. Once recognized, the insurance scheme is automatically subject to the KUVG and the implementation regulations. The most varied sectors of sickness insurance are more or less thoroughly regulated by this special legislation. For example, it includes regulations about the circle of people insured, the law on doctors and hospitals, the law on benefits, freedom of action and administration of justice. Nevertheless, sickness insurance schemes have a high degree of autonomy: they can settle many questions under their own charters and regulations. Both public sickness insurance schemes, i.e. those run by cantons or communities, and private sickness insurance schemes can gain recognition; the latter only if—under private law—they possess the legal form of an association, a cooperative or a foundation. Since the revision of the KUVG of 13 March 1964 they also have power, like branches of that public administration, to stipulate laws and duties in concrete cases by means of unilateral decree; this decree assumes formal legal force, like a court verdict, if not repealed judicially.

The KUVG empowers only the cantons and not the federal government to declare sickness insurance compulsory for the entire population or for certain sections of it. The cantons can transfer this authority to the communities. This ruling has led to extremely varied arrangements: in some cantons there is no obligation, in other cantons practically the whole population is subject to it and in yet other cantons there exists only partial obligation which usually covers people with low incomes. Although only about 25 percent of the Swiss population is subject to this obligation, some 94 percent of it subscribed to a sickness insurance scheme in 1976.

Sickness insurance is fundamentally an individual insurance. At the same time, since its revision in 1964, the KUVG also provides for the possibility of collective insurance; for example, an employer can collectively insure his staff against sickness.

Sickness insurance schemes are to insure the sickness risk. They are free to choose whether or not to cater at the same time for accident insurance—with limited benefits—without pension insurance for death and disablement. Maternity ranks equally with illness since a special maternity insurance has not yet been introduced in Switzerland.

The KUVG determines the minimum benefits. Sickness insurance schemes must provide benefits for medical care or sick pay. If a supplementary premium is paid, they often grant additional benefits beyond the scope of the compulsory benefits, as provided in their charters and rulings.

Sickness insurance is primarily financed by the contributions of the insured persons plus subsidies from the public authorities, especially from federal government.

Since the revision of 1964, litigation between the insured and the sickness insurance schemes is usually decided by the cantonal insurance courts of first instance and by the Federal Insurance Court on further appeal.

Since the drastic revision of the KUVG of 13 March 1964 several attempts at developing and restructuring sickness insurance have failed. The Federal Department of the Interior is currently working on improvements within the existing system. In November 1978 it published a 'report and draft' on the 'partial revision of sickness insurance' for this very purpose.

In 1960 there were still over 1000 recognized sickness insurance schemes, in 1979 there were only 548. This reduction—predominantly affecting small insurance schemes—is undoubtedly because sickness insurance is becoming more complicated and its finance increasingly difficult.

Accident Insurance [10]

The KUVG provides a single insurance institution, responsible for accident insurance. This is the SUVA (Schweizerische Unfallversicherungsanstalt—the Swiss Accident Insurance Institution) in Lucerne. This is largely self-administered by the employers and employed persons who subscribe to it; it has its own administrative board and legal personality. Numerous types of business, for example, factories, and transport firms have to be covered by accident insurance. People employed in such concerns are automatically insured against industrial and non-industrial accidents as well as against certain types of occupational illnesses. This is a 'class-oriented law' as it only applies to employed persons. [10a] The KUVG stipulated the benefits which are extensive: medical care, sick pay, disability pensions and pensions for surviving dependants, etc. Finally, it does not just provide for minimum benefits as in the case of sickness insurance. Accident insurance is financed by premiums. These are paid by the employers for industrial accidents and by the employed, i.e. the insured, for non-industrial accidents. There are no state subsidies. Litigation arising from insurance is predominantly decided at the cantonal insurance courts of first instance; an appeal against their decisions can be made at the Federal Insurance Court.

As far as accident insurance is concerned, the KUVG has been frequently modified but never fundamentally. A bill on total revision is currently before the National Assembly for deliberation. One of its main points is the extension of compulsory insurance to all employed persons as to date only about two-thirds are subject to compulsory insurance. Furthermore, the bill provides for two separate laws on sickness and accident insurance in future. Private insurance schemes are to be authorized to be insurance institutions within the framework of the extended compulsory insurance.

Old Age and Surviving Dependants' Insurance [11] (AHV)

A federal law on insurance for old age and surviving dependants, the 'Lex Schulthess', was accepted by the federal councils on 17 June 1931 but rejected by a plebiscite of 6 December 1931. The present Federal Law on Old Age and Surviving Dependants' Insurance did not come into being until after the Second World War, on 20 December 1946; the voters accepted it with an overwhelming majority on 6 July 1947. It came into force on 1 January 1948. Since then it has been modified by nine numbered and several unnumbered amendments. Use was only made once of the referendum, namely against the ninth of these revisions; however, the people voted in its favour on 26 February 1978.

Old age and surviving dependants' insurance, the AHV, is the largest social institution in Switzerland. Primarily it is implemented by over 100 'Ausgleichskassen' (compensation institutions) which were founded during the Second World War in accordance with the decree on wage and income substitution for servicemen. There are about eighty 'Verbandsausgleichskassen', i.e. institutions which were founded by professional associations of employers and self-employed persons, as well as twenty-six cantonal and two federal 'Ausgleichskassen'. These 'Ausgleichskassen' are institutions under public law. They collect contributions from the employers and the insured and provide benefits when required. The Central Income Substitution Office (Zentrale Ausgleichsstelle) in Geneva is responsible for settling accounts between the 'Ausgleichskassen' and for keeping a central register of insured persons and pensioners. Ultimately, financial compensation is provided through the compensation fund (Ausgleichsfonds) of the AHV which has its own legal personality. Moreover, this also acts as a collective emergency reserve, the 'fluctuation fund', of the AHV. This is financed by an allocation procedure (Umlageverfahren) as a matter of principle.

The AHV is an insurance of the people which covers the whole resident population. Swiss citizens living abroad can subscribe to it voluntarily.

The AHV grants pensions — indemnification in some cases — to widows and orphans of a deceased insured person and also to insured persons who have reached a certain age. Thus, insured 'risks' are the death of the insured person and the attainment of a certain age.

The system of benefits is somewhat complex: here is a brief introduction. Ordinary pensions are paid out if contributions have been paid for at least one full year. Otherwise, only extraordinary pensions can be considered; these usually presuppose destitution. They are no longer of great significance nowadays. Ordinary pensions are either full or partial. Full pensions are granted if the insured has paid compulsory contributions since the age of 20 or since the AHV was introduced in 1948. If there are gaps in contributions, partial pensions are paid out. These are calculated according to a simplified 'pro-rata-temporis' method. Single old age pensions (ordinary full pensions) form the basis of the Swiss pension system. Single women receive a pension at the age of 62 and men at the age of 65. The maximum pension is currently twice as much as the minimum pension (from 1 January 1980: 1110 Fr./550 Fr. per month). The pension level depends on the average yearly income on which contributions have been paid during the compulsory payment period. In 1979, for example, people already received the maximum pension who had paid their contributions on an average annual income of about 16 500 Fr.

Apart from the single old age pension there is also an old age pension for married couples. The couple have a right to such a pension as soon as the husband has reached the age of 65 and his wife the age of 62 or is 50 percent disabled. Old age pensions for married couples amount to 150 percent of the single old age pension. The wife can demand that half of the pension be paid directly to her. If she has reached the age of 55, but not yet 62, her husband can claim a supplementary pension in addition to his single old age pension. Old age pensioners who still have children under-age receive a children's 'pension' in addition to their old age pension in certain circumstances.

Destitution compensation is paid monthly to destitute old age pensioners. In addition, old age pensioners have a right to financial assistance if they need this to travel in order to keep in touch with the world around them etc. Pensions for surviving dependants are calculated on the basis of the single old age pension. Thus, a widow's pension amounts to 80 percent, the half-orphan's pension to 40 percent and the full orphan's pension to 60 percent of the relevant old age pension. Childless widows can only claim pensions in certain circumstances; otherwise they can only demand an indemnification, currently amounting to a maximum of just over 50 000 Fr.* Pensions have been indexed in part since 1 January 1979. Thus, they are adjusted partly to reflect price developments—usually increases—and partly wage developments.

The AHV is financed by contributions from employers and insured persons, by federal government and cantonal subsidies and by the profits of the 'Ausgleichsfonds' (compensation fund). The contributions of wage earners, i.e. persons who are not self-employed, are fixed as percentages of the wage paid, and are borne half each by the employer and the employed person.[11a] There is a special ruling on contributions for the self-employed and for those not gainfully employed. Gainfully employed old age pensioners also have to pay contributions in certain circumstances since 1 January 1979. Ordinary pensions are paid out regardless of whether the pensioner is still earning or not and whether he is needy or not. At this point, one of the peculiarities of the Swiss contribution system should be mentioned: earned income is subject to the compulsory contribution system without any upper limit. Thus, contributions also have to be paid on those parts of the income which no longer influence the pension level. Such contributions are known as 'solidarity contributions', for the benefit of those insured persons in lower income brackets. This system has made it possible to have relatively high pensions while keeping contribution rates relatively low.

Insurance litigation arising from the AHV is judged by the cantonal authorities as first court of appeal and by the Federal Insurance Court as the supreme court of appeal.

The tenth AHV revision is already being prepared. This will include *inter alia*, the position of women in the AHV as well as a flexible retirement age.

Disability Insurance (IV)[12]

The Federal Law on Disability Insurance of 19 June 1959, which has been in force since 1 January 1960, closed the last major gap in the social security system. Disability insurance (IV) is closely linked with the AHV both from an organizational and structural point of view. It is implemented by various agencies of the AHV. It has special agencies of its own: the IV Commissions and the regional offices. The IV Commissions are above all responsible for clarifying the insured person's ability to become integrated and, if necessary, to make a plan for integration as well as to assess disability and helplessness. They cannot issue rules; this is done by the competent 'Ausgleichskasse'. The regional office is a specialized agency which acts in the field of integration upon the IV Commission's instructions and keeps in contact with the disabled.

Exactly the same people are covered by disability insurance as are covered by the AHV. Disability is the insured risk. Disability is understood as the inability to earn a living in the case of gainfully employed persons and the inability to work

---

* When calculating old age pensions for married couples or pensions for surviving dependants, the average annual income of the husband is taken as a basis. However, to increase the annual average, any income which the wife may have earned and on which contributions have been paid before or during the marriage, are added to the husband's income.

in the case of persons who are not gainfully employed such as housewives. Inability to work means 'the impossibility of carrying out one's previous duties which is equivalent to inability to earn a living' (IVG 5 §1).

Disability insurance provides two types of benefits: measures to integrate the disabled into working life and pensions, including destitution compensation. Integration has priority over pensions as a basic principle. Pensions are to be granted only if integration does not succeed or is not far-reaching enough or if there seems to be no chance of success right from the start. Integration measures are divided into five categories: medical measures; [12a] measures relating to work (for example, retraining and job placement); measures for special schooling and the care of helpless minors; the issue of financial assistance; the payment of daily allowances during the integration period. A claim to a pension exists only in cases of qualified disability, namely to half a pension if at least 50 percent disability exists; in so-called cases of hardship if one-third disability exists; and to a whole pension if the insured person is at least two-thirds disabled. Disability pensions correspond to old age pensions, i.e. the single disability pension corresponds to the single old age pension and the disability pension for married couples to the old age pension for married couples. A supplement is granted for younger disabled persons. Moreover, in certain circumstances supplementary pensions for wives, children's 'pensions' and destitution compensation in cases of helplessness of disabled persons are paid out.

Disability insurance is financed — with slight variations — according to the same principles as the AHV. The legal provisions of the AHV also apply analogously for the administration of justice.

Regulation of Supplementary Benefits to the AHV/IV (EL) [13]

On 1 January 1966 the Federal Law on Supplementary Benefits to the AHV/IV of 19 March 1965 came into force. According to this law the Swiss Government grants the cantons subsidies if they pay out supplementary benefits to those AHV/IV pensioners who do not reach certain levels of income and means. These pensions for the needy are to ensure that through the AHV/IV pensions and supplementary benefits, the pensioners receive an income that provides them with a secure existence. This institution is rapidly losing its significance as the ordinary full pensions are designed at least to provide a reasonable standard of living since the fifth AHV revision. With this revision the pensions were more than doubled in two phases, namely from 1 January 1973 and 1975 onwards.

Income Compensation (EO) [14]

In the text of 3 October 1975, the Federal Law on Income Compensation for Persons Doing Compulsory Military Service or in Civil Defence accords men and women who are doing their military service or are in civil defence a claim to compensation, for example, housekeeping compensation for married persons, compensation for single persons, allowances for children and even compensation for persons who are not gainfully employed such as students. The benefits are financed by contributions which are collected principally from those persons who pay compulsory contributions to the AHV. The Swiss government does not grant any subsidies. Income compensation is implemented mainly by the agencies of the AHV. The provisions of the law on the AHV also apply analogously for the administration of justice.

Unemployment Insurance (AlV)[14a]

The Federal Law on Unemployment Insurance of 22 June 1951 largely took over the provisions which had already been laid down in the authorization act (Vollmachtenbeschluss) of the Federal Council of 14 July 1942. This proved to be inadequate when the recession began in 1975, particularly as it did not provide for nationwide compulsory unemployment insurance. On 13 June 1976 the people and the state councils accepted the new BV 34novies: according to this, unemployment insurance is compulsory for employed persons as far as the government is concerned. In view of the uncertain economic outlook, the National Assembly passed a provisional ruling (the so-called 'Übergangsordnung') by federal decree of 8 October 1976 on the introduction of compulsory unemployment insurance. This ruling is limited to 5 years and expires on 1 April 1982 at the latest as a new law on unemployment insurance ought to exist before then. The details are regulated by decree of the Federal Council. According to this provisional ruling, the existing recognized unemployment insurance institutions are to continue to be responsible for paying out benefits to the unemployed. Now, however, the AHV 'Ausgleichskassen' are to collect contributions which are owed by the employers and the employed (at 1 January 1980: 0.8 percent). The wage level, in line with AHV legislation, is decisive for this; in contrast to this legislation, however, the wage is only subject to compulsory contributions up to a maximum of 46 800 Fr. per annum. The federal law mentioned above continues to apply in part, for example, in the field of benefits, in procedural matters and with reference to job placement through the cantonal labour exchanges.[15]

Family Allowances (FLO)[16]

The Federal Law on Family Allowances for Agricultural Workers and Smallholders of 20 June 1952 — thus reads the title of the law that is currently in force — which was last amended on 14 December 1973, largely took over the provisions of the decree which the Federal Council had brought in during the war by an authorization act (Vollmachtenbeschluss). The revision of the law of 16 March 1962 provided for the inclusion of independent smallholders in the lowlands as well as the mountain farmers covered hitherto. Housekeeping and child allowances are granted. Time has shown that there is no urgent need for a federal law which would make, for example, all employed persons, i.e. not only those working in agriculture, subject to the ruling on family allowances, for all cantons passed laws on child allowances between 1943 and 1963. The FLO is partly financed by contributions of the employed person and his employer and partly by subsidies and is implemented by the cantonal 'AHV-Ausgleichskassen'.[17]

Military Insurance (MV)[18]

The Federal Law on Military Insurance of 20 September 1949 has frequently been amended but is nevertheless still valid in principle. It covers persons during military service or civil defence against accident and sickness, in some exceptional cases against accident only. Benefits are similar to those of compulsory accident insurance, and are thus well-developed. The federal government finances military insurance entirely from public funds in accordance with the allocation procedure. The Federal Office for Military Insurance (Bundesamt für Militärversicherung) is responsible for its implementation. Various efforts have been made from 1972-1976 to revise completely the law. For the time being, the very idea of total or even partial revision of the law is not being followed up. [19]

Administration of Justice [20]

Where the laws are found

Rulings on the administration of justice in this area are scattered and not easy to survey. Regulations are chiefly found in the social insurance laws themselves, in the Federal Law on Administrative Procedure of 20 December 1968 (VwG or VwVG), in the Federal Law on the Organization of Federal Administration of Justice (in the version of 20 December 1968) and in cantonal decrees in which instances of administration of justice and appropriate procedure are laid down. Only a few such details will be provided here.

Social Insurance Courts — First Appeal

The various social insurance laws stipulate that the cantons have to establish a court of first appeal, for example, an insurance court each for accident, sickness and military insurance and a further appeal court each for the AHV and the branches linked to it, such as EL, EO, FLO etc. Cantons are authorized to co-ordinate legal decisions in a single court; this is what individual cantons have done. The federal government has created only one court of first appeal, namely the Federal Appeal Authority (Eidg. Rekursbehörde) for persons living abroad in accordance with AHVG 84 II. The social insurance laws instruct the cantons at several points on how they are to arrange their procedural law for the cantonal insurance courts in order to guarantee uniform practice in social insurance law. The social insurance courts are bodies of administrative jurisdiction as they have to judge litigation arising from federal administration laws, i.e. the social insurance laws.

Federal Law on Administrative Procedure (VwG)

The VwG provides for procedural regulations on the administration and issuing of injunctions — known as 'administrative acts' (Verwaltungsakte) in Germany — and for appeal procedures, i.e. such injunctions at superior administrative offices. However, the VwG does not apply to all social insurance institutions which have to make rulings. Furthermore, it rescinds any procedural regulations found in social insurance law, if there is inconsistency. Only a few of its provisions are applicable to cantonal insurance courts. Thus, in many respects the VwG complicates procedural law for social insurance.

Federal Insurance Court (EVG)

Rulings of first appeal social insurance courts can usually be taken to the Federal Insurance Court (Eidg. Versicherungsgericht — EVG) in Lucerne. In accordance with the Federal Law on Sickness and Accident Insurance of 1911, the EVG was created as an independent court, in addition to the Federal Law Court in Lausanne. Procedure was governed by a federal decree. The much cited amendment to the Federal Law on the Organization of Federal Administration of Justice of 20 December 1968 designates the EVG 'as the social insurance section of the Federal Law Court which is independent from an organizational point of view', with its headquarters in Lucerne, and integrates it chiefly into federal administration jurisdiction. The EVG is currently composed of seven full-time federal judges[20a] and nine part-time substitute judges as well as a total of thirteen clerks of court and secretaries who draw up the judgments.[21] It is also authorized to investigate whether federal law has been contravened (*revisio in iure*); insofar as the granting or refusal of insurance benefits is concerned, however, the EVG is allowed to examine the subject matter and its reasonableness.

EMERGENCE AND DEVELOPMENT OF SOCIAL INSURANCE IN SWITZERLAND

PART I: FROM THE FOUNDATION OF THE SWISS CONFEDERATION UNTIL THE END OF THE FIRST WORLD WAR (1848–1918)

THE FEDERAL CONSTITUTIONS OF 1848 AND 1874[22]

The Federal Constitution of 12 September 1848

When the Napoleonic empire collapsed, Switzerland emerged from the former French protectorate. The cantons agreed on the federal treaty (Bundesvertrag) of 7 August 1815 which established a confederation of states. The Diet ('Tagsatzung' – an assembly of representatives of the cantons) was to conduct any joint transactions. Switzerland's perpetual neutrality was expressly acknowledged at the second Paris Peace Conference held on 20 November 1815. The July Revolution in France, 1830, triggered off a strong liberal movement in Switzerland. In the majority of cantons, the liberal parties improved the democratic rights and strived for increased federal power and authority. Disputes, predominantly of a religious nature, persuaded the seven Catholic cantons to liaise and form the 'Sonderbund' (The Separatist League) in 1845. In the Swiss Civil War of 1847 (Sonderbundkrieg) the Diet forced the Separatist League to dissolve with the help of federal troops commanded by General Dufour. Thereafter, federal reforms could be implemented without disturbance. On 12 September 1848 the cantons accepted a federal constitution which transformed Switzerland from a confederation of states into a federal state.

Initially, no Socio-political Powers for the Federal Government

The parliamentary system of two houses, based on the American model, was designed to create a balance between centralistic and federalist tendencies. However, the new constitution gave the federal government relatively modest powers. Still, it enabled the government to abolish internal customs duties, road and bridge tolls and to standardize weights and measures as well as postal services. Thus, important conditions were created for the economy to flourish. The federal government had no powers at a socio-political level, not even to legislate on civil law.

The Federal Constitution of 29 May 1874

A liberal-oriented party, known as the 'Freisinnig-Demokratische Partei' today, dominated both the National Council and the Federal Council for decades. It did not lose its majority until 1919 when a proportional voting system was introduced for the National Council. Shortly after the federal state was founded, this party began to work for a stronger central government and for standardization, for example, of the civil law. Although the first attempt totally to revise the federal constitution of 1848 failed in the plebiscite of 1872, the federal authorities continued their revision work. A new draft of the constitution with less centralistic tendencies was accepted by the people on 19 April 1874. It was brought into force by the National Assembly as the new federal constitution on 29 May 1874. The latter has not been totally revised since then.

Article 34, still Valid Today

Here are a few of the innovations of the federal constitution of 1874:[23] the facultative statutory referendum;[24] the firm establishment of the principle of free trade and enterprise which had already been included in the constitutions of numerous cantons; federal government authority in the sphere of the law of obligations, including commercial law and the law of exchange;[25] the federal government was also responsible for making liability laws and stated matters.

Article 34, which is still valid today, is of major significance for the future development of social legislation. Paragraph 1 reads as follows:[26]

> The federal government is authorized to draw up uniform regulations on the employment of children in factories and on the working hours of adults in the same. It is also entitled to issue regulations to protect workers against industrial activities which are a threat to their health and safety.

Paragraph 2 then subordinated the commercial pursuits (of emigration agencies) and of 'private enterprises in the field of insurance . . . to the supervision and legislation of the federal government'.

Paragraph 1 is designed primarily to protect human health from being endangered and is thus of a police nature; however, it already contains roots from which modern social insurance was later to grow. Private insurance companies were also important for the further development of social insurance; paragraph 2 created the basis for their healthy growth.

1875–1890

Industrialization and Industrial Workers[27]

The Beginning of Industrialization

The spinning jenny, the predecessor of the modern power loom, which had been invented in England, was introduced to Switzerland as early as 1800. The industrial boom in Switzerland in the first half of the nineteenth century was largely due to the textile industry which included the cotton, silk and embroidery industries.[28] Other economic branches which developed greatly because of the rapid progress of mechanization were the watch- and clock-making industry and — in the second half of the century — the engineering and machine industry and later the chemical industry. Towards the end of the century, exports also rose considerably. From 1888–1913 the total foreign trade (exports and imports together) increased from about 1500 million to 3300 million Francs. In 1888 some 600 000 people were working in industry and crafts; in 1910 this figure amounted to 811 000.[29] Industrialization drew large numbers of workers away from agriculture in particular and created a new class within the population, namely the industrial labour force[30] which included both factory workers and workers in cottage industries in Switzerland.

Towards the end of the century the building trade also expanded; this was largely due to industrialization and the construction of road and railway networks. Railway construction met with considerable difficulties in Switzerland as the federal government was not assigned control of the railways until the Railway Act was passed in 1872. At the end of 1880 there were 2440 kilometres of railway tracks; in 1950 there were about 5700 kilometres. In 1882 the Gotthard railway was put into operation.[31] This north-south link was and is of supreme importance as Switzerland has no raw materials of her own of any note — apart from water — and must import them from abroad. This also applies to coal. Switzerland thus began at an early date to harness waterpower for generating electricity. The first electricity works were opened as early as 1886.

Social Situation of Industrial Workers

Industry was prone to crises. Thus, new tariff protection policies of neighbouring states could paralyse whole branches of industry within a short time.[32] Numerous companies which had been started without an adequate financial or technical basis during a spate of feverish business promotion and development in the last couple of decades of the nineteenth century, disappeared from the scene again. The threat of unemployment was always at hand, even if only latently.

Workers' wages were modest. However, they gradually rose as many companies grew economically stronger. Hauser[33] has tried to record in a table the development of average real wages for certain years between 1830 and 1955. At the same time he has calculated how long a worker had to work to be able to buy a pound of bread, beef and butter. Here are the figures in hours and minutes for 1860, 1880 and 1955. Bread: 2 hours; 1 hour 5 minutes; 7 minutes. Beef: 4 hours 30 minutes; 3 hours; 1 hour 7 minutes. Butter: 6 hours 18 minutes; 5 hours 32 minutes; 1 hour 44 minutes. Thus, the actual wage has risen steeply over the course of 100 years. However, it was still extremely modest in 1860 and in 1880. This explains why women and even children worked in industry; the whole family had to earn a wage to ensure an adequate family income.[34] Recurrent price increases which, for example, were often caused by poor harvests in Switzerland or in neighbouring countries, made life very hard. Prices for important foodstuffs, such as bread, could double or even treble in next to no time, only to drop again later. Wages were not adjusted to price increases; thus, great hardship might be caused.[35]

The Emergence of Swiss Trade Unions and Trade Associations

Trade unions emerged rather late in Switzerland, compared with in England. Beginnings were to be found in different industrially developed cantons or towns in the first half of the nineteenth century. However, the trade unions of the different economic branches did not become fully developed until the second half of the century. The Swiss Trade Union Congress (Gewerkschaftsbund) was founded in 1880. At first only twelve branches joined with a total of 133 members. Now it has about half a million members.[36] In the same year, quite independent of this, the Swiss Social Democratic Party was founded. Social Democratic parties had been founded earlier in some of the cantons. Fusion into a single Swiss party had failed previously because of ideological disputes and differences of opinion on the party programme. Marx' and Engels' ideas played a considerable role; however, they contributed more towards splitting than uniting the labour force. [37] In the 1880s the Social Democratic Party just managed to exist in the background. In its stead, the 'Grütliverein' (Grütli Association) considered itself to be the true representative of the working man's interests. [38] Furthermore, both the Liberal and the Conservative Party in Parliament had their own 'left' wing which pursued social policies. Trade and industry had organized themselves at national level before the labour force. The Swiss Trade and Industry Association (Schweizerische Handels- und Industrieverein) (Vorort) was founded on 12 March 1870. [39] Employer associations came after the trade unions, namely at the beginning of the twentieth century. In 1908 they amalgamated to form a central organization. [40]

No Major Social Unrest in Switzerland

Since the founding of the federal state, industrialization has not led to any major social unrest in Switzerland. The early days of industrialization were hard for workers: long hours, low wages, the danger of unemployment, no compensation for price increases. Plenty of factory owners succeeded in accumulating great wealth and of these many not only treated their workforce in a patriarchal manner, as was customary at that time, but were positively despotic. Thus, it is amazing that there were very few strikes in the factories. [41]

The Factory Act and Factory Liability
Legislation — Cantonal Social Laws — Workers' Self-help
and Other Welfare Institutions

From 1875–1890 the federal government only passed laws to safeguard industrial workers against the economic consequences of industrial accidents and diseases. There were the Factory Act of 1877 and the Factory Liability Acts of 1881 and 1887. No federal laws were enacted for other social risks such as unemployment, old age, disablement and sickness. Cantonal laws and community rulings were the exceptions. For example, Lucerne, in 1876, converted an institution for the care of the sick, which had been run by the town council and by master craftsmen in earlier centuries, into a general municipal sickness insurance scheme for workers which all workers had to join. [42]

There were numerous private institutions which provided assistance if, for example, members fell on hard times due to illness. These were based on the idea of voluntary social work. Basel was a shining example of this. All the charitable foundations and associations there had funds amounting to 22 million Francs in 1880 which yielded some 4 million Francs interest per annum, almost as much as the national revenue. [43] In the same year, an average of one out of every 13.6 inhabitants was a member of a relief society which granted assistance in acute or chronic cases of hardship on the principle of reciprocity. [44]

Workers also had recourse to self-help by establishing relief funds. By 1880 there were already 1085 of these funds; most of them provided benefits in cases of sickness and some of them also or only covered other risks such as disablement, death, or old age. Relief and sickness schemes of this type gradually developed into trade unions. [45]

Factory insurance schemes, which mainly provided sick benefits for workers, were widespread. In 1880 there are said to have been 350–400 factory insurance schemes with some 45 000 members; these accounted for about 50 percent of all the workers employed in concerns subject to the provisions of the Factory Act.[46]

Unemployment insurance schemes started quite early. The workers began with self-help. The typographers founded the first private unemployment insurance scheme in Switzerland in 1884. The first public unemployment insurance schemes in Europe were founded by the cities of Bern in 1893 and St Gallen in 1884.[47]

Organized old age pension schemes developed relatively late. Modest beginnings are perhaps to be noted in the 1870s when large companies, such as Sulzer, took out collective insurance for their staff with the 'Schweizerische Rentenanstalt' (Swiss Pension Institution).[48] Later pension schemes were established for civil servants, in 1888 in the canton of Basel-Stadt, followed by the canton of Geneva in 1893/99 and then by the Swiss railways for their staff in 1907. A general scheme for assistance in old age was started for the whole population in the cantons of Neuchâtel (1898) and Vaud (1907) but was not compulsory.[49]

Although there were all kinds of relief funds, people could nevertheless fall on hard times. Relatives were of course obliged to help to a certain extent, but even this help was frequently bound to fail. The home community was the 'last resort'. Since about the sixteenth century it had been the community's duty to assist needy citizens.[50] However, the poor were mostly looked down upon. For a long time the antiquated opinion prevailed that poverty was one's own fault or even God's punishment for evil conduct.[51] Mass poverty — so-called 'pauperism' — has undoubtedly existed in every century. It has been estimated that in the middle of the last century it affected 20 percent of the population in, for example, England, Holland and Belgium. Since then it has receded quite considerably in Switzerland at any rate; in 1870 an official enquiry showed that 4.6 percent of the population drew on poor relief.[52] Numerous communities with modest financial resources had large numbers of poor to support. Poor communities could only grant modest assistance. Thus, they welcomed the establishment of an industry as this at least provided sources of revenue. It is not known which section of the population had the highest percentage of poor people on average in the medium term towards the end of the last century.[53]

The Factory Act of 1877[54]

Liberalism

Liberalism, as expressed in the constitution, for example, in terms of free trade and enterprise, encouraged the entrepreneurial spirit to the full; Switzerland has largely to thank this very spirit for her industrialization and the construction of the railways. Its postulate that the state should not interfere with the economy — *laissez faire et laissez aller* — [55] had also led to social injustices, namely the ruthless exploitation of labour of men, women and children in factories. Furthermore, machines without adequate safety devices and long working hours causing fatigue were a frequent source of accidents.

The employment of women and children had been widespread in earlier centuries. It continued and even increased in the factories in the nineteenth century. In his early writings, even Pestalozzi expressed the view that children could be employed in industry from the age of 6 onwards as they had to get used to working. However, children were not to be overworked and school was to have priority. Abuse was particularly bad in the first decades of the nineteenth century. Children had to work 13–15 hours a day in conditions which caused grave damage to health.[56] In 1868 9505 children worked in a total of 664 factories in Switzerland. The age range of 9017 children was 12–16, 436 were 10–11 year olds and 52 were under 10.[57]

Cantonal Legislation on Worker Protection

Some cantons had laws on protection for workers before federal legislation on this was passed. As early as 1815 in the canton of Zürich a law stipulated that children were not to work in factories before the age of 10 and that they were to work for a maximum of 12–14 hours. The canton of Glarus is particularly noteworthy as there laws had to be made at the annual assembly of the canton's citizens (Landsgemeinde). About one-third of its inhabitants worked in the factories, especially in cotton mills and in cloth printing works.[58] There had been earlier legislation on the protection of workers; however, the cantonal Factory Act of 1866 was truly innovatory: this was probably the first law on the continent which reduced working hours for adults to a maximum of 12 hours per day. In 1872 the canton went one step further by introducing an 11-hour working day.[59] Both these laws served the federal government as a model for its Factory Act.

The Factory Act of 1877

In accordance with Art. 34 which had been incorporated in the federal constitution of 29 May 1874, the federal authorities passed the Factory Act with astonishing speed. After careful preparation by a board of experts and after numerous views had been considered, the Federal Council passed the draft bill on the new law on 2 November 1875 and presented it to the National Assembly on 6 December 1875.[60] The National Assembly accepted the draft, which was amended in only a few points, on 23 March 1877 and thus accepted the Federal Law on Work in Factories,[61] more briefly called the '1877 Factory Act'. As a referendum was demanded, a plebiscite took place on 21 October 1877. The law was only just passed after a fierce struggle with 181 204 votes for and 170 857 votes against.[62] It was primarily opposed by industry and industrial organizations which thought they would be at a disadvantage compared with foreign competition; the law was supported by the employed and their organizations. However, there were considerable exceptions on both sides. Thus, several far-seeing industrialists spoke in the National Assembly decisively for shortening working hours, for example, as this would increase working capacity. At the same time many workers voted against the bill in the plebiscite as they feared wage reductions which did not in fact occur.[63]

The law provides for an 11-hour working day for adults and prohibits night work but includes regulations on exceptions. It provides pregnant women and women after delivery a respite period of 8 weeks both before and after the birth. It raises the minimum age for child labour to 14 and limits the working hours of 14–16 year olds to 11 hours per day including schooling and religious instruction. It also intervenes in the employment contract, for example, by regulating the method of wage payment and the annulment of employment contracts in favour of the employed. Moreover, it is important that the law provides for state employed factory inspectors who are to check that the law is carried out in factories. The labour force owes these inspectors a considerable debt particularly with regard to factory hygiene and accident prevention.[64]

The Factory Act contains a series of rules which influenced later federal legislation on social security for the labour force over many years. These included:

Article 1 §2 and the Factory Register (Fabrikverzeichnis). The law defines the term 'factory' which, of course, had to be specified more exactly by decrees of the Federal Council.[64a] Furthermore, in Art. 1 §2 it stipulates that the Federal Council is to decide in cases of doubt whether an industrial concern is a factory and thus subject to the law. The Federal Council also had to draw up and keep up to date a factory register. Factories listed in this register were later automatically subject to compulsory accident insurance in accordance with the KUVG of 13 June 1911.

Preventive Measures. The law also contains regulations on the prevention of accidents and illness. These 'prophylactic' measures later formed an authoritive section of compulsory accident insurance law.

Article 5 §2b: Causal Liability in the Case of Industrial Accidents. Provisionally, until the Liability Laws were passed, Art. 5 §2 lit. (b) of the Factory Act introduced the principle of causal liability in the case of accidents at work.[65] According to this, the employer is liable even if he or his staff are not at fault when a worker has an accident. He can only be freed from liability if, for example, he proves that the accident was an act of providence. If the person involved in the accident is partially at fault, liability to pay damages is reduced. With causal liability for industrial accidents the legislator established a system which lasted for about 50 years.

Article 5 §2d: Industrial Illnesses. According to lit. (d) of the same article, the Federal Council is 'furthermore to designate those industries which, according to evidence, give rise to certain dangerous illnesses to which liability is to be extended'. Lit. d was specified in more detail in the Federal Council's resolution of 19 December 1887, in which it drew up a list of dangerous substances which 'produce certain dangerous diseases'.[66] This set a pattern for the rule which the KUVG introduced later in compulsory accident insurance with regard to industrial diseases.

With the Factory Act of 1877 the federal government had for the first time intervened successfully in the sphere of social policy. Of course, it only included a small minority of the working population in its initial phase — in 1888 some 160 000 workers were subject to the Factory Act,[67] as large groups of people working in the cottage industries and trades were excluded. The federal government preferred modest progress instead of jeopardizing its bill with a particularly bold plan.[67a]

The Factory Liability Acts of 1881 and 1887[68]

The Federal Law on Factory Liability of 25 June 1881

The Federal Council submitted a draft for a federal law to the National Assembly in its communication of 26 November 1880.[69] Such a law was to regulate liability according to Art. 5 of the Factory Act more specifically. The National Assembly accepted the Federal Law on Factory Liability on 25 June 1881. As a referendum had not been petitioned, the Federal Council could put the law into force on 11 October 1881.[70]

The Factory Liability Law predominantly confirms the liability already set forth in Art. 5 of the Factory Act. According to Art. 2 the factory owner is subject to causal liability and thus he is even responsible for accidents which occur by chance, if his worker suffers 'bodily injury or death on the premises of his factory or during the course of work in the same'. However, he can be exempted from liability if he proves that the accident or industrial illness, for example, is an act of providence or has been caused exclusively through the fault of the worker. In such cases, the employer is only partly liable 'if the damaged person is partly at fault for the accident (or illness in accordance with Art. 3)'. This law impairs the worker's position with regard to liability quite considerably compared with Art. 5 of the Factory Act. In Art. 5 it limits liability as this 'is not to exceed six times the annual income of the person concerned, nor the sum of 6000 Francs . . . in the most severe cases'.[71] This maximum does not apply if 'injury or death has been caused by an action liable to criminal prosecution on the part of the employer'.

In its communication the Federal Council sets forth that it must take special account of smaller and financially weaker factories:

> The factory owner in whose establishment a major accident has occurred and who has to pay damages to several people could easily go bankrupt. This would be no less disadvantageous to those entitled to damages and to the other workers than to the employer himself. As the misfortune of the one usually brings about the misfortune of the other, the payment of damages to the extreme would lead to the misfortune of both parties. (pp. 543–570)

The Federal Council refrained from bringing in compulsory liability insurance as the premium for concerns 'in which the manufacturing profit is extremely slight . . . can be relatively high' (p. 571).[72] After all, it intended encouraging factory owners to take out insurances. Art. 9, which was included in the law upon the instigation of the Federal Council, stipulated that benefits from accident insurances, sickness insurances etc. were to be taken into account when assessing compensation for damages, provided the factory owner had paid at least half the premium.

The Federal Law on the Extension of Liability
and the Amendment of 26 April 1887 of
the Federal Law of 25 June 1881

The Federal Law on the Law of Obligations of 14 June 1881 adhered to the principle of liability for intentional and negligent acts for contractual and non-contractual injuries. It only provided for causal liability for certain situations. Thus, concerns which were not subject to the Factory Act were only liable for their workers' accidents if they or their assistant staff were at fault. Large circles of people considered it an unjustified privilege that factory workers, but not other employed persons, could claim damages for accidents and industrial illnesses even if their employer was not at fault. Thus, the National Council accepted the following Klein motion on 25 March 1885:

The Federal Council is invited:

1. to revise the laws on liability of 1st July 1875 and of 25th June 1881 with a view to extending liability and to facilitating the validity of claims to damages;
2. to examine the question, and to draw up an appropriate report, whether general compulsory workers' accident insurance should be aimed at.

Klein had been inspired to ask the question, proposed under 2 above, by the German law on workers' accident insurance, passed at Bismarck's instigation in 1884 (cf. p. 406).

The Federal Council fulfilled these demands with its communication of 7 June 1886 and tabled the draft bill for a Federal Law on the Extension of Liability.[73] On 26 April 1887 the National Assembly passed the Federal Law on the Extension of Liability and the Amendment of the Federal Law of 25 June 1881. As a referendum was not demanded, the Federal Council could put the law into force on 1 November 1887.

In Art. 1, the law names those types of concern for which the regulations on liability under the Factory Liability Act are to be applied. According to paragraph 2 these are most varied types of business — for example, the building trade — 'if the employer concerned employs an average of more than 5 workers during working hours'.

Moreover, Art. 6 commits the cantons to make provisions which guarantee needy persons administration of justice free of charge, including legal aid free of costs, for law suits concerning liability. Articles 8 and 9 are also noteworthy as they bind employers to report accidents to the competent cantonal authorities. If the supervisory officials ascertain that the person who has had an accident 'cannot receive the damages due to him amicably, then they must report immediately to the cantonal government. The latter will order an enquiry to be made and will inform the interested parties of the result'.

On p. 697 f. and 703 the communication explains these regulations: There have been frequent complaints that the law of 25 June 1881

> is not applied or only inadequately applied in many places. . . . Compensation for damages is not paid at all, or only very small amounts are paid, as the worker accepts the sum he is offered for fear of losing his job because he has not the means to go to court to sue for his rights, due to a lack of knowledge, etc.

Such complaints are well-founded, thus 'remedial measures are urgently required'. 'Such injustice can only be counteracted by the proposed official supervision . . .' (p. 704).[74]

On p. 694 the communication states that the question of compulsory accident insurance still requires extensive preparatory work. One must beware of taking haphazard steps linked with the welfare of the whole country which could have serious consequences. Moreover, the federal constitution would inevitably have to be revised in order to introduce compulsory insurance. On p. 692 the communication mentions that industries in general 'are in the midst of a difficult crisis'; at present it is important to avoid 'burdening them with more than they already have to bear with the existing Liability Law'.

Supercession of the Factory Liability Law by the KUVG

The system of causal liability for accidents at work, laid down in the two laws of 1881 and 1887, was in force until the end of March 1918. On 1 April 1918 it was replaced by compulsory accident insurance in accordance with the KUVG which will be discussed later.

Swiss Private Insurances [75]

Most insurance companies played a considerable role in the origins and development of social insurance. Thus, it seems appropriate to discuss some aspects of their history and other features.

Fire Insurance — the First Type of Public Insurance

As homelessness in winter was as hard to bear in Switzerland as famine, fire insurance developed at an early stage. The first public fire insurance scheme was founded in the canton of Aargau in 1805. Other cantons soon followed suit. It is surely not accidental that the oldest Swiss private insurance company which still exists belongs to the fire insurance sector (Mobiliarversicherung 1826).

Failure of the First Life Insurance Companies

Life insurance companies had been founded in Switzerland by the first half of the nineteenth century. However, most of them had to be liquidated after a short time. Only companies established after 1850 survived. [76]

Origins of Private Insurance Companies

In the first decades following the foundation of the federal state, numerous companies emerged which flourished and still exist. As examples, here are a few of these companies with the year of their foundation: The 'Rentenanstalt'—the largest life insurance company—1857; 'Helvetia-Feuer' 1861; 'Schweizerische RückversicherungsGesellschaft'—today the largest re-insurance company in the western world—1863; 'Basler' 1864; 'Schweiz' and 'Neuenburger', both 1869; 'Zürich'—today the largest direct insurance company on the continent—1872; 'Winterthur' 1875; 'Pax' (life) 1876; 'Patria' (life) 1878; 'National' 1883; 'Union Suisse' 1887; 'Vaudoise' 1895.

Statistical Comparison

According to official statistics, 118 insurance companies were licenced in Switzerland in 1877/8; ninety-seven of these were foreign, particularly German, French and English. [77] It is amazing that about 100 years later, namely in 1975, only ninety-three companies were licenced.

Pacesetting Role of Private Insurance

This almost feverish trend of founding insurance companies from about the middle of the nineteenth century onwards can be accounted for by several reasons. First, there were new needs for insurance as industrialization progressed. Then, the transition from an agricultural to an industrialized state led to an expansion of the money economy without which private insurance is hardly conceivable. Finally, the introduction of a system of insurance agents, following the American pattern, had major repercussions on the expansion of the insurance sector. The insurance agent was tantamount to a new sort of peddlar who went from house to house seeking new orders for insurance policies. The incentive to do such work consisted in considerable commissions paid to the agents from the beginning of the 1870s with the conclusion of every policy. The agents made the population — and the politicians — aware of the idea of insurance. Thus, indirectly, they helped to pave the way for the introduction of social insurance.

Deficiencies of Early Insurance

The rapid growth of the insurance business in the last century also had its drawbacks. There were not enough competent experts available so some companies went bankrupt or had to be wound up. The expansion of the network of agents meant that often people with unsuitable characters were employed who promised all sorts of things before concluding a policy which were not realized when a claim under the insurance was made. In Switzerland — as in Germany and in other countries — private insurance did not always have a very good reputation. [78] One must not forget that the financial basis — e.g. in free and untied reserves — could not be firm in the face of such fast growth.

Insurance Supervision by the Federal Law of 1885 and the Law on Insurance Policies of 1908

The Federal Law of 25 June 1885 made private insurance companies in Switzerland subject to effective state supervision. [79] This led to notable discipline within the insurance sector. The supervisory authorities are especially to watch that the companies remain solvent and do not demand excessively high premiums. Thus, one of the most important prerequisites was created enabling Swiss private insurance to develop into one of the largest 'insurance exporting countries' in the world. The insurance policy was regulated for the whole of Switzerland by the Federal Law on Insurance Policies (VVG) of 2 April 1908 which still applies today.

Liability Laws and Private Insurance

The Liability Laws of 1881 and 1887 led to a considerable boom for numerous insurance companies. These turned workers' insurance into a special business branch. They developed collective accident insurance which covered workers of a single concern against accidents and combined it with liability insurance. Compensation from accident insurance was to be counted towards claims arising from liability. Accident insurance permitted the rapid regulation of damages as benefits were standardized; thus, in the majority of cases the question of liability no longer needed to be discussed. Because of the laws on liability, the insurance companies in Switzerland learnt a great deal about workers' insurance. This enabled them to enter the field of workers' insurance in other states also, [80] even if the laws there were somewhat different. Thus, with their business drive they have gradually taken on a task whose nucleus already had clearly socio-political traits.

Private Insurance Companies as Social Insurance Institutions?

As social insurance developed and expanded later on, the federal government was often confronted with the question whether private insurance companies could and should be used as social insurance institutions. This idea was originally rejected upon the introduction of compulsory insurance for employed persons with the KUVG in which the federal government gave preference to a state monopolized institution. In the last few decades technical and legal solutions have been recognized which gradually permitted another attitude. Thus, nowadays it is uncontested that a subject under public law can be granted similar jurisdiction to that of public administration itself. This is also possible for insurance companies. Thus, based on special legal regulations, they can be used as insurance institutions under public law.[81] Furthermore, it is technically and legally possible to use them for the implementation of compulsory insurance. Of course, from a political point of view it is then imperative to closely limit their profits and administrative costs. Moreover, the legislator must fix financing systems and make certain other provisions to prevent insured persons etc. from being adversely affected when an insurance company is dissolved as the latter does not fulfil the conditions of permanence — unlike insurance institutions which are borne or guaranteed by the state.[82] Finally, however, it will always remain a political question whether private insurance companies should be used to solve socio-political problems or not.

Bismarck's Social Insurance Legislation[83]

In some ways Bismarck's social insurance legislation had a lasting influence on Swiss legislation. Thus, it is worth examining his 'work' in some detail. It is expedient at this point to indicate solutions which were already evident in Bismarck's social insurance legislation and which were then realized in part some time later in Switzerland.[84]

The Kaiser's Message of 17 November 1881

After the German victory over France in the war of 1870/1 the new German Reich was founded. Wilhelm I, proclaimed Kaiser in Versailles on 18 January 1871, appointed Otto von Bismarck, the former Prussian Minister-President, as Chancellor.

As early as 7 June 1871 the Reichstag passed the Liability Act (Reichshaftpflichtgesetz). This applied, inter alia, to factories (for workers' accidents). Liability was linked to the negligence of the employer or his representatives; thus, this law did not introduce causal liability.[85] The legal position of the worker was not improved much with this law.

After Lasalle's death (1864) the German Social Democratic Party adopted a Marxist line under the leadership of Bebel and Liebknecht. Bismarck considered the Social Democratic Party a danger for the new Kaiserreich; thus, he forbade all Socialist associations and publications with an emergency law, the Anti-Socialist Law, of 1878. In order to counteract the political commotion which this law caused with a constructive policy, at least partly to solve the 'social question' and to reconcile the labour force with the monarchic state, Bismarck created the social insurance laws: the Sickness Insurance Law of 1883, followed by the Accident Insurance Law of 1884 and the Law on Disability and Old Age Insurance of 1889. These laws were mainly restricted to the labour force and introduced compulsory insurance for the first time organized in the form of an institution under public law. Young Kaiser Wilhelm II brought about Bismarck's downfall in 1890. He resigned from all his offices and thus could not realize his insurance plans for widows and orphans of deceased workers. Such an insurance was not established until 1911 within the framework of the 'Reichsversicherungsordnung' (Insurance Decree). This combined all laws on social insurance in a single law (codification). The basic structures which Bismarck had created continue to exist in the Federal Republic of Germany to this very day. [86]

The Kaiser's message of 17 November 1881 to the Reichstag has become famous. It is frequently called the Magna Carta of German social insurance. It contains motives and programmes for social insurance laws. It begins thus: 'Already in February this year We expressed our conviction that the curing of social ills is not exclusively to be found in the repression of Social Democratic excesses but also in the furtherance of the workers' well-being'. [87]

With his three laws Bismarck was the first in the world to establish social insurance in a more or less compact system of social security. Problems with which he had to come to terms and solutions which he firmly established in laws are in the main still topical today. Thus, some of these will be discussed briefly with particular reference to the present.

Repercussions of Bismarck's Three Laws

Compulsory Insurance. Bismarck frequently expressed his views on what he considered 'the most basic of all single questions', namely whether insurance companies should be responsible in any way for the new social insurance, i.e. accident insurance. He always decisively rejected this idea for various reasons. He did not believe 'that the insurance companies are prepared to give up their shares and dividends in the interest of the workers'; 'whatever else, no private concerns (i.e. insurance companies) with dividends and bankruptcy'. Indeed, he wanted to nationalize the most important branches of the insurance sector 'because of its public utility and the moral interest which the state has in preventing profiteering exploitation'. He also refused to build up social insurance on the basis of voluntary subscription as hardly anyone could maintain that that would be as successful as compulsory insurance. Furthermore, he limited insurance to the labour force initially but soon planned to extend it to other groups of the population, at least with regard to old age and disability insurance. [89]

Switzerland has largely regulated compulsory accident insurance with the KUVG according to the above-mentioned principles: insurance under public law; limitation to employed persons; compulsory contributions, a state-run institution; exclusion of private insurance companies. [90] The old age and surviving dependants' and disability insurance schemes (AHV/IV) are organized along the same lines except that they cover not only the employed but the whole population. The 'Lex Forrer' on sickness insurance was also largely based on Bismarck's legislation. As this law was rejected by the people — cf. below p. 410 — sickness insurance took a different course of development: no compulsory subscription throughout Switzerland; licensing of private insurance institutions so that the insurance relationship was originally regulated in accordance with principles of private law, [91] but nevertheless exclusion of private insurance companies. There is still debate on making sickness insurance compulsory.

Contributions and State Subsidies. The contributions paid by employers and employed and state subsidies represented the main sources of financing for Bismarck's legislation. Insurance against accidents at work was to be financed by the employer alone. This principle has made headway in Switzerland and in most other Western countries. As regards sickness insurance, Bismarck's legislation provided for one-third of expenditure to be covered by employers' contributions and two-thirds by the insured persons' contributions. According to the KUVG 2 I lit. (c) the employers cannot be forced to make compulsory contributions in Switzerland. This question is topical again now. Bismarck used all three sources to finance old age and disability insurance. Originally he wanted to introduce a state monopoly on tobacco in order to build up an old age pension scheme for the whole population (citizens' pensions) from its revenues. However, he had to refrain from this project.[92] The AHV/IV is also financed by all three sources in Switzerland. According to the AHVG 104 the federal government finances 'its contributions from revenues which it receives from taxes on tobacco and spirits'. Thus, it adopted and put into practice the idea of using tobacco to finance the AHV/IV.

Wage-related Contributions. Bismarck anchored the concept of wage-related contributions — wage percentages — in his laws.[93] The Swiss legislature has also adopted this rule for various branches. It has recently been proposed again for a particular aspect of sickness insurance.[93a]

A System of Multiple Institutions. The German legislature did not decide on a single insurance but on a division of social insurance into various branches. Moreover, insurance was not to be borne by a single institution, for example by a 'Reichs-versicherungsanstalt' (Insurance Institution), but by several institutions.[94] The Swiss legislature largely adopted these principles of multiple institutions and de-centralization — separation from state administration — for example in sickness insurance and the AHV/IV, and of late they are also being planned for com-pulsory accident insurance. Bismarck granted the insurance institutions a high degree of administrative autonomy for the parties concerned, particularly for the employer and employed in sickness insurance. This is amazing, as by so doing Bismarck — the enemy of political democracy[95] — incorporated an extremely democratic element, a right of co-determination so to speak, into social in-surance. The Swiss legislature followed this example by granting various institu-tions — SUVA (the Swiss Accident Insurance Institution), 'Ausgleichskassen' (compensation offices) etc. — administrative autonomy right from the start, or by letting them continue to have their own administration, as in the case of sickness and unemployment insurance institutions.

Accident Insurance Instead of Employers' Liability. Bismarck did not want to solve the problem of safeguarding workers against accidents at work by making more stringent laws on employers' liability — the introduction of causal liability or liability for negligent acts with a reversed onus of proof, whereby the employer would have to have proven that he was not at fault. Bismarck insisted from the start on replacing the liability system with accident insurance whose institutions were also to be responsible for accident prevention.[96] The Swiss legislature, however, first passed the Factory Liability Acts — with causal liability on the employer — and only proceeded at a later date introducing compulsory accident insurance for employed persons which is also responsible for accident prevention. Thus, it made a detour to come to the same solution as Bismarck, albeit with some delay.[97]

**First Legislative Competence of the Federal
Government with Regard to Social Insurance**[98]

Forrer's Memorandum of 1889

The Federal Council quickly undertook the task which had resulted from the Klein motion.[99] It extended its work to include the examination not only of accident insurance but also of sickness insurance. Upon the instigation of the Federal Council, the mathematician, Prof. Kinkelin, drew up a report on both subjects in Basel, dated 25 October 1889, and Forrer, a member of the National Council, drew up a long legal 'Memorandum on the Introduction of Swiss Accident Insurance', covering over 1000 pages, in Winterthur, dated 15 November 1889.[100] Forrer describes the liability system and its practical application at that time with which he had become acquainted as a lawyer during the course of numerous litigated cases (p. 856). He was extremely critical of the situation. Causal liability was incomplete as the owner of a works could plead that the accident was entirely the worker's fault; this made a reduction or even the complete rejection of the worker's claim possible. If the owner of the concern had not taken out insurance and was unable to pay, the injured person did not receive any compensation as insurance was not compulsory. The injured party had to take his employer to court. Thus, Forrer stated 'that the current liability system incites workers and employers against one another' (p. 878). He used the slogan which was then to play such an important role in the plebiscite: 'Insurance is the new watchword. Liability means disputes, insurance means peace' (p. 901).

Obviously inspired by Bismarck, he did not think private insurance companies were suitable to run workers' insurance (p. 889 f.). In a special section, he describes the basic features of a Swiss state-run accident insurance. Once again he expresses his earlier opinion: 'The basic features of the German system ought to be adopted and modified to suit our republican democratic principles' (p. 859 below).

The Communication (Botschaft) of 28 November 1889

With its communication of 28 November 1889 'on the introduction of legislation on accident and sickness insurance' the Federal Council submitted a draft for a new Art. 34bis to the National Assembly, which was to supplement the federal constitution.[101] It raised the question whether governmental jurisdiction should be restricted to sickness and accident insurance, or extended to disability and old age insurance, rather as in Germany. However, it rejected the idea as experience had to be gained first in sickness and accident insurance. It was thought that it would take some time before the idea of controlling other branches and of completing the constitution with a new article on jurisdiction could be considered.[102] The Federal Council recommended as a matter of urgency that the term 'workers' insurance' should be dropped and replaced by the more general term 'accident and sickness insurance' (p. 840 f.). It quoted verbatim some of the arguments of the German draft bill on accident insurance and also some of the 'explanatory remarks' on the corresponding Austrian draft bill (p. 831 f.). Furthermore, in Appendix III to its communication it submitted the texts of the German and Austrian 'Laws on Workers' Insurance' (p. 961–1014). This somewhat unusual procedure was partly due to the fact that many Swiss Germans at that time

thought highly of the two neighbouring 'Kaiserreiche'. Originality of ideas may
have sometimes suffered from this. The communication already used the term
'general social insurance' (p. 838) which was later changed to social insurance. [102a]

Article 34bis of the Federal Constitution (BV)

The National Assembly amended the draft of the Federal Council in major
respects. The federal government was not only 'competent to legislate' but actually had a legislative mandate. [103] The National Assembly revoked the restrictive
ruling that the federal government was authorized 'to declare that membership of
a sickness insurance association was obligatory for all wage earners' and provided
for the authorization of the introduction of a comprehensive compulsory insurance system. The text of Art. 34bis BV is as follows:

> In the course of legislation the federal government will establish sickness
> and accident insurance, taking existing sickness insurances into account. It
> can declare that membership is either universally compulsory or only com-
> pulsory for individual sections of the community.

The new article was accepted in the plebiscite of 26 October 1890 with a large
majority, 283 228 votes for and 92 200 votes against and by eighteen whole and
five half cantons. [104] Thus, for the first time the federal government had both the
competence and a mandate to legislate on social insurance. Art. 34bis BV is still
valid. [105]

1891–1918

Lex Forrer [106]

Referendum of 20 May 1900

After the plebiscite the Federal Council immediately began to prepare for the
new laws. In 1891 it sent a delegation to Germany and Austria to study the
sickness and accident insurance schemes there. The national councillor, Forrer,
was commissioned to work on the draft bill. Then Forrer had to interrupt his
work, since the 'Arbeiterbund' (Workers' League), led by its secretary, Hermann
Greulich, took steps for a constitutional initiative. This concerned the inclusion
of a regulation in the federal constitution whereby the whole population should
have a claim to medical treatment and care free of charge. [106a] This was to be
financed by introducing a state monopoly on tobacco. However, the petition for a
referendum did not gather the required number of signatures. In 1893 Forrer
was able to submit his first draft. It was revised by a board of experts. The
Federal Council submitted the drafts of a federal law on sickness and accident insurance to the National Assembly with its communication of 21 January 1896. [107]
    The National Assembly reshaped both the form and content of the bills quite
considerably. The National Assembly summarized them in a single law and also
incorporated a section on military insurance in it. The bill which had a total of
400 articles was passed on 5 October 1899. [108]
    Only a small group of journalists in Bern and a textile industrialist from
Eastern Switzerland petitioned for a referendum. Although all parties spoke in
favour of the bill's acceptance, it was rejected by a large majority in the plebiscite

of 20 May 1900: 341 914 votes against and only 148 035 for. Forrer was deeply disappointed; he resigned from his post as national councillor and lawyer to devote himself to other activities. Two years later, however, he was elected to the Federal Council; thus, he could work on a new bill on sickness and accident insurance. [109]

Provisions of the Lex Forrer

The Lex Forrer, rejected by the people, had provided for both compulsory sickness and accident insurance. From the age of 14 onwards, all people who were employed and received an annual income not exceeding 5000 Francs were to be compulsorily insured. There was the strongest opposition to compulsory sickness insurance which was partly to be implemented by public sickness insurance institutions to be set up by the cantons. The existing sickness insurances in particular feared for their future. The bill was said to represent the 'beginning of state Socialism' and was considered to be 'centralistic'. These were the main arguments. [110] There was very little opposition to a state accident insurance institution and to military insurance.

Military Insurance

As just mentioned, there was practically no opposition to the inclusion of a section on military insurance; the National Assembly drew up an independent law on military insurance and passed it on 28 June 1901. [111] The latter came into force on 1 January 1902.

At this point some details are given of both the previous and later developments in military insurance. As early as 7 August 1852 a federal law had obliged the federal government to grant persons who had had an accident during military service, or their dependants, certain benefits. When the new federal constitution was accepted, this law was replaced by the Federal Law on Military Pensions and Compensation of 13 November 1874. Illnesses were treated the same way as accidents. As the benefits were generally considered inadequate, the federal government concluded a private 'Collective Military Accident Insurance' with the 'Zürich' insurance company in 1887. Against payment of a premium, soldiers could insure themselves voluntarily with this company. Then, on 24 January 1893, the National Assembly authorized the Federal Council to take over the premiums of the 'Zürich' for all soldiers, at the expense of the Federal Treasury. This was done by Federal Council decree of 15 January 1895. With its communication of 28 June 1898, the Federal Council submitted the draft of a new military insurance law to the National Assembly; this was incorporated into the Lex Forrer [112] and — as already mentioned — finally became a separate federal law on 28 June 1901. However, it was not to be satisfactory for various reasons, for example, because of inadequate benefits. Thus, in the first year of the First World War the National Assembly passed the new Federal Law on Military Insurance of 23 December 1914. The Federal Council, however, never brought the complete law, but only individual articles, into force, namely with regard to the active service of the army during the First World War. The parallel existence of two laws which complemented one another at various points and which were further supplemented by decrees, made military insurance law so complicated that it was sometimes called a 'secret science'. [113]

The Federal Law on Military Insurance of 28 June 1901 is the first law with which the federal government took action in a sphere which nowadays is thought to belong to federal social insurance. Of course, this label was not used at that time. [114]

The Federal Law on Sickness and Accident Insurance of 13 June 1911 (KUVG)

Draft of the KUVG of 1906

After the people had rejected the Lex Forrer so decisively, there was a certain amount of perplexity about how to continue. The Swiss Association of Legal Practitioners (Schweizerische Juristenverein) passed a resolution at its annual meeting on 23/24 September 1901, recommending the development of legislation on liability. More concerns were to be included in it, compensation was to be improved and employers were to be required to effect a liability insurance. The Swiss Workers' League (Arbeiterbund) made a similar petition. The Federal Council also received numerous petitions from individuals and groups asking for a new bill on sickness and accident insurance to be elaborated. The Federal Council decided to take steps in this direction. It commissioned Dr E. Cérésole, a lawyer, to elaborate a draft bill. This was only to provide a law on promotion and subsidies for sickness insurance and was not to be linked with any federal obligation. Sickness insurances were only eligible for subsidies if they fulfilled certain minimum requirements, for example, if they provided certain prescribed minimum benefits. [115] Based on two bills of 1904 and 1905 — one each for sickness and accident insurance — the Federal Council adopted a resolution on the communication regarding the draft for a federal law on sickness and accident insurance on 10 December 1906. [116] On page 247 the communication states that the new draft is based on the twin principles of compromise and of a step by step course of action. As far as sickness insurance is concerned, it departed from the German model as it gave up the idea of 'class insurance', i.e. limited to the labour force: every Swiss citizen was to be allowed to be a member of a sickness insurance scheme as a matter of principle. A complete and final solution to the problem of sickness insurance could not be expected at the first attempt,

> even less as the conditions which are peculiar to our country, our current legislation, our institutions, the temperament of our people and our very needs make it impossible simply to transplant a system from somewhere else. We need an independent solution in practically every respect.

Nevertheless, the Federal Council decided to model accident insurance largely on the German pattern and to introduce compulsory state-run accident insurance for the employed who were already subject to liability legislation and for other concerns. It proposed that the insurance was not only to cover accidents at work but also other accidents of the insured. In this respect, Swiss legislation deviated from all the known rules of foreign legislation which only included accidents at work in workers' accident insurance. The Liability Laws were to be repealed with the introduction of accident insurance. The work's owner was no longer to be subject to causal liability for accidents at work but to a far less severe form of liability for negligence. [117]

Plebiscite on the KUVG of 4 February 1912

The National Assembly made amendments to several items in the draft. It wanted to strengthen the self-administration and autonomy of the accident insurance which was to be newly established. Both the employer and the employed were to be represented in the governing body. The National Assembly also differentiated more clearly between insurance for accidents at work and for other accidents; the employers had to finance the former completely while premiums for the latter were to be paid by the insured, but the federal government was, of course, also to pay subsidies. [117a] The National Assembly accepted the draft bill on 13 June 1911. A petition had been made for a referendum; this was held on 4 February 1912. The people accepted the bill by a slight majority: 287 565 for and 241 426 against it. The KUVG with some 131 articles almost completely separates sickness and accident insurance. Fundamentally, it still applies today although several major and minor amendments have been made to it since then. [118]

Establishment of the Federal Office for Social Insurance
(Bundesamt für Sozialversicherung)

The federal government now had to establish an office to carry out the tasks prescribed in the KUVG — supervision, fixing of subsidies etc. In 1912 it set up the 'Bundesamt für Sozialversicherung' which was of major significance for the later development of various branches of social insurance. [118a]

Creation of the SUVA (Schweizerische Unfallversicherungsanstalt —
Swiss Accident Insurance Institution)

The federal government could put the section on sickness insurance into force as early as 1 January 1914 as the sickness insurance institutions had already existed for some time. However, the introduction of compulsory accident insurance required extensive preparatory work as an insurance institution had to be established first of all. This, namely the SUVA, began its work on 1 April 1918. The Federal Insurance Court (Eidg. Versicherungsgericht) which had been created as a supreme court to judge litigations arising from compulsory accident insurance — not, however, from sickness insurance — also went into operation at the same time.

The Supplementary Law (Ergänzungsgesetz) to the KUVG of 1915

The legislator had obviously not realized that countless works which were now subject to compulsory accident insurance were tied to insurance companies with accident and liability insurance policies. This was presumably the primary reason why the so-called 'Ergänzungsgesetz' to the KUVG was passed on 18 June 1915. This stipulated that such policies are no longer valid as soon as a concern is subject to accident insurance, without either party having to pay compensation (Art. 1 I and Art. 2 II). The 'Ergänzungsgesetz' also regulates other matters which are not dealt with here. [119]

Consequences for Private Insurance

Several private insurance companies lost a considerable part of their portfolio because of the introduction of state accident insurance. [120] However, they survived. Moreover, they could console themselves with the fact that they had gained considerable knowhow through workers' insurance; that facilitated their progress in business both at home and abroad.

First Use of the Term 'Social Insurance' (Sozialversicherung)

After the KUVG had come into force, the term 'Sozialversicherung' began to gain a footing in Switzerland, as had happened in Germany. The Federal Council used it several times in its communication of 21 June 1919 on incorporating an Art. 34 quater BV (AHV/IV — legislative competence). [120a]

Other Significant Laws of That Era

Codification of Private Law

The first two decades of the twentieth century were not only of major significance for the development of social insurance. On 10 December 1907 the federal councils unanimously accepted the Civil Code and on 30 March 1911 — also unanimously — the Law of Obligations which replaced several laws of 1881, including the Law on Employment Contracts[121] which was part of the Law of Obligations. There was no petition for a referendum. Both laws came into force on 1 January 1912. Thus, the federal government had codified private law; most of the cantonal laws on private law became void.

The codification of private law is characterized by uniformity and compactness. It followed on from a thousand-year-old legal tradition. In contrast, social insurance law was completely new to the legislature which had to feel its way slowly and pragmatically as it tried to develop social insurance legislation. Thus, social insurance law lacks the uniformity and compactness of private law. It will undoubtedly take many decades before the legislature manages to codify social insurance law in such a way that it is at all comparable with private law. [122]

Legislation on Workers' Protection (Industrial Safety)

The Factory Act of 1877 was repealed by the Federal Law on Work in Factories of 18 June 1914. This law paid greater attention to health protection regulations, made new provisions for work and rest hours and extended protection for women and young people. The federal government developed industrial safety legislation in stages, once its authority had been extended by the partial revisions of the federal constitution of both 1908 and 1947. Today, the Federal Law on Work in Trade and Industry (Arbeitsgesetz) of 13 March 1964 applies. The parties concerned had striven for this law for decades. [123]

PART 2: THE INTER-WAR YEARS (1919–1939)

BACKGROUND

The First World War

The First World War ended on 11 November 1918 when the Germans accepted the terms of the armistice. The monarchies of Germany and Austria collapsed and were replaced by republican state constitutions. The November Revolution in Germany marked the transition from war to peace. The Communists had already begun the Russian Revolution, which brought them to power, a year earlier on 7 November 1917. Their leader, Lenin, had lived as an emigrant in Switzerland during the war. He had already left Switzerland by 9 April 1917 to return to Russia. [124]

Repercussions on Switzerland

Switzerland was spared the rigours of war. The principle of armed neutrality had proved its worth once again. Nevertheless, in November 1918 Switzerland experienced the most difficult political and social upheavals since the federal state had been founded in 1848. General price rises which were only slowly balanced out by wage increases, if at all, [124a] the shortage of foodstuffs and to some extent their unjust distribution and unemployment caused grave social tensions. A severe epidemic of influenza aggravated the situation. The Russian Revolution also sparked off revolutionary tendencies in Switzerland. On account of these circumstances, on 11 November 1918 the Social Democratic Party, the Swiss Trade Union Congress (Schweizerische Gewerkschaftsbund) and the Social Democratic faction of the National Council, together with the Olten Action Committee headed by Robert Grimm, called for a general strike. This was to continue until the federal authorities had accepted a minimum programme of nine points. [124b] The Federal Council and the National Assembly rejected this ultimatum and decided to bring in troops to maintain law and order. On 13 November 1918 the Federal Council presented the Olten Committee with an ultimatum to end the strike that very day. The strike ended somewhat later and thus civil war was avoided. The outcome of this trial of strength had been decided in favour of the federal authorities and thus of the middle classes and farming population. [125] The Olten Committee gradually disintegrated. [126]

Consequences of the Strike

Initially, the nationwide strike intensified class warfare and deepened the split between the workers and the middle classes and farming population. The Social Democratic Party was, for example, subsequently averse to national defence as the troops had played a decisive role in breaking the general strike. [127]

Growth of Socio-political Awareness

The middle class became increasingly aware that it had done too little in the social sector and that this was one of the reasons for the social upheavals. [128] Perhaps it was because of this awareness that the federal authorities realized several of the nine demands over the following years which had been made in the form of a minimum programme when the strike was called out. Thus, by passing appropriate legislation, they introduced proportional representation for National Council elections and the 48-hour week. In the summer of 1919 the Federal Council submitted a bill to the National Assembly for the adoption of a provision in the federal constitution which authorized the federal government to introduce old age and surviving dependants' insurance. [128a] This was followed by a Federal Law on the Payment of Contributions to Unemployment Insurances in 1924. In the long term the general strike increased social awareness among the population and is thus at the root of the growth and development of social insurance — even if this occurred much later.

From Confrontation to Cooperation

The threat presented by National Socialism in Germany in the 1930s did much to promote the idea of class reconciliation in Switzerland. After the unfortunate confrontation of 1918, cooperation began to develop steadily and was expressed in the Peace Agreement (Friedensabkommen) of 19 July 1937. This Peace Agreement was signed by the President of the Federation of Swiss Machine and Metal Industrialists (Arbeitgeberverband Schweizerischer Maschinen- und Metallindustrieller), Ernst Düby, and Konrad Ilg, [129] President of the Swiss Metal and Watch and Clock Workers' Association (Metall- und Uhrenarbeiterverband) which was the largest trade union. It was based primarily on good faith as far as relations between employers and employed were concerned and it promoted the idea of a partnership between these two groups in industry in other economic branches also. Moreover, it assured Switzerland labour peace for decades and considerably improved the social position of the workers. The Nazi threat also made the social Democratic Party support national defence again in 1935 and to remain faithful to this stance during the Second World War. [130]

The World Economic Crisis

During the inter-war years Switzerland was also shaken by economic crises. In 1922 there was an average of 67 000 completely unemployed. [131] The world economic crisis, which began with the Wall Street crash on 29 October 1929, reached its climax in Switzerland in 1936 when the number of unemployed rose to 120 000. The federal authorities were kept extremely busy with this development. Furthermore, they had to concern themselves at that ominous time with economic war provisions. They had to build up the military as well as the will to carry out national defence. Thus, the inter-war years were not propitious for the development of social insurance, as we shall see shortly. [132]

FEDERAL FUNDS FOR THE UNEMPLOYED

Unemployment Relief

The federal government had already made numerous provisions for unemployment relief during the war — with federal acts or Federal Council resolutions. It allowed cantons and communities certain amounts so that they could give assistance to the unemployed. Thus, with its resolution of 24 March 1917, the Federal Council established a 'Fund for Unemployment Relief' which it financed from the war profit tax. [133] It also made contributions to unemployment insurance schemes after the war. In 1923, sixty insurance institutions were entitled to subsidies; eighteen of these were public, established by cantons and communities, four were based on a footing of equality and thirty-eight were associations' insurance schemes. [134]

In Spite of the Federal Law of 17 October 1924;
No Satisfactory Regulation of Unemployment Insurance

In 1923 the number of unemployed gradually declined. Thus, the federal government decided to reduce unemployment relief and to make new rulings for subsidies to unemployment insurances. With this in mind, the Federal Law on the Payment of Contributions to Unemployment Insurances was passed on 17 October 1924. [135] This sets forth the conditions which an insurance institution must fulfil in order to be entitled to federal contributions. Thus, the institution had to charge its members contributions (premiums), stressing its character as an insurance. This was a law on subsidies or promotion which bore similar features to the KUVG with regard to sickness insurance. Of course only later decrees used the expression 'recognition': the Decree VI of 19 January 1937[136] settled the 'recognition of insurance institutions' in a special section. An institution desiring federal contributions first had to apply to the government for 'recognition'. As the cantons remained responsible in principle for arranging unemployment insurance as they thought best, for example, for introducing total or partial compulsory insurance for employed persons, this branch of insurance continued to be marked by great diversity.

When unemployment increased again in 1930 affecting, for example, the watch and clock and embroidery industries, the afore-mentioned law proved inadequate. The government passed various resolutions to develop unemployment relief again, apart from insurance, for example, 'on crisis assistance for the unemployed' in 1931, 'crisis support for the unemployed', 'welfare for older unemployed persons' in 1939. These resolutions were conceived to support those unemployed persons who had no claim to insurance benefits from unemployment insurance schemes, either because they were not insured at all or because the 90-day period of eligibility for benefits laid down by federal law had expired. The parallel existence of both federal and cantonal resolutions governing both insurance and relief in the most varied ways led to an almost intolerable fragmentation of the law which continued right into the Second World War. The federal government did not succeed in finding a satisfactory solution to unemployment insurance between the two wars.

OLD AGE, SURVIVING DEPENDANTS' AND DISABILITY INSURANCE

Plebiscite on Article 34 quater BV of 6 December 1925

With its communication of 21 June 1919 'on the introduction of legislative law on disability, old age and surviving dependants' insurance and on the procurement of federal funds required for social insurance', [137] the Federal Council submitted a motion to the National Assembly to make several additions to the federal constitution. Art. 34 quater was to empower the federal government to introduce disability, old age and surviving dependants' insurance and Articles 41 ter and quater were concerned with the financing of the insurances. The communication has no less than 210 pages and also has an appendix of 12 pages. It portrays the state of legislation on this subject of numerous foreign countries and of the cantons, and sketches solutions for future Swiss legislation etc. In a supplementary communication the Federal Council went into detail on levying death duties.[138] The National Assembly amended several points of the drafts. It did not want to know anything about the federal government's death and gift taxes as these ought to be reserved for the cantons; it also rejected the proposed beer tax. Art. 34 quater, to which it agreed, committed the federal government to the introduction of old age and surviving dependants' insurance and also authorized it to set up disability insurance afterwards. The financial contributions of the federal government and the cantons were not to exceed half of the insurance's total requirements. Thus, the other half was to be financed through contributions, stressing the character of insurance. The net revenue from future taxes on tobacco and alcoholic beverages was reserved for old age and surviving dependants' insurance. At the same time a new Art. 41 ter authorized the federal government 'to tax raw and processed tobacco'.

The people accepted the proposals for the constitution on 6 December 1925 by a large majority 410 988 votes in favour and 217 483 against. [139]

Failure of the 'Lex Schulthess'; Increased Old Age and Surviving Dependants' Relief

With its communication of 29 August 1929 the Federal Council submitted a draft to the National Assembly for a federal law on old age and surviving dependants' insurance. This was accepted by the National Assembly almost unanimously, with a few amendments, on 17 June 1931. [140] The draft provided for compulsory insurance for everyone. Every canton was to set up a special insurance institution. Men had to pay fixed contributions of 18 Francs and women 12 Francs per annum. Thus, the contributions did not depend on social factors — level of income or wealth. Employers had to pay 15 Francs per employed person. The old age pension of 200 Francs per annum was to be granted from the age of 66 onwards. Moreover, provisions were made for widows' pensions of 150 Francs per annum and orphans' pensions of 50 Francs per annum per child.

A petition was drawn up for a referendum against the draft bill. The people rejected it on 6 December 1931 with 510 695 votes against and 338 838 for. [141] This 'Lex Schulthess', named after the member of the Federal Council responsible, was hardly a good solution from today's point of view. As already mentioned, the contributions were not graded according to social considerations and, furthermore, the pensions would have been too low even by the standards of the day. The reason for its rejection, however, probably lies elsewhere: most people were scared of an experiment with new levies as economic crisis spread.

After the bill's rejection, the federal government improved old age and surviving dependents' relief by granting state subsidies to private foundations for the aged and later for young people and to the cantons. [142] However, this did not provide sufficient financial security for the old, surviving dependants and the disabled. The present arrangement did not come into force until after the Second World War. Thus, the legal regulation of AHV was initially just as much of a failure as that of sickness and accident insurance.

PART 3: THE SECOND WORLD WAR (1939–1945)

SPECIAL AUTHORIZATION ACT (VOLLMACHTENBESCHLUSS)

On 30 August 1939 the National Assembly gave the Federal Council extraordinary authorization by federal act to take steps to protect the country and to maintain Swiss neutrality. [142a] These powers were not only used for economic and military purposes but also for socio-political measures. Indeed, the Federal Council passed several acts which formed the basis for the almost turbulent development after the war. Regulations which were made could be tried out in practice during the war and if they proved successful they were to be incorporated in regular legislation later on. The common threat and the experience of active service in the militia brought different strata of the population closer to one another and they began to understand each other better. [143] The socio-political measures which the Federal Council implemented on the basis of its special powers also helped decisively to preserve Switzerland during and after the war from the turmoil it had experienced in November 1918.

RULING ON INCOME SUBSTITUTION (LOHN- UND VERDIENSTERSATZORDNUNG)

Military Relief During the First World War

During the First World War servicemen did not usually receive a wage during their long service and otherwise only earned very low army pay; thus, they and their families often became destitute. According to OR 335 (rev. OR 324a) the employer was only bound to continue paying a wage for a relatively short time when a person he employed did military service as the employer did not usually have the means to pay for longer periods. If servicemen had dependants to support they could apply to the community concerned for 'military relief'. This had been introduced by the military organization of 1907.[144] This relief was considered a form of poor relief and as such it was unsatisfactory as the difficulties themselves were caused by compulsory military service. Thus, this system had to be replaced by a more efficient solution at the beginning of the Second World War, namely by the Ruling on Income Substitution.

The Reform of 20 December 1939 and Other Resolutions During the Second World War

Based on its special authorization, the Federal Council issued a 'Resolution on the Provisional Settlement of Income Substitution for Employed Persons in Active Service' on 20 December 1939. This ruling did not come into force until 1 February 1940. Briefly, it provided as follows:

Each firm had to deduct 2 percent from wage payments and contribute the same amount itself. From these amounts, compensation payments were to be made to men in active service normally employed in that firm. This compensation was precisely regulated by the Ruling on Income Substitution and graded according to essential family commitments. The employer arranged 'equalization' by settling contributions and compensation together and only squaring up in full with the 'Ausgleichskassen' (equalization schemes). He could draw the necessary amounts from these if compensation exceeded contributions at this first level of equalization; conversely he had to reimburse the 'Ausgleichskassen' in cases of an active balance. The 'Ausgleichskassen', to which numerous firms were attached, carried out equalization at the second level. They had to hand over surpluses to the Swiss central 'Ausgleichsfonds' (equalization fund) and in the case of a debit balance they could demand the missing amounts from this fund. Thus, the third level of equalization took place at the central 'Ausgleichsfonds'. However, both this and the 'Ausgleichskassen' had first to be created. Professional associations of employers set up association equalization schemes (Verbandsausgleichskassen). Moreover, each canton had to organize a cantonal 'Ausgleichskasse' which covered employers who were not part of a 'Verbandsausgleichskasse'. The 'Ausgleichskasse' was a body corporate; it gained this status when granted a licence to function and upon recognition by the competent government administrative authority. The central 'Ausgleichsfonds' was established by the federal authorities. As the social partners were already prepared to cooperate among themselves and with the federal authorities, this system could be built up within a short time so that it fulfilled the tasks in hand.

During the war the Federal Council passed further resolutions finally resulting in four systems: the Wage Substitution Rule for the Employed; Income Substitution Rules for People Employed in Trade and in Agriculture; the Rule on the Interruption of Studies for Students.[145]

The rule described above was a decisive breakthrough in the development of Swiss social insurance. This applies especially to the newly founded underwriters, the 'Ausgleichskassen', as these could be used to implement AHV, IV and other branches after the war. The rule on contributions—whereby all gainfully employed persons had to pay certain percentages of their earnings without an upper limit and regardless whether these consisted of a wage or another form of income—proved successful.[146]

Unemployment Insurance

On 14 July 1942 the Federal Council largely standardized unemployment insurance by authorization act. It maintained the system of subsidizing unemployment insurance schemes; however, it settled questions of insurability and eligibility to claims. Furthermore, it set up an equalization fund for insurance schemes to be able to grant more heavily burdened insurances equalization supplements (compensation for risks).[147] With the same act, the Federal Council also laid down the basic features of unemployment assistance. It passed another act on 23 December 1942 regulating details. The first mentioned act was altered three times. It remained in force until it was incorporated in the regular body of laws with the Federal Law on Unemployment Insurance of 1 January 1952.

Rules on Family Allowances (Familienzulageordnung)

Agricultural workers and mountain farmers are among the socially weaker groups of the Swiss population. Their importance for the country's provision with foodstuffs became evident during the war. There was the danger that farmers would give up their jobs to earn more money in trade and industry; thus, the Federal Council passed a resolution on 9 June 1944, based on its special authorization, granting agricultural workers and mountain farmers financial assistance in the form of household and child allowances. The cantonal 'Ausgelichskassen' were to put this resolution into operation. This was the first time that the Federal Council had laid down a rule on family allowances at federal level for a particular branch of the economy.[148]

Part 4: Development of Social Insurance Since the Second World War (Since May 1945)

Economic and Social Policy

Economic Boom Since 1945

The expected unemployment after the Second World War did not occur. Switzerland experienced an economic boom to an extent unknown hitherto, lasting from 1945 until the recession began in 1974/75. As the productive apparatus was sometimes overburdened, there began to be signs of an overheated economy; thus, for example, a socially and economically dangerous evil grew in the form of general price inflation.

Statistical Data

A few figures will illustrate the developments. Between 1948 and 1978 the price index rose from 100 to 235.5.[149] General price increases reached an all-time high in 1974 with 9.8 percent. Wages increased even more considerably. From 1948–1978 growth amounted to 769 percent in nominal terms and 269 percent in real terms[150] based on consumer prices in 1948. The AHV wage index is used for wages which are subject to AHV contributions. If this index showed the figure 100 for 1948, it had risen to 557.4 by the end of 1977.[151] In 1948 the gross national product amounted to 19 220 million Francs and in 1978 it was 156 900 million Francs. If one computes this in terms of prices in 1970, the figures for 1948 are 36 055 million and 100 075 million Francs for 1978. This means a real increase of 178 percent. The number of completely unemployed persons reached its highest level in 1976 with an average of 20 703 (1948: 2971) compared with some 120 000 in 1936.

The Problem of Foreign Workers in Switzerland

During various phases of the overheated economy there was an acute shortage of labour. This was largely met by employing foreign workers (so-called 'Gastarbeiter'). Thus, the proportion of the foreign population in Switzerland greatly increased. At the end of 1950 there were 285 446 foreigners in a total population of 4.714 million and at the end of 1975 these figures had risen to 1.043 million foreigners in a total population of 6.333 million. This proportion has dropped slightly since then (898 000 at the end of 1978, i.e. 14.4 percent). The steady growth of the foreign population caused many problems including those of a psychological nature. A constitutional initiative took place, demanding the drastic reduction of the number of foreign workers in Switzerland.

This 'Ueberfremdungsinitiative'[152] (an initiative against large numbers of foreigners in Switzerland) was rejected by a narrow margin in the plebiscite of 7 June 1970. Following this the federal authorities took measures to reduce gradually the foreign proportion of the population. Moreover, the high number of foreign 'guest workers' meant that Switzerland concluded social insurance agreements with numerous states in order to solve the guest workers' most urgent problems of social insurance.

Turbulent Development of Social Insurance

Social insurance has developed turbulently since the Second World War. Apart from the KUVG which had been passed before the First World War, all the more important laws on social insurance which are now valid were passed after 1945. Here are some of the reasons: compared with other West European industrialized states Switzerland lagged behind in the social insurance sector. Thus, it had to make up for lost time. Favourable economic developments provided plenty of scope for socio-political discussions and decisions and kept the population's fear of experiments at bay. As already mentioned, the Second World War had increased mutual social understanding between different groups of the population; among the political parties there was a broad consensus of opinion that social insurance had to be further developed and on how this was to be done. Finally, it should be stressed that the competent federal administrative authorities — the 'Bundesamt für Sozialversicherung' (Federal Office for Social Insurance) — showed remarkable application in the preparation and execution of laws and decrees.[153]

Incorporation of Authorization Acts into Regular Law

In order to be able to incorporate the authorization acts of the Federal Council into regular legislation, the federal authorities first had to create a constitutional basis for this in several respects. Reference will be made to the new provisions of the federal constitution in the appropriate place. The order of the following portrayal is largely determined by the dates when a federal law concerning social insurance was either passed or radically amended.

OLD AGE AND SURVIVING DEPENDANTS' INSURANCE[153a]

The Federal Law of 20 December 1946

After the rejection of the 'Lex Schulthess', attempts to create the AHV stagnated for the time being. Apart from the Saxer motion in the National Council in 1938, most parliamentary advances — of which there were many — date from the period following the introduction of the rule on wage and income substitution. This 'social achievement' paved the way for the AHV to be introduced satisfactorily and without major difficulties.[153b] There was a constitutional initiative on 25 July 1942. Furthermore, several cantons made petitions for initiatives to establish the AHV. Those of the cantons of Berne and Aargau induced the Federal Council to propose to the National Assembly that the Federal Council should table an appropriate bill. This motion was unanimously adopted as a resolution by both councils.[154] The 'Eidg. Volkswirtschaftsdepartement' (Federal Ministry of Economic Affairs) engaged a board of experts on 11 May 1944, led by Dr Arnold Saxer, a former national councillor and now director of the 'Bundesamt für Sozialversicherung' (Federal Office for Social Insurance), which was to clarify the situation for the introduction of the AHV and to elaborate proposals. The board of experts concluded its work with a comprehensive report dated 16 March 1945. Its proposals showed the shape that the draft bill was to take. On 24 May 1946 the Federal Council submitted the communication and draft of a Federal Law on AHV to the National Assembly.[155] A special communication of 29 May 1946 explained the 'financing of AHV with public funds' and linked it to appropriate draft laws.[156] The councils essentially combined the two bills and agreed to the Federal Law on Old Age and Surviving Dependants' Insurance within an amazingly short time, on 20 December 1946. This was only possible because the organization and provisions on contributions were based on the well-tried solutions of the Rule on Wage and Income Substitution. There was a referendum against the law. However, politically active citizens (women did not have the vote at that time) accepted it on 6 July 1947 by 862 036 votes for compared with 215 496 against. A bill had never been accepted with such a large majority since the federal state had been founded in 1848.[157] The law came into force on 1 January 1948.[158]

Extension of the AHV

In contrast to the rejected 'Lex Schulthess', the law on the AHV is based on a 'flexible' rule on contributions. Contributions are not 'fixed' but are 'wage-related' and are characterized by the solidarity of the financially stronger groups in the population. Furthermore, as the AHV is financed according to a contributory system which is linked with a fluctuation fund, it could expand without major difficulties. Economic prosperity encouraged further development. From 1 January 1948 to the end of 1979 there were no less than nine constitutional initiatives on the AHV. Of course, the people only had to vote on a few of these as the initiators withdrew most of them; their requests were usually accounted for in amendments to legislation or, in one case, in a counter proposal of the National Assembly. So far the Law on AHV has been subject to nine numbered and three unnumbered revisions. There was only a referendum against the ninth AHV revision. The people voted in favour of the bill on 26 February 1978. Over 200 parliamentary motions in the federal councils also dealt with the AHV; most of these aimed at its gradual development.[159]

Statistical Data

The following figures will help to shed light on the development of the AHV until the end of 1979.[160] Originally, the minimum pension (single old age pension) amounted to 480 Francs and the maximum pension to 1500 Francs per annum. At the end of 1979 these were 6300 Francs and 12 600 Francs respectively. Thus, minimum pensions have risen about 13-fold and maximum pensions about 8.4-fold. As maximum pensions have been raised less in percentages than minimum pensions, it looks as if the development of old age pensions is gradually turning towards a uniform pension as the 'Lex Schulthess' had proposed. At the same time prices have risen by about 2.4-fold. Thus, the purchasing power of old age pensions has increased substantially. During the same period earned incomes which are subject to AHV contributions have increased about 5.5-fold.[161] Originally, contribution rates for employers and employed for AHV alone were 4 percent and at the end of 1979 they were 8.4 percent of the wage; for the self-employed these percentages were 4 percent and 7.8 percent respectively.

The 'Drei-Säulen-Prinzip' (Three Pillar Principle)
of the new Art. 34 quater of the Federal Constitution

In the referendum of 3 December 1972 the people voted in favour of a new Art. 34 quater of the federal constitution.[162] This article concerns not only matters of jurisdiction but also sets forth guidelines on how old age, surviving dependants' and disability pensions are to be shaped in future. The Three Pillar Principle is anchored in it *'de facto'*. The first pillar, namely the state AHV and IV, is to cover requirements for existence; the second pillar, i.e. schemes connected with work — staff pension funds, pension insurances etc. — is designed, along with the first pillar, to enable all employed persons to continue their usual mode of life in an appropriate way; the third pillar consists of the citizen's own provisions which the government and cantons are to further with appropriate fiscal and property policies.[163] A draft bill on the second of these pillars has been submitted to the federal councils;[164] however, hardly any provisions have been made yet for the third pillar. The government has to a large extent reached its goal of a pension which provides a secure existence with the far-reaching eighth AHV revision. The revision led to more than doubling the pension in two stages. This came into force on 1 October 1973.

AHV Revisions

Here are some notes on the AHV revisions:[165]

The First AHV Revision

With the first AHV revision of 21 December 1950, in force from 1 January 1951,[166] the federal authorities aimed at relieving cases of hardship. They extended the circle of persons who had a claim to a transitional pension. They also somewhat improved the regressive scale of contributions for the self-employed by raising the income limit.[167]

The Second AHV Revision

Wages and prices did not develop as had been expected in 1947. Thus, compared with the original forecasts, there was a surplus in the AHV fund. The second AHV revision of 30 September 1953, in force from 1 January 1954 onwards,[168] provided for pension increases. Both the ordinary minimum and maximum pensions as well as the transitional pensions were raised. The contribution for people who were not gainfully employed was raised from the previous amount of 1–50 Francs to 12–600 Francs. Compulsory contributions for gainfully employed persons over the age of 65 were completely abolished.[169]

The Third AHV Revision

According to the original rule, people belonging to the 'transitional generation', i.e. those born before 1 July 1883, were only eligible for a transitional pension if their income did not exceed a certain level (a pension depending on needs). They had not paid any contributions. The third AHV revision of 22 December 1955, in force from 1 January 1956,[170] abolished the income level requirement. Thus, transitional pensions were paid from that time onwards without considering need.[171]

The Fourth AHV Revision

The fourth AHV revision of 21 December 1956, in force from 1 January 1957, brought many changes, some far-reaching: regular pensions were increased by using a new pensions formula and partial pensions were raised by counting double the number of contributory years.[172] The legislature lowered the pension age for women eligible for a single old age pension from 65 to 63. Widows' pensions were uniformly fixed at 80 percent of the single old age pension; previously they had been between 60 percent and 90 percent depending on the age of the woman when widowed. Orphans' pensions were also raised. The sinking scale of contributions was improved once again in favour of the self-employed.

'Adaptive Revision'

Linked with the introduction of the IV (cf. below p. 431), the Law on the AHV was again revised (an unnumbered revision) on 19 June 1959. The amendments came into force with the Law on Disability Insurance of 1 January 1960.[173] It was designated an 'adaptive revision' (Anpassungsrevision) as it was being adapted to the IV. The most important amendment consisted of the introduction of the pro-rata-temporis ruling for partial pensions. If contributions had not been paid over a sufficiently long period, there was no longer a claim to a full pension but only to a partial pension. This was particularly significant for insured foreigners as they form the largest group with incomplete contribution periods. Transitional pensions were to be called extraordinary pensions from then on.[174]

The Fifth AHV Revision

The fifth AHV revision of 23 March 1961, in force from 1 January 1962 onwards, brought average nominal pension increases of 28–29 percent and contribution relief for self-employed persons with modest incomes by modifying the sliding contribution scale. It also reorganized state contributions from 1978 onwards and stipulated that pensions and the financial situtation of the AHV were to be re-examined every 5 years.[175]

This revision was partly instigated by a petition for a referendum of the Swiss Social Democratic Party on 22 December 1958 and of a non-party committee for higher AHV pensions on 22 May 1959. Both petitions were withdrawn in 1961[176] as the fifth AHV revision largely fulfilled their demands.

The sixth AHV Revision

The sixth AHV revision involved many amendments which were introduced by the Federal Law of 19 December 1963, in force from 1 January 1964.[177] For example: old and new pensions were raised by at least a third. The pensionable age for women was lowered from 63 to 62. From then on old age pensioners received supplementary pensions for wives between the ages of 45 and 60, amounting to 40 percent of the single old age pension, and for children who were still under age or receiving full-time education. The sinking contribution scale was modified once again in favour of the self-employed with low incomes by raising the income limits. The contribution rate remained at 4 percent. However, the legislature raised the state contribution considerably. Anticipated additional expenditure exceeded that of all the previous revisions put together.

Constitutional initiatives of the Swiss Committee of the Association of Old Age, Surviving Dependant and Disabled Pensioners (Vereinigung der Alters-, Hinterlassenen- und Invalidenrentner) of 7 June 1962 and of the 'Schweizerische Beobachter' of 12 July 1962 had given rise to the revision. They were withdrawn in 1965.[178]

A federal law of 6 October 1966, in force from 1 January 1967, increased pensions by 10 percent to compensate for price increases. This was an unnumbered AHV revision.[179]

The Seventh AHV Revision

On 25 August 1966 the Christian National Trade Union Congress (Christlichnationale Gewerkschaftsbund) submitted a constitutional initiative. It demanded *inter alia* an increase in pensions by one-third as well as the annual adjustment of pensions to general price increases and real income developments (indexing). This led to the seventh AHV revision of 4 October 1968, in force from 1 January 1969.[180] This affected eighty articles of the AHV law and decree. Here are a few of the many amendments. Compared with the sixth AHV revision, new pensions were raised by 50 percent to 60 percent and old pensions by one-third. Thus, the legislature differentiated between old and new pensions for the first time. Minimum and maximum pensions were now fixed at 200/320 Francs per month for old pensions and 200/400 Francs per month for new pensions. It introduced the institution of postponed old age pensions which did not attain any

significance. Old people in need also received compensation who had not received anything from the IV before reaching pensionable age. The relationship
between pensions and prices was to be investigated every 3 years and between
pensions and earned income every 6 years at the latest. For the first time the
legislature raised the contribution rates, from 4 percent to 5.2 percent. The self-
employed were granted a modest contribution discount of 0.6 percent so that they
only had to pay 4.6 percent instead of 5.2 percent. Furthermore, the sliding contribution scale was eased. The contributions of those who were not gainfully
employed were raised — more than three-fold — and now amounted to between 40
and 2000 Francs per annum. Government contributions were also reorganized.
Finally, a measure was taken which served to improve coordination among the
individual branches: works accident pensions of the SUVA and military insurance pensions were to be reduced if together with the AHV pensions they exceeded the last assumed annual income.[181]

With a federal law of 24 September 1970, in force from 1 January 1971, AHV
pensions were raised by 10 percent. This was not a numbered revision.[181a]

The Eighth AHV Revision

With the acceptance of the new Art. 34 quater of the federal constitution, the people had paved the way for the future development of the AHV: pensions were to
cover subsistence requirements whereas they had previously formed only the
basis to which more benefits had to be added until a reasonable standard of living
was secured. With the eighth AHV revision of 30 June 1972, which partly came
into force on 1 January 1973,[182] the federal authorities attained their new goal to
a great extent. Further development followed in two stages. From 1 January
1973, the single old age pension amounted to a minimum of 400 (previously 200)
and a maximum of 800 (previously 440) Francs per month. This was an increase
of 25 percent; thus, the minimum pension amounted to 500 and the maximum
pension to 1000 Francs per month. The old pensions were adjusted to the level of
the new pensions.[182a]

The massive increase in pensions made it seem expedient to adjust the level of
individual types of pensions to the single old age pension. An old age pension for
married couples now amounted to 150 percent (formerly 160 percent) and the
supplementary pension for the wife to 35 percent (previously 40 percent) of the
single old age pension. The amounts budgeted for widows', children's and orphans' pensions remained unchanged.

The position of women regarding statutory insurance was improved with the
eighth AHV revision. Since then, a woman can demand that half of the married
couple's pension is paid to her personally, without giving any reasons. The position of widows and divorced women was also improved in a number of
respects.[183]

Alterations to the level of benefits made an adjustment to contribution rates
unavoidable. Contributions for employed persons (half of which is paid by the
employer and half by the employed) were raised from 5.2 percent to 7.8 percent
and those for the self-employed from 4.6 percent to 6.8 percent of earned income.
The sliding contribution scale for the self-employed with lower incomes reduced
their contribution rates.[184] The contributions of persons who are not gainfully
employed were almost doubled; the new minimum amounted to 89 Francs and
the new maximum to 9000 Francs per annum. State funds were to finance a

quarter of the AHV from 1978 instead of from 1985 onwards. According to the new rules the 'Ausgleichsfonds' (compensation fund) was not to be lower than 1 year's expenditure.

Federal Acts (Bundesbeschlüsse) Prompted by the Recession

In 1974 the economic boom came to an end and recession began. The government had to change over to a deficit budget policy. From 1975–1977 it passed urgent and non-urgent federal acts providing for various measures during this period. *Inter alia*, it reduced the federal contribution to the AHV while having to adjust pensions in keeping with general price rises. Details of these complex acts are not to be included here.[185] It is important to mention, however, that the single old age pension was raised by about 5 percent to compensate for general inflation: the minimum pension amounted to 525 Francs and the maximum pension to 1050 Francs per month from January 1977.[186]

On 10 April 1975 Progressive Organizations of Switzerland (POCH/PSA) submitted a proposal for a referendum to reduce the retirement age from 65 to 60 for men and from 62 to 58 for women. This proposal was rejected by a large majority in the plebiscite of 26 February 1978.[187] The voters were aware that realizing such demands would involve considerable contribution increases.

The Ninth AHV Revision

The ninth AHV revision of 24 June 1977, brought into force in stages from 1 January 1979,[188] involved several significant amendments. These did not serve to develop benefits further but to consolidate social services from a long-term point of view. They also regulated numerous details in various sectors. As a referendum had been demanded, voting was held on 26 February 1978. The people voted for the bill by a large majority.[188a]

Some of the amendments deserve mention.[189] According to Art. 33 ter I AHVG, the Federal Council now has the mandate and competence to adjust 'ordinary pensions — usually every two years at the beginning of the calendar year — to wage and price developments' by re-assessing the pensions index. This 'is the arithmetic mean of the wage index computed by the Federal Office for Trade, Industry and Labour (Bundesamt für Industrie, Gewerbe und Arbeit) and of the national index of consumer prices' (§2). 'The Federal Council can adjust ordinary pensions later if this index has risen less than 5% within two years' (§4). Pension adjustments for the AHV and the IV are regulated by two supplements in the transitional rulings on the ninth AHV revision. Thus, pensions have been indexed in part by also being adjusted to wage developments with the pensions or mixed index. This is known as 'prozentuale Dynamik' (percentage indexing).[190] With its decree of 17 September 1979, the Federal Council adjusted pensions in accordance with the new ruling for the first time and fixed the single old age pension at a minimum of 550 Francs and maximum of 1100 Francs per month as of 1 January 1980.[190a]

The ninth AHV revision made no provisions for government contribution. Furthermore, it introduced limited compulsory contributions for old age pensioners who are gainfully employed.[191] It provided for a contribution-free amount of 750 Francs per month. Contributions for persons who are not gainfully employed were doubled.

The minimum age for a supplementary pension for a wife was raised from 45 to 55. The supplementary pension now amounts to only 30 percent (previously 35 percent) of the single old age pension. The pension for married couples will only be paid out in future when the wife has reached the age of 62 (previously 60). The AHV also provides assistance for disabled old age pensioners. Furthermore, it will also grant assistance to promote old age welfare. Since 1 January 1975, for example, it has been contributing towards the building of homes for old people.

When the AHVG was passed, no ruling was made — this was presumably an oversight — for cases where the same event gives rise both to AHV pensions — for example, of the widow and children — and also to a claim against a liable third party. Thus, the damaged party could accumulate these claims. After the increase in pensions due to the eighth AHV revision, this occasionally resulted in extreme 'overcompensation'. Thus, the ninth AHV revision introduced the right of simultaneous recourse to the AHV and also to the IV: some claims to damages are transferred to the AHV/IV if and insofar as this compensates the damages with its benefits in accordance with the law on liability.[192]

The ninth AHV revision finally gave the Federal Council the competence to make the necessary regulations to prevent unjustified accumulation of benefits and to regulate relations with other social insurance branches.[193] Thus, it created a basis for the improvement of coordination within the social insurance system.

The Tenth AHV Revision — in Preparation

Preliminary work for the tenth AHV revision has already begun. The demands of women are to be the central issue of this revision. These are *inter alia*: a flexible age level for old age pensions; abolition of the institution of old age pensions for married couples and the introduction of an independent pension claim for the wife; re-examination of the question of the pensionable age of the wife if the flexible age level is not introduced. Old age pensions of divorced women ought also to be reformed.[194]

Repercussions of the AHV Revisions on Other Laws

Practically every AHV revision involved amendments to other branches of social insurance. Usually the IV was most affected as it is closely linked with the AHV.

MILITARY INSURANCE[195]

Partial Revision of the Federal Law on Military Insurance (MVG) by Resolution of the Federal Council on 27 April 1945

Between the two world wars the government made several attempts to pass a new law on military insurance, to no avail. Thus, during the Second World War the Federal Law of 1901 and several provisions of the Federal Law of 1914 still applied. However, the Federal Council made full use of its powers and amended the existing law. In September 1944 the head of the Federal Military Department (Eidg. Militärdepartement) submitted a draft for a new law which was revised by a committee of experts. The latter came to the conclusion that it was impossible to totally revise the Federal Law on Military Insurance (MVG) within a reasonable period and thus only the most urgent demands were to be realized.

The Federal Council followed this proposal and, using its special powers, it passed the Resolution of 27 April 1945 on the Partial Revision of the MVG.

The MVG of 20 September 1949

Dr Arnold, a federal judge, was commissioned shortly after the war by the Federal Military Department to draw up another bill. The Federal Council presented this to the National Assembly with its communication of 22 September 1947; the MVG was passed on 20 September 1949 and is still valid today. As a referendum was not demanded, the law could be put into force on 1 January 1950.[196]

Adjustment of Benefits through Partial Revisions of the MVG

Since then, the MVG has been amended by five partial revisions.[197] These served predominantly to adjust benefits to general price increases. The revision of 19 December 1963 is particularly noteworthy. With this revision the federal government introduced the law of liability institution of satisfaction into the MVG and thus into social insurance (Art. 40bis). The MVG has also been affected several times by other federal laws. Thus, Art. 48 of the Civil Defence Law of 23 March 1962 stipulates that persons doing civil defence service are insured with the MV.

Preparatory Work for a New MVG

From 1972 to 1976 preparatory work was done for a new law. First of all the Division (Abteilung) — now the Federal Office (Bundesamt) — for Military Insurance worked on a preliminary draft. Then a board of experts made its report to the Federal Military Department in 1976.[198] However, since then the idea of total or even of partial revision of the law has been abandoned.[199]

UNEMPLOYMENT INSURANCE[199a]

Legislative Powers of the Federal Government

On 6 July 1947, the people accepted the new economic article of the federal constitution and Art. 34ter at the same time. The latter gave the federal government legislative powers in the field of unemployment insurance and unemployment welfare, with considerable restrictions of course, since, for example, the cantons alone continued to be competent to establish public unemployment insurance schemes and to introduce compulsory insurance.

Federal Law of 22 June 1951

Now that the federal government had this new competence, it appointed successive boards of experts to work out drafts for an unemployment law. To do this they could build upon the Authorization Act of the Federal Council of 14 July 1942 as this had proved largely successful. With its communication of 16 August 1950 the Federal Council presented its draft for a new law to the National Assembly. The latter passed the bill on 22 June 1951. As there was no referendum the law came into force on 1 January 1952.[200] Of course, unemployment insurance did not play an important role in the following two decades because of the economic boom. In 1971 and 1972 claims made on unemployment insurance reached an all-time low as it only paid out money to 1000 insured persons.[201]

Compulsory Unemployment Insurance According to the Federal Act of 8 October 1976 (the so-called 'Übergangsordnung' — Interim Ruling)

The legal provisions proved inadequate when the recession began in 1975. The National Assembly thus took numerous measures by means of emergency federal act. On 13 June 1976 the people accepted a new Art. 34novies BV on unemployment insurance which replaced the relevant provisions of the previous Art. 34ter. It states that unemployment insurance is compulsory for all employed persons as far as the government is concerned. With the Federal Act of 8 October 1976 the Federal Assembly decided by means of the so-called 'Übergangsordnung' on the introduction of compulsory unemployment insurance for all employed persons. This rule is limited to 5 years.[202]

FAMILY ALLOWANCES[202a]

Article 34 Quinquies BV

On 13 May 1942 the action committee 'Für die Familie' (For the Family) handed in a constitutional initiative demanding that the federal government was to have the competence to legislate on family assistance. The initiative prompted the National Assembly to elaborate a counterproposal. The latter was accepted in the plebiscite of 26 November 1945 as Art. 34 quinquies BV. According to §2 the federal government can set up 'Familienausgleichskassen' (family compensation schemes) and declare compulsory membership either for everyone or for individual sections of the community. Thus, it is competent to introduce rulings on child and family allowances. The initiative was withdrawn.

The Federal Law of 20 June 1952

After the war the federal government incorporated the Federal Council's Authorization Act of 9 June 1944 on family allowances for agriculture into the ordinary law with the federal acts of 20 June 1947 and of 22 June 1949. In this way it gained time for the issue of the Federal Law of 20 June 1952 which is still valid today although several slight amendments have been made to it in the meantime.[203]

No Comprehensive Federal Government Ruling

On 16 August 1957 the Federal Council commissioned a board of experts to examine the question whether a federal law on family allowances was to be created. In its report of 27 February 1959 the board approved the issue of a general 'Federal Law on the Compulsory Payment of Child Allowances to Employed Persons'. However, this suggestion met with stiff opposition. The Federal Department of the Interior returned to this idea again later and asked on 11 November 1968 for the cantons' and leading associations' opinions on it. These showed that there was no need for such a federal law as the cantonal provisions were adequate. Thus, the federal government continued only to pay out family and child allowances for a small section of the population, namely agricultural workers and smallholders. Special regulations exist for federal officials which is part of civil service law.[204]

INCOME COMPENSATION[204a]

When the economic article of the federal constitution was revised — accepted by the plebiscite of 6 July 1947 — Art. 34ter was also revised. It grants the federal government, *inter alia*, the power to issue regulations on wage and income compensation for persons doing military service. Thus, the federal government was empowered to integrate into regular legislation rulings made during the war by the Federal Council's various authorization acts. With the Federal Law on Compensation for the Loss of Earnings of Persons Doing Military Service (EOG) of 25 September 1952,[205] the federal government condensed the four compensation systems into a uniform compensation system.[206] The law was revised several times to adjust to changed economic conditions. Art. 22 bis BV, accepted by the plebiscite of 24 May 1959, granted the federal government the competence to legislate on civil defence (civil defence article). On 23 March 1962 the federal councils voted in favour of the Federal Law on Civil Defence (Zivilschutzgesetz).[207] It grants persons in civil defence a claim to compensation for their loss of earnings. The EOG was not given an appropriately amended title until the revision of 18 December 1968. This was amended again by the revision of 3 October 1975; the title now reads 'BG über die Erwerbsersatzordnung für Wehrund Zivilschutzpflichtige' (Federal Law on Income Compensation for Persons Doing Military Service and Civil Defence).[208]

DISABILITY INSURANCE[208a]

Origins of the Law on Disability Insurance (IVG)

According to the original text of Art. 34 quater BV, the federal government was bound to establish old age and surviving dependants' insurance but was, however, only authorized — and not bound — 'to introduce disability insurance at a later date'. Once the AHV had been established, the Federal Council could turn its hand to preliminary work on disability insurance. It commissioned a board of experts on 13 September 1955; the latter delivered its report, dated 30 November 1956. This provided the Federal Council with the basis for a draft bill which it presented to the National Assembly in its communication of 24 October 1958.[209] The National Assembly passed this bill surprisingly quickly, on 19 June 1959, as the Federal Law on Disability Insurance. The close link between the IV and the AHV, regarding organization, financing and pensions, eased the legislative passage. A referendum was not demanded. Thus, the law came into force on 1 January 1960.[210] Beforehand, however, on 13 October 1959, the Federal Council had to pass a resolution on the introduction of disability insurance which was primarily intended to establish the institutions required for the implementation of disability insurance. These are the IV commissions and the IV regional agencies. However, the regulations on implementation still had to be worked out. This was not done until the law came into force on 17 January 1961. The Federal Council's resolution on disability insurance regulates the wide-ranging material in 117 articles.[211]

Art. 85 IVG made extremely good provision for persons who were already disabled on 1 January 1960. They were insured as they were 'entitled to a claim in accordance with the statutory provisions'. 'It is assumed that disability existed when this law came into force'. If the legislature had only provided for benefits for persons who became disabled after the said date, disability insurance would not have become fully effective for several decades. Thus, in 1960 the IV commissions received 91 523 applications, whereas in 1961 these numbered only 48 453. It soon became clear that there were far more disabled persons in Switzerland than the authorities had assumed when drafting the law.[212]

Amendment of the IVG

Amendments to AHV legislation regularly affected the IV; thus, with time IV pensions had to be raised considerably. Legislation on disability insurance was also thoroughly revised. In the autumn of 1964 a board of experts, commissioned by the Federal Department of the Interior, examined questions regarding revision. The board's report was published in September 1966. The Federal Council adopted most of the proposals in its communication to the National Assembly of 27 February 1967 and in its draft bill. The law was passed on 5 October 1967 and came into force on 1 January 1968.[213] The revision covered practically every sphere of IV without affecting the structure. It led to the amendment of about 100 articles of the IVG and the IVV.[214]

The New Article 34 quater BV and the IV

Art. 34 quater BV which had been accepted by the plebiscite of 3 December 1972 now forms the basis at constitutional law for both old age and surviving dependants' pensions and disability pensions. Thus, the 'Three Pillar Principle' anchored in it also applies to disability insurance. It is important to specifically mention §7: 'The federal government promotes the integration of the disabled. . . .' Thus, the idea of integration is also reflected in the federal constitution.[216]

SICKNESS INSURANCE[217]

Fundamental Revision of 13 March 1964

Ever since the KUVG had been in force, the competent department of the Federal Council had tried on several occasions to revise the first section concerning sickness insurance. Drafts for a revision, elaborated at its instigation in 1921 and 1954, failed.[218] After disability insurance had been introduced the Federal Department of the Interior began to try again. It drew up principles for the revision of sickness insurance and submitted them with an explanatory report, dated 25 May 1960, to the cantons and associations for their comments.[219] Thereafter, the Federal Council could submit the draft of a Federal Law on the Amendment of the First Section of the KUVG to the National Assembly with its communication of 5 June 1961. This law excluded the so-called 'Doctors' Law' which covers the triangular relationship between sickness insurance schemes, the insured and the doctors as the Federal Council thought this would have posed too great a threat to the bill's success. Only the State Council requested proposals on its regulation. The Department of the Interior succeeded in finding a compromise solution by negotiating with representatives of the medical profession and the sickness insurances. However, this solution was rejected later by the Swiss

Medical Society (Schweizerische Aerztekammer). The Federal Council submitted a draft for the reform of the Doctors' Law with its supplementary communication of 16 November 1962.[220] Several items of the draft were amended by parliament. The amending law was passed on 13 March 1964. It was not contested by a demand for a referendum. This was the first far-reaching revision concerning sickness insurance to be made since the KUVG first came into being in 1911. Numerous rulings on implementation also had to be amended. The sickness insurances had to adapt their charters and regulations to the new law by 1 January 1966 at the latest. The amending law did not become fully effective until this date although it predominantly came into force on 1 January 1965.[221]

Reform of the Administration of Justice

The amendment brought numerous improvements, particularly for the insured, relating, for example, to personal liberty, statutory minimum benefits, the complex Doctors' Law[222] and state contributions. The reorganization of the administration of justice was of major significance. Instead of the previous fragmentation of laws, the law was largely standardized by federal law. Thus, litigation between insured and the sickness insurances is now settled by the cantonal insurance courts in the first instance and thereafter by the Federal Insurance Court as the supreme court of appeal. The recognized sickness insurance schemes have the competence to issue regulations and thus, as far as the government is concerned, they have sovereign power, similar to public administration.[223]

'Flimsermodell'

In the years following the revision of 1964, demands were frequently made in parliament for further fundamental amendment of the KUVG. The Federal Department of the Interior thus commissioned a large board of experts, comprising fifty-five members, to draw up proposals for the reform of sickness insurance. The board presented a thorough written report on 11 February 1972. Its proposals have become known as the 'Flimsermodell' as the board had held most of its meetings in the spa of Flims. It proposed introducing nationwide compulsory insurance for certain aspects, such as for hospitalization and sick pay. This 'Flimsermodell' inspired numerous groups of the population to draw up their own models – about a dozen in all.[224]

The 'Double No' of 8 December 1974

Long before the report was presented, on 31 March 1970, the Swiss Social Democratic Party submitted a constitutional initiative 'for a social sickness insurance' with which it demanded a new Art. 34bis. This contained a wide-ranging programme for the reform of sickness insurance which also involved nationwide compulsory insurance in many other respects. Subsequently, the National Assembly adopted a counterproposal for the revision of Art. 34bis and integrated important points in it from both the 'Flimsermodell' and the initiative mentioned above. However, in the plebiscite of 8 December 1974 the people clearly expressed their two-fold rejection of the initiative and of the counterproposal. The people did not want federal compulsory insurance for hospital care. A new board of experts also made no headway with its report of 5 July 1977.[225] This board wanted to introduce a levy of a percentage of the wage to provide an additional source of finance for hospital care insurance. There was great opposition to this. Thus, the Federal Department of the Interior dropped the matter. Under the title 'Teilrevision Krankenversicherung' (Partial Revision of Sickness Insurance) the Federal Department published the 'report and preliminary draft, 1978'. It is not aiming at 'the systematic reform of sickness insurance but is limiting itself to improvements in the present-day system, namely in the sphere of persons insured, of benefits, of cost reduction and financing'. There are plans for the Federal Council to submit a communication and a draft to the National Assembly in 1980 on the partial revision of the KUVG.[226]

REGULATION OF SUPPLEMENTARY BENEFITS TO THE AHV/IV[227]

The Federal Law of 19 March 1965

According to the original concept, the AHV/IV was only to be a basic insurance. Further benefits had to be added to the AHV/IV pensions to ensure that pensioners had a sufficient income to live on. Works' and other pension schemes had to be borne in mind. However, even after the introduction of the AHV/IV there was uncertainty as to when an appropriate federal law would be passed. Thus, a solution suggested itself which could be realized relatively quickly: supplementary benefits. These were to be paid to persons who were still 'needy' despite the AHV/IV pensions. The Federal Law on Supplementary Benefits to the AHV/IV of 19 March 1965[228] was passed as a law on subsidies: the federal government grants the cantons allowances if these pay AHV/IV pensioners, whose income and wealth does not exceed certain limits, supplementary benefits. The basic difference between ordinary AHV/IV pensions and these supplementary benefits is that the supplementary benefits are linked to a means test. Thus, they closely approach the idea of welfare while differing from it as they are 'standardized', i.e. fixed by law so that their level can be determined in the individual case.

There is no doubt that supplementary benefits have met a great social need and have provided relief for countless people; only their sting, the means test to prove true need, has hurt a great many entitled persons and deterred them from making a claim to benefits which are due to them.

Since the ordinary full pensions have been designed to provide a reasonable standard of living, supplementary benefits have decreased in importance. Nevertheless, plenty of people in Switzerland do not receive full pensions but only partial pensions. They are often still dependent on supplementary benefits.[229]

CANTONAL RULINGS

Several cantons make use of an authorization of the Federal Law on Supplementary Benefits to grant old age, surviving dependants' and disability assistance in various forms, in addition to supplementary benefits, to assist needy pensioners.

ADJUSTMENTS TO BENEFITS

Legal provisions on determining 'a reasonable standard of living' — for example, income levels — have been frequently changed and adapted in line with general price increases.[230] If the federal government raised AHV/IV pensions above the level of inflation, supplementary benefits sometimes had to be cut. Occasionally the recipients were rather bitter about this.[231]

Revision of Compulsory Accident Insurance (UVG)[232]

'Minor Revisions'

Several 'minor revisions' have been made to the KUVG with regard to accident insurance; these affected only a few provisions and did not change the structure of the law at all. They served, for example, to adapt benefits to the general price rises by increasing the insured wage. The Federal Law on Cost-of-living Bonuses for Pensioners of the Swiss Accident Insurance Institution and of the Military and Civil Labour Service of 20 December 1962 committed the SUVA to pay cost-of-living bonuses to its pensioners 'in accordance with this law' on top of already fixed pensions.[233]

Total Revision

In 1967 the Federal Department of the Interior commissioned a board of experts to draw up proposals for the revision of accident insurance. The board presented its report on 14 September 1973. The Federal Council submitted the draft of a new accident insurance law to the National Assembly with its communication of 18 August 1976.[234] Based on the afore-mentioned report, the Federal Council proposed the total revision of the law; sickness and accident insurance were to be treated in a separate law.[235]

Accident insurance was now to be declared compulsory for all employed persons. The previous monopoly of the SUVA is to be replaced by the principle of multiplicity of insurance institutions. Thus, in future, private insurance companies and sickness insurance schemes can participate. Improved coordination with other insurance branches, i.e. with AHV/IV, is aimed at in the benefits sector.

The National Council accepted the bill with a few insignificant amendments in March 1979. The board of the State Council has started to confer but has not finished its consultations yet. The State Council will only deal with the bill in the course of 1980. The new law should come into force, if at all, on 1 January 1982 at the earliest.

Works' Old Age, Surviving Dependants' and Disability Pension Schemes (BVG)

The Present Ruling

Within the framework of the 'Three Pillar Principle' works' or staff pension schemes are to form the second pillar which, along with the first pillar, the state AHV/IV, enables all employed persons to continue to enjoy their usual standard of living, insofar as this is reasonable, when faced with the risks of old age, disablement and death. In Switzerland, there are over 16 000 private staff pension schemes, usually in the legal form of foundations. In addition, there are also staff pension schemes under public law for civil servants and employees of the community. Together these institutions have funds exceeding 30 000 million Francs.[237] The federal government has passed some rulings on staff pension schemes; for example, Art. 331–331 (c), Art. 339 (d) OR, in the text of 25 June 1971 (Revision of the Law on Employment Contracts) and Art. 89bis ZGB, which designates staff pension foundations as a special type of foundation.[238] However, this ruling does not fulfil the legislative mandates of the federal government as stipulated in Art. 34 quater in §3 and 4 of the federal constitution.

Draft for the Federal Law on Works'
Old Age, Surviving Dependants' and
Disability Pension Schemes (BVG)

A board of experts, appointed by the Federal Department of the Interior, proposed the introduction of federal compulsory insurance for staff pensions in its
report of 16 July 1970. At the beginning of 1972 the AHV/IV commission set up
a committee for staff or works pension schemes. This committee drew up the
'Report and Principles with regard to a Federal Law', dated 25 September 1972,
and at the end of 1974 it submitted a preliminary draft on the subject, including a
short report. The Federal Council incorporated much of this preliminary draft in
its own bill which it presented to the National Assembly in its communication on
the Federal Law on Works' Old Age, Surviving Dependants' and Disability Pension Schemes of 19 December 1975 (BVG).[239] The National Council approved
the bill in the autumn session of 1977. Since then the commission of the State
Council has been working on it. It is investigating solutions which deviate fundamentally from the plan of the Federal Council and the National Council and
which are less perfectionist. It is impossible to predict at the moment when the
State Council will concern itself with the bill and what the outcome will be. In addition, there are indications that a referendum will be demanded. The fate of the
BVG is uncertain at present.

CONCLUDING REMARKS

Having discussed Swiss social insurance with regard to currently valid law and its
history in the first two sections, a few individual points will be considered in the
following section.

GENERAL

Swiss social insurance has not been built up on the basis of a master plan. Indeed,
the federal government has proceeded pragmatically by passing individual laws
to regulate, step by step, those sectors which seemed favoured at the time by the
prevailing trends. The initial development and expansion of social insurance is a
good example, showing that the federal government cannot mould social policy
according to doctrine but has to do whatever pragmatic political thinking considers possible and feasible in a given situation. This special feature of Swiss
politics is deeply rooted in the institutions under constitutional law which are now
to be explained.

STATUTORY REFERENDUM AND CONSTITUTIONAL INITIATIVE

Their legal structures have already been sketched (cf. above p. 385) and the way
they work has been shown in the context of the history of the various laws. Here,
once again, are some of the main features.

Facultative Referendum

The facultative referendum has held the emergence and development of social insurance very much in check and has, in part, channelled it along lines which was
not 'programmed' by the authorities. This applies equally to the plebiscites of

1900 and 1931 which rejected both the 'Lex Forrer', designed to regulate sickness and accident insurance, and the 'Lex Schulthess', aiming at the introduction of an old age and surviving dependants' insurance. The KUVG, regulating sickness and accident insurance, was not adopted by the people until the plebiscite of 4 February 1912, i.e. 12 years after the plebiscite on the 'Lex Forrer'. The second bill on the AHV did not meet with the people's approval until 16 years after the plebiscite on the 'Lex Schultess', on 6 July 1947. The ruling on sickness insurance in the KUVG provided a completely different solution from that of the failed 'Lex Forrer'. Instead of a comprehensive sickness insurance, a law only on subsidies and promotion came into force which, moreover, did not make insurance compulsory throughout Switzerland. So far all attempts to make sickness insurance compulsory for all have failed. In other branches of social insurance, however, such as accident insurance and AHV/IV, insurance has become compulsory. According to the law currently in force, the AHV also deviates fundamentally in major spheres from the solutions proposed by the 'Lex Schulthess' for example in methods of financing benefits and insurance institutions.

The referendum casts its shadow before it actually takes place. This is noticeable when boards of experts or the competent Department of the Federal Council prepare a legal bill. It is often apparent whether certain proposals will meet with opposition or not. This applies particularly if the competent Department submits its proposed solutions for a new bill to interested circles for comment. The 'Report and Preliminary Draft, November 1978' of the Federal Department of the Interior gives a vivid picture of the thorny partial revision of sickness insurance. On p. 2 it describes the proposals of a board of experts and on p. 3 f. the reactions to these proposals, some of which were unfavourable. On p. 8 ff. the conclusions drawn by the Department from these reactions are described. Thus, clearly hinting at a referendum, the Department indicates on p. 8 that the draft bill 'would be strongly incriminated politically' by federal compulsory hospital care insurance for everyone; and on p. 9 it renounces the idea of partial financing of insurance for hospital care by percentages of wages because such a proposal had 'only met with occasional approval' (p. 4) when submitted to interested parties for comment.[240]

The facultative referendum makes Swiss democracy a democracy of consensus, particularly in the sphere of social insurance; it is imperative that federal authorities have the approval of the most important groups in the population whenever decisive reforms are to be realized.[241]

Constitutional Initiative

The constitutional initiative first became important for social insurance after the Second World War. From 2 December 1969 to 13 April 1970, for example, no less than three initiatives were handed in on the further development of old age, surviving dependants' and disability pensions. These stimulated the Federal Council and National Assembly to draw up a counterproposal at constitutional level which was presented to the people with the constitutional initiative on 3 December 1972. The people accepted the counterproposal and rejected the initiative. The three constitutional intiatives made the Federal Council and the National Assembly decide to accelerate the above-mentioned development considerably. Furthermore, they largely fulfilled the function of the non-existent statutory initiative; each contained a complete programme for the future arrangement of the named sectors which stipulated terms to the legislature. The constitutional initiative of 31 March 1970 also fulfilled this function. It proposed a new Art. 34bis BV on sickness and maternity insurance. It also set out a programme to commit the legislature to a specific arrangement of these branches. Furthermore, this initiative was intended to make the legislature accelerate the revisionary work already in progress. However, it was rejected, along with the National Assembly's counterproposal, in the plebiscite of 8 December 1974.

Recently the constitutional initiative has acted like a motor giving the federal authorities the push to act on social insurance. In cases where they set out a programme for the legislature, they led, to a certain extent, to the population being able to form an opinion on this programme during the preliminary stages of voting. As the last-mentioned initiative on sickness and accident insurance was rejected, it is quite likely that the disputed items of the programme, for example federal compulsory insurance for hospital care, will not be carried through for some time.[242]

DIVERSITY IN SOCIAL INSURANCE[243]

The great diversity which is so characteristic of Swiss social insurance is already apparent from previous references.

Institutions

The large number of different institutions points to this diversity.[244] Let us first examine the difference between single and multiple institutions. The SUVA has the monopoly in its sector, excluding other institutions from compulsory accident insurance. The role of the Federal Office for Military Insurance is similar. At the other extreme is sickness insurance: numerous sickness insurances compete, at least partially, with one another to enlist individual members and to conlude collective policies amongst the same population groups. This applies in a similar fashion to unemployment insurance also. The 'Ausgleichskassen' (compensation institutions) are midway between these two positions. They are also to be graded as multiple institutions but they do not compete with one another as each has its own sphere of competence.[245]

The legal forms of insurance institutions are also marked by diversity. Many institutions are public; some have and others do not have legal status. Those with legal status include, for example, the SUVA and the 'Ausgleichskassen'; those without legal status are several of the public sickness insurance schemes as well as unemployment insurance schemes which are integrated into communal or cantonal administration. Public corporations must also be mentioned as sickness insurances frequently take this form, i.e. public sickness insurances which are based on membership. Numerous sickness and unemployment insurances are subjects of private law, namely associations, cooperatives or foundations. These are usually called private sickness and unemployment insurances to differentiate them from public insurance schemes.

If one wants to apply the terms direct and indirect state administration[246] it is obvious that most of the institutions must be counted among those subject to direct state administration: they are administrative units which have been separated from federal administration itself. There are only a few exceptions to this, for example, the Federal Office for Military Insurance as well as the two federal government 'Ausgleichskassen'. In Switzerland, social insurance is the most obvious example of direct state administration.

The creation of a single, hierarchically ordered administrative apparatus — the 'standard insurance' — would hardly be consistent with the federalist structure of Switzerland. Moreover, it cannot be proved that such a 'standard insurance' would be 'cheaper', i.e. entail less administrative costs, than the present system.

The idea of a single institution particularly goes against Swiss tradition which bases innovation on developments of the past. Art. 34 bis §1 BV stipulates for sickness insurance that the legislature has to take existing sickness insurances into consideration. The legislature must also consider existing private and public unemployment insurances when organizing unemployment insurance. Recourse must also be taken to the already existing 'Ausgleichskassen' established during the Second World War for the implementation of AHV/IV. The federal government envisages maintaining the order of existing staff pension schemes (the second 'pillar') of both private industry and the public authorities. There are also plans to allow sickness insurances and even private insurance companies to act as the implementing institutions for more extensive compulsory accident insurance of the employed.

The Insured

The circle of persons insured differs in the individual branches. This is due partially to the juxtaposition of voluntary and obligatory insurance.[247] For example, the oldest existing law on social insurance, the KUVG, does not make sickness insurance compulsory from the federal government's point of view. However, the cantons are entitled to bring in compulsory insurance for the whole population or for individual classes. Accident insurance is compulsory for certain groups of employed persons from the federal government's point of view. At the same time the KUVG provides two voluntary accident insurances for other groups of persons; one of these insurances strongly resembles liability insurance. However, these voluntary insurances have never been brought in. Fundamentally, the AHV/IV is compulsory for the whole population; however, contributions to it are only voluntary for Swiss people living abroad.

According to the current transitional regulations, unemployment insurance is basically compulsory for employed persons. According to the new Art. 34novies BV the federal government is also to deal with voluntary insurance for the self-employed.

Social insurance is both for certain classes and for the people as a whole.[248] AHV/IV is designed as the people's insurance, covering the entire population. The KUVG offers sickness insurance to the whole population in principle, though the same law has established accident insurance as one for employed persons and thus a 'class insurance'. Unemployment insurance in its present form is also a 'class insurance', limited to employed persons. However, as already mentioned, this is later to be available for the self-employed. Family allowances were established as a 'class insurance'; however, apart from agricultural workers it includes smallholders and self-employed persons.

Financing

The financing side of social insurance is also marked by great diversity. This applies to the financing systems.[249] The allocation procedure (Umlageverfahren) is laid down for military insurance. A variation of the level premium system (Kapitaldeckungsverfahren), namely a pensions funding system known as the 'Rentendeckungsverfahren' or 'Rentenwertumlageverfahren', had already been provided by the KUVG when compulsory accident insurance was brought in. Most of the other branches of social insurance, i.e. AHV/IV and sickness insurance, are financed by means of the allocation procedure with a fluctuation fund.

The accident insurance funds come only from premiums, in military insurance they come from taxes. In the AHV/IV, sickness insurance and other branches, however, mixed systems exist; thus, these insurances are financed by premiums (contributions) and public funds (taxes), i.e. by contributions from the public authorities.[250] The amount of contributions from the authorities differ from branch to branch.

The contributions or premiums are fixed according to different criteria. From the very beginning, the KUVG fixed a wage-related premium for the SUVA, following the German pattern, while in sickness insurance only the individual premium existed at first, replaced later by the wage-related premium with the statutory introduction of collective insurance. Wage-related premiums became the norm in most other branches in which contributions are paid. In AHV/IV other factors, including property, had to be considered for persons who are not gainfully employed.

The principle of equivalence, i.e. equilibrium between the premiums on the one hand and the risks and the insurance benefits on the other, plays a large part in some cases for example in compulsory works' accident insurance, and only a minor or no part at all in others, for example in AHV/IV. The principle of solidarity only came into the foreground when the AHV/IV was introduced. The earned income on which contributions are based has no upper limit so that persons with higher incomes pay contributions in favour of persons with lower incomes. In this respect the contribution is no longer a premium in the insurance sense but a form of public tax (a so-called 'Gemengsteuer').[251] There are also considerable differences with regard to persons who owe contributions. However, these will not be listed here.[252]

Eligibility for Benefits

Eligibility for benefits[253] is also extremely varied in scope. Different principles govern the legal or statutory aspects. In many branches, benefits have been greatly developed since the Second World War, for example, the AHV/IV pensions have been increased far above general inflation rates. Benefits have also been considerably increased in sickness insurance due, for example, to the revision of the KUVG of 13 March 1964 but also due to the insurances' own action, i.e. without legal compulsion.

LEGAL TRENDS

Move Away From Private to Public Law

When the KUVG was passed it recognized insurance conditions both under public and private law. Insurance situations in compulsory accident insurance and in sickness insurance for public sickness insurances were governed by public law, while private sickness insurances were governed by private law. Originally both solutions also existed in unemployment insurance, as in sickness insurance.

The Federal Law on Unemployment Insurance of 22 June 1951 was innovatory in this respect. It granted private unemployment insurance schemes the competence to issue orders in individual cases and thus to fix both the rights and duties of the insured unilaterally. Such decrees can gain formal legal force. With this ruling the federal government granted subjects under private law — associations and cooperatives — sovereign power. This development was continued with the KUVG revision of 13 March 1964 whereby private sickness insurances were also granted the competence to issue orders and thus have sovereign power. The federal government is following the same trend with its current revision of the KUVG with regard to accident insurance, for it wants to grant private insurance companies which are licenced as accident insurance institutions sovereign power. In the other branches, the insurance condition was conceived in accordance with public law right from the beginning.

This move away from private to public law has also been reflected in the administration of justice. Originally the civil courts were responsible for judging litigation arising from insurance situations under private law. With the change to public law, the legislature also reorganized the administration of justice by replacing civil courts with administrative courts — cantonal insurance courts, appeal courts, etc. This development found its ultimate expression in the Federal Insurance Court, the supreme court for the whole of social insurance, and in the fact that social insurance jurisdiction was integrated into administrative jurisdiction with the amendment to the Federal Law on the Organization of Federal Administration of Justice of 20 December 1968.

Swiss social insurance indeed sets an example by giving subjects under private law sovereign power and by changing institutions under private law into institutions under public law.

Problems of Coordination

The pragmatic regulation of social insurance through individual laws has shown up deficiencies of coordination increasingly clearly over ten years. Such deficiencies are primarily to be seen in the rulings on eligibility for benefits but also on contributions and in the relation of social insurance law to liability law. Similar questions have been settled differently, and sometimes not at all, in the various branches. This applies, for example, to the statute of limitations, to forfeiture, to the reclaim of unowed payments, to time limits and to the interplay of various benefits. The time has now come for the legislature to pay greater attention to those problems by coordinating parallel regulations better, by creating a General Section, or by closing insurance gaps.

Pending Legislative Mandates of the Federal Constitution

Apart from articles on competence, the federal constitution also contains mandates for the federal legislature concerning social insurance.[254] The legislature has not yet fulfilled its mandate to regulate staff or works' pensions schemes (the second 'pillar') in accordance with Art. 34 quater BV. However, a bill has been brought before the National Assembly for consideration. The Federal Council has not yet drawn up a draft bill for the third pillar (on personal provisions), as stipulated in section 6 of the same article. Furthermore, according to Art. 34 quinquies section 4 BV the federal government is committed to establishing

'statutory maternity insurance'. An appropriate bill is not yet under consideration. The KUVG includes a few provisions on maternity; however, these do not
fulfil the constitutional mandate.

BIBLIOGRAPHY

In most cases only the name of the author and abbreviated titles from this list are quoted in the
notes; other bibliographic references are to be found in the notes.
Aubert, J.F. (1967). *Traité de droit constitutionnel suisse,* 2 Bände, Neuchâtel/Paris.
Bassegoda, J. (1976). *75 Jahre Militärversicherung, 1901–1976,* Bern.
Benöhr, H.P. (1977). *Crise et législation sociale: l'exemple du 19ᵉ siècle.* Université de Neuchâtel,
Conférences universitaires.
Bigler-Eggenberger, M. (1979). *Soziale Sicherung der Frau,* Bern und Frankfurt a.M.
Burckardt, W. (1931). *Kommentar der schweizerischen Bundesverfassung vom 29. Mai 1874,* 3. Aufl., Bern.
Fleiner, F. (1923). *Schweizerisches Bundesstaatsrecht,* 1. Aufl., Tübingen.
Fleiner, G. (1949). *Schweizerisches Bundesrecht,* Neubearbeitung der ersten Hälfte des
gleichnamigen Werkes von F. Fleiner, Zürich.
Furrer A. (1952). *Entstehung und Entwicklung der schweiz. Sozialversicherung,* Freiburger Diss.
Gautschi, W. (1968). *Der Landesstreik 1918,* Zürich.
Graf, J. (1979). 'Aus der Geschichte der AHV', *ZAK,* S. 291, 386 und 525.
Grobéty, D. (1979). *La Suisse aux origines du droit ouvrier,* Freiburger Diss.
Gruner, E. (1968). *Die Arbeiter in der Schweiz im 19. Jahrhundert.* Soziale Lage, Organisation,
Verhältnis zu Arbeitgeber und Staat, Bern.
Hauser, A. (1961). *Schweizerische Wirtschafts- und Sozialgeschichte,* Zürich und Stuttgart.
Holzer, M. (1954). *Kommentar zum Bundesgesetz über die Arbeitslosenversicherung,* Zürich.
Hug, W. (1963). Privatversicherung und Sozialversicherung, *SZS,* S. 1, 98 und 175
Hug, W. (1971). *Kommentar zum Arbeitsgesetz,* Bern.
Hug, W. (1979). Die Kodifikation des Arbeitsrechts, *SZS,* S. 161 ff.
Landmann, J. (1904). *Die Arbeiterschutzgesetzgebung der Schweiz,* Basel.
Maurer, A. (1963). *Recht und Praxis der schweizerischen obligatorischen Unfallversicherung,* 2. Aufl., Bern.
Maurer, A. (1974). *Grundriss des Bundessozialversicherungsrechts, Ringbuch,* Zürich.
Maurer, A. (1975). *Kumulation und Subrogation in der Sozial- und Privatversicherung,* Bern.
Maurer, A. (1976). *Einführung in das schweizerische Privatversicherungsrecht,* Bern.
Maurer, A. (1979a). *Schweizerisches Sozialversicherungsrecht,* Band I, Allgemeiner Teil, Bern.
Maurer, A. (1979b). Die soziale Altersicherung der Frau in der Schweiz, *SZS,* S. 187 ff.
Müller, S. (1978). *Entstehung und Entwicklung der AHV von 1945–1978,* Freiburg.
Oertli, U. (1955). Unfallversicherung, obligatorische, in *Handbuch der schweizerischen Volkswirtschaft,*
Band II, Ausgabe, S. 463 f.
Pfluger, A. *Juristische Kartothek der Krankenversicherung,* 2. Aufl., Solothurn.
Piccard, P. (1917). *Haftpflichtpraxis und soziale Unfallversicherung,* Zürich.
Saxer, A. (1977). *Die soziale Sicherheit in der Schweiz,* 4. Aufl., Bern/Zürich.
Schaeppi, C.H. (1974). *Der Anspruch auf Kinderzulagen, unter besonderer Berücksichtigung der sanktgallischen
Gesetzgebung,* Berner Diss.
Schatz, B. (1952). *Kommentar zur Eidgenössischen Militärversicherung,* Zürich.
Schweizerische Unfallversicherungsanstalt (1968). *50 Jahre SUVA 1918–1968, Denkschrift.*
Tschudi, H.P. (1965). 25 Jahre Ausgleichskassen, *SZS,* S. 89 ff.
Tschudi, H.P. (1977). 'Ziele und Stand der Sozialversicherungsrevisionen', *SZS,* S. 179 ff.
Tschudi, H.P. (1979). 'Die verfassungsrechtlichen Grundlagen der Sozialversicherung', *SZS,* S. 81 ff.
Vogel, W. (1951). *Bismarcks Arbeiterversicherung. Ihre Entstehung im Kräftespiel der Zeit.* Braunschweig.
Wannagat, G. (1965). *Lehrbuch des Sozialversicherungsrechts,* Band I, Tübingen.
Zacher, H. (1979). 'Das neue Sozialgesetzbuch – der Einbau der Sozialversicherung in das Sozial-
leistungssystem', *SZS,* S. 249 ff.

NOTES

1 For these and further statistical data cf. *Statistisches Jahrbuch der Schweiz,* 1979 as well as
references at footnotes 149–152.

2 Women were not granted political rights (the vote) at governmental level until the plebiscite of 7 February 1971, culminating in an appropriate amendment to the Swiss constitution. Female suffrage has been introduced in nearly all cantons but has not actually been realized in every canton. In the Grisons there are still about sixty communities where it has not yet been introduced. Thus, a female Swiss could not become a member of the local council there but could, for example, become a member of the Federal Council or of the Federal Court. Cf. Maurer (1979), *SZS* p. 188.

3 In favour of this: Saladin Peter, *Grundrechte im Wandel*, 2.A., p. 241; against it: Gysi Peter, *Die sozialpolitische Begrenzung* . . . pp. 112 and 121. Cf. for German law e.g. Wannagat, *Lehrbuch* p. 171 ff.

4 For more details of this concept see Gysi, pp. 35 and 61.

5 Maurer, *Sozialversicherungsrecht*, after note 87.

6 There are countless definitions of the concept 'insurance'; so far none of them has earned general recognition. Furthermore, there is no superordinate term for 'insurance' which applies both to private and social insurance. Cf. Maurer, *Sozialversicherungsrecht* at note 92 and *Privatversicherungsrecht* p. 115 with recommended reading.

7 Thus, public insurance can exist with and without compulsory contributions. 'Public insurances which do not require contributions' are traditionally equated with the idea of 'relief' in the Federal Republic of Germany. This concept has only had a weak echo in Swiss writings on the subject and has hardly ever been used in legal decisions. The term also seems to be disappearing gradually in the Federal Republic of Germany and is being replaced by other concepts. Cf. Maurer, *Sozialversicherungsrecht* at notes 59 and 57a. (It is important to stress that the expression 'social insurance' has a special meaning for each country and each particular time in history.)

8 Maurer, *Sozialversicherungsrecht* before note 126a. The term 'social law' or its synonym 'social legislation' is also controversial in Switzerland. Social insurance law would seem to be the narrower and social law the broader of two concentric circles. The following fields which are part of social law and social insurance are named: labour law; social assistance for trade and farmers; measures concerning employment policies and protection for tenants; welfare. Cf. details in Maurer, *loc. cit.*, §1, III, especially lines 1 and 2, with recommended reading. In the present work these spheres of law will only be mentioned inasmuch as they make the historical development of social law easier to understand and they serve to complete the picture of it.

8a Cf. at note 106.

9 Bigler-Eggenberger, *Soziale Sicherung* p. 142; Maurer, *Grundriß*, p. 3; Pfluger, *Kartothek*; Saxer, *Die soziale Sicherheit* p. 116; SJK, *Karten Krankenvers*.

10 Maurer, *Recht und Praxis*; Maurer, *Grundriß* p. 56; Saxer, *Die soziale Sicherheit* p. 147; SJK, *Karten Unfallversicherung*.

10a Art. 115–119 which provide for voluntary insurance have never been put into force. Thus, the owners of insured concerns cannot be voluntarily insured with the SUVA: Maurer, *Recht und Praxis* p. 22 and p. 59; also relevant Bigler-Eggenberger, *Soziale Sicherung* p. 160.

11 Bigler-Eggenberger, *Soziale Sicherung* p. 100; Maurer, *Grundriß* p. 109 ff.; Maurer, *Alterssicherung der Frau*, SZS 1979 p. 187 pp.; Saxer, *Die soziale Sicherheit* p. 23; SJK, *Karten AHV*.

11a The contribution rates for employers and employed are currently (1 September 1979) fixed as follows (the figures in brackets are for the self-employed):

old age and surviving dependants' pension (AHV):	8.4%	(7.8%)
disability insurance (IV):	1.0%	(1.0%)
income compensation (EO):	0.6%	(0.6%)
Total	10.0%	(9.4%)

12 Bigler-Eggenberger, *Soziale Sicherung* p. 119; Maurer, *Grundriß* p. 150; Saxer, *Die soziale Sicherheit* p. 64; SJK, *Karten Invalidenversicherung*.

12a According to IVG 13, under-aged insured persons have a right to the necessary medical treatment of congenital abnormalities. In the decree of 20 October 1971 all congenital abnormalities for which such measures are granted are defined.

13 Maurer, *Grundriß* p. 149; Saxer, *Die soziale Sicherheit* p. 90; SJK, *Karte Alters- und Hinterlassenenfürsorge*.

14 Saxer, *Die soziale Sicherheit*, p. 219; SJK, *Karten Erwerbsersatzordnung*.

14a Holzer, *Kommentar*; Saxer, *Die soziale Sicherheit* p. 208; SJK, *Ersatzkarte Arbeitslosenversicherung*. Tschudi, *Sozialversicherungsrevisionen*, (1977) SZS p. 184.

15 For more details of this complicated ruling see SJK, *Ersatzkarte* no. 1147.

16 Saxer, *Die soziale Sicherheit*, p. 195; Schaeppi, *Kinderzulagen* pp. 37 and 45; Vasella, (1971) *SZS* p. 127; Tschudi, (1977) *SZS* p. 191.

17 Cf. also Maurer, *Sozialversicherungsrecht* at notes 169 and 181 f.

18 Saxer, *Die soziale Sicherheit* p. 231; Bassegoda, J. (1976), 75 *Jahre Militärversicherung*, Bern 1976; Schatz, *Kommentar;* SJK, *Karten Militärversicherung.*

19 Maurer, *Sozialverischerungsrecht* at notes 179 and 583a.

20 Maurer, *Sozialversicherungsrecht* §§22–25 with bibliographic references.

20a Their number is to be increased to nine shortly.

21 Contrary to the supreme courts in the Federal Republic of Germany, the Swiss federal judges do not draw up the judgments themselves. The number of clerks of court and secretaries is to be increased to a total of twenty-three shortly. The Federal Council has already informed the National Assembly accordingly.

22 On the historical development cf., for example, Aubert, *Traité I* pp. 17 and 34; Fleiner/Giacometti, *Bundesstaatsrecht* p. 4.

23 Compilation in Aubert, *Traité I* p. 48 ff.

24 The law concerning initiatives by the people for partial revision was not introduced until 1891.

25 The federal government did not receive legislative powers in the other spheres of civil and penal law until after the plebiscite of 13 November 1898; the former Art. 64 was amended and a new Art. 64bis was added to the federal constitution.

26 Cf. Benöhr, *Crise et législation sociale*, p. 12; Burckhardt, *Kommentar* p. 280; Landmann, *Arbeiterschutzgesetzgebung* p. XXVI etc.

27 Further reading: Benöhr, p. 2 ff.; Bergier, Jean-François (1974). *Naissance et croissance de la Suisse industrielle*, Bern; Bodmer, Walter (1960) *Schweizerische Industriegeschichte, Die Entwicklung der schweizerischen Textilwirtschaft im Rahmen der übrigen Industrien und Wirtschaftszweige*, Zürich; Dällenbach, Heinz, (1961) *Kantone, Bund und Fabrikgesetzgebung (1853–1877)*, Berner Diss., Zürich; Grobéty, *La Suisse*; Gruner, *Arbeiter in der Schweiz*; Hauser, *Wirtschaft und Sozialgeschichte*; Hobi, Emil (1920) *Die Entwicklung der Fabrikgesetzgebung im Kanton Glarus*, Berner Diss.; Maurer, *Sozialversicherungsrecht* §5, II; Rappard, William E. (1914) *La Révolution industrielle et les origines de la protection légale du travail en Suisse*, Bern.

28 Gruner p. 52; Hauser, p. 199.

29 Hauser p. 194.

30 Gruner, p. 51. He estimates that they accounted for 279 000 in 1880 (p. 81) of the total population of 2.8 million.

31 Hauser p. 291.

32 Hauser p. 329.

33 Hauser p. 323.

34 More details in Gruner p. 113.

35 During the Franco-German War of 1870/1 the prices for certain foodstuffs in Switzerland trebled, indeed even rose five-fold, within a few weeks; Hauser p. 328.

36 Gruner, p. 877; he describes the development of the trade unions in the nineteenth century in different sections. The Christian Social Trade Union Congress of Switzerland (Christlichsoziale Gewerkschaftsbund) was founded in 1907.

37 Gruner, p. 769. On p. 790 he portrays Karl Moor and Otto Lang as the true fathers of Swiss Marxism (Communism). In a Social Democratic programme of 1878, for example, the abolition of private property and of inheritance was put forward.

38 Gruner p. 796, 802 and passim.

39 Wehrli, Bernhard (1970). *Aus der Geschichte des schweizerischen Handels- und Industrie-Vereins*, Zürich, p. 27. On p. 24 he points out that in 1863 the federal administration did not have special civil servants to deal with trade affairs.

40 Hauser, p. 350. For more details on employers in the last century cf. Gruner, p. 954.

41 For further information on employers and strikes cf. Gruner, p. 959, 920 and 925 (with tables of strikes).

42 Gruner, p. 253; he mentions that a limited, statutory compulsory membership scheme had been introduced in the canton of Zürich as early as 1844; he also describes the efforts which failed in Basel in 1881 to create compulsory sickness insurance for all employed persons.

43 Gruner, p. 1001.

44 Gruner, p. 1003.

45 Gruner, pp. 1004, 1005 and 1008.

46 Gruner, p. 1018; the oldest factory sickness insurance scheme was started in 1827 by the

Ebauches works (p. 1016)—in 1903 there was a total of 2006 mutual sickness insurance schemes; Furrer, *Entstehung und Entwicklung*, p. 54.

47 Maurer, *Sozialversicherungsrecht* at note 157. Gruner p. 256 assumes that unemployment in Switzerland was not such a dreadful scourge as in other countries as the Swiss worker could live on a subsidiary income from agriculture—if he lived in the country. Indeed, many workers had small fields and kept small animals such as goats and pigs in particular.

48 Gruner p. 1015.

49 Maurer at note 158.

50 Fleiner, *Bundesstaatsrecht*, p. 526.

51 Hauser p. 188 and 330.

52 On pauperism in detail: Gruner p. 16, and p. 28, note 31.

53 Recently the principle of domicile has increasingly ousted the principle of the native community in Switzerland; thus, the community of domicile has to assist its poor. One also speaks less and less of 'poor relief'; this term has been replaced by 'welfare' or 'social assistance'. Cf. Maurer p. 59.

54 Cf. literature cited in note 27 and Landmann, *Arbeiterschutzgesetzgebung* p. XXX; Schiwoff, Victor (1952) *Die Beschränkung der Arbeitszeit durch die kantonale Gesetzgebung und durch das erste eidgenössische Fabrikgesetz von 1877*, Berner Diss (rer-pol.).

55 Cf. the summary of Adam Smith's more important ideas, e.g. in Hauser, p. 192.

56 Hauser p. 331.

57 Gruner p. 114.

58 Dällenbach, p. 72 with details on the employment of women and children; Grobéty, *La Suisse* p. 53.

59 Dällenbach, p. 89, briefly describes the turbulent assembly of the citizens of the canton of 29 September 1872; Grobéty, p. 88.

60 *BBl* (1875) IV p. 573 and 921; cf. the text to BV 34 at note 26. The communcation to the National Assembly is still remarkable in some ways as it reflects that era, dares to forecast the future and describes foreign legislation—German, French and English.

61 AS (n.F.) 3 p. 241.

62 Gruner, p. 248; he, like numerous other authors, mentioned in notes 27 and 54 portrays the interesting history of its emergence; cf. also Grobéty p. 169.

63 Cf., for example, Benöhr p. 14, and Gruner p. 237.

64 Dr Fridolin Schuler from the canton of Glarus deserves special mention. He offered to work as a factory inspector and later distinguished himself with his publications on protection for the workers and on sickness insurance; cf., e.g., *Erinnerungen eines Siebzigjährigen*, Frauenfeld 1903 and *Die obligatorische Krankenversicherung in der Schweiz*, Zürich 1891.

64a The definition was extended on several occasions to include further types of factories.

65 The Federal Council sheds light on the ruling of the German Liability Act of 1871, which is less stringent than that of the Factory Act, in its communication (Botschaft), p. 941.

66 AS (n.F.) 10, p. 397. This is the first 'list of poisons' drawn up by the Federal Council.

67 Benöhr, p. 21.

67a Later the Federal Council often followed this policy of small steps; cf., for example, *BBl* (1886) II 700 on the extension of the Factory Liability Law to agriculture: 'It is in all events more useful to ensure slight progress than to endanger it completely. . . .'

68 Literature: Landmann, *Arbeiterschutzgesetzgebung* p. LIV and XCIV; Piccard, *Haftpflichtpraxis*; Scherer (1908), *Die Haftpflicht des Unternehmers aufgrund des Fabrikhaftpflichtgesetzes und des Ausdehnungsgesetzes*, Basel; Zeerleder (1888). *Die schweiz. Haftpflichtgesetzgebung*, Bern.

69 *BBl* (1880) IV p. 541 (communication) and 584 (draft).

70 AS (n.F.) 5 p. 562.

71 On p. 573 the communication notes that a foreman receives an annual wage of almost 1500 Francs or a daily wage of 5 Francs.

72 The communication compares the draft both with the Federal Law on the Liability of the Railways of 1 July 1875 and with similar foreign laws, especially with those of Germany and England.

73 *BBl* (1886) II p. 689 (communication) and p. 705 (draft); part of the Klein motion is to be found on p. 689. With reference to the question of compulsory accident insurance it states, *inter alia*, that it is preferable to merely extending liability 'as it is capable of the greatest expansion—both extensively and intensively—as on the one hand the opposition of the small employers ceases and on the other hand the plea of an act of providence can be eliminated, that of the person's own fault can be limited to the severest cases and the insurance can cover

accidents of all types' (quoted in Landmann, p. LVII note 2). Thus, Klein portrayed possible rulings which were realized later in the KUVG.

74 In its communication on p. 704 the Federal Council also takes the insurance companies to task: the supervisory bodies were to control that workers who were entitled to damages were 'not paid ridiculously low amounts, or even nothing at all, by the employer or the insurance companies, such as is often the case'.

75 Mahr, Werner (1951). *Einführung in die Versicherungswirtschaft*, Berlin; Manes Alfred (1930). *Allgemeine Versicherungslehre* I, 5.A., Leipzig und Berlin; Maurer, *Privatversicherungsrecht mit zahlreichen Literaturhinweisen;* ders., 'Zusammenhänge mit der Entwicklung der Privatversicherung' p. 355, in H.F. Zacher (ed.) (1979): *Bedingungen für die Entstehung und Entwicklung von Sozialversicherung*, vol. 3 der Schriftenreihe für internationales und vergleichendes Sozialrecht, Duncker & Humblot, Berlin; some of the following information has been gleaned from this.

76 Patria (1978). *Panorama eines Jahrhunderts Lebensversicherung 1878-1978*, p. 9, Basel.

77 *BBl* (1885) I p. 120; Maurer, *Privatversicherungsrecht* p. 39 note 30 (This should read: 1878).

78 Cf., for example, the remark in a communication by the Federal Council, quoted in note 74.

79 Germany did not have a law on the supervision of insurance companies until the beginning of this century. Today the 'Versicherungsaufsichtsgesetz' (Federal Law on the Supervision of Private Insurances) of 23 June 1978 applies. This has replaced the law of 1885. For the constitutional basis cf. after note 26.

80 Cf. the noteworthy comments on the subject by Sprecher, Andreas, *75 Jahre 'Zürich', Aus der Werkstatt der 'Zürich' 1872*, p. 25.

81 Maurer, *Sozialversicherungsrecht* §10, II, 2.

82 The federal government is currently concerned with these and similar questions as it must decide whether it wants to permit private insurance companies to function as insurance institutions for compulsory accident insurance for employed persons and also for staff pension schemes. More details in the essay by Maurer mentioned in note 75.

83 Cf. Maurer, *Sozialversicherungsrecht* §5, III, with references for further reading, from which the following information has been predominantly gleaned; see also essay mentioned in note 75.

84 In many respects it is impossible, or else only possible with an exceptionally broad study of sources, to judge whether the same solution was found 'by chance' in Switzerland or whether German legislation really had provided the impetus.

85 Cf. above note 65.

86 On the origins of German social insurance laws: Vogel, *Bismarcks Arbeiterversicherung*.

87 Text, e.g., in Wannagat, *Lehrbuch* p. 63. Bismarck largely composed the message himself; Vogel, p. 134 note 3. The Social Democrats were highly critical of social insurance legislation; some of them rejected it entirely. For example, they voted against the Sickness Insurance Law. However, they supported the development of legislation on industrial safety for workers; Vogel pp. 53, 55, and 57.

88 Vogel, pp. 152, 138, and 169. Bismarck was called a 'state socialist' who wanted to go as far as socializing all means of production—despite his basic Conservative attitude.

89 Vogel, p. 176; Wannagat p. 71.

90 Private insurance companies are to be allowed to be responsible within a certain framework after the current total revision of accident insurance; cf. after note 232.

91 With the revision of the KUVG of 13 March 1964, the insurance relationship is subject to public law and to administrative jurisdiction; the private sickness insurances—associations, cooperatives, foundations—received power of jurisdiction.

92 Wannagat, p. 71 and Vogel p. 176. In Switzerland attempts were made to create a sickness insurance free of charge for the whole population and to finance it by introducing a monopoly on tobacco; cf. at note 106a.

93 Wannagat, pp. 65, 69, and 73.

93a Cf. after note 225.

94 Wannagat, p. 73. Recently authors have again proposed that all social insurance should be implemented as a single insurance in the Federal Republic of Germany; cf. Maurer (1977), *SZS* p. 86.

95 Vogel, p. 142. This contradictory policy is also apparent in that the patriarchal land and factory owner, Bismarck, fought the Socialists while realizing state socialism with public social insurance. He was primarily a 'Realpolitician' and not a political doctrinarian.

96 Vogel, pp. 33 and 96. The German Social Democrats spoke out for a solution in liability legislation for a long time; Vogel, pp. 51, 54.

97 Cf. further on, p. 412.
98 Denkschrift, p. 13; Furrer, *Entstehung und Entwicklung*, p. 58; Oertli, *Unfallversicherung*, p. 463.
99 Cf. note 73.
100 Both documents are printed in *BBl* (1889) IV p. 843 and 855.
101 *BBl* (1889) IV p. 825 (communication) and p. 842 (draft)
102 The question is once again topical whether the federal government should be granted legislative jurisdiction on social insurance and basic social laws by a general clause or only for certain individual branches or basic laws, i.e. according to the enumeration method; cf. Maurer, *Sozialversicherungsrecht* note 40. The Federal Council's forecast was right: it took a long time, some 35 years, before the federal government was commissioned in accordance with the constitution to introduce old age and disability insurance.
102a Cf. at note 120a.
103 For the difference between legislative competence and legislative mandate: Maurer, *Sozialversicherungsrecht* at note 238a.
104 *BBl* (1896) I p. 190; Furrer, p. 59 note 27.
105 A petition for a referendum and a counter-proposal by the National Assembly on replacing Art. 34bis with a new one were rejected in a plebiscite of 8 December 1974; cf. before note 225.
106 Denkschrift, p. 14; Furrer, p. 59; Maurer, *Recht und Praxis*, p. 3.
106a This anticipated the idea which later played a central role in the English Beveridge Plan; cf. Maurer, *Sozialversicherungsrecht*, note 57.
107 *BBl* (1896) I S. 189 (communication with details on history) and p. 465 (draft bills) as well as (1906) VI p. 229 ('Historischer Überblick').
108 *BBl* (1899) IV p. 853.
109 Denkschrift, p. 14.
110 Furrer, p. 61.
111 *BBl* (1900) III p. 367, AS (n.F.) 18 pp. 803, 849, and 940 as well as Bassegoda, *Militärversicherung*, p. 11.
112 More on the history of military insurance in Bassegoda, *Militärversicherung*, p. 7; Piccard (1965) *SZS* p. 233; lit. *75 Jahre 'Zürich'*, p. 39 one reads:

> 'even if the outer trappings look warlike, conditions in the good old days were quite idyllic with regard to the former accident insurance for the Swiss army. Based on an agreement with the Federal Military Department, all soldiers, from the colonel with cock's plumage on his headgear to the last common soldier in leather trousers, were protected by the 'Zürich' insurance when they were in service. Anyone who did not wish to be insured had to report this at the first roll-call.'

This private insurance contract, by the way, is said to have led to the institution being called 'military insurance'. This term was applied in all later legislation; cf. Schatz, commentary p. 19.
113 Maurer, *Sozialversicherungsrecht*, note 162.
114 Cf. at notes 8, 18, and 102a as well as at 120 a.
115 The Federal Council's concept of only passing a promotional law (Förderungsgesetz) for sickness insurance was a happy solution as it helped sickness insurance develop far more than had been expected — without compulsory insurance throughout the country and without state insurance institutions prescribed by the government.
116 *BBl* (1906) VI p. 229 (communication) and p. 405 (draft) with a summary of the Lex Forrer (p. 233) and events following the plebiscite (p. 237).
117 Cf. further details, e.g., in Furrer p. 61; Denkschrift p. 17, and Maurer, *Recht und Praxis* p. 3.
117a These subsidies were abolished by the Federal Law of 5 October 1967; AS 1968 p. 64.
118 Cf. the basic features of the KUVG at notes 9 and 10. The current total revision of accident insurance provides that both branches are to be regulated by respective laws, as the Federal Council had proposed with its communication on the Lex Forrer; cf. at note 107.
118a The 'Bundesamt für Sozialversicherung' is an adminisrative section of the Federal Department of the Interior since 1 January 1955; previously it had been part of the Federal Department of Economics; *SJK* Ersatzkarte Nr. 1313, *Krankenversicherung I*, p. 7.
119 Maurer, *Recht und Praxis*, p. 48.
120 Cf. publication mentioned in note 80, *75 Jahre 'Zürich'*, p. 30.

120a *BBl* (1919) IV p. 1 ff. Cf. at notes 114 and 102a. Fleiner, *Bundesstaatsrecht* p. 533 also used the
      term 'Sozialversicherung'; cf. also Hug (1963), *SZS* p. 103.
121   Cf. more details on the development of labour law in Hug (1979), *SZS* p. 170. The Law on
      Employment Contracts has been newly regulated by the Federal Law of 25 June 1971. Since 1
      January 1972 the tenth section of the Law of Obligations applies. This regulates the employ-
      ment contract in Art. 319–362.
122   The Federal Republic of Germany also aims at having a Social Code in the long term. It is
      impossible to forecast at the moment whether it will ever attain such an aim. Cf. also Zacher
      (1979), *SZS* p. 255.
123   More details in Hug, commentary p. 11 ff. and (1979), *SZS* p. 168.
124   For more details on Lenin's role in Switzerland and on his departure see Gautschi,
      Landesstreik, pp. 43 and 64.
124a Gautschi, p. 46.
124b Gautschi, p. 281.
125   Gautschi, p. 276.
126   Gautschi, p. 359.
127   Gautschi, p. 369.
128   Gautschi, p. 371.
128a The Federal Council had already thought of introducing an old age and surviving dependants'
      insurance in 1889; however, it could not decide on a schedule; cf. earlier at note 102. One can
      assume that the general strike accelerated the federal government's preparations for the crea-
      tion of provisions based on constitutional law.
129   He had belonged to the Olten Action Committee.
130   Gautschi, p. 71, and 384 note 5. Members of the Olten Action Committee later held highly
      honourable positions in the state: Ernst Nobs was the first Social Democratic federal coun-
      cillor in 1943 and Robert Grimm presided at the United National Assembly in 1946;
      Gautschi, p. 378, note 58.
131   *BBl* (1924) II pp. 538 and 520; at the end of April 1923 there were still 35 512 completely
      unemployed and 17 767 partially unemployed.
132   Maurer, *Sozialversicherungsrecht* p. 97.
133   Compilation of numerous decrees in Furrer, *Entstehung und Entwicklung*, p. 125; on p. 122 f.
      the author portrays earlier unsuccessful efforts to introduce unemployment insurance by
      federal law.
134   *BBl* (1924) II 538. The federal government paid 143 million Francs in unemployment relief
      from 1917 to 1923 but only 7.6 million Francs to unemployment insurance schemes. Thus,
      one can conclude that the unemployment insurances did not play an important role at that
      time. Cf. Saxer, *Soziale Sicherheit* p. 208, with a table on p. 210 on the development of
      unemployment insurance from 1924 to 1975; in 1936 there were 204 schemes (an all-time
      high) and in 1975 there were 131.
135   AS 41 p. 235.
136   AS 53 p. 45.
137   *BBl* (1919) IV pp. 1–210 (communication), p. 211 f. (draft) and pp. 213–224 (appendix).
138   *BBl* (1920) III p. 706.
139   *BBl* (1925) II p. 679 (text of the bill), (1926) I p. 1 and (1946) II p. 365.
140   *BBl* (1931) I p. 1000 (bill on which the vote was taken).
141   *BBl* (1946) II p. 366 and (1932) I p. 1 with slightly differing figures.
142   Furrer, p. 108; *BBl* (1946) II p. 366; no. 2 of the reports published by the 'Bundesamt für
      Sozialversicherung': *Die Alters- und Hinterlassenenversicherung und -fürsorge in der Schweiz bis Ende
      1943*, Bern (1944).
142a Both the Federal Diet and the National Council voted unanimously in favour of the Special
      Authorization Act. The Social Democrats were not represented in the Federal Council at that
      time (cf. earlier, note 130). Nevertheless, two Social Democrats and two communists ab-
      stained from voting. For more details see Georg Kreis, (1979). *Die Einführung des Vollmachtenre-
      gimes vor 40 Jahren*, Neue Zürcher Zeitung no. 201, p. 35, with pointers on the controversial
      question whether the Authorization Act complied with the constitution or not. A permanent
      commission appointed by each chamber of the National Assembly had to ensure that the
      Federal Council did not make undesirable use of its powers.
143   Maurer, *Sozialversicherungsrecht*, p. 98.
144   Furrer p. 84; Tschudi (1965), *SZS* p. 90 ff.
145   For more details see Furrer p. 88; Peter Saxer (1953). *Die AHV-Ausgleichskassen als neue*

Organisationsform der schweizerischen Sozialversicherung, Berner Diss. p. 94.

146 Saxer, *Soziale Sicherheit*, p. 219. The wage-related premium had already been introduced by the KUVG for compulsory accident insurance. However, there is an upper limit for compulsory contributions. Furthermore, only part of the working population is covered by compulsory accident insurance.

147 Bigler-Eggenberger, *Soziale Sicherung* p. 93; Maurer p. 100; Furrer p. 129.

148 Saxer, *Soziale Sicherheit* p. 196; Schaeppi, *Kinderzulagen* p. 37.

149 Cf. also Müller, AHV. p. 149.

150 Dr R. Ehlers of the Schweizerische Kreditanstalt in Zürich provided me with most of the figures quoted here. I should like to thank him at this point for his help.

151 Müller p. 149. The Swiss workers are said to have one of the highest wage levels of all countries.

152 This was also known as the 'Schwarzenbach-Initiative' after its initiator. It is not exclusively a Swiss phenomenon that large numbers of foreigners trigger off defensive mechanisms among the indigenous population.

153 The following federal councillors contributed decisively to the development of social insurance in their capacity as heads of the departments concerned: Dr W. Stampfli (in office from 1940 to 1947) and Prof. H.P. Tschudi (in office from 1959 to 1973).

153a Cf. at note 11 and for historical details see Jakob Graf (1979), *ZAK* pp. 291, 386 and 459.

153b In *BBl* (1946) II p. 366, the various proposals are summarized, also in no. 3 of the reports mentioned in note 142.

154 *BBl* (1946) II p. 369.

155 *BBl* (1946) II p. 365 (Botschaft) and p. 555 (Gesetzesentwurf).

156 *BBl* (1946) II p. 589–694.

157 Saxer, *Soziale Sicherheit*, p. 24. More historical details in Furrer p. 109; Granacher (1958), *SZS* p. 240; Greiner (1958), *SZS* p. 58; Müller, AHV p. 53.

158 More details on the structure of AHV at note 11. SR 831.10.

159 Maurer, *Sozialversicherungsrecht* p. 102 with bibliographic references in note 173.

160 Maurer p. 103.

161 Cf. at note 151.

162 Cf. at note 139. On the same day the people rejected a constitutional initiative of the 'Partei der Arbeit' 'For a Real People's Pension' of 2 December 1969 and accepted the National Assembly's counterproposal which brought about the currently valid ruling of the federal constitution. The counterproposal contained elements which were present in two other constitutional initiatives, i.e. that of the Swiss Social Democratic Party and the Swiss Trade Union Congress of 18 March 1970 and another of a non-party committee for up to date old age pensions of 13 April 1970. Both these initiatives were withdrawn in 1974. Cf. Müller AHV pp. 116 and 165.

163 Maurer p. 131 note 244a.

164 Probably about 80 percent of the employed are insured in a staff pension scheme, even if for very different benefits.

165 The term 'AHV Revision' means that legal regulations on the AHV (the AHV Law, etc.) have been amended, added or abolished. Thus, these revisions are amendments made by federal law which usually make amendments necessary at statutory level.

166 *BBl* (1950) II 185; AS (1951) p. 391.

167 Müller, AHV p. 67, suspects that with this revision parliament 'only brought in an 'alibi exercise' because of the elections in 1951'. With the degressive or sinking scale of contributions, the contribution rates for the self-employed whose incomes do not exceed a certain level are graded downwards. The income level was fixed at 25 200 Francs at the end of 1979. The self-employed who earned this much did not have to pay the full contribution of 7.8 percent but only 7.4 percent and someone who earned, for example, 4200 Francs only had to pay a contribution of 4.2 percent.

168 *BBl* (1953) II 81; AS (1954) p. 211.

169 The ninth AHV revision re-introduced a modified version of this. For further details cf. Müller, AHV p. 71; new minimum pension of 720 Francs and maximum pension of 1700 Francs per annum.

170 *BBl* (1955) II p. 1088; AS (1956) p. 651.

171 Müller, AHV p. 75; Granacher (1957), *SZS* p. 69.

172 *BBl* (1956) I p. 1429; AS 1957 p. 262. The new minimum pension amounted to 900 Francs

and the maximum pension to 1850 Francs per annum (1957), *SZS* pp. 77 and 278 as well as (1959) p. 310.

173 *BBl* (1958) II p. 137; AS (1959) p. 854.
174 Müller, AHV p. 80; Salathé (1960), *SZS* p. 223.
175 *BBl* (1961) I 213; AS (1941) p. 491; Müller, AHV p. 80; Achermann (1962), *SZS* p. 297.
176 Müller, AHV p. 80 and 165.
177 *BBl* (1963) II 517; AS (1964) p. 285; Müller, AHV p. 87; Achermann (1964), *SZS* p. 297. The communication describes the 'Three Pillar Principle' for the first time: Müller p. 87.
178 Müller, AHV p. 87 and 165.
179 AS 1967 p. 19; Gfeller (1968), *SZS* p. 60; Büchi (1967), *SZS* p. 227; Müller, AHV p. 93.
180 *BBl* (1968) I 602; AS 1969 p. 111; Gfeller (1970), *SZS* p. 37; Müller, AHV p. 103.
181 According to an amendment of 27 September 1973, in force from 1 January 1974 onwards, a corresponding ruling now applied for pensions for accidents which did not occur at work. *BBl* (1973) II p. 571. For the first time the communication also dealt with proposals which the national councillor, Dr A.C. Brunner, made on reorganizing the pensions system. He made further proposals in the following years and thus enriched discussions on the AHV. Naturally, the legislature rejected most of these proposals. Numerous details in Müller: AHV pp. 94, 98.
181a AS (1971) p. 27; Maeschi (1971), *SZS* p. 268.
182 *BBl* (1971) II p. 1057; AS (1972) p. 2483; Müller AHV p. 118; Maeschi (1973), *SZS* p. 188.
182a A federal law on the amendment to the Law on AHV of 28 June 1974 settled this second increase, deviating somewhat from the eighth AHV revision. Moreover, it guaranteed the pensioners double the amount of pension due in September 1974 as an immediate improvement to compensate for the rise in prices. Müller (1976), *SZS* p. 41.
183 For current ruling cf. Maurer (1979), *SZS* p. 200.
184 The government raised contributions for the employed to 7.8 percent in 1973 and to 8.4 percent, the currently valid rate, on 1 July 1975; similarly, the rate for the self-employed was first raised to 7.3 percent and then by the ninth AHV revision to the present rate of 7.8 percent.
185 Cf. the reports by Büchi and Müller in (1975) *SZS* p. 135, (1976) pp. 40 and 265, (1977) p. 220, (1978) pp. 194 and 282.
186 Müller (1977), *SZS* p. 220.
187 Müller (1978), *SZS* p. 282. 1 451 220 against the proposal and 377 017 for it.
188 *BBl* (1976) III 1; AS (1978) p. 391.
188a 1 192 144 voters were in favour of the bill, 625 566 were against it. Büchi (1978), *SZS* p. 284.
189 For more details see Büchi (1977), *SZS* p. 268; Müller (1978, *SZS* p. 195, and Müller, AHV p. 122.
190 Maurer, *Sozialversicherungsrecht* p. 319. The mixed or pensions index was fixed at 100 for the time when the national index of consumer prices had reached the level of 175.5 points.
190a AS (1979) p. 1365. Details in Büchi (1979), *SZS* p. 281.
191 This type of compulsory contribution had been abolished by the second AHV revision; cf. at note 169.
192 More details on the complex right of recourse or subrogation in social insurance in Maurer §20; Maurer, *Kumulation und Subrogation*, p. 45.
193 Müller (1978), *SZS* p. 197; Maurer §21.
194 Büchi (1979), *SZS* p. 281; Maurer (1979), *SZS* p. 207.
195 Cf. at notes 18 and 113. For more historical details see Furrer, *Entstehung und Entwicklung* p. 28, and Bassegoda, *Militärversicherung*, p. 11.
196 *BBl* (1947) III 97; AS (1949) p. 1697; SR 833.1.
197 Bassegoda p. 13 enumerates them.
198 The author is Prof. E. Fischli. Maurer p. 104.
199 Büchi (1976), *SZS* p. 195 and (1977) p. 282.
199a Cf. at note 14a.
200 *BBl* (1950) II 525; AS (1951) p. 1163; SR 837.1. More on history in Holzer, *Kommentar* p. 17, and Furrer p. 130.
201 Saxer, *Soziale Sicherheit* p. 210 (table).
202 Cf. at note 14a; SR 837.100. The competent department has already drawn up a bill for a new unemployment insurance law and this has been submitted to various interested bodies for comment.

202a Cf. at note 16.
203 Cf. at notes 16 and 148. SR 836.1.
204 Cf. Saxer, *Soziale Sicherheit* p. 195; Tschudi (1977), *SZS* p. 191; Maurer p. 105; Vasella (1971), *SZS* p. 127.
204a Cf. at note 14 and p. 419.
205 *BBl* (1951) iii p. 297; AS (1952) p. 1021; SR 834.1.
206 Cf. at note 145.
207 Shortened title, introduced by the Federal Law of 7 October 1977, AS (1978) p. 50; SR 520.1.
208 Gfeller (1970), *SZS* p. 46; Müller (1976), *SZS* p. 295; Saxer, *Soziale Sicherheit*, p. 222.
208a Cf. at note 12.
209 *BBl* (1958) ii 1137; AS (1959) p. 827; SR 831.20.
210 Granacher (1960), *SZS* p. 64, and Salathé (1960), *SZS* p. 224.
211 AS (1961) p. 29; SR 831.201. Granacher (1961), *SZS* p. 71; Achermann (1962), *SZS* p. 298.
212 Graf (1962), *SZS* pp. 161, 165 with numerous indications on the introduction of IV.
213 *BBl* (1967) i 653; AS (1968) p. 29; Büchi (1967), *SZS* p. 231 and (1966) p. 213.
214 Büchi (1968), *SZS* p. 278 and Gfeller (1969), *SZS* p. 42. A few individual points of the IVG were also amended later, quite separately from an AHV revision, for example, by the Federal Law of 9 October 1970 (AS (1971) p. 54). Various minor amendments were also made to the IVV as well as to the resolution on congenital abnormalities. Survey in Büchi (1974), *SZS* p. 144.
215 Cf. at note 162.
216 The regulation of supplementary benefits sketched in p. 434 applies both to AHV and to IV.
217 Cf. at note 9 and p. 412.
218 Achermann (1966), *SZS* p. 54.
219 Granacher (1961), *SZS* p. 73 and (1960) *SZS* p. 65 (History of origins).
220 Communication of 5 June 1961 and supplementary communication of 16 November 1962 in *BBl* (1961) p. 264 and (1962) p. 646. Büchi (1963), *SZS* p. 151, and Granacher (1962), *SZS* p. 222.
221 AS (1964) p. 965; Achermann (1966), *SZS* p. 53.
222 Cf., for example, Maurer, *Grundriss* p. 40.
223 Maurer, *Sozialversicherungsrecht* p. 106.
224 Maurer, *Grundriss* p. 53; Maurer, *Sozialversicherungsrecht* p. 107.
225 Büchi (1977), *SZS* p. 276 and (1978) p. 290; Tschudi (1977), *SZS* p. 186 ff.; Maurer, *Sozialversicherungsrecht* p. 107.
226 Büchi (1979), *SZS* p. 292 compiles the points of the revision.
227 Cf. at note 13.
228 *BBl* (1964) ii p. 681 (communication of 21 September 1964); AS (1965) p. 537; SR 831.30.
229 Maurer (1979), *SZS* p. 194: only about 15 percent of all old age pensioners currently still receive supplementary benefits. All cantons have adopted the system of supplementary benefits. Gfeller (1968), *SZS* p. 61 and Saxer, *Soziale Sicherheit* p. 90.
230 Cf., for example, the Federal Law on the Amendment of the ELG of 9 October 1970 (AS (1971) p. 32) and on this: Maeschi (1971), *SZS* p. 271 and Büchi (1971), *SZS* p. 137.
231 Büchi (1970), *SZS* p. 138 and — on the latest adjustment — (1979), *SZS* p. 291.
232 Cf. at notes 10 and 118
233 AS (1963) p. 272; SR 832.25; Maurer, *Sozialversicherungsrecht* p. 318.
234 *BBl* (1976) iii p. 141.
235 In detail: Seiler (1977), *SZS* p. 6; Maurer (1977), *SZS* p. 162; Berenstein (1979), *Semaine judiciaire* p. 122; Büchi (1977), *SZS* p. 280, (1978) p. 293, and (1979) p. 296.
236 Cf. at notes 162–164.
237 Maurer (1979), *SZS* p. 190 and (1978) p. 77.
238 Maurer, *Privatversicherungsrecht* p. 351 with bibliographic references.
239 *BBl* (1976) i p. 149; Frischknecht (1976), *SZS* p. 73; Büchi (1976), *SZS* p. 163, (1977) p. 269, (1978) p. 284 with indications of origins and (1979) p. 282. Maurer, *Sozialversicherungsrecht* p. 108.
240 On p. 3 the report mentions that the Federal Ministry of the Interior has invited ninety-five different bodies to submit remarks and proposals concerning the report of the board of experts. About half of these bodies have made use of this invitation.
241 Maurer (1973), Problem der schweizerischen Sozialversicherung, *VSSR*, p. 167.
242 Maurer, *Sozialversicherungsrecht* p. 109, and — on the differentiation between legislative competence and legislative mandate under constitutional law, linked with a programme — p. 126 ff.

243 Cf. in particular Gysin (1958), Mannigfaltigkeit und Koordination in der Sozialversicherung, *SZS* p. 1.
244 More details on organizational law in Maurer, *Sozialversicherungsrecht*, p. 242.
245 Maurer, p. 245.
246 Maurer, p. 239.
247 More details in Maurer, p. 264.
248 Maurer, p. 263.
249 Maurer, p. 357.
250 Maurer, pp. 354 and 363.
251 Maurer, p. 378. The solidarity contribution serves the vertical redistribution of income.
252 Maurer, p. 373.
253 More details in Maurer, p. 292.
254 Cf. Maurer, p. 126.

ABBREVIATIONS

AHV	Alters- und Hinterlassenenversicherung (Old Age and Surviving Dependants' Insurance)
AHVG	BG über die AHV (Federal Law on the AHV)
AlV	Arbeitslosenversicherung (Unemployment Insurance)
AlVG	BG über die AlV (Federal Law on the AV)
Art.	Article
AS	Amtliche Sammlung der Bundesgesetze (Official Collection of Federal Laws) (indicated as 'Neue Folge' (n.F.) — new series — since 1874)
BBl	*Bundesblatt* (Federal Government Bulletin)
BG	Bundesgesetz (Federal Law)
Botschaft	Communication of the Federal Council to the National Assembly (on draft of a BG etc.)
BRD	Bundesrepublik Deutschland (Federal Republic of Germany)
BV	Bundesverfassung (Federal Constitution)
Diss.	Dissertation
eidg.	eidgenössisch (federal)
EL	Ergänzungsleistungen (Supplementary benefits)
ELG	BG über Ergänzungsleistungen zur AHV und IV (Federal Law on Supplementary Benefits to the AHV and IV)
EO	Erwerbsersatzordnung (Income compensation)
EOG	BG über die Erwerbsersatzordnung für Wehrund Zivilschutzpflichtige (Federal Law on Income Compensation for Persons Doing Compulsory Military Service or in Civil Defence)
EVG	Eidg. Versicherungsgericht (Federal Insurance Court, Lucerne)
FLG	BG über die Familienzulagen für landwirtschaftliche Arbeitnehmer und Kleinbauern (Federal Law on Family Allowances for Agricultural Workers and Smallholders)
Fr.	Francs
IV	Eidg. Invalidenversicherung (Federal Disability Insurance)
IVG	BG über die IV (Federal Law on Disability Insurance)
IVV	VO über die IV (Decree on IV)
KUVG	BG über die Kranken- und Unfallversicherung (Federal Law on Sickness and Accident Insurance)
MV	Militärversicherung (Military Insurance)
MVG	BG über die MV (Federal Law on Military Insurance)
MO	BG über die Militärorganisation (Federal Law on Military Organization)
n.F.	neue Folge (new series (see AS))
Note	footnote (references are made to the text where the note is to be found)
OG	BG über die Organisation der Bundesrechtspflege (Federal Law on the Organization of Federal Administration of Justice)
OR	BG über das Obligationenrecht (Federal Law of Obligations)
SJK	Schweizerische juristische Kartothek (Swiss Legal Catalogue, Geneva)
SR	Systematische Sammlung des Bundesrechts (Systematic Collection of Federal Law)

SUVA	Schweizerische Unfallversicherungsanstalt (Swiss Accident Insurance Institution, Lucerne)
SVZ	*Schweizerische Versicherungs-Zeitschrift*, Bern (Swiss insurance periodical)
SZS	*Schweizerische Zeitschrift für Sozialversicherung*, Bern (Swiss journal for social insurance)
UVG (E)	Entwurf zu einem BG über die Unfallversicherung (Draft for a Federal Law on Accident Insurance)
VO	Verordnung (Decree)
VSSR	*Vierteljahresschrift für Sozialrecht*, Berlin (quarterly journal for social law)
VwG (or also VwVG)	BG über das Verwaltungsverfahren (Federal Law on Administrative Procedure)
ZAK	*Zeitschrift für Ausgleichskassen*, Bern (journal for 'Ausgleichskassen')
ZGB	Schweizerisches Zivilgesetzbuch (Swiss Civil Code)

Index

Contents

A. Name index (selection)

B. Systematic Index

I, Terms, institutions, principles	Germany	France	Great Britain	Austria	Switzerland
allocation of benefit rights between divorced spouses	78 f				
compensation, social -	3f,18,20,49,67,75	100	226f,	268,351,365	440
compulsory insurance	1f,20f,22,23f,25, 27f,32,37f,40f,44, 54,68f,71,74	95,97,101,106,109f 112ff,116ff,120,124, 126,133f,135,141f	154f,175,177,180, 184,186,206,233f	265,277,284,287f, 292,295,302ff,320, 347f,350	389,292,298,402f, 407,410,412,418, 429f,433,435f,439
contributions -employers/employee contributions	19f,22,26,27f,32, 49f,53,68	117f,119,127,136	155f,174,182ff,187, 189,192ff,200f, 223ff,227f,233,240	269,285,287,301 303	387,413,419f,422, 427
-compulsory contributions	20f,N,50,22,49	109f	155,222ff	285,287,292f,301	387,407f,413,419f, 422,427
employers' liability	18f	112ff	151,173ff,224,227	283f,292,294ff,364	401ff,408f,412
European social policy	73f				
family income	31,66	135	152		420
freedom of the will	21f	97,100f,107f,114, 117f,120,141	194	346,350f	407,412
guaranteed income	3f,31,63f,81f	100f,138,143,144	240.	265,269	392,423,434
harmonization of social security systems	27,37f,41,43,47,58, 66,72,74	123f,126ff,131f,135, 141,142	190,194,200,216,229f	266,327f,331f,339ff	424,426,428,431, 435,441
inexcusable fault		114			
insurance	20f,49,84		176f,183f,186,189, 192,198,200f,222, 226,234f	265	386,416f,440
just wage		95,106f			
minimum benefits	81	140	192,201,228	361	389,426
mutualité		115f,126,128			

	Germany	France	Great Britain	Austria	Switzerland
solidarity	20,22	96,104,108,123f, 129,131,136	186,193,230	342	440
subsidiarity, principle of -		110f	201	348	
subsistence minimum	51f,67,68,81,83	111,123,129,143	151,154,162,191, 194,217,219,235,240	269,359	392,423,426,434
unity of social insurance	27,33,37f,47,58	96,123f,126ff, 130f,135f,141f	155,190,216f,223, 229f	265f,327f,340f	408,439
voluntary insurance	1,44,54,74f	114	154,182,185f,206 217f	note 440,344	389f,407,412,439
voluntary organizations	17,	101,104	163,234		398
II. Systems					
accident insurance	23ff,28ff,32,38, 44f,54,69,75	121,134,140f	155,173ff,213ff, 218,223,227	268,294ff,315ff, 326ff,344ff	387,389,note 73, 403f,409ff,412ff,435
bankruptcy allowance	73				
contribution credits		108			
dependants' insurance	39f,44f,82	132,140	190,210ff	309,326ff,341	387,389ff,417f,422ff
family benefits	66	96,106f,110f,118f, 122,126,129,132,135	153f,191f,198, 199f,220	319,357	387,393,420,430
friendly societies		94,97,99,115f,121f, 125,139f			
health insurance	25f,28ff,32f,38f,44ff, 54f,69f,74f,84ff	124,128f,131f,133f, 140	152,154,184f,189f, 192,206,217,223,	267f,302ff,306f, 318f,324f,345ff	387ff,398f,409ff 412ff,432ff
income insurance of					
- farmers	2,67f,74	109f,117f,126,134 141f	222	347ff	387
- military personnel	2,21f,43,45,45	note 54,136	153		387,393f,410ff
- miners		note 57,72		307ff,317f,330f	
- notaries, notaries' clerks		105		266,329,345	
- public servants		note 54,57		266,324f,344f	399
- seamen	2				

	Germany	France	Great Britain	Austria	Switzerland
- self employed persons	28,54,68,81	124,133f,136f,142	155,127	265f,346,354,350	439
- white collar workers	2,28f,40f,44,46, 75,77f,82	124f,129	155,206ff,217ff	313,319f,328,354	439
- workers	2,28f,32,75,77f,	109f,116ff,141f	155,206ff,217ff	313,328f,354	389ff,439
income replacement					387,392,419f,428f, 431
invalidity insurance see also accident insurance	32f	132ff	182	309,320f,328,330 342,358f	391f,417f,424f, 431f
maternity insurance	29,42,45	124,133f,135,141	208	268,319,357	388
occupational welfare benefits	75,82	95,105f,109f,117	155f,197f,201,218, 240		423,434,436,441
old age insurance	4,36,67	106f,125f,130,132, 135f	153,177ff,190,209f, 217	268f,320ff,326,358f	387,389ff,417f,422ff
poor relief see public welfare provision					
private insurance	20,82	106,104f	164f,174f		387,398f,404ff,411
- accident	19	106			411,413f
- fire	20				404
- life	20,54	106,140f	226		404
public welfare provision	17f,33,43,49,51f,67 143	95f,100f,108,110f, 195f	151,153f,161ff,180ff	324f,329ff	399,416,418,434
unemployment benefits	43,49ff,72	120,135f,138	151f,154f,164,184ff, 189,202ff,216f,222f	329ff,	387,393,416f,429f
war benefits	42,51f,60	127	153		755,783f,795f
III. Risks					
accident see also industrial injury	44	104,130,134,136,140		327	389,412
bankruptcy, earning loss through -	73	106			

	Germany	France	Great Britain	Austria	Switzerland
care, need for -			152		
death	39f,41,44f,66	120ff,126,140	155f,157,163f,195,210ff,215f,227	356ff	390,398,402,435
disability	83f	111,139	206,220f	226	
dismissal		106,117			
fire		115			404
industrial disease	3,38,45,69	123,126,134	151,157,173ff,213f,218	327,357	398,401
industrial injury	3,19,28f,54	105f,112ff,120ff,126,134f,140f,note 113	151,155,157,173ff,213f,218	268,294ff,316ff,357	389,393,398,401f,411f
- commuting accident	45		214	316,318,357	
- reduced ability to work	3,45f,57		155,215,221	268,316,358	392
invalidity	3,32f,40,41,52,57,66,83	104f,120f,126	152f,155f,157,206,212,214f,219,220f	269,316,320f,330,342	391f,398,431f,435f
- incapacity for employment	29,41,45,66,68	129f	206f,212,214f,	268f,316f,342f,356ff	391f
liability	19	94,106,112ff,121,141	173ff,213,227	294ff,364	401ff,409,412
maternity	29,42,45,75	96,120ff,124,126,131,133f,135,1441,143f	155,195,208f	356f	388
old age	3f,29,41f,45,66,75,78f,82	96,106ff,109,111,119ff,124,126,131,142,144	153,156,177ff,190,209f	268f,320ff,329,	390f,398f,418,424f,427f,435f
retirement	67		155,209f		
short time working		139			
sickness	3,28,33,72,74f,83ff	96,98,104ff,109ff,119ff,125f,129ff,133f,140f,144	152,155,163,180f,184,206,219	267f,343,356,365	388,note12a,393,398,411
unemployment	31f,43,45,66	104,120,122,138f,143,144	151f,154f,164,180,185ff,189,202ff,216f,219	325f,343	416f

IV. Insured individuals	Germany	France	Great Britain	Austria	Switzerland
general remarks	1f,32,36,81	121,125ff,131f,138	216ff,	265f	389,407,411,439
artists	2,54			347,354	
authors		127			
blind			152		
casual workers			217		
children	66f,75	134,139	152f,199f,220		425,430
craftsmen	54,68,82	96,115,130,142		317,319	
disabled persons	3,32f,40,66	127	196f,202,206f	309,320f,330	390ff,411
employees	1,28,38f,40f, 44f,74,82	106,117,121,124, 130f,note 103,140, 142	217	324,328,342 344,354,358	
family dependants see also children, spouses, surviving dependants, widowers	28,31,36,66,74	118,note 87,139	152,154f,191f, 199f,217,219f, 238	265,319,321,330, 347f,357	387,389f,393f, 420,430
farmers	54,67f,74,82	96,130f,134,141		344,347ff,354	393,420,430f
farm workers	32,38,75,81f	96,114,130,134,141f	155,216	297f,303ff,317,320, 328,329f,344,358	393,420,430
forest workers	32,75			265,298,303ff,320, 328,329f,358	
handicapped people	2,59,75,79,84	111,135,139	152f,196,200,220f	266	
household servants	38,			319,329	
housewives	2		153,200,202,218, 238f	266	392
itinerant trades people	38				
live savers	44			364	
living together, persons -		96,132,135		327	
midwives	54				
military personnel	42,52,60	127,136,142	152f,216f,223		392,411,419f,428f

	Germany	France	Great Britain	Austria	Switzerland
miners	45,47	117,note 54,71		298,302f,307f, 309f,317f,358	
national service				266,329,345	392,431
notaries, notaries' clerks notaries'		note 57,72			
old people	3f,29,41,75,78f	108,138f	151,153f,162,209f	269,358f	390,425
one wage earners		126,135			
orphans see surviving dependants					
pensioners	51f,54,74		204,209,217		753
people not gainfully employed	49f				391f,
persons providing caring service in the home			152,156,200		
poor people	51	108	151f,161f,180ff, 196,217		434
prisoners	59f,	96,132,135			
prostitutes		96,132			
public servants	32	105,note 71, 136,142	216ff	268,324f,344f	399,431,435
railway workers		117,136	217	265,303,315f,340	399
school children, people looking for their first job	75	132,135	153	344	
seasonal workers			202,223		
self-employed persons see also craftsmen, farmers	1f,81	96,115,124,126, 130f,133f,141f	155,195,217,224	266,321,336,339 346f,354,359	439
sick persons	30,36f	108,111	152f,162,196f 215,217f	268,318f,324f	388,note 21a, 412
single parents		135,	153,197,200,210f,239		

	Germany	France	Great Britain	Austria	Switzerland
spouses	42,54,79	134f	155f,209,217,220		390,425,428
s.a. family dependants housewives					
students	75	127,142	195,204,217f	344	420
surviving dependants	39f,41,45,51f79	127,135	151,153ff,190, 202,210ff,215f	268,301,309,321, 357f	390,418,424
trades people	28,38,54			315	
transport workers					
unemployed persons	49f,72f	120,138	151f,216ff,	325f,358f	393,416f,429f
voluntarily insured people	28,54,74f		154,217f	344,346,354	390,439
widowers	79		212,216,238	266,301,357	
widows see surviving dependants					
women	45,78f		155f,209,217,219, 227	339	390f,424ff,428
V. Benefits					
1. benefits in kind and services					
- general remarks	45f,83				
- early medical diagnosis	74,83,84	139		267,344,356,365	
- education		103			
medical care	3f,29,33,46,53,54, 69f,75,83,84f	94,111,129 137,139	152,154,180, 184f,206	267f,303,325,342, 343f,356,365	note 12a, 392
. benefits payable					
a. non current benefits (lump sum benefits)					
- additions	76		220		
- capitalized compensation	40,45			583,321,327 303,309,325	391
- death benefit				309,357	
- funeral grants		140f	155,213,220,227		
- reimbursement of		105			
- reimbursement of contributions	39,71		212,223		
- reimbursement of costs		111,125,128,131,255		342	

	Germany	France	Great Britain	Austria	Switzerland
b. current benefits					
aa. short term benefits					
- bankruptcy	73				
wages guarantee					
- benefits for wrongful dismissal		117,140			
bb. medium term benefits					
- continued payment of wages by employer	3,70,72,74	129f,140		268,325,356	
- housing allowance	67,73	129			428
- maternity/pregnancy allowance	42,45,54,84	126,134	154,155,207,208	268,325,357	388
- sick pay	3,29,36,46,72,74f, 82	129f	154,155,206f	268,303,309,325, 344,356f	388
- unemployment insurance benefits/ unemployment assistance benefits	49,50f,72	138	152,154f,186,202ff	320,325	393,416f
- working/household assistance	68,74f,83,84	134			393,420
cc. long-term benefits					
- general remarks	36,63 54,65,68f,75		201f,218ff,226f	269,339,341f, 358,359,365	390f,424
- calculation					
-- indexing	4,45,54,57,59,64ff, 68,69,73,78,82	129	202,220,226,240,	269,343,359,365	391,424ff,427,429, 432,434
-- minimum	57			362	390,424,426ff
-- accident see disablement					
- childrens' allowance	46,66f,73	94,101,112f,129,134, 140	153,200		390,430
- disablement	3,29,36,45f,69		152f,155,200,206f, 215,219ff	268,316,318	389,391f,431f
- ex-servicemen	51f,73		153		
- old age	4,36,46,67f	118,121,129f	153,154,178,209f	269,329f,343	340f,424ff
- partial					424
- poor relief	see public welfare provision				

	Germany	France	Great Britain	Austria	Switzerland
- public welfare provision	51,67	111,139	200	329	418,434
- supplementary	52,68	152,215	268f,342,343f,358, 359	390,427f,434	
- surviving dependants	3,29,39,41,45,46, 41f,57,84	127,135	153ff,210ff,227	268,309,357	389ff,418,424ff
- transitional			154,227		423f,432
3. complex benefits					
- accident prevention	29,30f,33,69,75,83	113,127,134f,144	160,173	344,357	292,396,399,401
- rehabilitation	33,45,66,68,75,83,84	131		268,343,357,365	432
- vocational assistance	3,45,69,73			357	392
4. Others					
- labour exchange	49,50,73		151f,179f		
- maternity leave	122,134			357	400
- tax allowance exemption	108		153		
VI. Organization					
administration	26f,39,50,43,60f	119f,123f,126ff, 132f,136,144f	162,228	267,296,304	438
associations	36f,55,61			334,338	438f
church	17	104,109f			
collective agreement between doctors and sickness insurance funds	3,29,36f,47f,54,61, 76,85	122,128,140	185		132
consultative bodies			230f		
employment exchanges			180,186,190,229		
friendly societies		94f,99,101,107f, 114ff,134,140	185,190,229		
- approved societies			145,185,190,192, 206,207f,219,229f		
local and regional authorities	17f,20f,38,49,51	95,104f,108,110f, 121f,128,139	151f		388,399,400,416,434
medical profession	3,37,47f,54	119f,122,128,133,137	185		432f

	Germany	France	Great Britain	Austria	Switzerland
ministry	49,54	112,128	153ff,229f	296,301,304,347	385,437
private insurance	38f	106,128			404ff,435,438
self administration	2f,26ff,30,39,41,47,50,53f,55,61	119,123f,126f,130f,132,136	229,230	267,296,304,321,338,363	389,408,443,438f
social insurance institutions	2f,25ff,29ff,36,38,40f,47,49f,53,55,60f,67f,72f,74	105,107,110,112,117ff,121ff,126ff,130f,132ff,139f,141		266ff,303,306ff,318,319,329,338,343f,345ff,353	385,388ff,393f,408,411,413,419,420,422,429,438
social security legal institutions (tribunal)	31,33,39,60f		200,230,231f	267,296,334,338,342	385,387,389,391,392,394f,413,433,444
Supplementary Benefits Commission			197,230		
trade unions	49		229,230	325	
Unemployment Assistance Board			229		
Unemployment Insurance Statutory Committee			229		
VII. Financing					
budgetary assessment procedure	29,36,45f,64,71			269,270,301,327,361	393,423,439
capital coverage	note 75,30,31,46,55			301,327	440
contributions					
- additional	28,32				388
- calculation	29f,59	125	155f,200f,218,221ff	346	408,420,note 146, 421,422f,440
- ceiling		124,129,130			390f,393,417,419
- collection	50,59	122	156		
- compulsory see I. contributions					
- employed people	3,26,27,29,41,49,50,58,72	105,109f,117f,122,note 64,137	155f,186,197,201,223ff	269f,285,296,310,332,344,360ff	388ff,392f,417f,419,427

	Germany	France	Great Britain	Austria	Switzerland
- employers	3,26,27,29,41,49,50, 72	105,109f,117f,119, 122,143	187,201,223ff	269f,303,310,332, 360ff	389ff,392f,413,418f
- late payment	75				
- level	3,78	122	201	270,360	418,419,427
- limit	28,32,38,59	137			427
- rate	3,29f,36,41,50,58, 59,66,71, note 163, 76,78	122	197	270,296,344,360	note 11a,391,393, 423,42ff,note 184
- self employed people	67	137	155,224	346	391,420,423ff
- setting of individual		127	222ff		
- system		138	222ff		439f
cost reduction	46f,50f,76ff	137		331	
cost sharing	49	104			
costs of social insurance systems	1f,46f,76,82f	111,124f,128	190,198	268	note 134
doctors' remuneration	37,48,77	122,128,137			
financial adjustment	33,55,71f,77,83	118,124,128,132, note 94,136f,138	370,331,343,344	390,419	
financial administration	71f	132f	225f		425
financial deficit	50,77	136f	225f	331	
financing of social insurance systems	3,24f,26f,29f,33,41, 45f,48,49ff,54ff, 66,71,72,76ff	107ff,111,117f,120, 125,128f,137f,140, 142f	153,178,186,189f, 192f,200f,205f,213f, 222f,224ff,227	265,269f,296,331f, 338f,359ff	387,388ff,407f,411, 413,416ff,439f
part payment by the individual	46,69,70	131,140			
pension funds		105	155,225		390f,422f,427,440
reserves	29,36,57,66,71,77, 78		197		390,423,427,440
state subsidies	3,26f,30f,41,46,49f, 55,66,68,71,78	108,136,138	182,185f,198,225	388f,392,393,413	416,425,426f,434,440
surpluses	33,36,45f,55,57,75		225		424

VIII. Former systems	Germany	France	Great Britain	Austria	Switzerland
benevolent funds see also relief funds	12,18ff,49			285ff,353	298f
factory insurance schemes	18f			285ff	398f
fraternities	20	93		284f,295,303,307ff, 330,353	
friendly societies			163f,177,182,184f, 213,233		
guild financial provision	20	99		284	
miners' provident funds	20,21f,24				
mutualité		99,115f			
relief funds	12,FN38,18f,20f,25	99,104f,197f		287f,303,306f,353	398f
trade association sickness funds				286,292,303,353	
unemployment insurance schemes					399
Bismarck's social policy	9ff,12ff,80f	94,104,108,112,119, 143	150,165,168,172f, 177,236	269,280,292ff,305, 351ff	403,406ff,409
church	17	103,106f,109,118	158,163		
collectivism			158ff,165,168f,171f, 180,182f,194,201, 232f,239		
competition, spirit of -					386,399
currency - inflation	42f				
- reform	42,56	118f			
democracy	80	103		277	437
dependancy on wages, increasing	5f,34,42,57,80,81f	102	156	396	
economic - boom	42,52,56f,72,82		187,195	278,281f,314,333,337	396,420f
- crisis	16,42f,45,56f,70f,76,82	95f,119,135,141ff	187f	278,281f,323,329	397,415,416,420f

	Germany	France	Great Britain	Austria	Switzerland
economy policy	16,39f,42f,46	123	187,191,240	281ff,315	395f
empire, the second		102f,105			
European Economic Community	73f	142f			
factory legislation, reform of	5,11,20f			272f,281,287,391f, 303f,351	
Federal Republic of Germany-foundation of	56				
German Reich, foundation of the -	10,80f				
individualism s.a. liberalism	15,80	123f	159ff,163,169,171f, 174,177,181ff,191, 194,201,233ff,239f	273	
industrialization	6f,33f,42,80	93	156f,189	271,281ff,337	396ff,404
influences, foreign - and international comparison - general remarks					
- Austria - Germany	40				
- Austria - Switzerland				265f,280,351	410
- Britain - Austria				288,304	
- Britain - France		95f,119f,142			
- Britain - Germany	note 62		158,165		
- France - Belgium		113			
- France - Germany	13				
- France - Switzerland		113			
- Germany - Austria	note 91			292ff,302,315,333	
- Germany - Britain			173,179,182,184f		
- Germany - France		108,112,114,120,141			
- Germany - Switzerland					403,406ff, note 84,410 note 106a
- Switzerland - Britain			186		
labour law	18f,43,73,79		183	283,291,323,351	396,400
labour movement	9ff,35	102ff	170,188f	274ff,287f,302	397f,415

	Germany	France	Great Britain	Austria	Switzerland
legal system			158ff,235f		414,436ff
legislation	44,59ff		235f		384ff,395f,400,436ff
s.a. individualism	10,14,15ff,80	93,101ff,109,119	169f,191	271f,278f,349	395,399f
migrant workers	76				421
monarchy		102		271ff	
national socialist oppression	43,47,52ff	120		324,332f	
Paris commune		94,102f,112			
paternalisme patronal		115			
political associations			198f,220		427
- parties	10,34f,39f,50	123f	198ff	311ff	395,397f,415
-- social democratic	11ff,34f,42f,50,62,70,73	103,123	188,198,201	302,305,311ff	397f,415,425,433
population growth	5,34,56,80		156ff,189		
poverty	8	102	161f,167,177,180ff,195f,200	283	399
republic s.a. Weimar Republik - second		102			
- third	120f,126f	102,111,115,116			
- fourth	121,125,131f,136,140				
- fifth					
revolution, 1848	10	99	163	271f	
social christianity		101,104,106f,109,118		279f,289,300f,351	
social reformers	14f,23	103	167ff,190ff	277,279f,294f	
Social sciences, influence of -	71,79		166ff,195f		
social structure	5f,8,82	107			
standard of living	5,8f,34,52f	108	157,196	283	397

	Germany	France	Great Britain	Austria	Switzerland
trade unions	11f,34f,41f,43,49, 53,56,60,70	94,97,102ff,116, 117ff,123f,133	158,164,168,174f, 177,184,186,188, 190,199,203,205,214	315,325,345	397f,415,425
Unemployment	5,7,42f,49,50f,57, 70,76	102	189	272,282,323f,325f, 331,333	note 47,415,416f, 421,429
urbanization	5,34,42,80		156		
Weimar republic	42				
Women and children, employment of -	8,14,34	157,160	281	397,399f	
worker associations	10f	102ff	164	272,274ff,287f,311f, 315	397f,412
World War					
- First	41f	110,119	187	313,315	414f,419
- Second	56ff	95,119		335	419,421

Notes on the Contributors

Herbert Hofmeister is Professor of Law at the University of Vienna. His main publication is *Die Grundsätze des Liegenschaftserwerbes in der österreichischen Privatrechtsentwicklung seit dem 18. Jahrhundert*, Vienna, 1977.

Alfred Maurer is Professor of Law at the University of Berne, and former director of the "Zürich — Versicherungsgesellschaft". He is the author of *Schweizerisches Sozialversicherungsrecht*, Band I, Allgemeiner Teil, Berne (Stämpfli), 1979.

Anthony Ogus is Professor of Law at the University of Newcastle upon Tyne. He has published (with E.M. Barendt) *The Law of Social Security*, London (Butterworths) 1978 (updated edition).

Yves Saint-Jours is Maître-Assistant, Faculty of Law, University of Paris I. He is the author of *Traité de Sécurité Sociale*, tome I: Le droit de la Sécurité Sociale, Paris (L.G.D.J.), 1980 (updated edution).

Detlev Zöllner is Professor of Law. He has held the position of assistant deputy minister to the German Federal Ministry for Social Affairs and director of the branch-office of the International Labour Organization, Bonn. His main publication is: *Öffentliche Sozialleistungen und wirtschaftliche Entwicklung*, Berlin (Duncker & Humblot), 1963.